"All who are not offended by me are blessed."

Luke 7:23

"In the last days, difficult times shall come.
Men shall be lovers of themselves and will be covetous.
They will be proud, braggarts, blasphemous, disobedient,
ungrateful, and they will be wickedly unholy. They will lack natural
affection for others and be trucebreakers, false accusers,
and have no self-control. They will be fiercely savage,
and hostile towards anyone that is virtuous.
They will be traitorous, self-willed, self-conceited,
and they will love recreation (pleasure) more than they will love God;
Some will have the appearance of godliness,
but they will reject the power to live a godly life.
Be sure to turn away from these types of people."

2 Timothy 3:1-5

"But you Daniel, close up the words and the book will be sealed until the time of the end, when many will travel to and fro, and knowledge shall be greatly increased… Go your way Daniel, for the words are kept secret until the time of the end."

Daniel 12:1-9

Table of contents

Truth

The New Testament Scriptures:

Knowledge & Wisdom

Introduction

In 2000, I started on a journey that would change my life forever. Having been a "Christian" all of my life, growing up in a Christian church, going to Christian school, believing the bible and trusting in God, I began to see that there are many different kinds of Christians in the world of whom hold many differing beliefs and traditions. This started me on an extensive study into the history of Christianity and the many Christian church denominations and factions that exist, in order to see a full picture of modern Christianity and to come to understand, if it were possible, what the true Christian doctrines originally were and are.

In my research, I held one main criteria, of which was to be completely honest before God in all things, at all times. I began my study by researching many denominational churches and factional variants of churches that consider themselves Christian, in order to understand what each holds as doctrine concerning many topics. I also began to research the history of the early Christian churches, starting with the apostles and those that followed after them, in order to have a solid basis for what Christianity was at that time and what doctrines were held as true in the early days of the Christian church. It may be a surprise to many Christians that there are many writings that have been preserved from the late first century from men like Barnabas, Ignatius, Clement, Hermas & others, some of whom we find their names are written in the bible. From the second century many writings from Origen, Theophilus, Iranaeus, Justin Martyr and many others also exist. From the third century there are many more who took the time to write, as did so many others throughout history, right on up to today. In studying these ancient writings, it is possible to understand what many of the church leaders believed as doctrine at any given point in time, and it becomes easy to recognize when alterations in doctrine began to appear within the early Christian churches.

As I began to look closely to the writings of the early churches in the first few centuries, I was surprised to see that there were some small differences in doctrine that had begun to become evident in the early churches as early as the late first century! By the early third century, just 175 years after the resurrection of Jesus Christ and his ascension into the heavens, and just 100 years after the last living apostle John had died, Christianity was already in chaos, with many of the prominent apologists of that time already at odds with each other concerning many doctrines. From the early writings of the third century, each one seemed to hold his own set of doctrinal positions that differed from all the others concerning many topics. It was common for the men of that time to debate amongst themselves, much like as is often seen today.

"For the time will come when many will not continue in true doctrine,
but according to their own lustful desires, they will gather unto themselves
teachers to teach what their itching ears want to hear.
They will turn their ears away from hearing the truth
and they will be turned to believe many myths and lies."
2 Timothy 4:3

About 150 AD, a group of independent sects began to arise of which thought to combine the teachings of Platonism, Orientalism and paganism with Christianity. These sects called themselves Gnostics (the knowledgeable ones). The underlying principal for Gnosticism is that knowledge is considered the basis for attaining eternal salvation and that faithfulness was not important. By the early part of the third century, some of these gnostic sects began to gain in popularity and many Christians brought their debates against them. Because the Christians held many differing doctrines one from another and many diverse Gnostics also considered themselves to be Christians, there was never anything accomplished but to debate. Each individual church had at that time already strayed into teaching what was suitable unto themselves, whatever it took to bring the people in the doors! This created a great need for clarity as to what the original doctrines were and what makes a true Christian.

In 306 AD, Constantine took over the reign from his father. He was outwardly sympathetic to the Christians, so he legalized Christianity in 313 AD, but the debate as to what the true Christian doctrines were raged on. In 325 AD, the Council of Nicea was arranged in order to establish a universal set of doctrines that were to be held by all Christians. This council voted on what doctrines would be held as true and which would be dismissed and held as heretical. Within 50 years after the Council of Nicea, the doctrines which had been established in 325 AD were already being altered, and with the rise of Augustine, a former Manichean Gnostic, new doctrines began to arise within Christianity that would greatly prevent freedom of religion in many parts of the world for over 1000 years and would change the most basic principles as to what Christianity is, many of which still remain within Christianity today. One of these new doctrines was that the Roman church would hold the power to coerce and even kill, through means of torture, anyone that held any other doctrinal beliefs than what the church held. They claimed that it was the duty of the Roman church to kill all who they deemed to be heretics. Many of the Christian leaders at that time were executed for holding to the earlier held doctrines! With such a strong weapon, the Roman church was able to silence all dissenters and challengers. This was also the foundation for the Crusades. With such power the RCC could not easily be challenged and they would then go on to use their power to keep the people in submission and to use them for political power and financial gain for many centuries.

Another thing that Augustine brought into Christianity was the belief that everyone is a sinner, and that to be forgiven of our sins, all that was needed is to confess them. Though there is biblical truth to this doctrine concerning sins committed unintentionally, (Hebrews 10:26-29; Numbers 15:28-31; 1 John 5:16-17) he extended this doctrine to all sins, allowing for unbridled lust (Jude 1:4). You see, in the Greek language, of which the new testament scriptures were originally written, there are three different words used for the word "sin", identifying the different types of sin, of which have not been properly translated into the English bibles, where only one is often used and no distinction is typically made. Augustine began to blur the lines of sin and even today it is not often recognized by Christians that different types of sin exist. Because of this, most Christians now recognize that we all make mistakes and generally call their mistakes "sin", yet most tend to also extend what they call "sin" to deliberate choices to do what they know to be wrong, making no distinction between "unintentional sin" and "defiant sin". Such mindset goes all the way back to Augustine, however the bible does make the distinction, as do the modern-day courts. There is always a much greater penalty for intentionally choosing to do what is known to be wrong. In law, such is called premeditated crime. The bible sometimes uses the terms "presumptive sin", "defiant sin", "willful sin" or "iniquity" which is to commit sin while knowing that it is wrong and to presume that God will forgive you.

After centuries of corruption within the Roman church, a few brave men broke away in an attempt to establish a better system of doctrines. They faced death but wanted to address the easily seen errors of the Roman church. Their efforts created the first denominational churches. They called themselves Lutherans, Methodists, Baptists and there were also several others. Generally, they were called Protestants because of their protest against the Roman church, but even between these first Protestant denominations, they did not agree among themselves concerning the original doctrines of Christ.

Since the establishment of the first denominational churches, there were some congregants that differed in their opinions as to the true doctrine and interpretation of scripture, so some began to split off to create their own churches in order to hold to their own preferred doctrines. This happened time after time, each time some of the people broke off to create their own denominational churches of whom began teaching their own set of doctrines. The result of all of this is the reason why there are many thousands of different denominations in existence today, all of whom hold to their own specific set of teachings and doctrines. So to an outsider, Christianity looks much like a buffet; If you find one that you can digest - just ignore the rest! Just find a church that you like, one that you can fit yourself into as you are, and then close your eyes and enjoy the show! If we are being honest, as a whole, modern Christianity is utter chaos, as each church teaches so many different things from one another! There is generally no uniformity among the churches. Is Christ now the minister of all of this confusion? No, he is a God of order and of truth. Truth is not relative for each of us to establish as we might want or think, but there is only one true doctrine and all else are doctrines of men. (Matt 15:9)

One of the most surprising things that I have found, is that many times, churches, after having set their doctrinal positions at the establishment of their church, later change their doctrinal positions! Some have stated that they needed to update for the times or cater to the people. This might be good business, but it is a red flag when it comes to sincerity, honesty and truth, because God is the same yesterday, today and forever. (Hebrews 13:8; Malachi 3:6) Even as far back as the times when the apostles still lived, there were some within the churches who made changes in doctrine and many times they even altered the scriptures!

"For I know this, that after my death, grievous wolves will enter in among you that will not care for the people of God. Even from among yourselves men shall arise and speak corrupt things to draw away disciples after themselves."
Acts 20:29

This may be a difficult topic for some Christians who might ask, if the scriptures are altered, what can be trusted? Actually, anyone who is honest with themselves before God and does a study on the history of the bible can ascertain without question that the scriptures have been and are still being altered even today!

It might surprise some Christians that the bible was not available as a book that was accessible to the common man until the 1600's. In the early churches, most non-Catholic Christians were lucky to have a small portion of the bible held within their gathering. They were often forced to gather in secret. Early on, the RCC had translated the scriptures into Latin and prevented the people from gaining access to them; Additionally, the people were prevented in most cases from learning to read, a time known as the dark ages. This was done to force the people to go through the Roman church in order to learn about God and to limit their understanding to the Roman Catholic perspective. This is the reason some motivated people, including John Wycliffe who died as a martyr, began to raise their voices and call for change.

It is recognized by historians and scholars that some of the books of the new testament were being altered even into the early third century or later. Scribes many times added their notes to the texts, written in the margins, and translators sometimes used the words of the scribes, even in place of the biblical text! Translators often weakly translated the scriptures to offer a generic meaning of which could then be interpreted in many different ways by the reader. This allowed for more sales of their bibles, of which would be accepted by many people with differing ideologies. Very often in the scriptures, the Greek words that were originally used were compound words of which have been translated incompletely. Other times the phrasing is reversed, of which changes the meaning of a text. Many times the Greek words are miscategorized in the concordances and are listed incorrectly. There are many corruptions and contradictions in the bible that date back to inaccurate testimony when texts were originally written, copying errors, translation errors and many other types of errors. Yet with this, the true doctrine of Christ remains evident in the scriptures, if you can see through the fog. Many of the alterations, inaccuracies and contradictions have been pointed out and corrected in this book.

In 1611, the first widely distributed English bible was offered to the people. The King James bible has been used for over 400 years in America and many other parts of the world. It wasn't until the mid-1800's that other significant versions began to appear. Today there are over 1000 different versions of the bible in the English language, all of which offer different phrasing and support differing ideologies, often expressing very different things one from another. Many churches choose to use their preferred version of the bible which helps them support their preferred doctrines; This is evidence that the scriptures are still being altered to support preferred doctrines, as they have been all along.

"In all of his letters he spoke of these things, some of which are difficult to understand for those that are unlearned and they are not able to be understood by those that are unstable, so they pervert them, as they do with all of the other scriptures, of which shall lead them unto their own eternal destruction."
2 Peter 3:16

Now if we were to look at today's Christianity from an outsider's perspective, what would we see? It would be a difficult thing to grasp what true Christianity is, because each church is teaching differently from all of the other churches. It would look like Christianity is whatever someone wants it to be. It would look like all you need to do is claim that you get your doctrines from the bible and mention the name Jesus Christ a few times and that is all it takes to be a Christian.

If one was coming from an unbiased perspective to try to decide which church is teaching God's truth in all things, it would be a long journey in order to research the many differences between all of the denominational churches and compare them. How would one choose? You might have a better chance winning the lottery than to pick the true church from the modern-day churches! That is because, since the churches all hold so many different doctrines, there is at best only one church that could possibly hold all of God's truth, though evidence shows all have brought in some doctrines of men, distorting the truth to some degree or another. So which denominational church would you pick? Typically, one's own bias makes the decision for them and people tend to choose the church they feel that suits them the best! So one might ask, what is wrong with that? Well, to fit yourself into a church based upon your own ideologies and preferences (terms/rules), that is to play God; It is to exclude the creator from your form of religion! Doing so is to make your own decision as to what the true doctrine is, instead of submitting yourself to the true doctrine that God has set and to conform yourself to his way. This is fundamentally important to get right, because we are not going to be judging ourselves on judgment day, but God is the ultimate judge of each man and woman. Don't you think it would be better to live by God's truth and his terms, than to choose for yourself which set of doctrines you hold to be true and then fit yourself into a church that is comfortable for you? True doctrine is immensely important and everyone should reevaluate what they hold as true and not just continue in what they presently choose to believe and hold as truth. (2 Corinthians 13:5)

"If anyone brings unto you any set of doctrines (gospel) that is different than that which you have already received from us, let him be cursed!"
Galatians 1:9

Some might ask, isn't truth relative to your own perspective? Actually, God's truth is eternal and never changes. Sometimes referred to as "the word of God", or more properly, "the instructions of God", true doctrine begins with Christ Jesus. No matter how much one might believe something, if it is not God's truth, it's error and the one holding such position will be greatly sorrowful on judgment day. It must be said that the bible is not what is being referred to as the word of God, but God's true doctrine is.

**If the bible is the word of God, God speaking to you,
then whose version of what it says is the word of God
and why do the publishers keep changing what he has to say?**

It isn't one's own interpretation of the scriptures that matters, but without question it can only be the original intent of the scriptures, of which is the true doctrine of Christ that matters when one is concerned with God's truth and true doctrine.

It can be very confusing for an onlooker, because so many preachers say that they are teaching right from the bible, yet they teach so many different and sometimes contradicting messages from one another concerning the very same verses! You see, one teaches a doctrine of a pre-tribulation rapture, yet another promotes a doctrine of a post-tribulation rapture; Another may claim no rapture at all and another might teach that the rapture has already happened! Then each church and minister claims to be using the scriptures to prove their case! What we must ask is, what is God's truth on the matter! Only God's truth should matter to a true Christian.

Again, in today's churches, concerning baptismal doctrine, one teaches that baptism is necessary for salvation and another teaches that baptism is not necessary for salvation; Both claiming to be using the scriptures! They even debate as to what a true baptism is; If it is only spiritual or if it is by water, if one must be submerged or just a drop on the forehead. There are differences concerning what repentance is and if it is necessary for salvation. There are differences in what is taught concerning salvation, prophecy, the godhead and all other doctrinal topics within Christianity, with someone teaching practically every possible niche of every topic! There are so many variants of what is being taught in the churches today on every conceivable topic - yet each one claims to get their directives from the bible - but how can this be? It is because the bible has been misused, altered, misinterpreted and greatly misapplied by many people for nearly 2000 years!

You see, the majority of preachers and theologians don't go to the scriptures to understand what they say and then teach what is written as a whole; They tend to gather an idea or doctrine and then go to the scriptures to misuse and misapply them so that they can try to prove what they choose to teach, claiming it is right there in the bible. This is what the scriptures call "the doctrines of men". But those doing so always need to ignore other scriptures that contradict their doctrine or they greatly distort the meaning of those scriptures in order to misapply them also. Many times they make them say the exact opposite of what they so clearly say! They have also altered the bible itself with the many hundreds of different versions that now exist, of which change the wording of the scriptures to assist in altering their meaning.

Example:
1 John 3:8 - KJV vs. NIV (commit vs. practice) The Greek is G-4160 ποιῶν = to commit (present participle active – "a single action moving forward")

16

Furthermore, when translation was done, the translators often translated many Greek words into a single generalized English word of which can hold many different meanings. The preachers just use the definition of the word that best suits their doctrine!

An example of this is the word "faith" of which is represented in the Greek by four different Greek words, all of which hold a specific meaning and place of speech. When generalized into English, the reader is forced to determine the proper meaning of the word and its proper place of speech! In English, the word "faith" can hold seven different meanings and can be used as a noun or a verb! The word "saved" is represented in Greek by over 20 different Greek words, many of which are compound words, yet they are translated simply to the nondescript word "saved" in the modern bibles. There are also many other generalized words that hold multiple meanings that are used in the English translations of the New Testament, of which are most often misinterpreted!
Some examples of these are the words "grace", "law", "believe", "beast", "works", "flesh", "body", "faith", "saved", and "spirit".

The scriptures certainly are true if understood properly; However, true doctrine must hold the correct definition and the proper placement of speech for each word, then clarify whether the text is meant literally or figuratively, physically or spiritually.

What is true doctrine? It is an understanding of God and his truth. It is not relative to each of us to decide for ourselves, but it is eternal and never changes. It is God's offer unto each man and woman for what his terms are for living this life. It is always pure, honest, sincere and usually very hard. It tends to go against what one might naturally desire, because it is not of this world, but of the higher eternal world.

Remember, God's ways are above our ways. True doctrine is to always do what is right while having a sincerely pure heart, knowing that God is always watching. This is what leads to being righteous (*right + just*) and in the end, can bring eternal life.

This book re-establishes the truth of the new testament scriptures keeping the original intent by fully translating the Greek text, based upon a full understanding of the scriptures as a whole. Included are many references that help to establish true doctrine concerning every conceivable topic. When compared to the earliest doctrines that are expressed in the writings of the early church leaders, the Epistle of Barnabas, 1 & 2 Clement, the books of Hermas, Papias, Polycarp and Ignatius, it can easily be seen that what is written in this book is an extremely accurate picture of the original intent of the scriptures of the bible, which clarify and promote the original doctrine of Jesus Christ and true Christianity.

Do you hear the call?

The authentic doctrine of Jesus Christ

The doctrine of Jesus Christ is simple, but needs some explaining, so to cut through the many doctrines of men that have clouded the minds of Christians everywhere. It begins with the law of God, of which is simple:

"...you shall love your God with all of thy heart (emotions),
with all of thy mind (thoughts), with all of thy soul (body)
and with all of thy strength (efforts);
And you shall love your neighbor (others) as yourself"
Deuteronomy 6:5 & Luke 10:27

It is necessary to keep the law of God at the forefront of your mind when considering the many sub-doctrines that make up the doctrine of Christ. It is also important to understand the purpose of God's plan for this world and all that he has created, of which was to create a people that might choose to love him by their own free choice to do so. God chose to offer mankind freewill to choose, each one for himself, the choices that they might make while living in this life; We must choose whether to live unto our own cares and desires, or to live to honor God and live in accordance to his instructions. Freewill is the key to conquering in this world and without it, no one could act independently of the way that he or she was created. Without freewill, the sin that one might commit could not be attributed to him, because he only acted in accordance to the way that he was created. Without freewill, no one could choose to love God or defy him, but would only act in accordance to their "programming". Without freewill, commandments and doctrine are pointless, as is the concept of religion. Animals act by instinct and have no religion, but they live and they die with no thought of doing what is right or wrong; Without freewill, mankind would be no different. However, because of freewill, each man and woman can now choose to live in accordance to the law of God or to defy him. Without freewill, there could not be a judgment day, in which everyone will be judged for what they have done in this life.

"Paul took the time to explain thoroughly concerning righteous living,
self-control and the coming judgment that will soon come upon every man."
Acts 24:25

"... for that day of judgment and the revealing of the righteous judgment of God;
He will deliver unto every man and woman according to what each had done
in their life. Unto those who live truly continuing patiently in doing that which is good
and living incorruptibly, they shall receive wealth, honor and everlasting life.
But unto those that are contentious against God and disobey his ways,
and remain confidently continuing in unrighteousness, they will receive the anger and
indignation of God; Distress and fire shall come upon everyone who continues in
wickedness... But honor, wealth and peace unto every one that continues faithfully doing
that which is good; First with the Jews and the same with the gentiles."
Romans 2:5-10

There are some that believe that there is no freewill or that freewill is limited, but such ideas are based upon the observances of some people and might be desirable to others, because if true, this would relieve them of the guilt and the punishment for their sins, at least to some degree. However, though it must be admitted that people have addictions and many just can not overcome their sin, the addiction was always the result of a freewill choice at one time earlier in their life and the slavery to sin is always based upon one's choice when they had originally committed that sin for the first time.

"And Jesus said, I tell you the truth, whoever commits sin is a slave to sin,
but the slave shall not abide in the house of God forever...
But he that the son sets free is completely set free."
John 8:34-36

It is the act of first choosing to commit a sin that enslaves a man or woman, causing addictions and prevents people the ability to overcome many sinful acts. Everyone at some point in their lives does choose to do what they know is wrong and does become a slave to some sins; But if you are set free by Jesus Christ, the slavery of sin is broken and freewill is restored.

"By what a man is overcome, the same is he also enslaved."
2 Peter 2:19

But some might say, we are all sinners, everyone sins and we always will be sinners while we live in this world. Though this may be true, as we all do make errors in judgment and act without thinking and we certainly all make mistakes, it must be brought to light that the bible makes a difference between the types of sins, some being sins that are forgivable, and some which are not forgivable.

"Whoever takes action against what is taught by the son of man,
it can be forgiven of him; But whoever blasphemes the holy spirit
can never be forgiven, not in this life or the next."
Matthew 12:32

"If anyone becomes aware of a brother having committed a sin not unto death, they shall ask
God for forgiveness and God will give life unto those that commit a sin not unto death.
There is a sin that is unto death, for such, I do not say that you should pray for it."
1 John 5:16

Clearly, in these scriptures there is a distinction made between two types of sin, one being less severe of a transgression against God and the other a mortal sin. In our modern bibles it can be very difficult to find understanding and clarity on the subject, but at the time of the writings of these above quotes it was commonly understood what was meant by the differences between sins, as it is written in the old testament scriptures and was expressed in the Greek language in which the scriptures were written. All we need to do is look there for understanding.

*"When one commits a sin in ignorance before the Lord, atonement shall be made
and it shall be forgiven unto him. You shall have one law for all that sin ignorantly
for both those that are born among the children of Israel and also for the foreigner (gentile).
But the one that sins defiantly (presumptuously), whether native born or a foreigner (gentile),
he blasphemes the Lord and he must be cut off (H-3772 -killed), because he has despised the
Lord's instructions and broken his commandments,
his sin shall remain upon him."*
Numbers 15:28-31

This verse very clearly defines blasphemy of the holy spirit (*God*), what a sin unto death
is and also what sin not unto death is. When we have this in mind, we can then start to
understand many other scriptures.

*"Because if we willfully commit sin, after we have come to understand the true way,
there is no longer a sacrifice remaining for such a defiance against God;
But there is a certainty of terrifying judgment and the fiery anger of God that shall consume
all that defy him. Anyone who disregarded the law of Moses was put to death without pity at
the testimony of two or three witnesses; How much harsher of a punishment is then due, if
someone pushes the son of God down under their feet and chooses to defile the blood of
Christ and the covenant by which they had been cleansed,
and also chooses to defy the spirit that has brought unto them the assistance of God?"*
Hebrews 10:26-29

*"Even though I had at one time been a blasphemer and persecuted the people of Christ,
I received the grace of God abundantly
and I received forgiveness, because what I did, I did in ignorance."*
1 Timothy 1:13

*"Because the wrath of God is revealed upon all ungodliness and unrighteousness of every
man that knows what is right, yet chooses to do that which is unrighteous."*
Romans 1:18

When we look to the original Greek language for the word "sin" we find that three
different words were originally used, each with a specific meaning of which defines a
different type of sin. Greek word G-264 is a defiant sin, a sin unto death, whereas Greek
word G-265 is a sin committed in ignorance and Greek word G-266 is a general non-
specific offense. It truly is a shame that these more complete and clear meanings were not
more fully translated and carried over into English bibles, as it would have helped bring
many more people to the original meaning of many scriptures.

In the modern churches, biblical repentance, biblical baptism, the terms of the new
covenant and true biblical conversion are not being taught properly. Thus, the conversion
that you may have received is most likely without the power to free you from your sin.
The evidence of this is that you are still choosing to commit sin. This is evidence that a
true conversion is still needed!

*"For they are false apostles, deceitful workers that have disguised themselves
as apostles of Christ; Do not be surprised, because even Satan makes himself appear
as an angel of light. Why then is it any great thing for his servants to transform
themselves into the image of ministers of righteousness,
of which their end judgment will be according to their deeds."*
2 Corinthians 11:13-15

*"In the final times, most people will fall away from living a faithful life of dedication unto
God. They will attach themselves to imposters that will deceive them and unto doctrines
of demons. They will be hypocritical liars, distorting what they perceive as truth..."*
1 Timothy 4:1-2

*"...there will also be many false teachers among you, of whom will secretly bring in
damnable heresies of destruction, living in a contradicting way unto the Lord who
redeemed them, of which they lead themselves unto eternal damnation. There will be
many who will follow their damnable ways, of whom will speak evil of the true way."*
2 Peter 2:1-2

Do you ever do something that you know is wrong? I'm not talking about an error in judgment or an honest mistake, or even an action that you know is wrong but did without thinking. If you are choosing to commit sin that you know is wrong, even once in a while, you are not in Christ.

*"We know that whoever is regenerated of God does not choose to commit sin,
because he that is regenerated by God guards himself
and the devil does not corrupt him."*
1 John 5:18

It is important to remember the words of Christ Jesus; *"whoever commits sin is the slave to sin."* If you were to go back to your sin after having truly been cleansed and converted by Christ, of which very few modern Christians have done properly, you would again become a slave to your sin and there is no way for you to be cleansed again. The forgiveness of God is brought at conversion and then he assists us to help us remain faithful to him going forward! Conversion is the second chance to get right with God. The prodigal son was prodigal only once.

*"For those that have been illuminated...and held the expectation
of the world to come, if they fall away,
it is impossible to renew them again unto repentance.
As they would need to re-crucify themselves and put the son of God to an open shame."*
Hebrews 6:4-6

*"What then can be said? Shall we continue to commit sin
so that God's grace might be multiplied? No, it is forbidden!"*
Romans 6:1

"No man can serve two masters. Either he will love one and hate the other
or he will hold strong to one and despise the other."
Matthew 6:24

"Your sins are forgiven unto you, go and sin no more."
John 8:11

There is only one pathway unto salvation and it is through the blood of Christ Jesus, of which cleanses us from our sins when we are converted. This also breaks the slavery to sin, restores freewill and gives us the power to choose to live as God requires. There is only one way to access the blood of Christ, through a true repentant heart and baptism which cleanses us from all previously committed sins. (Romans 3:25).

"Therefore, have godly sorrow that brings forth true reformation before God
and be converted for the pardon of your sins,
so that the rebirth may bring upon you the presence of the Lord."
Acts 3:19

"Brothers, what must we do to be saved?
And Peter said to them, everyone must have godly sorrow that brings forth true
reformation unto the deliverer and be baptized unto God in the name of Jesus Christ for
the pardon of your sins, and you shall receive the gift of the holy spirit."
Acts 2:37-38

Peter twice spelled out the pathway of conversion. Jesus also made it clear as his ministry was all about repentance. He explained that to be converted was to become as a little child (*reborn*) and then he clarified what is expected of a new convert.

"...and he (Jesus) said, truly, if you do not convert and become as a small child, there is
no possibility for you to enter into the kingdom of above. Whoever shall humble himself
in this way to become as a child, he shall be elevated into the kingdom of above.
Whoever shall receive the message of one of these coming in my name, he shall receive
me. But whoever of these that believe on me and again choose to offend me, it would be
better for him if a large millstone were hung around his neck and he be thrown into the
deepest sea. Woe unto all in the world that commit such offenses against me, though it is
necessary that temptations occur, yet woe to the one that commits an offense against me.
Therefore, if your hand or your foot cause you to do that which is evil, cut it off and throw
it far from you; For it is better for you to enter into eternal life maimed or crippled, than
for you to have two hands and two feet but be cast into the eternal fire.
If your eye causes you to commit an offense against me, pluck it out and throw it far
from you; For it is better for you to have only one eye when entering into eternal life,
than for you to have both eyes and be thrown into the eternal lake of fire.
See that no little ones (converts) bring an offense against me, because I tell you, the
angels above see everything and bring news of it before the Father above."
Matthew 18:2-10

23

Jesus also spoke about the method of baptism as the act of conversion and the way to receive forgiveness of sins. He never spoke of baptism being a sacrament or only as an outward sign of an inward change, as is taught commonly in the churches today. Any change that has happened must not only be inward, but also in how we choose to live! Baptism is the method of accessing the blood of Christ, to die with him and be born a new creation, to no longer be a slave of sin, but the servant of Christ. (Romans 6:1-23)

"Except a man be reborn through water and the spirit,
he is in no way able to enter the kingdom of God."
John 3:3-5

"Those that believe, baptize them unto God and they shall be reserved by God"
Mark 16:16

"You shall go into all nations, disciple them and baptize them in the name
of the Father and Son, and into the Holy Spirit.
Teach them to observe all things that I have taught unto you."
Matthew 28:19-20

The simplicity of the doctrine of Jesus Christ is this:

You must have godly sorrow unto true reformation before God (*Yehovah*) and be baptized (G-907 *baptizo -submerged in water*) in the name of Jesus Christ (*Yehowshuwa*) for the remission of your sins, and you shall receive the helper, the holy spirit, who will guide you, strengthen you and help you live a holy life, to go and sin no more.
For all transgressions (*sins*) that one might commit unintentionally, confess them before God and you will be forgiven. Do not be found to defy God, not even once after you have been converted, but remain faithful, to honor and obey him and you will receive eternal life.

"I send you out to be my witness unto all nations;
To open the eyes of the blind and turn them
from the ways of darkness unto the Light;
From the deeds of Satan unto the deeds of God;
They will be offered the remission of their sins
and an inheritance among all that are sanctified
through faithfulness unto me."
Acts 26:17-18

Life as a true Christian

*"So then, do not be stressed nor anxious worrying about what you will eat or drink
or wear. For these things are what those who do not know God are seeking.
Your Father above knows that you have need of all of these things.
But seek first for that which is of the kingdom of God and to be righteous before him, you
will be supplied with all of what you have need of. So then, do not be stressed
or anxious for what you will need in the future, because tomorrow will bring its own
troubles. It is meant to be that each day have its own difficulties."*
Matthew 6:31-34

*"He that does not take up his own cross to follow after me, he is not deserving of me.
He that works to establish his life (in this world) shall lose it.
But he who surrenders the good of this life for my name sake, he shall find life (eternal)."*
Matthew 10:39

After conversion, the quest for the real life begins. The scriptures make it clear that everyone who comes to Christ must suffer much hardship and will be hated by the world. This is because once one has been converted into Christ, the work begins to ready you for the kingdom of God and to test you to find if you will be faithful unto Christ and live as he requires. There is only two possible options as to how to live this life; One can live to go out and conquer the world, live for one's own self and satisfy every desire, or one can throw all of the cares of this life away to serve Christ. It is impossible to serve Christ and one's own desires for things in this world.

"No man can serve two masters… You can not serve God and worldly gain."
Matthew 6:24

It all comes down to whether one truly believes in what Christ offers. We all have a choice to make. Do you believe in what Christ has promised, enough that you are willing to trade the cares of this life away for the eternal? Will you remain faithful unto him through any challenge that comes your way? We are not to make this world our home nor live to gather treasures here in this life, but to be as a stranger passing through. If anyone chooses to not choose and continues living this life in the normal way, that is a choice in itself; To not do as God commands is evidence of unbelief in Christ.

This is not an effort to offer an acceptable message that will be received as inviting by most people, but is the honest picture of what should be expected of those who convert to Christ for real. Life in Christ is necessarily difficult, so be prepared for persecution and much difficulty, unto some more than others. Remember the words of Paul: *"To live is for Christ and to die is gain."* Each of us who come to Christ must keep our focus on him and his promise of the eternal life in a better world, and know that whatever suffering and difficulty we endure is for our own eternal good. We need to always remember that the difficulty and persecution are only a part of the test and are temporary.

"And you shall be hated by all men for my name's sake...
The disciple is no better than his teacher, the servant is not above his lord...
If they have called the master of the house Beelzebub,
how much worse shall they call those that are of his household?"
Matthew 10:22-25

Jesus was betrayed and rejected by his own people. He was scourged and crucified next to two criminals. He was mocked, spit upon and beaten. The Apostles also suffered greatly, many of them dying gruesome deaths as Martyrs. Paul wrote of his immense hardship:

"Of the Jews, five times I received forty lashes less one;
three times I have been beaten with rods; Once I was stoned;
three times I suffered shipwreck; I spent a night and a day in the deeps of the sea...
I have been in danger in the cities and in the wilderness; I am always in danger
of false brethren; I have been worn out (tired) and suffered much pain.
Many times I have been... hungry and thirsty, often not having food to eat;
I have been in the cold and not properly clothed..."
2 Corinthians 11:24-27

The Apostle Paul suffered greatly so that you might be able to receive the truth of the Gospel and that you might know how to receive eternal life, if you might choose it! The great amount of suffering that he endured might make some wonder if it is worth it! Paul had his focus on the eternal, to do the will of God. It did not matter what suffering he needed to endure, for he knew that this life is only temporary and the suffering but momentary in comparison to the bliss of the eternal life that is promised to all who are proven faithful. The Apostle Paul was given the truth by Jesus and he was given the responsibility to preach to the world; He did so, no matter the difficulty that he had before him, even in the face of death. Paul is a great example who demonstrates the appropriate mindset that each of us as true Christians must have.

"... urging them to continue in their dedication...
...that only through many difficulties, hardships and persecutions (tribulations)
will we enter into the Kingdom of God."
Acts 14:22

"... we told you that you shall suffer much affliction."
1 Thessalonians 3:4

"If the world hates you, know that it hated me before it hated you. If you were
of the world, the world would love you, because it loves its own; But you are not of the
world... therefore the world hates you... The servant is no better than his master.
If they have persecuted me, they will also persecute you: They will do these things unto
you because of me, and because they do not know the one that sent me."
John 15:18

"Let us not become tired in doing good:
for in due time we shall reap if we faint not."
Galatians 6:9

"If you are without correction and education, of which every son must share in,
then God does not treat you as a son, but as fatherless."
Hebrews 12:8

There are many scriptures that tell us that those who come to Christ will suffer much difficulty and affliction. We must understand that the purpose of the hardships and difficulties are for testing us and instilling the proper qualities within us that are required by God. If he is our Lord, then whatever he chooses each of us to suffer, we must know that he loves us and he knows what is best for each of us. The Apostle Paul gives us guidance as to how we must deal with such difficulties:

"... I take pleasure in physical pain, in injury, when I am in need, when I am persecuted
or in anguish for Christ's sake: For when I am weak, then I receive power."
2 Corinthians 12:10

We must embrace the difficulty and hardship, the times of trouble and the physical pain, knowing that we suffer for a purpose that is mandated by God, for our benefit and the benefit of others. We must suffer, yet remain faithful to Christ in all things. He that endures faithfully until the end of life shall receive eternal life.

"If anyone will come unto me, he must deny himself,
take up his own cross and follow me."
Matthew 16:24

"Truly I tell you, only through much difficulty can a wealthy man
enter the kingdom of above... All who have turned away from houses, brothers, sisters,
father, mother, wife, children, or lands for my name sake,
they shall inherit a hundred times... and receive eternal life."
Matthew 19:24-29

The things that are so very important to many in this life are the very things that are used against us in the test of life. Whether it be security, riches, the best health insurance, the prettiest wife or husband, the biggest house or fastest car, these are all worthless in the eyes of God and work against us in many ways. In the end, even one's family will be used against each of us if Satan believes it might be enough to get us to fail the test. My wife and I have seen this first hand. For the Apostles, many walked away from their families, friends and livelihoods, and they followed Christ. Jesus said to the Apostles, *"follow me"* and they dropped everything to do so. That does not mean that today you need to do so because the Apostles did or because the scriptures say so, but each of us must obey Christ when he personally speaks to each of us. If the spirit of Christ lives in your heart, that is where he will speak to you and where you must listen for his voice.

"Do not be unequally joined together with those that are unfaithful:
What fellowship do the righteous have with those that are lawless?
What relationship does light have with darkness?
What do Christ and Belial have to agree upon? What part has a believer with an
unbeliever? What principal does the temple of God have with idolatry?
For you are the temple of the living God... Therefore, come out from among them, you
must separate yourselves from them...Touch not anything impure, and I will accept you."
2 Corinthians 6:14-17

We are to have no part with those who do not love and obey our God. We are to be separate from them. This does not mean in the street, and does not mean to fail to bring the Gospel to the lost. It means in dealings of a personal nature and in doing business or trade. We are not to get together with unbelievers, not even for the purpose of family gatherings, reunions or for old time sake! We must keep at the forefront at all times, to bring the Gospel to the lost when meeting with others. We do not gather together in the false churches who teach the doctrines of men; We must not debate nor reason with them! We do not have lunch or play a round of golf with an old college buddy for old time sake, but only to be an example of Christ in us and to bring the gospel unto others. Anything that is not edifying unto Christ is not proper. When it becomes clear that he/she is not interested in hearing the Gospel, it is time to cut them off. Whether in the middle of dinner, or on the second hole. We have one purpose in dealing with unbelievers; To bring Christ Jesus to them. If they don't give you the respect to talk to them about what you are passionate about and give an honest ear, then it will only lead you into temptation and hardship.

"But avoid absurd challenges, genealogies, arguments and debates of law;
They are vain and not beneficial. Reject those that remain as heretics
after the first and then second warning"
Titus 3:9-10

Evangelism is meant only for the mature in Christ. The young in Christ and the immature, these are not to enter into the den of wolves, but to gather the milk of true doctrine and grow into maturity in Christ, where they will not be deceived nor drawn away into error.

"Do not build up treasures for yourselves here on the earth,
where moth and rust cause them to decay, and where thieves break in and steal.
But lay up for yourselves treasures in the heavens, where moth and rust do not corrupt,
and where there are no thieves to break in to steal.
For where your treasures are, there your heart will also be."
Matthew 6:19-21

These are the words of Jesus. Though they may be very difficult to grasp, there is wisdom in them that will make living the true Christian life much less difficult, no matter how difficult things may be. The key is to keep your focus where it needs to be, on the eternal. It is obvious that everything in this life is temporary, but the eternal things are perfect, forever and will not decay. We must endure without making it about what we gather in this life or how good we have it, but to keep the eternal focus in mind at all times. Each of us must remember that this life is only a test, and the test only comes to an end when each of us die. In every situation, we must keep in mind that the circumstances that each of us face are temporary, no matter how good or bad we might have it, no matter joyous or painful; If our focus is on the eternal, we will overcome and pass this test of life and shall receive the prize of eternal life.

"Everyone that is born of God overcomes the world."
1 John 5:4

"These things I have told to you that you might have peace.
In the world you shall have tribulation, but be of good cheer,
for I have overcome the world."
John 16:33

Interestingly, in the original Greek, the word for sheep is word G-4263 "probation". When one is converted into Christ he becomes a sheep of Christ, spiritually speaking. This offers the inheritance of eternal life, but the life that one lives in this world is the equivalent to being on "probation"; It is a test to see if you are serious and will comply with God's ways, and if you are faithful, you will receive the promise of eternal life. If you fail, you will violate your probation and be cast into the eternal prison.

"Therefore, if your hand or your foot cause you to do that which is evil,
cut it off and throw it far from you; For it is better for you to enter
into eternal life maimed or crippled, then for you to have two hands
and two feet but be cast into the eternal fire.
If your eye causes you to commit an offense against me,
pluck it out and throw it far from you;
For it is better for you to have only one eye when entering into eternal life,
than for you to have both eyes and be thrown into the eternal lake of fire.
See that no little ones (converts) bring an offense against me, because I tell you, the
angels above see everything and bring news of it before the Father above."
Matthew 18:8-10

"You must continue to patiently endure, because after you have
accomplished the will of God, you shall obtain the promise (eternal life)."
Hebrews 10:36

The Fruits of the Spirit

The fruits of the spirit are the qualities that one begins producing and brings forth from within themselves when they have the spirit of God in them. It might be better explained to understand the word "spirit" as a "demeanor". It is a perspective, a mindset and an attitude to face this world while living for the eternal world. It is to live with the hope of what will come, not what we presently see.

"Live according to the spiritual and you shall not commit the carnal lusts;
For the carnal lusts are against the spiritual and spiritual are against the carnal,
as they are contrary to one another; So you must not do what you would have done."
Galatians 5:16-17

What Paul is trying to convey is that we are not to live for the cares or lusts of what the body might crave for. This does not mean that we do not take care of our body, but that we are to live in a way that we produce good fruit and that which we do is righteous before God. Simply, that we are to obey what we know to be true through the guidance of the holy spirit of Jesus Christ and not give in to our own cares for the things of this world.

"But that which is produced by the spirit of God are these things; Love, joy, peace, patient continuance in truth, kindness, goodness, conviction, meekness, self-control, and there is no law against such things. Those that are in Christ have extinguished their own selfishness and the longing for that which is forbidden by God. Those that are in Christ have extinguished their own selfishness and the longing for that which is forbidden by God, through many hardships and sacrifices. If we live in the spiritual, we must also conform ourselves unto the spiritual ways of God."
Galatians 5:22-25

Love (agape) = (G-26)   = affection, benevolence, adoration, care for others
Joy   = (G-5479) = delight, cheerfulness, having hope, being positive
Peace   = (G-1515) = peacefulness within, quietness, rest
Longsuffering = (G-3115) = patient endurance in difficulty, having a long temper
Kindness   = (G-5544) = caring, being kind, excellence in treatment of others
Goodness   = (G-19)   = virtue, integrity, purity, moral excellence, chaste
Faith   = (G-4102) = loyalty, being trustworthy, being faithful
Meekness   = (G-4236) = humility, docile, gentleness, serenity, tame, mild, peaceful
Temperance   = (G-1466) = self-controlled, abstinence, moderation, self-denial

The Gifts of the Spirit

The gifts of the Spirit are supernatural gifts that are given by God to everyone who truly converts and begins living the true Christian life as Christ commands. These gifts are only given by the spirit of God at his discretion. Everyone who truly converts will receive at least one of the gifts, though some people receive more than one gift. But unto whom much is given, much is expected. The gifts of the spirit are to fulfill the necessary ministries within the body of Christ - the Ekklesia. They are meant to edify the whole body (people of God) and not for uplifting one above another. No one is meant to take glory unto themselves or get wealthy because of the gift that he has received. Each gift is given by God accordingly as he desires to give and each gift is to be used for his glory and his purposes.

"There are also different ministries that are all from our master.
There are varieties of things to be done, but our God is effectively
working through each one to accomplish all of the necessary things.
Each one is given a bestowment of the spirit of God so that each may contribute.
For unto one, the spirit gives the message of wisdom, but unto another, the message of
knowledge is given; Unto another, the true doctrine is given,
again by the spirit; Another receives the gift of healing by the spirit;
Unto another, the ability to do miracles; Unto another the gift of prophecy, but another
shall receive the discernment of spirits; Another receives the gift of languages,
and unto another the interpretation of languages.
Through all that are in Christ, all of the necessary actions are accommodated by the
same spirit who distributes privately unto each one as he chooses."
1 Corinthians 12:5-11

The gift of wisdom - knowing how to do what is right in every circumstance
The gift of knowledge - a supernatural knowledge
The gift of understanding the true doctrine - having full understanding of all God's truth
The gift of healing - supernatural healings
The gift of miracles - supernatural actions
The gift of prophecy - supernatural predictions and correction in truth
The gift of discernment of spirits - the ability to see the dispositions and intents of others
The gift of languages - the supernatural ability to speak foreign languages
The gift of interpretation of languages - supernatural ability to interpret foreign languages

The scripture also states that we should crave to receive the better of these gifts, but be satisfied with what is given. Unto the one who is faithful in the little things, more will be given unto him. Keep this in mind and you will be given according to your ability.

The deeds of the flesh

*"Now the deeds of the flesh (carnal) are clear to recognize and they are
adultery, fornication, filthiness, lustfulness, idolatry, sorcery, hatred, strife,
covetousness, passionate rage, self-promotion, double mindedness, heresies,
ill will towards others, murder, drunkenness, verbal abuse, and other like things;
As I have already warned you and clearly told you in the past,
those that do any of these things shall not inherit the kingdom of God."*

Galatians 5:19-21

Adultery   = (G-3430) sexual contact against a husband or wife with another
Fornication   = (G-4202) pornography, sexual contact when unwed
Uncleanness   = (G-167) impure, not fully dedicated to truth, morally spotted/dirty
Lasciviousness = (G-766) filth, to please oneself without care of consequences
Idolatry   = (G-1495) to leave truth, worship a false god, put anything above God
Witchcraft   = (G-5331) sorcery, magic, spells, drugs, getting high, altering the mind
Hatred   = (G-2189) hostility, enmity
Variance   = (G-2054) argument, debate, discord, fighting
Emulations   = (G-2205) competition, jealousies, striving against others, self-exalting
Wrath   = (G-2372) fierceness, indignation, anger, rage
Strife   = (G-2052) contention, superiority above others, rivalry
Seditions   = (G-1370) rebellion against God, insurrection, spitefulness against truth
Heresies   = (G-139) to come against truth, unbelieving, trusting in falseness
Envying   = (G-5355) jealousy, envy
Murders   = (G-5408) murder, killing for gain, lust or anger
Drunkenness   = (G-3178) intoxication, influenced by alcohol or other intoxicant
Reviling   = (G-2970) using foul language, to demean others, gossip

*"The fearful, unbelieving, abominable, all murderers, whoremongers, sorcerers,
idolaters and liars shall find themselves in the lake that burns with fire
and brimstone. This is the second (eternal) death."*

Revelation 21:8

What Hell will be like

Many times, Jesus used the term "weeping and gnashing of teeth" to describe what it will be like for those who will be rejected and sent to an eternity in hell.

References: Matthew 8:12; 13:42; 13:50; 22:13; 24:51; 25:30 & Luke 13:28

Gnashing (G-1030) = to grind the teeth together as in anguish and great pain.
Weeping (G-2805) = shedding tears of great sorrow, lamentation, wailing.

This should make it clear that Jesus was offering a serious warning to all who would reject him, that they will be greatly sorrowful for eternity because of the choices that they had made in this life. The scriptures give us a picture of what judgment day will be like:

"Then he shall say to them on the left, depart from me, you are cursed,
descend into the everlasting fire...
Just as ye did not do good unto the least of these,
you did not do good unto me. Go away into everlasting punishment,
but the righteous shall go unto everlasting life."
Matthew 25:41-46

"And many (H-3605 - the whole, all, everyone)
that sleep in the dust of the earth shall awaken,
some to everlasting life, and some to shame and everlasting contempt
(H-1860 - rejection, repulsed, abhorrence)"
Daniel 12:2

"...the carcasses of the men that have transgressed against God,
for their worms (H-8438 - flesh eating maggots) shall never die,
neither shall their fire ever be quenched; They shall be an abhorrence unto all"
Isaiah 66:24

Modern society has become accustomed to such horror. Because of this, it can be hard for some to see this is the certain reality of many. If and when it is personal it will be much more relevant; But at that time, it will be too late for anyone to change course.

If anyone has any difficulty as to comprehending hellfire and wants a mild preview of what hell will be like, imagine bringing a large pot of water to a heated boil then put your hand into the water for several seconds. (*If anyone actually does this, take your hand out and soak it in ice water.*) Can you feel the pain!!! Though this is not a recommendation to anyone, it is only an extremely mild and temporary example of what hell will be like.

Now picture your whole body being in that forever!

The eternal life in the heavens

For those who are found to be righteous, they will receive everlasting life; They will spend forever in a world that will have no evil in it. It will be a place that only those who are proven to be faithful and fully committed to God can enter. There will be no decay, no corruption, no selfishness, no rot and no rust. There can be no one that is defiled nor any thieves, nor any abomination, nor liars. There will be no aging nor time. No more curse and no more sorrow, no crying and no pain. This place seems too good to be true and it is in this life, but it is the picture that the scriptures give to us of the eternal world for all who obey the Gospel of Jesus Christ, love him and remain faithful until the end.

"And God shall wipe away all tears from their eyes,
and there shall be no more death, neither sorrow, nor crying,
neither shall there be any more pain: For the former things are passed away."
Revelation 21:4

"And there shall in no way enter into it anything that is defiled,
neither anyone that commits an abomination or makes a lie,
but only those who are written in the Lambs book of life."
Revelation 21:27

What road will you choose?

Do you truly believe?

Matthew

Chapter 1

1. The written account of the life of Jesus Christ, the son of David, the son of Abraham.
2. Abraham brought about Isaac, Isaac brought about Jacob; Jacob brought about Judah and his brothers;
3. Judah brought about Pharez and Zarah of Tamar; Pharez brought about Hezron and Hezron brought about Aram; (Ruth 4:18-22) Aram brought about Amminadab
4. and Amminadab brought about Nahshon; Nahshon brought about Salmon;
5. Salmon brought about Boaz of Rahab; Boaz brought about Obed of Ruth and Obed brought about Jesse;
6. Jesse brought about David the King. David the King brought about Solomon out of the wife of Uriah and Solomon brought about Rehoboam;
7. Rehoboam brought about Abijah and Abijah brought about Asa; Asa brought about Jehoshaphat
8. and Jehoshaphat brought about Jehoram; Jehoram brought about Uzziah;
9. Uzziah brought about Jotham and Jotham brought about Ahaz; Ahaz brought about Hezekiah and
10. Hezekiah brought about Manasseh; Manasseh brought about Amon and Amon brought about Josiah; Josiah brought about Jehoiachin and his brothers during the time of the Babylonian captivity.
11. After the captivity in Babylon, Jehoiachin brought about Shealtiel
12. and Shealtiel brought about Zerubbabel;
13. Zerubbabel brought about Abiud and Abiud brought about Eliakim; Eliakim brought about Azor;
14. Azor brought about Sadoc and Sadoc brought about Achim; Achim brought about Eliud;
15. Eliud brought about Eleazar and Eleazar brought about Matthan; Matthan brought about Jacob;
16. Jacob brought about Joseph the husband of Mary, from out of whom was born Jesus, the Christ.
17. Truly all the generations from Abraham unto King David are fourteen generations; From King David unto the Babylonian captivity are fourteen generations and from the Babylonian captivity unto the Christ are fourteen generations.

**It must be noted concerning lineage,
the Luke chapter 3 account contradicts the account here in Matthew.
This is properly explained in the Luke 3 account.**

18. This is the way that the birth of Jesus Christ came to be; When his mother Mary was engaged to Joseph, before they had been physically joined together, she was found to be pregnant by the holy spirit of God. (Luke 2)
19. Joseph, her husband to be, being a righteous man and not being willing to embarrass her publicly, proposed to put her away in secret.
20. And while he thought on these things an angel of the Lord came unto him in a dream and said, Joseph, son of David, do not fear to take Mary to be your wife. That which is growing within her is brought about by the spirit of God and is holy (*without blame*). (Psalms 22:10)
21. She will bring forth a son and you shall call his name Jesus, because he will save the people from their sins. (John 1:29 -Yehowshua - *salvation of Yehovah*)

Verses 22-23 look to have been added by a scribe and not a part of the original text.
22. And all of this happened that it might be fulfilled which was spoken by the Lord through the prophet, saying;
23. Behold, a virgin will conceive in her womb and will bear a son and they will call him Emmanuel, which being translated is to mean, God with us. (Isaiah 7:14)

24. When Joseph was awoken from his sleep, he did as the angel of the Lord had commanded of him and he took Mary to be his wife,
25. but he did not touch her until after she brought forth her firstborn child, and he was named Jesus.

Matthew 2

1. Jesus was born in Bethlehem, Judaea, in the days of Herod the king. At that time, wise men from the east arrived at Jerusalem. They asked, where is he, king of the Jews?
2. We saw his star in the eastern sky and have come to worship him.
3. Hearing of this, king Herod felt threatened and many in Jerusalem were feeling the same;
4. So Herod gathered all of the high priests and the record keepers of the people to enquire of them where the Christ was to be born.
5. They told him that the Christ would be born in Bethlehem, Judea, as it was written by the prophets.
6. "And you, oh Bethlehem, in the land of Judaea, you are in no way the least of the provinces in Judaea; For out of you there shall come a leader who will shepherd my people Israel." (Micah 5:2)
7. Then Herod privately called for the wise men and asked of the exact time that the star had appeared.
8. Herod then said unto them, be on your way to Bethlehem and seek diligently for the child and when you have found him, bring me the information of his location so that I may go there to worship him also.
9. And when they had heard the words of the king, they went on their way, the star in the east led them until it stood above the place where the young child was.
10. Seeing the star, they were exceedingly full of joy.
11. When they came into the building, they saw the child and Mary his mother, they fell down and worshipped him. Then they opened up the treasuries and they presented unto him gifts of gold, frankincense and myrrh. (Isaiah 60:6)
12. In a dream from God, they were warned to not return to Herod, so they returned unto their own country by a different way.
13. When they had departed, a messenger of the Lord appeared unto Joseph in a dream; He said: Rise up! Take the child and his mother and flee to Egypt! Remain there until I bring you another word. This is because Herod is seeking to kill the child.
14. When he woke up, he took the child and his mother, traveling that very night heading to Egypt.
15. They remained in Egypt until the death of Herod.

This part of verse 15 was added by a scribe, is misapplied and not a part of the original text.
So that it would be fulfilled, that which was spoken by the Lord through the prophet; Out of Egypt I have called my son. (Hosea 11:1-3)

16. When Herod had seen that he was ignored by the wise men, he became greatly angered and he ordered that all male children in every district of Bethlehem under the age of two years old at the time that he had spoken to the wise men, that they all be killed.

Verses 17 & 18 look to have been added by a scribe and not a part of the original text.
17. In this the prophecy of Jeremiah was fulfilled, saying;
18. "A voice was heard in Ramah, weeping and wailing and in great mourning; Rachel weeps for her children, not willing to be comforted because they are no more." (Jeremiah 31:15)

19. When Herod had died, an angel of the Lord again appeared unto Joseph in Egypt;
20. He said, arise and take the young child and his mother and travel back into the land of Israel; For he who was seeking the life of the child has died.
21. So he arose and took the child and his mother to the land of Israel.
22. But when he had heard that Archelaus now reigned over Judaea in place of Herod his father, he was afraid to go therein: Being warned by God in a dream, he went instead into Galilee.
23. He then chose to live in the city of Nazareth.

The remainder of verse 23 looks to have been errantly added by a scribe and not a part of the original text. No old testament prophecy reference could be found.

In this the prophecy was fulfilled as spoken by the prophets, that he shall be called a Nazarene.

Matthew 3

1. In the days that followed, John the baptizer began to speak in the wilderness of Judaea.
2. He said, repent, the pledge for the kingdom of above is approaching. ("Eggike" = G-1448 + G-2427)

Verse 3 looks to have been added by a scribe and not a part of the original text.

3. *This is the one who was spoken of by Isaiah the prophet when he said; "The voice announcing in the wilderness, to prepare the way for the Lord and to make his way clear." (Isaiah 40:3)*

4. John wore clothing made of camel fur and he wore a leather bag on a belt tied around his waist, and he ate locusts and honey.
5. All of Judaea went out to see him, as well as all of the people from the regions of Jordan.
6. Many were baptized in the Jordan river, having confessed with sorrow for all of the sins that each one had committed.
7. But when he saw the Pharisees and Sadducees coming forth unto the baptism, he said to them; You are the offspring of vipers! Who has warned you to run from the coming wrath? (Luke 3:7; Matt 12:34; 23:33)
8. Produce the fruit that is necessary for repentance! (2 Corinthians 7:9-10; Acts 26:20)
9. Do not think to say unto yourselves that you have Abraham as your father; (John 8:39) For I tell you that God is able to raise up these stones to be children of Abraham! (John 8:39-41)
10. The axe has already been laid into the root of the tree. (*cut off* - Daniel 9:26; Romans 11:14-20) Every tree that is not producing good fruit shall be cut down and thrown into the fire! (Luke 3:9, Zachariah 11:10) I baptize you in water unto repentance,
11. but he who will follow (*arise after*) me is stronger than me, of whom I am not worthy to carry his shoes. He will also baptize you in the holy spirit of God and by fire! (1 Peter 1:7)
12. The fork used to separate the wheat from the chaff is in his hand; He will completely cleanse the grain and he will gather up the grain into his barn, but the chaff he will gather to be burned in the (*eternal*) fire.
13. Soon after this, Jesus arrived from Galilee at the Jordan river to see John and to be baptized by him. (Isaiah 9:1)
14. But John refused him saying; I need to be baptized by you, so why do you come to be baptized by me?
15. But Jesus said unto him, back down now; For it is necessary for us to complete all of the requirements. John then gave in.
16. While being baptized, Jesus came up out of the water and immediately the sky opened up and they saw the spirit of God descend upon him as a dove; There was a voice from the heavens that said:
17. "This is my beloved son, in whom I am delighted." (Psalms 2:7; Hebrews 5:5)

In the Matthew 4:1 account, Jesus went into the wilderness after he was baptized to be tempted for forty days. In the John 1:35 account, Jesus met Andrew and then Simon Peter after he was baptized. On the surface this looks to be a contradiction, though it is not. Jesus met Andrew and Simon Peter just following his time of being tempted in the wilderness.

Matthew 4

1. Jesus was led by the spirit of God and he came to a place void of people. There he was tested by the devil.
2. After he had fasted for forty days and forty nights, he was hungry.
3. The tester came near and said to him, if you are the son of God, command that these stones become bread.
4. He answered saying, it is written, man shall not live by bread alone, but according to every word that is spoken by the mouth of God. (Matthew 2:12; Deuteronomy 8:3)
5. Then the devil took him to the holy city and set him upon the highest part of the temple,
6. and he said to him, if you are the son of God, throw yourself down: For it is written that the angels shall have power to protect you and with their hands they will catch you, and you will not as much as strike your foot against the stones. (Psalms 91:11-12)

7. Then Jesus said unto him, it is also written; Do not tempt the Lord your God. (Deuteronomy 6:16)

8. Again the devil led him to a very high mountain to show him all of the kingdoms of the world and their glory.

9. Then he said, I will give unto you all of this if you will fall down and continually serve me.
(John 14:30; John 16:11; Ephesians 2:2; Acts 26:18; Revelation 12:12 - *How did Satan receive this to give them? God gave it to mankind but each man has given it to Satan by committing sin - Genesis 1:26*)

10. Then Jesus said unto him, leave me Satan! For it has been written, only the Lord God Almighty shall one serve and him alone. (Deuteronomy 6:13)

11. Then the devil departed from him.

12. When Jesus had heard that John had been arrested, he went to Galilee,

13. and having left from Nazareth, he lived at Capernaum near the sea, in the regions of Zebulun and Napthali.

Verses 14 - 16 look to have been added by a scribe and not a part of the original text.

14. So that it might be fulfilled which was spoken by the prophet Isaiah, who stated;

15. In the land of Zebulun and Nepthali along the sea, beyond Jordan, Galilee of the nations

16. The people who were sitting in darkness saw a great light, and unto all who were in the region and shadow of death, light appeared to them. (Isaiah 9:1)

17. From that time Jesus began to proclaim and speak; Repent! The pledge for the kingdom of above is approaching. (Jonah 3:8-10)

18. Jesus was walking along the sea of Galilee when he saw two brothers, Simon nicknamed Peter, and his brother Andrew as they were casting nets into the sea; They were fishermen.

19. Then he said to them, come follow me and I will make you fishers of men.

20. Immediately they left their nets and followed him.

21. And going from there he saw another two men, James son of Zebedee and John his brother in the boat with their father repairing their net, and he called to them. (Luke 5:10)

22. Immediately they turned away from the boat and their father and they followed him.

23. Jesus went all around Galilee teaching in their synagogues and announcing the gospel of the kingdom. He also healed all types of sickness and diseases that the people had.

24. The news of him spread all the way to Syria: They brought the sick who had all types of diseases and torments of whom had been suffering. Even those possessed by devils, the mentally impaired and those who were paralyzed; He healed all of them!

25. Large crowds of people followed him from Galilee, Decapolis, Jerusalem and all of Judaea, and even from beyond the Jordan river.

Matthew 5

1. Seeing the crowds, Jesus went up upon a hill and he sat down there with his disciples.

2. He then opened his mouth and began to teach them and said;

3. Fortunate are those who are humble in spirit, because the kingdom of above is for these.
(1 Peter 5:5-6; James 4:6; Matthew 18:1-4)

4. Fortunate are those who are suffering, for they shall be comforted. (1 Peter 4:16-19; Hebrews 11:25)

5. Fortunate are the gentle, because they shall receive an inheritance of the land. (1 Peter 3:4)

6. Fortunate are those who hunger and thirst to be righteous, because they shall be satisfied.
(Zephaniah 2:3; Psalms 15)

7. Fortunate are those who are merciful, because they shall receive mercy.
(Matthew 6:12-15; Mark 11:25-26; Luke 6:37; Luke 17:4)

8. Fortunate are those who have a pure heart, because they shall see God.
(Philippines 4:8; Psalms 24:4; James 3:17; 1 John 3:3)

9. Fortunate are those who make peace with God, because they shall be called sons of God.
(1 John 3:1; Romans 5:1; Colossians 1:20; 2 Peter 3:14)

10. Fortunate are those who are persecuted for being righteous; The kingdom of above is for these.
(John 15:20)

11. Fortunate are you when you are hated and persecuted, and when others speak evil against you in lies because of me. (John 15:20; Luke 21:12; Romans 12:14; 1 Thess 3:4; John 16:33; Acts 14:22; Rev 1:9)

12. Be very happy and excited, because great is your reward in the heavens. For this is how the prophets were also persecuted in earlier times.

13. You are the salt of the earth; But if the salt has lost its taste, how will it again become salty? Then it is good for nothing except to be discarded, thrown to the ground and walked upon by men.

14. You are to be a light unto the world; A city is not able to become hidden when it is built upon the top of a hill.

15. No one lights a candle and places it under a basket, but they put it on a candlestick so that it will give light to all; (Psalms 18:28; Mark 4:21; Luke 11:36; Luke 8:16)

16. Shine your light in the presence of all people so that they may see your good ways and that they may glorify your Father above.

17. Do not think that I have come to destroy the law of Moses or the words of the prophets.
I have not come to take away from them but to bring the fulfillment (*completion*) of them!

18. With certainty I tell you, until the earth and the heavens are no more in existence, not the smallest part of the law of God shall pass away, not a single letter or point, until all is completed.

19. Whoever shall relax the smallest part of the precepts of God (Matthew 22:36-40) and teaches men to do so, he shall fall short (G-2807+G-2344 - *be locked out*) of the wealth of the kingdom of God.

20. I tell you the truth, if your righteousness does not surpass the righteousness of the scribes and the Pharisees, in no way will you enter into the kingdom of God.

21. In times past you have heard it said, you shall not murder, whoever commits murder is deserving of damnation;

22. But I tell you, the one who is angry with his brother without a valid cause, he shall be guilty of judgment: Whoever shall say to his brother, you are worthless, he is liable unto the Sanhedrin, but whoever shall treat his brother as though he is worthless, he shall be guilty unto the eternal fire.
(Matthew 22:40; Leviticus 19:18; Luke 10:27; Mark 12:30; 1 John 2:9-11)

23. If you bring a gift to the altar, and while you are there you remember that your brother has something against you,

24. leave your gift in front of the altar and go to first be reconciled with your brother, then come to offer your gift.

25. Settle with your adversary quickly while you are still speaking with him so that your adversary will not take you to the judge, and the judge send you to the officer to be thrown into prison.

26. Surely I tell you, in that place, you will not ever be released until you have repaid every last bit.

27. You have heard that it was said in the distant past, do not commit adultery.
(Exodus 20:14; Deuteronomy 5:18)

28. But I say unto you, anyone who looks at a woman with eyes of lust has already committed adultery with her in his heart.

29. If your right eye causes you to commit sin, tear it out and throw it from you; It is better for you to have parts of your body destroyed, than for your whole body to be cast into the eternal fire.

30. If your right hand brings you to commit sin, cut it off and throw it away from you. It is better for you to have parts of you destroyed, than for your whole body to be cast into the eternal fire.
(Matthew 18:9; Mark 9:47)

31. It has been said in past times, whoever divorces his wife, let him give her a bill of divorcement.
(Deuteronomy 24:1)

32. But I tell you that whoever divorces his wife except for a matter of fornication, does himself commit adultery. Whoever shall come unto him also commits adultery. (Matthew 19:9; 1 Corinthians 7:15)

33. Again, you have heard it said in the past, do not make a false oath, but give your oath unto the Lord.
(Leviticus 19:12; Numbers 30:2)

34. But I tell you, do not make any other oath. Do not make an oath by the heavens, because they are the throne of God; Neither by the earth, because it is his footstool; Nor by Jerusalem, because it is the city of the great king. (Isaiah 66:1; Psalms 48:2)

36. Do not make an oath by your own head, because you can not control the function of even one hair.

37. Make your words, yes when you mean yes, or no when you mean no; Anything more than that is evil.

38. You also have heard it said, an eye for an eye and a tooth for a tooth.
(Exodus 21:24; Deuteronomy 19:21, Leviticus 24:20)

39. However I tell you, do not seek vengeance for a wrong against you if the one that is against you is malicious; But if they strike you on the right cheek, turn unto him your left cheek also.

40. If anyone chooses to bring a lawsuit against you to take away your shirt, also give him your coat.

41. Whoever will pressingly ask for you to go a mile with them, go with them two miles.

42. Give to him who asks of you, and unto the one who looks to borrow, if you have the ability to give, do not refuse him.

43. You have heard it said, you shall love your neighbor and hate your enemy;

44. But I say unto you, show love unto your enemies, bless those that curse you, do good to those who hate you and pray for those who abuse you and persecute you;

45. In this, you will become the son of your Father above. (1 John 3:1) It is he who makes the sun to rise on both the good people and the evil people and he sends rain on the just and the unjust.

46. If you love only those who love you, what reward will you have? Do not do as the tax collectors do.

47. If you only welcome your brethren, what exceptional thing do you do that is different than others?

48. You must be perfect, the same as your Father above is perfect.

(1 Peter 1:16; 1 Thessalonians 3:13; Romans 6:22; 1 John 3:8; 1 John 5:18; Numbers 15:28-31)

Matthew 6

1. Be careful to not make your merciful deeds known unto other people or to be seen by them. If you do, there will be no reward for you in the heavenly realm.

2. So when you do good deeds, do not announce them as the hypocrites do, in the streets and the synagogues, that they may be honored by men. Truly, I tell you, they have already received their reward.

3. When you do good deeds, do not even let your left hand know what your right hand is doing,

4. so in this, your good and merciful deeds shall be secret, and your Father above will see in secret and he will repay you in a way that all will see.

5. When you pray, do not be as the hypocrites; They love to pray in the synagogues and openly in the streets in order that they might be seen by many people. Truly I tell you, they have received their reward.

6. But when you pray, go into your room and shut the door and pray in secret unto the Father, and he will see you in secret and will reward you openly.

7. When you pray, do not use pre-scripted words of vanity as those who do not know God use. They believe that due to their continual repetition they might be heard.

8. Do not be like them; Your Father knows what you have need for even before you ask of him.

9. When you pray, do so in this way: Our Father who is above, your name is above all others.

10. May your kingdom come and your will be accomplished here on the earth, the same as it is in the heavens.

11. May you give us today that which we have need of to eat,

12. and forgive our transgressions *(mistakes)*, as each of us also forgive the trespasses of others against us. (Numbers 15:22-29; Matthew 7:1)

13. Do not allow us to fall when temptations come, but deliver each of us from all evil. Because it is your kingdom, your power and for your glory, forever. (2 Peter 2:9)

14. For if you forgive the *(unintentional)* trespasses of others against you, your Father will also forgive your *(unintentional)* trespasses against him. (Numbers 15:28-31; Mark 11:25; Matthew 18:35)

15. But if you do not forgive others of their trespasses, your Father will not forgive you of your trespasses.

16. When you fast, do not do as the hypocrites with sadness showing in your face; They disfigure their faces to show to others that they are fasting. They have their reward.

17. But when you fast, wash your face and anoint your head with oil,

18. so not to appear unto others that you are fasting. Your Father above will see what is in secret. When he sees you in secret, he will reward you openly.

19. Do not build up treasures for yourselves here on the earth, where moth and rust cause them to decay, and where thieves break in to steal. (1 Timothy 6:9)

20. But lay up for yourselves treasures in the heavens, where moth and rust do not corrupt and where there are no thieves to break in to steal. (Luke 12:21)

21. For where your treasures are, there your heart will also be.

22. The light of the body is the eyes. If the eye is unwavering in purity, your whole body is full of light.

23. But if your eyes are wicked, all of your body is in darkness. If your light is dim, the darkness in you is very abundant.

24. No man can serve two masters. (Luke 4:8; 16:13) Either he will hate one and love the other, or he will hold strong to one and despise the other. It is not possible to serve both God and worldly gain (*unto yourself*). (James 4:3)

25. Because of this I tell you, do not be stressed out about things pertaining to this life; What to eat and drink, or for what to wear. Isn't your life much more than what you eat and drink or what you wear?

26. Look at the birds in the sky; They do not sow nor reap nor gather into barns, yet your Father who is above feeds them! Are you not more valuable unto God than they are?

27. Who by being stressed-out is able to make himself one inch taller?

28. Concerning your clothing, why should you be anxious? Consider the lilies in the meadows, how they grow, yet they do nothing laborious.

29. I tell you that even Solomon, in all of his wealth was not clothed as one of those lilies.

30. But if God clothes the lilies that are here today and in a short time are dried up in the summer heat, how much more will he clothe you? Do you lack confidence in him?

31. So then, do not be stressed nor anxious, worrying about what you will eat, or drink or wear.

32. For these things are what those who do not know God are seeking. Your Father above knows that you have need of all of these things.

33. But seek first for that which is of the kingdom of God and to be righteous before him, you will be supplied with all that you have need of. (John 14:13; John 16:24)

34. So then, do not be stressed or anxious for what you will need in the future, because tomorrow will bring its own troubles. It is meant to be that each day have its own difficulties.

Matthew 7

1. Do not condemn others, so that you will not be condemned; (Matthew 6:12)

2. In the same measure that you bring forth judgment, you will also receive judgment.

3. Why do you look at the sliver in your brother's eye while you yourself have a stick in your own eye?

4. How can you say to your brother, allow me to help you with your fault, while you yourself struggle much more than he with the same fault? (Romans 2:1)

5. You are a hypocrite! First take that stick out of your own eye, then you might be able to see to take out the splinter out of your brother's eye.

6. Do not give that which is holy unto the dogs (*those always looking to feed themselves*). Do not offer your pearls unto the pigs (2 Peter 2:22) or they will trample them over with their feet and then turn to charge at you. (Proverbs 23:9)

7. Ask and it shall be given unto you; Seek and you will find; Knock and it will be opened unto you. (Isaiah 55:6)

8. Each one who asks, receives and he who seeks, finds; The one who knocks, it shall be opened unto him.

9. What man who has a son, if he asks for bread will give him a stone;

10. Or if he asks for a fish will give him a snake?

11. If then, you who are sinners know how to give good things to your children, how much more will your Father from above give that which is good unto his children when they ask of him?

12. In the way that you would prefer to be treated by others, treat them in that very same way. For this is the way of the law of God and what the prophets spoke about. (Matthew 22:37; Mark 12:30; Luke 10:27)

13. Enter in through the narrow gate; Because wide is the gate and broad is the way that leads to destruction, yet most people will attempt to enter through it.

14. Narrow is the gate and straight is the way that leads to life, and very few there will be who find it. (John 3:32; Luke 13:23; Psalms 146:8; Psalms 147:11)

15. Beware of the false prophets (*false teachers*) that make themselves appear to be as sheep, because inwardly they are ferocious wolves; (2 Corinthians 11:13-15; 2 Peter 2:1-22; Jeremiah 14:14; Jude 1:4; Matthew 24:5-11; Jeremiah 23; Micah 3:11-12; 2 Timothy 4:3)

16. You will know them by their fruits (*their deeds*). Do men gather grapes from thorn bushes or figs from thistles?

17. Every tree that is good produces good fruit; But a corrupt tree produces corrupted fruit. (John 15:2)

18. A good tree can not produce corrupt fruit; Neither can a corrupt tree produce good fruit. (Hosea 9:16)

19. Every tree *(everyone)* that does not produce good fruit is cut down and cast into the fire; *(eternal fire)*

20. Therefore, every man shall be known by their fruit.

21. Not everyone who says to me, master! Master, will enter into the kingdom of above. Only those who do the will of the Father above. (1 John 2:17; Matthew 21:28-31; Psalms 119:1-2; Galatians 1:4; John 8:42-47; James 4:17; Luke 12:47; Romans 1:21-32; Luke 18:8)

22. On judgment day, many will say to me, master! Master! Did we not prophesy in your name, in your name cast out devils and in your name, done many mighty things? *(speaking of false Christians)*

23. And then I will declare unto them, all who continued to defy me, I do not know you. (Psalms 119:21; Proverbs 28:13; Numbers 15:30-31; Hebrews 10:26; Romans 6:16)

24. Everyone who hears my words and complies with them, he is a prudent man who builds his house upon the rock *(Christ)*. (Matthew 16:18; Psalms 119:44; 1 Corinthians 10:4)

25. When the rains come and the floodwaters arise and the winds blow *(difficulties and temptations)*, the house is strong and withstands the storm, because it is built upon the rock.

26. Everyone who hears my words and does not comply with them, they are as a foolish man who builds his house upon the sand: (John 8:21)

27. When the rains come and the flood waters arise and the winds blow against that house *(difficulties and temptations)*, that house shall not stand, but will fall *(away)* in a mighty way.

28. And when Jesus finished his teaching, the crowds were astonished at his doctrines.

29. Jesus taught them as one who holds authority, not as the scribes do.

Matthew 8

1. When Jesus came down from the hill, large crowds followed him;

2. He noticed a leper had come to worship him and said, Lord, I know that you are able to heal me, would you do so?

3. Jesus reached out his hand, touched him and said, I will; Be cleansed! Instantly he was cleansed from his leprosy!

4. Then Jesus said unto him, make sure that you do not tell anyone, but go to the priests and give the offering that is commanded by the law of Moses; This will be a testimony unto them.

5. And Jesus then went into Capernaum and a centurion *(Roman military leader)* began to desperately call out to him;

6. Lord, my son is laying in my house, paralyzed and in terrible pain.

7. Jesus said unto him, I will come to heal him.

8. The centurion said, master, I am not worthy for you to enter into my home, but if you would just say the word, I know that my boy will be healed.

9. I am a man of authority having many soldiers under me. I tell one to get something and he goes and gets it. I tell another to come and he comes, and I tell my servant to do something and he does it.

10. Hearing this, Jesus was astonished and said this: Truly I tell you, in all of Israel I have not found such great trust and dedication.

11. I tell you with certainty, that many will come from the east and from the west *(non-Jews, gentiles)* who will sit down with Abraham, Isaac and Jacob in the kingdom of above, (Hebrews 11:9)

12. but the sons of the kingdom of Israel will be cast into the outer darkness where they will be grinding their teeth and weeping in great pain *(hell)*. (Daniel 9:27; Romans 11:19-22; John 8:39-44)

13. Then Jesus said unto the centurion, Go! As you have put your trust in me, so shall it be unto you; And in that same hour he saw that his son was healed.

14. Then Jesus went to Peter's house and he saw Peter's mother in law laying down, sick with a fever;

15. He touched her hand and the fever left her and she arose to serve them.

16. When evening had come, they brought unto him a man possessed by many demons. Jesus spoke a word and all of the demons were cast out. Many people there had diverse sicknesses and he healed all who were sick.

Verse 17 was errantly added by a scribe and is not a part of the original text.

17. In this, he fulfilled that which was spoken by the prophet Isaiah when he said, he bore our infirmities and healed our weaknesses. (Isaiah 53:5; 1 Peter 2:24)

18. When Jesus saw a large gathering of people surround him, he decided to go to the other side of the lake;
19. But one scribe came near to him and said, teacher, I will follow you wherever you go.
20. Jesus said to him, the foxes have holes and the birds of the sky have roosts, but the son of man does not have a place to rest his head.
21. One of the disciples said unto him, Lord, allow me to go and bury my father.
22. But Jesus said unto him, follow me and let those who are dead (*spiritually*) bury those who have (*physically*) died without eternal hope.
23. Then Jesus entered into a boat with his disciples
24. and there came upon them a great storm that arose upon the sea. The boat began to be covered by the waves, while Jesus was sleeping.
25. One of his disciples went unto him and awoke him, crying, Lord, save us! We are about to die!
26. And Jesus said unto him, why are you afraid? Do you lack confidence in me? Then Jesus rose up and he rebuked the winds and the sea. The winds and sea began to be calm.
27. The men on the boat were shocked and said, what kind of man is this, that even the winds and the sea obey him?

In the Mark 5:1-17 and Luke 8:26-40 accounts of the following story,
the land was called Gadarenes and
it was only one man who was demon possessed.

28. Coming by sea into the land of the Gergesenes, he encountered two men who were demon possessed coming out of a graveyard. They were very violent and were preventing any man from passing by them.
29. And they called out and said, what do we have need of from you, Jesus the son of God? Have you come for the purpose to torment us?
30. In the distance there was a herd of many pigs grazing.
31. The demons began to beg Jesus that if he was going to cast them out, that he would allow them to go into the herd of pigs.
32. And Jesus said, go! And they came out and went into the herd of pigs. Immediately the herd of pigs ran off of the cliff and fell into the sea and they all died.
33. Those who were tending the pigs went into the city and told the people all of what had happened with the pigs and of the demon possessed men.
34. Immediately all who were in the city came to see Jesus and when they saw him they begged him to leave their land.

Matthew 9

1. Jesus entered into a boat and he went to his home city.
2. He noticed that they were bringing him a paralyzed man who was laid out on a bed and he also saw that they had belief in him; So Jesus said to the paralyzed man, be comforted, your sins are forgiven. (Luke 5:20; John 5:14; John 8:11; Mark 2:5; Luke 7:48)
3. Then some of the scribes spoke among themselves saying, this man is speaking blasphemy.
4. Jesus, knowing their thoughts said unto them; Why do you have evil in your hearts?
5. Is it easier to say that your sins are forgiven of you or to say rise up and walk?
6. So now you know that I hold the power to forgive sins. (Romans 6:1-23) Then Jesus said to the paralyzed man, rise up, take your bed and walk back to your home.
7. Then the man got up and walked to his home.
8. But when the gathering of people saw this, they were greatly amazed and they glorified God for giving so great a miracle unto him.
9. As Jesus passed by, he saw a man sitting at the tax office named Matthew. He said unto him, follow me! Then Matthew got up and followed him.

10. It came to be that Jesus was invited to his home where he could relax and have a meal; There were many tax collectors and sinners in that place sitting with Jesus and his disciples.

11. The Pharisees said to his disciples, why does your teacher eat with tax collectors and with sinners?

12. Jesus overheard them and replied; The healthy do not need to be healed, but those who are sick are in need of being healed.

13. Now understand that this means, I would rather for you to be obedient than for you to make a sacrifice; (1 Samuel 15:22, Micah 6:6-8; Proverbs 21:3; Matthew 12:7; Hebrews 10:5) I did not come to call the righteous ones unto repentance, but the unrighteous. (Hosea 6:6; Proverbs 21:3)

14. Then the disciples of John the Baptizer came unto him and asked, why is it that both we and the Pharisees are often fasting, yet your disciples do not fast?

15. And Jesus replied, why would the children of the bridal party mourn while the bridegroom is still there with them? The day will come when the bridegroom will be taken from them, then they will fast.

16. No one puts a new patch on an old piece of clothing, because it would take away from the strength of the clothing and a worse rip will happen.

17. Men do not put new wine into old wineskins, because the old wineskins, being reused will weaken and break and the new wine will be spilled. But men put new wine into fresh wineskins and they are well preserved together.

18. As Jesus was speaking, a powerful ruler entered into the house and he worshipped Jesus; Then he said, my daughter has just died. Please come and lay your hands upon her so that she might live again!

19. Then Jesus arose and his disciples followed him. (Luke 8:42)

20. Then a woman who had a bloody wound for over twelve years came up behind him and touched the fringe of his robe;

21. She had said in her heart, if I am able to touch his robe I will be cured!

22. Jesus then turned to see her and said, be comforted daughter, your conviction has cured you. And the woman was healed in that moment. (Hebrews 11:1)

23. Then Jesus entered into the house of the powerful ruler and he saw a flute player and a group of people that were in chaos and greatly disturbed.

24. Jesus said unto them, get yourselves out of there for the girl is not dead, but is sleeping. They laughed and scoffed at him.

25. When the people were made to leave, he entered the room of the girl and took her hand; The little girl awoke!

26. This news was spread throughout all of the land.

27. Then, as Jesus was leaving that place, two blind men followed after him and cried out saying, have pity on us son of David. (Psalms 22:24)

28. As he came into the house, they came close to him and Jesus said to them, do you believe that I am able to heal you? And they said, yes Lord.

29. Then he touched their eyes and said, according to your dedication and trust in me, may it be unto you.

30. And their eyes were opened. Then Jesus said, do not tell anyone of this.

31. But when they left, they told everyone they came across.

32. As they left the house, there was a man who could not speak, being possessed by a demon.

33. When the demon was cast out, the man was able to speak again. The crowds were in awe and they said, never has anything like this been seen at any time anywhere in Israel.

34. The Pharisees said, he casts out demons by the power of the prince of demons.
(Luke 11:15; Mark 3:22)

35. Jesus went into all of the cities and villages, teaching in their synagogues and announcing the gospel of the kingdom. He healed all types of sickness and injuries that existed among the people.

36. Seeing the large crowds, he was moved with pity because they were worn down and tired, like sheep without a shepherd. (Zechariah 11:17; Ezekiel 34:5; 2 Chronicles 18:16-18)

37. Then he said unto his disciples, the harvest surely is abundant but the workers are so very few.

38. Pray that the Lord of the harvest might send more workers to assist his harvest. (Revelation 14:16; John 4:35; Luke 10:2; Mark 4:29)

Matthew 10

1. Then Jesus called his twelve disciples to him and he gave unto them authority over unclean spirits and to cast them out, and to heal every disease and infirmity.
2. The names of the twelve Apostles are: Simon who is nicknamed Peter and Andrew his brother; James and John, the sons of Zebedee;
3. Philip and Bartholomew, Thomas and Matthew the tax collector; James the son of Alphaeus and Labbaeus who was called Thaddeus; (Luke 6:15; Acts 1:13)
4. Simon the Canaanite and Judas Iscariot, the one who betrayed him. (Mark 3:16-19)

In the Luke 6:15 and Acts 1:13 the names of the disciples differ
from the account given here in Matthew (circa - 37 AD)
and in Mark (circa - 56 AD).
It must be noted that the Luke and Acts accounts were written many years later
by second and third hand testimonies (circa - 110 AD) and look to be in error.

5. These twelve were sent out by Jesus, commanding them to not go unto the gentile nations nor unto the cities of the Samaritans at this time.
6. But go only unto the lost sheep of the house of Israel; (Amos 5:4)
7. Go and announce, the pledge for the kingdom of above is approaching. (Matthew 3:2)
8. Go and heal those who are sick, cleanse the lepers, raise those who are spiritually dead and cast out demons. Freely give unto others that which you have freely received.
9. Do not take any money nor a travel bag with you.
10. Do not take two coats nor shoes with you nor a staff, because the worker is deserving of what he has need of.
11. And whatever city or town you enter into, seek out one who is open to this message and remain at his home until you leave that city. (Hebrews 13:2)
12. When you enter into a house, feel welcome there.
13. If this household truly is deserving, feel at peace and get your rest there. But if you find that it is not deserving, do not feel at peace and do not rest at that place.
14. Whoever does not receive you nor hear the message that you bring, leave that house. When you leave that city, shake off the dust from your feet as you leave that place. (Luke 9:5; Mark 6:11; Acts 13:51)
15. Truly I tell you, it will be more tolerable for the cities of Sodom and Gommorah on the day of judgment than for that city.
16. Be aware, because I send you out as sheep in the midst of wolves; So be as cautious as a predator and as harmless as a dove.
17. Beware of the people, because they will betray you; Some will turn you over to the Sanhedrin and you will be taken unto their courts and you will be scourged in their holding places.

Verses 18-22 are out of context in this place and look to have been taken from Matthew 24:8-9
and errantly put in this place by a scribe. They are not a part of the original Matthew 10 text;
They are nearly word for word to the parallel accounts of Mark 13:11-13 and Luke 21:12-19.
In this book they have been restored to their proper placement.

23. But when they persecute you in one city, leave that place and go to another city. You will not have gone to every city in Israel by the time the son of man has completed his purpose.
24. The disciple is not above his teacher, nor a servant above his lord.
25. It shall be that the disciple shall be as his teacher and the servant as his master. (1 John 3:3) If they have called the master of the house Beelzebub (*a devil*) how much worse shall they call those that are of his household? (1 Peter 2:21; Luke 6:40)
26. Do not be afraid of them; Because there is nothing that can be hidden of which will not be made known and all that is done in private shall be seen by all.
27. That which I now speak that is obscure, you will explain clearly unto others. What you hear from me, announce it from the housetops.

28. Do not be afraid of those who can kill your body but not harm your soul; Fear the one who can destroy both your body and soul and throw them into the eternal fire. (Psalms 2:11-12; Philippines 2:12)

29. Are two small birds not sold for a small amount of money? Yet one does not fall out of the nest without my Father knowing about it.

30. Likewise, the number of hairs on your head are all counted.

31. So do not be afraid, because you are much more valuable than many little birds.

32. Whoever shall rise up and remain in covenant with me while still living in this life, I will acknowledge unto my Father who is above.

33. But whoever defies me and contradicts my instructions while alive in this life, they will be rejected by my Father who is above. (Hebrews 10:26; Numbers 15:30-31; 1 Samuel 15:23; 1 John 5:16-17)

34. Do not think that I have come to make peace on earth. I have not come to bring peace, but a sword!

35. I have come to divide a man against his father, daughter against her mother and a wife against her mother in law; (Psalms 27:10)

36. To make a man's enemies to be of his own family. (Micah 7:6)

37. He who loves his father or mother more than he loves me, he is not suitable unto me. He who loves his son or daughter more that he loves me, he is not deserving of me.

38. He that does not take up and carry his own cross to follow after me, he is not deserving of me.

39. He that works to establish his life in this world shall lose it; But he who surrenders the good in this life for my name sake, he shall find life (*eternal*).

40. He who receives you receives me and he who receives me receives the one who sent me. (1 John 2:23)

41. He who accepts the words of a prophecy that is come from a true prophet, he shall receive benefit from that prophet. *(Example: Nineveh accepted the words from Jonah and received the benefit, not destroyed.)* He who becomes righteous in the name of the righteous one (*Christ*) will receive the benefit of being a righteous man.

42. Whoever drinks one small cupful concerning these things and becomes a disciple (*of Christ*), truly I tell you, he will not lose what he has gained. (John 4:36)

Matthew 11

1. When Jesus finished instructing his twelve disciples, they went to teach in their designated cities.

2. When John the baptizer was in prison, he heard of the things that Christ had done, so he sent two of his disciples to ask of him;

3. Are you he that was to come or shall we continue to look for another?

4. And Jesus said unto them, go and tell John what you have seen and have heard.

5. The blind receive their sight and the lame ones now walk; The lepers are cleansed and the deaf can now hear; The dead have been raised and the distressed ones are given the good news;

6. Blessed is he who is not offended by my words. (Luke 7:23)

7. Then as they left, Jesus spoke to the crowd about John the baptizer, and he said: What did you go into the desert to see? Certainly, a reed shaken by the wind.

8. What did you go there to see? Not a man wearing soft clothing! Truly those who wear soft clothing are those who live in the house of the king.

9. But what did you go there to see? A prophet? Yes, but I tell you, John is much greater than a prophet.

10. For he is of whom it has been written: "Come and see, I send out my messenger to confront you and he shall prepare the way before the Lord." (Malachi 3:1: Isaiah 40:3; John 1:21-23)

11. Surely I tell you, of all who have been born of a woman, none have arisen to be greater than John the Baptizer; Yet the least in the kingdom of above is greater than he!

12. From the days that John began to preach until today, the kingdom of above has been violently treated and the powerful have kept it from you. (*this remains true today*)

13. The prophets and the Jewish law prophesied of John,

14. and if you can receive truth, he is the one prophesied of by Isaiah; He is the one that he said would come. (Isaiah 40:3; John 1:21)

15. Let the ones who have ears, allow them to hear.

16. What shall I compare this present nation (*of Israel*) to? It is like a group of children at the town square, sitting and calling unto their friends and saying;

17. We have played music for you, but you did not dance. We have cried for you, but you have not taken it to heart.

18. John did not come to take in unto himself, yet you say that he is demon possessed!

19. If the son of man came eating and drinking and taking unto himself, they would say that he is a gluttonous drunkard, a friend of tax collectors and of sinners. A man's understanding is shown by what he produces (*says and does*).

20. Then he began to speak against the cities in which many of his powerful miracles had been done, because they had not turned from their evil ways.

21. He said, Woe to you Chorazin! Woe to you Bethsaida! If the powerful miracles that happened in you had been done in Tyre and in Sidon, they would have turned from their evil ways long ago and repented in great mourning for the great evils that they had committed.

22. It will be more tolerable for Sidon and Tyre on the day of judgment than it will be for you!

23. And you, Capernaum, you being so powerful and wealthy, exalted into the heavens; Yet you shall be brought down to hell! Because if the miracles and great wonders done in you had been done in Sodom, it would still be here today. (Isaiah 12:13-15)

24. I tell you with certainty, for those in the land of Sodom it will be more tolerable on the day of judgment than for you.

25. Then Jesus looked upward and said, I thank you Father, Lord of the heavens and the earth, because you have hidden these things from the cunning but have revealed them to the simple and uneducated.

26. Yes, oh Father, this is pleasing unto you.

27. All things were given to me by my Father and no one fully knows the son but the Father; No one fully knows the Father but the son and those who the son is willing to reveal him to.

28. Come to me, all who are tired and carrying great burdens; I will give you rest.

29. Take my yoke upon you and learn from me, I am gentle and humble in my heart. You will find peace in your spirit.

30. What you are obligated to is useful and the necessary services you will be required of is light.

Matthew 12

1. Jesus went on the Sabbath day and walked through the grain fields and his disciples were hungry, so they began to pick some of the grain heads and eat them.

2. Some of the Pharisees saw them and said unto him, look! Your disciples are doing that which is not lawful for them to do on the Sabbath day.

3. But Jesus said unto them, have you not read what David and those with him did when they were hungry?

4. How he went into the house of God and he ate the bread that was offered which is not lawful for them to eat, but only for the priests? (1 Samuel 21:6) Have you not read that even the priests in the temple desecrate the Sabbath, yet they are guiltless?

6. I say to you, one who is much greater than the temple is now here.

7. If you would have understood this scripture, "I would rather your obedience than for you to make a sacrifice", you would not have condemned the guiltless.
(1 Samuel 15:22; Hosea 6:6; Proverbs 21:3; Micah 6:8; Matthew 9:13; Hebrews 10:5)

8. For the son of man is also the Lord over the Sabbath day.

9. When he left that place he went unto their synagogue.

10. There was a man there with a crippled hand and they then asked him, is it lawful to heal on the Sabbath? Their purpose was to accuse him of breaking the law, no matter how he might answer.

11. Then Jesus replied to them, which one of you men that have sheep, if one was to fall into a hole on the Sabbath would not go and pull it out?

12. How much more important is a man than a sheep! It is lawful to do good deeds on the Sabbath.

13. Then he said to the man, reach out your hand; And when he extended forth his hand it was healed, as good as his other hand.

14. But the Pharisees gathered together and held a council against him, looking for a way to destroy him.

15. Jesus, knowing all things, left that place. Many people followed him and he healed all who had need.

Verses 16 - 21 were errantly added by a scribe and are not a part of the original text.
In Christ there was no fulfillment of the Isaiah 42:1-4 prophecy.
The prophecy states that he would bring judgment unto the gentiles, however Christ did not bring judgment unto the gentiles, but he did bring salvation unto the gentiles.
The scripture states that he would not cry out nor have his voice heard in the streets;
However, Jesus himself said that his voice was heard in the streets.
(Luke 13:26; John 18:20; Luke 4:14-21, 37; Luke 7:17; Isaiah 42:13; Mark 6:14)
Additionally, Matthew 14:1 & Mark 1:28 contradict the claim that Jesus was to be unknown,
though he did choose for a time for it to remain a secret that he is the Christ. (John 7:26)
Therefore, the claim that the Isaiah 42 prophecy was fulfilled in Christ is an error.
Isaiah 42:1-4 speak of a future prophet & Isaiah 42:13-18 speak of the return of Jesus Christ.
For these reasons, these verses have been excluded.

22. Then a man was brought unto Jesus who was possessed by demons; He was blind and could not speak. Jesus healed him so that he could again speak and see.

23. The crowds were amazed and they asked, how could this not be the prophesied son of David?

24. But the Pharisees that overheard those in the crowd said, this man does not cast out demons but through Beelzebub, the ruler of demons.

25. Jesus knew what they were thinking and said unto them, every kingdom that is divided shall be brought to ruin. Every city or house that is divided against itself will fall.

26. If Satan was to cast out his own demons that he has sent, would he not be divided against himself! If that is the case, then how can his kingdom exist?

27. And if I, by the power of Beelzebub cast out demons, by whom do your sons cast them out? Let them judge you! *(their sons do not cast out demons)*

28. If I cast out the demons by the spirit of God, know that the power of God has come down upon you.

29. How can a thief enter into the house of one that is strong in an attempt to steal from him, if he does not first tie up the strong man?

30. All who are not in compliance with me are against me. All who do not do as I instruct, pierce me and work against me.

31. I tell you this, that every sin and blasphemy that a man might commit can be forgiven, except if a man blaspheme the holy spirit, it can never be forgiven, not in this life or the next.
(Ephesians 4:31-32; Numbers 15:30; 1 John 5:16-17; 1 Samuel 15:23; Hebrews 10:26-29; Acts 3:17)

32. Whoever takes action against what is taught by the son of man it can be forgiven of him. But whoever blasphemes the holy spirit of God, it can in no way be forgiven of him, not in this life nor in the eternal life. (Isaiah 63:10; Numbers 15:28-31; 1 Samuel 15:22-23; 1 John 5:16-17; Hebrews 10:26-27; Hebrews 6:4-9; 1 John 3:9; Romans 6:1-2; Ezekiel 33)
(you must not choose to defy God, not even one time after coming into covenant with him - Acts 2:38).

33. You will make your tree good and its fruit will be good or you will make your tree corrupt and the fruit thereof will be corrupt. A tree is known by the fruit that it produces. (Matthew 7:18; John 15:2)

34. You Pharisees are the offspring of vipers! How can you who are corrupt speak that which is honest? (Matthew 23) It is by the overflowing of what is in the heart that brings the mouth to speak.

35. A good man has good treasure in his heart, from which he brings forth that which is good; But a corrupt man, due to the evil that is in his heart brings forth that which is corrupt and evil. (Romans 6:16)

36. But I tell you, that every instruction that I speak unto mankind that goes inactive in you, you will need to give an account for it on the day of judgment.

37. Because by my words each man will be justified, but by my words you will be condemned.

38. Then some of the scribes and Pharisees asked, teacher, may we see a sign from you?

39. Jesus answered and said, a nation that is evil and adulterous demands to see a sign, but there shall be no sign given unto you, except for the sign of Jonah the prophet.

Jesus died on Wednesday afternoon before the Passover Sabbath, Thursday
and he was raised before daybreak on the first day of the week, Sunday.
This is not taught in the churches who honor Good Friday and Easter Monday,
of which are pagan holy days, and only allow 2 days for Jesus to be in the grave.

40. Just as Jonah was in the belly of a whale for three days and three nights, so also will the son of man spend three days and three nights in the heart of the earth. (Jonah 1:17)

41. The men of Nineveh shall rise up in judgment against this generation and will condemn it, because they repented at the correction given by Jonah. Today there is one much greater than Jonah among you.

42. The queen of the south will also rise up in judgment against this generation and will condemn it; She came from the outermost part of the earth to hear the wisdom of Solomon. Take notice, one who is greater than Solomon is now here!

43. When an unclean spirit goes out of a man, it travels through dry places longing for a new home, but when he does not find it,

44. it chooses to try to return to its old house from which it was taken out of. When it returns, it finds him empty, having been cleansed and he is very attractive. (John 8:34-37)

45. Then it goes and finds seven other spirits that are more evil than itself and they enter in to make him their home. Then, the latter is then much worse than at first. (2 Peter 2:20-22) It will also be the same with this evil nation!

46. While Jesus was still speaking, his mother and his brothers awaited in the distance to speak to him;

47. Then someone said unto him, your mother and your brothers are waiting to speak to you. (Mark 3:32) *(likely to tell him that the husband of Marry, their father Joseph had died - Matthew 14:13)*

48. He answered and said unto them, who is my mother and who are my brothers?

49. Then he stretched forth his hands unto his disciples and he said, look and see, these are my family;

50. Whoever does the will of my Father above, it is these who are my family. (Matthew 7:21)

Matthew 13

1. That same day, Jesus came out from a house and he went to sit by the sea. (Matthew 14:13)

2. A large crowd began to gather around him, so Jesus went up into a boat and sat down and all of the people on the shore stood there nearby.

3. Jesus spoke to them in many parables and he said; A sower went out to plant. (John 15:2; Mark 5:3)

4. While he spread the seed, some fell along the roadway and birds came and ate all of those seeds.

5. Some seeds fell upon the rocky ground where there was very little soil and they grew up quickly ,

6. but because it did not have proper roots in the soil, when the sun beat down was scorched and dried up.

7. Some seed fell near thorn bushes, but the thorn bushes grew and choked them out and they died.

8. Some fell upon good ground and they grew up and produced good fruit, some a hundred, some sixty and some thirty.

9. He who has an ear, allow him to hear. (Isaiah 43:8)

10. Then the disciples came near and asked, why do you speak in parables?

11. And Jesus answered them and said, it is for you to know the mysteries of the kingdom of above, but unto others it has not been given for them to know;

12. Because whoever holds the truth within him, unto him more understanding will be given; But to he who does not have, what little he does have will be taken away from him.

13. This is why I speak in parables, because they see but do not perceive; And though they hear my words, they do not understand.

Verses 14-15 look to have been added by a scribe and not a part of the original text.

14. This is the fulfillment of the prophecy spoken by Isaiah which says: "Though they hear, they will not understand, and though they will see, they will not perceive.

15. Because the hearts of the people have grown pompous, their ears have grown dull and their eyes are now closed. They can not see with their eyes nor hear with their ears. If they did understand with their heart, they would be converted and I would heal them." (Isaiah 6:9-10)

16. But you are blessed, because with your eyes you can perceive and with your ears you can hear.

17. But I speak the truth unto you; Many prophets and righteous men have wanted to see what you now see and hear what you are hearing;

18. I will now further explain the parable of the sower unto you.

19. Anyone who hears the message of the kingdom and does not understand it, the evil one takes away that

which would have been planted in his heart. This is the seed that had fallen along the roadway.

20. The seed that had fallen upon rocky ground, they are those who hear the message and receive it with great joy,

21. but they have no roots and are temporary, because when difficulty or persecution come upon them because of the message, they stumble and fall. (Hebrews 6:4-6; 2 Timothy 2:23)

22. The seed that is fallen near thorn bushes are those who hear the message, but the anxieties of this world and the deceit of wealth choke that which was planted and they become unfruitful. (1 Timothy 6:9)

23. But the seed that fell upon good ground, these are they who hear the message and understand it; They grow to bring forth good fruit, some a hundred, some sixty and some thirty.

24. Jesus then brought forth another parable unto the people; He said, the kingdom of above resembles a man who plants good wheat seed in his field.

25. Then while he was resting, an enemy came and dropped weed seeds among the good seed and then left.

26. When the wheat had sprung up, the weeds also began to appear.

27. Then the servants of the owner of that field came unto him and said, master didn't you plant good seed in your field? Where have all of these weeds come from?

28. And he said unto them, an enemy did this! The servants then asked him, shall we go out and gather the weeds up?

29. Then the master replied, no, because in gathering up the weeds, you will uproot the wheat also.

30. Allow both to grow together until the harvest; (Revelation 14:14-20) and at the time of the harvest I will say to the harvesters, first gather up the weeds and tie them in bundles in order to burn them. Then I will gather the wheat and put it in my barn. (*analogy to the second coming of Christ - no pretribulation rapture*)

31. And Jesus told them another parable and he said, the kingdom of above is like a grain of mustard seed which a man took and planted in his field;

32. Surely it is the smallest of all seeds but when it grows it becomes a large tree and the birds of the sky come to rest in its branches.

33. Then he gave another parable: The kingdom of above is like yeast that a woman took and mixed with three scoops of flour and let it sit until all of it was raised.

Verses 34-35 look to have been added by a scribe and not a part of the original text.

34. Jesus spoke all of these things in parables unto the people and he did not speak unto them in any other way than in parables.

35. This is the fulfillment of the prophecy which says: I will speak parables from my mouth and I will speak of things that have been secret from the beginning of the world. (Psalms 78:2)

36. Then Jesus sent the people away and went into a house and the disciples came unto him and asked; Will you explain to us the parable of the weeds.

37. Jesus said unto them, he who plants the good seed is the son of man (*Christ*); The field is the world;

38. The good seed are the children of the (*eternal*) kingdom; The weeds are the children of the evil one;

39. The enemy who planted them is the devil (*Satan*). The harvest is the end of this world and the harvesters are the messengers of God.

40. The way that the weeds are gathered and burned in the fire, it will be the same at the end of the world.

41. The son of man will send forth his messengers and they will gather together all who have gone against him and all who do not obey his law; (Matthew 22:37-40)

42. And he will cast them into the eternal fire, where there will be wailing and the grinding of their teeth due to the great pain. (Psalms 112:10)

43. At that time, those who are righteous will shine forth like the sun in the kingdom of their Father. He who has ears, allow him to hear. (Daniel 12:3)

44. Again, the kingdom of above is like a treasure that is hidden in a field. When a man finds a small part of it, he joyfully goes and sells all that he has and buys that field.

45. The kingdom of above is again like a merchant who is looking for pearls of great quality.

46. And when he finds one of great value he sells all that he has so that he could buy it.

47. The kingdom of above is much like a fisherman's net that is cast into the sea. When it is drawn up, it has in it many different kinds of fish.

48. When it is full, it is taken to shore. Then they sit down and gather the good into bins, but the unwanted are discarded.

49. It will be done in this way at the end of the world. The messengers will come forth and take the corrupt away from the righteous, (*This is evidence against a pre-tribulation rapture*)

50. and they shall be thrown into the eternal fire where there will be wailing and grinding of their teeth because of the great pain.

51. Then Jesus asked them, did you understand all of these things that I spoke unto you? And they all answered, yes Lord.

52. Because of this, all of you who write so to instruct others how to enter into the kingdom of above, are like the master of a house who opens up his wealth unto others. (John 17:20)

53. When Jesus finished giving these parables, he left that place

54. and he went into his hometown and he taught them in their synagogue. They said in astonishment, from where did he gain this wisdom and power?

55. Is this not the son of Joseph the carpenter? Is his mother not Miriam and his brothers James, Simon, Joseph and Judas? (John 14:22; Jude 1:1)

56. And his sisters, are they not all with us? So from where could he have gained all of this knowledge?

57. They were offended and did not believe in him. But Jesus told them, a prophet is not disrespected, except in his hometown and by his own family.

58. Jesus did very few miracles there because of their unbelief.

Matthew 14

1. At that time, Herod, a powerful ruler, he had heard of the fame of Jesus,

2. so he said unto his servants, this must be John the baptizer; He must have been raised from the dead! Look at the mighty things that he has the power to do!

3. Previously Herod had arrested John and threw him into prison to please Herodias, the wife of his brother Philip.

4. He did so because John had said that it is not lawful for him to have her for himself.

5. So Herod wanted to kill him but he feared the crowd who thought of John as a prophet.

6. But on his birthday, at a dinner that he held, the daughter of Herodias danced for them, pleasing Herod.

7. Herod then swore an oath, to give unto her whatever she might ask for.

8. The young girl was pressured by her mother to say, give me the head of John the baptizer on a platter.

9. The king was greatly distressed, but because of his oath and the witnesses that were there, he gave the order for it to be done.

10. Those that he sent beheaded John in the prison.

11. His head was then brought on a platter and was given to the girl, and she brought it to her mother.

12. The disciples of John then came and took his body and buried it, then they came and told Jesus.

13. When Jesus heard the news, he wanted to be by himself and planned to take a boat to a deserted place. When the people heard this, they followed after him walking out of the city. (*Jesus also wanted to be alone after his brothers and mother came to see him* - Matthew 12:47-13:1)

14. As he was leaving, Jesus saw the large crowd and he had pity on them, so he healed all who were sick.

15. In the evening the disciples came to him and said, this is a desolate place and the day is now over. Dismiss the crowd so that they can go and buy provisions for themselves.

16. But Jesus said unto them, they have no need to go away, give unto them so that they can eat.

17. They answered and said, we have only five loaves of bread and two fish!

18. Then Jesus said, bring them to me.

19. Then he commanded the people to sit down on the grass, and he took the five loaves and two fish and he looked up to the heavens and he blessed the food; Then he divided it and gave the bread to his disciples and the disciples gave unto the people.

20. Everyone ate and was filled: Then they gathered up the leftovers and there were twelve baskets full remaining.

21. The number of men that had eaten were about five thousand, plus their women and children!

22. Then Jesus immediately compelled his disciples to get into a boat and to go without him to the other side while he sent the people home.

23. When he had sent the people away, he went up on a hill to pray. When the evening came, he was alone.

24. Later, the boat was in the middle of the sea, being tossed by the waves. The wind was against them.

25. In the latter part of the night Jesus came unto them, walking upon the water.

26. When the disciples saw him walking upon the sea, they were troubled and said, it is a phantom! Out of fear they cried out!

27. But then Jesus spoke to them and said, be comforted, it is I, do not fear.

28. Then Peter said unto him, Lord, if it is you, allow me to walk on the waters and come to you.

29. And Jesus said, come! When Peter came down from the boat, he walked on the water and began to walk to Jesus!

30. But when he noticed that the wind was strong, he began to sink and he cried out, Lord help me!

31. Immediately Jesus stretched out his hand and took a hold of him and said, you lacked confidence, why did you doubt?

32. When they came into the ship, the wind stopped.

33. All that were in the ship worshipped him.

34. When they came to shore, they entered the land of Gennesaret.

35. When the people of that country came to know that Jesus was there, they gathered all of those from their whole country that needed healing and brought them to him.

36. They begged that they might only touch the fringes of his clothing; All who touched his clothing were healed!

Matthew 15

1. There was a time when the scribes and the Pharisees from Jerusalem came to Jesus and asked him;

2. Why do your disciples violate the traditions of the elders? They do not wash their hands before they eat.

3. Then Jesus said unto them, why do you violate the precepts of God through your traditions?

4. God commanded, revere (*hold as precious, have value for*) your father and your mother, and he who curses his father or mother, let him be put to death. (Exodus 20:12; 21:17)

5. But you say, anything that you might gain from me is a gift; (*nothing is to be expected of me*)

6. However, a man does not bring honor unto his father and mother in this way. By this, you have annulled the commandment of God through your traditions.

7. You are hypocrites! To be honest, Isaiah did prophesy of you when he said,

8. "These people come unto me with their mouth and with their lips they honor me, but they push me away in their hearts.

9. In vain they worship me, teaching as doctrines the ordinances of men." (Isaiah 29:13 – *parallel to today*)

10. Then Jesus called the crowd to come near to him and he said, hear and understand:

11. It is not what enters the mouth of a man that defiles him, but it is that which comes forth out of a man that defiles the man. (Matthew 12:34-35; Romans 14:2; 1 Corinthians 8:7-13)

12. Then the disciples came unto him and asked him; Do you know that the Pharisees that heard what you said were offended?

13. Then Jesus answered and said, every plant that my Father from above has not planted shall be uprooted.

14. Have nothing to do with them! They are blind leaders of the blind; If the blind lead the blind, both will fall into the abyss (*hell*). (2 Corinthians 6:14-18)

15. Then Peter asked him, will you explain this parable?

16. Then Jesus said, are you really that unintelligent Peter?

17. Do you not understand that everything that enters through the mouth enters the stomach and is expelled into the privy?

18. But that which a man produces (*says/does*) is brought forth from the heart and that is what defiles a man! (Galatians 5:19-21)

19. Because from out of the heart is where such evil things come from: Planning to do evil, murder, adultery, fornication, theft, speaking lies and blasphemy. (Numbers 15:30-31- *premeditated sin*)

20. These are the things that defile a man but to eat with unwashed hands does not defile a man.

21. Then Jesus left that place and went to Tyre and Sidon.

22. A Canaanite woman who lived near the border of her country cried out unto him and said, have pity on me master, son of David. My daughter is badly demon possessed.

23. But Jesus did not say a word unto her. Then his disciples requested that he send her away, because in the past she yelled evil things at them.

24. Jesus said unto her, I was only sent unto the lost sheep out of the house of Israel.

25. Then she came and worshipped him at his feet and said; Lord, please help me!

26. Jesus answered and said, it is not good to take the bread of the children and throw it to the dogs.

27. She replied, this is true, but even the dogs eat the crumbs that fall off of the table of their masters!

28. Then Jesus said unto her, oh woman, you have strong convictions. Then he said, may it be as you desire. Then he went and healed her daughter.

29. After this, Jesus left that place and went to the sea of Galilee and went up on a hill and sat down.

30. Many people began to gather together and they brought the lame, blind, dumb, maimed and many others to him and they dropped them before the feet of Jesus and he healed them all!

31. The crowds were amazed when they saw the dumb ones speak, and the maimed ones made whole, and the lame ones walk and those who were blind that could now see! They glorified the God of Israel.

32. Jesus called the disciples toward himself and said, I am full of pity for these people, because for three days they have been with me without any food. I do not want to send them away hungry, or they might get weak along the way.

33. Then the disciples said to him, from where in this desert can we find enough bread to feed this large gathering of people?

34. And Jesus asked them, how many loaves do you have? And they said, seven loaves and a small fish.

35. And he told the people to sit on the ground.

36. Then he took the seven loaves and the fish and he gave thanks and he broke it and gave it to the disciples to distribute it unto the people.

37. All of the people ate and were filled. Then they took up that which was left over and there were seven baskets full.

38. The number of the people that ate were four thousand men, along with their women and children.

39. Then he sent them away and got into a boat and went unto the land of Megdala.

Matthew 16

1. When Jesus arrived there, the Pharisees and the Sadducees approached to tempt him. They asked for him to show them a sign in the heavens.

2. Jesus said, nightfall is approaching and you might say it is a fair sky. The sky will become reddened and the reddening is because the sky will become cloudy; In the morning there will be a storm with rain.

3. You are hypocrites; You understand how to discern the weather by the appearance of the sky, but you are not able to discern who I am by the miracles I do?

4. Only an adulterous and wicked people seek a sign, but a sign will not be given except for the sign of Jonah the prophet. Then Jesus turned and he walked away from them. (Jonah 1:17; Matthew 12:40)

5. Jesus said unto the disciples, take notice and beware of the leaven of the Pharisees and Sadducees.

6. When the disciples caught up with him, they realized that they had forgotten the food.

7. Then they asked each other, did he say this because we did not bring the food?

8. When Jesus noticed this he said unto them, why are you distressed, in that you did not bring the food? Do you still have no confidence in me?

9. Do you not remember the five loaves and the five thousand people? How many baskets of food was left over?

10. Do you not also remember the seven loaves and the four thousand people? How many baskets of leftovers were there after that?

11. How is it that you do not understand the meaning when I said unto you, beware of the leaven of the Pharisees and Sadducees?

12. Then they knew that Jesus did not speak of the leaven of bread, but of the teachings of the Pharisees and Sadducees. (1 Corinthians 11:18-34; John 6:27-60; Luke 14:15)

13. Then Jesus went unto a part of Caesarea near Philippos and he asked the disciples; Who do the people say that I am?

14. They said, some say that you are John the baptizer; Others say Elijah, Jeremiah or one of the other prophets.

15. Jesus replied and said, who do you say that I am?

16. Simon Peter said, you are the Christ, son of the living God.

17. Jesus answered and said unto him, you are fortunate Simon son of Jonah, because no one of flesh and blood told you this, but the Father who is above made you understand this. (1 Corinthians 2:11)

18. Then Jesus said, you (*Simon*) are petros (*a small piece of stone*). It is upon this bedrock that I will construct my people, and doors of temptation will not deceive them. (1 Corinthians 10:4; Matthew 21:44)

19. I will give you (*plural, my people*) the keys of the eternal kingdom (*the holy spirit*) (Ezekiel 36:27). Whatever temptations my people overcome on the earth shall surely be defeated in the eternal kingdom; But whatever temptations ensnare them on the earth shall surely keep them enslaved in the eternal kingdom. (John 20:23; Matthew 18:18)

20. Then Jesus told his disciples that they should not yet announce to anyone that he is the Christ.

21. At this time Jesus began to explain to his disciples that it is necessary for him to go to Jerusalem and suffer many things because of the elders, chief priests and scribes, and that he would be killed, but on the third day he would be raised.

22. But Peter took Jesus close to him and began to admonish him saying, you need to be cheerful Lord; You shall in no way suffer like this!

23. But Jesus then turned and said; Get away from me Satan! (Luke 4:8) You bring temptation for me to stumble and fall, because you do not set your mind upon the things of God but on that of men. (verse 18)

24. Then Jesus said unto his disciples, if anyone will come unto me, he must deny himself, take up his own cross and follow me. (Luke 14:27; Mark 8:34; 2 Timothy 1:9)

25. Whoever lives for the cares of this world, he will lose his life eternally; But he that offers up the cares of this life on my account, he will obtain life everlasting.

26. What benefit is it for anyone to gain the whole world but forfeit the eternal life? What will a man exchange for his own soul?

27. I shall return with the angels, having great power and the honor of the Father; I will give recompense unto each man for what he deserves, according to the deeds that he had committed in this life. (Hebrews 10:31; Psalms 62:12; Romans 2:6-11; Revelation 20:13)

28. Surely I tell you, there are many here in this place that will not experience death until they see the son of man establish his kingdom. (Acts 1:2-2:47)

Matthew 17

1. Six days later, Jesus took Peter, James and his brother John up on the top of a high mountain to be in private.

2. While there, Jesus was physically changed in their presence and his face shined as the sun; His clothes were as bright white as a light. (Matthew 28:3)

3. Know this, Moses and Elijah were seen there with him and they talked together.

4. Then Peter said, Lord, it is good for us to be here. Would you like for us to build three huts, one for you, one for Moses and one for Elijah?

5. While he was speaking, a brightly lighted cloud overshadowed them. Take notice, a voice said from out of the cloud, this is my beloved son, in whom I am delighted; Listen to him. (*obey him*)

6. When they heard the voice, the disciples fell on their faces and were extremely alarmed.

7. Then Jesus came to them and touched them and said, stand up and do not be afraid.

8. As they stood up, they looked and they saw no one but Jesus alone.

9. As they came down from the mountain, Jesus said, tell no one of what you saw until after I have risen from the dead.

10. Then the disciples asked him, why do the scribes say, the one prophesied of by Isaiah must first come?

11. Jesus answered and said, surely he is to come first and he shall disclose all things;

12. But I tell you, he has already come but they did not recognize him, then they mistreated him according to what they had in their hearts. In the same way, the son of man shall also suffer because of them. (Isaiah 40:3; John 1:21)

13. The disciples then understood that he spoke of John the baptizer.

14. When they came upon a crowd, a man came unto him and kneeled down before him,

15. and said, Lord, have mercy on my son; He is mentally impaired and he suffers miserably. Sometimes he falls into the fire and even into the water!

16. I brought him unto your disciples, but they were not able to heal him!

17. Jesus answered him and said, oh how these people are untrustworthy and with absolutely no understanding! How much longer will I be with you? How much more of you can I withstand? Bring him unto me.

18. Jesus rebuked the child and a demon came out of him and the boy was healed from that time onward.

19. Then the disciples came up to Jesus privately and asked him, why were we not able to cast him out?

20. Jesus said, it was because of your unbelief. Truly I tell you, if you have the dedication as a grain of mustard, you will say unto a mountain, go away and it will move and nothing will be impossible for you.

21. This type of unbelief can not be overcome without much prayer and fasting.

22. And while they were staying in Galilee, Jesus said unto them, it is almost time that the son of man shall be delivered up into the hands of men,

23. and they will kill him; But after the third day he will be raised. They were extremely upset.

24. When they came to Capernaum, those that receive the tax approached Peter and said, does your teacher pay the tax?

25. Peter said, yes! And as he was coming into the house, Jesus stopped him and he said, what are you thinking Simon? From where do the kings of the earth receive their collections for taxes? From their own children or from strangers?

26. Peter answered and said, from strangers. Jesus said unto him, then the sons are certainly free!

27. But so that we not offend them, go to the sea and throw in a hook; The first fish that comes up, take it and open its mouth and you will find a silver coin. Take it and give it to pay the tax for you and me.

Matthew 18

1. At this time, some of the disciples came to Jesus and asked him, who shall be the highest rank in the kingdom of above.

2. And Jesus called a small child unto him and sat him near him,

3. and he said, truly, if you do not convert (Acts 3:19; Acts 2:38 John 8:31-36; Ecclesiastes 7:29) and become as a small child (*reborn*), there is no possibility for you to enter into the kingdom of above.
(1 Peter 2:1-2; Romans 9:11; John 3:3)

4. Whoever shall humble himself in this way, to become as a small child (*pure - innocent*), he shall be elevated into the kingdom of above. (Isaiah 66:2; Ecclesiastes 7:29)

5. Whoever shall receive the message of one of these coming in my name, he shall receive me.
(*be converted and receive the holy spirit of Christ*) (Acts 2:38; Acts 3:19)

6. But whoever of these that believe on me and again choose to offend me, it would be better for him if a large millstone were hung around his neck and he be thrown into the deepest sea.
(2 Peter 2:20-22; Hebrews 10:26-27; Titus 2:11-12; Psalms 19:13; Luke 17:1)

7. Woe unto all in the world that commit such offenses against me, though it is necessary that temptations occur, yet woe to the one that commits an offense against me. (Numbers 15:28-30; 1 John 5:16-17)

8. Therefore, if your hand or your foot cause you to do that which is evil, cut it off and throw it far from you; For it is better for you to enter into eternal life maimed or crippled, than for you to have two hands and two feet but be cast into the eternal fire.

9. If your eye causes you to commit an offense against me, pluck it out and throw it far from you; For it is better for you to have only one eye when entering into eternal life, than for you to have both eyes and be thrown into the eternal lake of fire. (Matthew 5:29; Mark 9:47; Hebrews 9:14)

10. See that no little ones (*converts*) bring an offense against me, because I tell you, the angels above see everything and bring news of it before the Father above.
(Hebrews 4:13; Romans 2:6-10; Revelation 20:12-15)

11. Understand that the son of man has come to save those that have been lost.

12. What do you think? If a man has a hundred sheep and one is lost, does he not leave the ninety-nine and go to look for it?

13. If he finds it, surely, he is happier for that one sheep than for all of the other ninety-nine that did not go astray!

14. In the same way, it is not the desire of the Father that any are lost and die eternally.
(*yet all have freewill to choose for themselves*)

15. So if your brother commits a trespass, go and talk to him about it between you and him alone.

If he shall listen, then you have strengthened your brother. (1 John 5:16)

16. But if he will not listen to you, take two or three brothers, that by the mouth of two or three witnesses every word be confirmed to be true. (Deuteronomy 19:15; 1 John 5:16-17)

17. But if he fails to hear them, tell the whole gathering. If he refuses to hear it from the whole gathering, consider him the same as a pagan or a tax collector.

18. Truly I tell you, whatever you overcome on the earth shall surely be defeated in the eternal kingdom; Whatever ensnares you on the earth shall surely keep you enslaved for eternity.
(Matthew 16:19; John 20:23; Revelation 22:11)

19. Again I tell you, if two or more of you come into agreement concerning anything that they might have need of, it will be given unto them by my Father above. (John 14:13; John 16:23; James 4:3; Matthew 21:22)

20. Because where there are two or three gathered together that are of me, I am there.

21. Then Peter approached Jesus and said, Lord, how many times shall a brother commit trespasses against me and I have need to forgive him? Seven times?

22. Jesus said unto him, not only seven times but seven times seventy.

23. The kingdom of above is much like a king that decides to bring into account all that he is owed.

24. When he had started accounting, there was a man that owed ten thousand talents of silver and he was brought before him.

25. The man did not have the ability to repay what he had owed so the king commanded that he be sold, and his wife, and his children, and all that he owned in order to repay the debt.

26. The man fell down and kneeled before the king and said, please have patience with me, I will repay all that I owe you. *(He showed sincere repentance)*

27. Then the king was moved with compassion and he released him and forgave all of his debt.
(this is what Christ offers to do for us at conversion - John 8:34-37, Acts 2:38; Romans 6:1-4; 3:25)

28. But when the man went home, he came across a neighbor that owed him a hundred denari of brass. Then he took a hold of him and grabbed him by the throat and said, pay back unto me all that you owe!

29. Then the man fell at his feet and begged that he have patience and that he would repay in full.

30. But the man would not have pity on him and had him thrown in prison until such time that he repays the entire debt that was owed. *(a comparison of the one who converts and then goes back to his former sin)*

31. So when the people had found out what this man had done, they were greatly disturbed; So they went to the king and reported the happenings unto him, all that had occurred.

32. Then he called the man unto him again and he said unto him, you are an evil man! I had forgiven you all of your debt because you asked of me:

33. Shouldn't you have had the same compassion upon your neighbor, the same as I had mercy upon you?
(Do unto others as you would want them to do unto you.)

34. The king was angry and sent him to the torturers, because he could not repay his debt. (2 Peter 2:20)

35. It is also the same with your Father above, he will also do the same unto you, if from your heart you do not forgive each one of your brothers of their trespasses against you.

Matthew 19

1. When Jesus had finished speaking, he left Galilee and went across the Jordan river to a border area of Judea.

2. There were large crowds that followed him and he healed many.

3. But the Pharisees approached him in an effort to tempt him and they said: Do you allow a man to divorce his wife for any reason he wishes?

4. Jesus answered them and said, did you not read in the scriptures: In the beginning, God created male and female?

5. For this purpose, a man shall leave his father and mother and shall be joined to his wife, and the two shall become one. (Genesis 1:27; 2:24; 1 Corinthians 7)

6. Moving forward they are no longer two bodies, but one; What God has joined together, do not separate.

7. And they said unto him, so why did Moses instruct to give a document of divorcement and to divorce if you choose? (Deuteronomy 24:1)

8. Jesus said unto them, it is because of your lustful and hardened hearts that Moses permitted you to divorce your wives, but it was not intended for it to be this way.

9. I tell you in truth, that whoever divorces his wife for any other reason than because she had committed fornication, if he wed another, he commits adultery. If she wed after divorcing, (*except for her husband committing fornication*) she also commits adultery. (Matt 5:32; 1 Cor 19:9; Luke 16:18; Romans 7:2)

10. His disciples said unto him, if this is the fault of being wed, what is the benefit of matrimony?

11. Then he said unto them, all men do not have the ability to hear this, so it is only intended for those that are able to receive it.

12. There are some men that are impotent from birth and there are some men that were made to be impotent by other men (eunuchs). There are also some who have made themselves to be impotent to help them remain in compliance with the kingdom of above. He who is able to receive this, may he receive it.

13. Then some little children were brought unto Jesus so that he might hold their hands to pray, but the disciples attempted to chase them away.

14. Jesus said, allow the children; Do not stop them from coming to me. It is only ones such as these that shall enter into the kingdom of above. (Matthew 18:1-4)

15. And he touched their heads softly and prayed with them, then he left that town.

16. Take notice, a man came near to Jesus and asked him, good teacher, what must I do to inherit everlasting life?

17. Jesus said unto him, why is it that you say that I am good? (*Did the man know that Jesus is the Christ?*) You know there is only one that is good and that is God. But if you shall receive life, obey his commandments. (Psalms 19:7)

18. And the man asked him, which? Jesus said, do not murder, do not commit adultery, do not steal,

19. do not lie, revere and value your mother and father, and have affection and benevolence for others, the same as you would want to receive from them. (Exodus 20:12-16; Deuteronomy 5:16-20)

20. The man said unto him, all of these things I have obeyed my whole life, but do I still lack something?

21. And Jesus said unto him, if you want to be made perfect, take your belongings and distribute them unto everyone who is in need and you will have much wealth in the eternal life.
Then come follow and me. (Luke 18:22; Mark 10:21)

22. But when he heard this, the man was truly grieved in his heart, because he had an abundance of many acquired things that he loved.

23. Then Jesus said unto his disciples, truly I tell you, only through much difficulty can a wealthy man enter into the kingdom of above.

24. Again I tell you, it is with less difficulty to walk a herd of camels through a small chasm then for a wealthy man to enter into the kingdom of above.

25. Having heard this, the disciples were greatly astonished and asked, then who can have the possibility of being eternally saved?

26. Jesus turned and said to them, with men it is impossible, but with God all things are possible. (Philippines 4:13)

27. Then Peter said to him, we have turned away from all things to follow you; What shall we receive?

28. Jesus said unto them, truly, those that have followed me and are regenerated, when the son of man sits in his majesty and power, you will sit upon thrones and will judge the twelve tribes of Israel. (Rev 4:4)

29. All who have turned away from houses, brothers, sisters, father, mother, wife, children or land for my sake, they shall inherit a hundred times what they had given up and shall receive eternal life.

30. Many that are foremost in this life will be the lowest for eternity; Many that are the lowest in this life will be of the highest in the eternal life. (Psalms 27:10)

Matthew 20

1. The kingdom of above is like a man that is the owner of a vineyard who went out early to find workmen to hire to work in his vineyard.

2. When he had agreed with each of the workers, a piece of silver for a day's wages, he took them into his vineyard.

3. About three hours later he saw more men looking for work, standing in the market place doing nothing;

4. So he said to them, come into my vineyard to work and that which is due I will pay you.

5. They agreed and went to the vineyard to work. Then he went in the afternoon and did the same.

6. In the early evening, he again found more men doing nothing, so he said to them, why do you stand around all day doing nothing?

7. They said, because no one has hired us. So he said, go into my vineyard to work and whatever is due, I will give to you.

8. So when nightfall came, the owner of the vineyard said unto his head manager, call the workmen and pay them their wages. Start with the ones hired last and then unto those hired earlier.

9. Those that came to work in the early evening received one piece of silver.

10. But when the ones hired first came, they thought that they would receive more; But they also received one piece of silver.

11. When they had received it, they grumbled against the owner of the vineyard

12. and they said, those that were last worked for only one hour, but you have given them the same as us, yet we worked hard in the heat all day long!

13. The owner of the vineyard said to them, friends, I have done no wrong to you. Did I not agree with you to pay you a piece of silver for a day of work?

14. Take what you have earned and go home. I have chosen to give unto those that came last the same as unto you.

15. Is this unlawful for me to give what I have as I choose? Is your eye evil because I choose to do good?

16. So those that are the least shall be foremost and those that are foremost shall be least. Many are called but very few shall be chosen.

17. Then Jesus, heading to Jerusalem, pulled his disciples aside to be in private and he said unto them;

18. Take notice! We are going to Jerusalem! I will be turned over to the high priests and the scribes and they will condemn me to death;

19. They will deliver me unto the gentiles, so that I may be mocked, scourged and crucified. But on the third day, I will rise again.

20. Then the mother of the sons of Zebedee came near to Jesus, bringing her sons with her as she worshipped him. She wanted to ask something of him.

21. Jesus asked her, what do you want? So she said unto him, will you allow for these two sons of mine to sit, one on your right hand and one on your left hand in your kingdom.

22. Then Jesus said unto her, you do not know what you ask for. Is it possible for you to drink the cup that I am about to drink? Can you be baptized with the baptism of which I am baptized? They said, we surely are willing!

23. Jesus said unto them, indeed the cup that is mine you will also drink of (*they were both also martyred*) and the baptism that I am baptized with, you will also be baptized with *(holy spirit)*: But to sit at my right and my left hand, that is not mine to give, but is for who it has been prepared for by my Father.

24. And when the other disciples heard this, they were aggravated about what the two brothers had asked.

25. Then Jesus called them near to him and said, you know that the rulers of nations exercise lordship over the people and their powerful leaders hold much authority over them.

26. It shall not be like this among you. Whoever desires to be the greatest, it is he that serves the most.

27. Whoever wants to be the highest among you, he shall be as a slave. (Romans 1:1)

28. It is the same with the son of man, "I did not come to be served, but to serve and to give my life to be the ransom for many." (Isaiah 35:10; Isaiah 51:10; Jeremiah 31:11)

29. As they were leaving Jericho, a large crowd followed them.

30. Take notice, there were two blind men sitting near the road that had heard that Jesus was passing by and they cried out and said, have mercy upon us Lord, son of David.

31. But the crowd told them to shut up and not speak! But with this, they cried out even louder and said, Lord, son of David, have pity on us.

32. Jesus stopped walking and called to them and he said, what is it that you desire I do for you?

33. They said to him, that you might open our eyes!

34. Jesus had compassion upon them and he touched their eyes; Immediately they received their sight and they followed him. (*We must also have similar compassion unto others if we are of Christ*)

Matthew 21

1. As they came close to Jerusalem, they came into Bethphage near the mount of olives. Jesus called two disciples and he said to them:

2. Go into the village and you will find an ass and her colt tied up. Loosen them and lead them to me.

3. If anyone says anything to you, tell them the almighty has need of them. He will return them very soon.

Verses 4-5 look to have been added by a scribe and not a part of the original text.

4. And this was the fulfillment of the prophecy spoken by the prophet:

5. "Tell the daughter of Zion, your king comes unto you meekly, riding on an ass, even the colt, the foal of an ass." (Zechariah 9:9)

6. So the disciples went and did as Jesus had ordered them to do.

7. They led the ass and the colt and they put their robes on them for Jesus to sit upon.

8. A large amount of people laid down their robes on the ground along the way and others were cutting branches from the trees and spreading them on the ground as well.

9. The crowds of people, those going in before him, as well as those following him cried out and said: Hosanna to the son of David. Blessed is he that comes in the name of the Lord. Hosanna in the highest! (Psalms 118:25-26)

10. When Jesus had entered into Jerusalem, the whole city was shaken, saying, who is this?

11. The crowds were saying, this is Jesus, the one that was spoken of by the prophets; He is the one from Nazareth of Galilee.

12. Then Jesus entered into the temple of God and he threw out all who were buying and selling in the temple. He overturned the tables of the money takers and the seats of those selling doves!

13. Then he said, it is written that this house shall be a house of prayer, but you have turned it into a den of thieves. (Isaiah 56:7; Jeremiah 7:11)

14. Then those that were blind and lame came to him and they were healed there in the temple.

15. But when the scribes and high priests saw the miracles that Jesus did and the children yelling out, "hosanna to the son of David"; They were greatly displeased,

16. so they said unto him, do you hear what they are saying? And Jesus said to them, yes! Did you never read "Out of the mouths of babes and sucklings you shall have perfect praise?" (Psalms 8:2)

17. Jesus left there and went out of Jerusalem unto Bethany and found lodging there,

18. but he returned to Jerusalem early the next day, as he was hungry.

19. Then he saw a fig tree along the way and he went to it, but he found no fruit on the tree but only leaves. Jesus said unto it, never again shall you bring forth fruit. And the fig tree immediately dried up! (Luke 3:9; Hosea 10:15; Jeremiah 11:16; Isaiah 9:14-19 - *the fig tree represents ancient Israel*)

20. After having seen this, the disciples were amazed and said, how could this fig tree dry up so quickly?

21. And Jesus said unto them, truly I tell you, if you have complete dedication and exactness and you are completely convinced, say to a mountain, get up and throw yourself into the sea, and it will be done!

22. All that you have need of, speak in earnest prayer; Be completely trusting in me and you will receive. (John 14:13; John 16:23; James 4:3; Matthew 18:19)

23. And when Jesus again came into the temple, the high priests and some elders came to him while he was teaching the people and they asked him: By what authority do you do these things? Who gave you authority to do this?

24. Jesus answered and said, I will ask you one question and if you answer me, I will tell you by what authority I do these things.

25. The baptism of John; Was it from God above or of men. They reasoned amongst themselves and they said, if we should say from God, he will say, then why did you not believe him!

26. But if we should say from men, we fear the crowd because they hold John to have been a prophet.

27. They then answered Jesus and said, we do not know. Then Jesus said unto them, so I will not tell you by what authority I do these things.

28. Consider this: A man had two sons and he called the first and said, go today and work in my vineyard.

29. But he said, no I will not. Afterwards having regretted it, he decided to go and he went.

30. Then the man came unto his second son and instructed the same. He answered his father and said, I will go, but then he did not go. (*the first represents gentiles and the second the Israelites*)

31. Which of the two sons did the will of his father? (Matthew 7:21) And they answered him and said, the first. Jesus said unto them, truly the tax collectors and the harlots will enter into the kingdom of God instead of you.

32. John came to you teaching the way of righteousness, but you did not believe him; Yet the tax collectors and the harlots did believe him. Previously they did not see, but regretted afterwards and believed in him.

33. Here is another parable for you to hear: A man who was the owner of a piece of good land planted a vineyard and put a fence around it, built a winepress and constructed a tower, then turned it over to the workers to work it. Then he traveled to a faraway country: (Isaiah 5:1-7; Mark 12:1; Luke 20:9)

34. When the time of the harvest was approaching, he sent his loyal servants to receive the harvested fruit.

35. Then the workers took his loyal servants and beat one, killed another and threw stones at the others. (Matthew 23:31 - *the prophets*)

36. Then he sent more loyal servants, more than the first time, but they did the same unto them.

37. Finally he sent his son unto them, and he said, surely they will revere my son!

38. But when the workers saw his son, they talked among themselves and said, this is the heir; If we kill him, then we will have his inheritance.

39. So they took him and threw him out of the vineyard and they killed him. (*Jesus*)

40. When the owner of the vineyard comes, what will he do to those workers?

41. Surely he will horribly destroy those worthless workers (*ancient, unconverted Jews*) and he will find other workers (*gentiles*) who will give unto him that which was due, the good fruits of the vineyard.

42. Jesus asked them, didn't you ever read in the scriptures, "the stone that was rejected by the builders, but came to be the head of the corner." This is from God, yet is it not understood by you! (Psalms 118:22-23; Isaiah 28:16)

43. Because I tell you these things, the kingdom of God shall be taken from you and given to another people that will produce the good fruits (*deeds*) of which are expected and necessary. (Acts 26:20)

44. The one who falls on this rock (*Christ*) will be broken (*transformed*) by the power of it; But he that it falls upon shall be pulverized and destroyed. (1 Corinthians 10:4; Matthew 7:24)

45. When the high priests and Pharisees heard these parables they knew that he was speaking about them,

46. They looked to take a hold of him but they feared the crowds, because they held him to be a prophet.

Matthew 22

1. Then Jesus again spoke to them in parables and said:

2. The kingdom of above is like a king that made a wedding feast for his son.

3. So he ordered his servants to send out invitations to those that were to be invited (*the ancient Jews*), but they chose not to come.

4. Then he sent out other servants to announce that the feast was ready; Tell them that I have butchered the oxen and the fattened calf and all things are ready; Come now to the wedding feast!

5. Yet they did not care and they went their own ways, one to his own field and one to his occupation.

6. Some of the others seized his servants, insulted them and they even killed some. (*the prophets*)

7. When the king heard of this, he was greatly angered, so he sent an army to destroy those murderers, and to burn their city. (Daniel 9:24-27 - *Prophecy was fulfilled in 70 A.D.*)

8. Then he said to his servants, the feast is ready but those that were first invited were not worthy.

9. Go now, travel the roadways unto the distant places and invite all that you find (*gentiles*), call them to come to my wedding feast. (Revelation 19:9)

10. And when his servants went out unto the distant places, they gathered as many as they could find who would come, both those that were good and those that had in the past been evil; They filled the wedding feast with them and they sat down to eat.

11. And the king examined the guests as they were sitting at the tables getting ready to eat and he saw a man that was not properly dressed for the wedding. (*did not have on a white robe - Revelation 7:13*)

12. He said to him, how were you able to enter, not being dressed properly for the wedding? But the man was speechless! (Revelation 19:8)

13. The king said to his servants, tie this man up, both hands and feet and throw him into the outer darkness where there will be great wailing and grinding of teeth due to the great pain he shall suffer in that place. (Revelation 19:7; John 10:1-10; Psalms 112:10)

14. Many are called, but very few shall be chosen (*elected*).

15. Then the Pharisees held a meeting to see how they might ensnare him.

16. So they then sent their pupils along with the Herodians unto Jesus and they asked, teacher, we know that you are truthful and that you teach the true way to God, and that you do not favor any man because you do not concern yourself with the outward appearances of men. *(how they show themselves to be).*

17. So tell us, what do you think; Is it lawful to pay taxes unto Caesar? Or is it not?

18. But Jesus knew the evil in them and he said, why do you tempt me? You are hypocrites!

19. Then he said, show me the coin that is due for the tax. So they brought him a copper coin.

20. Then Jesus said unto them, whose image and inscription is on the coin?

21. They said, it is of Caesar. Then Jesus said unto them, give unto Caesar that which is Caesar's, but give unto God that which is God's.

22. When they heard him say this, they were amazed and they walked away from him.

23. That same day, some of the Sadducees, those that say that there is no resurrection (Revelation 20:12; Daniel 12:2) came unto him and questioned him.

24. They said, teacher, Moses said that if a man dies without having any children, his brother shall take his wife and she shall raise up offspring unto his brother. (Deuteronomy 5:5)

25. But if there were seven brothers and the first who was her husband died without any children, then the next brother took her and then died,

26. then the third, unto the seventh, none of them having any children with her;

27. But then finally, the woman died as well;

28. In the resurrection, which of the seven brothers shall have her as his wife? Since they all had her!

29. Then Jesus answered and said unto them, you have erred. You do not know the scriptures nor the power of God.

30. In the resurrection, none shall be joined in wedlock. They shall all be as the messengers (*angels*) of God from above.

31. But as concerning the resurrection of the dead, have you not read that which was spoken unto your people by God, when he said;

32. "I am God of Abraham, Isaac and Jacob; I am not the god of the dead, but of the living." (Exodus 3:16)

33. When the crowd heard this they were amazed at what he had taught.

34. When the Pharisees had heard that Jesus had silenced the Sadducees, they gathered around Jesus.

35. Then one who was an expert in the Mosaic law tested him and said;

36. Teacher, what commandment is the highest in the law? *(Jesus gives them the law of God - the highest law)*

37. And Jesus said unto him, you shall love your God with all of your heart, all of your soul and all of your mind. (Deuteronomy 6:5; Psalms 119:34)

38. This is the first and greatest commandment.

39. The second is very much like it; You shall offer affectionate benevolence (*love*) unto your fellow man, the same as you care for yourself. (Leviticus 19:18; Luke 10:27; Mark 12:30)

40. These two commandments hold all that is in the law (*of God*) and everything spoken by the prophets. (Psalms 19:7)

41. With so many of the Pharisees gathered together, Jesus asked them a question:

42. What do you think concerning the Christ? Whose son is he? And they answered and said, David's.

43. Then he asked them, then how does David call him Lord (*master*)?

44. When he wrote, "the Lord (*God, the Father*) said into my Lord (*Christ*), sit at my right hand, until I shall put those that are hostile unto you to be trampled upon under your feet." (Psalms 110:1)

45. If David calls him (*Christ*) Lord, how can Christ be his son?

46. But no man was able to answer him, not a word. No one did dare to question him ever again.

Matthew 23

1. Then Jesus spoke to the crowd and his disciples and he said;

2. The scribes and Pharisees are appointed over the power structure given by Moses.

3. What they teach you should observe and do; But do not do as they do, because they do not live that which they teach. (*This is only for those under the Mosaic law, not in the new covenant*)

4. They put many heavy burdens on the shoulders of men which are too difficult to bear (Acts 15:10); Yet not even with a single finger do they have any interest in bearing those burdens upon themselves.

5. All that they do, they do to be seen by men. They even leave their notes hanging out of the scripture texts and put fringes on the clothes that they wear.

6. They love to sit in the honorable seats at large dinner gatherings and in the synagogues;

7. They adore being greeted in the streets and to be called "Rabbi" by men. (*a title - "my master"*)

8. Do not call anyone Rabbi, as there is only one master teacher and that is Christ and all of you are brothers. (John 16:13; Jeremiah 31:34)

9. Do not call any man your spiritual father here upon the earth. For there is only one spiritual father and he is Christ.

10. Do not be called a master leader, because there is only one and that is Christ.

11. He that is the greatest shall be a servant unto all.

12. Whoever shall promote himself shall be humiliated, but he that is humble shall be greatly exalted up.

13. Woe unto you scribes and Pharisees, you are hypocrites! You close the door unto the kingdom of God for many people. You truly shall not enter and neither shall they who might have, except for you having prevented them from entering therein. (*This also applies to all modern-day false teachers*)

14. Woe unto you scribes and Pharisees! You are hypocrites! You steal away the houses of widows, but for an outward appearance, you offer a long prayer for their well being. For this, you will receive great damnation. (Psalms 10:8-11)

15. Woe unto you scribes and Pharisees! You are hypocrites! You travel on both land and sea to find one convert (*unto Judaism*), but when you have converted him, you make him double the child of hell that you yourselves are.

16. Woe unto you, you are blind leaders of the blind. You are those who say that whoever swears by the temple is nothing, but whoever swears by the money in the temple is obligated to keep his word.

17. You are blind fools! What is greater, the gold in the temple or the temple which sanctifies that gold?

18. You also say that whoever swears at the altar, it means nothing, but whoever swears by the gift that they offered on the altar is obligated to keep his word.

19. You are fools and you are blinded! Which is greater, the gift on the altar or the altar that makes the gift to be sacred?

20. Whoever makes a promise at the altar, does so before the altar and also all that is offered upon it.

21. He that makes a promise by the temple, does so by the temple, but also by he that abides within it!

22. He that makes a promise, he has sworn unto the heavens and he does so by the throne of God and by he who sits upon the throne.

23. Woe to you scribes and Pharisees, you are hypocrites! You offer tithes of mint, anise and dill, but you have abandoned the more important things of the law of Moses, which are justice, mercy and faithfulness unto God. Though it is right to bring the tithes (*under the Mosaic law*), you ought to have also kept the other more important things as well.

24. You are blinded leaders; You are the ones who strain out a gnat (*to purify your water*) but yet you swallow the camel dung!

25. Woe unto you scribes and Pharisees, you are hypocrites! You cleanse the outside of a glass and bowl, (*your outward appearances*) but within you are full of robbery and self-indulgence.

26. You blind Pharisees, first cleanse all that is within you, then all that shows outward will also be clean.

27. Woe unto you scribes and Pharisees, you are hypocrites! You are like a tombstone that has been cleaned, but underneath you are full of the bones of the dead and completely unclean.

28. Even though you outwardly appear to be righteous, within you are destitute, full of hypocrisy, wickedness and filth.

29. Woe unto you scribes and Pharisees, you are hypocrites! You have built up beautiful gravestones for the prophets and you decorate their graves;

30. You say that if you had been there in the days of your forefathers, you would not have been complicit in shedding the blood of the prophets;

31. Yet in this, you fully admit that you are the children of those who murdered the prophets of God! (Matthew 21:35; John 8:44)

32. But you are guilty just as well, but only slightly to a lesser degree than they are.

33. You are serpents, the offspring of vipers! How do you think that you can escape the judgment and the eternal lake of fire?

34. Be aware, it was I that sent the prophets unto you, unto the wise and unto the record keepers. *(those that wrote the old testament scriptures)* Some of them you have killed and crucified, and some you have beaten in your synagogues and have chased from city to city; (Matthew 21:35)

35. Upon you shall fall the punishment for all of the righteous blood of the whole earth, from Abel unto Zechariah the son of Barachia whom you murdered between the temple and the alter.

36. Truly I tell you, all of the punishments for these things will soon come upon this nation! (Daniel 9:24-27 - *The destruction of Jerusalem in 70 A.D.*)

37. Jerusalem, Jerusalem, you have murdered the prophets and have thrown stones at those that have been sent unto you! How much I have desired to gather your children unto me, in the same way a bird gathers her young ones under her wings; But you would not allow it! (Isaiah 30:15)

38. Know this, your temple shall be made desolate. *(will be destroyed* - Jeremiah 22:5; Jeremiah 7:24-34; Daniel 9:26-27; Amos 5:1-2)

39. I tell you with certainty, you shall not in any way come to the truth that I bring, unless you come to admit you were truly blessed by the one who has come in the name of Jehovah.

Matthew 24

1. Jesus walked away from the temple and his disciples came to talk with him about the architecture of the buildings;

2. Then Jesus said, do not admire these things. I tell you the truth, not any of this will remain, because very soon all of these stacked stones will be demolished. (70 AD)

3. Then they sat down at the Mount of Olives and his disciples came unto him privately and they asked, tell us; What will be hereafter and what will be the sign of your return and the end of the world?

4. Then Jesus said unto them; Beware, do not let anyone mislead any of you; (2 Thessalonians 2:11)

5. Many will come and claim to be of me, they will even say that I am the Christ, yet they will deceive many and lead them into great error. (2 Thessalonians 2:9-10; Isaiah 30:10; 2 Timothy 4:3-4; Zephaniah 3:4; Jeremiah 23:1-40; Isaiah 56:10-11; Ezekiel 22:28; 1 Peter 2:1-22; Jude 1:4)

6. You will hear of many battles and reports of war. Take notice, but do not be afraid; These things must happen, but the end will not be immediately at that time.

7. Nation will arise against nation and uprisings with kings against their own people! And there will be shortages of food, plagues and earthquakes in many various places.

8. But all of these will be the beginning of sorrow.

The proper placement of the verses from Matthew 10:18-22
brought here from Matthew 10;
They have been returned in their proper place.
Mark 13:11-13 and Luke 21:12-19

18. Some of you (*my people*) will be brought before governors and before kings because of your testimony of me, to be a witness of truth against them and against all people.

19. When they take you to be questioned, do not be anxious or stressed about what you will say,

20. because it will not be you who will speak, but the spirit of the Father within you that will speak through you. (1 Corinthians 3:16-17; 1 Corinthians 6:19; Ephesians 2:21-22)

21. Brothers will betray their own brothers unto death and fathers will betray their own children: Children will rise up against their parents and cause them to be put to death. (2 Timothy 3:1-5)

22. And you will be hated by all people because of me; But the one who endures faithfully until the end shall be eternally saved.

9. Then they shall arrest and persecute you (*the faithful*) and they shall kill many of you; You will be despised by all people because you are of my name.
(2 Timothy 3:12; Revelation 6:9-10; James 5:6; Psalms 116:15; Psalms 11:2; Revelation 13:7)

10. Then they shall scandalize many. *(lead astray and reserve them unto Satan)* People will hate and betray one another. (Revelation 13:16; Daniel 11:31)

11. Very many false teachers and false prophets shall arise and they shall deceive many, leading them to destruction. (2 Thessalonians 2:11; 2 Corinthians 11:13-15; 2 Peter 2; Jude 1:4; 1 Timothy 4:1-3)

12. Because wickedness shall be greatly multiplied, the natural affection and care that people have for one another will evaporate and disappear; (2 Timothy 3:3)

13. But those that remain faithful unto God until the end of their life, *(even through much difficulty and testing)* only these shall be reserved by God to receive eternal life. (Hebrews 6:15; Romans 6:16-22)

14. The gospel of the kingdom shall be published in all of the world (Revelation 14:6) as a witness against all nations and all peoples, and then the end of the world shall come. (Isaiah 42:1)

15. So when you see the detestable thing that strips away and devastates (*abomination of desolation - mark of the beast*) spoken of by Daniel the prophet, abiding in the sacred places, (1 Corinthians 3:16) may he that reads this understand well; (Daniel 11:31; Mark 13:14; Revelation 13:16)

16. Those that are of Jehovah, (Romans 2:28-29) run for your escape to the mountains. (Ezekiel 7:16)

17. Those that are in the mountains, do not go back to gather needed things from civilization.

18. Those that are in the countryside, do not even enter a town to gather clothing.

19. Woe to them that are pregnant or nursing young ones at that time.

20. Pray that your departure not occur in the wintertime nor on a holiday; *(when much is closed down.)*

21. Because at that time there will be great persecution (*the great tribulation*), such that has not ever occurred in the history of the world. (Revelation 3:10; 6:11; 13:15-16; Daniel 7:21; Daniel 11:33-12:1)

22. Except if those days are shortened (Revelation 16:1-21; Revelation 8:1-10:11; Matthew 24:29), no one who is in Christ would remain alive, but for the sake of the elect (*the 144000, the first fruits*) those days will be shortened. (Revelation 8:5-9:1; Psalms 116:15; Revelation 13:7)

23. At that time, if any man shall say unto you, here is Christ, or there is Christ, do not believe them.

24. Many false christs, false teachers and false prophets shall arise; Some will show great signs that they claim to be the fulfillment of ancient prophecies, so to attempt to deceive even the elect of God, if that was possible. (2 Peter 2:1; Acts 20:29-30; Matthew 24:4-5, 11; 2 Thessalonians 2:10-12; Galatians 2:4-5; Jude 1:4)

25. Take notice, as I have already told you these things in the past.

26. So if they say to you that Christ is in the deserted place, do not go there! Or if they say that he is in a private building, do not believe them!

27. Because as lightning flashes across the sky to light up the entire sky, so shall my coming (*return*) also be. (Psalms 97:4)

28. Wherever the wholesome ones are, they will be gathered together with the eagles (*in the air*). (1 Thessalonians 4:17; Luke 17:37)

29. Immediately after the persecution of those days (*great tribulation*), the sun will be darkened and the moon shall not give its light, because stars shall fall from the sky and powerful forces of the heavens shall violently shake all of the earth. (*This event shortens the great tribulation*) (Isaiah 13:9-13; 24:23; 29:6-7; Ezekiel 32:7; 38:20; Daniel 7:13; 12:1; Joel 2:10, 31; 3:15; Revelation 6:12; 8:5-12; 16:1-10)

30. Signs will appear in the sky; They are the signs of the return (*coming*) of Jesus Christ, and all races on earth shall mourn greatly as they see him coming on the clouds of the sky, with great power and honour.

31. And he shall send forth his angels and the great trumpet of God shall sound; (1 Thessalonians 4:16; Revelation 10:6-7) then they shall gather together all of the elect of God, from the four corners of the earth, from one side of the sky unto the other. (Revelation 14:12-16)

32. Understand therefore the parable of the fig tree: When the branches become tender and it brings forth its leaves, you know that the summer is near;

33. Just the same, when you see all of these things happening, know that the time is very close, as he is standing at the door. (1 Thessalonians 5:4)

34. Surely, the generation that shall see these things begin to happen, they shall not all die until all things are completed. (Daniel 12:7)

35. The heavens and the earth shall come to their end, but my words shall never lose their life.

36. But concerning the day and the hour, no one knows when it will come, not even the angels in the heavens! Only my Father above knows the exact day when it will be.

37. But as it was in the days of Noah, it shall also be similar at the time of the return of Christ Jesus.

38. Because in the days before the great flood, the people were eating and drinking, having weddings and planning for their future, right up until the time that Noah entered the ark;

39. But they did not know until the flood came upon them and killed them all; It shall also be the same at the return of the son of man. (1 Thessalonians 5:2-4)

40. At that time two shall be in the country. One shall be received by God and the other shall be forsaken. (Luke 17:35)

41. Two shall be grinding in the mill, one shall be received by God and the other shall be forsaken.

42. Be vigilant, because you do not know the moment that your Lord shall return.

43. But know this, that if the man of the house knew when the thief was coming, he would be vigilant and would not allow his house to be broken into.

44. Who shall be the faithful and wise servant who the Lord shall appoint to care over his people and give them nourishment (*spiritual nourishment*) when it is needed? (Luke 12:42-44; Daniel 12:1)

46. Fortunate is he who the Lord finds doing so when he returns.

47. Surely I tell you, he shall appoint him over all that he possesses.

48. But if an unwise servant says in his heart that the Lord will delay his return,

49. and he begin to abuse (*mislead*) his fellow servants and eat and drink with the drunkards;

50. The master of that servant will come in a day that he does not expect and at a time that he is not aware

51. and he will cut him in two; Then he will throw both halves in with the hypocrites where there will be weeping and grinding of the teeth. *(due to the immense pain) (Psalms 112:10)*

Matthew 25

1. The kingdom of above is comparable to ten maidens that took lamps and went out to meet a bachelor that was looking for a bride to wed.

2. Five of them were prudent and five were foolish. (Matthew 24:40-41)

3. The foolish ones took their lamps, but did not take oil with them.

4. The prudent ones took lamps and brought enough oil with them.

5. But the bachelor delayed his coming so they all laid down and slept.

6. In the middle of the night the notification came, come see! The bachelor is arriving shortly; Go out to meet him!

7. Then all of the maidens rose up and began to prepare their lamps.

8. The foolish maidens said to the prudent ones, give us some of your oil, our lamps are not able to be lit.

9. The prudent maidens said no, we do not have enough for both us and you. But go to those who sell the oil and buy some for yourselves.

10. So they went to buy some, but while they were gone the bachelor came and the ones that were ready went with him to the wedding feast and the door was shut.

11. Later, the other maidens came and said, master of the house, open up the door for us!

12. But he said no, because I do not know who you are. (Matthew 7:23)

13. So watch and be ready, because you do not know the day nor hour that the son of man will come.

14. The kingdom of above is like a man who was about to travel abroad. So he called his servants unto him and he gave some money to them.

15. He gave five silver talents to one; Then he gave two silver talents to another and he gave one silver talent to the other one, each according to his ability, then he went on his journey.

16. The one that had received five talents worked them and he made an additional five talents of silver.

17. Likewise the one that had received two talents, he made an additional two silver talents.

18. But the one that received one talent went his way and dug into the ground and buried the silver that was entrusted to him by his master.

19. After a long time, the master returned and took them to account.

20. He that was given five talents brought another five talents and said, master you gave me five talents and I was able to gain an additional five talents.

21. His master then said unto him, well done my good and faithful servant. You have been faithful over a few things, I will now set you over many things.

22. The one that received two talents said, master, with the two talents that you delivered to me, I was able to gain an additional two talents of silver for you.

23. The master said unto him, well done; You are a good and faithful servant. You have been faithful in a few things, now I will set you above many. Enter in unto the joy of your master!

24. Then he that was given one talent of silver said, master, I know that you are a hard man that harvests that which you did not plant and gathering that which you did not scatter;

25. I was afraid, so I went and hid your talent in the ground! Here it is and you have that which is yours.

26. His master then said unto him, you are a derelict and wasteful servant. You knew that I harvest where I did not plant and gather where I did not scatter.

27. Why did you not at least give my silver to the bankers, where you could have gained interest? Then I would have received that which was mine with interest!

28. Therefore, take this talent from him and give it to the servant that now has ten talents.

29. Unto the one who has (*and is faithful*), more will be given, but to he that does not have, even what he has will be taken from him. (Matthew 13:12) (*This goes for the gifts of the spirit as well*)

30. Now throw that worthless servant into the outer darkness where there will be great weeping and the grinding of teeth. (*due to enormous pain*) (Psalms 112:10)

31. When the son of man comes in his glory and all of his holy angels with him, he will sit on his throne of honor; (Zephaniah 3:15; Revelation 14:14-19)

32. Assembled in front of him shall be those of all the nations and he will separate them one from another, as a shepherd separates the sheep (*obedient*) from the goats. (*disobedient*)
(Ezekiel 34:17-22; Zephaniah 1:12)

33. He will set his sheep to his right and the goats on his left. (Revelation 20:12-15)

34. Then the king will say, those on the right of me, come, you are blessed by my Father. You shall inherit that which was prepared from the beginning of the world. (Daniel 12:2)

35. Because when I was hungry you gave me meat; When I was thirsty you gave me a drink, and when I was a stranger you took me in;

36. When I was naked, you gave me clothing; When I was sick, you helped me; When I was in prison, you came unto me. (Matthew 22:40)

37. Then the righteous will answer him and say, master, when did we see you hungry and feed you, or thirsty and gave you drink?

38. When did we see you as a stranger and take you in; When did we see you naked and give you clothing?

39. When were you sick or in prison and we helped you?

40. And the king shall answer and say, truly I tell you, that which you did for one of the least of my brethren, you did so unto me. (*Because Jesus lives within those that are his*)

41. Then he shall say to them on the left, depart from me, you are cursed; Descend into the everlasting fire, because you have prepared yourselves for the devil and his demons. (Matthew 7:23; Daniel 12:2)

42. When I was hungry, you did not give me anything to eat; When I was thirsty, you did not give me a drink. (James 2:15-17)

43. When I was a stranger, you did not give me a place to sleep; When I was naked, you did not give me any clothing; When I was sick and in prison, you did not come to visit or help me. (Matthew 22:40)

44. Then they will say unto him, master, when did we see you when you were hungry, or thirsty, or a stranger, or naked, or sick, or in prison, and not offer assistance unto you?

45. Then the master shall say, truly I tell you, just as you did not do good unto the least of these, you did not do good unto me.

46. Go away into everlasting punishment, but the righteous shall go unto everlasting life. (Romans 2:5-11)

Matthew 26

1. When Jesus had finished his teachings, he said to his disciples;

2. Know that in two days the Passover begins and the son of man shall be betrayed and will be crucified.

3. At that same time, there was an assembly of high priests, scribes and some of the elders. They gathered in the court of the high priest Caiaphas.

4. They consulted how they might deceive him, so to be able to arrest and then kill him.

5. But they agreed to not do so on the feast day, so the people would not start an uprising.
(Acts 18:21; 21:30)

6. Jesus was at that time in Bethany at the house of Simon the leper; (John 12:3; Mark 14:3; Luke 7:36)

7. A woman approached him there, having an alabaster jar with very precious ointment in it and she poured it over his head as he was sitting down.

8. But when one of his disciples saw this, he was not pleased and he said, what a waste this is!

9. This ointment could have been sold for a lot of money that could have been used to assist the poor.

10. When Jesus heard this, he asked, why do you cause trouble for this woman? She has done a good thing unto me.

11. The poor will always be with you, but you will not have me (*in body*) with you for much longer.

12. She has anointed me with this ointment to prepare my body for its burial. This is why she did it.

13. Truly I tell you, wherever this gospel is given in all of the world, she will be remembered and this will be spoken of as a memorial unto her.

14. Then Judas Iscariot, one of the twelve disciples went unto the high priests;

15. He asked them, what will you give unto me if I deliver him up to you? They contracted with him for thirty pieces of silver. (Zechariah 11:12-13)

16. From that time he looked for an opportunity to betray him.

17. On the first day of the feast of unleavened bread, the disciples came unto Jesus and they asked him, where would you like for us to prepare to eat the feast of Passover?

18. And Jesus said, go into Jerusalem and speak to a certain man; Tell him that the master has said, the time is close and my disciples and I will eat the passover feast at his home.

19. The disciples did as Jesus had instructed of them and they prepared the Passover.

20. In the evening, Jesus sat down with the twelve disciples.

21. While they were eating he said unto them, truthfully I tell you, one of you will betray me.

22. When they heard this, they were very saddened and each of them began to ask him, Lord, is it I?

23. Jesus said, it is the one who is dipping his hand with me in the bowl; He will betray me.

24. Truly the son of man shall depart in the same way that it is written of him in the scriptures. But woe to the one that betrays him. It would have been better if he had not been born. (Matthew 18:6; Titus 1:16)

25. Then Judas said, it is I Rabbi. And Jesus said unto him; It is true.

26. Then Jesus took the meat and he blessed it, cut it up and he dispersed it among the disciples, and he said, this is for my body, accept this and eat it. (John 6:53; Romans 6:1-23)

27. Then Jesus took the pitcher and he gave thanks and he said unto them, drink all of this.

28. This is for my blood and the new covenant (*contract offered*) that shall be brought forth for the sake of many and will completely free them of sin. (John 8:34-36; Acts 2:38; Acts 3:19; Romans 6:1-23)

29. I tell you, I will not drink again from the fruit of the vine until the day when I drink it with you in the kingdom of my Father. (*the eternal kingdom that is yet to come* - Revelation 21-22; 1 Corinthians 15:24)

30. After this they sang a hymn and went to the mount of olives.

31. Then Jesus said unto them, tonight you will all abandon me. It is written, "the shepherd shall be struck down and his sheep will be scattered." (Zechariah 13:7)

32. But after I have been raised, I will go into Galilee and wait for you there.

33. Then Peter said unto him, even if they all lose their devoutness in you, I will never doubt nor fail you.

34. Jesus said, truly I tell you, this very night, before the rooster crows you will deny me three times. (Luke 22:34; Mark 14:30)

35. And Peter said unto him, if I was to die with you, I in no way will deny you. The other disciples also said the same of themselves.

36. Then Jesus brought them to a place called Gethsemane and he said unto his disciples, you stay here while I go to pray over there.

37. He took along with him Peter and the two sons of Zebedee and he began to grieve and be distressed; (Psalms 22:14)

38. Then he said unto them, my soul is deeply grieving concerning my death. Stay here, watch with me.

39. Jesus walked a little further and he fell upon his face; He prayed and said, Father, if it is possible, may this fate be taken away from me; Though not my will be done, but your will be done.

40. Then he went unto the disciples and found them sleeping and he said unto Peter; Do you not have the strength to watch with me for even one hour?

41. Watch and pray that you do not fall when you are tempted; Your spirit within you is willing, but the physical body is weak.

42. Again, a second time Jesus walked off a little distance and he prayed: My Father, if it is not possible for this fate be taken from me; May your will be done. (John 17)

43. And he again came and found them sleeping, as their eyes were very heavy.

44. So he left them and as he walked away a third time, he again prayed in the same way.

45. Then he came back to his disciples and he said, go ahead, sleep and get your rest.

46. Be aware, the hour has come that the son of man shall be delivered into the hands of sinners. (*a short time passes and then*) Rise up and awaken! The one that shall betray me is coming.

47. While he was still speaking Judas appeared and there was a large crowd of people with him holding swords and clubs; There were also many elders and high priests. (Mark 14:43; John 18:3; Luke 22:47)

48. Judas had given them a sign of which was, the one that he would kiss, it is he. Arrest him.

49. Immediately Judas came to Jesus and said, farewell Rabbi! Then he strongly kissed him.

50. Then Jesus said, friend, why have you done this? Then they came and seized him and took him away.

51. But Look! One of those with Jesus stretched out his hand with a drawn sword and struck a servant of the high priest, taking off his ear.

52. Then Jesus said unto him, put your sword back in its proper place; All who fight with the sword shall die with the sword. (Revelation 13:10)

53. Do you think that I am not able to call upon my Father and have him send more than twelve regiments of angels?

54. But then, how should the scriptures be fulfilled? Know that this must be.

55. Then Jesus said to them, why did you come to take me with swords and clubs like you would a thief? I sat with you and I taught in the temple, yet you did not arrest me then!

The first sentence of verse 56 looks to have been a scribal error and is a repeat of verse 54.

56. But all of this has occurred so that the scriptures of the prophets would be fulfilled.

56. Then, all of the disciples ran away and abandoned him. (Isaiah 53:3)

57. Those who seized Jesus took him to Caiaphas the high priest where the scribes and priests had gathered.

58. Peter followed them at a distance all the way to the court of the high priest and he went inside and sat with a younger servant of Christ (*John*) so that he could see what would happen. (John 18:15)

59. The high priests, elders and all of the Sanhedrin looked for false witnesses against Jesus so that they could put him to death, but they could find no one.

60. There were many false witnesses that came forward, yet they did not find anyone credible. Finally, there came two false witnesses that said;

61. This man said that he is able to destroy the temple and to rebuild it in three days.

62. Then the high priest stood up and said unto Jesus; Do you have nothing to say? What do these witnesses have against you?

63. But Jesus did not speak. Then the high priest said, I put you under oath before the living God, tell us if you are the Christ, the son of God.

64. Jesus said unto him, you have it correct; I will also tell you that you will watch as the son of man is sitting at the right hand of power when I come on the clouds in the sky. (Daniel 7:13; 1 Thessalonians 4:17; Revelation 14:14)

65. Then the high priest tore his clothes and screamed, he blasphemes! We have no more need of any further witnesses. Take notice, now you have heard his blasphemy.

66. What do you think? They answered and said, he is deserving of death;

67. Then they spit in his face and beat him with their fists; As they beat him they said,

68. prophesy unto us, who is it that is striking you?

69. Then, as Peter was sitting outside of the court, a slave-girl came to him and said, you were with that Jesus of Galilee!

70. But Peter denied in front of them and he said, I do not know what you are talking about.

71. When he was leaving, while he was in the entry way, another saw him and said to the crowd, this one was with Jesus the Nazarean.

72. But Peter again denied with an oath, saying, I do not know this man.

73. A little while later another came and said, surely you are of them! Even your accent tells that you are.

74. Then Peter began to invoke curses and he swore an oath, I do not know this man. Then immediately the rooster crowed. (John 18:27)

75. At that moment Peter remembered the words of Jesus when he said, before the rooster crows you will deny me three times. Immediately he realized what he did and he went outside and cried with deep regret.

Matthew 27

1. When the morning had come, all of the high priests and many of the Sanhedrin held a meeting against Jesus so to put him to death. (Psalms 22:16)
2. After they tied him, they led him to Pontius Pilate, the governor.
3. Then Judas, the one who betrayed him, saw that he was condemned to death; He was greatly sorrowed, so he went and gave back the thirty pieces of silver to the high priest and the elders (Zechariah 11:12-13)
4. and he said, I have sinned by betraying innocent blood. But they said, that is nothing to us!
5. Then he threw the thirty pieces of silver into the temple and he left. Then he went and threw himself off of a cliff. (G-520 + G-1824 - Acts 1:18)
6. The high priests took the silver and said, it is not lawful to put this money into the treasury, since it is the price of blood. (*of which they had paid - making them guilty anyway*)
7. They held a meeting and chose to purchase the field of the potter for the burial of foreigners.

Verses 8-10 were certainly added by a scribe and are not a part of the original text.
8. *So that field was called the field of blood, and still is today. (obviously added by a scribe at a much later date.)*
9. *This was the fulfillment of the prophecy spoken by Jeremiah (**actually Zechariah**) the prophet who said: "he took the thirty pieces of silver, the price of the Messiah is paid, the sons of Israel did set a price*
10. *and gave the silver for a field of the potter, as my master gave command." (Zechariah 11:12-13)*

11. And Jesus stood before the governor and the governor asked him, are you the king of the Jews? Jesus said I am.
12. When he was accused by the high priests and scribes, he said nothing.
13. Therefore Pilate said to him, do you not hear what they have testified against you?
14. But Jesus did not answer him nor speak a single word. (Isaiah 53:7) The governor admired him greatly for this.
15. At a feast, the governor offered the release of one prisoner to the crowd, one of their choice.
16. They held a prisoner that was notorious, who was named Barbaras.
17. Then they assembled and Pilate said unto them, who shall I release unto you, Barbaras or Jesus, the one who is called Christ?
18. He knew that they brought him because of their envy.
19. When he sat down upon the judgment seat, his wife said unto him, have nothing to do with this righteous man. I have suffered many things today because of a dream that I had of him.
20. But the high priests and elders had persuaded the crowd that they should ask for Barbaras and for him to kill Jesus. (John 18:40)
21. The governor said unto them, which do you choose for me to release unto you? And they said Barbaras!
22. Then Pilate asked them, what shall I do with Jesus the Christ? And they all said unto him, crucify him!
23. Then the governor asked, what evil has he done? But they cried out louder and said, crucify him!
24. When Pilate saw that he could not convince them but instead there was an uproar, he took clean water and washed his hands in front of the crowd and he said, I am innocent of the blood of this righteous man. You will see his power in the end!
25. And all of the people *(unbelieving Jews)* said, may his blood be upon us and upon our children!

In this, the Jews cursed themselves and their offspring,
and sadly, most religious Jews still reject Christ, even today!

26. Then he released Barbaras and had Jesus whipped, then he sent him to be crucified.
27. The soldiers of the governor took Jesus into the interrogation room and surrounded him with soldiers.
28. Then they took all of his clothes off of him. They put on him a red colored robe,
29. braided a crown of thorns, put it upon his head and they put a reed in his right hand: Then they bowed before him and mocked him and they said: Hail unto the king of the Jews.
30. Then they spit on him, took the reed and beat him on his head.
31. After this, they mocked him, took off the robe and put his clothes back on him, then they led him to the place where he was to be crucified. (Isaiah 53:5)

32. As they started making their way, they saw a man named Simon, a man of Cyrenia. They compelled him to carry the cross that Jesus would be crucified upon. (John 19:17)

33. They came to a place called Golgotha, which in Hebrew (H-1538) means the place of skulls.

34. They gave him vinegar mixed with poison to drink. But when he tasted it he would not drink it.

35. They crucified him and then they competed for his clothing.

This part of verse 35 looks to have been added by a scribe and not a part of the original text.
This was the fulfillment of the prophecy; They would throw stones for my clothing. (Psalms 22:18)

36. Then they sat down and watched over him.

37. They put a sign over his head that read the charges against him: Jesus, King of the Jews.

38. Two thieves were crucified with him, one on his right and one on his left. (Isaiah 53:12)

39. Those that passed by blasphemed Jesus and shook their heads (Psalms 22:7-8)

40. and they said, the one who said that he would destroy the temple (1 Corinthians 3:16-17) and again rebuild it in three days, save yourself! If you are the son of God, come down off of that cross.

41. The high priests and scribes also mocked him, and the elders said;

42. He helped other people, but he is not able to help himself. If you are the king of Israel, come down from your cross and we will believe you.

43. They also said, he relied upon God, so let God come now and rescue him if he will; He did say that he is the son of God, did he not?

44. The two thieves (*transgressors, rebels*) that were crucified with him also mocked him.
(*This contradicts the Luke 23:39-43 account --- Hebrews 12:3; Mark 15:27; Isaiah 53:12*)

45. At midday or thereabout the land was covered with darkness, of which lasted about three hours.

46. Then Jesus cried out with a loud voice and said; Eli, Eli lama sabachthani? He spoke in Hebrew, which translates to say, "My God; My God, why have you left me? (Psalms 22:1)

47. Some that were there thought he spoke in Greek and misunderstood thinking he called for Elijah.

48. Immediately, one took a sponge, put it on a reed and dipped it in sour wine then reached up to give him a drink. (Psalms 69:21)

49. Some of the onlookers said, get away from him, let us see if Elijah will save him. (Psalms 22:7-8)

50. Jesus again cried out with a loud voice, then he allowed his spirit to depart.

51. Take notice of this! Immediately the veil of the temple was ripped into two pieces from top to bottom, and there was a strong earthquake and the bedrock was split wide open.

Verses 52-53 were errantly moved into this place by a scribe.
These verses were taken from the original placement of between verses 28:2 and 28:3.
This was done so to promote a false understanding and false time placement of the
Daniel 12:2 prophecy portraying as though the eternal resurrection had already occurred.
(2 Timothy 2:18; 2 Thessalonians 2:2)
These verses have been properly translated and put in their proper place.

54. Now the centurion and those with him keeping watch over Jesus, when they saw the earthquake and all that happened, they were greatly frightened and they said, truly this was the son of God! (Mark 15:39)

55. Many women that were on-looking from a distance who had followed Jesus from Galilee, they came to offer service unto his body,

56. of whom were Mary Magdalene, the mother of James & Joseph and mother of the sons of Zebedee.

57. When nightfall came, a wealthy man by the name of Joseph from Arimathaea who was also a disciple of Jesus, (Luke 10:1)

58. went unto Pilate and asked for the body of Jesus. Pilate then ordered that the body be given to him.

59. When Joseph took the body, he wrapped it in clean linen cloth

60. and placed it in a tomb that was freshly cut into the bedrock, then he rolled a large stone in front of the doorway of the tomb to seal it.

61. Mary Magdalene and the other Mary sat across from the grave.

62. The following morning after the crucifixion, the high priests and Pharisees went before Pilate.

63. They said, we remember when he was alive, the imposter said that he would rise from the dead after three days.

64. Please command that the grave be made secure, so that his disciples do not come at night and steal away his body and then tell the people that he has risen. If this was to happen, the aftermath would be worse for us than before!

65. Pilate said unto them, have your guards, now go and make it as secure as you can.

66. So they went and made the grave as secure as was possible and they placed guards to watch over it.

Matthew 28

1. Late in the evening, at the dawn of the first day of the week (*Sunday*), Mary Magdalene and the other Mary were coming to see the grave

2. when a strong earthquake occurred at that time; An angel of God descended from above and came to roll away the stone from the door of the grave

The proper placement of 27:52-53.

52. and the tomb was opened; The restored physical body that had died was raised.

53. He came forth out of the tomb resurrected, and he entered into the holy city and appeared unto many people.

3. His face was like lightning and his clothing were as white as snow. (Matthew 17:2; Mark 9:3)

4. The guards shook with great fear because he (*Jesus*) had been awakened (G-1453) from the dead.

5. When the women came to the tomb, the messenger (*angel*) of the Lord said unto the women, do not fear, the one that you are looking for, Jesus, he is not here.

6. He is risen, just as he said that he would. Come and see the grave where the master was laid.

7. Then the angel said, go quickly and tell his disciples that he has risen from the dead! He has gone into Galilee and waits for you there. (John 20:2)

8. So they went quickly from the tomb, both afraid and joyfully excited and they ran to tell his disciples.

9. As they went, they looked and saw Jesus coming towards them, and he said, be at peace.

10. When they approached him, they hugged him around his feet and they honored him.

11. At that time those guards came into the city and reported what they had seen unto the high priests;

12. Then they held an assembly with the elders to decide what to do. They took a large amount of silver and offered it to the soldiers

13. and they said, you shall say that his disciples came in the night and took his body away while you were sleeping.

14. If the governor hears of this, we will persuade him and free you from any further burden.

15. So they took the silver and did as they were instructed.

The following sentence was obviously added by a scribe.

Their report is still reported by the Jews even today.

16. And the eleven disciples went into Galilee, to the hill where Jesus had determined.

17. There they saw him and honored him, but some were hesitant.

Verses 18-20 were stated by Jesus just before his ascension.

18. Jesus talked with them and he said, the highest authority in the heavens and the earth has been given unto me. (Revelation 1:11)

19. You shall go into all nations, disciple them and baptize them in the <u>name</u> of the Father and Son, and into the Holy Spirit. (1 John 5:6-8, Acts 2:38; Psalms 22:27)

(Yehovah = {H-3068} -*Jehovah*; Jesus = Yehowshuwa = {H-3068 + H-3467} = Jehovah salvation)

20. Teach them to observe all that I have taught unto you, and know that I will be with you every day unto the end of the world. (John 14:18)

An overview of the book of Matthew

The book of Matthew was the earliest written of the four gospels, written about 34-37 AD, just a few years after the events. The accounts in Matthew are generally very accurately preserved as a whole, with the exception of some alterations and additions that were done by scribes in the following decades, of which, most have been pointed out in this translation. The book of Matthew should be considered as more reliable than the books of Mark or Luke, because Matthew was a first-hand eyewitness and participant in many of the events recorded herein.

John

Chapter 1

1. In the beginning there was a purpose (*spoken topic - for the creation of the world*); The purpose was in accordance with God and was God's plan. (Isaiah 55:11; Genesis 1:2, 6, 9, 11, 14, 20, 24, 26 - *the spoken word*)

2. It was this way in the beginning with God

3. that everything came into being through him, and nothing was created without him. (Genesis 1:1; Isaiah 44:24; Isaiah 51:13)

4. In him (*God*) the light (*Christ*) exists, and through the light, life is offered unto all of mankind. (John 3:20; 8:12; 9:5; 12:46; 14:6; Psalms 27:1; 1 Thessalonians 5:5)

5. The light shines in the darkness and the darkness can not overpower it. (Exodus 14:20)

6. There was a man named John that was sent by God;

7. He came to be a witness to testify of the light (*Christ*), so that all might come to put their trust in him;

8. John was not the one who is the light, but he did testify concerning the light.

9. He that is the light (*Christ*) enlightens every man that comes into this arrangement (*covenant*). (John 14:26)

10. Though the world was created by him, he came into the world, yet those of the world did not recognize him.

11. He came unto his own people, but they did not receive him.

12. But all that do receive him, he gives them authority to become the children of God, unto all those that continue believing into his name; (1 John 3:1-3)

13. They are not of blood (*physical descent*), neither do they follow after the lustful desires for that which is evil, neither do they follow after the desires of this world, but are regenerated and reserved by God.

14. For this purpose, he came into a body and he lived among us, and we saw his glory. Glorious in the manner of the only one produced from within the Father; He is full of the power of God and the revealed truth.

15. John became a witness unto him and he announced this, saying: This is he whom I spoke of; He that comes after me is much greater than I, because he is the highest above all.

16. And through all that Christ Jesus did, we can receive the assistance of God, in contrast to living by our own ability. (*new covenant vs. old covenant*)

17. Because the Mosaic law was given through Moses, but the assistance of God and the revealed truth has come into being through Jesus Christ.

18. No man has continually pleased (G-2193+ G-699) God throughout a full lifetime; (Deut. 34:10) The only begotten son is of the substance of the Father and he has announced the terms. (*of the new covenant*)

19. And this is the witness of John, when the Jews commissioned priests and Levites, they would ask him, who are you;

20. He acknowledged and did not deny, but he fully acknowledged, I am not the Christ.

It must be noted that in most modern bibles, verse 21 creates a contradiction with Matthew 11:14; Matthew 17:11; Mark 9:12; and Luke 1:17-21 of which have been corrected in this book.

21. And they again asked him, who are you then? Elijah? (Malachi 4:5) And he said, No! Then they asked, are you a teacher? And he answered, No!

22. And they said unto him, who are you? Tell us, so that we can go and tell those who sent us. What do you say about yourself, who are you?

23. Then John said, I am the voice announcing in the wilderness, I am the one Isaiah spoke of, and I have come to make the way straight for the Messiah. (Isaiah 40:3; Malachi 3:1)

24. Those that were sent unto John were sent from the Pharisees,

25. and they asked him, why do you baptize if you are not the Christ, nor Elijah, nor a teacher?

26. Then John said, I baptize in water, but standing among you is one that you will not recognize.

27. It is he that shall come after me, but he was also before me and I am not worthy to untie his shoes.

28. All of these things happened in Bethabara, across the Jordan river where John was baptizing.

29. The following day, John saw Jesus coming toward him and he said: Look! The Lamb of God! He shall make a way to take away the transgressions (*sins*) of the world. (Matthew 1:21)

30. This is he whom I told you would come after me, the man who was also before me, because before me he existed.

31. I did not know who he was, except that he would be revealed unto Israel. He is the reason that I came unto the water to do baptisms!

32. And John was a witness unto this, and he said; I have perceived a spirit coming down from out of the sky, as a dove, and it remained upon him.

33. But I truly did not know who he was, but he that sent me to baptize in water said to me, upon whomever you see the spirit descend and remain upon, it is he that is saturated with the holiest spirit.

34. And I have seen and I have witnessed, that this is he that is the son of God.

35. On another day, John stood with two of his disciples watching Jesus walking, *(Matthew 4:18)*

36. and he said, look! The lamb of God! (*this happened after Jesus returned from the temptation of Satan*)

37. And two disciples of John heard him speaking, and they followed Jesus.

38. Then Jesus turned and looked at them as they were following him and he said to them, what are you doing? And they said, Rabbi, (*teacher*) where do you live?

39. And Jesus said to them, come and see. They came with him and saw where he lived and remained there with him until about the tenth hour of the day.

40. Andrew, the brother of Simon Peter was one of the two who had heard John and then followed him.

41. Then he went and found his brother and said, Simon, we have found the Messiah!

42. Then he led him to Jesus, and he looked at them and said, you are Simon the son of Jonah. You shall be called Cephas. (*Cephas in Hebrew, Petros in Greek, Peter in English = means a small piece of stone*)

43. One day, Jesus had a reason to go into Galilee, and he found Philip there, and said to him, follow me.

44. Philip was from Bethsaida, the same city that Andrew and Simon Peter were from.

45. Then Philip found Nathaniel and said unto him, we have surely found him; He that gave the written ten commandments unto Moses and the prophets spoke of, he is Jesus the son of Joseph from Nazareth!

46. Then Nathaniel said unto him, out of Nazareth? Can anything good come out of that place? Then Philip said, come and see.

47. Then Jesus saw Nathaniel coming towards him and said unto him; Look, truly an Israelite in whom there is no deceit!

48. Then Nathaniel said to him, from where do I know you? Jesus answered and said, before Philip called you, you were under the fig tree and I saw you.

49. Nathaniel answered and said, rabbi, you are the son of God and you are the king of Israel.

50. Jesus then said to him, because I said that I saw you under a fig tree you believe in me? You will see much greater things than this!

51. Then he said unto him, truly I tell you, hereafter you will see the heavens open up and the angels of God ascending and descending unto the son of man.

John 2

1. On the third day, there was a wedding in Cana of Galilee and the mother of Jesus was there.

2. Jesus was also invited along with his disciples to go to the wedding.

3. They came to be short of wine, so the mother of Jesus told him that they do not have enough.

4. Jesus said to her, why should that be a concern to you or me? My time has not yet come.

5. His mother said to the servants, whatever he tells you to do, do it.

6. And there were six stone water jars setting there according to the custom of purification of the Jews, and each one had the capacity to hold two or three measures (*gallons*).

7. Jesus said unto them, fill the jars with water. So they went and filled them up to the top.

8. Then he said to them, draw some out and take it to the chief of the feast; They did as they were instructed.

9. But when the chief of the feast tasted the water, it had become wine! He did not know from where the wine had come, but his servants that drew the water knew. The chief of the feast called the bridegroom

10. and he said to him, everyone puts the good wine out first and then it settles; When they have become

intoxicated, then they give out the lesser quality wine; Yet you have kept the good wine until now?

11. This was the beginning of the miracles of Jesus, in Cana of Galilee. This revealed his glory and his disciples began to establish trust in him.

12. After this, Jesus went to Capernaum with his mother, his brothers and his disciples. He remained there for many days.

13. The Passover of the Jews was near and then Jesus went up to Jerusalem.

14. In the temple he found sheep, oxen and doves being sold, and the money takers were there sitting.

15. He made a whip out of long grasses and he threw all of them out of the temple, the sheep, the oxen and the money takers, spilling the money and overturning the tables!

16. Unto those who were selling the doves he said, get these things out of here! Do not make my Father's house a house of merchandising.

17. The disciples later remembered what is written: "The zeal of your house consumes me." (Psalms 69:9)

18. The Jews then said to him, give us a sign (*omen*) to justify unto us that which you have done.

19. Jesus said unto them, I will destroy this temple and in three days I will raise it up again.

20. Then the Jews said, it took forty-six years to build the temple, and you will raise it up in three days?

21. But he himself spoke about the temple of his body. (1 Corinthians 3:16-17)

22. At the time that he was raised from the dead, the disciples remembered that he had said this unto them, and they believed that which was written of him and the words that Jesus had spoken.

23. As Jerusalem was having the feast of Passover, many believed in his name, seeing the many miracles that he did.

24. But Jesus himself did not establish trust in them because he knew all things. (John 6:66)

25. He had no need that any be witnesses, for he knew what was within every man's heart.

John 3

1. There was a man of the Pharisees named Nicodemus, a ruler of the Jews. (John 19:39) He came to Jesus in the night time (*in secret*) and asked him; Rabbi, we know that you are a teacher that is come from God;

2. No one can do the miracles that you are able to do if God is not with them.

3. Jesus responded unto him and said, truly, truly I tell you, if a man is not reborn (*regenerated*) from above, he will not be able to see the kingdom of God. (Matthew 18:1-3; Acts 3:19; 2:38; Romans 6:1-23)

4. Then Nicodemus said unto him, how is a man able to be reborn when he is old? Is he able to climb into his mother's womb to be birthed a second time?

5. Jesus said to him, truly I tell you, except a man is reborn through water (*cleansing of baptism*) and of the spirit, he is not able to enter the kingdom of God. (1 Corinthians 12:13; Acts 2:38; Acts 3:19; 1 John 5:6; Psalms 51:2,7)

6. For those that are living according to the lustful desires (*flesh*), they are carnal (*flesh*). Those that are truly living a regenerated (*reborn*) life through the character of God, they have the spirit of God. (*in them*)

7. Do not be confused because I said to you that you must be reborn from above. (Matthew 18:1-10)

8. The wind blows where it will and you hear its sound, but you do not know from where it comes or where it goes. Similar are all who have been regenerated (*reborn*) by the spirit of God.

9. Nicodemus then said unto him, how is it possible for this to happen?

10. Jesus answered and said, are you not a teacher of Israel, but yet you do not understand these things?

11. Truly, I tell you, I certainly speak what I know to be true, and I truly am a witness of what I know to be valuable, but my testimony you do not receive?

12. If you do not believe the things that I have told you that are of the earth, how will you believe if I told you about the things from above?

13. No one shall ascend up into the heavens, except if that which is from the heavens is brought into you, the son of man (*Christ*) who is from above. (1 John 4:1-5)

14. The same as Moses lifted up the serpent in the wilderness, so also must the son of man be lifted up;

15. In this, everyone who commits themselves unto him will not be destroyed, but receive eternal life.

16. This is the way that God is affectionate unto his creation; He offers his only born son, so that all that continue believing unto him shall not be destroyed, but are able to receive life everlasting.
(1 John 4:9; Romans 10:11; Hosea 14:9; Psalms 133:3; Psalms 145:13)

17. God did not send his son unto mankind to condemn them, but that they might be rescued through him.

18. Those believing into him shall not be condemned, but all that are not believing into him are already condemned, because they have not committed their trust in the only born son of God.

19. This is the reason for judgment day: The light has entered into the world, but men love the darkness (*sin*) more than the light (*Christ*), because their deeds are evil.

20. For all that continue doing wickedness hate the light, and they refuse to come into the light, so that they not be convinced and corrected from their wicked deeds. (1 John 3:3-10; 2 John 1:9-11)

21. But he that lives according to the truth (*God's ways*) does come into the light, and his good deeds shall be made known, that they are according to God. (Acts 26:20; 1 John 3:3; Philippines 3:9; John 4:24)

22. Soon after this, Jesus came with his disciples unto the land of Judea and he remained there with them and they were baptized.

23. At that time, John was baptizing in Aenon near Salem, because there was much water there, so they came and were baptized.

24. For at this time John had not yet been thrown into prison.

25. Then one of the disciples of John discussed with the Jews concerning purification *(being cleansed of sin)*

26. They came to John and asked him, Rabbi, who was it that was with you across the Jordan? The one whom you witnessed and saw, he is now baptizing and everyone is coming to him! (Romans 6:1-23)

27. John answered them and said, no man is able to take hold of anything (*concerning eternal life*) unless he has committed himself to live according to the ways of God. (1 John 3:3)

28. You yourselves are witnesses that I said clearly that I am not the Christ, but I am the one that was sent to come before him.

29. He that comes for the bride is the bridegroom, but the friend of the bridegroom stands by and can hear him, is joyful and happy because he has heard the voice of the bridegroom; In this, my joy has been made complete.

30. He must increase, but I must decrease.

31. The one who is come existed from the beginning and he is above all. Those who are concerned with things that are earthly are carnal and they speak of carnal things. Those that abide in the one that is from above holds a much higher place, above all others.

32. He that experiences and understands this, he is a witness, and this witness (*evidence*) few others get a hold of (*understand and commit to*). (Matthew 7:14; Luke 13:23)

33. He that receives this testimony in himself is a witness that God is true.

34. For the one sent of God (*Jesus*) speaks the words of God and God does not limit the spirit unto him. (John 6:51; 1 Corinthians 11:27)

35. The Father loves the son, and all things have been given unto his hands.

36. He who is committed *(obedient)* unto the son shall receive everlasting life. He that is disobedient unto the son will not see life, but the wrath of God shall come upon him (verse 18; Hebrews 10:26; Romans 2)

John 4

1. When Jesus had heard that the Pharisees were aware that he was making more disciples and baptizing more than John had, (John 3:26)

2. though Jesus himself did not baptize, but his disciples were baptizing,

3. he decided to leave Judea and he went again to Galilee;

4. It was necessary for him to go through Samaria.

5. When he came into a city of Samaria that is called Sychar, which is near the piece of land that was given by Jacob to Joseph his son, there was a well there, the well of Jacob.

6. Jesus was tired from his journey and he sat down at the well. It was about the sixth hour of the day.

7. A Samarian woman came to draw water and Jesus said to her, please offer me a drink. (Isaiah 46:12)

8. His disciples had gone to the city to purchase food.

9. Then the woman of Samaria said, how is it that you who are a Jew ask me for a drink, I being a woman of Samaria? For Jews do not have any dealings with we Samaritans.

10. Jesus answered her and said, if you knew the gift of God and the one who is asking you for a drink, you would have asked and I would give unto you the living water.

11. And the woman said to him, master, you have no vessel and the well is deep; From where will you draw living water?

12. Are you greater than our forefather Jacob who gave to us this well, out of which he drank from, the same as his sons and their livestock.

13. And Jesus answered and said unto her, everyone who drinks of this water will again thirst;

14. Whoever drinks of the water that I give will never thirst again, but the water that I give will spring up like a fountain of uplifting living water unto eternal life!

15. The woman said, master, give me of this water so that I will no longer thirst nor come here to draw.

16. Jesus said unto her, go and call for your husband and bring him here.

17. But the woman said, I do not have a husband. Then Jesus said unto her, your words are true that you do not have a husband! This you have spoken is truth;

18. But yet you have had five husbands and now the one that you accompany is not your husband.

19. Then the woman said to him, master, I perceive that you are a prophet;

20. Our forefathers worshipped on this hill, but you say that Jerusalem is the proper place to worship.

21. Then Jesus said unto her, woman, trust me; There will soon come a time when not on this hill nor in Jerusalem will anyone worship the Father. (*a prophecy of 70 AD.*)

22. You do not know what you worship, but I surely worship what is true; Salvation belongs to the Jew (Jesus, *those who belong to Jehovah*) (Romans 2:29)

23. But the time is approaching and now is, when the true worshippers will worship the Father in spirit (*disposition - heart*) and in truth (*evidence*). Because the Father seeks for such ones to serve him.

24. For God is spirit, and those who worship him must do so in spirit (*character*) and truth (*evidence*).

25. Then the woman said to him, I know the Messiah is coming, the one who will be the Christ; When he comes, he will make all things known.

26. Then Jesus said to her, I who am speaking to you, I am he!

27. Then his disciples came and were surprised that he was speaking to the woman, though no one asked, what are you seeking for or why are you talking with her?

28. Then the woman left her water jar there and she went into the city, and she announced to the men:

29. Come and see! There is a man who told me all of what I have done! Is this not the Christ?

30. So they went out from the city and came unto Jesus,

31. meanwhile the disciples recommended unto him, teacher eat.

32. But he said unto them, I have food to eat that you are unaware of.

33. Then the disciples said to one another, no one brought him anything to eat!

34. But then Jesus said, my food is that I do the will of he who has sent me, that I finish his work.

35. Do you not say, in four months there will be a time to harvest? Look, I tell you now, lift up your eyes, and look at the fields, for they are already white and ready to harvest!

36. The one who continues harvesting will receive what he has earned and he will gather fruit unto everlasting life; He that sows will rejoice together with the ones who harvest. (Matthew 10:42)

37. For these words are true; There is one that sows and another that reaps.

38. I have sent you to harvest that which you did not labor over. Others have labored, and you have come in unto their labor.

39. Many of the Samaritans in that city put their trust in him because of the word that was testified of the woman; "he told me about all that I have ever done."

40. Then the Samaritans came to him and they invited him to remain there with them, and he stayed there for two days.

41. Many others believed upon him through his words.

42. They then said to the woman, we no longer believe because of your word, but because we ourselves have heard and we know that this truly is the one, the Christ, the saviour of the world!

43. After two days, Jesus left that place and he went to Galilee.

Verse 44 has been misplaced by a scribe and is out of context in this place. Jesus was from Nazareth but this context is of Samaria.

44. *Jesus demonstrated that a prophet has no respect in his own native town.* (Matthew 13:57)

45. Then when he came into Galilee, the Galileans received him seeing all of the things that he had done in Jerusalem at the feast, as they had also gone to the feast.

46. Then Jesus came again unto Cana of Galilee, the place where he had turned the water into wine. There was a noble man there in Capernaum that had a son that was very sick.

47. When he had heard that Jesus was coming into Galilee, he went unto him and asked him if he would come and heal his son because he was close to death.

48. Jesus said unto him, if not for signs and the fulfillment of prophecies you certainly would not believe.

49. The noble man said, Lord please come before my child dies!

50. Jesus said unto him; Go, your son shall live! So the man believed the words that Jesus said unto him and he went away.

51. When he was on his way, his servants came running to meet him and told him; Your child lives!

52. Then he asked him in what hour that he had recovered; They told him, it was yesterday about the seventh hour when his fever left him.

53. That is when the father of the boy knew, that was the time in which Jesus had told him, your son shall live, the very time that he believed; Henceforth his whole house believed with him!

**Verse 54 looks to have been added by a scribe and not a part of the original text
Jesus did not come to Galilee from Judea but from Samaria. (verses 39-43)**

54. This was the second miracle that Jesus did when coming from Judea into Galilee.

John 5

1. After these things there was a Jewish feast and Jesus went up to Jerusalem.

2. At the sheep gate in Jerusalem, there is a pool with five terraces that in Hebrew is called Bethesda.

3. Lying in there were a large number of people who had sicknesses, the blind, lame and crippled and they were waiting for the waters to begin stirring up.

4. For a angel of God occasionally would come and stir up the waters, and the first one to enter therein after the stirring of the waters would be healed from whatever infirmity he might have.

5. There was a man there who for thirty-eight years suffered with infirmity.

6. When Jesus saw him lying there and already knowing that he had been suffering for such a long time said to him, do you want to be healed?

7. The man suffering the infirmity answered him and said, Lord, I have not found any man who would throw me in the pool after the waters become stirred up. While I am making my way towards the water, there is always another who comes and enters therein before I can get there.

8. Jesus said unto him, rise up! Take your bed and walk! (Psalms 22:24)

9. Instantly the man was healed and he took up his bed and he walked away!

10. And this happened on a Sabbath day. Then the Jews went to the man who had been healed and said, it is the Sabbath; It is not lawful for you to carry your bedding.

11. He answered them and said, he that healed me told me to take up my bedding and be on my way.

12. Then they asked him, who is the man that told you to take up your bedding and go on your way?

13. But the one that was healed did not know who he was and Jesus had left the immediate area and there was a large gathering of people in that place.

14. Jesus later found him in the temple and said unto him, be aware, you have been made whole; Go and sin no more or a worse thing will come upon you. (2 Peter 2:20-22; Hebrews 10:26; Numbers 15:30; John 8:11; Luke 5:20)

15. Then the man went out of the temple and reported to the Jews that it was Jesus who had healed him.

16. Because of this, the Jews began to persecute Jesus and they were looking for a way to kill him, because of the things that he did upon the Sabbath day.

17. But Jesus said unto them, the deeds of my Father are being done through me.

18. Because of this, they wanted much more to kill him, not only because he broke the Sabbath, but calling God to be his Father, thus making himself to be equal to God. (Isaiah 9:6 - *everlasting Father*)

19. Then Jesus said unto them, truly I tell you, I am not able to do anything of myself, but I am only able to

do what I have seen the Father instructing; Whatever he instructs, these are the things that I do.

20. The Father loves the son and shows unto him all things that he instructs, and he will show unto me much greater things so that you might admire (*wonder*).

21. For just as the Father shall raise up the *(spiritually)* dead to give life unto them, so the son must also bring life unto those who he chooses. (Matthew 22:11-14, Daniel 12:1-2; Revelation 19:7)

22. Because the Father shall judge no one; All judgment is given unto the son.

23. In this, they might all honor the son just as they honor the Father. The one that does not honor the son does not honor the Father who has sent him. (John 12:45; 1 John 2:22-23)

24. Truly I tell you, those that hear my words, obey them and continue to live fully committed unto me, they are qualified to receive everlasting life; Condemnation shall not come upon them, but they gain the ability to be changed from death unto life. (John 3:16)

25. Truly I tell you, there will come a time that is now beginning, when the (*spiritually*) dead will understand the instructions of the son of God, and those that will take heed will live forever.

26. For just as the Father in himself is life, the same is given unto the son and he has life in himself.

27. He also gave for him to be the bringer of justice, because he is the son of man.

28. Do not be surprised, because there will come a time when all that are in the tombs will hear his call

29. and they will come out; Those that have done good, unto the resurrection of life everlasting, and all those that have done evil, unto the resurrection of damnation. (Daniel 12:2; Revelation 20:12; Romans 2:6-10)

30. I am not able to do anything by myself! But as I hear, I determine (*judge*), and my judgment is righteous. I am not looking to fulfill my own will, but the will of the Father who sent me. (verse 19)

31. If I am my own witness, my witness is not trusted to be true;

32. But there is another witness of me and his testimony is true.

33. You have seen John before me and he was a witness of the truth.

34. I do not require the testimony of any man, but I tell you these things that you might be saved.

35. He was a lamp that burned and glowed, and you were willing to be joyful in your weakness in his light for a short time.

36. However, I have a witness that is greater than John; The deeds that the Father has given unto me to do, I will complete them. These deeds that I do are an evidence that the Father has sent me.

37. My Father is also a witness of me. His voice you have never heard and his face you have not seen.

38. His instruction you do not have living in you, because the one that he has sent unto you, you do not believe (*commit to*).

39. Search the scriptures because you think that in them you shall receive everlasting life; They testify (*are a witness*) of me,

40. yet you do not choose to come to me so that you might receive life!

41. I do not recognize the honor given by men.

42. I perceive that the love of God is not in you. (verse 30)

43. I have come in the name of my Father, but you do not receive me. When another comes in his own name, you will strongly receive him. (Daniel 11:24; Matthew 24:24 - *speaking of the antichrist*)

44. How is it possible for you to believe (*commit unto me*)? You receive honors from one another that satisfy you and you do not have any desire to seek for the honor of God!

45. Do not think that I shall have need to accuse you before the Father; For there is one that accuses you, that is Moses, the one in whom you claim to be committed!

46. Therefore, if you truly trusted in Moses, you would have recognized and trusted in me, because it is I whom Moses had written about.

47. You certainly do not trust in what Moses wrote, so then how could you trust in my words?

John 6

1. After this, Jesus left that place and crossed the sea of Galilee, also called the sea of Tiberias.

2. There was a large crowd that followed him, because they saw the many healings and miracles he did.

3. So Jesus went up upon a hill and sat there with his disciples.

4. This was a time near the Passover feast of the Jews.

5. When Jesus looked outward, he saw the crowds gathering together, all coming to see him; Then he said unto Philip, from where can we gather enough food to feed all of these people?

6. But Jesus said this to test him, because he already knew what he would do.

7. Philip answered and said, two hundred denarii of food is not enough to feed all of them, even if each one was to receive a very little!

8. And one of the disciples, Andrew, the brother of Simon Peter said;

9. There is a young boy who has five small barley loaves and two fish, but there are so many people gathering here!

10. Then Jesus told them to have the people sit down on the ground, because there was much grass in that place. Therefore, the people sat down and the number of them was about five thousand.

11. And Jesus took the loaves and gave thanks, then he gave it unto the disciples and they distributed unto those sitting down on the grass. Then the same was done with the fishes, and they all ate as much as they desired to eat and were filled.

12. Then he said unto his disciples, gather up the leftovers so that nothing is wasted.

13. So they gathered them up and there were twelve baskets with pieces of the barley bread, that were left over after they had all eaten.

14. Then the men saw what Jesus had done and they said, this truly is the Messiah that was to come.

15. Jesus knew that they were about to come, take him and make him a king, so he withdrew unto a solitary place alone.

16. In the evening the disciples went down to the sea

17. and they entered into a boat and went across the sea of Capernaum; It had become night and Jesus had not yet returned to them.

18. Soon a strong wind came upon the sea.

19. After having already traveled a certain distance, about 25 or 30 stadia, they saw Jesus walking on the water and as he came close to the boat they became afraid.

20. But he said to them, it is I! Do not fear

21. They wanted to get him into the boat, but instantly the boat struck land at the place where they were intending to land. (*this seems to be incomplete compared to other similar accounts*)

22. The following day, the crowd of people that were standing across the sea who saw the boat that the disciples had entered in, and they knew that there was no other boat and that Jesus had not gone with the disciples in the boat, but they went alone;

23. It happened that other boats from Tiberias had come near to the place where they had eaten and given thanks unto the Lord;

24. When the crowd saw that Jesus was not there, nor were his disciples, they entered into the boats and they came to Capernaum seeking to find Jesus there.

25. And when they had found him, they asked, Rabbi (*teacher*), how did you get here?

26. Then Jesus answered them and said, truly you seek me not because you see the evidence *(that I am the Messiah)*, but because you were given the food and were filled.

27. Do not be concerned with the food that is temporary and decays, but concern yourselves with the food that abides unto everlasting life, of which the son of man shall give unto you; Know that my Father God is within me. (Luke 14:15; 1 Corinthians 11:18-34)

28. Then they said unto him, what can we do in order to do the deeds of God?

29. Then Jesus said unto them, it is necessary that you completely commit yourselves in the one whom he has sent. (Matthew 22:37; Mark 12:30)

30. And they asked, what sign will you do that we might both see, believe and put our trust in you? What is your evidence (*deeds*)?

31. Our forefathers ate mannah in the wilderness, just as it has been written, and they lived. He gave to them the food out of the heavens to eat! (Psalms 78:24)

32. Then Jesus said to them, truly I tell you, it was not Moses who gave unto you the bread from the heavens, but my Father that gave it to you.

33. For the bread of God is the one who came down from the heavens and offers life unto all in the world. (John 1:4)

34. Then they said to him, the master always gives unto us our food.

35. And Jesus said unto them, I am the bread of life; The one that commits unto me shall never hunger, and the one that continues trusting in me shall never thirst.

36. But I have said that you have seen me, yet you do not believe (*trust and commit*). (John 3:19-20)

37. Everything that the Father has committed unto me shall remain with me, and those that come unto me

shall not be rejected.

38. For I have descended from the heavens, not to do my own will, but to do the will of he that sent me.

39. This is the will of the Father who has sent me, that all that he has given unto me shall be raised up on that final day (*judgment day*).

40. The will of he that has sent me is that everyone who can perceive the son and fully commit unto him should receive everlasting life and I will raise them up in that final day. (John 3:16; Romans 2:10)

41. Therefore the Jews murmured concerning him because he said "I am the bread that has come down from the heavens".

42. They said, is this not Jesus the son of Joseph, of whom we know his father and his mother? How can he say that he has come down from the heavens?

43. Then Jesus answered them and said, do not murmur with one another;

44. No one is able to come before me if the Father does not guide him to me. Only these will I raise up on the final day.

45. It is written by the prophets, and they shall all be taught by God, each one who can understand shall learn from the Father, all that come unto me. (Isaiah 54:13; Jeremiah 31:33-34)

46. None have seen the Father except those that are near unto God; Only these have perceived the Father.

47. Truly, he that commits unto me shall receive everlasting life. (John 3:16; Romans 2:10)

48. I am the bread of life.

49. The forefathers ate the manna in the desert, but they died.

50. He that has come down from the heavens, if anyone shall consume of him, they shall eat and not die.

51. I am the living bread that came down from the heavens; If anyone shall eat of this bread, he will live forever. Truly, the bread that I offer is my body (*crucified and risen*) (Romans 6:1-23), of which I will offer on the behalf of those in this world so that they might live. (1 Corinthians 11:18-34; Luke 14:15; John 3:34)

52. Then the Jews argued among themselves and said, how can this man offer unto us his body to eat?

53. Then Jesus said unto them, truly I tell you, if you do not consume (*be engulfed in*) the body of the son of man and partake (*be reconciled*) in his blood, you have no life in yourselves. (Romans 6:3-8)

54. He that is consuming my body and drinking of my blood, he has the promise of everlasting life and I will raise him up on the final day. (1 Corinthians 11:18-34; Luke 14:15)

55. Because my body surely is the (*spiritual*) food, and my blood truly is the drink (*baptism*); (Acts 2:38)

56. He that continues eating of my body and drinking my blood shall remain in me and I in him.

57. Just as the Father has sent me and I live through the Father, the same is the one that partakes of me, he must also live through me. (1 Corinthians 11:18-34; Luke 14:15)

58. This is the bread that has come down from the heavens; Not the same as when your forefathers ate manna and eventually died; He that eats of this bread shall live forever.

59. He said these things while teaching in the synagogue in Capernaum.

60. Thereafter many of his disciples that had heard these words said, this message is difficult; Who is able to understand it?

61. But Jesus knew they were murmuring among themselves, so he asked them, does this offend you?

62. What if you had seen the son of man ascend to the place from where he had first come?

63. It is the spirit that brings life but the body does not bring eternal benefit, not at all! These words that I have spoken unto you are spiritual (*spiritual analogy*) and offer life.

64. But there are some here who are not believing. Jesus knew from the beginning those that are believing, but he also knew who would betray him.

65. He said, this is why I told you that no one is able to come unto me unless my Father has offered for him to believe and remain committed unto me.

66. At this time, many of his followers reverted back (*fell away*) and no longer walked with him. (John 2:24)

67. Then Jesus said unto the twelve, do you want to leave also?

68. Then Simon Peter said unto him, master, unto whom shall we go? You hold the instructions of life!

69. We have completely come to trust that you are the Christ, the son of the living God.

70. Then Jesus said, did I not choose you twelve? Yet there is one devil among you! He spoke of Judas Iscariot, the son of Simon, the one that would betray him. He was one of the twelve.

John 7

1. And after those things, Jesus was spending his time in Galilee. He did not want to go to Judea because the Jews were seeking to kill him there.

2. The Jewish feast of tabernacles was near.

3. Then his brothers said to him, leave here and go to Judea so that your disciples there can see all of the mighty deeds that you do.

4. For no one does anything in secret if he desires to be made known. If you can do these things, then reveal them unto the whole world!

5. For not even his own brothers believed him.

6. But Jesus said unto them, the time for me has not yet come, yet your time is always awaiting. Because I tell you the truth, I am disrespected. But I am a witness of myself and the deeds are undeniable.

8. You go up to this feast, but I will not go, because my time has not yet been completed.

9. And after he said these things unto them, he remained there in Galilee;

10. But when his brothers went up to the feast, he also went with them, secretly, not publicly.

11. The Jews looked for him at the feast and they said, where is he?

12. And there was murmuring among the crowds; Some said that he is good, while others said no; He only deceives the stupid people.

13. No one publicly spoke of him for fear of the Jews.

14. But at about the midpoint of the feast Jesus went up to the temple and taught.

15. The Jews were shocked and said, how is it that he knows the scriptures, being that he is uneducated?

16. And Jesus answered them and said, my teachings are not mine own, but are of he that sent me and he made them evident unto me.

17. If anyone wants to do his will (*of the Father*), then they will know whether this teaching is of God or if I am speaking for myself.

18. He who speaks of his own, he seeks for honor unto himself, but the one who seeks honor unto the one who has sent him, this is the true one and there is no unrighteousness in him. (1 John 3:3; 1 John 1:5-7)

19. Didn't Moses give you the (*Mosaic*) law, yet why don't any of you live by his law and why do you seek to kill me?

20. Then the crowd answered and said, you have a demon. Who is it that seeks to kill you?

21. And Jesus answered and said, I did mighty deeds and you all admired.

22. This is why Moses offered unto you circumcision, though it was not of Moses but of your forefather (*Abraham*), yet now on the Sabbath you go and circumcise a man!

23. So if a man receives circumcision on the Sabbath, does he not break the law of Moses? Yet now you are angry because I healed a man on the Sabbath? You are hypocrites!

24. You do not judge righteously, but you judge by appearance!

25. Then some of those of Jerusalem said, is this not the one that they are looking to kill? (verse 20)

26. Now he is speaking publicly and they have nothing to say unto him? Perhaps the rulers truly know that this is the Christ! (John 9:25)

27. But we know from where this man originated, yet when the Christ comes, no one shall know from where he is out of. (Hebrews 7:3; John 8:58; Psalms 110:4)

28. Then Jesus announced in the temple as he taught, he said, you not only know who I am, but you also know from where I have come and that the one who has sent me is true, though you do not know him!

29. But I know him because I am of him and he has sent me. (John 1:18)

30. Then they thought to arrest him, but no one laid a hand upon him, because his time had not yet come.

31. But there were many in the crowd that believed in him, and they said, could there be greater indication that he is the Christ more than what this man has already done?

32. And the Pharisees heard the crowd murmuring concerning these things said about him, so they sent some Pharisees and the under officers of the high priests to attempt to seize him.

33. Then Jesus said unto them, for a short time I will remain here with you; Then I will go unto he that has sent me.

34. Then you will seek for me but you will not find me. Where I will be, you are not able to follow.

35. Then the Jews said unto themselves, where could he go that we could not find him? To the Diaspora (*Jewish people living abroad*) in gentile nations, will he go and teach into the Greeks?

36. What is it that he has said, you will seek me and you will not find me, and where I am you are not able to follow?

37. On the great final day of the feast, Jesus stood and announced aloud saying, if anyone thirst let him come unto me and drink.

38. He that puts his trust in me, just as it is said in the scriptures, rivers of living water shall flow out of his belly. (1 Corinthians 11:25)

39. But this was speaking of his spirit that would be received by all those that continue to put their trust in him. At that time, the spirit of the holy one was not yet given, (Acts 1:1- 2:40) because Jesus had not yet had his glory (*life*) taken away. (*he had not yet been crucified, risen and ascended - the holy spirit is the spirit of Christ Jesus*)

40. Therefore, many in the crowds heard the message that he gave and they said, truly this is the prophet.

41. Others said, this is the Christ. Yet others said, no, for Christ shall not come from out of Galilee.

42. Do the scriptures not say, that from out of the seed of David and from out of Bethlehem, the very village of David that the Christ would come?

43. Then began a great division among the crowd concerning him.

44. Then there were some that wanted to seize him, but no one laid a hand upon him.

45. That is when the under officers of the high priests returned to the Pharisees and they said to them, why did you not bring him?

46. And the under officers said, there has never been a man who has spoken as this man speaks!

47. Then the Pharisees said, you have not also been deceived, have you?

48. None of the powerful ones have trusted in him and neither have any of the Pharisees!

49. But those in the crowd are cursed because they do not know the law (*traditions of the Jewish law*).

50. But after he had spoken with Jesus in secret, Nicodemus, being himself a Pharisee said unto them; (John 3:1-3)

51. The Jewish law does not judge a man if it does not hear him first and knows what he is doing.

52. They then answered and said unto him, you are not also from Galilee, are you? Search and see if any prophet has risen up from Galilee.

John 8

1. And they went, each one to his own house, but Jesus went unto the mount of Olives.

2. Again at dawn he came unto the temple and all of the people came to him. Jesus taught them while sitting there.

3. Then the scribes and the Pharisees brought unto him a woman that was arrested while taking part in adultery, and they stood her in front of Jesus.

4. Then they said unto him, this woman was arrested while in the act of committing adultery.

5. According to the law of Moses, it is commanded for us to stone her to death; What do you say?

6. They said this to tempt him, so that they might be able to accuse him. Then Jesus bent down with his finger and wrote in the soil as though he did not hear them.

7. And they continued to question him, and he straightened himself back up and then said;
He that is sinless (*not guilty of the same thing*) should cast the first stone. (*Where is the man?*)

8. Then he again bent down and wrote upon the earth.

9. But when they heard, and because their consciences were convicted, one by one they went away, beginning with the oldest unto the last one. Jesus was left alone and the woman stood in front of him.

10. Jesus stood back up, having seen no one but the woman and he said unto her, woman, where are your accusers? Is there anyone remaining to condemn you?

11. And she said, there is no one remaining my master. And Jesus said unto her, your sins are forgiven unto you, now go and sin no more. (1 John 3:3-10; Luke 5:20; John 5:14; verses 31-36)

12. Then Jesus again began to speak to the people gathering around him, and he said, I am the light of the world. (John 1:4-7) He that chooses to follow me can not abide in darkness (*sin*), but will have the light unto life. (John 1:4; Romans 6:1-2, 16; 1 John 2:8; 1 John 3:3-10; 2 Peter 2:20-22; Hebrews 10:26; 1 John 1:5-7)

13. Then the Pharisees said, you are a witness for yourself and your testimony is not true (*you are lying*).

14. Jesus answered and said, even if I testify for myself, my witness is true because I know from where I am from and unto where I am going. But you do not know where I am from, nor where I shall go.

15. You make your judgment according to your own selfish desires, but I have not misled anyone.

16. If I make a judgment, my judgment is true, for I am not alone, but the Father who sent me is with me.

17. It is written in the law of Moses, that the witness of two men is true. (Numbers 15:35; Hebrews 10:29)

18. I am a witness unto myself and the Father who has sent me is also a witness unto me.

19. And they asked him, where is your Father? Jesus answered and said, you do not know me nor my Father. If you had known me, you would also have known my Father. (1 John 2:23; 2 John 2:9)

20. Now Jesus spoke these words in the treasury while teaching in the temple, yet no one arrested him, because his time had not yet come.

21. Then again Jesus said unto them, I will be leaving here and you will seek for me, but you will die in your sins. Where I will go, you are not able to come. (*God's chosen people? - Malachi 2:2-3*)

22. Then the Jews mocked, will he kill himself? He says, where I am going you are not able to follow!

23. And he said unto them, you are from below (*hell*), but I am from above! (Matthew 23:13-39) You are of this world, but I am not of the world. (1 John 2:15-16)

24. That is why I said to you, you will die in your sins. Because if you do not fully commit yourselves unto me and know that I am he, you will die in your sins.

25. And they asked him, who are you? Jesus answered them and said, this I will tell you; I am the highest power. (Revelation 1:8)

26. I have many things to speak to you concerning your eternal condemnation, because he that has sent me is true and I tell the world all that I have heard from him.

27. They did not know that he spoke of the Father above.

28. Then Jesus said unto them, when the son of man has arisen, you will know that I am above all; Then you will know that I am (*the Christ*). I do nothing for my own purposes, but I speak that which the Father has instructed unto me.

29. He that has sent me is with me. The Father has not left me to be alone, because I always do that which is pleasing unto him. (John 14:18-20)

30. When he said these things, many began committing their trust in him.

31. Then Jesus said unto the Jews that had committed their trust in him, if you continue according to my instructions, you will truly be my disciples,

32. and you will know the truth and the truth shall set you free.

33. Then they said, we are of Abraham's seed and no one has ever held us as slaves! How is it that you can say that we will be made free?

34. And Jesus said, I tell you the truth, whoever commits sin (*defiance - Numbers 15:30*) is a slave to sin. (Matthew 18:2-10; 1 John 3:8; 5:16-18; Romans 6:22)

35. But the slave will not abide in the house (*of God*) forever, but the son shall live forever; (Galatians 4:22-26)

36. But he that the son sets free is completely set free!
(Matthew 26:28; 1 John 3:3-10; Acts 2:38; Romans 6:16; Matthew 18:3-4)

37. I know that you are the physical descendants of Abraham, but you are seeking to kill me, because my words find no place in your heart. (Jeremiah 18:23)

38. That which I have experienced with my Father is what I speak, but you also do that which you have seen from your father.

39. Then they responded and said, our spiritual father is Abraham. But Jesus said unto them, if you were the (*spiritual*) children of Abraham, you would be doing the deeds according to Abraham. (Isaiah 51:1-2; Matthew 3:9; Galatians 3:27-29)

40. But now you are seeking to kill me, a man who has told you the truth, of which I was instructed by God! Such is not according to what Abraham instructed!

41. You do the deeds of your father. Then they said unto him, we are not generated by fornication, but we have one father, God.

42. Then Jesus said, if God was your Father, you would love me; For I have been taken from within God and he is with me; I did not come for my purposes, but for the purposes of he that has sent me to do.

43. Why do you not understand my words? It is because you are not able to hear my instructions.

44. You are of your father the devil (1 John 3:8; Romans 6:16) and the desires that your father craves for, you also desire to do. He was a murderer of men from the beginning, and the true way was never established in him because the truth is not in him. (John 3:21) When he speaks, he lies, because he can only speak in his own ways, because he is a liar, the father of lies! (Revelation 21:8)

45. But because I speak the truth, you do not believe me.

46. Who of you can offer correction unto me concerning sin? But if I tell the truth, why will you not believe me?

47. He that is of God hears the instructions of God, this is why you can not hear *(understand),* because you are not of God! (*speaking to the Jews*)

48. Then the Jews answered and said unto him, it must be that you are a Samaritan and demon possessed!

49. Jesus responded and said, I do not have a demon, but I honor my Father! Yet you dishonor me!

50. I do not look for my own honor, but there is one who is watching and he will judge. (Matthew 18:10)

51. Truly I tell you, if anyone keeps my instructions, death will not be recognized for them, not ever.

52. Then the Jews said unto him, now we know that you have a demon; Abraham died and so have all of the prophets! But you say, if anyone keeps my instructions they will never taste death, forever!

53. You are not greater than our father Abraham who did die! The prophets also died! Who do you think you are?

54. Jesus answered and said, if I honor myself, then I have no honor. It is my Father who honors me, of whom you say that he is your God!

55. Truly, you have not known him, yet I know him. If I was to say that I do not know him, then I would be a liar just like you; But I do know him and I keep his instructions.

56. Abraham your forefather would have leaped for joy to have seen my day. He did foresee it rejoicing.

57. The Jews said unto him, you are not even fifty years old, yet you claim to have seen Abraham?

58. Jesus said unto them, truly I tell you, before Abraham existed, I existed! (John 1:1-3)

59. Then they gathered stones so that they might throw them at him, but Jesus was concealed and he went away from the temple walking right past them.

John 9

1. As Jesus went, he came across a man that had been blind since he was an infant.

2. The disciples asked him, teacher, who was it that sinned, this man or his parents, in that he has been blind since he was born?

3. Jesus said, it is neither that he sinned nor his parents, but he is blind so that the power of God might be revealed through him.

4. I must do the deeds of the one who sent me while it is daytime, because the evening is approaching quickly, when nothing will be able to be done.

5. While I am in the world, I am the light of the world. (John 1:4)

6. While he was speaking, he spit on the ground and made clay from the spittle, he took it and anointed the eyes of the blind man. (Psalms 22:24)

7. Then he said unto him, go and wash in the pool of Sliloam, which translated means "living to be sent out." So he went and washed and was made able to see!

8. Those nearby and those that saw him previously said, he was blind! Is this not the one who would sit and was always begging?

9. Others said, this is he, while yet others said, it looks like him. Then the man said, I am he.

10. Then they asked him, how is it that you have been made to now see?

11. And he said, the man called Jesus anointed my eyes with clay and told me to go to the pool of Sliloam; While I washed there, I looked up and I could see!

12. Then they asked him, where is this Jesus? He said, I do not know.

13. Then they arrested the man and took him before the Pharisees.

14. It was on the Sabbath day when Jesus made the clay and opened his eyes.

15. Then the Pharisees began to ask him how it was that he can now see; He said, Jesus put clay in my eyes and I washed, now I can see.

16. Then some of the Pharisees said, but he is not of God; He does not even keep the Sabbath! Others said, how can a man that is a sinner be able to do such miracles? A division then broke out among them.

17. Then they asked the blind man again, what do you have to say concerning him (*Jesus*), in that he healed your eyes? The man said, he is a prophet.

18. The Jews refused to believe him, that he was blind but could now see. Then they called the man's parents concerning having received his sight.

19. Then they asked them, is this your son? Has he been blind since the day he was born? How is it that he can now see?

20. The parents of the man said, certainly this is our son and he was born blind!

21. How he is now able to see we do not know. We don't know the one that has opened his eyes. Our son is of age to testify, let him tell you.

22. They said these things because they had fear of the Jews, because they had already established that if anyone would acknowledge him as the Christ, that they would be expelled from the synagogue.

23. This is the reason that his parents said, he is of age, ask him.

24. Then they called the man who had been blind to come out a second time and they said to him, give honor unto God, we know that this man is a sinner.

25. Then he answered and said, whether or not he (*Jesus*) is a sinner, I do not know. What I do know is that I was blind, but now I can see!

26. Then they again asked him, what did he do to you and how did he open your eyes?

27. Then he answered them again and said, I already told you! Have you not heard me? Why do you want me again to repeat myself? Are you wanting to become his disciples?

28. Then they were angered at him and said, you are one of his disciples, but we are disciples of Moses.

29. We know that Moses spoke to God, but for him (*Jesus*) we do not know where he originates.

30. Then the man said unto them, there certainly is something here to wonder about, since you do not know where he is from, yet he has healed my blindness!

31. We know that God does not hear the prayers of sinners; But if a man is God fearing and does his will, then God hears him. (Isaiah 1:15; Romans 8:27 - *this destroys sinners prayer theology and repetitive repentance every time one commits sin theology* - Matthew 7:21-23; Proverbs 15:29; Isaiah 58:9; 59:2)

32. In all of history it has never been heard of any man having been healed from blindness if they had been born blind.

33. If he is not from God, then he could not do such a thing!

34. They answered and said to him, you were born submerged in sin, but you think to teach us? Then they threw him out of the building.

35. Jesus had come to hear that they had thrown him outside, so he went and found him and said unto him, do you commit your trust unto the son of God?

36. The man answered and said, who is the master so that I might commit my trust unto him?

37. And Jesus said to him, you can now see him and he is speaking with you; I am he.

38. The man said, I do commit my trust unto you master. And he began to worship him.

39. Then Jesus said, this is the reason that I came into the world, so that those who could not see might now be able to see, and that those who thought that they could see, would show (*prove*) that they are blind.

40. Those Pharisees that were close by and heard this said unto him, we are not blind!

41. And Jesus said unto them, if you were blind you would not be guilty of sin unto death,

(James 4:17; Numbers 15:30; Hebrews 10:26-27; Romans 1:18; Mark 9:42-43; Psalms 19:13)

but you say that you can see, so thereby your sin shall remain upon you. (Numbers 15:28-31; Psalms 19:13; 1 John 5:16-18; Matthew 12:31-32; 1 Corinthians 6:9-10; Mark 7:21-23; Galatians 5:19-21; Ephesians 5:5-7; 2 Timothy 3:1-5)

John 10

1. Truly I tell you, anyone that does not enter through the door into the gathering of my sheep, but tries to enter in any other way, they are thieves that come to plunder.

2. But he that enters through the shepherd's door (*Christ*) is one of my sheep.

3. The gatekeeper opens for them, leads them and calls his sheep by name; The sheep hear his voice.

4. When he gathers his sheep, he goes before them and his sheep follow him, because they know his voice.

5. They will never follow a stranger, but they will run away, because they do not know the voices of strangers.

6. Jesus had spoken unto them in an allegory, but they did not perceive all that he had explained to them.

7. So Jesus again said unto them, truly I tell you, I am the door of the sheep.

8. All that come against me are thieves that came to plunder, but the true sheep do not follow them.

9. I am the door; If anyone enters through me, he will be reserved (*saved*) and will be made free (*from sin*). He will obtain all that he has need of. (John 8:34-37)

10. Thieves only come to steal, kill and destroy. I have come to offer the ability to have eternal life.

11. I am the good shepherd; The good shepherd will lay down his life for the benefit of his sheep.

12. The hirelings (*paid preachers*) are not of the shepherd and the sheep are not their own. When they see the wolf coming, they abandon the sheep and run away, and the wolf overcomes (*corrupts*) them; (*the hirelings*) Then the sheep are scattered. (2 Corinthians 11:15; 2 Peter 2:3)

13. The hirelings run because they are only wage earners and they do not have true concern for the sheep, as they matter nothing to them.

14. I am the good shepherd. I know all those that are mine and I am known by all that are mine.

15. Just as the Father knows me, I also know the Father, and I will lay down my life for my sheep.

16. I also have different sheep that are not of this gathering (*gentiles*); It is also necessary for me to lead them and they will hear my voice, and all will become one gathering with one shepherd. (Galatians 3:27-29)

17. This is why my Father loves me, because I will lay down my life, so that they may have life. (*eternal*)

18. No one takes my life from me, but I willingly lay it down. I hold the authority (*power*) to lay it down, and I also hold authority (*power*) to receive it again. This assurance I have received from my Father.

19. Again there erupted a division among the Jews because of these words.

20. Many said that he has a demon and that he is insane. Why would anyone listen to him?

21. Others said, these can not be the words of a man that is demon possessed, because a demon can not heal the blind eyes of any man, so that he might now see!

22. The dedication feast in Jerusalem was soon to take place and it was wintertime.

23. Jesus walked into the temple, coming to the porch of Solomon.

24. There he was encircled by the Jews and they said to him, do not keep us in suspense, tell us plainly, are you the Christ?

25. Jesus answered them and said, I have already told you, (John 7:26)

26. yet you refuse to commit yourselves unto me; This is because you are not my sheep! (John 8:44)

27. Just as I have told you, my sheep hear my voice and I know them. They understand and are in accord with me. (Isaiah 40:11)

28. I offer unto them everlasting life, that they shall not perish. No one can steal them away from me. (*from my jurisdiction*)

29. My Father has given them to me and he is more powerful than all others; No one is able to steal them from out of his hands (*jurisdiction*). (Romans 8:39)

30. My Father and I are one.

31. Then again, the Jews began gathering up stones so that they could throw them at him.

32. Then Jesus said, I have shown unto you many good deeds and miracles that have been done through me from my Father. For which of these good deeds do you plan to kill me?

33. But the Jews answered him and said, we will not kill you concerning anything that you have done, but for blasphemy! You are only a man, yet you make yourself to be as God!

34. Jesus answered and said, is it not written in the scriptures, "I said that you are gods?" (Psalms 82:6)

35. If he said that they were gods that were in possession of the instructions of God, how can these scriptures be broken?

36. You have said that the one the Father has sanctified and sent into the world has blasphemed, because I have said that I am the son of God.

37. If I had not done the deeds of my Father, then do not believe me.

38. But I have done the deeds of my Father! If you do not believe my words, then believe for the sake of the deeds that I have done, then you will know that I am he and that the Father has sent me.

39. They again thought to arrest him, but he escaped from their hands.

40. Jesus then went across the Jordan river again, unto the place where John had first began baptizing,

41. and he remained there. Many came unto him and asked him, John did not do any miracles, but all the things that John had to say about this one (*Jesus*) are true.

42. Many there committed their trust in Jesus.

John 11

1. And there was a certain man who was very sick by the name of Lazarus from Bethany, the same village as Mary and her sister Martha.

2. It was Mary that anointed the Christ with expensive ointment and then wiped off his feet with her hair, and it was her brother Lazarus that was sick. (John 12:3)

3. The sister sent a message unto Jesus that said, master, know that one whom you love is very sick.

4. When he heard this, Jesus said, the sickness has not yet killed him; It is for the purpose to bring glory unto God and that the son of man may be glorified by it.

5. Jesus loved Martha, her sister Mary and also Lazarus.

6. After Jesus had heard that Lazarus was sick, he remained in that same place for two more days. (*Jesus remained there to allow time for Lazarus to be put in the grave*)

7. After that he said to his disciples, let us go to Judea again.

8. Then the disciples said to him, the Jews are now looking to kill you, yet you want to return there again?

9. Jesus answered and said, are there not twelve hours in the daytime? If anyone is to walk in the daytime he does not stumble because he can see by the light of the world.

10. If one is to walk in the nighttime he will stumble because the light is not there unto him.

11. After he said these things, he said, our friend Lazarus has fallen asleep; I must go and awaken him.

12. Then the disciples said, master, if he has fallen asleep he will recover.

13. But Jesus had spoken that Lazarus had been put in the grave, but they thought that he said that he was sleeping.

14. Then Jesus said unto them plainly, Lazarus has been put in the grave;

15. But I am joyful for you, that in this, you will fully commit your trust. We shall go to him.

16. Then Thomas asked for permission to stay behind, saying to the fellow disciples, if we go, we will all surely die with him!

17. Then when Jesus finally came, they were told that he had been dead inside of the tomb for four days.

18. Bethany was near Jerusalem, about fifteen stadion (*furlongs*).

19. Many of the Jews had come earlier unto Martha and Mary in order to offer comfort concerning their brother's death.

20. When Martha heard that Jesus was coming, she went to meet him, but Mary remained in the house.

21. Martha said unto Jesus, master, if you were here, my brother would not have died.

22. But I know that whatever you ask God for, he will give unto you. (James 4:3)

23. Jesus said unto her, your brother will rise up again.

24. Then Martha said unto him, I know that he will arise in the resurrection, on the last day. (Daniel 12:2)

25. But Jesus said to her, I am the resurrection and the life; He who commits his trust in me, even if he dies he shall live. (1 Thessalonians 4:13-18; Romans 2:4-11; Revelation 20:5-15)

26. All that live according to me and commit their trust in me shall never die. Do you trust in this?

27. And she said to him, yes master, I have committed my trust and know that you are the Christ, the son of God that has come and lived in this world.

28. And after these things were said, Martha went and called Mary her sister and said to her secretly, the teacher is calling for you. (*secretly because of the Jews that were still there*)

29. When she had heard this, she rose up quickly and went to him.

30. Jesus had not yet come into the village, but had remained in the place where he had met with Martha.

31. Then the Jews that had been in the house consoling her, because she quickly rose up and left the house, they followed her, thinking that she would go to the tomb so that she could cry there.

32. When Mary came to the place that Jesus was, when she saw him, she fell at his feet and she said to him, master, if you were here, my brother would not have died.

33. And as Jesus saw her crying in great sorrow and that the Jews were also crying; He became upset in his spirit and was troubled,

34. and then he said, where have you buried him? And they said, master, come and see.

35. Then Jesus began crying.

36. And the Jews said, look at how much brotherly affection he had for him.

37. Some of them said, he (*Jesus*) was able to open the eyes of the blind, but he was not able to prevent this one from dying!

38. Jesus again became upset in his spirit, but then he came to the tomb. It was a cave with a stone covering the opening.

39. Then Jesus said, take away the covering stone, but Martha, the sister of the one who had died said, master, it is the fourth day and by this time he will stink terribly!

40. Then Jesus said to her, did I not tell you, that if you commit your trust in me, you will see the power and glory of God? (*It takes complete trust and dedication to receive a miracle*)

41. And they lifted the stone where the dead one was laid and Jesus raised his eyes upwards and said, Father, I thank you, because you have heard me.

42. I know that you always hear me; It is because of the crowd of people here that I said, "so that you will commit your trust"; This is why you have sent me.

43. Then he cried out with a very loud voice and said; Lazarus! Come outside!

44. And the one that had died came forth, being tied around the feet and hands with grave sheets and his face was wrapped in a cloth! Then Jesus said, untie him and allow him to be released.

45. Thereafter, many of the Jews who had come to see Mary, after having seen what Jesus did, they believed upon him! (*This is symbolic of how those who are completely dedicated to and trust in Jesus will be raised up unto the eternal life.*)

46. There were some that went away to the Pharisees and told them what Jesus did.

47. The high priests and the Sanhedrin said, what shall we do? This man does many miracles!

48. If we leave him alone, all will eventually commit their trust in him and the Romans will come and they will take our place and our nation from us.

(This is evidence that they knew that Jesus is the Messiah yet decided to kill him anyway!)

49. But there was a man named Caiaphas, the high priest for that year that said to them, do you know nothing at all?

50. Do you not consider that it is better if one man is to die for the benefit of all of the people, than for the entire nation to be destroyed? (*of which happened anyway 40 years later at 70 AD*)

51. He did not speak this for himself, but being the high priest that year he prophesied that Jesus was going to die on behalf of the nation,

52. But not for that nation only, but also for all of the children of God that were scattered, that they might all be gathered together in one body. (Galatians 3:27-29)

53. From that day they began planning on how they would kill him.

54. Therefore Jesus no longer walked among the Jews, but he left that place and went into a country near the solitary place of Ephraim where there was a small town, and he stayed there with his disciples.

55. The Passover of the Jews was coming soon and many would go to Jerusalem from other nations before the Passover so that they could be purified.

56. Some looked for Jesus and said to one another while standing in the temple, what do you think of this, that he has not come to the feast?

57. The high priests had also given commands that if anyone knew where he was, they must be told of it, that he might be arrested.

John 12

1. Before the six days of Passover came, Jesus went to Bethany where Lazarus lived, the one who Jesus had raised from the dead. (Matthew 26:6)

2. They prepared a feast for him and while Lazarus rested with them, Martha served them.

3. Then Mary took a pound of expensive pure spikenard ointment and rubbed it upon the feet of Jesus, and then she wiped it with her own hair upon his feet. The house was filled with the fragrance of the ointment. (Matthew 26:7)

4. Then one of the disciples, Judas Iscariot the son of Simon, the one who would soon betray him said,

5. why was this ointment not sold for three hundred denarii and given to the poor? (Matthew 26:9)

6. But he did not say this because he cared for the poor, but because he was a thief, and it was he that carried the money bag; If it had been put in, he would have taken it.

7. Therefore Jesus said, pardon her, for she has been saving up for it so to anoint me for the day of my burial. (Matthew 26:12)

8. You will always have the poor among you, but I shall not always physically be here with you.

9. There was a large crowd of Jews that knew that he was there. They did not come into the house because Jesus was there and that Lazarus might see them.

10. But they gathered to discuss the matter. The high priests also discussed whether they should kill Lazarus as well,

11. because with his life from death, many Jews turned away from them to commit their trust in Jesus!

12. The following day, there was a very large crowd that was on their way to the feast. They had heard that Jesus was coming into Jerusalem,

13. so they took branches of palm trees and went out to meet him. They cried out, hosanna, blessed be the one that comes in the name of God, the King of Israel! (Psalms 118:26)

14. Jesus was given the colt of an ass and he sat upon it, just as it has been written;

15. "Do not fear, oh daughter of Zion; Take notice, your king has come sitting upon the foal of an ass." (Zechariah 9:9; Isaiah 40:9)

16. But the disciples did not know the prophetic scriptures at that time, but after Jesus had been glorified they found that these things had been written, of which were the very same things that they had witnessed.

17. Then all of the crowd saw and witnessed Lazarus, the man that Jesus had called out from the tomb when he raised him from the dead.

18. For this is why the crowd came to him, because they had heard of this great miracle that he had done!

19. Then the Pharisees said unto themselves, watch that you are not convinced of anything! Take heed, because there are many that have left us to follow him!

20. There were also some Greeks that went up to the feast so that they could worship.

21. Some of them approached Philip who was from Bethsaida, Galilee, and they asked him, master, we would like to see Jesus.

22. Then Philip told Andrew and they both came to tell Jesus.

23. Jesus said unto them, the time has come that the son of man shall be glorified.

24. Truly I tell you, if a grain of wheat falls to the earth and dies, it remains alone; But if it dies, it produces new growth rendering much fruit.

25. He that loves his life in this world shall lose it, but he that hates the life in this world shall find life everlasting. (1 John 2:15)

26. If anyone chooses to serve me, he must be the same as I am (1 John 3:3; 2 Timothy 2:11) and where I am, there my servant will also be. If anyone chooses to serve me, my Father will value him.

27. Now my heart troubles me, so what shall I say? Father please deliver me from this day, though I know that this is the reason that I have come.

28. Father, glorious is your name. Then a voice was heard in the heavens: "How glorious and honorable!"

29. Those who were standing there had all heard this! Some said that thundering had just happened! Others said that a messenger (*angel*) of God had just spoken!

30. Jesus said, this voice was not for me, but for you.

31. Now a decision shall be given unto everyone: The ruler of this world can be cast out away from you. (Satan - John 14:30; John 16:11; 1 Corinthians 2:6; Ephesians 2:2; Acts 26:18; Matthew 4:9; Revelation 12:12)

32. When I have been resurrected up from the cross, I will call all people unto me. (Galatians 3:27-29)

33. He said this to signify what kind of death he would soon suffer.

34. Then the people in the crowd said, we have heard that the Christ shall live forever! How can you say that it is necessary for the son to be resurrected?

35. Then Jesus said unto them, only for a short time will the light remain here with you. Begin to walk while you still have light so that darkness will not overcome (*take*) you. He that walks in darkness does not know where he is going. (1 John 1:5-6)

36. While you have the light, commit your trust unto the Light so that you might become sons of the Light. (John 1:1-3)

37. Jesus spoke these things, then he hid himself and went away from them. But even though he did many miracles and healings in their presence, they refused to commit their trust in him!

The following verse looks to have been added by a scribe and not a part of the original text.

38. In this the words of Isaiah were fulfilled, which said; "And the power of the Messiah has been revealed, but who has believed his announcement?" (Isaiah 53:1)

39. This is the reason that they wouldn't commit their trust; Through the words of Isaiah it is said,

40. "Their eyes are blinded so that they can not see, nor understand with their heart to be converted, so that I might make them whole (*take away their sins*)." (Isaiah 6:10, Isaiah 48:4; Acts 2:38; Acts 3:19)

41. Isaiah said this when he saw his glory and then spoke about him.

42. Still, even with this there were many of the rulers that had confirmation that he is the Christ, but because of the Pharisees, they refused to confess, that they would not be thrown out from the synagogues.

43. You see, they loved the glory of men more than the glory of God.

44. Then Jesus announced, the one who commits their trust in me does not only believe in me, but also in he that has sent me.

45. Those that recognize me, recognize the one that has sent me. (1 John 2:23, John 5:23)

46. I have come to bring Light into the world, so that all that commit their trust in me shall not continue to remain living in the darkness (*sin*). (John 3:16-21; 1:4; 1 John 1:5-7)

47. If anyone hears my words and does not commit their trust, I do not condemn him; I did not come into the world to judge the world, but so that I could offer salvation unto everyone in the world. (Romans 11:26,32; Titus 3:5)

48. Those that reject me and do not receive my words, they have the words that I spoke of which will judge them, and they will be judged by them on the last day. (Revelation 20:13-15; Romans 2:6)

49. I did not speak for myself, but I have spoken for the one that sent me, my Father. He gave these instructions to me, all that I have said and announced.

50. I know that his instructions bring everlasting life. I speak the things exactly as my Father has told me.

John 13

1. Before the feast of Passover came, Jesus knew that his time had come and that he would be taken from this world to take his place before the Father. He knew those that were his and those who loved them.

2. When the time came for the dinner, the devil had already established in the heart of Judas Iscariot, the son of Simon, that he would betray him.

3. Jesus now knew that everything was in the hands of the Father and that he had come from God and he knew that he would soon return to be with him. (*after his ascension*)

4. He then got up from dinner, took his clothing and put them aside, and he wrapped himself in a robe.

5. Then he put some water into a basin and he began to wash the feet of the disciples; Then he wiped off their feet with the robe that he was wearing.

6. When he came to Simon Peter, Simon said unto him, master, are you going to wash my feet?

7. Jesus said unto him, that which I am doing, you do not understand, but you will understand very soon.

8. Then Peter said unto him, you shall not wash my feet, now nor ever! Then Jesus said unto him, if I do not wash you, you shall have no part with me. (Acts 2:38; Mark 16:16)

9. Simon Peter said unto him, master, don't wash only my feet but wash my hands and my head also!

10. Then Jesus said unto him, having already been completely cleansed and living completely clean, there is no need for anything other than your feet to be washed (*symbolically - to remain clean*). (John 3:22; Acts 2:38; Acts 3:19) You are clean, but not all of you are clean;

11. For he knew that one would betray him; This is why he said not all of you are clean.

12. So after he had washed their feet and took his own clothes, then he sat down and said to them, do you know what I have done for you?

13. You call me teacher and master and you are right.

14. So if I, the teacher and master have washed your feet, you must also wash each other's feet. (Matthew 18:21-22 - *forgive one another for all trespasses, to help others remain clean*)

15. This is an example, as I have done, you do also.

16. Truly I tell you, the servant is not better than his master, nor is the messenger greater than the one that has sent him.

17. If you understand these things then you are blessed, but only if you live accordingly.

18. I am not speaking to all of you, as I know who has been plucked out. The scriptures shall be fulfilled, as there is one that is eating the bread with me that will lift up his foot against me. (Hebrews 10:29)

19. Before it happens, I have told you, so that when it happens, you shall have confirmation that I am he.

20. Truly I tell you, those that receive the one that I send (*the holy spirit*) shall receive me and the one that sent me. (1 John 4:1-5)

21. After he said these things, Jesus was troubled in his heart, then he said, truly I tell you, one of you will betray me.

22. The disciples looked confused about what he was saying.

23. As he was sitting down, one of his disciples that Jesus loved laid his head upon his chest.

24. Then Simon Peter asked, who could it be that he is speaking about?

25. Then the one that was leaning on the chest of Jesus said, master, who is it?

26. Jesus said, the one that I give this piece of bread to. Then he spit upon the bread and gave it to Judas Iscariot, the son of Simon.

27. After the bread was given to him, Satan rose up in him and he said, whatever you plan to do, do it quickly!

28. But none of the other disciples heard this, because he had said it to him privately.

29. Some had thought that he spoke to him concerning the money bag that Judas was holding, for Jesus to tell him what things they had need of for the feast, or for the poor, of what he should give.

30. After he had eaten, Judas left in the night!

31. When he had gone out, Jesus said, now the son of man shall be glorified and God shall be honored through him.

32. Then Jesus said, if God is honored through me, he will glorify me through himself and will continue to honor me. (*It is the same with the faithful*)

33. Children, for only a short time I will be with you. You will seek me; But as I told the Jews, where I am going, you are not able to come.

34. I also tell you and I emphatically remind you of the command that I have previously told you. You must have much love (*affection and benevolence*) for one another, just as I have loved you, you must love one another. (John 2:9; Matthew 22:37-39; Mark 12:30-31; 1 John 2:7-9)

35. This is how everyone will know that you are my disciples, if you have affection and benevolence (*love*) for one another.

36. Then Simon Peter said, master, where are you going? Jesus answered him and said, where I am going you are not able to go with me, but eventually you will follow me there.

37. Then Peter said unto him, master, why am I not able to go with you now? My life is for you and I will lay down my life for you.

38. Then Jesus said to him, you will lay down your life for me. But truly I tell you, the rooster will not crow before you deny me three times!

John 14

1. Do not be troubled in your heart, commit yourself unto God and commit yourself unto me.

2. In my Father's house there are many places to live. Whether or not I tell you of this, I am going to prepare a place for you.

3. If I go to prepare a place for you, I will come again to receive you unto myself, and where I will be, you will also follow. (Matthew 24:30)

4. You know where I am going and you know the way. (Acts 2:38; Romans 6:1-23)

5. Thomas said to him, master, we know where you are going, but how will we know the way?

6. And Jesus said to him, I am the way, the truth and the life, no one shall come unto the Father, except through me. (John 1:4)

7. If you have known me, you have also known my Father, and from this day forward you shall be aware of him and shall discern him.

8. Then Philip said to him, master, show us the Father and that will be enough for us.

9. And Jesus said to him, I have been with you so long now, yet you do not know me Philip? If you have seen me, you have seen the Father. So how is it that you say, show us the Father?

10. Are you not believing that I am in the Father and the Father is in me? These words that I speak to you, I do not speak for myself, but for the Father who is living within me. It is he that does the mighty deeds.

11. Commit your trust and know that the Father is in me and I am in the Father. If not, then trust in me because of the mighty deeds.

12. Truly I tell you, those who commit their trust in me, the mighty works that I have done, they will also do, and even greater they will do, because I am going unto my Father. (Mark 16:16-20)

13. And whatever you have need of, ask in my name and I will give to you, that the son may honor the Father. (James 4:3)

14. So if you ask therefore in my name, I will give it unto you. (*if it is according to the will of God*)

15. If you love me, keep my commandments.
(Mark 12:30; Luke 10:27; Deuteronomy 6:5; Lev. 19:18; Matthew 22:37; Psalms 119:44; Proverbs 4:4)

16. I will ask the Father and he will send you the helper (*advocate - spirit of the holy one*), and he will abide with you until the final day. (Psalms 145:20; Ezekiel 36:27)

17. It is the spirit of truth whom the world is not able to receive, because they can not perceive and do not recognize him; But you know him because he has lived with you and will live within you. (*spirit of Jesus*)

18. I will not leave you to be orphans; I will come unto you. (*Jesus states that the holy spirit is his spirit*)

19. In just a little while the world will no longer perceive me, but you shall perceive me, and because I live, you shall also live.

20. In that day, you shall know that I am in my Father, you are in me and that I am in you. (1 John 4:1-4)

21. He that knows and understands my instructions and keeps them, it is he that loves me. He that loves me will be loved by my Father and I will love him and I will reveal myself unto him. (*by his holy spirit*)

22. Then Judas, (*the brother of Jesus - Matthew 13:55; Jude 1:1*) not Iscariot, asked him, master, why is it that you are able to reveal yourself unto us but not to the world?

23. Then Jesus answered and said, if anyone loves me he will keep my words (*instructions*) and my Father will love him, and we will come and make our abode (*dwelling place*) in him.
(1 Corinthians 3:16-17; 1 Corinthians 6:19; Ephesians 2:21-22)

24. He who does not keep (*live by*) my instructions does not love me. (Proverbs 28:13; John 3:19) These words are not my own, but they are of my Father who sent me.

25. I have spoken these things unto you while I am with you.

26. But the helper, the spirit of the holy one, who the Father will send in my name, he will teach you all things and remind you of everything that I have spoken unto you. (Isaiah 48:17-18)

27. I send you forth with peace, my peace I give unto you; I do not give unto you as the world gives. Do not let your hearts be troubled and do not be fearful.

28. Understand that I told you that I am going away, but that I will return unto you. (Matthew 24:30) If you love me, then you should be joyful that I am going to my Father, because my Father is much greater than I am.

29. Know that I have told you these things before they happen so that you will continue to commit your trust in me.

30. I will speak few additional things unto you, for the ruler of this world is coming, but he does not have anything on me. (John 12:31; John 16:11; 1 Corinthians 2:6; Ephesians 2:2; Daniel 11:36-45; Revelation 12:12)

31. But the world knows that I love the Father, and as he has commanded unto me, that I do. Now get up and let us leave this place!

John 15

1. I am the living root and my Father is the Lord of the vineyard. (Luke 20:9-13)

2. Every branch in me that is not bringing forth good fruit, he cuts it off; Every branch that is bearing fruit, he prunes it so that it might bear more fruit. (Matthew 7:17; 12:33; 13:3-26; Romans 11:20)

3. You are already clean, because you have heeded the instructions that I have spoken to you.

4. Live according to me and I will live in you. (John 14:23; 1 Corinthians 6:19) Just as the branch is not able to produce fruit by itself if it is not connected to the root, you can not either, if I do not live in you.

5. I am the root and you are the branches. He that lives by me, I live in him and he will produce much good fruit. Apart from me you are not able to become accomplished. (*reach the destination*)

6. If any man does not live according to my words, they are cut off like a branch and they dry out and are gathered up and shall be cast into the fire and burned. (Romans 11:17-24; Hebrews 6:4; Revelation 20:15)

7. If you live by me and if my instructions are alive in you, whatever you have need of, ask and it shall be given unto you. (James 4:3)

8. In this, my Father is glorified, because you are my disciples and you bring forth much good fruit.

9. Just as the Father loves me, I have also loved you; Live by my love.

10. If you keep my instructions, you will remain in my love (*affection and benevolence*), just as I have kept the instructions of my Father and have remained in his love.

11. I have repeatedly spoken these things so that you might remain in my joy and it might be complete.

12. This is my commandment (*instruction*), that you love one another, just as I have loved you. (Matthew 22:37-39 - - *This destroys the Hebrew Roots doctrines of obeying parts of the Mosaic law*)

13. No one has greater love than this; That a man shall lay down his own life for his friends.

14. You are my friends if you do what I have commanded unto you. (Romans 6:16)

15. I will no longer call you slaves, because a slave does not understand the purposes of their master. (John 8:34-36) I call you friends, because I have told you everything that I have been given by my Father.

16. You have not drawn (G-1828+G-1823) me unto your radiance, but I have dragged you out and led you forth (G-1828 + G-1806 + G-3303) unto me, and I have established you so that you might go out there and bring forth good fruit and that your good fruit remain. (John 14:21-23) Whatever you shall ask the Father in my name (*that you have need of*) he will give unto you. (James 4:3)

17. I command this unto you, that you love one another.

18. If the world hates you, know that it hated me before it hated you. (1 John 2:15)

19. If you were of the world, the world would love you, because it loves its own. But you are not of the world, because I have surly dragged you forth and led you out of the world. Therefore the world hates you.

20. Remember the words that I have spoken to you; The servant is no better than his master. (Matthew 10:24-25; Luke 6:40) If they have persecuted me, they will also persecute you. If anyone of them live by my instructions, they will also receive you.

21. They will do these things unto you because of me, and because they do not know the one that sent me.

22. If I had not come and instructed them, they would not have committed defiant sin (*unto death*). But now they don't have any excuse. (James 4:17; Hebrews 10:26; Numbers 15:28-31)

23. All these things they do unto you because of me, because they do not know the one that sent me. All who reject me also reject my Father. (1 John 2:22)

24. If I did not do the works (*miracles*) that were witnessed by them, of which no one else could do, they would not be guilty of sin unto death. (1 John 5:17; Numbers 15:30-31) But even though they have known (*that I am the Messiah),* they hate (*reject*) both me and my Father. (1 John 2:23)

The following verse looks to have been added by a scribe and not a part of the original text.
25. But in this, the words that have been written in the old testament scriptures were fulfilled; "They hated me without a cause." (Psalms 69:4)

26. When the helper comes (*spirit of the holy one*) who I will send unto you from the Father, of whom is the spirit of the truth that proceeds from out of the Father, the spirit shall be the evidence of me. (*in you* - 1 John 4:1-4)

27. You shall also hold the evidence, because you and I are of the highest (*the Father*). (1 John 4:4)

John 16

1. I have repeatedly told you so that you do not stumble to fall away from God.

2. They will throw you out of the synagogues, and there will come a time when all who kill you will think that they are doing a service unto God.

3. They will do these things unto you because they do not know the Father nor me.

4. But remember that I have told you of this; When the time comes, you will think on my words, that I told you these things from the beginning; But know that I will be with you. (1 John 4:1-4)

5. Now I will be going unto the one who sent me and none of you shall ask me, where are you going?

6. But now, because I have told you these things there is grief filling up in your hearts.

7. But I am telling you the truth, because it is to your advantage that I go away; If I do not go away, the helper will not come unto you. But when I go, I will send him to you.

8. And when he is come, he will bring correction unto the world concerning their sins, concerning righteousness and concerning justice. (John 14:17)

9. Concerning sin, because they do not commit their trust unto me. (John 3:18-19)

10. Concerning righteousness (Jeremiah 31:33-34), because I am going unto the Father and you will no longer see me.

11. Concerning justice, because the ruler of this world shall be condemned. (1 Corinthians 2:6; Revelation 12:12; Revelation 19:20; Revelation 20:2)

12. Yet there are many things that I would like to tell you, but you are not yet able to carry them just yet.

13. But when he comes, the spirit of truth will assist/guide you into complete truth (*to discern and live it*); (1 John 2:27; 1 John 4:1-4; Ezekiel 36:27; 1 Corinthians 2:10) He will not speak for himself, but whatever is true he will speak and he will announce the things that are coming unto you.

14. He will honor me, because he will receive of me and then he will speak unto you. (1 John 4:1-4)

15. Everyone that is mine also has the Father, this is why I said, he shall receive from me and then he will instruct you. (Isaiah 44:7; Jeremiah 31:31-36)

16. In a short time you will not see me (*the cross*), but then in a short time you will see me again (*the resurrection*), then I will go unto my Father (*the ascension*). (John 20:17)
(The previous verse along with John 20:17 destroys the errant Luke 23:39-43)

17. Then the disciples said unto one another, what is it that he is saying to us, that in a short time you will not see me, then in a short time you will see me; Also, then I am going unto the Father?

18. They said, what does he mean by saying, in a short time? We do not understand what he is saying!

19. Jesus knew that they wanted to ask him, so he asked them, do you want to ask me questions about this, because I said, in a short time you will not see me, then in a short time you will see me again?

20. Truly I tell you that you will cry and you will mourn and the world will be cheerful. You will be grieving, but your grief will be turned into great joy.

21. When a woman is bringing forth a child, she is distressed; But when the child is born, she does not think of the distress, because of the joy that is generated in bringing a life into the world.

22. You will soon truly have grief, but I will see you again and you will be joyful in your hearts with such joy that no one can take away from you.

23. And on that day you will not be needful of anything. Truly I tell you, that whatever you have need of, ask the Father in my name and he will give it to you. (John 14:13; James 4:3)

24. Until now, you have not asked for anything in my name; Ask if there is a need and you will be given; You will surely have joy in this confidence.

25. I have spoken unto you in allegories (*parables*); There will come a time when I will not continue to speak to you in allegories, but I will make known unto you plainly the things concerning the Father.

26. That is the day that you will ask for what is needed in my name; I will have no need to petition the Father for you;

27. The Father shall have affection for you, because you have loved me and you have committed your trust that I am the one who has come forth from God.

28. I came forth from the Father so that I could come into the world. I tell you again, soon I shall leave this world and return unto my Father. *(verse 16, John 20:17)*

29. The disciples said unto him, look, you have spoken with clarity and you are not speaking in an allegory *(parable)*, you did not use one!

30. We know that you know all things and there is no need that anyone teach you. This is why we committed our trust that you are of God.

31. Jesus said unto them, have you committed your trust?

32. Be aware, the hour is coming and is now upon us, that you will be scattered; Each of you will turn your own way and you will leave me alone, though I will not be alone, because my Father is with me.

33. These things I have told to you that you might have peace. In the world you shall have tribulation (*hardship*), but be of good cheer, for I have overcome the world. (1 John 4:4; 1 Thessalonians 3:4; Revelation 1:9; Acts 14:22; Isaiah 59:15)

John 17

1. Jesus spoke these things and lifted up his eyes towards the heavens and said,

Verses 2 & 3 were added by a scribe and are not a part of the original text.

2. Father, the time has come. Make your son glorious and also that you be honored by him. Even as you have given him authority over all people, that he may give unto them life everlasting unto all that you have given unto him.

3. And he is everlasting life, and in him they may know that you are the only true God, and that you have sent Jesus Christ. (these verses are a third person account; the text returns to first person below.)

4. I honored you on the earth and I accomplished all that you gave for me to do.

5. Now you shall glorify me unto yourself, Father, with the glory that I had before the world existed when I was with you.

6. I have made your name known unto the men that you have given to me from out of the world. They are yours, and you offered them unto me and they have kept your instructions.

7. Now they know everything that you have made known to me is from you.

8. The instructions that you gave to me, I have given unto them and they received them, and they truly know that I was sent from you and they have committed their trust and know that you sent me.

9. I offer a request for their benefit; I do not ask for those of the world, but only those whom you have given unto me, for they are yours.

10. All that is mine is yours; All things that are yours are mine; I shall be made glorious within them. (1 John 4:1-5)

11. I shall no longer be in the world, yet they will remain in this world, but I will be coming to you. Holy Father, keep all whom you have given unto me in your name so that they might become as we are.

12. While I have been in the world I have kept them according to your name. I protected those that are yours and not one of them is lost, except for the son of destruction, so the prophecies have been fulfilled.

13. Now I shall come unto you and I have spoken these things so that the joy in me may be made fully alive within them.

14. I have given them your instructions, and for this the world hates them, because they are not of the world, even as I am not of the world.

15. I do not ask that you take them out of the world, but that you protect them from wickedness.

16. They are not of the world, just as I am not of the world.

17. Purify them through your truth. (*that they understand your truth and live accordingly*) Your words are truth.

18. Just as you have sent me into the world, I have now also sent them out into the world. (Matthew 28:18-20)

19. I have kept myself pure (*holy*) for their sake, (*To be a worthy sacrifice that would take away their sins*) so that they would also be made pure through the way (*offer*) you have made.

20. My request is not only for these, but also for everyone who shall commit their trust in me through their words; (*the scriptures are their words, not God's words - Matthew 13:52*)

21. That each one may become one with you, as you are in me and I in you, that they may live through us and that they commit their trust that you have sent me.

23. I in them and you in me, so that they may live perfectly and be at one with us. In their testimony the world may know that you have sent me and that I have loved them, the same as you have loved me.

24. Father, those whom you have given unto me, I ask that they might also be able to come to where you are and where I shall soon be, so that they may see my glory which you have given unto me, because you have loved me even before the foundations of the earth were laid.

25. Righteous Father, the world did not recognize you, but I have known you and these few are aware that you have sent me.

26. I have made your name known unto them, so that the affection that you have for me might also be in them and that I also be in them.

John 18

1. After Jesus had said these, things he went with the disciples across the brook of Kidron where there was a garden. He and his disciples entered therein.

2. Judas, the one that would betray him knew the place because Jesus and his disciples gathered there many times previously.

3. Judas gathered together a squad and soldiers from the high priests and Pharisees and they came with torches, lamps and weapons. (Matthew 26:49; Mark 14:43; Luke 22:47)

4. At that time, Jesus knew all that was about to happen to him, so he came forth and asked them, who are you looking for?

5. They said to him, Jesus of Nazareth. Then Jesus said to them, I am he! And Judas, the one that betrayed him also stood with them.

6. Again he said to them, I am he! Then they went up behind him and fell to the ground.

7. Jesus asked them again, who are you looking for? And they said Jesus of Nazareth.

8. Again Jesus said, I am he. If you are seeking me, allow the others to go free.

Verse 9 looks to have been added by a scribe and not a part of the original text.

9. In this, the scripture was fulfilled which says, "Those that you have given unto me, not one was lost."

10. Then Simon Peter drew his sword and struck a slave of the high priest and cut off his right ear. The name of that slave is Malchus. (Matthew 26:51; Mark 14:47; Luke 22:50)

11. And Jesus then said to Peter, put your sword into its sheath; Shall I not drink from the cup that the Father has given unto me?

12. Then the soldiers, officers and servants of the high priest seized Jesus and tied him,

13. First they took him to Annas. He was the father in law of Caiaphas the high priest that particular year.

14. Then he was taken to Caiaphas, the one that had instructed the Jews when he told them, it is better for one man to die for the benefit of the nation. (John 11:49-50; Matthew 26:57)

15. Simon Peter and another disciple (*John*) followed Jesus. The other disciple was acquainted with the high priest and he went with Jesus into the courtyard of the high priest; (Matthew 26:58)

16. Peter stood at the entrance outside. Then the disciple that was acquainted with the high priest spoke to the gate keeper and he brought Peter inside.

17. The maiden, a gate keeper said unto Peter, are you not one of the disciples of this man? And Peter said to her, no I am not.

18. The servants and the officers were standing near a fire that they had made because it was cold outside, and they were keeping warm. Peter was there with them standing and keeping himself warm.

19. At this time the high priest questioned Jesus concerning his disciples and concerning his doctrine.

20. Jesus answered him and said, I publicly spoke to the people; (Luke 13:26, Matthew 12:19) I regularly taught in your synagogues and in the temple where the Jews always gather together. I spoke nothing in private gatherings. (Matthew 12:16-21 Isaiah 42:1-4)

21. Why are you questioning me? Question those that had heard what I had spoken unto them! Truly they know what I have said.

22. But when he said these things, an under officer slapped Jesus and said, is that the way that you should answer the high priest?

23. Jesus said unto him, if I spoke anything corruptly bring your evidence forth, but if I am innocent then why do you beat me?

24. Then Annas had him bound and sent him to Caiaphas the high priest. (Psalms 2:1-3)

25. While Simon Peter was standing there warming himself, they said unto him, are you not one of his disciples? But he again denied and said, I am not.

26. One of the servants of the high priest, a family member of the one whose ear Peter cut off, he said, did I not see you there in the garden with him?

27. And a third time Peter denied, then immediately the rooster crowed. (Zechariah 13:7; Matthew 26:74)

28. It was early when they led Jesus to the Praetorium, but they did not enter in so that they not become defiled, so that they could eat the Passover meal.

29. Then when Pilate came out to them he said, what is the complaint that you bring against this man?

30. They answered and said, if he was not an evil one we would not have delivered him unto you.

31. Then Pilate said to them, you take him and judge him according to your Jewish law. Then the Jews said to him, it is not lawful (*under Roman law*) for us to crucify anyone. (John 19:7)

Verse 32 looks to have been added by a scribe and not a part of the original text.
No reference to crucifixion could be found.

32. In this, the scriptures were fulfilled which said the type of death that he would die.

33. Then Pilate went into the Praetorium again and he asked Jesus, are you the king of the Jews?

34. Jesus answered him and said, are you questioning me yourself or did others ask this of me?

35. And Pilate said to him, I am not a Jew. The Jewish nation and the high priests delivered you to me, so what did you do?

36. Then Jesus answered him and said, my kingdom is not of this world. If my kingdom was of this world my servants would have fought and protected me and I would not have been taken by the Jews. But my kingdom is not of this world.

37. Then Pilate said to him, truly are you not a king? Jesus answered and said, you have said that I am a king. I have been born for this and this (*to die*) is the reason that I have come into this world, that I could testify to the truth; All that are in the truth hear my voice. (*understand and obey my words*)

38. Pilate said to him, what is truth? And when he had said this, he again went out to the Jews and said to them, I do not find any crime in him.

39. It is a custom that I release one prisoner for you at the Passover; You decide who I should release, the king of the Jews?

40. And they all cried out again and said, not him; Release Barabbas. Barabbas was a thief. (Matthew 27:20; Mark 15:15; Luke 23:18) (*In other accounts, Barabbas was also a murderer*)

John 19

1. Therefore, Pilate took Jesus and scourged (*whipped*) him.

2. The soldiers weaved a wreath out of thorns and they put it upon his head as a crown, and threw a purple robe upon him.

3. They said, hail unto the king of the Jews. They also beat him with their hands.

4. Then Pilate went outside again and said to them, look, I bring him outside so that you may know that I have found no fault in him.

5. Then Jesus was brought outside wearing a thorny wreath and the purple robe; Then Pilate said unto them, look, here is the man!

6. When the high priests and the officers saw him, they yelled out loudly, crucify him! Crucify him! Then Pilate said to them, you crucify him; I have found no fault in him!

7. But the Jews answered and said, we have our law, and under the Jewish law he must die because he has called himself to be the son of God. (John 18:31)

8. When Pilate had heard this, he became alarmed.

9. He then entered into the Praetorium and said unto Jesus, where are you from? Jesus did not answer him.

10. Then Pilate said to him, why do you not speak to me? Do you know that I have the power to have you crucified and I have the authority to release you?

11. Then Jesus said unto him, you have no authority over me, none whatsoever, unless it has been given unto you from above; But this is the reason that those who brought me unto you have committed the greatest sin. (*Because Jesus said that he is the son of God*)
(Numbers 15:30-31, Psalms 19:13; 1 John 5:17; Hebrews 10:26; Matthew 12:32)

12. Because of this Pilate again tried to release him, but the Jews screamed out, if you release him, you are no friend of Caesar! Everyone who makes themselves to be a king creates a dispute against Caesar!

13. Then after hearing these words, he led Jesus outside and he sat down upon the throne. This was at the place called mosaic patio, but in Hebrew is called Gabbatha.

14. It was the day of preparation before Passover, and it was about the sixth hour of the day, and he said to the Jews, look! This is your king!

15. They screamed out loudly, away, away! Crucify him! Then Pilate said to them, do you want me to

crucify your king? Then the high priests answered and said, we have no king but Caesar!

16. This is why they gave him up to be crucified. And they took Jesus and they led him away,

17. carrying his own cross; He was led out to the place that is called the place of the skulls, which in Hebrew is called Golgotha. (Matthew 27:32)

18. There they crucified him along with two others, one on his left side and one on his right side with Jesus in the middle. (Isaiah 53:12; Matthew 27:38)

19. Pilate wrote a title and put it on the cross and it read, Jesus of Nazareth, the king of the Jews.

20. Many of the Jews read this title because it was a place near the city in which Jesus was crucified. It was written in Hebrew, Greek and Latin. *(the political reason - to quiet potential future insurrections)*

21. Then the high priests of the Jews said unto Pilate, do not write king of the Jews, but write that he said that he is the king of the Jews.

22. Pilate answered and said, what I have written is written and shall remain.

23. When the soldiers had crucified Jesus, they took his clothes and made four lots and each of the four soldiers received their share. His coat was seamless and was woven all around.

24. They had said to one another, let's not tear it, but we should cast lots to see who shall receive it.

The following part of this verse looks to have been added by a scribe and not a part of the original text.

In this the scripture was fulfilled which says, they divided the clothing and for my coat they cast lots. Truly the soldiers did these things as the scripture prophesied. (Matthew 27:35; Psalms 22:18)

25. But the mother of Jesus and her sister stood by the cross with Mary the wife of Clopas and Mary of Magdalene.

26. When Jesus saw his mother and one of the disciples that he loved standing by, he said to his mother, woman, that is your son.

27. Then he said to the disciple, that is your mother. And from that very time onward, that disciple took her into his own home *(to care for her)*.

28. Jesus knew that he had accomplished what was necessary for the scriptures to be fulfilled, then he said, I am thirsty.

29. There was a vessel that was full of vinegar, and they filled a sponge with vinegar and used a hyssop branch to offer it up to his mouth.

30. Then Jesus took the vinegar and he said, the acquiescence *(perfect demonstration)* of mercy. *(speaking of his sacrifice for them)* (tetelestai = G-2309+G-1653); Then he looked downward and yielded up his spirit.

31. Since it was the day of preparation for the Jews, so that he not remain on the cross on the sabbath day, because that sabbath was a great day *(not the weekly Sabbath but Passover)*, they asked Pilate that his legs be broken and that he be taken away.

32. Then the soldiers that crucified him came and they broke the legs of the others *(the two thieves)* that were crucified with him.

33. But when they came upon Jesus, they saw that he was already dead, so they did not break his legs,

34. but one of the soldiers stabbed him and pierced his side; Immediately out spilled water and blood. *(the water represents the washing away of all previous sins during water baptism - the blood represents the sacrifice that is necessary for all who come to Christ, to faithfully endure all hardships and suffering.* John 3:5; 1 John 5:6; Romans 6:1-23)

35. And I am a witness of the suffering *(myself experiencing the suffering personally)*; I am a true witness, and I write knowing the truth first hand, so that you may believe. *(commit yourself unto him)*

Verses 36-37 look to have been added by a scribe and not a part of the original text.
36. In this, the scriptures were fulfilled, that not a bone was broken. (Exodus 12:46)
37. Again in a different scripture it says, they shall look back upon the one that they have pierced. (Zechariah 12:10)

38. And after this, Joseph from Arimathea, living in hiding, for fear of the Jews because he was a disciple of Jesus, he asked Pilate to take the body of Jesus, and Pilate allowed it. So he came and took the body.

39. Then Nicodemus, the one who came unto Jesus in the night (John 3:1-21), he brought a mixture of myrrh and aloe, about a hundred pounds.

40. And they took the body of Jesus and they wrapped it in linens and spices, as is the custom according to Jewish burials.

41. And in the place where he was buried, there was a garden, and in the garden there was a newly cut tomb which no one had ever been laid in.

42. Because this was the day of preparation of the Jews, the tomb in which they laid Jesus was close by.

John 20

1. On the first day of the week, Mary of Magdalene came early while the darkness was still covering the tomb and she saw the stone was removed from the tomb,

2. so she ran and came to Simon Peter and another disciple who loved Jesus, and she said to them, they took the master out of the tomb and we do not know where they put him! (Matthew 28:7)

3. Then Peter and the other disciple went to the tomb. (Luke 28:3; Mark 16:5)

4. The two ran together, but the other disciple ran more quickly and came to the tomb first.

5. He bent down and looked into the tomb and saw the linen wrappings, but he did not go in.

6. Then Simon Peter came up behind him and he did enter the tomb; He also saw the linens lying there.

Verse 7 looks to have been added by a scribe and not a part of the original text.

7. The face cloth that was lying on his head was there also, but it was not with the linens, but was wrapped up in a place away from them.

8. Then the other disciple, the one who came to the tomb first went in as well, but they did not believe that he had been raised from the dead,

9. because they didn't yet know the prophetic scriptures which state that he must be raised from the dead!

10. Then the disciples went back to their homes,

11. but Mary remained at the tomb crying dearly outside. As she was crying, she bent down and looked into the tomb

12. and she saw two angels wearing white clothes; They were sitting down, one at the head and one at the feet where the body of Jesus had been laid.

13. They said to her, woman, why do you weep? She replied to them, because they have taken my master and I do not know where they have put him!

14. After she said this, she turned behind her and she saw Jesus standing there, but she did not know that it was him!

15. Jesus said to her, woman why do you cry? Who are you looking for? She, thinking that it was the gardener said to him, if you have carried him to somewhere else, please tell me where you have put him, and I will care for his body.

16. And Jesus said to her, Mary! And she turned and said, teacher!

It must be noted that John 20:17 and John 16:16, both first-hand accounts of John, overcome Luke 23:39-43, by which many false doctrines are based upon.

17. And Jesus said to her, do not touch me, because I have not yet ascended to my Father, but go to my brethren and tell them that I will be going to my Father, our Father; Unto my God and your God.
(Jesus was risen from the dead but had not yet ascended to the heavens)

18. And Mary of Magdalene brought the message to the disciples that she has seen the master and of the things that he told her.

19. It was the evening of the first day of the week, and the doors where the disciples were gathered were locked because they had fear of the Jews. Then Jesus appeared in the room with them and he said unto them, be at peace!

20. And when he said this, he showed them his hands and his side, and the disciples were overjoyed. The disciples had seen the master!

21. Then Jesus said unto them again, be at peace! Just as my Father has sent me, I also send you. (Matthew 28:19)

22. Then he breathed on them and said, soon you shall receive the spirit of the holy one.

23. Anyone who uses this power *(ability - Acts 2:38; Acts 3:19)* to remit their trespasses, their sins are forgiven unto them; (Romans 3:25; Romans 6:1-23; 1 Peter 4:17; Acts 2:38) But whoever refuse to do so, their sins shall remain. (Numbers 15:28-30; John 8:21)

24. Thomas, one of the twelve, nicknamed "twin", he was not with them when Jesus appeared,

25. but the other disciples told him, we have seen the master! But he said to them, if I do not see his hands and the scars from the nails, and be able to put my finger upon the nail scars and put my hand upon his side, I will not believe. (Zechariah 13:6)

26. Eight days later the disciples were again inside *(the house)* and this time Thomas was with them. Again, the doors were locked, but suddenly Jesus appeared and stood there with them, and he said, be at peace!

27. Then he said to Thomas, bring your finger here and observe my hands and touch my side with your fingers! The one that did not believe immediately believed! (Luke 24:41)

28. Then Thomas said unto him, you are my master and my God!

29. Then Jesus said unto him, because you have seen me, you have believed. Fortunate are they that commit themselves wholly unto me without seeing.

30. Jesus also did many other miracles in the presence of the disciples that are not written in this book.

31. But these things are written for you to believe that Jesus is the Christ, the son of God, and that if you continue believing *(obeying - John 3:16-21)* you shall receive *(everlasting)* life in his name.

John 21

1. After this, Jesus showed himself again unto the disciples at the Sea of Tiberias when he revealed himself in this way:

2. Simon Peter and Thomas were together with Nathaniel, the one from Cana of Galilee, the sons of Zebedee and two of the other disciples.

3. Then Simon Peter said, I am going fishing, and they said to him, if you don't mind we will come along with you. So they went and quickly got themselves into the boat. That evening they caught nothing.

4. In the early morning, Jesus came and stood on the shore, but the disciples did not know that it was him.

5. Then Jesus said to them, children, do you have anything to eat? They answered and said, no.

6. And he said to them, cast your nets on the other *(right)* side of the boat and you will be successful. So they threw their nets off of the other side of the boat and they did not have the strength to pull it in, because of the great amount of fish in it. (Luke 5:4-7)

7. Then the disciple who loved Jesus said unto Peter, it is our master! When Simon Peter had heard that it was the master, he tied on his fisherman's coat because he was naked and he threw himself into the sea.

8. And the other disciples in the little boat came because they were not far from the land, but only about two hundred yards from the shore, and they dragged the net with the fish.

9. When they went up onto the land they saw a fire of hot coals with a fish lying upon them, and there also was bread.

10. Then Jesus said unto them, bring over some of the fish that you have caught.

11. Simon Peter went up and he drug the net on to the land and it was full of fish, a hundred fifty-three, yet the net did not tear even though there were so many!

12. Then Jesus said unto them, come and let's eat the dinner. None of the disciples dared to ask him any questions, because they knew they were with the master.

13. Then Jesus came, took the bread and gave it to them, and also the fish in the same way.

14. This was the third time that he revealed himself unto the disciples after he was raised from the dead.

15. When they were eating, Jesus said unto Simon the son of Jonah, do you love me more than the others? And Peter said, yes master, you know that I have great affection for you. And Jesus said unto him, care for my lambs.

16. Then he said it again a second time, Simon, son of Jonah, do you love me? And Peter said, yes master, you know that I have great affection for you. Then Jesus said unto him, then be a shepherd unto my sheep.

17. Then, a third time Jesus asked him, Simon, son of Jonah, are you my friend? And because he said this a third time, Peter said unto him, master, you know all things and you know that I have great affection for you. And Jesus said, care for my sheep.

18. Truly I tell you, you have cared for yourself and you went where you chose to go, as you grow old, you will reach out your empty hands and another will care for you and he will take you to where you do not want to go.

19. He said this to indicate the kind of death he would have, that he would honor God through it. After this he said, follow me (*be as I am*).

20. When he turned, he saw the disciple who loved Jesus following, it was the same disciple that leaned upon his chest at the dinner and asked, master, who is it that is betraying you?

21. When Peter saw him he said, master, what is he doing?

22. And Jesus said unto him, if I choose for him to remain until I return, what is that to you?
Follow me (*be as I am*).

23. Then the message went out unto the other disciples that this brother would not die. But that is not what Jesus said, that he would not die; But Jesus did say, if I desire that he not die until I return, what is that to you?

The final two verses look to have been added by a scribe.

24. This is the testimony of the disciple (John) concerning these things and he has written them so that we know the truth from an eyewitness who was there with Jesus. (because many have altered the truth)

25. But there are also many other things that Jesus did, that if they were completely written down, I suppose that the world itself could not contain all of the scrolls.

An overview of the book of John

The book of John looks to be the first-hand account of the apostle John, written to clear up many of the inaccuracies and false doctrines that had already began to spread at the time of his writing (90 AD). John's account must be considered the most reliable of the four gospels due to him being an eyewitness and participant of the events. Though there have been some alterations made to the book over the past 1900+ years, the book of John is the most unaltered of the four gospels. Of the disciples, John was one of only three who was there to see all of the events, such as the transfiguration, of which Matthew was not.

The book of John has been moved ahead of the books of Mark and Luke due to its relevance, but also because Luke and Acts are two parts of one story that needed to be chronologically connected, both written to Theophilus.

Mark

Chapter 1

1. The establishment of the gospel of Jesus Christ, the son of God.

2. As it has been written by the prophets, for the record! "I shall send my messenger unto you to confront you. He will prepare the way before me.

3. The voice of the one crying in the wilderness, he shall prepare the way of the Lord. He shall make the way straight (*clear*) unto him." (Malachi 3:1; Isaiah 40:3)

4. John arose baptizing in the wilderness and announcing the baptism of repentance for the remission of sins. (Acts 2:38)

5. Very many people of the country of Judea and of Jerusalem came and were baptized of him in the Jordan river, having confessed their sins.

6. John was wearing clothing made of camel hair with a belt made of leather around his waist; He ate locusts and wild honey.

7. He announced and said, he that is more powerful than I is coming, he shall come after me, of whom I am not worthy to bend down and loosen the clasp of his sandals.

8. I have come to baptize you with water, but he shall also baptize you with his holy spirit. (John 3:5)

9. In those days, Jesus came from Nazareth of Galilee and he was baptized by John in the Jordan river.

10. As he came up from out of the water, the sky was opened up and the spirit came down upon him as if it were a dove.

11. Then there was a voice that was heard coming from out of the sky: You are my beloved son, in whom I am delighted. (Psalms 2:7)

12. The spirit of God drove him into a deserted place.

13. He remained there in the wilderness for forty days to be tested by Satan. He was with the wild animals and afterward the angels attended unto him.

14. After John had been arrested and thrown into prison, Jesus came into Galilee, proclaiming the gospel of the kingdom of God.

15. He said, the time has now come, the kingdom of God draws near; Repent and be completely committed unto the gospel of God. (Acts 2:38)

16. And while he was walking along the sea of Galilee, he saw Simon and Andrew his brother as they were throwing a small net into the sea; They were fishermen.

17. Jesus said unto them, come follow me and I will make you to be fishers of men;

18. So they left their nets and followed him.

19. Walking on a little further, he saw James the son of Zebedee and his brother John as they were in the boat mending their nets.

20. And when he saw them, he directly called out to them and they left their father Zebedee in the boat with the hired servants and they followed him.

21. They crossed the border into Capernaum, then entered into the synagogue and Jesus taught.

22. The people were amazed at the doctrine that he taught because he was teaching as though he was the authority, not as the scribes teach.

23. There was a man in the synagogue that had demonic spirits in him and he screamed out loudly:

24. Oh, who are we unto you, Jesus of Nazareth? Have you come to destroy us? We know that you are the holy one of God.

25. But Jesus forbid him to speak and said, be quiet and come out of him!

26. The man began convulsing and the unclean spirit screamed with a loud voice, then came out of him.

27. All of the people were astonished at what they saw! They began to discuss among themselves and say, who is this? What new thing was done here that even the demonic spirits are commanded by him and they obey him?

28. The news of him quickly spread into all of the regions of Galilee!

29. When they left the synagogue, they came unto the home of Simon and Andrew; James and John came along with them.

30. Simon's mother in law was laying down with a fever and they spoke to Jesus concerning her.

31. So Jesus came unto her and took her hand and lifted her up; Instantly the fever left her, and she began to

serve them.

32. The evening had come and as the sun set, they brought unto him all of those that were badly sick and injured and some that were demon possessed;

33. And the whole city had gathered at the door.

34. Jesus healed many that had various diseases and he cast out many demons, but he did not allow them to speak, because the demons knew who he was.

35. And Jesus arose up early the next morning while it was still dark and he went unto a deserted place and there he prayed.

36. Simon and the others began to search for him,

37. and when they found him they said to him, all of the towns people are seeking you!

38. Jesus said unto them, we shall go unto the neighboring towns so that I may also announce there:
For this is the reason that I have come.

39. There he preached in their synagogues throughout Galilee and he cast out many demons.

40. There was a leper that came unto him and begged him as he fell upon his knees, and he said unto him, if you would, I know that you can cleanse me.

41. Jesus, full of pity, reached out his hand and touched him and said, I am willing, be made clean!

42. And when he spoke to him, instantly the leprosy left him and he was cleansed!

43. Then Jesus sternly warned him and immediately pulled him away with him,

44. and he said unto him: See no one and tell not a thing of this, but go yourself unto the priests and offer that which is commanded by Moses concerning having been cleansed to be a witness unto them.

45. But as he left, he began to announce what had happened and tell many, but the news of the matter spread so greatly that Jesus was no longer able to openly enter into any other cities, so he went outside to the deserted places and they came unto him from every direction! (*Jesus was famous* - Matthew 12:17-20)

Mark 2

1. Jesus again entered into Capernaum. After several days it was rumored that he was in a certain house.

2. Immediately the people began to assemble and Jesus spoke to them of the kingdom of God, but with so many people there, there was no way to open the door;

3. They brought unto him a paralyzed man, four men carrying him on a cot,

4. but they were not able to come near to him because of the crowd; So they took a part of the roof off of the house, and as they dug through, they lowered the man on a cot!

5. And Jesus saw the dedication that they had and he said unto the paralyzed man; Child, your sins are forgiven of you. (John 8:11; John 5:14; Luke 5:20)

6. Now there were some of the scribes sitting there and they disputed in their hearts,

7. and they asked themselves, why does this man speak blasphemy? Who is able to forgive sins, except for God alone? (*Certainly not a priest!*)

8. Instantly Jesus knew their thoughts in his spirit and he said unto them: Why do you reason these things in your hearts?

9. What is easier to say, your sins are forgiven of you, or rise up, pick up your cot and walk?

10. But now you know that the son of man (*Jesus*) has the authority to forgive sins on the earth; Then he said unto the paralyzed man,

11. rise up and pick up your cot and walk unto your own house!

12. Quickly the man arose up and grabbed his cot and he left as the people watched. They were all astonished and they began to glorify God and said, no one has ever seen anything like this before!

13. Then Jesus went for a walk along the sea, but the crowd kept following him, so he kept teaching them.

**Verse 14 is in error and contradicts Matthew 10:3 and Mark 3:18
where it is said that James is the son of Alphaeus.**

14. As Jesus was walking, he saw Levi (*Matthew*) *the son of Alphaeus* sitting at the tax office. Jesus said unto him, follow me, and he arose up and he followed him. (Matthew 10:3; Mark 3:18; Luke 5:27)

15. When Jesus was relaxing in his (*Matthew's*) home, there were many tax collectors and sinners relaxing there with Jesus and his disciples;

16. The scribes and the Pharisees saw him eating with the tax collectors and with sinners, and they asked his disciples, why does he eat and drink with the tax collectors and sinners?

17. And Jesus overheard them and said unto them, there is no need for a strong healer, except for those that are badly sick. I have not come to call the righteous unto repentance, but the sinners.

18. Some of the disciples of John and some of the disciples of the Pharisees were fasting, and they came and asked him, why do the disciples of John and the Pharisees often fast, but your disciples do not fast?

19. And Jesus said unto them, are the sons of the bride chamber able to fast while the bridegroom is with them? As long as the bridegroom is with them they can not fast.

20. But the day shall come when the bridegroom will be taken away from them and then they shall fast.

21. No man sews a new patch on an old piece of clothing; Because if they do, it would take away the performance of it and a worse rip will occur.

22. No one puts new wine into old wineskins, otherwise they burst and the new wine is spilled out and the wineskins are worthless; But they put new wine into fresh wineskins.

23. Jesus had moved along and he came unto some grain fields on the Sabbath day, when his disciples began to pluck some of the grain heads and eat them.

24. The Pharisees said unto him, look! Why do they do on the Sabbath day that which is unlawful (*under the Jewish law*)?

25. And Jesus said, did you never read what David and those with him did when they were hungry?

26. How he entered into the temple in the days of Abiathar the high priest and they ate the bread of presentation, of which is not lawful (*under the Jewish law*) for them to eat? It was only for the priests, but he gave it unto those that were with him.

27. Then Jesus said unto them, the Sabbath was created for man, not man for the Sabbath;

28. So now you know that the son of man is also the Lord over the Sabbath.

Today we have laws, that are interpreted by statutes, which are enforced by codes.
The law is the law to be adhered to, but the statute is an interpretation of the law;
The code is a lower level application of the statute.
In old covenant times, the law was given by God,
but the _Mosaic law_ was the equivalent of a statute
in that it was an interpretation of the _law of God_.
Then you have the _Jewish law_, of which was a lower level application of a statute,
equivalent to a modern-day code.
English bibles seldom make a distinction.
Jesus had told the Pharisees that through their traditions (_Jewish law_),
they make the law of God to no effect,
by making it enforce the opposite of that which was intended.

Mark 3

1. Then Jesus entered into the synagogue and there was a man there with a crippled hand.

2. The Pharisees watched him to see if he would heal on the Sabbath, so that they might accuse him.

3. Jesus told the man with the crippled hand to stand up in front of him;

4. Then Jesus said unto them, is it the right thing to do good on the Sabbath, or to do evil? To save a man, or to let him die? And they were silent.

5. Then he looked around at them with passionate indignation (*anger*), being greatly grieved because of the hardness of their hearts, and he said to the man, reach your hand out toward me; And when the man did so, his hand was completely restored as good as the other.

6. And when they left, the Pharisees immediately held a meeting with the Herodians, so to come against Jesus and plan how they might kill him.

7. but Jesus left the area with his disciples and they went to the sea; There was a large gathering of people that followed him from Galilee and from Judea.

8. People also followed him from Jerusalem, from Idumea, beyond the Jordan river and there were some from Tyre and Sidon; They gathered a great crowd that had heard of the many miracles that he had done, and they came unto him.

9. Then he instructed the disciples to remain near the boat so that the crowd would not engulf them.

10. He healed many, so they crowded him so that they might be able to touch him, all that had infirmities.

11. And those with demonic spirits fell in front of him when they saw him and they cried out and said, you are the son of God!

12. He instructed them to not reveal that he is the Christ.

13. Jesus went up on a high mountain, and he called those that he chose and they went with him.

14. He picked twelve that would remain with him, that they should be sent to announce (*the kingdom*).

15. He gave them authority to heal those that were sick and to cast out demons.

16. And he gave a name unto Simon, the nickname, Peter (pebble).

17. James, son of Zebedee and John his brother, Jesus nicknamed them the sons of thunder;

18. He also chose Andrew, Philip, Bartholomew, Matthew, Thomas, James the son of Alphaeus, Thaddeus, Simon the Canaanite,

19. and Judas Iscariot, the one that did betray him. (Matthew 10:1-4; Luke 6:15; Acts 1:13)

20. And Jesus came into a house, and a crowd came together again; It was so packed with people that they could not even eat the meal.

21. But when those who were trying to arrest him had heard of this, they said, he is out of his mind!

22. And the scribes came down from Jerusalem and said: He has Beelzebub; The ruler of the demons is by who he cast out demons. (Luke 11:15; Matthew 9:34)

23. Jesus called them unto him and he spoke to them in parables: He said, how is Satan able to cast out Satan?

24. If a kingdom is divided against itself, it is not able to remain a kingdom.

25. If a house is divided, that house is not able to continue together any longer.

26. If Satan is against himself, he is divided, he is not able to remain, but his kingdom is come to its end.

27. No one is able to steal the treasure of a strong man, nor enter into his home to steal, unless he first ties up the strong man, and only then can he go to take what he will.

28. Truly, all sin that one might commit and all vilification that one might speak, can be forgiven;

29. Except whoever takes action against the spirit of our holy God, it shall not be forgiven of him in this life, and he shall receive eternal damnation. (Numbers 15:30-31; Matthew 12:31; 1 John 5:16-17)

30. Because of this, they said that he has an unclean spirit.

31. Then the mother and brothers of Jesus came and were standing outside, and they sent word to him, calling for him to come to them. (*This is likely when Joseph the husband of Mary had died*)

32. And a large crowd gathered around him and they said to him, be aware that your mother and your brothers are seeking for you to come to them over there.

33. Jesus answered them and said, who is my mother and who are my brothers?

34. He looked circling around those that were surrounding him and he said, Look! My mother and my brethren!

35. Whoever does the will of God, these are my family. (Matt. 7:21; 21:28-32; 1 Peter 2:15; 1 John 2:17)

Mark 4

1. At another time, Jesus again began to teach near the sea and a large crowd gathered near him, so he entered into a boat to sit on the water. All of the crowd were on the land facing the sea,

2. and he taught many things to them in parables and as he taught them, he said;

3. Hear my words. A man went out to plant his grain. (Matthew 13:3)

4. While he was sowing the seed, some fell along the roadway, and the birds came and ate it up.

5. Other grains fell upon rocky ground where there was not much soil. It sprung up quickly, but because it did not have depth in good soil, the sun arose and scorched it;

6. It did not have good roots and it dried up.

7. Some seed fell into thorn bushes, but the thorn bushes grew up and choked them out and they did not produce any good fruit.

8. Some seed fell upon good ground and it grew and produced good fruit, and some produced one hundred, and some sixty and some thirty.

9. Then Jesus said unto them, he who has ears, let him hear.

10. And when he was away from the crowds, those who were in his company, including the twelve

disciples, they asked him about the parable.

11. Jesus said unto them, it is determined for you to know the mysteries of the kingdom of God; But for those who do not have good intentions, it is not for them to know; This is why I speak in parables.

12. In that they can see, but while seeing, they do not perceive; While they hear, they do not understand, therefore they are not converted nor do they have their sins forgiven of them. (Isaiah 6:9-10)

13. Then Jesus said unto them: Do you not understand this parable? How will you understand the other parables that are more difficult to understand?

14. The one who plants, he spreads the instructions of God.

15. Those that are by the roadway, these are they in which the words are sown, but when they hear it, immediately Satan comes and takes it away from them, to prevent it from growing in their hearts.

16. They that are similar to those that fell on the rocky places, they are those who when they hear the word of instruction, immediately they receive it with joy,

17. but they do not have any roots in themselves and they are temporary; Then when trouble or persecution comes because of the message, they stumble and fall away.

18. There are also those that fell into thorn bushes; These are those who have heard the word,

19. but the cares of the things of this life, the deceitfulness of wealth and their own lusts come and choke the message and they become unfruitful. (Matthew 7:17-19; Matthew 13:18-23)

20. And those that fall upon good ground are those that hear the instruction and welcome it and they bring forth good fruit; One thirty, one sixty and another a hundred times.

21. And he said, is a candle meant to be put under a bushel basket or under a bed? Is it not meant to be put upon a candlestick?

22. Know that there is nothing that can be hidden of which will not be made known and nothing shall be kept secret, because everything shall be exposed by the light.

23. If anyone has an ear, may he hear.

24. Then he said unto them, understand that which you hear and in whatever amount you measure, it will be measured unto you the same in return and it will be given abundantly unto you that understand this.

25. Unto whoever has an abundance of understanding, more shall be given; But whoever does not have, the little that he does have will be taken from him.

26. Then Jesus said, the kingdom of above is much like a man that spreads seed on the ground;

27. Then for many days he does not watch it, but the seed sprouts and grows.

28. The earth itself brings forth its fruit, first the green, then the head and then the full grain within the head.

29. But when it brings forth its fruit, he goes out with the sickle because the harvest is ready.

30. And he continued and said, unto what shall we compare the kingdom of God, or in what parable can we make a comparison?

31. It is as a grain of mustard seed that is planted in the ground, at which time it is of the smallest of all seeds in all of the earth.

32. But when it is planted, it grows up and becomes larger than all of the other plants, and it has large branches that are able to bring shade, and in its branches the birds roost.

33. And Jesus spoke to them in many other parables to teach them, as much as they could bear.

34. He did not speak to them other than in parables, but he explained all things privately to his disciples.

Verses 35-40 offer a different account than Matthew 8:28, and Luke 8:26.

35. That same day, when the evening had come, Jesus said unto the disciples, let us go to the other side.

36. Then he dismissed the crowd and they got into the boat. There were also other small boats that followed them.

37. Then a strong wind began to blow and a storm came upon them, and the waves were thrown over the boat and it became nearly full of water.

38. Jesus was sleeping on the stern of the boat, so they woke him up and said to him, teacher, does it not matter to you that we are about to die?

39. Then Jesus arose and forbid the wind and the waves, and he said to the sea, be silent, be still! And the winds subsided and there was a great calm.

40. But they were afraid with a great amount of terror and they said to one another: Who is he, that even the wind and the sea obey him?

Mark 5

1. And they came to the other side of the sea, into the land of the Gadarenes.

2. As they got out of the boat, a man with a demonic spirit came from out of the graveyard to meet them.

3. The man lived in the graveyard and he could not be bound, even with chains.

4. He had often been bound in chains and he had broken the chains each time, shattering them, and no one had the strength to subdue him.

5. He was always among the hills and in the graveyard, both day and night, and he cut himself with sharp stones often and he screamed loudly. (Psalms 22:24)

6. Jesus saw him coming from a distance as the man ran down the hillside and fell at his feet.

7. He yelled loudly and said, what do you want with me Jesus, the son of the most high God? I ask you to swear that you will not torment me!

Verse 8 is misplaced and belongs after verse 12 and has been put there below.

9. Then Jesus asked him for his name, and he answered and said, Legion, because we are many.

10. And the spirit begged him, that he not send him out of the physical world.

11. Nearby there was a heard of pigs feeding;

12. The demons begged Jesus and said, allow us to go into the pigs.

* 8. Jesus said unto the man, come out! And immediately the demonic spirits came out of the man!

13. He ordered the demons to enter into the pigs, and when they did, they immediately ran down the hillside and ran off of a cliff and fell into the sea! And there were about two thousand pigs that were drowned in the sea.

14. The men that were tending the pigs ran and told those in the nearby city of what had happened, and they came to see what had occurred.

15. When they came to Jesus, they saw the man that had been demon possessed sitting there with a robe on and was mentally stable.

16. Because of what had been done concerning the demon possessed man and the pigs,

17. the people began to beg them to leave their land!

In the Matthew 9:28-34 account of the previous story,
the land was called Gergesenes and it was two men that were demon possessed.
Matthew was an eyewitness, but Mark was not.

18. Then Jesus and his disciples entered into the boat and the man who had been possessed by the demons began begging Jesus that he come with him.

19. But Jesus did not allow him to go with them, but told him to go unto his family home and tell them of what the Lord has done because he had pity on you.

20. And the man went and proclaimed unto the people of Decapolis all of the things that Jesus had done for him; All that heard him speak were astonished!

21. When Jesus crossed back to the other side, there was a large crowd by the sea waiting there for him.

22. And take notice, the leader of the synagogue was there waiting for him. His name was Jairus and when he saw Jesus, he fell at his feet.

23. He begged him saying, my little daughter is very sick and is dying. Will you come unto her and lay your hands upon her to heal her so that she may live?

24. Jesus went with him and a huge crowd followed them and were pressing in on them from all sides.

25. And there was a woman who had a bloody wound that had not healed for twelve years.

26. She had made many efforts to be healed and gone to many healers in the past. She had spent all of her money trying to find a way to be healed, but the bleeding had gotten worse even through all of her efforts;

27. When she had heard of Jesus, she came from within the back of the crowd and she reached with all of her efforts to touch the robe of Jesus!

28. She had said in her heart, if only I might just touch his robe, I will be healed.

29. And immediately upon touching his robe, the bleeding stopped and she knew that her body was healed.

30. But Jesus immediately knew within himself that some power had gone forth from him, so he turned unto the crowd and said, who touched me?

31. The disciples said unto him, with all of these people pressing in upon you, you ask, who touched me?

32. And he looked around to see the one who had done this.

33. But the woman was afraid and she trembled knowing what had happened unto her, so she came and fell in front of him and told him the truth.

34. And Jesus said unto her, daughter your convictions have healed you. Go in peace and be completely healed from your plague.

35. While Jesus was still speaking, a message came from the home of the leader of the synagogue which said, your daughter has died; There is no reason for you to trouble the teacher about this matter anymore.

36. When Jesus heard this he said unto Jairus, do not fear, but only trust in me.

37. Jesus did not allow anyone to go with him except Peter, James and John.

38. They came to the house of Jairus and they saw a commotion and there were many that were crying, mourning greatly.

39. And Jesus entered the house and said unto them, why do you make so much noise and mourn? The child has not died, but she has only fallen asleep!

40. But those in the house scoffed, laughed at him and mocked him. But Jesus had everyone taken out of the house and took the father and mother of the child and those whom he had chosen; They went in unto the child and saw her lying there.

41. Then Jesus took a hold of the hand of the child and he said unto her, talitha koumi (Aramaic), which translates to mean, little girl, rise up!

42. Immediately the little girl arose and she stood up and walked around. She was about twelve years old. All of the people were amazed and greatly pleased with great passion.

43. Jesus said, give her some food, that she might eat.

Mark 6

1. Then Jesus went away from that place and he came unto his homeland. His disciples came with him.

2. When the Sabbath day had come, he began to teach in the synagogue and those that heard him were astonished. They said, from where have these doctrines come. From where did he get this wisdom and from where have all these powerful deeds that he has done originate?

3. Is he not the son of a carpenter, his mother Mary, and his brothers James, Joseph, Simon and Judas? Are his sisters not here with us? They stumbled at these things and did not believe in him. (Rom 9:32)

4. But Jesus said to them, a prophet does not go without honor, except in his home town and by his own family.

5. He did not do many miracles in that place, with the exception of a few of the sick of whom he laid his hands upon them and they were healed.

6. He was shocked and wondered at their disbelief. So then Jesus went around about unto all of the surrounding towns and villages, teaching unto them.

7. He called the twelve unto him and began to send them out in pairs. He gave them authority over the demonic spirits.

8. He commanded them to take nothing with them except a staff only; Not a bag, no food and no money.

9. But only that they should put on shoes and take a coat.

10. Then he said unto them, whenever you enter into a house, remain there until you leave that town.

11. All that do not receive you, nor are willing to hear your message, leave that place and shake off the dust from your feet to be a testimony against them. (Luke 9:5; Matthew 10:14; Acts 13:51)
Surely I tell you, that it will be more tolerable for those who lived in Sodom and Gomorrah on the day of judgment, than for that place.

12. When they went, they began to preach the message of repentance. (Jonah 3:8-10)

13. They cast out many demons and touched many with olive oil. Those that were sick were healed.

14. King Herod had by now heard of him, for Jesus was well known (*famous*). And Herod said, has John the Baptizer risen from the dead? This man does many mighty things! (Matthew 12:16-21; Isaiah 42:1-4)

15. There were others that thought of him as Elijah, yet others said that he is a prophet, possibly one of the past prophets come back to life! (Luke 9:8, 19)

16. When Herod heard these things he said, I had beheaded John, this one must be John having been raised from the dead!

17. It was Herod that had arrested John, chained him and threw him into prison; He did this because of Herodias, the wife of his brother Philip, of whom he had taken as his own wife,

18. John had said unto Herod, it is not lawful for you to have your brother's wife.

19. But Herodias held a grudge against him and she wanted him to be killed, but was not able to do so.

20. Herod respected John, knowing that he was a righteous man and holy unto the Lord, and he had kept him safe. Herod was also influenced by John to do many things after having spoken with him.

21. So Herodias waited for the opportunity, and she saw her chance at a birthday feast for Herod in which many influential people were invited, including the colonels and the political leaders of Galilee.

22. So Herodias sent in her daughter to dance for them and she pleased Herod and his guests; The king said unto the girl, ask of me whatever you wish and I will give it to you.

23. He swore unto her, whatever you might ask, up to half of my kingdom.

24. As she was walking out she asked her mother, what shall I ask? She said, the head of John the baptizer.

25. Then the girl entered in haste unto the king, and she said, I desire that you give to me the head of John the baptizer on a plate.

26. The king became deeply grieved, but because of his oath and because of all of his guests, he could not refuse her.

27. So immediately he dispatched an executioner and ordered that they bring unto him the head of John. So the man went and beheaded him in the prison;

28. The head was brought unto him on a platter and it was given to the girl; Then the girl gave it to her mother.

29. When John's disciples had heard of this, they went and took his body and placed it in a tomb.

30. Then his disciples went unto Jesus and gave him the news of all of the things of what had been done.

31. Jesus said unto them, come with me to this deserted place and we will rest a little while. There were many people passing by and it was so busy that they could not even find a place to sit and eat.

32. So they went by boat to a deserted place so that they could be in private;

33. But the crowds saw them going, because many had recognized them, so they went on foot; People from all of the city followed them and gathered together before him.

34. And Jesus saw the huge crowd coming towards them and he had compassion on them because they were as sheep without a shepherd. So he began to teach them many things. (Numbers 27:17; Ezekiel 34:5)

35. And the time came when his disciples came near to him and said, this is a deserted place and we have been here for many hours!

36. Send them away so that they can go back to their villages, that they might buy themselves some food, because they have nothing to eat here.

37. But Jesus answered and said unto them, give them what you have! And they asked him, where shall we go and buy two thousand denarii of bread to give to them?

38. And Jesus said, go and see how many loaves you have. But they already knew, and they said, five loaves and two fish.

39. Then Jesus ordered them to have the people sit down on the grass and gather themselves into groups;

40. So they sat down in rows; A hundred in some rows and fifty in others.

41. Jesus took the five loaves and the two fish and looked up into the sky, and he thanked the Father for what he was about to give. Then he broke the loaves and gave the pieces unto his disciples, and they placed the baskets in front of them. Then he cut up the fish and divided pieces unto all of the people,

42. and they all ate and were satisfied.

43. When they gathered up the leftovers, there were twelve baskets full, including some fish!

44. There were about five thousand men who ate.

45. Then, quickly he gathered the disciples unto himself and they entered into the boat and he told them that they should go to the other side unto Bethsaida, but that he would stay to dismiss the crowd.

46. When they had gone, he went up to a hill to pray.

47. And the evening came and the boat was out in the middle of the sea. Jesus was alone on the land.

48. In the distance, Jesus saw that they were having difficulty rowing, as the wind was against them. In the middle of the night he came unto them, walking on the water; He wanted to approach them,

49. but when they saw him walking on the sea, they thought that he was a phantom and they were afraid and began screaming!

50. They had seen him and were all greatly distressed. Then Jesus spoke to them and said, have courage, it is I, do not fear!

The accounts of verses 51-52 contradict
the accounts of Matthew 14:29 & Luke 8:25 and should not be held as valid.

51. He came unto them, and as he came up into the boat the wind died down. They were amazed, awestruck and speechless!
52. They did not understand the miracle of what had happened with the loaves and the fish, because their hearts were blinded.

53. When they had crossed over, they came unto the land of Gennesaret and they anchored there.
54. As they were getting out of the boat the people there recognized who they were,
55. so they ran unto all of the neighboring towns and they began to bring unto him the sick people laying on cots and they carried them unto him.
56. Wherever Jesus entered into a village, a city, the countryside or the markets, they brought unto him those that were ailing. They begged him that they might only touch his robe and all that touched it were healed.

Mark 7

1. The Pharisees gathered together in a place where Jesus was, and some of the scribes came from Jerusalem.
2. They saw that some of his disciples were eating with unwashed hands, and in this they found a way to accuse them.
3. You see, the Pharisees and all of the Jews do not eat unless they have washed their hands, keeping according to the traditions of the elders.
4. When they come in from the town square (*gathering places*), they do not eat unless they first dip their hands in water. They wash many other things before they might choose to hold them in their hands, for example, cups, utensils, pots and dishes.
5. Then the Pharisees and the scribes began to question him; Why do your disciples not do according to the traditions of the elders? They are eating with unwashed hands!
6. Then Jesus said unto them, Isaiah prophesied concerning you hypocrites! As it has been written, these people honor me with their lips but their hearts are far from me. (Isaiah 29:13 - *same as today*)
7. In vain they worship me, teaching for doctrines the commandments of men!
8. You forsake the commands of God to keep the traditions of men; By immersing your utensils and cups and other things, as many of you do,
9. you completely set aside the commandments of God, so that you might keep your own traditions.
10. Moses said, respect and care for your father and your mother, and that whoever curses his father or mother must die! (Deuteronomy 5:16; Exodus 21:17)
11. But you say that a man can say unto his father or mother, corban; That is to say, whatever you gain by me is a gift (*nothing shall be expected of me*).
12. You no longer require him to do anything for his father or mother!
13. You make the law of God of no effect by the traditions that you hold; You also do many similar things.
14. Then Jesus called the crowd to come near to him and he said to them, hear my words and understand:
15. There is nothing from outside of a man, that when it enters into him will defile him; It is only that which is produced by a man that can defile him. (1 Corinthians 8:26-33)
16. If anyone has an ear to hear, let him hear.
17. Jesus entered a house to get away from the crowd and one of his disciples asked him about the parable.
18. Then Jesus said, are you that unintelligent? Do you not understand that anything a man might eat can not defile him before God? (Colossians 2:16, Romans 14:13-23)
19. What a man eats does not enter into his heart but into his stomach, and then it goes out unto the privy!
20. And he said, that which is produced by a man, it is that which can defile him.

21. From within the heart of a man is where evil is produced, things such as wicked thoughts, adultery, fornication,

22. murder, theft, selfishness, deception, lust, malice, blasphemy, pride, recklessness, and all types of willful defiance against the things that are right; (Numbers 15:30-31; Hebrews 10:26)

23. Evil actions come from the heart and when they proceed out from a man he is defiled.

24. Then Jesus rose up and went unto the border areas of Tyre and Sidon. He entered a house hoping that no one would know that he was there.

25. But a certain woman had heard that he was there, and she came unto him because her young daughter had a demonic spirit and she fell at his feet.

26. The woman was Greek, a Syrian-Phoenician. She asked if he would cast out the demonic spirit from her little daughter.

27. But Jesus said unto her, first allow the children to be satisfied, for it is not good to take the food away from the children and throw it to the dogs.

28. Then she answered and said unto him, yes Lord, but even the dogs are under the table and eat the crumbs that fall from the children.

29. Jesus said unto her, go, the demon has now gone from your daughter!

30. And when she went, she saw that the demon had gone out of the girl and she was laying on the couch.

31. Jesus left the area of the border of Tyre and Sidon and he came to the Sea of Galilee, unto the center of Decapolis.

32. They brought unto him a deaf man that could barely speak; They begged him that he might put his hands upon him.

33. Jesus took him away from the crowd to be in private, put his fingers on the man's ears and he spit, putting it on his tongue.

34. Then he looked up to the heavens and he groaned and said, Ephphatha! (*Aramaic for*) Be opened!

35. Instantly his ears were opened! His tongue was freed and he spoke correctly.

36. He ordered that he should not tell anyone, but the more he ordered that they should not tell, the more they proclaimed.

37. And they were extremely amazed and said, all these things he has done, that even the deaf are made to hear and the dumb can now speak!

Mark 8

It seems that some of the earlier parts of this story that should have proceeded 8:1 are missing. To have proper understanding and context, refer to Matthew 15:29-39.

1. Then a very large crowd gathered together and they had nothing to eat. Jesus called his disciples unto him and he said; I have pity for the people

2. because they have been here with me for three days and have had nothing to eat.

3. If I send them back to their homes without eating, they will grow weak along the way, and some have come from great distances.

4. His disciples said to him, from where shall we gather enough food to satisfy all of these people, being that we are in a deserted place?

5. And he asked them, how many loaves do you have? And they said, seven.

6. Then he ordered the crowd to sit down upon the ground and then he took the seven loaves and he gave thanks unto the Father, and he broke them and gave in to the disciples so that they might begin to serve it unto the people.

7. They also had a few fish, and Jesus then blessed them and ordered they these also be served.

8. Everyone ate and were filled, and they gathered the leftovers and there was enough to fill seven baskets!

9. There were about four thousand that were fed! Then Jesus sent them back to their homes.

10. Then Jesus and the disciples began to enter into a boat and went into the region of Dalmanutha.

11. Then the Pharisees gathered together near Jesus and began to dispute with him. They asked to see a sign (*evidence*) in the sky, tempting him.

12. Jesus sighed and asked, why does this nation demand to see a sign? Truly I say unto you, if I will give a sign unto this nation…

Again, it seems that this story is incomplete. (Matthew 16:1-4)

13. Jesus left and he again got into the boat and he went unto the other side;

14. But the disciples had forgotten to take food, not even a single loaf was with them on the boat.

15. Jesus ordered the disciples to distance themselves from the Pharisees and he said, beware of the leaven of the Pharisees and of the Jewish leaders.

16. The disciples asked one another, did he say this because we have no food with us?

17. Aware of this Jesus said, why are you concerned that you have no food? Is your heart still in unbelief?

18. Your eyes, can you not see with them? Your ears, can you not hear with them? Don't you remember?

19. I broke the five loaves and it was made to feed five thousand men! How many baskets did we have leftover? They answered and said twelve.

20. Do you not also remember the seven loaves and the four thousand people that it was made to feed? How many baskets of leftovers were there remaining after that? They answered and said, seven.

21. Then he said unto them, how do you still not understand?

22. Then Jesus went unto Bethsaida, and there he was greeted with some men that were carrying a blind man, bringing him unto Jesus; They asked in sincerity, will you touch him?

23. So Jesus touched the hand of the blind man and walked him unto a place outside of the village. Then Jesus spit into his eyes, then he laid his hands upon him and asked if he can see anything.

24. And the man said, I see men upright like trees and they are walking around.

25. Then Jesus again placed his hands upon his eyes and told him to look up. Then the man was completely restored and saw everything clearly.

26. Jesus sent him to his own house and said, do not go into the village; Do not tell anyone of this.

27. Then Jesus went with his disciples unto the villages near Caesarea in the land of Philippi. On the way he asked his disciples, whom do men say that I am?

28. They said, some think you are John the Baptizer, others think you are Elijah or one of the prophets.

29. Then Jesus said unto them, who do you say that I am? Simon (*Peter*) answered and said, you are the Messiah, the Christ.

30. And Jesus said, tell no one of this at this time.

Matthew 16:13-20 offers a more complete account of the above conversation.

31. Then Jesus began to explain to them that he must suffer greatly and he would be condemned by the elders, high priests and the scribes, and that he would be killed; But after three days, he would rise again.

32. Jesus spoke clearly unto them, but Simon (*Peter*) pulled him aside and began to rebuke him;

33. Then Jesus turned around and he rebuked Simon in the presence of the disciples and said, get behind me Satan! You do not have the will of God at the forefront of your mind, but the will of men!

34. Then he called the people to gather near him and he said; Whoever shall desire to approach God, he must deny himself, take up his own cross and follow me. (Luke 14:27; Matthew 16:24; 2 Timothy 1:9)

35. Whoever desires to live for this life shall lose it, but whoever loses his life for my sake, he shall find life everlasting.

36. What would it benefit a man if he gained all of the wealth of the whole world, yet he was to lose his own soul?

37. What can a man give in exchange for his own soul? (Psalms 22:29)

38. For all of you who are adulterous and sinful people, whoever rejects me and my instructions, the son of man will also reject him when he comes with his holy angels in the honor and power of the Father.

Mark 9

1. Jesus then said, truly I tell you, there are some of you that are standing here who shall not experience death before seeing the powerful liberty (freedom from sin – G-1658) of the kingdom of God. (Acts 1; Matt 16:28)

2. Then after six days, Jesus took Simon Peter, James and John up upon a tall mountain to be alone with them in private and he was transformed in their presence. (Matthew 17:1-3)

3. His clothing shined bright white, much like fresh snow; Nothing on earth is able to whiten them in such a way!

4. Elijah and Moses then appeared with Jesus and they spoke with him.

5. Then Peter said unto Jesus, teacher, it is good that we are here! Shall we make three huts, one for you, one for Moses and one for Elijah?

6. Peter did not know what to say because he was afraid.

7. Then a cloud came over them and a voice came from out of the cloud and said; "This is my beloved son in whom I am delighted. Obey him!"

8. Suddenly they looked around and saw no one but Jesus, again alone with them.

9. Then they descended from the mountain and Jesus commanded them to tell no one of what they saw until after the son of man has risen from the dead.

10. And they asked themselves what it meant, to be raised from the dead!

11. Then they asked him and said, the scribes say that the one prophesied of by Isaiah must come before the Messiah. (John 1:21; Isaiah 40:3)

12. Jesus said unto them, surely he must come first, to re-establish all things (*the truth of God's way*). It has also been written that the son of man must suffer many things and be hated.

13. But I tell you that he has already come (*John the baptizer*) and they did what they chose unto him, just as it is written of him.

14. And they approached the other disciples and saw a large crowd was gathered and the scribes were arguing with them.

15. Instantly the crowd saw Jesus and they were greatly surprised and they ran up and greeted him.

16. Then Jesus began to question the scribes and he asked, what are you arguing with them about?

17. One man from the crowd said, teacher, I have brought my son unto you because he is not able to speak, having a demonic spirit within him;

18. Whenever it takes him, it cuts into him and he begins to foam at the mouth grinding his teeth; He is wasting away (dying). I told your disciples that they should cast it out, but they were not able.

19. Jesus answered and said unto them, oh, you are an unbelieving nation! How much longer shall I be here with you? How much longer can I endure you? Bring him to me.

20. And they brought him unto Jesus. And when it saw him, immediately the spirit began to make him convulse and he fell to the ground and he rolled around and began foaming at the mouth.

21. Then Jesus questioned the father of the boy and asked him, how long has this been going on? The father replied, since he was an infant!

22. Many times it has thrown him into the fire and also into the water, trying to kill him. Is there anything that you can do to help us? Have pity upon us.

23. Jesus said unto him, if you believe, all things are possible.

24. Immediately the father of the boy cried out with tears and said, I believe Lord, strengthen me to believe!

25. When Jesus looked at the people as they were gathering a crowd together, he cast out the demonic spirit and said, you dumb and deaf spirit, I command you to come out of him and you shall never again enter into him.

26. The spirit cried out and made him convulse, and the spirit came out of the boy and the boy laid there as if he was dead, and many said that he was dead!

27. But Jesus went to him and took his hand and lifted him up.

28. Then the disciples entered into a house with Jesus and asked him, why were we unable to cast out the demon?

29. Jesus said unto them, this kind of unbelief can not be taken away except by much prayer and fasting.

30. Then they went from there and passed through Galilee and Jesus did not want anyone to know.

31. He taught his disciples and said, the son of man shall be delivered up into the hands of men and they

shall kill him; After he has been slain, he shall arise after three days!

32. But they did not understand what he spoke of and they feared to ask him about it.

33. Then they came unto Capernaum, and coming into a house he questioned them and said, what is it that you were all discussing along the way?

34. But they did not answer because they asked among themselves who is greater!

35. Then as they sat, he called the twelve unto himself and he said unto them, if anyone wants to be first, he shall be the least and the servant of all.

36. Then he took a child and sat him in the middle of them and he embraced him. Then he said to them;

37. Whoever receives me and becomes as one of these little children, they are in my name. Whoever receives me also receives my Father, the one that has sent me. (Matthew 18:1-4; 1 John 2:23)

Verses 38-40 look to have been added by a scribe and contradict Matthew 7:21-22.

38. And John said, master, we saw others casting out demons in your name but we stopped them because they were not of us.

39. But Jesus said, do not stop them. For no one can do a work of power in my name and yet commit evil (defiant sin) against me.

40. Because whoever does not go against me, I am with him. (1 John 3:3-10)

Verse 41 is out of context and should be understood through the light of Matthew 10:42.

41. Whoever of you shall give a cupful of water (true doctrine), because you are teaching Christ, truly I tell you, you will not lose what you have gained.

42. Whoever of these little ones that believe on me, if they offend me (*choose to commit sin*), it would be better for them if a large millstone were hung around their necks and be thrown into the deepest sea.

43. Therefore, if your hand causes you to do that which is evil (*offends me*), cut it off and throw it far from you; For it is better for you to enter into eternal life maimed or lame, than for you to have two hands but be cast into the eternal fire. (Matthew 18:6-9; Hebrews 10:26-29; Romans 1:18; James 4:17)

44. There, the flesh-eating maggots shall never come to their end, and the fire shall never be quenched.

45. Therefore, if your foot causes you to do that which is evil (*offends me*), cut it off and throw it far from you; For it is better for you to enter into eternal life maimed or lame, than for you to have two feet but be cast into the fire that will never be quenched. (Matthew 5:29; Matthew 18:9; Romans 1:18; Hebrews 10:26-29)

46. There, the flesh-eating maggots shall never come to their end, and the fire shall never be quenched.

47. If your eye causes you to commit an offense against me, pluck it out and throw it far from you; For it is better for you to have only one eye when entering into eternal life, than for you to have both eyes and be thrown into the eternal lake of fire. (Matthew 5:29; Matthew 18:9; Romans 1:18; Hebrews 10:26-29)

48. There, the flesh-eating maggots shall never come to their end, and the fire shall never be quenched. (Isaiah 66:24; Matthew 18:1-10)

49. For everyone will be tested for their value by fire, and every sacrifice shall be tested for its value against defilement. (1 Peter 4:12-13; James 1:3)

50. Prudence is good, but if your prudence becomes insipid (*lacking in quality*), how will you be prepared? Have within yourselves prudence and live peaceably with one another.

Mark 10

1. Then Jesus got up and he went to the border of Judea on the other side of the Jordan river and the crowds again gathered around him; As he usually did, he taught them.

2. And the Pharisees came near to him to ask him the question; Is it lawful for a man to divorce his wife? They were testing him.

3. Jesus answered and said; What did Moses command?

4. They answered and said, Moses allowed a book of divorcement to be kept and that one should go forth with the divorce.

5. Jesus said, it was because of your hardheartedness that he wrote that instruction for you.

6. However, from the beginning of creation, God made there to be male and female.

7. This is the reason that a man shall leave his mother and father to be joined to his wife;

8. The two shall become of one purpose, so moving forward they are no longer two, but one.

9. So that which is conjoined by God, no man should want to separate.

10. They then went into the house and his disciples asked him about the same thing.

11. Jesus said unto them, whoever divorces his wife and then goes to be wed to another, he commits adultery against her; (1 Corinthians 7:15; Matthew 5:32; Matthew 19:9; Luke 16:18)

12. If a woman divorces her husband and is wed to another, then she commits adultery.

13. Then some young children were brought unto him, that he might touch them, but the disciples began to rebuke those that were bringing them.

14. When Jesus saw this, he was greatly displeased and he said unto them, allow the children to come unto me and do not prevent them. For the kingdom of God is for ones such as these. (Matthew 18:2)

15. Truthfully I tell you that whoever does not properly enter into the kingdom of God as a little child shall in no way enter therein. (1 John 3:3; Matthew 18:1-4; Acts 3:19; 2:38)

16. Then he took them into his arms and touched them and blessed them.

17. When Jesus was leaving that place, a man came running up to him and kneeled down before him and asked him, good teacher, what shall I do to inherit everlasting life?

18. Jesus said unto him, why do you say that I am good? There is only one that is good and that is God.

19. You know the commandments; Do not commit adultery, do not murder, do not be a thief, do not be a false witness, do not defraud, hold value for your father and mother...

20. The man said, teacher, I have kept all of these things my whole life!

21. Then Jesus looked at him with affection and said, there is one thing that you lack: Go and begin giving the things that you have; Give to those that are in need. (Matthew 19:21; Luke 18:22) Do this and you will have treasure in the heavens, then come, take up your own cross and follow me.

22. But the man was very sad at these words that he heard because he had many beloved possessions, and he went away grieving.

23. Then Jesus looked around and he said unto his disciples, how difficult it is for a wealthy man to enter into the kingdom of God.

24. The disciples were astonished at his words. Then Jesus said to them, children it is very difficult for those that trust in the riches of this world to enter into the kingdom of God.

25. It is easier to lead a herd of camels through the eye of a needle than for a wealthy man to enter into the kingdom of God.

26. They were extremely astonished and said to themselves, who is able to be eternally saved?

27. Then Jesus looked intently and said, for men it is impossible, but for God nothing is impossible. (Philippines 4:13)

28. Then Peter began to say to him, look, we turned away from everything to follow you!

29. Jesus said, I tell you the truth, anyone who has turned away from a house, or brothers, or sisters, or father, or mother, or wife, or children, or land for my sake and the sake of the gospel of God,

30. those who do so shall surely receive a hundred times in the world to come.

Mark 10:30 has been altered by a scribe, adding that we shall receive our rewards in this life.
Such would create much contradiction in the previous verses and in verse 31.
To match Matthew's account, the following has been corrected.

31. Many that are the highest in this life shall be at the bottom in the eternal life. Many that are at the bottom in this life shall be at the top in the eternal life.

32. So they were making their way unto Jerusalem and Jesus went in front of them. They were greatly amazed but they were afraid. Jesus took the twelve disciples aside and began to tell them about what would soon happen to him.

33. He said, look! We are heading unto Jerusalem and the son of man shall be given up to the high priests and the scribes. They will condemn him unto death and will turn him over to the gentiles.

34. They will mock him, flog him, spit on him and will kill him; But on the third day he shall arise again!

35. James and his brother John, the sons of Zebedee came up to Jesus and asked, teacher, we ask that you grant unto us that which we desire.

36. And Jesus asked them, what is it that you desire of me?

37. They said unto him, we ask that we may sit, one of us at your right hand and one of us on your left hand in your kingdom.

38. Then Jesus said unto them, you do not know what you are asking for. Are you able to drink of the cup that I will drink and are you able to be baptized with the baptism that I am baptized with?

39. And they said, we are willing! And Jesus said unto them, surely the cup that I drink of, you will also drink of as well, and the baptism that I have received of, you will also receive of;

40. But to sit at my right hand or my left hand, that is not for me to give, but is for whom it was prepared.

41. And after hearing this, the other disciples were angry at James and John.

42. Then Jesus called them all near to him and said, you know that those who hope to rule over a nation hold power over the people and the powerful ones also hold authority over them;

43. But that is not the way it shall be among you; Whoever desires to be the greatest among you, he must be the servant of all.

45. Even I, the son of man did not come to be served, but to serve and to give my life as the ransom for many. (Matthew 20:28; 1 Timothy 2:6; Isaiah 51:10; Isaiah 35:10; Jeremiah 31:11)

46. And they passed through Jericho. When they were leaving, a large crowd of people surrounded them, and a blind man named Bartimaeus, the son of Timaeus sat by the roadside begging.

47. When he heard that it was Jesus of Nazareth, he began to cry out: Jesus the son of David, please have mercy on me!

48. There were many people that told him to be quiet, but he cried out even louder, son of David please have pity upon me!

49. Jesus stood still and told the people to bring him. So they brought him and then they said, be comforted and stand up, Jesus has called you to come to him.

50. So he threw down his coat and stood up and walked over unto Jesus.

51. And Jesus said unto him, what do you wish that I do for you? And the blind man said to him, my master, I pray that you might make me see again.

52. And Jesus said unto him, go! Your conviction has healed you. Instantly the man was healed and he could see again, then he followed Jesus!

Mark 11

1. When they came near to Jerusalem, they entered into Bethphage and Bethany near the Mount of Olives; Jesus said unto two of his disciples, go into the village over there, and immediately on the left there will be a colt tied up, which no one has sat upon before. Loosen it and bring it to me;

3. If anyone asks you what are you doing, tell them that the master has need of it and will return it soon.

4. So they went and found the colt tied near the door outside at the crossroads, and they untied it.

5. Some that were standing nearby said, why are you untying the colt?

6. And they said that which Jesus commanded, so they let them take it.

7. They led the colt to Jesus and they threw their coats over it, and he sat on it.

8. The people began throwing their coats on the roadway, others cut and laid branches along the way.

9. They cried out from all around and sang, hosanna, blessed is he that is come in the name of the Lord!

10. Blessed be the kingdom of our forefather David; Blessed is he that comes in the name of the Lord. Hosanna in the highest.

11. When Jesus entered into Jerusalem he went into the temple. He looked around at the happenings going on there, but because it was late, he returned unto Bethany with his twelve disciples.

12. The following morning he was hungry, so he left Bethany.

13. On the way, he saw a fig tree in the distance that had leaves on it. He came unto it hoping to find fruit to eat. When he approached it, he found no figs but only leaves on it.

14. Jesus said to the tree, never again shall you bring forth fruit. His disciples heard him say this.
(fig tree is representative of ancient Israel)

15. And they came into Jerusalem and Jesus came into the temple and he began to throw out those that were buying and selling in the temple; Then he overturned the tables of the money takers (*cashiers*), as well as the seats of those that were selling doves!

16. He did not allow any man to carry any goods into the temple.

17. Then Jesus said, it is written that my house shall be a house of prayer unto all nations, but you have turned it into a den of thieves! (Isaiah 56:7)

18. The scribes and high priests heard this and looked for a way that they could kill him, but they were afraid because the crowd was accepting of his doctrine.

19. When the evening came, he again went out of Jerusalem.

20. Then early the following morning, they again walked past the fig tree and it was dried up to the roots.

21. Then Peter remembered and said to Jesus, teacher look and see! The fig tree that you cursed has dried up and withered away! (*representative of ancient Israel* - Hosea 1:4-10)

22. And Jesus said, have total dedication unto God.

23. I tell you truly, whoever tells a mountain to be cast down into the sea, if he does not doubt in his heart, but he believes that what he says will occur, whatever he says, it will be done. (*if it is the will of God*)

24. Because of this, I tell you, whatever you have a serious need for, ask and have confidence that you will receive and it will be given unto you.

25. When you are praying, forgive whatever you might have against anyone, so that your Father may also forgive your violations against him. (1 John 2:1; 1 John 5:16; Numbers 15:22-31)

26. If you do not forgive, neither will your Father above forgive you of your transgressions against him. (*speaking of unknown sins* - 1 John 2:1)

27. Then they came to Jerusalem and Jesus walked around in the temple and the high priests and scribes as well as some elders surrounded him.

28. They asked, by what authority do you do these things and who gave you authority to come here?

29. Jesus answered them and said, I will ask you one thing; Answer me and I will tell you by what authority I do these things.

30. The baptism of John, was it from above or was it of men? (*a time of silence occurred*) Answer me!

31. They debated among themselves and said, if we say from above, then he will say why didn't you believe him.

32. If we say of men, we fear that the people will rise up against us, as they hold John to have been a prophet of God!

33. And they answered and said unto Jesus, we do not know! And Jesus said unto them, you have not answered my question and therefore I will not tell you by what authority I do the things that I do.

Mark 12

1. Jesus taught them in parables: A man planted a vineyard, put a fence around it, dug in a winepress, built a castle, turned it over to the workers and then he went away.
(Isaiah 5:1-7; Matthew 21:3; Luke 20:9)

2. Later he sent a servant unto the workers so that he might receive the fruit of the vineyard,

3. but they took him, beat him and turned him away empty handed.

4. Then he sent another servant to them but they threw stones at him, one striking him in the head! Then they sent him away while insulting him.

5. Then again he sent other servants, but they beat them and even killed some. (Matthew 23:31)

6. Then the man sent his own beloved son to go to them, and he said, surely they will respect my son.

7. But the workers of the vineyard talked among themselves and said, this is the heir. Come and let's kill him and we will receive possession of the vineyard for ourselves.

8. So they then took him and killed him and threw his body outside of the vineyard. (Jeremiah 18:23)

9. What do you think the owner of that vineyard would then do? Surely, he will come and utterly destroy those workers and he will give the vineyard unto others. (Daniel 9:24-27; Jeremiah 7:30-34; Isaiah 5:6-7)

In this parable, the man is God; The first workers are the Jews;
The vineyard is Jerusalem; The castle is the temple in Jerusalem;
The servants are the prophets; The son is Christ Jesus;
The utter destruction was the 70 AD destruction of Jerusalem; The others are the gentiles.

10. Didn't you ever read in the scriptures? "The stone that the builders rejected shall become the foundation stone that connects two walls!" (Psalms 118:22-23; Isaiah 28:16)

11. This is the Lord's doing. Isn't it wonderful in your eyes?

12. Then they wanted to seize him, however they feared the crowd; But they knew that the parable was a condemnation of themselves. They then left him and walked away.

13. So they sent unto him some of the prominent Pharisees and Herodians to try to catch him in his words.

14. When they came, they said teacher, we know that you are in truth and that you do not care who it is that you speak to, because you do not look to the appearance of a man, but you teach truth and the way to God; So is it lawful to pay taxes unto Caesar, or is it not?

15. But Jesus knew their hypocrisy and he said unto them; Why do you test me? Bring unto me a silver coin, so that I might look at it.

16. So they handed one to him. Then Jesus said to them, whose image and inscription is on that coin? And they said unto him, Caesars!

17. Then Jesus said unto them, give back unto Caesar that which is Caesar's, but give unto God all that is due unto him. And the people were astonished!

18. Then the Sadducees came; They believe that there is no resurrection of the dead, (Daniel 12;2; Revelation 20:12-15) yet they asked him:

19. Teacher, Moses wrote that if a man has a brother that dies and he leaves behind a wife but no children, that he should take his brother's wife and raise up offspring unto his brother.

20. So if there are seven brothers, and the first took the wife but then died with no children,

21. then the second did the same, then the third likewise;

22. So if all seven had her the same and none of them left any children and eventually the woman also dies,

23. in the resurrection, when all are raised, whose wife will she be since she was the wife of each one?

24. Then Jesus answered them and said, is this why you have come to be in error? Do you not know the scriptures nor the power of God?

25. When they rise again from death, they shall not take wives nor be given unto wedlock, but they shall be as the messengers (*angels*) in the heavens.

26. Concerning the dead and the resurrection of the dead, did you not read in the books of Moses, at the burning bush, when God spoke to him he said, "I am the God of Abraham, Isaac and Jacob. I am not the God of the dead, but the God of the living." (Exodus 3:6) Therefore, you are in much error.

27. Then one of the scribes came to Jesus and asked him, what is the foremost commandment?

29. Jesus said, the first of all of the commandments, hear this oh Israel, God is your master and he is one;

30. You shall love him with all of your heart, all of your soul, all of your mind and all of your strength. (Luke 10:27; Deuteronomy 6:5; Leviticus 19:18; Matthew 22:37)

31. This is the first commandment, and the second is much like it: You shall love your neighbor (*others*) as yourself. There are no greater commandments.

32. The scribe then said unto him, well teacher, you say the truth, that there is only one God and that there is no other but him,

33. and that we must love him with a whole heart, all of our understanding, with all of our soul and all of our strength and that we must love others as ourselves. (Matthew 22:37; Luke 10:27) This is more important than all of the burnt offerings and sacrifices! (Hosea 6:6)

34. Jesus saw that he was intelligent so he said, you are not that far from the kingdom of God.

35. Then Jesus asked the scribes, how is it that you say that the Christ shall be the son of David?

36. For David himself said by the spirit; "The Lord (*the Father*) said to my Lord (*Christ Jesus*), sit at my right hand, until I place your enemies below your feet." (Psalms 110:1)

37. You see, David himself calls him Lord, so how can he be his son? And the large crowd was happy to hear these words. No one dared to ask him anything else.

38. And Jesus also said to them, watch out for the scribes that dare to walk about in robes to receive greetings in the public places;

39. They love the best seats in the synagogues and the best seats at dinners.

40. Yet they are the ones that steal the houses away from widows (*foreclosure*), and to cover their evil, they offer long prayers on behalf of them! They will receive a much harsher judgment. (James 2:14-17)

41. Then Jesus sat down on the other side of the treasury as he watched the crowd toss copper coins into the treasury. There were many wealthy people that threw some in as well.

42. But there was a poor widow that threw in two lepta, which is about two half cents.

43. So Jesus called the disciples unto himself and he said unto them, truly I tell you, this poor widow gave more than all of the others that gave to the treasury.

44. For the others threw in out of the abundance of what they had, but she threw in all that she had, even in her poverty. It was all that she had to live on!

Mark 13

1. When he was leaving the temple, one of his disciples said to him, teacher, look at these wonderful buildings and the beautiful stones that they are constructed with!

2. And Jesus said to them, do you see all of these large buildings? Not one stone shall remain upon another and all shall be destroyed. (Matthew 24:2)

3. While they were sitting on the Mount of Olives across from the temple, Peter, James, Andrew and John asked him in private,

4. will you tell us when these things will be? What will be the indication when everything shall be completed (*the end of the world*)?

5. Jesus answered them and said, beware that no one deceives you.

6. Many shall come in my name saying that I (*Jesus*) am the Christ, yet they will lead many astray. (2 Peter 2:1-23; 2 Timothy 3:5; 4:3-4; Jeremiah 23; Acts 20:29; Jude 1:4; Ezekiel 22:28; Isaiah 56:10-11)

7. When you hear of fighting and news of wars, do not be alarmed; These things must first happen, but the end is not yet come.

8. Nation shall rise against other nations and kings shall come against their own people. There will be earthquakes in many scattered places, and there will be famines and there will be many other disturbing things that happen; These are only the beginnings of the hardships that shall come. (Matthew 24:8)

9. But you yourselves must watch carefully, because they will turn you (*believers*) over to the military tribunals and the courts of the people, and you shall be beaten. You (*those of me*) will be brought before rulers and kings because of me, to be a testimony against them.

10. The (*authentic*) Gospel must be announced unto all nations and peoples. (Matthew 24:14)

11. When they shall lead you (*believers*) away, delivering you up, do not be anxious or think about what you should say. It shall be given unto you at the proper time. For it shall not be you that speaks, but the holy spirit of God speaking through you.

12. Brother shall betray brother unto death, and fathers shall betray their own children; (Psalms 17:10) Children shall rise up against their own parents and have them be put to death! (Matthew 10:36; Micah 7:6; Luke 21:16)

13. You (*believers*) will be hated by everyone because of my name in you, but he that faithfully endures until the end (*of life*) shall be eternally saved.

14. When you see the detestable thing that strips away and devastates (*abomination of desolation – mark of the beast*) spoken of by Daniel the prophet, abiding in the sacred places (Daniel 11:31; Revelation 13:15), may the one that reads this understand well, those that shall be true Jews, (Romans 2:28-29) run for your escape to the mountains. (Ezekiel 7:16)

15. Those that are in the mountains do not go back to gather needed things from civilization.

16. Those that are in the country, do not even enter into a town to gather clothing.

17. Woe to them that are pregnant or nursing young ones at that time.

18. Pray that your fleeing not occur in the wintertime (*bad weather*), nor on a holiday (*much is closed*).

19. Because at that time there will be great persecution, such that has not ever occurred in the history of the world. (Revelation 6:9; 13:7; Daniel 11:33-35; 12:10-11; Matthew 24:21)

20. Except if those days are shortened, no one who is in Christ would remain alive, but for the sake of the elect (*first fruits*) those days will be shortened.

21. If any man tells you, over here is Christ, do not believe him. Or, he is over there, do not believe him.

22. There shall be many false messiahs and also very many false prophets and false teachers; They will show signs claiming to be the fulfillment of prophecies; If it was possible, they would fool even the elect of God. (Matthew 7:15; 24:5)

23. Be aware and be careful, because I have warned you of these things in advance!

24. In the times following that great affliction (*tribulation*), the sun shall be darkened, and the moon shall not show her light. (Matthew 24:29; Joel 3:15; Ezekiel 32:7; Isaiah 13:9-13; Revelation 6:12; 8:5-12; 16:1-11)

25. The stars in the sky shall fall and the forces in the sky shall shake the whole world. (Rev. 8:5-12)

26. Then they shall see the sign of the son of man coming on the clouds, with much power and honor.

27. And he shall send his messengers to gather together the elect (*chosen, remnant*) from out of the four corners of the earth, and bring them up into the sky. (1 Thessalonians 4:15-17; Matthew 24:31)

28. Now learn the parable of the fig tree. When the branch is tender, it is getting ready to bring forth leaves and you know that summer is near.

29. You must also know that when these things begin to happen, it is near, I am even standing at the door!

30. Truly I tell you, the generation that notices these things begin to happen, they shall not all die before all things have been accomplished.

31. The sky and the earth shall have their end, but my words shall not ever pass away.

32. As for the day and the instant, no one knows, not the messengers of God nor the son, only the Father.

33. Look out! Be awake! Pray! For there shall be no warning that the time has arrived.

34. As a man when he is going away leaves his home and gives his servants authority, each one receives responsibility and the doorkeeper is ordered to watch;

35. So you who have understanding, watch, for no one knows the exact time when the master of the house shall return, whether it be in the evening, at midnight, when the rooster crows or at the dawn.

36. Watch so that when he comes, he does not find you sleeping! (1 Thessalonians 5:4)

37. What I have said unto you, I also say unto all. Therefore watch!

Mark 14

1. Two days later began the Passover and the days of unleavened bread; The high priests and scribes were searching for a way to deceive Jesus so that they might entrap him and kill him.

2. They agreed that they would not do it on the feast day so not to create an uprising among the people.

3. Jesus was in Bethany in the house of Simon the leper. While he was resting, a woman came with an alabaster jar full of very expensive oil of which she emptied, pouring it upon the head of Jesus.
(John 12:3; Matthew 26:7)

4. But there were some that were offended by this, saying unto themselves, what a waste this was of the valuable oil!

5. It could have been sold for a good price of three hundred silver coins and it could have been used to help the poor. There was one that was greatly angry.

6. But Jesus said, do not trouble her; Why do you have anger towards this woman? She has done a good thing unto me.

7. You shall always have the poor among you, and when you are able you will do good for them, but you shall not always have me standing here with you.

8. What this woman did was to anoint my body for its burial! (Matthew 26:12)

9. Truthfully I tell you, wherever this gospel is preached in all of the world, so also shall the good deed of this woman be proclaimed as a memorial unto her.

10. Judas Iscariot, one of the twelve disciples then went to the high priests and he negotiated with them to betray Jesus. (Matthew 26:14)

11. When they spoke to him, they were very happy and promised to give him silver as a reward.
He began to look for the opportunity to betray him.

12. On the first day of unleavened bread, when the passover had been killed, Jesus asked his disciples, where do you plan to have the Passover meal?

13. Then he called two of his disciples to him and said, go into the city, there you will meet a man carrying a pitcher of water, follow him.

14. Wherever he enters, tell the housemaster that the teacher asked for the use of your guestroom for us to eat the Passover meal. May we eat there?

15. He will show you the guest room already set up. There you shall prepare the meal.

16. So the disciples went into the city and found the man that Jesus had spoken of. They prepared the Passover feast at that man's home.

17. That evening Jesus came unto them

18. and they sat down and they ate, and Jesus said, truly I tell you, one of you that is here eating with me shall betray me. (Matthew 26:21)

19. They were saddened, and one by one they began to say unto him, Lord is it I?

20. And Jesus answered and said, it is the one that is currently dipping with me in the dish.

21. Truly the son of man shall go, just as it has been written about him in the prophecies, but woe unto the one through whom the son of man is betrayed; It would have been better for him if he was never born.

22. While they sat, Jesus took the food and blessed it, divided it and gave it to them and he said: Take and eat, this is for my body.

23. Then he took the cup, and he gave thanks and he gave it to them and they all drank from it.

24. And he said, this is for my blood bringing in the New Covenant, and through it many shall surely be poured out upon (*receive of it*).

25. Truly I tell you, that I shall not drink of the fruit of the vine again until that day when in the kingdom of God, we shall drink together.

26. Then they sung a hymn and went to the Mount of Olives.

27. Jesus said unto them, you will all be offended because of me tonight, because it is written, I shall strike the shepherd and the sheep will be scattered. (Zechariah 13:7)

28. But after I have risen, I will be waiting for you in Galilee.

29. Then Peter said unto him, even if all of the others are offended, I shall not be.

30. Jesus said unto him, truly I tell you, tonight before the rooster crows, you Simon Peter will deny me three times. (Luke 22:34)

31. But Peter spoke out even more adamantly and said, if I am to die with you, I will never deny you; All of the others agreed the same.

32. So they came to the place called Gethsemane. Then he said to his disciples, sit here while I pray.

33. And Jesus took Peter, James and John with him, and he began to be greatly distressed and afraid.

34. Then Jesus said unto them, my soul is deeply troubled that I shall be killed. Remain here and watch.

35. Then Jesus walked a little way and fell on his face and asked the Father; Is it possible that this might pass from me at this time?

36. Then he said Papa, Father; All things are possible for you. Will you remove this cup from me? But not my will be done, your will be accomplished.

37. Then Jesus got up and found them sleeping, and he said to Peter, Simon, are you sleeping? Couldn't you be strong enough to stand with me for even one hour?

38. Watch and pray, that you not fall when you are tested! Truly the spirit is willing but the body is weak.

39. Then again Jesus went away and prayed the same words.

40. When he returned, he again found them sleeping, as their eyes were heavily weighted. They did not know what to say to him.

41. Then he came a third time and said to them, sleep now and rest. It is all right and the time is now come. The son of man is now going to be delivered up into the hands of sinners.

42. Rise up and go now! Look, the one that has betrayed me is coming!

43. Then immediately as he was speaking, Judas, formerly one of the twelve came walking towards him with a large crowd that had many swords and clubs, including the scribes, high priests and many elders. (Matthew 26:47; John 18:3; Luke 22:47)

44. Judas had given a sign that whoever he would kiss, he is the one and that they should arrest him and lead him away securely.

45. Immediately, Judas came to Jesus and said, teacher, teacher, and then he forcefully kissed him.

46. Then they grabbed a hold of him and seized him;

47. One of the disciples drew a sword and cut off the ear of the servant of one of the high priests.

The verse 47 account above is incomplete. (Matthew 26:51; Luke 22:50-5; John 18:10)

48. And Jesus said, why do you come out with swords and clubs to take me as though I was a thief?

49. I was with you regularly teaching in your temple. Why did you not seize me then? It is so that the scriptures may now be fulfilled.

50. The disciples then abandoned him and were scattered.

**Verses 51-52 are with no doctrinal point to be made and
are certainly not a part of the authentic text.
No supporting evidence of this account is spoken of anywhere else in the scriptures.
Therefore, these verses have been removed from this text for the sake of decency and necessity.**

53. They took Jesus away unto the chief of the high priests and all of the high priests, scribes and elders came together.

54. Peter followed them at a distance, until they entered into the court of the high priest. He sat with one of the petty officers to warm himself near the fire.

55. The high priests and all of the Sanhedrin looked for testimony against Jesus for which they could put him to death, but they did not find any.

56. There were many that testified falsely against him but their stories did not match each other.

57. And some stood up falsely and said:

58. We heard him say that he would tear down the temple that was made by the hands of men and rebuild it without the use of hands in three days!

59. But their testimonies were not the same.

60. Then the high priest stood up in front of them and he questioned Jesus and said, do you have nothing to say? Not a word? Why do they testify against you?

61. But Jesus remained silent and did not answer him a single word. Again the high priest asked another question: Are you the Christ, the blessed son?

62. And Jesus said, I am! And you will see the son of man seated at the right hand of power when he comes in the clouds of the sky! (Matthew 24:31; 1 Thessalonians 4:17; Revelation 14:14)

63. The high priest tore his clothes and screamed; Why do we need any further testimony?

64. You have heard his blasphemy! What does it look like to you? And they all gathered and condemned him to death.

65. Some began to spit on him and they also beat him with their fists and said, prophesy; Who is it that is hitting you? Even the petty officers hit him with slaps.

66. Peter was in the front of the court when one of the female slaves of the high priest came in.

67. She saw Peter by the fire and she looked closely at him and said, you were with Jesus of Nazareth.

68. Peter denied and said, I do not know nor understand what you are talking about. Then he went into the alley way. The female slave saw him again and began to say to those that were there, he is one of them.

70. But Peter again denied. Then a little while later, there were some that were near Peter who said, truly you are one of them, as you even have a Galilean accent in your speech!

71. Then Peter began to curse them and swear that he was not; He said, I do not know the man that you speak of!

72. Immediately the rooster sounded and Peter remembered what Jesus had said: Before the rooster crows, you will deny me three times! And as he realized this, he began to mourn deeply. (Numbers 15:27-28)

Mark 15

1. First thing the following morning, the high priest held a counsel and he invited the scribes, elders and all of the Sanhedrin. They had Jesus tied and they led him into the court before Pilate.

2. So Pilate questioned him and said, are you the king of the Jews? Jesus responded, you have it right.

3. Then the high priests accused him of many things, but Jesus did not say a word.

4. So Pilate again asked him; Do you have nothing to say? Do you see that there are many witnesses here that testified against you?

5. Still, Jesus did not say a word and Pilate admired him for that.

6. At the feast, he offered to release one prisoner, whichever one they desired.

7. There was one called Barabbas, of whom was found with those who had made an insurrection. He had committed murder during one of the insurrections.

8. The crowd began to beg for him, and he also did for them.

9. Pilate said, do you wish that I release the King of the Jews?

10. He knew that it was because of envy that they had brought Jesus before him.

11. But the high priests riled up the people to say that they would ask for Barabbas to be released.

12. Then Pilate asked them, what shall I do with the one that is called the King of the Jews?

13. And they cried out, crucify him!

14. But Pilate said to them, what evil thing has he done? Then they cried out even louder, Crucify him!

15. So Pilate released Barabbas unto them and he sent Jesus to be whipped and then to be crucified.

16. Then the soldiers led him away to the court that is called Praetorium. There they gathered together a group of men.

17. They put a purple robe on him and a weaved crown made of thorn bushes.

18. Then they began to salute him and say, hail, king of the Jews!

19. Then they beat him on the head with a reed and spit on him, and got on their knees mocking him, falsely worshipping him.

20. When they had finished mocking him, they took off the purple robe, put his own clothes on him and brought him out so that they could crucify him.

21. As they made their way, they saw a man, Simon of Cyprus, as he was coming in from the countryside. He is the father of Alexander and Rufus. He was compelled to carry the cross for Jesus. (John 19:17)

22. They brought him to Golgotha, which in Hebrew (H-1538) means, the place of skulls.

23. They gave him a drink that was spiced with myrrh wine, but Jesus did not drink it.

24. At the third hour of the day they crucified him.

25. After they crucified him, they took his clothes and gambled for who would have them.

26. His charges were posted, of which were put above him, "The King of the Jews!"

27. And with him they crucified two thieves (G-459 - *wicked men, rebels*); one on his right and one on his left. (Hebrews 12:3; Matthew 27:38; Isaiah 53:12)

Verse 28 looks to have been added by a scribe and not a part of the original text.
28. In this the scripture was fulfilled which says; With the lawless ones he shall be counted. (Isaiah 53:12)

29. Those that passed by blasphemed him and shook their heads and said, oh look, it is the one that said that he would destroy the temple and in three days rebuild it!

30. Save yourself and come down from that cross.

31. In the same way the high priests mocked him along with the scribes and they said, he helped many others but he is not able to assist himself.

32. Let us see Christ, the king of Israel come down from that cross so that we might see and believe! And the two that were crucified with him also insulted him. (Matthew 27:44- *these contradict Luke 23:39-43*)

33. In the sixth hour of the day, darkness fell over the land and it remained until the ninth hour.

34. In the ninth hour, Jesus cried out with a loud voice and said; Eloi, Eloi, Lama sabachthani? This being translated from Hebrew means: My God, my God, why have you forsaken me?

35. Some that were there thought that he called for Elijah (*in the Greek language*).

36. One that was there ran to fill a sponge with wine and put it on a reed, and reached it up for him to drink of it. Then some said, forsake him, let us see if Elijah will come and take him down.

37. Then Jesus let out a loud yell and he died.

38. Immediately the veil of the temple was torn in two, from top to bottom.

39. There was a centurion that was standing near to him when he died, and he said, surely this man is the son of God. (Matthew 27:54)

40. And there were women watching from a distance of whom included Mary Magdalene, Mary the mother of little James and Joses, and Salome.

41. They had also followed him and assisted him when he was in Galilee, and there were also many other women that had come there from Jerusalem.

42. When the evening had come, since it was a preparation day before the Sabbath (*Passover*),

43. Joseph from Arimathea came as an honorable counselor, of whom was also awaiting the kingdom of God and he courageously went to Pilate and asked for the body of Jesus.

44. Pilate was surprised that he had died so quickly, so he called a centurion and asked to verify that he had already died.

45. When he had double checked with a centurion that Jesus had died, he granted the body to Joseph.

46. Joseph had brought a linen cloth, wrapped him and them laid him in the tomb, of which had only recently been cut into the rock. Then he rolled a large stone in front of the door of the tomb.

47. Mary Magdalene and Mary of Joses watched the place where he was laid.

**The Passover holy day was on Thursday, of which the scriptures call the Sabbath,
and Jesus was raised on the day after the Sabbath, however this was speaking
of the weekly Sabbath, being raised early Sunday morning, the first day of the week!
This allows for three days in the grave, as the prophets predicted.
It must also be noted that the modern holidays of good Friday, Easter Sunday
and Easter Monday are fallacies and not representative of any holy day
related to Christ, but are pagan holidays related to Ishtar, the mother and wife of Nimrod.**

Mark 16

1. When the sabbath had passed, Mary Magdalene, Salome and Mary the mother of James had brought spices so that they might come and anoint him.

2. So very early on the first day after the sabbath they came to the tomb and the sun had already risen.

3. Then they thought, who will roll away the stone from the door of the tomb?

4. Then they looked up and saw that the large stone had already been rolled away from the tomb!

5. When they entered into the tomb they saw what appeared to be a young man seated on the right side; He was wearing a white robe and they were frightened.

6. He said, do not be afraid. The one you are looking for, Jesus of Nazareth who was crucified, he has risen! He is not here! See, this is the place that he had been laid!

7. Go and tell Peter and the other disciples that he is waiting for them in Galilee! You will see him there just as he had told you.

8. They ran out of the tomb because they were trembling and tremendously excited, and they were not able to speak clearly because they were afraid.

9. When he had arisen early on the first day of the week, he first appeared to Mary Magdalene, of whom he had previously cast out seven demons.

10. Then she went and told those that had known him, because they were mourning and weeping.

11. When they had heard her words saying that he was alive, they did not believe her.

12. But after this, two of them were walking in the countryside and he revealed himself unto them, though in a different way.

13. They went and told the others but they did not believe.

14. Later, as the eleven were relaxing, he revealed himself to them. He was disappointed by their unbelief and the hardness of their hearts, because they did not believe those who had seen him after he had risen.

15. Then he said to them: Go into all of the world and announce the gospel unto everyone.

16. Those that believe, baptize them unto God and they shall be reserved by God. Those that do not believe (G-569 - *disobedient*) will be damned. (Matthew 28:19)

17. The evidence of those that have fully committed themselves is that some shall cast out demons in my name and some shall speak new languages; (Psalms 51:2; John 13:8: 1 Corinthians 12)

18. They will properly refute the snakes (*false teachers*), and if anything deadly is received unto them, they will overcome. They shall lay their hands upon the sick and the injured, and they shall be healed.

19. After the Lord had spoken these things unto them, he ascended into the sky and he took his place at the right hand of God. (Acts 1:9; Revelation 12:5)

20. So they went out and preached everywhere, the Lord Jesus working in them (*by his spirit*), and the message was confirmed through the things they did.

An overview of the book of Mark

The book of Mark was written long after the happenings and were based upon the recollections of eyewitnesses and oral stories that were passed on. It can be assumed that the book of Mark most likely was written somewhere between 55-65 A.D. with the likelihood that it may have been altered as late as 400 AD. Its authorship is inconclusive, though may be assumed that it was written by the same Mark that traveled with the apostle Paul, of whom is mentioned in the book of Acts. It can be easily assumed that the writer of the book of Mark did not have the book of Matthew in hand when he wrote his own account, because if he did, his own accounts would have necessarily been much more complete and the order of events would have been more accurate. Based upon these clear and unarguable observations, the accounts in the book of Mark generally look to be true, though not in every detail. Though there seem to be some additional facts that are not included in Matthew's account, the book of Mark must certainly hold an inferior position of relevance when compared to the accounts of Matthew and John. Any part of the book of Mark that is incomplete, out of the proper chronological order or out of context when compared to Matthew or John's accounts must necessarily be considered as inaccurate or incomplete. The first-hand accounts of Matthew and especially John must be trusted above that which is recorded in the book of Mark when there is conflict. It must also be noted that there are at least hundreds of ancient accounts of the book of Mark, of which have many variations between themselves. I have done my very best to translate as closely as possible to the original intent and have pointed out additions, alterations, inaccuracies, conflicts and corruptions wherever possible.

Luke

Chapter 1

Verses 1-4 are an introduction and cover page.
They offer insight to the reason the book of Luke was written.

1. Since many have taken it upon themselves to write an account concerning the matters of he (*Christ*) who lived and walked among us,

2. just as it was offered (*spoken*) unto us by the eyewitnesses and servants that are living according to his instructions,

3. it seemed good for me to also write, since I have investigated everything from the beginning so that I could write unto you, my noble friend Theophilus, *(This is evidence that the book of Luke was not dictated by nor inspired by God, but is the work of a man using his own logic, based upon his research.)*

4. so that you might know that which you have been taught is true. (Acts 20:29-31)

The original beginning of the book of Luke.

5. In the days of Herod the king of Judea, lived a priest by the name of Zacharias, of the family of Abia, and his wife Elizabeth, one of the daughters of Aaron.

6. They were righteous (*innocent, equitable in character*) before God, living in obedience unto the commandments and ordinances, and they were blameless before the Lord.

7. They were without children because Elizabeth was not able to bear and they were growing elderly.

8. It was that while he was serving as priest, according to his responsibilities unto God,

9. in accordance with the practices of the priests, that he burn incense before entering into the temple.

10. Many people were praying outside at the time of incense

11. when a messenger *(angel)* of God appeared unto him and stood on the right side of the incense alter.

12. Zacharias was troubled when he saw this and he fearfully fell down.

13. Then the angel said to him, do not be fearful Zacharias, because you and your wife's prayers unto God have been heard. Elizabeth will bring forth a son and you shall call his name John.

14. He shall bring great joy and rejuvenation unto you and many will be joyous because of his nativity;

15. He will be great in the eyes of God and he will never drink wine nor strong drink; The spirit of God will be upon him, even from his mother's womb.

16. He will turn many of the sons of Israel unto the master, their God.

17. He will precede before the one *(Messiah)*. He will be the one spoken of by Isaiah; (Isaiah 40:3) "He will turn the hearts of the children unto the Father, and unto those that are disobedient unto the way of righteousness, he will show them to live in the ways of the Messiah." (John 1:21; Luke 9:8)

18. Zacharias said unto the angel, how can I believe this is true? For I am old and my wife is advanced in her life as well.

19. And the angel said unto him, I am Gabriel, (Daniel 8:16; Daniel 9:21) the one who stands in the presence of God; I was sent to speak this unto you and to announce the good news of these things.

20. You will be silent and not able to speak until the day that this happens, because you do not believe my words of which will be fulfilled in the proper time.

21. The people were expecting Zacharias and they wondered about why he was delayed in the temple.

22. When he came out, he was not able to speak to them and they perceived that he had seen a vision in the temple. He signaled to them but he remained unable to speak.

23. This happened as his days of service were being completed, so he went away unto his home.

24. Soon after that, Elizabeth his wife conceived and he hid her for five months and then he believed.

25. He said, God has allowed this unto me because it is the time that he has decided to remove my disgrace from the eyes of men.

26. In the sixth month, the angel of God, Gabriel was sent unto a city in Galilee that is called Nazareth,

27. unto a young virgin who was engaged unto a man whose name was Joseph. He was of the lineage of David; The name of the young virgin was Mariam.

28. The messenger *(angel)* entered the house and spoke unto her and said, be cheerful, the blessing of our

God is upon you. You are greatly beloved above all women.

29. When she saw him, she was greatly distressed by his words and she thought about what sort of greeting this could be!

30. The messenger said unto her, do not be fearful Mariam, because you are favorable unto God.

31. Be aware, you will conceive in your womb and you will bring forth a son and you will call him Jesus.

32. He will be great and he shall be called the son of the most high; God will give him the throne of David, his forefather.

33. He will rule over the house of Israel forever, because his kingdom will never come to an end.

34. Mariam said unto the angel, how can this be, I have never allowed any man *(to touch me)?*

(Isaiah 7:14)

35. The messenger *(angel)* said to her, the spirit of God shall come upon you and the power of the most high will surround you in a way that your first born shall be holy and called the son of God.

36. And know this! Your relative Elizabeth has also conceived a son in her elderly state and she is in her sixth month, previously she was unable to conceive.

37. Nothing is impossible if God commands it.

38. And Mariam said, servant of the master, let it be according to what you have spoken. Then the messenger *(angel)* left her.

39. When the daylight came, Mariam went to the hill country quickly unto a city of Judah,

40. and she came unto the house of Zacharias and she greeted Elizabeth.

41. When Elizabeth heard the greeting of Mariam, the child within her leaped in her womb and Elizabeth was full of the holy *(blameless)* spirit;

42. She yelled out with a loud voice and said, you have been blessed above all women and you have been blessed with fruit in your womb!

43. From where has the mother of our Messiah come unto me?

44. For I knew when I heard the sound of your greeting because the child within my womb leaped in excitement.

45. Blessed are those that shall commit their trust, because this is the fulfillment of the things that have been spoken unto me by our God.

46. And Mariam said, our lord has lifted up my heart *(spirit)*.

47. He has brought much joy and excitement into my heart, my savior.

48. Because he considered me even through my humility as his servant. Truly all generations will know that I am blessed;

49. Because the mighty one has done many great things for me. His name is sacred.

50. His compassion is from generation to generation, unto all who fear him.

51. He has done mighty things by his power. He has dispersed those that were proud in their hearts.

52. He has brought down rulers from their thrones *(Nebuchadnezzar)*, and he has exalted the lowly ones. *(David)*

53. He has filled those who hungered for that which is good, and the wealthy he has made to be desolate.

54. He helped his servant Israel establish mercy. (Exodus 1:1)

55. He even spoke unto our forefathers, unto Abraham and unto his children forever.

(John 10:1; Galatians 3:27)

56. Mariam remained with her for about three months, then she returned unto her own home.

57. But for Elizabeth, the time had come to bring forth and she bear a son.

58. And the neighbors and relatives heard that the Lord God had offered unto her great mercy and they were joyous with her.

59. When the eighth day had come and they were about to circumcise the child, they called the child after the father Zacharias.

60. But the mother said, this shall not be. He shall be called John!

61. And they said, there is no one in your family who has this name.

62. So they signaled unto the father to ask what he wanted him to be called.

63. They asked for a tablet, and he wrote, John is his name. All wondered at this!

64. But his mouth was then instantly opened, also his speech returned and he spoke a blessing unto God.

65. Then fear came upon those around them, and all those in the hill country talked about him.

66. All that could hear in their hearts said, who shall this child be? For the hand of the Lord is with him.

67. Zacharias was filled with the sacred spirit and he prophesied and said,

68. blessings unto our master, the God of Israel, because he has chosen and has brought redemption unto his people.

69. He is raising up a horn *(powerful weapon)* unto salvation for us, from the house of David his servant,

70. just as he spoke through the mouths of his prophets.

71. We shall be offered salvation from the enemy *(Satan)*, and we shall be brought out of the hands of those who hate us;

72. He will offer the mercy of the Father and remember his sacred covenant

73. that he swore unto Abraham our forefather with an oath;

74. To give to us *(the seed, Christ)*, so that we should no longer fear the hand of the enemy *(Satan)*, but that we would be able to overcome, to now serve him *(God)*. (John 8:31-36; Romans 6:16)

75. In this, we would be consecrated *(of right character)* and could live righteous before him all of the days of our lives! (1 John 3:3; 2 Timothy 2:11; 1 Thessalonians 3:13; Romans 6:22)

76. And you my child, you will be called a prophet of the most high God. You will precede in front of the face of the master and prepare the way unto him. (Malachi 3:1)

77. You will bring the knowledge of salvation *(from sin)* unto them, by the remission of their sins, (Acts 2:38, Acts 3:19; Mark 16:16; Romans 6:1-23; John 8:31-37)

78. through the sympathy of the mercy of God unto us, because he has seen us and given his Light from above. (John 1:4)

79. He shall appear unto those who are in darkness and sitting in the shadow of death (Psalms 23:4), to direct our feet into the way of peace *(with God)*.

80. And the child grew and became strong in the character *(spirit)* of God, and he lived in the lonesome places until the time that he was made known unto Israel.

Luke 2

1. And it came to be in those days that there went out a decree from Caesar Augustus that all of the world *(Roman empire)* should be accounted. *(census)*

2. This accounting first began when Cyrenius was the governor of Syria.

3. Everyone was made to give an account and each one was to go to his own home town.

4. Joseph also went from Galilee from out of the city of Nazareth unto Judea, the city of David, which is called Bethlehem because he was from out of the house of David.

5. He was to be accounted for with Mariam because she was engaged to him and pregnant.

6. And it came to be, that while they were there, her day to bring forth the child had come.

7. She brought forth her first born son and she wrapped him in a swathe *(a one piece garment)* and laid him in a manger *(animal feeder)*, because there was no place to be found for them to rent.

8. Now there were shepherds in the prairies *(uninhabited grasslands)* that lived off of the land; They were guarding their animals in the evening

9. when a messenger from God came unto them and his glorious illumination engulfed them and they were alarmed and greatly frightened.

10. The angel said unto them, do not be fearful, because I announce good news unto you; A great joy is come unto all people;

11. A saviour has been born today in the city of David and he is the Christ *(Messiah)*, our master.

12. I offer unto you a sign; You will find the child wrapped up in a cloth and lying in an animal feeder.

13. Suddenly a large number of heavenly beings appeared with the angel who were praising God and they said, glory unto the most high God!

14. He will bring the way unto peace *(with God)*, unto all the earth (Romans 2:10; 2 Peter 3:14) and will demonstrate his good will unto mankind. (Matthew 20:28; Mark 10:45; 1 Timothy 2:6)

15. As the angel went back up into the heavens, the shepherds said to one another, we should go into Bethlehem and see that which has happened, of which our God has made known unto us.

16. They came eagerly and they found Mariam and Joseph, the child was lying in the animal feeder.

17. They publicly announced unto everyone concerning what had been told to them about the child.

18. All who heard them wondered about those things that were spoken unto them by the shepherds.

19. But Mariam kept the topic secret, pondering it in her heart.

20. Then the shepherds returned to their homeland and they gave glory and praise unto God for all that was told unto them and what they had seen!

21. When the eighth day came and the child was to be circumcised they named him Jesus, just as the messenger *(angel)* had ordained before the child was conceived in the womb.

22. When her days of cleansing were completed, as is commanded by the law of Moses, they took him up into Jerusalem to present him unto God;

23. Just as it is written in the law of Moses. Every male child that comes out of the womb must be dedicated to be holy before our God. *(the roots of christening, of which is different than baptism)*

24. They also made the sacrifice that is required by the Mosaic law before God; Two turtledoves *(two nesting doves).*

25. There was a man named Simeon, a righteous man from Jerusalem that was devout and he was eagerly expecting the consolation *(purification)* of Israel; The sacred spirit of God was upon him.

26. It was made known unto him by the sacred spirit that he would not die before he would see the Christ.

27. So he came into the temple by the leading of the spirit, at the moment when they were bringing in the parents of the young child Jesus, to do as is the custom according to the Jewish law concerning the child.

28. Then he took the child into his arms and he blessed God, and he said;

29. Now release your servant in peace, my master, according to your promise unto me,

30. because my eyes have now seen our Messiah!

31. The one that you have sent to appear unto all people,

32. to be a light that will be revealed unto all nations (John 1:4) and be the glory of your people, Israel.

33. Joseph and his mother absorbed all these things that were being said about him.

34. And Simeon blessed them and said unto Mariam the child's mother, this one is appointed to bring the fall and resurrection of many within Israel. He shall do many things that will be spoken against.

35. Your heart will be pierced by the sword, but because of this, many shall understand with their hearts and minds.

36. There was also Anna, a prophetess, the daughter of Phanuel from out of the tribe of Asher; She was very old. She lived with her husband for seven years when she was a young woman,

37. but she had been a widow for about eighty-four years and she did not ever leave the temple. She served both night and day with fasting and prayers.

38. At that same time, she came to give thanks unto the Lord and she spoke unto everyone concerning the child, that he would offer himself as ransom unto Jerusalem.

39. As they had finished everything according to the Jewish law, they returned unto Galilee, unto the village of Nazareth.

40. As the child grew, he became strong in the disposition *(character of God)* and he was full of wisdom, and the grace of God was upon him.

41. His parents went every year unto the feast of Passover.

42. When he was twelve years old, they went up to Jerusalem according to the custom of the feast.

43. When they completed the days required and they were returning, the boy Jesus remained in Jerusalem and neither Joseph nor his mother knew.

44. They supposed that the boy was among their traveling companions. They had traveled for a whole day away from Jerusalem when they realized he was missing, so they began to look for him among the relatives and friends.

45. When they did not find him they returned to Jerusalem to look for him.

46. After three days they finally found him in the temple. He was sitting among the teachers and they were listening to him and asked him many questions. (Daniel 9:26 - *he cut off the old covenant*)

47. All that heard him were amazed at his intelligence and at his answers. (Zechariah 11:10)

48. When his parents found him, they were surprised, and his mother said unto him, child, why have you done this unto us? Your father and I were very distressed and have been looking for you!

49. The young Jesus said to them, why would you be distressed while looking for me? Why did you not know that I would be doing according to the purpose given of the Father (*Yehovah*)?

50. But they *(his parents)* did not understand that which he had spoken unto them.

51. Jesus then went with them and they returned unto Nazareth, and he lived in obedience unto them; Yet his mother kept all of these things in her heart.

52. Jesus continued to grow in his wisdom, in stature and in favor before God and also among the people.

Luke 3

1. In the fifteenth year, under the reign of Tiberius Caesar, while the governor Pontius Pilate was governing over Judea, and the ruler of Galilee was Herod, and his brother Philip was the ruler of Iturea and the country of Trachonitis, and Lysanias was the ruler of Abilene,

2. under the high priesthood of Annas and Caiaphas, the message came unto John, the son of Zacharias while he was living in a desolate place.

3. At that time, he began to travel unto all of the towns in Jordan and he proclaimed the baptism of repentance for the remission of sins, (Acts 2:38; Acts 3:19; Romans 3:25)

4. as it is written in the book of Isaiah the prophet, "the voice crying in the wilderness, he will prepare the way for the Messiah and he shall straighten his paths;

5. Every valley shall be elevated and every mountain and hill shall be brought down, and the perverse shall be set straight and the ways that are rough *(rocky)* shall be made smooth;

6. And all of mankind shall perceive the salvation of God." (Isaiah 40:3-5; Jeremiah 31:31-34)

7. He said unto some of the people (*the scribes and Pharisees*) that were coming unto him to be baptized, oh nation of vipers! Who has warned you to run from the coming wrath?

8. Produce the fruits that are necessary for repentance (Acts 26:20; 2 Corinthians 7:9-10), and do not begin to say within yourselves that you have Abraham as your forefather. (John 8:39-42; Galatians 3:29) Because I tell you that God is able to transform these stones and raise them up to be children of Abraham!

9. The axe has already been laid to the root of the tree (Daniel 9:26; Matthew 3:10; Hosea 9:16 - *The tree is ancient Israel, foretelling that the end of the nation was already decided, of which did happen at 70 AD)* Therefore every tree that does not produce good fruit shall be cut off and cast into the fire. (Matthew 7:19; 13:40; Mark 9:22; John 15:6; Luke 2:46)

10. And the crowd asked and said, what shall we do?

11. And he said unto them, if one has two coats, give one unto another who does not have one, and one that has surplus food, let him do the same.

12. Then the tax collectors came to be baptized, and they asked, what shall we do?

13. And John said unto them, you must do and continue to live as I have already commanded of you.

14. One of the soldiers asked, what else shall I do? And he said unto him, do not intimidate nor bring a false accusation against anyone, and be satisfied with what you have.

15. The people were anticipating and reasoning in their hearts concerning John and they wondered if he might be the Messiah.

16. But John answered them all and said, I baptize you in water, but there will soon come one who is much more powerful than I, of whom I am not worthy to unbuckle his sandals; When he comes, he will also baptize you with the holy disposition (*holy spirit*) and with fire.

17. The fan is in his hand and he will fully winnow the threshing floor and he will gather the wheat into the barn and the chaff will be burned up in the unquenchable fire. (Matthew 3:11; Matthew 25:32)

Verses 18-20 have been properly placed below verse 22.

21. And it happened while he was baptizing the masses of people that Jesus also came to be baptized, and when he was praying, the heavens opened up,

22. and the sacred spirit in a physical form, like a dove came down upon him; And there was a voice in the heavens (*sky*) that said, you are my greatly loved son and I am delighted in you.

The proper placement of verses 18-20.

18. John did correct the people concerning many things, and he preached the good news unto the people.

19. But when Herod, the ruler of that region had heard that John had brought a message of correction against him concerning Herodias, his brother's wife and also all of the evil things that he had done,

20. he proceeded to have John put into prison.

The following account of the lineage of Jesus contradicts the account given in Matthew 1.
(David through Joseph - 14+ generations)
The most likely reason for this is because the Matthew account was written about 34 AD
at a time when the temple was still operational in Jerusalem;

Luke's account was written about 110 AD, about 40 years after the temple
in Jerusalem had been destroyed, along with all of the records.
Luke was dependent upon the faulty testimonies of others and
must not have had the book of Matthew available to him when writing this account.

23. Jesus was almost thirty years old when he began and by Jewish law was the son of Joseph, son of Heli,
24. son of Mattatha, son of Levi, son of Melchi, son of Janna, son of Joseph,
25. son of Matthias, son of Amos, son of Nahum, son of Esli, son of Naggai,
26. son of Maath, son of Mattathias, son of Semei, son of Joseph, son of Judah,
27. son of Joannes, son of Rhesa, son of Zerubbabel, son of Salathiel, son of Neri
28. son of Melchi, son of Addi, son of Cosam, son of Elmodam, son of Er,
29. son of Joses, son of Eliezar, son of Jorim, son of Matthai, son of Levi,
30. son of Simeon, son of Judah, son of Joseph, son of Jonan, son of Eliakim,
31. son of Melea, son of Menam, son of Mattatha, son of Nathan, son of David, (Ruth 4:18-22)
32. son of Jesse, son of Obed, son of Boaz, son of Salmon, son of Nahshon,
33. son of Amminadab, son of Ram, son of Hezron, son of Pharez, son of Judah,
35. son of Jacob, son of Isaac, son of Abraham, son of Terah, son of Nahor, son of Serug, son of Reu, son of Peleg, son of Eber, son of Salah,
36. son of Cainan, son of Arphaxad, son of Shem, son of Noah, son of Lamech,
37. son of Mathuselah, son of Enoch, son of Jared, son of Mahalaleel, son of Cainan,
38. son of Enos, son of Seth, son of Adam, and created by God.

Luke 4

1. Jesus, being full of the holy spirit returned from the Jordan and was led by the spirit into the wilderness;
2. He was tested for forty days by the devil. He ate nothing during that time so when the time was finished he was hungry.
3. And the devil said to him, if you are the son of God, speak to these stones and they will become bread.
4. Jesus answered him and said, it is written, a man shall not live on bread alone, but on every utterance (*spoken word*) of God. (Deuteronomy 8:3)
5. Then the devil brought him to a very high mountain and showed him all of the kingdoms of the nation.
6. Then the devil said to him, I will give you jurisdiction over all of this and they will honor you; Because it has been given *(by them)* unto me and I can offer it all to whomever I choose. (1 Corinthians 2:6)
(John 12:31; 14:30; 16:11; Ephesians 2:2 - *Satan is the ruler of this world because God gave jurisdiction to mankind but mankind gave it to Satan* - Genesis 1:26 + Genesis 6:5)
7. If you will serve me, I will give it all to you.
8. Jesus answered and said, get behind me Satan! (Mark 8:33; Matthew 16:23) For it has been written, you shall only serve one master, God and only him. (Matthew 6:24; Luke 16:3; Deuteronomy 6:13)
9. Then Satan brought him to Jerusalem and he sat him on a pinnacle of the temple and he said unto him, if you are the son of God, throw yourself down from here;
10. For it has been written, he will command his angels and they will protect you.
11. They will catch you in their hands and you will not even hit your foot upon a stone. (Psalms 91:11-12)
12. Jesus answered him and said, it has been said, you shall not tempt almighty God. (Deuteronomy 6:16)
13. When every test was completed, the devil went away from him for a time. (John 13:27)
14. Jesus returned with the power of the spirit of God and he came to Galilee. There was news throughout all of that land concerning him. *(He was famous)*
15. He taught in their synagogues to live honorable towards everyone.
16. Then he came to Nazareth where he was raised, and he went according to the customs of that time into the synagogue on the Sabbath and he stood up to read.

17. He was handed a scroll of the prophet Isaiah and he unrolled the scroll and he read from the place where it is written,

18. "The spirit of our God is upon me, because he has anointed me to bring the announcement of the good news unto the poor; He has sent me to heal those that have lived with a broken heart and to preach unto the slaves of how to be freed (John 8:34-37; Acts 2:38) and for the blind to regain their sight.

19. Those that have been separated away and do mourn (*repentant heart*), a pardon shall be offered unto them; I announce that it is the appropriate year (*time*) of the Lord." (Isaiah 61:1-2)

20. When he rolled up the scroll, he returned it to the attendant and he sat down. And all of the eyes of the people were staring at him.

21. He then said unto them, today this scripture that you have heard has been fulfilled!

22. All of those that were there are witnesses of him and considered the words of God's grace that were coming from his mouth. They said, is this not the son of Joseph? (John 6:42)

23. But he said, it is not surprising that you will tell me, heal yourself with this parable! (They said) The things that we have heard in Capernaum, do them also in your home land!

24. And he said, truly I tell you that no prophet is accepted in his own hometown.
(Mark 6:4; Luke 4:24; John 4:44)

25. But I tell you the truth, that there were many widows in Israel in the days of Elijah, when the sky was shut off for three years and six months and there was a famine in all of the land.

26. Yet Elijah was not sent unto any of them except Zarephath of Sidon, unto a woman widow.

27. And there were many lepers in Israel during the time of Elisha the prophet, yet none of them were cleansed except for Naaman the Syrian!

28. They were greatly angered in the synagogue after hearing these things.

29. So they rose up and threw him out of the city; They brought him to the top of a cliff in which their city was built, with intentions to throw him down.

30. But he passed through the middle of them and he walked away from them.

31. Then he went into Capernaum, a city in Galilee and he taught them on the Sabbaths.

32. They were amazed at his doctrines, because there was authority in his speech.

33. In the synagogue there was a man that had a demonic spirit, and he cried out with a loud voice;

34. Leave me alone! What have we done to you, Jesus of Nazareth? Did you come to destroy us?
We know that you are the holy one of God!

35. Jesus rebuked him and said, be silent! Now come out of him. Then the demon threw him and it came out of him, but did not harm him.

36. Everyone was astonished and they all spoke unto one another and said, what message is this that even the demonic spirits are commanded by his authority and power and they come out!

37. The news went out about him unto every place in the region.
(*Jesus was famous - refutes* Matthew *12:16-21*)

38. Then Jesus rose up from the synagogue and he went unto the home of Simon (*Peter*). The mother in law of Simon had been taken by a high fever and they asked him concerning her.

39. He stood over her and rebuked the fever and it left her immediately, so she arose up and served them!

40. As the sun was setting, everyone that was sick and many that had various diseases were brought unto him; He laid his hands on each of them and they were healed!

41. Also, demons came out of many and they were crying out and saying, you are the Christ, the son of God. But Jesus rebuked them and did not allow them to speak, because they knew that he is the Christ.

42. The following day, he went out to a deserted place, but the crowds looked for him and they came unto him and they invited him to remain there!

43. He said unto them, it is necessary for the kingdom of God that I must also announce the gospel unto other cities, as this is one of the reasons that I was sent!

44. And he announced throughout the synagogues of Galilee.

Luke 5

1. The crowd was imposing upon him to hear a message of God, and he was standing by the lake near Gennesaret. He saw two boats resting at the edge of the lake

2. but the fishermen were not there, having gone to wash their nets.

The following account in verses 3-9 are given in John 21, after the resurrection.

3. Jesus entered into one of the boats that was owned by Simon and he asked him to set them out a little from the land. Then he sat and taught the crowd from the boat.

4. When he quit speaking, he said to Simon, let's go out into the deep waters so that we can let your nets out to gather a catch.

5. Simon said to him, master, we took nothing though we labored all night long. However, on your request we will let the nets down.

6. When they did this, they gathered a great amount of fish, so many that their net nearly broke. (John 21:3-6)

7. Then they signaled to their partners in the other boats to come and help them. When they came, they filled both of the boats so full that they were close to sinking!

8. Then Simon Peter fell on his knees and said to Jesus, abandon me my master, I have erred.

9. Simon was strongly amazed, as was everyone with them because of the great amount of fish that they had caught.

10. James and John, the sons of Zebedee were also partners with Simon. Then Jesus said to Simon, do not be stressed; From now on you will be a fisherman of mankind! (Matthew 4:17-19) *(this statement is out of context compared to Matthew's and John's account)*

11. And they brought the boats to the land, and they turned away from everything and followed him.

12. And it happened while they were with him in one of the cities, that there was a man full of leprosy. When he saw Jesus, he fell on his face and begged him and said, master, will you please heal me, I know that you can!

13. Jesus stretched forth his hand and said, I will. Be cleansed! Instantly the leprosy vanished from him!

14. Jesus said to him, tell no one of this! But go to the priest and show yourself and make an offering for your cleansing, just as Moses had commanded. This will be a testimony unto them.

15. But his fame was spread much more, and large crowds were coming to hear him and to be healed of their infirmities.

16. Jesus then left that place and went into a deserted place to abide there to pray.

17. On one of the days that Jesus was teaching, some who were becoming Pharisees and lawyers were coming from every village in Galilee unto Jerusalem. The power of God was there to cure the sick.

18. And there were men that were carrying a bed with a man that had been paralyzed, and they asked if they could bring him in and lay him before Jesus,

19. however they could not find a way through the crowd, so they went up on the housetop, broke through the tiles of the roof and they let the bed down from the roof in front of Jesus.

20. Jesus saw that they had great trust and dedication and said, man, your sins have been abolished *(forgiven of you)*. (Matthew 9:2; John 5:14; John 8:11)

21. The scribes and the Pharisees began to talk among themselves because of this, and they said, this man speaks blasphemy! Who is able to abolish *(forgive)* sins except for God? *(surely not a priest!)*

22. But Jesus knew what they were thinking and he spoke unto them directly and said, why do you reason this way in your hearts?

23. Is it easier to say, your sins have been forgiven unto you, or to say, rise up and walk?

24. But so that you know that I, the son of man, have the authority to forgive sins on the earth, then he said unto the paralyzed man, I tell you now, rise up and take your bed and walk; Go to your home.

25. Immediately he stood up in front of them and he took the bed that he had been laying upon, and he went to his home and glorified God!

26. Amazement was upon everyone that was there; They began to glorify God and said, we have seen an amazing thing here today!

27. Then after this, he went and saw a man who was a tax collector by the name of Levi *(Matthew)* who was sitting at the tax office. Jesus said to him; Follow me!

28. And he left everything and stood up and he followed him.

29. Levi made a large meal for him at his own home and he invited many who were tax collectors and many other sinners and they sat down to eat. (Matthew 9:9-10)

30. The scribes began to murmur with the Pharisees unto the disciples, and they said, why are you eating with tax collectors and sinners?

31. Jesus said unto them, there is no need for a healer except for those who are badly sick.

32. I have not come to call those who are righteous, but to call sinners unto repentance.

33. But they said, why did the disciples of John often fast (*go without food*) and continually pray? These things the disciples of the Pharisees also do; So why do your disciples both eat and drink?

34. Then Jesus answered them and said, the sons of the bride chamber are not able to fast while they are with the groom.

35. But there will come a day when the bridegroom will be taken away from them and when this happens, they will fast at that time.

36. He also told them a parable; No one puts a new patch on an old garment, otherwise they will tear because the old does not work well with the new.

37. No one puts new wine in old wineskins, otherwise the new wine will burst the old wineskins and it will spill out and the wineskins will be worthless. Both preserve each other together

38. No one that is drinking the old wine wants the new because they say that the old is better.

Luke 6

1. On the second Sabbath after Passover, Jesus was traveling along through some grain fields that were planted, and his disciples plucked some of the grain heads and were eating them, rubbing out the kernels with their fingers.

2. Some of the Pharisees then said to them, why are you doing that which is not lawful on the Sabbath?

3. Jesus said, did you not read what David and those with him did when they were hungry?

4. They went into the house of God and he took the show bread and he gave unto those that were with him, of which it is not lawful for them to eat, but only the priests?

5. Then he said unto them, the son of man is also the master above the Sabbath.

6. On another Sabbath he entered into the synagogue to teach; There was a man with a crippled hand.

7. The scribes and Pharisees were watching him closely to see if he would heal on the Sabbath so that they might bring charges against him;

8. But he knew what they were up to, so he said unto the man with the crippled hand, get up and stand before me! And the man stood up before him.

9. Then Jesus said unto them, I will ask you something: Is it lawful to do good on the Sabbath or to do evil, to save a life or to destroy one?

10. After he looked around at each one he said to the man, stretch forth your hand! The man did so, and he was completely restored!

11. But the Pharisees were filled with madness, and they convened together as to what they could do.

12. So the time came when he went to the mountain to seek the Father and he was spending the night there in prayer unto God;

13. When the daylight came, he called his disciples and chose out twelve from the group. These would become the apostles.

In verses 14-16, the names of the apostles are different than in Matthew 10:1-4; Mark 3:16-19.

14. Simon who he nicknamed Petros (Peter), and Andrew his brother; James and John; Philip, Bartholomew,

15. Matthew (Levi), Thomas, James the son of Alphaeus, Simon the one called Zealous, Judas the brother of James, (Acts 1:13)

16. and Judas Iscariot, the one who would betray him.

17. And he came down with them and he stood on a flat piece of ground. There were many followers and a large crowd was there from all around Judea and Jerusalem, and from the coastal countries of Tyre and Sidon.

18. They came to him to be healed from all of their many diseases. There were also some that were tormented by unclean spirits. They were all healed!

19. All of those in the crowd wanted to touch him, because the power went forth and healed everyone.

20. And he raised up his eyes to look at the disciples and he said, blessed are the poor, because the kingdom

of God is for you. (Matthew 5:3)

21. Blessed are those that are hungry, because you will be filled. Blessed are they that weep, because you will be joyful and laugh. (Matthew 5:5)

22. Blessed are you when men hate you, when they turn away from you, speak evil against you and say that your name is evil, all this because of the son of man.

23. You will rejoice on that day and be raised up, know that your reward is great in the heavens. Those are the kinds of things that your forefathers did unto the prophets. (Matthew 5:7)

24. But woe unto you who are wealthy, you have your comforts!

25. Woe unto those that are living in luxury needing nothing. You will be hungry! (James 5:1) Woe unto you who are laughing now, because you will mourn and be regretful!

26. Woe unto you when everyone is speaking well of you. This is the way that your forefathers treated the false prophets.

27. Understand this, love those who are hostile against you and do good unto those who hate you;

28. Bless those who curse you and pray for those that slander you.

29. If someone hits you on the side of your face, turn unto him the other cheek, and if one takes your coat, give him also the shirt off of your back.

30. Unto all that ask of you, give something. From those that you give to, do not ask for anything back.

31. In the way that you would want men to treat you, treat them in such a way. (Matthew 22:39; Mark 12:31)

32. If you love those that love you, what reward will you receive? Even sinners love those who love them.

33. If you do good unto those who treat you good, what reward is due unto you? Even sinners do this!

34. If you give to others in which you expect to receive back in return, how is this charity? Even sinners lend to others who will pay them back what is due!

35. Love those that are hostile unto you, treat them well and give expecting nothing in return, and your reward will be great; By living this way you will become a son of the most high! (1 John 3:1) For he offers his grace, even unto those that are unthankful and those that are evil. (Romans 11:26)

36. Therefore show mercy unto others, in the same way that your Father is merciful unto you.

37. Do not condemn others, and you will not be condemned. Do not condemn others, and you will not condemn yourself; Forgive and you will be forgiven. (Matthew 7:1; Romans 2:1)

38. Give and you shall be given what you have need of in adequate amounts, compacted, well mixed and overflowing. All that you have need of shall be given unto you. For in the same amount that you help others, it shall be given unto you.

39. Then he spoke in a parable unto them: A blind man is not able to guide another blind man, or they will both fall into the abyss (*hell*). (Matthew 15:14)

40. A disciple is not above his teacher, but when he is living perfectly one strives to be just like the teacher. (*Christ*) (Matthew 10:24; 1 Peter 2:21; 1 John 3:3)

41. How can you see the splinter in the eye of your brother, yet you not notice the log in your own eye?

42. How can you say unto your brother, allow me to take the splinter out of your eye, while you yourself have a log in your own eye? Hypocrite! First take the log out of your own eye so that you can see clearly in order to help take the splinter out of your brother's eye.

43. A good tree can not produce corrupt fruit and neither can a corrupt tree produce good fruit! (Matthew 7:16-19)

44. For a tree is known by the fruit that it produces. You do not gather figs from thorn bushes, nor do you gather grapes from thistles!

45. Good fruit is brought forth from out of the wealth in the heart of a good man, but corrupt fruit is brought forth from the evil lusts in the heart and produces that which is corrupt and evil. It is from out of the abundance of what is in one's heart that causes a man to do what he does.

46. Why do you call me Lord *(master)* and not do as I command of you? (Ezekiel 33:31-32)

47. Whoever comes unto me and hears my instructions and lives by them, I tell you that he is like a man that is building a house. (John 14:15; 1 John 3:3-10)

48. He digs it out and lays the foundation upon bedrock, and when the floods come and wash against the foundation of that house it will not be destroyed, because it is founded upon the bedrock.

49. But he who hears my instructions and does not live by them, they are like a man that builds upon sandy soil; When the floods come, that house will quickly fall and be destroyed.

Luke 7

1. When Jesus had finished giving his instructions unto the people, he went to Capernaum.

2. There, a certain centurion *(Roman military leader)* had a servant that was dear to him who was very sick and was about to die.

3. When he had heard about Jesus, he sent Jewish elders to come before him and ask for him to come, so that he could cure his servant.

4. When they came unto Jesus, they begged him earnestly and said, he for whom you should do this is worthy

5. because he loves our nation and he built a synagogue for us; Therefore, Jesus decided to go with them.

6. When he had not yet gotten to the house he was greeted by the centurion and his friends, and he said to him, master do not be troubled, because I am not worthy for you to enter in under my roof.

7. I myself am not fit to come unto you, but only say the word and my servant will be healed.

8. You see, I am a man who has lived with much authority and I have many soldiers under my power. I tell one to go and he goes, and to another, to come, and he comes. I tell my servant to do this and he does.

9. When Jesus had heard this, he was amazed and he turned unto the crowd that was following him and said, I tell you the truth, I have not found such dedication and trust in all of Israel, as with this man!

10. When the man's friends returned to the house, the servant had been healed!

11. The following day, Jesus and many of his disciples went into a city that is called Nain and a large crowd began to gather.

12. As he opened the gate into the city there was a young one who had died that was being brought out, the only son of his mother and she was a widow. There were many there with her that were from that city.

13. When the Lord saw her, he had pity and said unto her, do not cry! Then he went over and touched the coffin, those that were carrying it stood still. Then he said, young man, arise!

15. The one who was dead sat up and began to speak; Jesus then brought him to his mother.

16. All who were there were amazed and they glorified God and said, a great prophet has arisen among us and God has visited his people! (Isaiah 7:14)

17. Word of this was spread in Judea and throughout the whole region.

18. When the disciples of John reported all of these things unto him,

19. he called two of his disciples to come to him, then he sent them to Jesus to ask him, are you the Christ or should we expect another?

20. When the men came to him they said, John the Baptizer sent us to you to ask, are you the Christ or should we expect another to come?

21. That same hour Jesus had been healing many people of diverse diseases and casting out evil spirits, and healing the blinded eyes of many, allowing them to see. (Psalms 146:8; Isaiah 35:5)

22. Jesus responded unto them and said, take the report of what you have seen and heard unto John; The blind now see, the lame now walk, the lepers are now cleansed, the deaf can now hear, the dead are raised up and the poor are being given the good news! (Psalms 22:24)

23. All that are not offended by me are blessed.

24. When the messengers of John went away, Jesus began to speak about John to the crowd. He said, what did you go out there to see? A reed shaken by the wind?

25. What did you go there to see? A man who was teaching while wearing soft clothing? Beware, those that wear honorable clothing and live in luxury, they live in large houses and live like kings!

26. What did you go out there to see? A prophet? Yes! I tell you John is much greater than a prophet!

27. He is the one about whom it has been written; "Look, I send my messenger before your face, and he will prepare the way for you." (Malachi 3:1)

28. I tell you that no one who has ever been born of a woman is greater than John the baptizer, yet he is less than the least of those that will be in the kingdom of above!

29. All of the people that heard this that had been baptized by John, including the tax collectors said, God is righteous.

30. But the Pharisees, lawyers and the council of god, having rejected the baptism of John, they were greatly aggravated by this.

31. Then the master said, unto what shall I liken this nation? What are they like?

32. They are like children in the market place that are sitting and calling to each other saying, we have fluted for you but you have not danced; We have mourned you but you have not cried.

33. You see, John the baptizer came and did not eat bread nor wine, but you have said that he has a demon!

34. But I, the son of man have come eating and drinking, but you say, look, a gluttonous man who is a drunkard that keeps friends that are tax collectors and sinners!

35. Wisdom is justified by all that she produces. (Proverbs 14:6)

36. One of the Pharisees asked Jesus if he might have dinner with him. At the home of that Pharisee Jesus sat down to rest. *(The Pharisee was Simon the leper - Matthew 26:7, Mark 14:3; John 12:3)*

37. Take notice, a woman from the city that knew that Jesus was at the house of this Pharisee took an alabaster jar of ointment,

38. and she stood at his feet, and while behind him she began weeping. Then she wet his feet with her tears and with her hair she dried them while wiping and kissing his feet. Then she anointed him with the ointment.

39. When the Pharisee that had invited him saw this, he spoke within himself and said, if this man was a true prophet, he would have known as to what sort of woman this is that touches him and that she is a sinner.

40. Then Jesus said unto him, Simon I have something to say to you! Then he replied, go ahead teacher say what you will.

41. There was a creditor that had two debtors. The one owed five hundred pieces of brass and the other owed fifty pieces of brass.

42. Both were unable to pay, but the creditor completely forgave each of their debts. Which of the two do you think would love him more?

43. Simon answered and said, I would think that it would be the one who he forgave more. Jesus said unto him, you have judged correctly.

44. Then Jesus turned to the woman and said, do you see this woman? I came into your home but you did not wash my feet with water, however she washed my feet with her tears and dried them with her hair.

45. You did not give me a kiss, but when she came in she did not stop intently kissing my feet.

46. You did not anoint my head with oil, but she anointed me with oil.

47. I tell you, she is appreciative for having her many sins forgiven, as this is why she loves me so much. The one unto whom little is forgiven, loves little.

48. He said to her, your sins are forgiven unto you.

49. And when they sat back down they said within themselves, who does he think he is, that he is able to forgive sins?

50. Jesus said to the woman, your conviction *(evidenced by her action - she knew that Jesus is the Christ)* has saved you *(from your sins - Hebrews 11:1; Ephesians 2:8)*. Go in peace.

Luke 8

1. After this, Jesus traveled with his disciples into many cities and villages proclaiming and teaching how to live according to the gospel of the kingdom of God.

2. Some women who were cleansed from evil spirits and sicknesses also followed him. There was Mary of Magdalene, of whom seven demons were cast out;

3. Joanna the wife of Chuza was a manager for Herod; She and many others assisted him with many needed things that they gave.

4. A large crowd gathered and they were coming from the cities to see him and Jesus then told them a parable:

5. A man went out to scatter some seed on his fields. While he was scattering the seed, some fell along the roadway and was trampled, and the birds of the sky came and ate it.

6. Some fell on rocky ground and it grew up quickly, but it dried out because it did not have enough roots to bring moisture to it.

7. Some fell among thorn bushes, but when it was growing, the thorn bushes choked it out.

8. Now there was also some that fell upon good ground and it grew and produced good fruit, even a hundred times! After he said these things, he said, those that have ears to hear, may they understand. (Matthew 7:18)

9. Then his disciples asked him and said, why do you speak in parables and what does this parable mean?

10. And Jesus said, it is meant for you to know the mysteries of God; But when I speak in parables, some that see, do not perceive and some that hear, do not understand.

11. This is what the parable means: The seed is the instructions of God.

12. Those along the roadway hear, but the devil comes and takes the message out of their hearts, otherwise they would be saved (*from their sins*).

13. Those that fell upon the rocks, when they hear, they receive the message with joy, but they do not have good roots; While they are committed for a time, when difficulties come they fall away. (Hebrews 10:38-39)

14. The seed that fell among the thorns are those that understand, but they are more concerned with wealth and the pleasures of this life, so they live to pursue them, choking them from growing to maturity.

15. The seeds that fell on good ground are those who have a good heart and understand when they hear the message, and they keep to it; These bring forth good fruit through their faithfulness and patient endurance.

16. No one that has a lamp covers it with a pot or puts it under a bed; They put it on a lamp stand so that those who are coming can see the light!

17. Because when it is revealed unto you, it is not to be hidden, nor is it to be kept secret; It is to be made known to others when it has been revealed unto you.

18. Therefore, you must observe *(live)* what you know *(understand of the truth),* because whoever has, more will be given unto him, but whoever does not have (*understanding*), the little that he does have will be taken away.

19. Then the mother of Jesus came to him along with his brothers, but they were not able to get to him because of the crowd.

20. But it was made known to him that his mother and brothers were standing outside wanting to see him.

21. He answered and said to them, who are my mother and brothers? They are those who understand and live according to the instructions of God (*the faithful*).

22. Then Jesus entered into a boat with his disciples and he said, let's go over to the other side of the lake.

23. When they were making their way, Jesus fell asleep. Then a storm grew up around them with a strong wind crossing the lake and they were filling up with water, putting them in danger.

24. Then they came to Jesus and awoke him and said, master! master! We are about to die! And he gathered himself and forbid the winds and the roughness of the waters, and they became calm.

25. Then he said unto them, where is your dedication and trust? And they were in awe after fearing that they were about to die; And they said to one another, who is he, in that he is able to even command the winds and the water and they obey him!

In the Matthew 8:28-34 account of the following story, the land was called Gergesenes and it was two men who were demon possessed.

26. Then they sailed to the land of Gadarenes, which is across from Galilee.

27. And Jesus went out onto the land and a certain man from the city approached him. The man has been demon possessed for many years and did not wear any clothes, nor did he live in a house, but lived among the tombs.

28. When he saw Jesus he screamed out very loudly, what do you plan to do to me Jesus, son of the most high? I beg for you to not torment me.

29. Many times the people had commanded the unclean spirit to come out of the man and the people had arrested him but their chains and shackles could not hold him, even when he was being guarded he would break apart the bindings and he would run to the desolate places.

30. Then Jesus asked him, what is your name? And he said, legion, because there are many demons within him.

31. But the demons begged Jesus not to send them to the abyss.

32. However, there was a herd of many pigs that were feeding on the mountain and the demons begged him that he allow them to enter into the pigs, and Jesus allowed them.

33. Then the demons came out of the man and entered into the pigs! Immediately the herd ran down the side of the mountain, right off of the cliff, fell into the lake and were drowned!

34. The keepers of the pigs saw this as it happened and they ran away. Then they went to their city and throughout the countryside and told everyone all that had happened.

35. Many of the people came to see for themselves what had happened, and when they approached Jesus

and they saw the man that had been demon possessed, from which they were taken out and that he was clothed, of a sound mind and he was sitting at the feet of Jesus, they were frightened.

36. When they had seen all of this for themselves, that the demon possessed man was healed,

37. the people from that area of the Gadarenes asked Jesus to leave their land because of the large amount of fear upon them. Then Jesus entered into the boat and he returned.

38. But the man who had the demons taken out of him begged Jesus to go with him, but Jesus released him and said,

39. return to your family and tell everyone of what God has done for you! Then the man went away unto the city and announced the miracle that Jesus did for him!

40. When Jesus returned, there was a crowd that joyfully received him; They had been awaiting him.

41. And look! There was a man by the name of Jairus who was the chief of the synagogue. He fell at the feet of Jesus and begged him to come to his home;

42. His only daughter was about twelve years old and she was dying. But while they were on their way, the crowd pressed in close to him (Matthew 9:18)

43. and there was a woman that had been bleeding for twelve years, in which had spent all of her wealth with the healers (*doctors*), but they were not able to cure her.

44. The woman then came up behind him and she touched the edge of his clothes; Instantly the bleeding was healed!

45. Then Jesus said, who touched me? The people of the crowd denied, but Peter and those with him said, master, the crowd is pressing in upon you on all sides! But you ask, who touched me?

46. But Jesus said, someone touched me, because I know that power has gone out from me! (Matthew 9:20)

47. When the woman saw that she was not hiding, she came trembling and fell down before him and she told him the reason that she touched him and how she was cured instantly in the presence of all those people!

48. Then Jesus said, you are courageous daughter, your trust and dedication has healed you, go in peace.

49. While he was speaking, someone that was sent from the synagogue said to him, your daughter has died, do not trouble the teacher any further.

50. But Jesus overheard this and said, do not be afraid. Only trust in me and she will be cured.

51. Then Jesus came to the house, but he did not allow anyone to enter in except Peter, James, John and the mother and father of the girl.

52. They were all crying dearly and wailing for her. Then Jesus said, do not cry. The girl has not died, but is sleeping (*in a coma*); (Matthew 9:24)

53. But they ridiculed him because they were sure that she was dead.

54. Then Jesus told all of them to go, and he took her hand and called her name, and said, rise up child!

55. Her spirit returned *(she awoke from her coma)* to her and she began to stand up! Then he ordered that she be given some food. Then Jesus ordered them to tell no one of that which had happened.

Luke 9

1. And Jesus called his twelve disciples to him and he gave them power and jurisdiction (*authority*) over all demons and he gave them power to heal all diseases.

2. He sent them to announce the terms of the kingdom of God and to heal those in need.

3. Then he instructed them, take nothing with you, not a staff, nor a purse, nor food, nor money, nor extra clothing.

4. Whatever house you enter, remain there and go forth (*locally*) from there.

5. If you are not received in one place, leave that city and shake their dust from off of your feet to be a testimony against them. (Matthew 10:14; Mark 6:11; Acts 13:51)

6. So they went out and they traveled through many villages preaching the gospel and healing in every place they went!

7. Then Herod, the ruler of one fourth of the nation had heard these things were being done by Jesus, he was perplexed. This is because some were saying that he was John the baptizer back from the dead!

8. Some had thought that he was the prophesied appearance of Elijah, or that another one of the prophets had reappeared!

9. But Herod said, I beheaded John, so who is this one that I am hearing all of these things about? Then he began desiring to meet with him.

10. When the apostles returned, they told him of all the things they did. Then he took them away to a private place that was empty of people near the city of Bethsaida.

11. When the crowds found out where they were, they approached them and when they came upon him from the right side, he began to speak to them about the kingdom of God. All that were in need of being healed, he cured them.

12. But as the day came towards its end, the twelve said to him, send the crowd home unto the villages and their farms so that they may have lodging and supplies of food, since we are in this desert place.

13. But Jesus said, you must feed them. But they said, we only have five loaves and two fish! Shall we go buy food for all of these people?

14. There were about five thousand men. Jesus said to his disciples, have them sit down in groups of fifty.

15. They did so and all of the people sat down.

16. Then Jesus took the five loaves and the two fish and he broke them and gave them to the disciples to offer unto the crowds.

17. They all ate and were filled, every one of them! So when they gathered the leftovers, there was twelve baskets full.

18. Then Jesus went away from the people and began to pray alone with his disciples and he asked them; Who do the crowds say that I am?

19. They answered and said, some say John the baptizer and others say Elijah; There are also some that think that you are one of the ancient prophets who has arisen;

20. Then Jesus asked them and said, who do you say that I am? Peter answered and said, you are the Christ of God! (Matthew 16:16; Mark 8:29; John 6:68-69)

21. But Jesus ordered that they not tell anyone of this at that time,

22. and he said, it is necessary that the son of man suffer greatly and be rejected by the elders, high priests, scribes and to be killed. But after three days he will be raised up!

23. Then he said unto all of them, if anyone desires to come unto me, he must deny himself and take up his own cross every day and follow me. (Matthew 16:24; Mark 10:21)

24. Because whoever chooses to live for the cares of this life will lose his life; But whoever will turn away from the cares of this life for my purposes, he will receive life everlasting. (Matthew 6:19-21)

25. What benefit is it for a man if he should gain the whole world, but in the end is eternally lost and cast away?

26. Whoever will reject and disgrace me and my instructions, they will be rejected and disgraced when I return in the glory of the Father and the angels. (Revelation 20:12-15; Matthew 25:32)

27. But I tell you truly, there are some that are standing here who will not experience death until they see the kingdom of God begin to be established! (Acts 1-2)

Verses 28-32 are in error and contradict the accounts of Matthew 17:3 & Mark 9:2-8.
These other accounts say 6 days later, not 8 days later as in Luke's account
& neither mention these men falling asleep, but falling to the ground in fear!

28. And about eight days after these things were said, Jesus took Peter, James and John up upon a high mountain to pray.

29. While they were praying, the face of Jesus became different, and his clothing became brightly alighted and white.

30. Then two men appeared and spoke with him, of whom were Moses and Elijah.

31. They appeared in his glory and spoke of his departing of which he was about to fulfill in Jerusalem.

32. But Peter and those with him were very sleepy and laid down to sleep! When they awoke they saw his glory and two men standing there with him.

33. As they were about to leave that place, Peter said to him, master, it is a good thing that we are here with you; Should we make three houses, one for you, one for Moses and one for Elijah? Peter was not thinking about what he was saying.

34. As he said this, a cloud overshadowed them and they became very afraid as the cloud engulfed them.

35. A voice came from the cloud that said, this is my beloved son in whom I am delighted. Listen to him.

36. When the voice occurred, they saw that Jesus was alone (*Moses and Elijah were no longer there*). Then they became quiet and none of them told anyone of these things at that time concerning the things that they had seen.

37. On the following day as they came down from the mountain, a large crowd was there to meet them.

38. Then a man from the crowd yelled out, teacher, I beg you to take a look at my son, my only son.

39. Suddenly an evil spirit took a hold of his child and he cried out and he began convulsing with foam! It was very difficult but then it departed from him, though he was bruised.

40. I begged your disciples to cast it out, but they were not able!

41. Then Jesus said, oh this generation is perverse and untrustworthy! How much longer shall I be able to endure you? Bring your son to me.

42. As he was bringing him to Jesus, the demon cut him and he again began violently convulsing! Jesus cast out the unclean spirit and he healed the child and gave him back to his father.

43. Everyone was amazed by the great power of God and they all admired the things that he did.

44. Then Jesus said to his disciples, listen closely to my words; The son of man is soon going to be betrayed and given into the hands of men.

45. At that time the disciples did not understand what he was speaking about, as it had been veiled and kept from their understanding. They were afraid to ask him concerning his words.

46. Then they began to reason with each other as to which of them is the leader.

47. But Jesus saw their hearts through their reasoning, and he called a small child to come near to him. (Matthew 18:1-10)

48. Then he said, whoever receives the message of my children who come in my name, he receives me. Whoever receives me also receives the one that has sent me.

Verses 49-50 are completely out of context and unrelated to the topic.
For understanding, look to Matthew 18:1-10.

The least among you shall be the greatest!

49. Then John said, master, we saw someone who in your name was casting out demons, but we stopped him from doing so, because he is not among us!

50. And Jesus said to them, do not stop him, because whoever is not against us is with us.

51. The time was passing and the days were being completed that Jesus would soon be betrayed, and even his face looked as though he was readying himself to go to Jerusalem.

52. The Pharisees had sent messengers to go to apprehend him, and they went into the villages of the Samaritans to wait for his arrival,

53. but they did not arrest him because he was determined to go to Jerusalem.

54. James and John said, master, do you want for us to command that fire come down from the sky to destroy them, the same as Elijah did? (2 Kings 1:10-12)

55. Jesus rebuked them and he said, do you not know of what spirit you are?

56. I did not come to destroy mankind, but to offer salvation unto them! Then they went to another town.

57. As they were on their way, one man said to him, master, I will follow you everywhere you go.

58. Then Jesus said, foxes have dens and birds have nests; The son of man does not have a place to sleep!

59. Then he said to another one, follow me! But he said, master, first allow me to go and bury my father.

60. But Jesus said, let those that are eternally dead bury those who have physically died! You must continue to announce the terms of the kingdom of God!

61. Then another said, I will follow you master, but first allow me take care of my family matters!

62. But Jesus said to him, the one who puts his hand to the plow and then looks back to what is behind him, he is not fit for the kingdom of God.

Luke 10

1. Jesus appointed seventy disciples to go in pairs and sent them out into every city and place that he was planning to come.

2. Then he said to them, truly the harvest is large but the workers are very few; Pray that the master of the harvest will send forth many more workers to harvest for him.

3. Go, but know this; I send you out as lambs that are surrounded by wolves!

4. Do not carry a bag, nor any money, nor sandals, so that no one might harm you or take anything from you while you are on your way.

5. When you enter into a house, first ask yourself, is this a peaceful place?

6. If there is peacefulness in that home you should be at peace and get your rest there. If you do not feel at peace there, do not enter into that home.

7. Remain in that house, have them feed you and offer you something to drink; For the worker is due what is owed to him. Do not move from one house to another.

8. Whenever you enter into a city, if they receive you, eat whatever is brought before you.
(Colossians 2:16; Romans 14:2-3 – *dietary parts of the Mosaic law are not to be kept*)

9. Go and heal those that are sick and tell them that the kingdom of God is drawing near.

10. In whatever city you enter, if they do not receive you, go into their streets and tell them;

11. We shake off the dust from your city as we leave this place, but know that the kingdom of God shall come down upon you in judgment!

12. I must tell you, on that day, it will be better for Sodom than for your city!

Verses 13-15 do not fit the narrative.
The context changes from the instruction unto the seventy disciples,
to what Jesus is now saying to the cities that did not repent after he did miracles there.

13. Woe unto you Chorazin! Woe unto you Bethsaida! Because if the powerful deeds that were done in those cities were done in Tyre and Sidon, they would have repented long ago!
14. It will be more bearable for them on judgment day than for you!
15. Unto you Capernaum, you are raised up into the heavens with your power, yet you will be brought down unto hell! (Isaiah 14:13-15)

There is a return to the instructions unto the seventy.

16. Those who hear you also hear me, but those that reject you also reject me and the one who sent me.

17. Then the seventy returned joyfully and they said, master, even the demons are under our jurisdiction and power in your name!

18. Then he said to them, I perceive Satan as a falling star has fallen from the heavens!

19. Look! I give you authority to overcome the snakes *(false teachers)* and scorpions *(harmful people)*, and upon all of those that are empowered by the enemy *(Satan)*; Nothing shall cause you to fail.

20. Do not be joyful that the evil spirits submit to you, but be happy that your names are written in the book of life that is in the heavens. (Revelation 20:12-15)

21. At that time, the spirit of Jesus was encouraged and he said, I praise you Father, the highest master of the heavens and the earth. For you have hidden these things from the learned ones and the cunning, but you have revealed them unto the simple and uneducated. Yes Father, this is the way that is desirable unto you.

22. Everything that has been given unto me by my Father *(to do)*, no one understands except for the son and my Father. No one knows the Father except for the son, and whomever the son reveals him to.

23. Then he turned to the disciples privately and said, blessed are those eyes that can see what you can see. *(blessed are those that have understanding of what you now perceive)*

24. For I tell you, many prophets and kings have wanted to see what you now see, but they could not see, and to hear what you hear, but they could not hear!

25. Be aware! A certain lawyer stood up to test him and he said, teacher, what shall I do that I may inherit eternal life? (Matthew 19:16-22; Matthew 23;35-40; Mark 12:29-34; Romans 13:9)

26. Jesus said, what is written in your law? How do you understand it?

27. The man said, you shall love your God with all of your heart, all of your mind, all of your soul, and with all of your strength; And you shall love your neighbor as yourself. *(The law of God)*
(Deuteronomy 6:5; Leviticus 19:18; Matthew 7:12; Matthew 22:37; Mark 12:30)

28. Then Jesus said, you have answered correctly. Do this and you will live.

29. But the man wanted to justify himself and he asked Jesus, who is my neighbor?

30. Jesus replied and said; A certain man was going from Jerusalem to Jericho when thieves came upon him and stripped off his clothes, beat him badly and then they left him to die.

31. Then a priest came towards him who was heading in that direction, but when he saw him, he passed by

on the opposite side of the roadway.

32. Then a Levite also came upon that place and he did the same.

33. But then a Samaritan traveling by came upon him and saw him. He was full of sympathy,

34. He came near to the man and tended to his wounds with wine and oil. Then he put him on his own animal and took him to an inn and he cared for him.

35. The following day he took two denarii and gave them to the inn keeper and said to him, care for him; Whatever I shall owe you, I will give to you when I return. I will pay you.

36. Now I ask you, of these three men, which of them was a neighbor unto the man who fell to the thieves? (James 2:20-24)

37. And the man said, it was the one who was merciful unto him. Then Jesus said, go and do the same.

38. It happened that when he was entering into another village, a certain woman received him and brought him into her house.

39. She was the sister of Mary, of whom sat alongside of the feet of Jesus and listened to his words.

40. But Martha was distracted because she was busy serving. Then she came in and said, master do you not care that my sister has left me alone to serve? Will you tell her to help me?

41. Then Jesus said unto her, Martha, Martha, you are troubled by many things;

42. There is only need for one to do the serving, and Mary has committed herself to share in my goodness, of which will not be taken from her.

Luke 11

1. Jesus was in a certain place praying. When he finished, one of his disciples said to him, master, teach us to speak to God, just as John taught his disciples.

2. Then he said to them, when bringing a prayer, bring forth like this: Our Father who is in the heavens, your name (*Yehovah*) is the holiest. May your kingdom appear and may your will be accomplished on this earth the same as it is in the heavens.

3. Please give unto us the food that we have need of every day,

4. and forgive us of our trespasses, the same as we also forgive those who trespass against us. Do not allow us to fall when we are tempted (James 1:13), but protect us from those that are evil.

5. Then he said to them, if one of you has a friend that comes to you at midnight and asks, friend please give me three loaves of bread;

6. You see, a brother has arrived after a long journey and I have nothing to offer unto him!

7. Then if, from within your home you say, do not bother me, the door is already shut and the children are sleeping. I am not about to get up to give unto you! (*You would not be a true friend*)

8. I tell you, if you are a true friend, you will get up, even if you have nothing to give to him, and because of his shamelessness to come to ask of you, you should give whatever you have to offer.

9. I tell you, ask and it shall be given unto you; Seek and you shall find; Knock, it will be opened unto you.

10. Because everyone who has a need will receive, and the one seeking, shall find; If one is knocking, it will be opened unto him.

11. If a son asks for bread, will his father give unto him a stone? Or if he asks for a fish, will he give unto him a serpent?

12. Or if he asks for an egg, would he give unto him a scorpion?

13. Even those who live against the ways of God know how to give good gifts to their children; So how much more shall your heavenly Father give his sacred spirit unto those who ask?

14. Then Jesus cast out a demon that was dumb (*could not speak*). And when the demon came out, the man who was dumb was now able to speak and the crowds were astonished.

15. But some of them said, he casts out demons by Beel-Zebul, the chief of the demons. (Matthew 9:34)

16. Then others tempted him to give a sign in the heavens.

17. But he knew their thoughts and he said to them, every kingdom that is divided against itself will be brought to destruction. Every house that is divided will fall.

18. If Satan is divided amongst himself, how shall his kingdom stand? How can you say that I cast out demons by Beel-Zebul?

19. If I cast out demons by Beel-Zebul, by whom do your sons cast them out by? May they bring judgment upon you. (*Their sons do not cast out demons*)

20. But if I cast out demons by the power of God, then know that the kingdom of God has come down upon you!

21. When a man is living strongly armed and he is guarding his home, his belongings are safe.

22. But if one who is stronger comes and overtakes him, they take his weaponry as well. He gives over his defenses that he had trusted in.

23. Whoever is not with me is against me! He that does not gather with me is scattering.

24. When an unclean spirit comes out of a man, it goes to dry places seeking rest; But when it does not find a home, it says, I will return to my old home from which I have been taken out!

25. Then it finds him abiding clean and living with new furnishings.

26. Then it goes and finds seven more evil spirits who are more evil than itself and they enter in to live there. If this happens, the latter is worse than the beginning. (2 Peter 2:20-22)

27. While he was saying these things, a woman lifted up her voice from out of the crowd and said, blessed is the womb that bore you and the breasts that gave you suck. (*the worship of Mary is rejected by Jesus*)

28. But Jesus said, not so, but blessed is the one who hears these instructions of God and dedicates himself to live accordingly.

Verses 29-32 are out of context and make no sense in this place.

29. And the crowd gathered closely together, and Jesus began to speak; This is an evil nation. It seeks a sign, but I will not give a sign, except the sign of Jonah the prophet.

30. Just as Jonah testified in himself a sign unto the Ninevites, the same it will be with the son of man unto this generation.

31. The queen of the south will be awakened when the judgment comes, along with the people of this generation, and she will condemn them! She came forth from a great distance away to hear the wisdom of Solomon, and look! One that is greater than Solomon is now here!

32. Those of Nineveh will awaken at the judgment along with this nation and they will condemn you! They turned from their sins when Jonah brought the message to them! Know this, one who is greater than Jonah is now here!

33. No one lights a lamp and puts it in a secret place, nor under a barrel, but they put it on a lamp stand and those who come can then see by its light!

34. The eyes are the lamp of the body; When your eye is focused *(on truth)*, all of your body is full of light. But when your eye becomes corrupted, your whole body turns to darkness *(evil)*.

35. Be careful that your light not be turned unto darkness!

36. If your whole body is full of light and no part of you is in darkness, you will be completely full of light; just as a lamp when it shines its light upon you. (John 1:5-9)

37. A certain Pharisee asked if he would have dinner with him, so Jesus went in and sat down.

38. Then the Pharisee noticed and he asked him why he did not wash his hands before dinner.

39. But the Lord said to him, you Pharisees wash the outside of the cup and bowl, yet the inside is full of theft and other evils!

40. How is it that you cleanse the outside but do not make the inside to be clean?

41. But if you give compassionately from within, you will see that every part of you shall be clean.

42. Woe unto you Pharisees! You tithe with mint, anise and with every usable plant, but you ignore the justice and the love of God! Sure, you should do these things, but don't ignore the higher things.

43. Woe unto you Pharisees. You love to sit in the highest seats in the synagogues and to be warmly greeted in the marketplace. (Matthew 23)

44. Woe unto you scribes and Pharisees, you are hypocrites! You are as the unmarked tombs, and men walk over them but do not know.

45. Then one of the lawyers said to him, teacher, you are insulting us by the things that you are saying.

46. Then he said unto the lawyer, woe unto you lawyers! You put burdens upon men that are too difficult to bear, but you yourselves will not touch one finger upon them!

47. Woe unto you, because you build memorial stones for the prophets, but it was your forefathers who killed them!

48. You are witnesses against yourselves and you are pleased by the deeds of your forefathers. This is evidenced in that they killed them and that you build memorials for them!

49. It is because of this the wisdom of God says, "I will send unto them prophets and apostles, and they will

kill them and drive them out!"

50. It is because of this that this generation *(nation)* will bear all of the blood that has been shed by all of the prophets since the founding of the world! *(fulfilled in 70 A.D. with the destruction of Jerusalem)*

51. From the blood of Abel, until the blood of Zachariah, who was killed between the alter and the temple house; Yes, I tell you, all of this will be put upon this generation.

52. Woe to you lawyers, because you took the keys of knowledge, but you have not entered yourselves therein, and those who tried to live accordingly, you have prevented.

53. As he was saying these things to them, the scribes and Pharisees became terribly angry and began to provoke him to tempt him to misspeak concerning many things.

54. They laid in wait for him to say something, to catch something from out of his own mouth so that they could accuse him.

Luke 12

1. During an assembly of a great number of people, so many that they began to trample one another, Jesus began to tell his disciples, beware of the leaven of the Pharisees, they are hypocrites!

2. There is nothing concealed that will not be revealed, nor anything that is hidden that will not be made known before all.

3. Therefore, whatever you say in the darkness will be broadcast in the light; The secrets that are spoken in private rooms will be announced from the housetops.

4. I tell you, do not be afraid of those who can kill the body, because after that, there is no more that they can do.

5. But I warn you of who you must fear; Fear him who has the authority to kill you and cast you into hell. This is the one whom you should fear!

6. Five sparrows are sold for two copper coins, yet none of them are forgotten by God.

7. Even the hairs on your head are counted. Do not be afraid, because you are more valuable than many sparrows.

8. Everyone who will assent into covenant with me *(and live accordingly)*, the son of man will also bring acknowledgement of them in the presence of the messengers *(angels)* of God.

9. Anyone who lives in a contradicting way unto me in this life, he will be rejected by God in the presence of the messengers of God. (1 John 3:3-10; Hebrews 10:26-29)

10. Everyone who takes action against the sons of men, it can be forgiven unto them, but anyone who takes action against the spirit of the holy one, it will not be forgiven. (Numbers 15:30-31 - *blasphemy of God*)

11. When they bring you unto the synagogues *(courtrooms)* and before rulers and magistrates, do not be concerned with what you will say, nor what you may need to answer to;

12. The spirit of the holy one will give to you at that time that which you must say.

13. A man from the crowd said, teacher, instruct my brother to divide the inheritance with me.

14. But Jesus said, who appointed me to be a judge or a trustee over your matter?

15. Then Jesus said to him, beware that you do not become covetous. Because the value of one's life is not in what he possesses or owns.

16. Jesus spoke a parable to them; There was a certain wealthy man who produced much on his land;

17. So he reasoned within himself and said, what shall I do, because I do not have a place to store all of my gathered fruit?

18. Then he decided, I will build up new barns much larger than these, and I will gather the fruit that my fields produce and store them within. *(comparable to growing a business)*

19. Then I will say within myself, I have many goods that can be stored for many years, now rest and eat, drink and be happy. *(comparable to building a nest-egg for retirement)*

20. But God said to him, you are foolish! This very night your soul will be taken from you. All that you have stored up, unto who shall it go?

21. This is the way it is for those who build treasures for themselves in this life, they are not wealthy in the treasures of God. (Matthew 6:19)

22. He told the disciples, this is the reason that I tell you, do not be concerned for matters pertaining to this life, what you will eat, or what you will wear, nor concerns of the body.

23. This life is about much more than food, concerns of the body, or clothing.

24. Consider the birds, as they do not plant nor harvest, and they do not have a storehouse nor barn, but God feeds them! How much more important to God do you think you are?

25. And which of you who is anxious can add even an inch to his stature?

26. So if you are not even able to control the smallest things, why are you concerned with the big things that you can not control? (Page 370-371)

27. Look at the lilies, how they grow, yet they do not work nor spin. But I tell you, that even Solomon in all of his great wealth was not adorned as one of these!

28. The grass in the fields today is flourishing, but soon it will be dried out as in an oven and is withered. God cares for it, so how much more important are you? Do not lack confidence.

29. Do not be concerned with what you will eat or drink or wear; Do not be anxious.

30. These are the things that those who do not know God are concerned about and seek after, but your Father knows what you have need of.

31. But seek the kingdom of God and live righteously, and all of these things will be supplied unto you.

32. Do not fear little ones, because it is pleasing unto God to give the kingdom unto you.

33. Bring forth your possessions and give to those in need. Make yourselves bags that will never wear out, and build your treasures in the heavens, where there are no thieves there to steal and no moths to corrupt;

34. Because where your treasures are, your heart will also be. (Matthew 6:19-20)

35. Keep your fortitude and your lamp burning *(for God)*.

36. In your appearance before mankind, show that you are living in waiting for your master. When he returns, there will be a feast; For those who come and knock, it will be opened unto you. (Revelation 19)

37. Blessed are those servants who are awake when he returns. Truly I tell you that he will allow them to ascend, sit down and be attended to.

38. But if he comes in the second watch or the third, he must find you in this way; Blessed are the servants who will be ready.

39. But know this, if the master of the house knew when the thief was coming, he would have watched and not allowed the house to be broken into.

40. So then, you must be prepared, because the son of man will come at a time when he will not be expected.

41. Peter asked Jesus, master, are you speaking this parable unto us, or unto everyone?

42. And Jesus said, who is the faithful and prudent steward whom I will appoint over those of my household (Daniel 12:1), who will give unto them that which is needed at the proper time? (Matthew 24:44)

43. Blessed is the servant who the Lord finds doing in this way when he returns.
(Daniel 11:32-35; Daniel 12:3; Matthew 24:44)

44. Truly I tell you, he will appoint him over all that he has.

45. But if that servant says in his heart, the master will delay his coming, and then he goes and beats up the man servants under him, and the women servants, and goes and eats and drinks with the drunkards;

46. His master will come at a time that he will not expect and on a day that he will not know of, and he will cut him into two pieces and will throw both parts in with the unbelievers.

47. But if that servant who shall know the will of God within himself, if he does not do according to the will of God, he will have his place reserved unto great punishment.
(James 4:17; Romans 1:21-32; Matthew 7:21)

48. But those that have done that which is deserving of punishment but did not know better, they will be with lighter punishment. (Numbers 15:28-31; Hebrews 10:26; 1 John 5:16-18; Romans 1:18)
Unto the one to whom much is given, much will be demanded of him.

49. I will come and cast fire unto the earth, but what will I do if it is already burning?
(Revelation 8:5-11; Revelation 16:1-4)

50. I have a baptism to be immersed in, yet I have much strain upon me until it is completed!
(Romans 6:3-4)

51. Do you think that I have come to bring peace on the earth? No, I tell you, I have come to bring division!

52. There will be five in a house, and it will be divided, three against two.

53. The father shall be against his son and son against his father, mother against daughter and daughter against mother, mother in law against her daughter in law and daughter in law against her mother in law.

54. Jesus also said to the crowds, when you see a cloud rise up from the west, you know that rain is coming; So it happens.

55. When the south wind blows, you know that it will be hot outside; Then it occurs.

56. But you are hypocrites, because you know how to discern the signs in the weather, but how is it that you can not understand who I am (*by the miracles that I do*)?

57. Why are you not able to discern what is right? (Romans 1:28)

58. When you are taken to the courts by your adversary, do all that you can to settle with him so that he not drag you before the judge, the judge deliver you to the officer and the officer deliver you to prison.

59. I tell you, you will not leave there until every last farthing is paid! (Isaiah 27:5 -*Make peace with God*)

Luke 13

1. There were some there that told Jesus about the Galileans, of whom Pilate had exchanged blood for their sacrifices.

2. And Jesus said, do you think that those Galileans are the worst sinners of all because they suffered these things?

3. No! I tell you that if you do not repent (*turn away from your sins*), you will certainly perish (*eternally*). (Jonah 3:8-10)

4. Do you remember the eighteen people who the tower in Siloam fell on and killed, do you think that they were the worst sinners of all people who lived in Jerusalem?

5. No, I tell you that if you do not repent (*turn away from your sins*), you will all perish (*eternally*) .

6. Then he told a parable, a certain man had a vineyard that he planted; When he found a tree that did not have any fruit on it

7. he said to his servant, look, for three years I have come seeking fruit on this tree but it has not produced any fruit! Cut it down, because it is wasting ground!

8. The servant answered him and said, master, leave it for one more year and I will dig around it and fertilize it;

9. Surly it will make some good fruit, if not, then we will cut it down! (*the tree represents ancient Israel*)

10. Jesus taught in one of the synagogues on a particular Sabbath.

11. And look! There was a woman who had an evil spirit for more than eighteen years; She was bent over and not able to stand erect.

12. Jesus saw her and he called to her and said, woman, you are now loosened from your infirmity!

13. Then he put his hands upon her and instantly she was able to stand erect, and she glorified God.

14. But the ruler of that synagogue was very angry that Jesus had healed on the Sabbath, and he said to the crowd, there are six days in which to work; Come and heal on one of those days, but not on the Sabbath!

15. Then Jesus answered him and said, you are a hypocrite! Which of you does not loose his oxen or his horse and lead them to the water on the Sabbath?

16. This woman is an offspring of Abraham, in whom Satan had bound for eighteen years! But you are saying that it was not right to loosen her from his bond on the Sabbath?

17. And when he had said these things, those who had opposed him were put to shame. Those in the crowd were overjoyed at the wonderful things that they had seen happen.

18. Then he said, unto what shall I compare the kingdom of God?

19. It is like a grain of mustard seed of which a man threw into a field. When it grew, it became a very large tree in which the birds of the sky would come and roost in its branches.

20. Then he said, unto what shall I compare the kingdom of God?

21. It is like yeast, of which a woman takes and incorporates with three measures of dough; Therefore, the whole of it became raised.

22. Jesus traveled unto the cities and villages teaching, and he began making his way towards Jerusalem.

23. One of the disciples asked him, master, are there few who are being eternally saved?
(Matthew 7:13-14; John 3:32)

24. And Jesus said unto him, strive to enter through the narrow gate; Many will desire to enter in, but will not be able.

25. Because when the housemaster shuts the door, if you are found to be outside knocking at the door, saying master, master, open to us, he will say to you, I do not know you. (Matthew 7:13-23)

26. Then you will say, we ate with you and drank with you, and you taught in our streets!
(Matthew 12:16-21 - *this proves that Isaiah 42:1-5 is not speaking about Jesus*)

27. Then he will say, I tell you again, I do not know you; Get away from me all who continue to defy my instructions (*all that do unrighteousness*). (Psalms 112:10)

28. There will be great weeping and grinding of teeth (*from the great pain many will endure*), and you will see Abraham, Isaac, Jacob, and all of the prophets in the kingdom of God, but you will be rejected and remain foreigners.

29. Many (*gentiles*) will come from the east and the west, the north and the south, and they will sit down in the kingdom of God.

30. Know this, that the highest (*most noble and wealthy*) shall be least, and the least of these shall be first.

Verses 31-33 were errantly added by a scribe and are not a part of the original text.

31. Then some Pharisees came unto Jesus and said to him, get out and leave this place, because Herod is looking to kill you. (no evidence exists that Herod wanted him dead, but the Pharisees did - Luke 23:14)

32. Then he said, go and tell that fox, surely I cast out demons and I cure many. I cure many today and tomorrow, but on the third day, all will be completed.

33. But I must walk today, tomorrow and the following day, because it is not acceptable that a prophet is killed outside of Jerusalem. (Jesus was killed outside of the city, certainly this is error!) (Hebrews 13:12)

34. Jerusalem, Jerusalem! You have killed the prophets and you have stoned those who were sent unto you! How often I have tried to gather your children, the way that a bird gathers her chicks under her wings, but you would not have it! (Luke 19:41)

35. Know this! Your house shall be left unto you desolate! (Daniel 9:17, 27; Jeremiah 22:5) Never shall I ever recognize you unless you say, blessed is he who has come in the name of Jehovah.
(Mark 11:9; Psalms 118:26)

Luke 14

1. Then Jesus went to the home of one of the Pharisees on the Sabbath to have a meal, and they were carefully watching him.

2. They brought in a paralyzed man and set him near Jesus.

3. So Jesus asked the lawyers and Pharisees, is it lawful to heal on the Sabbath?

4. They did not answer him. Then Jesus took the man and healed him and let him leave the house.

5. Then Jesus said, which of you that has a horse or oxen, if one were to fall into a pit on the Sabbath day would not go and pull it out?

6. They had no ability to respond to him.

7. Then he told a parable unto those that were invited concerning how they were choosing who would sit in the high seats, and he said to them;

8. When you are invited by anyone unto a wedding feast, do not sit in the best seats if one who is more highly esteemed is invited.

9. If you do, the one that invited you will come to you and will say, give your place to this man. Then you will be ashamed and you will be put in the least seat.

10. When you are invited, go and sit in the least of the seats, and then the one who invited you may come to you and say, friend, let me take you to a better seat! In this you will be honored in the presence of those that are with you.

11. Everyone who promotes himself shall be humbled, and whoever is humble, he will be made honorable.

12. He then spoke to those that invited him; When you make a dinner, do not call your friends, nor your brothers, nor your relatives, nor your neighbors that are wealthy. This is because they will invite you as a return favor and you will have your reward (*repayment*).

13. When you have a banquet, invite the poor, the disabled, the lame and those that are blind.

14. In this, you will be blessed, because they do not have the ability to repay you. For this, you will be repaid at the resurrection of the righteous. (Revelation 20:12)

15. After hearing this, one of those that were sitting with him said to him, blessed is he that eats the bread in the kingdom of God. (1 Corinthians 11:18-34; John 6:27-60; Matthew 16:12)

16. But Jesus said to him, a certain man made a large dinner and he invited many people.

17. At the time that the dinner was ready he said to his servants, go out and tell those that have been invited

to now come, because it is ready for everyone! (Revelation 19:9)

18. Then each of them began to make excuses. The first said, I just purchased a field and I have the necessity to go out to see it. I ask that you excuse me.

19. Then another said, I just bought five yoke of oxen and I am going to test them out. I request that you excuse me. *(these men were focused on things of this world and not the eternal)*

20. Then another said, I have just taken a wife and I am not able to come.

21. Then the servant came close by and quietly told this to his master. Then the master grew very angry and said to the servant, go out quickly into the streets, and the alleys of the cities; Invite the poor and the lame and the disabled and the blind! *(these represent the lost of ancient Israel)*

22. Then the servant said, master, it has been done as you have ordered but there is still room for more!

23. Then the master said to his servant, go out into the roadways and beyond the borders of this land and request for them to come so that my house will be filled! *(these represent the gentiles)*

24. I tell you that those who were originally invited shall not taste of my food! (Zechariah 11:9-13; Malachi 2:1-3; Hosea 7:13; Isaiah 43:28 - *this represents the Jews who reject Christ*)

25. Large crowds gathered together before him, and he turned and said to them,

26. if anyone will come to me, he must turn away from his father, mother, wife and his children, his brothers and sisters, and even his own cares and desires, or he is not able to be my disciple. (Psalms 27:10)

27. Whoever does not carry his own cross to follow after me, he is not able to be my disciple. (Mark 8:34)

28. If one of you was planning to build a tower, you would first sit down to count the cost and see if you had the patient endurance to complete it!

29. This is so that after you have laid the foundations, you will not run out and lack the ability to finish it! Then all that see you would mock you and say, (Matthew 13:21-22)

30. this man began to build but did not have the ability to complete what he has started! (Romans 13:7)

31. What king after going out to encounter another king concerning war will not first sit down and consider whether he is able with his ten thousand men to defeat the army of twenty thousand that are set against him?

32. If not, yet while that king is still far away, wouldn't he send an ambassador to work out the terms of peace? (Isaiah 27:5; 2 Peter 3:14; Romans 2:10; James 3:18)

33. So then, know that everyone who does not forsake all, they are not able to be my disciple.

34. Salt is good. But if that salt becomes tasteless, how will you season your food?

35. It is not fit to be used as soil or manure, but only to be discarded. Let he who has ears, let him hear.

Luke 15

1. All of the tax collectors and sinners began to gather close to Jesus to hear him.

2. So the Pharisees and scribes complained and said, this one accepts sinners and eats with them!

3. Then Jesus spoke to them in a parable and said;

4. What man, if he has a hundred sheep, if one is lost, does not leave the other ninety-nine to go and find that one that is lost?

5. Upon finding it, he would put it on his shoulders and be overjoyed!

6. Then he would come to his house and tell the neighbors, rejoice with me, because I have found my sheep that had been lost!

7. I tell you that the heavens are overjoyed when one sinner turns away from his sin, much more so, than over the other ninety-nine that were not lost and have no sin to turn away from! (1 Peter 4:18; Proverbs 11:31; 1 John 3:8)

8. If a woman has ten gold coins, if she loses one, does she not get a lamp and sweep the floors of her house seeking to find what she has lost until she finds it?

9. When she finds it, she tells her friends and neighbors saying, be joyful for me; I have found the gold coin that I had lost!

10. This same joy is among the messengers (*angels*) of God when one sinner turns away from his sin. *(Yes, it is possible!* - Acts 2:38; John 8:11,31-36; Matthew 18:1-10; Romans 6:1-9; 1 John 3:8-9; 1 John 5:16*)*

11. Then Jesus said, a man had two sons.

12. The younger one said to his father, father, give me the share of your wealth that will be coming to me in the inheritance. So the father divided it and gave his share to him.

13. Then, not long after this, the young son gathered his wealth together and he went into a distant country, but there he wasted through his wealth while living in an improper and unwise way.

14. When he had burned through everything, a severe famine occurred throughout that country and he found himself in great need;

15. So he began to work for a man of that country and he sent him into the fields to feed the pigs.

16. But he was very hungry, so he filled his stomach with the husks from which the pigs ate, because no one gave him any food.

17. But then he came to himself and he said, the slaves of my father always have enough food, yet I am starving and will die here!

18. Then he got up and said, I will go to my father and I will say to him, father, I have done wrong and have sinned against you and against God;

19. I am no longer worthy to be called your son; Please forgive me and take me in as one of your slaves! (*this is the example of repentance - a one-time thing - he did not go prodigal again - Acts 3:19; 2:38*)

20. So he got up and came to his father, but while he was still far away his father saw him and he was very happy, and he was compassionate and he ran to him and began kissing him on his neck!

21. And the son said, Father, I have committed many great sins against you and against God; I am no longer suitable to be called your son; Please forgive me. (*God will forgive you but you must not turn back*)

22. But the father called his slaves and said, bring out some clean clothing and put a ring on his finger and get some sandals for his feet.

23. Now go and kill the fattened calf; Let us eat and celebrate;

24. My son who was dead, now lives again! He was lost, but is now found! So they began to celebrate. (2 Samuel ch.11-12; Romans 11:23)

25. The older son of that man was working in the fields and he came towards the house when he heard the music and saw dancing,

26. so he called one of the servants and asked, what is the reason for all of this?

27. The servant said to him, your younger brother came home! Your father killed the fattened calf, because he received his son back and he is well.

28. Then the older son became angry and did not want to go in, but the father came out and begged him to come in;

29. Then he answered and said to his father, all of these years I have honored you and I have never gone against any of your instructions, but you never even killed a goat so that my friends and I could celebrate!

30. Yet, my brother had wasted his inheritance and was living with the harlots, but when he came, you killed the fatted calf for him!

31. But the father said to him, son, you are always with me and all that I have is yours!

32. So let us celebrate and be joyful, as is right, because your brother was dead but now lives again. He was lost but is now found. (*a comparison to sinners that turn from their sin to convert unto Christ*)

Luke 16

1. Jesus said to his disciples, a certain wealthy man had a treasurer and he accused him of wasting his wealth.

2. So he called to him and said, I have heard something concerning you. Give an account of your stewardship, because it is possible that you can no longer be my treasurer.

3. The treasurer said within himself, what can I do so that my master not take away my position of treasurer from me? I do not have the ability to dig and I am too ashamed to beg.

4. What can I do, so that when I am removed from my position I might find someone to receive me into their home?

5. So he called each of the debtors of his master to come to him and he said to the first, how much do you owe my master?

6. The man said, a hundred gallons of oil. Then he said, take your statement and let's make it fifty.

7. Then he said to another debtor, how much do you owe? And he said, a hundred bushels of wheat; And he said to him, let's make it eighty!

8. So his master praised that unrighteous treasurer, because he acted prudently. You see, the children of this world are more practical than the sons of the light are in this world.

9. I tell you, if you make yourselves to be friends of unrighteous worldly gain, then you have failed to attain the everlasting life. (Matthew 25:34-36)

10. He that is faithful in the smallest things is also faithful in big things, and the one who is unrighteous in the least things is also unrighteous in the bigger things.

11. So if you have not been faithful to God concerning unrighteous worldly gain, (*to turn away from it*) why would he entrust you with the true *(eternal)* wealth?

12. If you have not been faithful with what is not yours, who shall give you something of your own? No servant can serve two masters;

13. Either he will hate one and love the other, or he will cling to one and will despise the other. You can not serve both God and worldly gain. (Matthew 6:24)

14. All of these things were heard by the money loving Pharisees, so they sneered at him.

15. Then Jesus said to them, you are those who justify yourself before men, but God knows your hearts; The things that men hold dearly and are highly prized are an abomination unto God.

Verses 16-18 do not work together and are out of context.
They are sayings of Jesus that are thrown in to get them into the book of Luke.

16. The Mosaic law and prophets foresaw John (the baptizer), and since that time the Kingdom of God is being announced. Everyone who enters therein (to the covenant), shall be treated very poorly (by those of the world). (Matthew 10:25; Luke 17:21)

17. It is easier for the heavens and earth to pass away, than for a single point of the law of God to fail.

18. Everyone who puts away his wife to be joined to another commits adultery, and everyone who weds the husband that put her away also commits adultery. (1 Corinthians 7:15; Matthew 5:31-32)

19. A certain wealthy man who regularly wore a purple robe of fine linen lived joyfully in luxury!

20. There was a man who was a beggar named Lazarus who laid down at the door of the wealthy man, and he was covered in sores!

21. Lazarus was hungry and longed to eat the crumbs that fell from the table of the wealthy man. The dogs came and licked his sores.

22. And it came to be that the poor man died and was carried away by angels unto Abraham's bosom, then the wealthy man also died and was buried.

23. The wealthy man found himself in hell, and he raised his eyes upward while being tormented and he saw Abraham at a great distance, and Lazarus was standing there near him.

24. And he called out saying, father Abraham, have pity on me, and please send Lazarus so that he can dip the tip of his finger in water to drip on my tongue to cool me down! I am in anguish in these flames!

25. But Abraham said, child, remember that you received the best of things your life and Lazarus received only the bad. But now, he is comforted and you are suffering. (Matthew 19:30)

26. Besides that, there is a great chasm between us that can not be crossed, and those who want to pass from here to where you are, they are not able, nor can those from where you are cross over to here!

27. Then the man said, please ask the Father if he will send Lazarus unto my father's house;

28. I have five brothers, so please send him so he might be a witness unto them so that they do not end up in this place of torment.

29. Abraham then said to him, they have Moses and the prophets as a witness, let them hear them!

30. But he said, no father Abraham, only if someone goes to them from the dead will they repent!

31. And he said to him, if they will not hear Moses and the prophets, they will neither be persuaded if someone comes to them from the dead!

Luke 17

1. Then Jesus said to his disciples, it is not impossible for one of you to fall and choose to commit an offence against me *(fall away, commit sin, stumble)*, but woe unto the one that does. (Matthew 18:4-10)

2. It would be better for you if the millstone of a horse were hung around your neck and that you be thrown into the deepest sea, than for one of you to bring the smallest offense against me. This is a warning unto all of you. (Hebrews 10:26-27; Numbers 15:28-31; 2 Peter 2:21-22)

154

3. If your brother commits an offense against you, speak to him about it; If he is truly sorry, forgive him.

4. If he trespasses against you seven times in a day, and seven times that day he sincerely says, I am sorry, then you must forgive him.

5. One of the disciples said to the Lord, give unto us more faith *(trust and dedication)*.

6. Then the Lord said, if you have the trust and dedication of a mustard seed, you will say to this tree, come up from your roots and plant yourself into the sea, and it will obey you!

7. If you have a servant plowing a field or shepherding, if you tell him to come here immediately,

8. and prepare a meal for you and to ready himself to serve you;

9. That servant is not given reward because he did the things that were expected of him to do.

10. It is also the same with you, that when you have done all that I have commanded, then I will say, you truly are obedient servants and you have done what you were required to do. (Hebrews 10:36; Acts 26:20)

11. On the way to Jerusalem, Jesus passed through the middle of Samaria and Galilee.

12. For a time, he remained there in a certain village and he encountered ten men that had leprosy and they stood at a distance,

13. yelling out to him saying, Jesus, master, have compassion on us.

14. Jesus said to them, go and show yourselves to the priests. And while they were on their way, they were cleansed!

15. But one of them, when he realized that he was healed, he returned to Jesus and with a loud voice he glorified God,

16. then he fell on his face at the feet of Jesus and gave thanks unto him; He was a Samaritan!

17. Jesus said to him, were there not ten of you that were cleansed? Where are the other nine?

18. Why have they not returned to give glory unto God, but only you?

19. Then Jesus said to him, may your spirit be uplifted because your dedication has cured you.

20. Then Jesus was asked this question by the Pharisees; When will the kingdom of God come? Jesus answered and said, the kingdom of God will not come with observation,

21. nor will it be said, look, it is here! Because the kingdom of God is within.

22. Jesus said to his disciples, the day will come when you will desire to see me, but you will not be able.

Verses 23-37 look to have been moved to this place and not a part of the original Luke 17 text. These verses have been returned to their proper place in Luke 21:24. (Matthew 24 & Mark 13)

Luke 18

1. Jesus then told a parable to explain that they should always pray and not grow tired.

2. He said, there was a certain judge in the city that did not fear God nor did he respect any man.

3. A widow that came before him said, give me justice from the one who is harming me.

4. But for a time he refused; After a while he said within himself, I do not fear God nor any man,

5. yet this widow troubles me again and again; I will give justice unto her so she does not continue to annoy me.

6. Then the Lord said, hear what this unrighteous judge had said.

7. Will God not bring justice unto his elect who cry unto him day and night in their longsuffering? (Rev 6:10)

8. I tell you that he will bring his justice unto them swiftly. But will I find any dedication *(unto God)* upon the earth when I return? (Matthew 7:21-23)

9. Then he told this parable unto some who trusted by their own judgment that they are righteous but they condemn everyone else. (Romans 2:1)

10. Two men went into the temple to pray; One was a Pharisee and the other was a tax-collector.

11. The Pharisee stood and said to himself while praying, Lord, I thank you that I am not like other people, thieves, adulterers, or even as this tax-collector.

12. I fast two times every week, and I tithe on every bit of gain that I receive. *(self-righteous and prideful)*

13. But the tax-collector stood in the distance and would not even lift up his eyes to the heavens, but he pounded his chest and said, God, be merciful on me, I have been a sinner. (Acts 2:38 - *a repentant heart*)

14. I tell you, this humble man went home that day justified, but all who exalt themselves will be humiliated; Those who humble themselves *(before God)* will be raised up. (Matthew 18:3)

15. There were many that were coming to Jesus with children so that he would spend some time with them.

But the disciples refused to allow them, and Jesus saw this.

16. Then he called them to come unto him and he said, allow the little children to come unto me, and do not reject them; For the kingdom of God is for such as these (*the innocent*). (Matthew 18:1)

17. Truly I tell you, whoever does not take hold of the kingdom of God as a little child will in no way enter therein. (Matthew 18:4; Acts 2:38; Acts 3:19; Romans 6:1-6; John 8:34-36)

The explanation of the previous verses is missing.
Look to Matthew 18:1-10 for clarity & understanding.

18. A certain ruler then asked him, good teacher, what must be observed to inherit everlasting life?

19. Then Jesus said, why is it that you say that I am good? *(did the man know that Jesus is the Christ?)* There is only one that is good, and he is God!

20. You know the commandments; Do not commit adultery; Do not commit murder; Do not commit theft; Do not bring any false testimonies; Revere *(value)* your father and mother.

21. Then the man said, I have kept these things since I was very young.

22. But Jesus said, there is one thing that you are lacking; Take and distribute your possessions unto everyone who is in need. (Matthew 19:21; Mark 10:21) In this you will have treasures in the heavens; Then come and follow me.

23. When he had heard this, he was greatly distressed, because he was extremely wealthy.

24. And when Jesus saw that he was brought to be greatly distressed by these words, he said, it is very difficult for those that have wealth to enter into the kingdom of God. (1 Timothy 6:9)

25. It is easier for a camel to go through the eye of a needle then for a wealthy man to enter into the kingdom of God.

26. All that heard this asked, then who is able to be eternally saved? (Mark 10:26)

27. Jesus said, the things that are impossible with men are possible when you are abiding near God.

28. Then Peter said, Look! We have turned away from everything to follow you.

29. Jesus said to them, truly I tell you, there is no one who has left his home or his parents, or his wife, or his children in this life for the sake of the kingdom of God

30. that will not receive a hundred times more in the approaching everlasting life.

31. Then he took the twelve aside and he said, we are going to Jerusalem and all of the things that have been written by the prophets about me will be fulfilled!

32. I will be given over unto the gentiles and will be mocked, insulted and spit upon;

33. After they have flogged *(whipped)* me, they will kill me. But after the third day, I will rise again! (Matthew 12:40; Jonah 1:17)

34. However, they did not understand what Jesus said at that time because it was hidden from them.

35. When he came close to Jericho, there was a blind man who was sitting on the side of the road begging.

36. When he heard the crowds passing through, he asked what was happening.

37. They told him that Jesus of Nazareth was coming this way.

38. Then the man cried out and said, Jesus, the son of David, have compassion for me! (Psalms 22:24)

39. But the people were yelling at him, telling him to be quiet. Because of this he only cried out much louder; Son of David, have compassion for me!

40. Jesus commanded him to rise up and to come unto him. As he came close to him Jesus asked him,

41. What do you want me to do for you? And the man said, master, that I might be able to see again!

42. Then Jesus said unto him, look up! Your conviction has healed you.

43. Suddenly the man was able to see and he followed Jesus and glorified God! All of the people that had seen this happen praised God.

Luke 19

1. Jesus entered into and then passed through Jericho.

2. There was a man by the name of Zacchaeus; He was the head tax collector and he was very wealthy.

3. He wanted to see who Jesus was, but he was not able because of the large crowd and because he was very short in stature.

4. But he ran up ahead of them and he climbed up into a sycamore tree so that he could see him, because

Jesus was going to pass by that way.

5. As Jesus approached that place, he looked up and saw him and he said, Zacchaeus, quickly come down from there; Today I will be staying with you at your home.

6. So he quickly came down and welcomed him joyfully.

7. When everyone saw this, they murmured and said, he will be lodging with a sinful man!

8. Standing near Jesus, Zacchaeus said to the master, half of my possessions I give to the poor; If I falsely accuse anyone, I repay four-fold.

9. Jesus replied to him, today salvation has come to your home and you shall be a son of Abraham. (Galatians 3:29; John 8:39)

10. I have come to seek out and offer protection *(salvation)* unto those who are lost.

11. After these things were said, Jesus added a parable, because he was nearing Jerusalem and many thought that the kingdom of God would immediately be revealed.

12. A certain noble man took a trip into a distant country to receive for himself a kingdom, and then planned to return again. (*A picture of Christ at his first coming and then at his second coming*)

13. So he called ten of his servants and he gave them ten silver minas, then he said to them, put them to use until I return.

14. But the people of that country hated him and they sent a delegation unto him to say, we will not have you reign over us.

15. When he returned after receiving his kingdom, he called his servants, those unto whom he gave the silver so that he would know what they did with that which they were given.

16. The first said, master, with your mina I gained ten more minas. (Matthew 25:15-28)

17. And then he said, well done my good and faithful servant, you have been faithful in the little things, now I will give you authority over ten cities!

18. Then the second came and said, master, with your mina I gained five more minas.

19. The master said, excellent, you will be given rule over five cities.

20. Then the other came and said, master, I have hidden away your mina in a cloth;

21. I feared because you are a calculating man, gathering that which you have not laid down and reaping where you did not sow.

22. So the master said to him, wicked servant, I will judge you by your own words. (Matthew 12:36) You know that I am a calculating man, that I take what I did not lay down and reap where I did not sow;

23. Why did you not give it to the table (*bankers*), where some interest may have been gathered?

24. The he said, take from him that mina and give it to the one that has ten!

25. And he said to him, but master, he already has ten minas!

26. I tell you, everyone that has, more shall be given; But he that does not have, even what he has will be taken from him. (*the minas represent God's wisdom*)

27. Concerning those enemies who would not have me reign over them, bring them to me and execute them before me. *(judgment day)*

28. After he said these things, he led them on his way to Jerusalem.

29. As he began to come near to Bethphage and Bethany, in the direction of the mount of Olives,

30. he sent two of his disciples to go into the opposite village from where they had entered, and he said, you will find a colt of which no man has ever sat upon; Loosen it and bring it to me.

31. If anyone asks what are you doing, tell them that the master has need of it.

32. Those that he sent went and found it, just as he told them.

33. When they loosened the colt, the owner said to them, why are you untying my colt?

34. They said, the master has need of it.

35. Then they led it to Jesus, and threw some of their clothing on the colt and they helped Jesus get on it.

36. As he was going, the people began throwing their clothing on the roadway.

37. As they drew near, he was already below the mount of olives and all of the multitude of disciples were rejoicing and praising God with loud voices concerning all of the powerful things that they had seen.

38. Then they sang, blessed is he who comes in the name of the Lord! Peace in the heavens and glory unto the highest places! (Psalms 118:26)

39. Some of the Pharisees from the crowd said to him, teacher, forbid your disciples.

40. Jesus answered them and said, I tell you, if they were to be silent, the stones will cry out!

41. As they came near with the city in sight, he cried over it and said; (Luke 13:34)

42. If only you would have known! Truly this day will be remembered, but the way unto peace *(with God)* has been hidden from your eyes!

43. Soon there will come a day when your enemies will prepare for a military siege against you. They will surround you and they will keep you in on all sides; (Daniel 9:25-27; Romans 9:27-28)

44. They will cut you down, as well as your children, and they will not leave one stone upon another, because you did not recognize the time of your visitation *(Christ)*. (Luke 21:6)

Verses 43-44 must be understood through the light of the prophecies
that are written in the old testament scriptures;
Daniel 9, Jeremiah 7 & Isaiah 10:21-23 give a more complete understanding of the subject.
Considering these prophecies is necessary in order to understand the happenings of 70 AD,
including the destruction of Jerusalem and the temple.
Here is one of the prophecies properly translated.
Now it all lines up perfectly.

Daniel 9:24-27

"...Seventy weeks (490 years) are set for this nation and upon Jerusalem,
to finish their transgressions, stop committing sin,
make reconciliation for defiance against God,
to establish everlasting righteousness, complete the old covenant, fulfill the prophecies,
and to anoint the most holy one (Christ).
...Know therefore and understand that from the command to rebuild Jerusalem
(after the Babylonian captivity 420 BC - 2 Chronicles 36:22-23)
until the arrival of the chosen military commander there shall be sixty-nine weeks;
The streets will be rebuilt again and the walls, even in difficult times.
In the last half of the sixty second week (431 years at 11 AD)
the Messiah (Jesus Christ) will cut off (bring an end to) the old (Mosaic) covenant
(Luke 2:42-47; Luke 3:9) but not because of his own negligence unto the covenant.
The troops of the military commander shall come and destroy the city and the sanctuary;
The end will be as an overflowing deluge
and the war of desolations are determined until all shall be completed.
And he (the military commander) shall make a peace agreement
with many for the final week
and in the last part of that seven-year period he will bring the sacrifices
and offerings to be stopped
because of the extreme filth and he will destroy
until the completion of all that is determined (by God)
will be poured out upon those that will be desolated (destroyed)."

Jesus was born – Sept/Oct 2 BC
Herod died – January 1 BC
Jesus in the temple – March/April 11 AD
Jesus' ministry begins – Jan-April 27AD-29 AD
Jesus put to death – March/April 30 AD
Military leader arrives in Jerusalem – August 63 AD
7-year peace agreement begins – December 63 AD
Jerusalem destroyed – August 70 AD

There was 40 years before entering the promised land.
There was also 40 years from Christ's resurrection until the destruction of Jerusalem.

45. Jesus entered into the temple, and he began to throw out those that were buying and selling. (Revelation 13:17 - *the faithful are not to be buying or selling in either instance*)

46. Then he said to them, it has been written, "this house is a house of prayer, but you have made it into a den of thieves!" (Isaiah 56:7; Jeremiah 7:11)

47. Jesus taught that day in the temple, even though the scribes and Pharisees and the elders of the people were seeking to kill him,

48. but they did not know how to, because the people were always near listening to him.

Luke 20

1. Jesus was teaching the people in the temple and announcing how to live according to the gospel, when the high priests, scribes and some of the elders approached him,

2. and they asked him, tell us, who gave you authority to do this? (*who gave you permission to teach*)

3. Jesus answered and said, I will ask you one question first;

4. Tell me, the baptism of John, was it ordained by God, or of men? (*Jesus makes a distinction*)

5. Then they deliberated among themselves saying, if we say it was ordained by God, then he will say, why did you not believe him?

6. If we say he was of men, the people will stone us because they are convinced that John was a prophet.

7. So they answered Jesus and said, we do not know!

8. Then Jesus said to them, neither will I tell you who gave me authority to do this.

9. Jesus began to speak a parable unto the people: A certain man planted a vineyard, and he turned it over to the husbandmen (*ancient Israel*), and then he went away for a period of time. (Isaiah 5:1-7; Matthew 21:33; Mark 12:1; John 15:1)

10. At the proper time, he sent a servant (*a prophet*) unto those husbandmen to receive the fruit of the vineyard but the husbandmen beat him and sent him away empty handed!

11. Then he sent more servants (*more prophets*), but they dishonored and beat them and sent them away empty handed.

12. But then he sent other servants (*prophets*), but they also did much harm to them and threw them out!

13. Then the master of that vineyard (*God*) asked, what must I do? I will send my own son (*Jesus Christ*), my beloved! Surely they will respect him. (John 15:1)

14. When those husbandmen saw him, they plotted among themselves and said, this is the heir; Let us kill him and we shall keep the proceeds for ourselves!

15. So they threw him out of the vineyard and they killed him! Now what do you think the owner of that vineyard will do to those husbandmen?

16. Surely he will come and destroy them *(70 A.D.)* and he will give the vineyard to others (*gentiles*). When they heard this they said, let it not be! *(they understood)*

17. And Jesus looked at them and he said, look, it is written in the scriptures; "The stone that the builders rejected, yet he will become the foremost foundation stone." (Isaiah 28:16)

18. Everyone that falls upon this stone will be gathered unto me and remolded, but whoever that stone comes down upon will be ground to powder (*destroyed*).

19. The high priests and the scribes were tempted to arrest him at that time, but they feared the people. They knew that the parable that he told was a condemnation of them.

20. So they watched him carefully, and they sent spies who were pretending to be righteous, so that they might catch him in his words, so they could deliver him up to the power and jurisdiction of the rulers.

21. So they asked him questions, saying, teacher, we know that you speak and teach the truth and that you do not look at the outward appearance of a man but that you teach the ways of God;

22. So is it lawful for us to pay taxes unto Caesar, yes or no?

23. Jesus perceived the slyness that was in them, and he said unto them, why do you tempt me?

24. Show me a silver denarius. Whose image and inscription is on that coin? They said, Caesar.

25. Jesus said unto them, give unto Caesar that which is Caesar's, but give unto God that which is God's.

26. They were not able to arrest him due to his words unto the people and they were shocked at his answer so they remained silent.

27. Then some of the Sadducees came unto him; They do not believe in the resurrection of the dead; They asked him a question and said;

28. Teacher, Moses wrote unto us that if any man has a brother that dies while having a wife, if she is childless, that he should take in his brother's wife and raise up offspring unto his brother.

29. So if there were seven brothers, and the first had a wife but he died childless;

30. Then the second took the wife and then he died childless; Then the third took her;

31. Then the same happened unto all seven and none of them left any children when they died;

32. Finally the woman also died;

33. In the resurrection, which of them shall have her as a wife, since all seven have had her as their wife!

34. Jesus answered them and said, the sons of this world go and become wed,

35. but those who are counted as being completely deserving of the world to come and unto the resurrection of the dead, they will not become wed nor will they be given to be wed;

36. They will be like the angels of God, as they will not be able to die; They will be the sons of God, being the sons of the resurrection. (1 John 3:1-2; Genesis 6:1-2)

37. But even Moses makes it clear at the burning bush that the dead will be raised; He calls the Lord, the God of Abraham, Isaac and Jacob! (Exodus 3:6)

38. God is not a god of the dead, but the God of the living! For all that are in him will live.

39. One of the scribes answered him and said, teacher, you have said truth.

40. They no longer dared to question him anymore, not a thing!

41. And Jesus said unto them, how can it be that it is said that the Christ is the son of David?

42. Even David himself said in the book of the Psalms, the Lord *(Father God)* says unto my Lord *(Jesus Christ)*, sit at my right hand,

43. until I make your enemies be put under your feet!

44. You see, David called him *(the Messiah)* Lord, so how can he be his son?

45. Then all of the people listened while Jesus told his disciples

46. to be very cautious of the scribes and those who love walking around in white robes, love to be greeted in the marketplaces and have the best seats in the synagogues and at dinner parties;

47. Quietly, they steal away the houses from widows, and under false pretenses they publicly say long prayers for those whose houses they have taken. They will receive much more severe damnation. (2 Peter 2:21-22)

Luke 21

1. Jesus looked up and saw some wealthy men taking their gifts to the treasury;

2. Then he saw a widow as she put in two small copper coins!

3. He said, truly I tell you, this poor widow has contributed more than all of the others,

4. because they have given out of their abundance of wealth, however she gave out of her poverty all that she had, to be a gift unto God.

5. Then some of the disciples began speaking about the temple and how it is decorated by many beautiful stones and has been adorned with many wonderful gifts.

6. But Jesus said, there will soon come a day when all that you see will be destroyed, and there will not be one stone remaining upon another. (Luke 19:43-44)

7. And they asked him and said, teacher, when will that happen, *(and what will be the sign of your return and the end of the world? - Matthew 24:3)*

Luke 21:8-28 note:
The book of Luke was written about 110 AD, well after the destruction of Jerusalem in 70 AD
The author of the book of Luke or a later scribe has misunderstood and misapplied
these prophecies that are meant for the time just before the return of Christ
and has errantly applied them to what they had seen
at the time of the destruction of Jerusalem at 70 AD
This is verifiable by the parallel accounts of Matthew 24 & Mark 13.
Where possible these errors have been corrected in the following text.

* In this chapter, the bold verses should be attributed to the destruction of Jerusalem in 70 AD.
All that is not bold should be understood to be in the final days.

8. And Jesus said, watch carefully so that you are not deceived, because many will come claiming to be of me, saying that I am the Christ; (*yet they will deceive many* - Matthew 24:5)
(Acts 20:30; Jeremiah 23:1-40; Jude 1:4; 2 Corinthians 11:13-15; Isaiah 56:10-11; Ezekiel 22:28)
9. When you hear of rumors of war and disorder, do not be afraid, because these things must first happen, but this is not yet the end.
10. Nations shall rise up against other nations, and kingdoms against their own people;
11. Great earthquakes will happen in many places and there will be famines and plagues (*pandemics*). There will also be fearful things happening in the sky. (Revelation 13:13)
12. They will lay their hands upon you and they will persecute you (*followers of Christ*) and take you unto their courts and send some of you to prison, and you will be taken before kings and governors, all because of your testimony of me! (Revelation 13:7)
13. They will look unto you for your testimony.
14. Do not think about what you will say before the time comes, so to make a defense.
15. I will give you wise words that those who oppose you will not be able to deny, nor argue against.
16. You will be betrayed by parents and brothers and relatives and friends, and they will put many of you to death. (Matthew 10:36; Mark 13:12; Micah 7:6; Revelation 13:7)
17. You will be hated by everyone, because of my name in you.
(Matthew 10:22; 24:9; Mark 13:13; John 15:18)
18. But the *(eternal)* crown on your head will not be taken from you.
19. Through your patient continuance (*faithfulness*), you will obtain your soul.
(Matthew 24:13; Revelation 14:12)
20. When you see armies encircling around Jerusalem, know that its destruction is close. *
21. Those who are of Jehovah, must flee to the mountains, and those in the remote places must not go back for supplies. (Ezekiel 7:16; Matthew 24:16; Mark 13:14)
22. Because these are the days of vengeance, and in them all of what is written concerning them will be fulfilled. * (Jeremiah 7; Daniel 9:24-27)
23. But woe unto those who are pregnant and with young children in those days, because there will be great distress throughout the whole earth, **and wrath upon these people. *** (*those of Judea*)
24. They will fall by the sword and be taken unto all nations, and Jerusalem will be trampled down by the gentiles until their occupation is completed. *(Daniel 9:25-27)

The proper placement of Luke 17:23-37...

23. Some will tell you, Christ is here, or he is there! Do not follow after them. (Matthew 24:26)
24. Just as lightning flashes and lights up across the whole sky, it will be similar in the day of my return. (Matthew 24:30; Acts 1:11)
25. **But first I must suffer many things and be rejected by my own people. ***
26. As it was in the days of Noah, it will also be similar in the days before I return. (Matthew 24:37)
27. They were eating and drinking, and taking wives, and planning for their futures, even until the day that Noah entered into the ark and the floods came, but it destroyed them all! (Matthew 24:37; Genesis 6)
28. It also was the same in the days of Lot, as they were eating and drinking and buying and selling, and planting and building;
29. But on the day that Lot went out from Sodom, it rained fire and brimstone from the sky, and it destroyed them all! (Revelation 8:10; Matthew 24:29)
30. It will be done in this way when the son of man returns.
31. On that day, those in the tall buildings, do not gather your belongings, nor take them with you; Those in the countryside must not return to the towns to get their things. (Matthew 24:17; Mark 13:15)
32. Remember Lot's wife!
33. Whoever seeks to save his own life will lose it, and those who lose their lives (*for my name sake*) will be preserved. (Matthew 10:39; Mark 8:35)
34. I tell you, in the night there will be two people in a bed, one will be forsaken by God and the other gathered unto immortality.

161

35. Two will be working together and one will be forsaken by God and the other will be gathered unto immortality.

36. Two will be in the fields, and one will be forsaken by God and the other gathered unto immortality.

37. Then Jesus said, wherever the wholesome ones are, they will be gathered together with the eagles (*in the air*). (1 Thessalonians 4:17; Matthew 24:28)

Continuing with chapter 21...

25. There will be signs in the sun, moon and the stars. There will be great perplexities on earth and the sound of the oceans will be great due to the raging waves. (Revelation 8:5-9; Revelation 16:3)

26. The people will be helpless due to the fearful anticipation of the things that are coming upon the earth; Because the powers in the sky will bring a great shaking. (Isaiah 13:9-13; Revelation 8:5-10:6; Matthew 24:29)

27. Then they will see the son of man coming in the clouds of the sky with much power and honor.

28. When these things begin to happen, stand up and lift up your heads, because your deliverance is close at hand.

29. Then he told them a parable: See the fig tree and all of the other trees; (Matthew 24:32)

30. When the leaves begin to sprout, know within yourselves that the summer is close.

31. Just the same, when you see these things beginning to happen, know that the kingdom of God is near.

32. Truly I tell you, that generation will not pass away until all things are completed. (Revelation 10:6; Daniel 12:7, 13)

33. The heavens and earth shall pass away, but my words will never fail.

34. Be careful to not be weighed down in your hearts with the cares of this world or drunkenness, nor the stresses of life, because that day will suddenly come. (2 Thessalonians 5:2-5)

35. It will come upon everyone that is living upon the face of the earth.

36. Be watchful at all times, live according to the way that is deserving to be spared from all of the things that will happen upon the earth. (Revelation 3:10) Therefore, stand honorably before the son of man.

37. Jesus went to the temple to teach, and at night he slept on the mountain called the mount of olives.

38. Many of the people rose up early to hear him in the temple.

Luke 22

1. The feast of unleavened bread was coming soon, of which is called Passover.

2. The high priests and scribes were conspiring as to how they could kill him, but they feared the people.

3. But the adversary arose up within Judas Iscariot; He was one of the twelve.

4. He went and spoke with the high priests and the leaders concerning how Jesus might be taken by them.

5. When they were satisfied, they came into an agreement to give him thirty pieces of silver.

6. Judas fully consented and looked for an opportunity to turn him over to them at a time when Jesus would be away from the crowds.

7. The day of unleavened bread came, of which was the day that the passover lamb must be killed.

8. Jesus sent Peter and John, telling them to go and prepare the Passover so they could eat.

9. They asked him, where shall we prepare it?

10. Jesus said to them, pay attention: You will go into the city and you will see a man carrying a pitcher of water; Follow him into the house he enters.

11. You will tell the master of the house, the teacher asks where your guest room is in which his disciples can prepare the Passover and they can eat it?

12. He will send his servant to show you the upper room that is large enough for you to prepare it.

13. When they went and found all as he had said, they prepared the Passover meal.

14. When the time came, he sat down with the twelve disciples.

15. Jesus said, with great longing I have looked forward to eat this meal with you before I shall suffer.

16. I tell you, never again will I eat until all is fulfilled concerning the kingdom of God. (verse 30)

17. He took the cup and he gave thanks and said, take this and divide it among yourselves;

18. I tell you that I will not drink from the fruit of the vine until the kingdom of above is established.

19. He took the bread and he gave thanks, then he broke it and gave it to them; H said, my body is given for you to live *(eternally)*, commit this unto your memory.

20. In the same way, he took the cup after they ate and said, my cup (*destiny*) is this: My blood shall be

poured out for you, this is for the new covenant *(contract offer between God and man)*

21. Be aware that the hand of the one who will betray me is with me at this table.

22. Truly the son of man shall go according to how it has been determined; But woe unto the man by whom he is betrayed! (Matthew 18:6-10; Numbers 15:30-31; Hebrews 6:4-6; Hebrews 10:26-29)

23. The disciples began asking among themselves, who could it be among us that could do such a thing?

Verses 24-34 are out of context in this place.

24. Then there arose a dispute among them as to which of them was the leader;

25. But Jesus said, kings of the gentiles lord over the people, those with authority are called benefactors.

26. But it shall not be that way with you. The greatest among you must be the least. The leader is the greatest servant.

27. Who is greater, the one sitting to a meal or the one serving him? It is not the one being served! I am here with you as a servant! (verse 19)

28. You are the ones that have remained with me through much difficulty and hardship;

29. Now I appoint you, the same as the Father appointed me,

30. so that you may eat and drink at my table in my kingdom; You will sit on twelve thrones judging the twelve tribes of Israel. (Revelation 4:4)

31. Then the Lord said to Simon, Simon, know that Satan demands that he grind you like wheat,

32. but I offer petitions on your behalf so that your dedication (*commitment*) not fail. When you have denied me, your brethren will strengthen you.

33. Simon (*Peter*) said to him, I am ready to go to prison with you, and even unto death!

34. But Jesus said, I tell you Peter, the rooster will not crow before you deny me three times. (Mark 14:30)

Verses 35-36 and 38 look to have been added by a scribe;
They are out of context, contradict many other scriptures
and are not part of the original text. (Matthew 26:52)

35. And Jesus said to them, remember when I sent you out without a bag, without money and without shoes? Were you needy of anything? They said, nothing!

36. And he said to them, but now if you have a purse or a wallet, bring it with you;
(Matthew 7:7; John 14:13; John 15:7) If you do not have a sword, sell your coat and buy one, you must have a sword. (Matthew 26:52; Revelation 13:10)

38. They said unto him, Lord, here are two swords. And he said to them, that will be enough.
(Matthew 26:52; Revelation 13:10; Romans 8:36; Luke 6:29; Matthew 5:39)

37. I tell you, all that has been written (*concerning the Christ*) is to be fulfilled in me, "he shall be counted with the wicked."
(Isaiah 53:12) These things *(prophecies)* that are concerning me have a conclusion. (1 Corinthians 13:8)

39. And Jesus, as he was accustomed to doing, went unto the mount of olives and his disciples followed.

40. When they had gotten there Jesus said to them, pray that you not fall when you are tempted (*tested*).

41. Then Jesus walked about a stone's throw away from them and he got down his knees and he prayed.

42. He said, Father, if you will, take this cup from me! But not my will be done, but your will be done.

The information in verses 43-44 is doubtful, as Matthew and John,
two of only eleven witnesses have not passed on this information, but these verses look
to be added by a scribe in the second century. Additionally, if the angel strengthened him,
why would he be more anguished; If the disciples were all sleeping, who was the witness to this?

43. And an angel appeared from heaven and strengthened him. (2 Corinthians 12:10; Habakkuk 3:19)

44. And he had become anguished, and he prayed more intently! And his sweat became as drops of blood as they fell to the earth.

45. As he rose up from prayer, he came to the disciples and found them sleeping,

46. Jesus asked, why are you sleeping? Get up and pray so that you do not fall when temptation comes!

47. But while he was speaking, a crowd was coming and Judas Iscariot, one of the twelve was leading them and he came close to Jesus and he kissed him. (Matthew 26:47; John 18:3; Mark 14:43)

48. But Jesus said to him, Judas, do you betray the son of man with a kiss?

49. When those with him saw what was about to happen, they said, Lord shall we fight with the sword?

50. Then one of them struck a servant of the high priest, cutting off his right ear. (Matthew 26:51)

51. But Jesus said, allow it to be; Then he touched his ear and healed him.

52. Then Jesus asked the commanders, high priests and the elders that came upon him, why did you come unto me as you would a thief, with swords and clubs?

53. Many times I was in the temple and you did not reach out your hands to take me? But now you take me under the cover of darkness (*night time*)!

54. When they arrested him, they led him away and took him to the house of the high priest, and Peter followed from a distance.

55. A fire was burning in the middle of the court, and Peter sat among them.

56. There was a female servant that saw him near the light of the fire; She began staring at him and said, this man was with him!

57. But Peter denied and said, woman I do not know him!

58. A short time later when seeing Peter, another said, you are one of them! But Peter said, I am not!

59. After an hour went by, another boldly charged him saying, truly I saw this man with him, and notice that he is also a Galilean!

60. Peter said, I do not agree with what you say. Immediately while he was speaking, the rooster crowed!

61. Then the Lord turned and looked at Peter. Then Peter remembered the prophecy that the Lord had said, that a rooster would not crow until you would deny me three times!

62. Then Peter went outside and cried bitterly.

(Peter denied Jesus afraid and without thinking - Numbers 15:28-31; 1 John 5:16-17)

63. The men that were guarding Jesus mocked him;

64. Having blindfolded him, they beat him, hitting him in the face and then they mocked him saying, prophesy unto us; Who is it that hit you?

65. They also blasphemed him concerning many other things.

66. When the daylight came, a group of elders, high priests and scribes took him before the Sanhedrin.

67. They said, if you are the Christ, tell us. And Jesus said, if I tell you, you would not believe me,

68. and if I answer you anything, you will not release me.

69. The son of man shall now be sitting at the right hand of the power of God.

70. Then they asked, are you saying that you are the son of God? And he said to them, you asked me that because you know that I am!

71. Then they said, why do we need of any further witnesses? For we have heard it from his own mouth!

Luke 23

1. Then they got up and took him to Pilate.

2. There they began to accuse him, and said, we found him perverting the nation and he refuses to pay tax unto Caesar, claiming that he himself is a king;

3. So Pilate interrogated him and asked, are you the king of the Jews? Jesus said, you have it correct.

4. Then Pilate said to the high priests and the crowds, I have found nothing! This man is blameless.

5. But they insisted and they said, he is from Galilee and has come unto this place to stir up the people and he teaches throughout all of Judea.

6. When Pilate heard that Jesus was Galilean, he asked, is he of Galilee?

7. Knowing that he was from Herod's jurisdiction, he decided to send Jesus to him, as Herod was in Jerusalem at that time. *(jurisdiction is very important - help in time of need page 372 - educational-legal)*

8. When Herod saw Jesus he was very pleased, as he was desiring to meet him for a long time due to the many things that he had heard about him. He hoped to see some miracle done by him.

9. So he asked him many questions, but Jesus did not answer him, not a word.

10. The high priests and scribes stood aggressively accusing him.

11. To humiliate him, Herod had his soldiers put upon him a luxurious robe, then sent him back to Pilate.

12. On that day Pilate and Herod became friends, but before this they were enemies against each other.

13. Pilate called the high priests and the elders of the people to come together

14. and he said to them, you have brought before me a man that you claim is perverting the people, but I have examined him in your presence and I have found nothing to accuse this man of concerning the charges that you have brought against him; Neither has Herod!

15. I sent him up to Herod and it is determined that he has done nothing deserving of death!

16. I will discipline him and then release him.

17. Due to a custom, he had the necessity to release one prisoner at the feast.

18. But the Jews shouted, kill him and release Barabbas!

19. Barabbas had been thrown in prison because he committed murder during one of the revolts in the city.

20. Then again Pilate tried to release Jesus;

21. But they shouted and yelled, crucify him; Crucify him!

22. And a third time Pilate said unto them, what evil has he done? I have found no cause for death in him, so I will discipline him and then release him!

23. But they started pushing harder and louder for him to be crucified! The voices of the high priests prevailed. (Isaiah 53:5)

24. So Pilate gave the sentence, that it should be accomplished according to their demands!

25. He released unto them the one who committed murder during the revolt and was thrown into prison, the one whom they asked for; Then he sent Jesus to be crucified as they had demanded.

26. As they took him, they grabbed a Cyrenian man named Simon who was coming in from the fields, and they coerced him to carry the cross of Jesus on his back. (John 19:17)

27. A large group of people followed behind him and the women were crying and mourning.

28. Jesus turned and said to them, daughters of Jerusalem, do not cry for me; Cry for yourselves and for your children!

29. Know this, there will soon come a day when they will say blessed are they that are unable to have children and the breasts that have never fed children.

30. "Because of sin, Israel shall be destroyed: (Daniel 9:24-27; Jeremiah 7:29-34) The thorn and thistle will come up upon their alters."

31. If they do these things when the living tree is with them, what will they do when the tree is dead?

32. There were two criminals that were put with him to be executed. (Jeremiah 7:29-34)

33. They were brought unto the place called skulls (*Golgotha*) and the criminals were crucified with him, one on his right and one on his left. (Matthew 27:38)

34. Jesus said, forgive them Father, because they do not understand what they are doing. *(speaking of the Romans* - Numbers 15:28-31; 1 John 5:16-17) And they divided his clothes and cast lots for his robe. (Psalms 22:18)

35. The people that stood watching scoffed at him, as did the leaders; They said, he helped others; If he is the Christ, the elect of God, let him help himself.

36. The soldiers also mocked him. Then vinegar was offered unto him.

37. Some said, if you are the king of the Jews, save yourself.

38. There was an inscription placed above him written in Greek, Hebrew and Latin which said; This is the king of the Jews.

**Verses 39-43 contradict the accounts of Isaiah, Matthew, Mark and John
and should be seen as unreliable. Luke himself was not a witness to these events. (Luke 1:1-3)
The book of Luke was written about 110 AD based upon second and third hand witnesses.
Because of this, these verses have not been included in this text.
(Matthew 27:44; Mark 15:27-32; Hebrews 12:3; Isaiah 53:12; John 19)
Additionally, it is often recognized in Christendom that no doctrine should be established based
upon only one scripture, that there must be at least two or three witness scriptures to establish a
doctrine. However, many false doctrines have been established, based upon these errant verses
with no secondary witnesses unto them, yet there are startling opposing witnesses!
For these reasons, these verses should not be used to establish any doctrine.**

Luke 23:43
"This day you will be with me in Paradise"

{Note: Greek word # 3857 "Paradeiso" is same as in 2 Corinthians 12:4}
After his death, Jesus went to hell to preach to the souls there, as stated in many other scriptures.
After he had risen, he told Mary Magdalene that he had not yet ascended to his Father.
In John 16:16 Jesus makes it clear that he will not go to the Father until after his resurrection.
Therefore, he could not have said what is stated in these now deleted verses, because he can not lie.
(John 16:16; John 20:17; 1 Peter 3:18-19; Psalms 16:10; Jonah 2:2;
Acts 2:27-33; Matthew 12:40; Matthew 27:44)

Furthermore, is it reasonable to believe that a self-admitted thief
would be a follower of Christ and that he would have more understanding
concerning Jesus and his kingdom than the disciples of Jesus had at that time?
Not according to the other accounts that clearly say that both criminals mocked him.

44. About the sixth hour of the day *(noon)*, darkness fell upon all the land until the ninth hour (3 PM).
45. The sun was darkened, and the veil in the temple was torn in two, right up the middle.
46. And yelling out with a loud voice, Jesus said, Father, I return my spirit into your hands.
When he had said this, he breathed out his spirit;
47. When the centurion saw this happen, he glorified God and said, truly this man was righteous.
48. All of the other people came together and after seeing what had happened they beat their breasts as they turned back *(they became prideful and arrogant)*.
49. All that had known him stood at a distance. The women that had accompanied him from Galilee saw all of this.
50. Be aware of this; A man by the name of Joseph of Arimathea was an advisor and was a righteous man
51. that did not agree with the decisions or the action of the council; He was eagerly expecting that he would enter into the kingdom of God;
52. He came before Pilate and requested that he be given the body of Jesus.
53. So he took him down and he wrapped him in linen cloth and placed him in a tomb that no one had ever been laid in.
54. It was the day of preparation, and the Sabbath holy day *(holiday)* was quickly approaching.
55. The women that came with him from Galilee chose to watch over the tomb that his body was laid in.
56. They brought with them, spices and ointment.

Luke 24

1. They rested on that Sabbath day, as was commanded in the law of Moses. On the first day of the week *(Sunday)* while it was still very early, they returned to the tomb and they brought the fragrances that they had prepared with them.
2. When they got there, they saw that the stone had been rolled away from the tomb.
3. Then they went in, but they did not see the body of Jesus,
4. and they became very upset at this. Then they saw two figures who were standing there in bright shining clothing. (John 20:12; Matthew 28:3; Mark 16:5)
5. They became terrified and put their faces to the ground. They said to them, why are you looking for the living among the dead?
6. He is not here, but has been resurrected! Remember when you were in Galilee he told you of this?
7. Remember when he said, the son of man will be given over into the hands of wicked men and he will be crucified, but on the third day he will rise again! (Psalms 22:16)
8. Do you remember his words?
9. When they returned from the tomb they told the news of these things to all of the eleven and everyone else that was there. (John 20:2; Matthew 28:7; Mark 16:8)
10. The women were Mary Magdalene, Joanna, Mary the mother of James and several other women who sat with them and they told the disciples of these things.

11. But their words seemed like worthless talk so they did not believe them.

12. Then Peter stood up and he ran to the tomb. When he bent down he saw the linens lying there, he went to a place alone to think about what might have happened! (John 20:2)

13. Two of them were heading to a distant village on that day of which was sixty stadia *(fifteen miles)* from Jerusalem, called Emmaus.

14. They talked to one another concerning all that had occurred.

15. As they were talking about these things, Jesus began to walk with them,

16. but their eyes did not look up to recognize him.

17. He asked them, what are you speaking about between yourselves and why do you appear so sad?

18. And one, whose name was Cleopas said to him, are you a stranger unto Jerusalem, not knowing of the things that have just happened in the past few days?

19. But Jesus asked, what things? And they said, all that happened to Jesus of Nazareth; The man was a prophet who did many powerful deeds and he spoke unto all of the people in the presence of God!

20. He was betrayed unto death by the high priests and the leaders of the people, then they crucified him!

21. We were hoping that he was the one who would free Israel. Today is only the fourth day since all of these things happened. (John 8:34-36)

22. Then this morning, some of the women astounded us after having gone to the tomb very early.

23. When they did not find his body they came and told us they had seen a vision of angels that said that he is alive!

24. Some of the others went to the tomb and they found it like the women had said, but he was not there!

25. Then Jesus said to them, oh foolish ones, you are slow in your hearts to commit your trust according to all of the things that the prophets have said!

26. Was the Christ not meant to suffer these things and to be made glorious?

27. From Moses and throughout all of the prophets, he explained unto them by all of the scriptures many things about himself.

28. As they were approaching the village where they were heading, he appeared to be continuing onward.

29. But they compelled him to stay and they said, stay with us, because it is almost evening time, the end of the day. And he went and stayed with them.

30. As he was sitting with them, he took the bread and blessed it, and he broke it and gave it to them,

31. and their eyes were opened and they recognized him, but then he disappeared from their sight.

32. Then they said to one another, our hearts were burning as he spoke to us on the road, and he opened up our understandings to the scriptures.

33. They immediately got up and headed back to Jerusalem and they found the eleven gathered together.

34. Then they said to them, the master truly is raised and he appeared to Simon!

35. He told us many things on the way and he was seen by them in the breaking of the bread!

36. As they were saying these things, Jesus himself appeared among them and he said, be at peace!

37. They were terrified, and fear overtook them as they thought that they saw a spirit!

38. Then he said to them, why are you so troubled? Why does doubt rise up in your hearts?

39. Look at my hands and my feet! I am he! Look closely at me, a spirit does not have flesh and bones like you can see that I certainly have. (Psalms 22:16)

40. Then he offered to them his hands and his feet.

41. Yet still they did not believe their eyes, but they were joyful and were admiring.

Verses 42-43 contradict the words of Jesus
written in Luke 22:16, Matthew 26:29 and Mark 14:25.
All was not yet fulfilled at this time, since Jesus had not yet ascended
to the kingdom of his Father, and his spirit was not yet given. (Acts 1-2)

And Jesus said to them, do you have anything to eat here?
42. And they gave him a broiled fish and a honey comb,
43. and he took from them and he ate.

44. He said, the words that I spoke to you, do you still remember them, that all of the things that have been written in the law of Moses and by the prophets and in the Psalms about me, they have been fulfilled.

45. So he opened up their minds to understand the scriptures;

167

46. Then he said to them, it has been written that the Christ must suffer and that he must be raised up from the dead after three days.

47. Then he explained repentance, baptism and the remission of sins through his name, (John 8:31-37; Acts 2:38; 3:19; Romans 6:1-23) and that they shall go forth unto all nations, beginning at Jerusalem. (Matthew 28:19-20)

48. You are witnesses of these things.

49. Be aware, I shall send forth the promise of the Father unto you *(the spirit of the holy one)*, but you must remain in Jerusalem until you are engulfed with the power from above.

50. He walked out with them unto Bethany and he lifted up his hands and he gave a blessing unto them.

51. While he was offering a blessing, he was taken from them and was carried up into the heavens.

52. They praised him and returned unto Jerusalem with great joyfulness,

53. and they continued living in the holy way, truly blessing and praising God.

An overview of the book of Luke

When considering the prophecies, (Acts 20:29-31) that corruption of the history and doctrines would soon happen, of which was already happening when the book of Luke was being written, and that the book of Luke was based upon the accounts of many unreliable second and third hand witnesses, it should be no surprise that there are many inaccuracies and contradictions in Luke when compared with other scriptures. Many of these accounts in the book of Luke were not put together in an organized way. Many of the teachings of Jesus have been thrown together with no storyline and are lacking correspondence from verse to verse in many places. There is also no order according to the chronological placement of events. Many verses within the book of Luke have been used to promote a variety of the false doctrines that made their way in to the churches as early as the early second century. It is also recognized by most scholars and seen in the early manuscripts that this book was altered by scribes continually for at least a century after it was originally written. In the book of Luke, it becomes obvious that an effort was made to be complete and list all of the sayings of Jesus, however many are inaccurate and incomplete, and are often forced together with no organized reasoning, nor purpose except to get them into the book. This is not to say that the book of Luke is not valuable, but that when there are inconsistencies, and there are many, we must trust the accounts that are from the eyewitnesses, Matthew and John. (John 14:26 - This was said to the disciples not the latecomers).

There was a man named Luke that is spoken of in the scriptures, though it is unlikely that the book of Luke was written by him.

The Acts of the Apostles

Chapter 1

1. Oh Theophilus, the first letter I wrote concerned all that Jesus did and taught,

2. and the precepts of how to live, that were given unto the apostles that he selected and taught until the day that he ascended up;

3. It also included all that he spoke about the kingdom of God. He showed himself alive with much certain evidence over forty days that were witnessed by many people after his suffering.

4. When Jesus came to them, he told them to remain in Jerusalem and not leave there, "but to await the promise of the Father, all of which you have been told of by me;

5. John baptized in water, moreover (G-1161), you will also be baptized by the spirit of the holy one, in not very many days." (John 3:5; John 20:22)

6. Then they came together and asked him, Lord, will you restore the kingdom of Israel at that time?

7. He said, none of you shall know the times and seasons that the Father has put under his authority.

8. You will receive ability *(power)* when the holy spirit comes upon you; (2 Timothy 3:5) You will be ambassadors in Jerusalem and unto all of Judea and Samaria, even unto the furthest places on earth.

9. He said this as they watched him being taken up into the clouds right before their eyes; (Mark 16:19)

10. As they looked to the sky, Jesus had just departed and two figures stood near them in white clothing,

11. and they said, Galilean men, why are you looking into the sky? This same Jesus that was taken up from you into the sky will return in the same way that you saw him ascend.

12. Then they returned unto Jerusalem from the Mount of Olives, which is close to Jerusalem, only a Sabbath's journey away. *(less than a mile)*

The names of the apostles in this account are different than in Matthew 10:1-4 & Mark 3:16-19.

13. When they came into Jerusalem, they entered into the upper room and they waited there. Peter, James and John, Andrew, Philip and Thomas, Bartholomew and Matthew, James the son of Alphaeus, Simon the Zealot, and Judas the brother of James;
(Judas is likely the brother of Jesus - Galatians 1:19; Jude 1:1; Matthew 13:55)

14. They were continually earnest with the same mindset, in prayer and in conversation. Mary the mother of Jesus and his brothers were also there.

15. In those days, Peter stood up in the middle of the disciples and a small crowd of about a hundred twenty people and he said, my brethren,

16. it is necessary for the scriptures to be fulfilled, that which was spoken through the mouth of David concerning Judas *(Iscariot)* who guided them to arrest Jesus;

17. He was abiding with us and he received a part of the ministry. (Hebrews 6:4-6)

18. But they bought a field out of the reward for his unrighteousness, then headfirst he fell, broken open in his middle parts and his bowels poured out. (Matthew 27:5)

19. And it was made known unto all that lived in Jerusalem that the field is in their own language called, Akeldama, which means field of blood.

20. It is written in the book of the Psalms, "May his estate be forsaken and he shall not live in it." (Psalms 69:25) and also, "May his days be few and may another take his position". (Psalms 109:8)

21. So then *(the replacement)* must be a man who was together with us all of the time, who came and went from among us unto the master Jesus,

22. beginning with the baptism of John, until the day that he was taken up from us; He must also be a witness of the resurrection to become one of us.

23. They chose two, Joseph of Barsabas, nicknames Justus, and the other was Matthias.

24. They prayed and said, you oh Lord know the hearts of everyone. Show out of these two which one you have chosen to take his share

25. in the ministry and apostleship that has fallen from Judas, who went to where he belongs.

26. So they gave lots *(dice)* unto them and the lot fell on Matthias, and he was counted with the eleven apostles. (Acts 9:15) *(the eleven picked Matthias to replace Judas Iscariot, but God picked Paul)*

Acts 2

1. When the day of Pentecost was completed they were all together in one place.
2. Out of the sky came a sound like a strong wind that blew through the house that they were gathered in.
3. Languages were sparked among them, and unto each of them was deposited the treasure. (Matthew 13:44; John 14:18-23)
4. They were all filled up with the wealth of the spirit of the holy one and they began to speak strange languages, accordingly as the spirit gave them the ability to speak.
5. There were devout men, Jews that were staying in Jerusalem who were from many nations.
6. So when the sound of this was heard, those Jews gathered together and they were greatly perplexed! This is because each of them heard the followers of Christ speak in his own language and dialect!
7. They were amazed and confused and they said to one another, are those that are speaking in this way all Galileans?
8. How is it that each of us can hear in our own language and dialect from where we were born?
9. Parthians, Medes, Elamites, and those of Mesopotamia, Judea, and Cappadocia, Pontus, the different places throughout Asia,
10. Pyrygia, Pamphilia, Egypt, the many regions of Libya and Cyrenia of the Romans;
11. Both those who were Jews and new converts to Judaism, from Crete and Arabia all heard them speaking in their own languages about the magnificence of God!
12. All were amazed and confused and they spoke to each other and said, how do you think that this could happen?
13. But there were some who ridiculed them and said, they took from the fermented wine and are drunk!
14. But Peter stood up, the eleven in union with him and he raised up his voice and he began speaking to them; Men of Judah and all that are staying in Jerusalem, listen to my words and it will be made known to you concerning these things.
15. It is not as you might think as we are not drunken; It is only the third hour of the day! (9 A.M.)
16. But what you have seen is that which was spoken by the prophet Joel;
17. "And it shall come to pass afterward, that I will pour out my spirit upon all regenerated people, and your sons and your descendants will speak of the mysteries (*prophesy*), your young men will be shown visions, and the old men will be given dreams. (Joel 2:28; Numbers 12:6)
18. I will pour out my spirit upon the men and women servants (*of God*)" (Proverbs 1:23; Galatians 3:28).

In the continuation of the prophecy from Joel 2:28-32, verses 19-20 are out of context as these verses do not pertain to the time of the early church, but to the time just before the return of Christ at his second coming, of which is very soon to come.

19. And the prophecy says that there will be fulfillments of prophecy (omens) in the sky and upon the earth, blood, fire, vapors and smoke, (Revelation 8:7 - none of which happened at that time)
20. and the sun will be turned into darkness and the moon will be reddened before the great and dreadful day of the Lord. (Revelation 6:12; Matthew 24:29; Malachi 4:5)

21. Everyone that is converted in the name of Jehovah will be reserved by God. (Isaiah 53:1-12; Acts 2:38; Acts 3:19)
22. Men of Israel, hear these words. Jesus of Nazareth, the son of God, while he lived, he demonstrated unto you powerful deeds and miracles and he fulfilled the prophecies, of which God did through him in your presence and you know this to be true!
23. It was predetermined for him to be reserved unto this and by the will of God, to be rejected and be taken at the hands of lawless men that killed him, having him crucified.
24. But God resurrected him from the power of death because it was not possible for him to be held by it.
25. For David said of him, "I can see the Lord in everything that is before me, because he is guiding my right hand so that I am not destroyed.
26. This is why I am joyful in my heart and I raise my voice, for my body shall live with hope,
27. because you will not leave my soul in hell, nor will you allow your holy one to touch corruption.
28. You have revealed the pathway unto life. You will fill me with joy in your presence." (Psalms 16:10)

29. Men and brothers, it is necessary to speak the words of our forefather David with boldness and clarity, because he died and was buried and his tomb remains with us even today.

30. In that he was a prophet, he knew that God swore an oath, that one of his descendants according to lineage would rise up to be the Christ and sit upon his throne.

31. Foreseeing this, he spoke of the resurrection of Christ, that he (*God*) would not leave his (*Christ's*) soul in hell, and that his body would not see corruption (*rot*). (1 Peter 3:17)

32. But God raised this Jesus up, of which we all are witnesses;

33. Then he ascended to the right hand of God, (Mark 16:19; Luke 24:28-51) and he has now poured out the promise of his holy spirit from the Father, which is what you now see and hear! (John 14:18, 23)

34. Because David did not ascend into the heavens, but he said; "My Lord (*Father God, Yehovah*) said unto my Lord (*Jesus, Yehowshua*),

35. sit at my right hand until I put those who were hostile to you under your feet." (Psalms 110:1)

36. Therefore with assuredness, let all of Israel know that God made him to be both the master and the Christ, this Jesus whom you crucified!

37. When they heard this, they were deeply sorrowful in their hearts and they asked Peter and the other apostles; Brothers, what must we do to be made right (*before God*)?

38. And Peter said to them, everyone must have godly sorrow that brings forth true reformation unto the deliverer (*Repent - G-3341 + G-2229 + G-4991*) and be baptized unto God (*G-907 + G-2320*) in the name of Jesus Christ (*Yehowshuwa =Yehovah salvation = H-3068 + H-3467*) for the pardon of your sins, and you shall receive the gift of the holy spirit. (John 3:5; Romans 6:1-23; John 8:31-36; Matthew 18:2-4; Colossians 2:12; Isaiah 53:11; Acts 22:16; Mark 16:16; Ezekiel 16:9; Ezekiel 36:27-31; Hosea 14:9; Jeremiah 33:8; Psalms 51:2, 7; Proverbs 16:6; John 13:8; Proverbs 28:13)

39. Because the promise is unto you and your children and everyone everywhere, all who shall be converted unto the name of the Lord. (Romans 9:8, 10:13; Galatians 3:14; Acts 1:4; Hebrews 6:13; Joel 2:28)

40. He spoke many other things and earnestly testified, then he brought comfort saying, turn away from this perverse nation. (*Israel*)

41. Those that truly welcomed within themselves this message were baptized. That day there were about three thousand added unto the faith.

42. They continued with dedication, according to the teachings of the apostles and they continued to fellowship with them and they ate together, keeping each other in prayer.

43. Unto each of them came a fear, because the apostles did many miracles and signs.

44. All of those that had been converted were together and they held everything in common.

45. Each went and gathered their goods and possessions and distributed them unto everyone, accordingly to the needs that each one had.

46. They continued daily, fully dedicated in one mind. They went to the temple and ate meals together from house to house and they shared their food happily with a purely sincere heart.

47. They praised God for the favor that he gave unto each of them, and the Lord added to the gathering daily, all who chose to be reconciled unto God.

Acts 3

1. Peter and John were on their way into the temple for the hour of prayer, the ninth hour (*3 PM*),

2. And there was a man there that was lame since he was born. Every day he was carried and laid at the gate of the temple called Beautiful to beg for handouts from the people that were going into the temple.

3. When he saw Peter and John about to go into the temple, he asked them for a donation;

4. Peter stared at him intently, as did John, and he said, look at us!

5. The man held his hand open as though he expected to receive some money from them;

6. But Peter said, I do not have gold or silver (*money*), but of that which I have, I give unto you! (*the holy spirit*) In the name of Jesus Christ of Nazareth, rise up and walk!

7. Peter took him by the right hand and he helped him get up, and immediately his feet and ankles were strengthened!

8. The man stood up and began excitedly jumping and he walked around; Then he went with them into the temple and continued walking around, leaping and praising God.

9. Some of the people saw him jumping and praising God, and they recognized him;

10. Because this was the man that always begged for handouts at the beautiful gate of the temple, everyone was amazed and bewildered at how such a thing could happen to him.

11. The healed man remained close to Peter and John, and many people came to them on Solomon's porch, and they were greatly excited.

12. When Peter saw this he said to the people; My fellow Israelites, why are you surprised at this? Why do you stare? It is not as though we did this by our own power or that by our own goodness he is now able to walk!

13. The God of Abraham, Isaac and Jacob, the God of our forefathers glorified his servant Jesus, the one who you rejected and delivered up unto the court of Pilate;

14. But he decided to set him free, though you again rejected the holy and righteous one and asked that a man that is a murderer be set free and given to you.

15. But then you killed the headmaster of life; However, God raised him up from the dead, of which we are witnesses. (Jeremiah 18:23)

16. Now, upon dedication unto his name, this man that you now see has been healed, and the commitment that this man has unto him gave him the complete healing that you now see before your eyes!

17. But my brethren, I know that what you did was done in ignorance.
(Numbers 15:28; Matthew 12:31; 1 John 5:16)

18. It was spoken in times past through the mouths of the prophets that Christ must suffer, and Jesus fulfilled all of the prophecies.

19. Therefore, have godly sorrow that brings forth true reformation unto God (Repent - G-3341 + G-2229 + G-4991) and be converted for the pardon of your sins, so that the rebirth may bring upon you the presence of the Lord; (Acts 2:38; Matthew 18:2-3; John 8:31-36; Romans 6:1-23; Galatians 3:27; Jonah 3:8-10; Jeremiah 33:8; Ezekiel 36:27; Hosea 14:9; Psalms 51:2; Ecclesiastes 7:29)

20. And he shall send unto you the one who lived with you and preached unto you, (*the holy spirit of)* Jesus Christ, (John 14:17-18)

21. who is in the heavens until the time of the restoration of all things. (Revelation 21-22) He is the one that God gave his holy prophets to speak about since the beginning.

22. Truly Moses said to the forefathers, "The Lord your God will rise up a prophet from one of your brothers like me; Listen unto him, every word that he speaks unto you.

23. And it shall be, that every soul who does not obey that prophet will be utterly destroyed along with the nation." (Deuteronomy 18:15-19 - *fulfilled in 70 AD)*

24. All of the prophets from Samuel and thereafter, as many as spoke, they also announced of these days *(in which they lived at that time this was written)*!

25. You are the offspring of the prophets and heirs of the covenant that God had given unto our forefather Abraham, when he said, "and through his seed, all of the families of the earth shall be blessed." (Genesis 15)

26. But God raised up his servant Jesus, first unto you, to bless you for the purpose of the turning away each one of you from your iniquities (*sins). (the purpose of the new covenant is to bring a powerful way for people who choose to love and obey God to live a holy life, to go and sin no more - Daniel 9:24)*

Acts 4

1. While they were speaking to the people, the priests, the governor of the temple and the Sadducees became greatly distressed

2. because they were teaching the people and announcing that Jesus had been resurrected from the dead.

3. Therefore they laid their hands on them and arrested them and held them until the following day, because it was already evening.

4. But there were many who heard the message that committed their trust in him (*Jesus Christ*). At that time the number of them (*the converts*) had grown to about five thousand people.

5. The following day they assembled the rulers, elders and scribes at Jerusalem.

6. The high priests Annas, Caiaphas, Jochanan, Alexander and all of the relations of the high priests also came to join them.

7. They displayed them in the middle of their assembly to interrogate them. Then they asked, who gave you permission, by what authority have you done these things? (Matthew 21:23)

8. Then Peter, being filled with the disposition of the holy one said, rulers and elders of the people of Israel,

9. if we are being examined for doing a good thing for this crippled man, by what power was he healed?

10. Let it be known unto all of you and unto all of the people of Israel, that in the name of Jesus of Nazareth, the Christ that you crucified, who God raised from the dead, it is because of him that this man stands before you and is healed!

11. This Jesus is the stone that was considered to be worthless by you, the builders, but he has become and is the head stone of the corner. (1 Peter 2:7; Matthew 21:42; Mark 12:10; Ephesians 2:20; Isaiah 28:16)

12. There is no salvation in any other; There is no other name that has been given unto any of mankind under the heavens in which one can be eternally saved. (*Yehowshuwa* (Jesus) - Matthew 28:18)

13. When they saw the boldness in Peter and John, and having recognized that they were illiterate and uneducated, they were astonished and they knew that they had been with Jesus.

14. But when they looked at the man that had been healed standing with them, they had nothing to argue against them.

15. So they commanded them to go outside, away from the Sanhedrin, then they talked with one another and they said;

16. What is there that we can do to these men? Truly there is a notable miracle that has been done through them and it is clear unto all of Jerusalem, and even we are unable to deny it!

17. But so that nothing more can be said to the people, we should threaten them to no longer speak of these things nor to anyone concerning this name (*Jesus of Nazareth*).

18. So they called for them and they ordered them to never speak nor teach concerning the name of Jesus! (1 John 2:23)

19. But Peter and John said, would it be right in the eyes of God for us to obey you, instead of God?

20. You decide! What we have seen and heard we can not be prevented from speaking!

21. So they threatened them again as they found no way in which to punish them. Because of this, the people all glorified God because of what had occurred.

22. The man who was healed had been crippled for over forty years.

23. When they were released, they went to the others to tell them all that the high priests and elders said.

24. Now when they had all heard, together they all opened up their voices unto God and they said, master, you are the God that made the heavens and the earth and the sea and everything that is in them;

25. Through the mouth of David you announced your servant; "Why do the heathen become enraged (*concerning Christ*) and the people revolve their lives around worthless things?

26. The kings and the rulers of the earth are assembled together to present themselves against the Lord and against his Christ;" (Psalms 2:1-2)

27. Because through Herod and Pontius Pilate, the gentiles along with the people of Israel, they gathered against your holy servant Jesus, the one who you have consecrated

28. to do all of the things that you have predestined and have intended to happen.

29. Now Lord, look at how these men have been threatened and yet your servants had the boldness to speak your message,

30. and you have reached out your hand to heal the crippled man, and the omens and miracles have happened through the name of your holy one, Jesus of Nazareth. (*the holy spirit is the spirit of Jesus*)

31. When they had finished their prayer, the place where they were gathered was shaken, truly a close encounter of the wealth of the divine spirit. They spoke the message of God everywhere with boldness.

32. Belief (*trust*) was growing in the hearts of the whole gathering, and they were of one mindset. None of them held any of their possessions to be their own, but all things were shared by each of them.

33. The apostles gave evidence of the resurrection of the Lord Jesus with great power and the gift of God was great upon all of them.

34. There was no one among them that was needy, because those coming into the gathering who owned land or houses sold them and brought the proceeds from that which was being sold,

35. and they placed it at the feet of the apostles, to be distributed according to what each one had need of. (*the offerings were distributed to the needy and not used by the leaders of the church for personal gain*)

36. Joses, the one that is called Barnabas by the apostles, which being translated means, the son of advocacy, a Levite, a Cypriot by race, when he was brought into the gathering,

37. he sold a field and brought the money and placed it at the feet of the apostles.

Acts 5

1. A man named Ananias and his wife Sapphira sold a possession

2. and secretly kept back some of the proceeds, and the wife was aware of it. He brought a part of the proceeds and laid it at the feet of the apostles.

3. But Peter said, Ananias, how is it that Satan has brought greed into your heart to make a weak attempt to deceive the spirit of the holy one and secretly keep back for yourself some of the proceeds from the sold possession? (*the fault of Ananias was that he lied - saying that this was all of the money from the sale.*)

4. While it was yours was it not yours to do with as you desired and in your power to sell? So why was this action contrived within your heart? You have not lied to men, but unto God!

5. When Ananias heard these words, he fell down and died! Then great fear came on all of those who heard of this. (*We must also have this same fear to defy God*)

6. So they wrapped the new member and carried him out and buried him.

7. It was about three hours later that the man's wife came in, not knowing what had happened.

8. And Peter said to her, tell me, did you sell the possession for that much? Then she said, yes, it was that much. (Revelation 21:8; Hebrews 10:26; Numbers 15:30-31)

9. Then Peter said to her, why have you also agreed to test the spirit of God? Know this, the feet of those that have buried your husband are at the gate and they shall carry you out the same!

10. Immediately she fell at his feet and died; As the men came in, they found her dead, so they carried her out and buried her beside her husband.

11. Great fear came upon the whole assembly and upon all who had heard of these things. (Proverbs 9:10)

12. Through the hands of the apostles many signs (*omens*) and miracles were accomplished among the people and they were all of one mindset and of the same purpose. As they sat on Solomon's porch,

13. many of the others there were not so courageous to accompany them, but they greatly respected them.

14. More and more believed in the master and were added unto them. There were many men and women;

15. It was that if some were sick, they would bring them into the streets and put them on beds and chairs, hoping that when Peter would walk by his shadow might fall upon them so that they be healed.

16. And the people assembled in the cities around Jerusalem, bringing those that were sick and those that were tormented by demons, and they were all healed!

17. The high priest and those with him, the sect called Sadducees, they were full of jealousy,

18. so they arrested some of the apostles, and they publicly put them in prison.

19. But in the night, a messenger of the Lord came and opened the doors of the prison and led them out and said;

20. Go stand in the temple and speak to the people everything that was taught by Jesus.

21. After hearing this, in the morning they went into the temple and taught. Meanwhile, the high priest and those with him called together the Sanhedrin and all of the elders of the people of Israel. They had already sent for the jailers to bring the apostles out before them.

22. But when the officers went into the prison and did not find them there, they returned and told it to them and said,

23. we went to the jail and all of the gates were closed and secured and the guards were standing outside at the door, but when we opened the door, we found no one inside!

24. When the high priests, the governor of the temple and the other priests heard this, they were confused as to what might have happened!

25. Then one who was there said unto them; Be aware, those men that you threw in prison are standing in the temple teaching the people!

26. Then the governor of the temple and his officers kindly asked for the apostles to come unto them, because they feared that the people might stone them to death (*if they arrested them again*)!

27. Then they were brought before the Sanhedrin and the high priest began questioning them,

28. and he said, did we not instruct you to no longer teach according to the name of Jesus? Yet you have filled all of Jerusalem with your teachings and you have attempted to put the blood of this man upon us! (Matthew 27:25)

29. But Peter and the other apostles said; We must obey God and not cater to the desires of men!

30. The God of our forefathers has raised up Jesus, the one who you assaulted and hung on the cross!

31. God has made him to be the highest ruler (Revelation 1:11) and the savior. He is been raised up to sit at the right hand of God, to offer repentance unto all of Israel and the forgiveness for your transgressions (*sins*). (Romans 11:26)

32. We are witnesses of his message and also of his holy spirit that God gives unto those who continue to obey him. (John 14:15-23; Hebrews 5:9 - *Do you still think that obedience is not necessary?*)

33. When they heard this, they were exasperated, so they held counsel to kill them as they did Jesus!

34. But one of the Sanhedrin stood up, he was a Pharisee by the name of Gamaliel, a teacher of the Jewish law (Acts 22:3) and he was respected by all of the people. He recommended that the apostles be put outside for a short time.

35. Then he said unto them, men of Israel, be careful for your own sakes concerning what you intend to do unto these men.

36. Remember in the past, the one named Theudas stood up; He claimed to be someone important and a group of about four hundred men were joined to him; When he died, everyone who had followed him were dispersed and nothing became of it.

37. Then there was also Judas from Galilee at the time of the census and he drew a considerable amount of people after himself; But when he died all that followed him were scattered.

38. Now I tell you, walk away from these men and allow them to go free; If their purpose is according to that of men, all that they do will come to nothing; But if it is of God, there is nothing that you can do to destroy it! You do not want to be found to be fighting against God! So they all listened to him.

40. Then after they had beaten the apostles, they ordered them not to speak concerning the name of Jesus, and then they released them.

41. When the apostles began walking away from the Sanhedrin, as they went, they were greatly joyful to be deemed worthy to suffer and be hated for their testimony in the name of Jesus! (Matthew 10:22; Luke 21:17; John 17:14)

42. Every day, from house to house and in the temple, they did not stop teaching and spreading the good news of how to live according to Jesus Christ.

Acts 6

1. But at the time when the number of disciples began to be greatly multiplied, there happened to be a complaining within the Greek converts against the Hebrews, because they were overlooking the daily needs of the widows that were among them.

2. So the apostles called some from among themselves and a group of disciples came together and said, it is not necessary for us to abandon the teachings of God to serve tables.

3. Select from among yourselves my brothers, seven men who are full of the holy disposition (*spirit*) and wisdom, of whom shall be appointed over this necessity.

4. As for us (*the twelve apostles*), we will continue in prayer, dedicated to bringing forth the Gospel.

5. Their words pleased all of the people, and they chose Stephen, a man that was full of dedication and the holy disposition (*spirit*); Then they chose Philip, Prochorus, Nicanor, Timon, Parmenas and Nicolas a new convert from Antioch. (*Nicholas* - Acts 20:30 - Revelation 2:6)

6. These men were set before the apostles, and they placed their hands on them and spent time in prayer and instructing them.

7. The message of God was being spread and the number of disciples in Jerusalem was growing very large, even a large amount of the priests became obedient unto the doctrine.

8. Stephen, full of dedication and power did many miracles and signs among the people.

9. But there were some from a synagogues that were called Libertines who were from Syria, Alexandria, and some of Sicily and Asia that disputed with Stephen.

10. They did not have the ability to stand up against the wisdom and spirit from which he spoke.

11. But they were stubborn men, and they testified that they have heard him speaking blasphemous words against Moses and God.

12. They began to stir up the people and the elders and scribes, and then they came and arrested him and took him before the Sanhedrin.

13. There were witnesses that stood there and said, this man does not ever stop speaking blasphemous words against this holy place and the Jewish law;

14. We have heard him saying that Jesus of Nazareth will destroy this place (*Jerusalem and the temple*) (Daniel 9:24-27; Luke 19:43-44; Jeremiah 7:29-34), and that he will change the customs of what Moses had delivered unto us. (Jeremiah 31:31-34)

15. And all of the Sanhedrin stared at him glaringly, and the appearance upon his face was like the face of an angel. (*brightly lit*)

Acts 7

1. Then the high priest said, do you now hold to these things?

2. And Stephen said, men, brethren and elders hear my words. Our glorious God appeared to our forefather Abraham when he was in Mesopotamia before he lived in Haran,

3. and he said to him, leave this land where your family has lived and go to a land that I will show unto you. (Genesis 12:1)

4. So he left the land of Chaldea and he made his home in Haran. When his father died, he went from there unto the land in which you now live.

5. But he did not give him the land to possess himself nor to walk in it, but he promised to give it to be occupied by his offspring; He said this at a time when he had no children!

6. Now God spoke this to him, that his offspring would be a foreigner in a strange land (*Egypt*), and that they would be enslaved and oppressed for four hundred years!

7. But God said, "I will condemn the nation in which they will be enslaved, and after that happens they will be brought out and shall serve me in this place. (Genesis 15:14; Exodus 3:12)

8. God made a covenant (*contract*) with Abraham to be circumcised; Then he fathered Isaac and he circumcised him on the eighth day. Then Isaac fathered Jacob, and Jacob fathered the twelve patriarchs.

9. But the patriarchs were full of jealousy, and sold Joseph their brother into the land of Egypt; But God was with him.

10. He took him out of his difficulties, gave him wisdom and brought him to be favored by Pharaoh the king of Egypt. He appointed Joseph to have governorship over Egypt and over his whole house.

11. But a famine appeared in Egypt and in all of the land of Canaan and it caused great burden upon the people. Our forefathers could not continue to feed themselves.

12. Jacob had heard that there was grain in Egypt, so he sent out our forefathers before him.

13. On their second visit, Joseph became aware of his brothers being there; It also became evident unto Pharaoh that those of Jacob's lineage were there.

14. Then Joseph sent for his father Jacob and all of his family, in all there were seventy-five of them.

15. So Jacob went down to Egypt and died there. Our forefathers transported him to Shechem,

16. and they placed him in a tomb which was purchased by Abraham for a certain amount of silver from the children of Hamor of Shechem.

17. So the time was drawing near for the promise that God swore unto Abraham, that his descendants would be greatly increased in Egypt.

18. But other kings arose who did not recognize Joseph.

19. Those kings lived deceitfully against our people and oppressed our forefathers, even ordering the killing of the infants, not allowing them to live.

20. At that time, Moses was born and he was cherished by God. He was raised for three months by his parents.

21. But when he was offered up, the daughter of Pharaoh raised him as her own son.

22. Moses was taught according to all of the wisdom of the Egyptians and he became powerful in his speaking and in deeds.

23. But when he was forty years old, it rose up in his heart to care for his brothers, the children of Israel.

24. When he saw one being abused, he defended, bringing vengeance upon the one doing the abuse, striking the Egyptian.

25. He thought that his brethren would understand that God, through his hands would bring unto them deliverance; But they did not recognize this.

26. The following day, he stopped two Israelites from fighting, bringing them to peace and he said to them; Men, you are brothers; Why are you doing harm unto one another?

27. But the one who did wrong unto his brother pushed Moses away and said, who appointed you to be our ruler and judge?

28. Do you now plan to kill me as you killed the Egyptian yesterday? (Exodus 2:14)

29. Because of this word, Moses left Egypt and he settled down in the land of Midian where he fathered two sons.

30. After forty years there were completed (*Moses was 80 years old*), the messenger of the Lord appeared unto him in the desert of Mount Sinai in a flame of fire upon a bush.

31. Moses was amazed at the sight, as he came towards it, he looked and the voice of the Lord spoke to him, I am the God of your forefathers, the God of Abraham, Isaac and Jacob. (Exodus 3:6, 15)

32. Moses was trembling and he did not dare look.

33. God said to him, take your shoes off, this is holy ground!

34. I have watched the affliction of my people in Egypt, I have heard their cries and I have come to rescue them; Go now, I send you into Egypt.

35. This same Moses who they rejected when they said, who appointed you to be our ruler and judge, God now sent to be ruler and deliverer, appointed by the hand of God appearing unto him in the burning bush.

36. So he led them out, doing many miracles and omens in the land of Egypt, in the Red Sea, and in the desert for forty years.

37. This Moses said to the sons of Israel; The Lord our God will rise up a prophet from your brothers like me; Obey him. (Deuteronomy 18:15)

38. This is he who was brought into the desert before the messenger that spoke to him upon Mount Sinai, and from whom our forefathers received the instructions of how to live, which they gave to us;

39. But our forefathers did not live by these instructions, but turned away from them and turned their hearts back to Egypt. (Exodus 4:19)

40. Then they said to Aaron, we will make gods for ourselves that will travel before us, for we do not know what has happened unto this Moses who led us out of Egypt.

41. So they made a golden calf in those days, and they brought forth a sacrifice unto their idol, and they were celebrating the creation of their own hands.

42. Therefore God turned against them and surrendered them to serve the lights in the heavens, just as it has been written in the books of the prophets: "Oh house of Israel, you did not bring unto me killed animals and sacrifices for forty years in the desert.

43. But you took upon yourselves the tent of Molech, and Remphan the star of your god and your idol resemblances that you create to worship; For this, I will send you into the far side of Babylon." (Amos 7:17; Jeremiah 7:29-34)

44. This habitation was evidenced unto us by our forefathers in the desert, just as it was commanded unto the one who reported this unto Moses, that it be made according to the pattern that God showed him.

45. This idolatry was again brought in when Joshua was head of the nation, having been inherited, of which was living within the forefathers, and they thrust God out from their presence until the time of David.

46. David found favor before God and wanted to find a home for the God of Jacob.

47. Solomon built a house for him,

48. but the most high God does not live in a temple that is built with hands, just as the prophet says;

49. "The heavens are my throne and the earth is my footstool; What kind of house do you think that you can build for me and how do you expect that I rest there?" This was said by God. (Isaiah 66:1-2)

50. "Did I not make all things with my hands?" (Isaiah 66:2)

51. You are stubborn headed and uncircumcised in your hearts and in your ears! You have always come against the spirit of holiness; Just as your forefathers did, you have also done.

52. Which of the forefathers did not persecute the prophets of God? (Matthew 23:31) They killed those who previously prophesied of the coming of the holy one *(Christ Jesus)*, the one that you betrayed and murdered.

53. But you received the law of God through this arrangement of messengers (*the prophets*), yet you do not keep it.

54. And when they heard these things they were deeply angered within their hearts and they grinded their teeth at him.

55. But being full of the spirit of holiness, he looked intently into the heavens and he saw the glory of God and Jesus standing at the right hand of God.

56. He said, I see the heavens have been opened up and the son of man standing at the right side of God!

57. But they cried out, screaming loudly and holding their ears; With violent passion they attacked him,
58. Then they threw him out of the city and they threw rocks at him until he was dead. And there was a witness of this, as they took off their robes they threw them at the feet of a young man named Saul. *(This young man would become, the Apostle Paul)* (Galatians 1:13; Acts 22:20)
59. They killed Stephen as he called out unto the Lord Jesus and said, my master Jesus, receive my spirit.
60. And he fell to his knees and cried out with a loud voice, Lord, do not hold this sin against them! (Numbers 15:28) When he had said this, he fell asleep *(died)*.

Acts 8

1. Saul consented to the killing of Stephen. Then it occurred that the gatherings *(called out ones)* were being heavily persecuted in Jerusalem, so they moved away from Judea and Samaria, dispersing themselves throughout many other countries, except for the apostles.
2. Devout men took the body of Stephen and were greatly mourning over him.
3. But Saul then began to ravage the people of God, going house to house, breaking in and dragging both men and women to prison;
4. But those that were dispersed abroad preached the message of the gospel wherever they went.
5. Philip went to a city in Samaria announcing Christ Jesus unto them.
6. The crowds paid attention to that which Philip said when they heard and saw first-hand the miracles that he was doing.
7. There were many that had unclean spirits that were taken out and many that had been paralyzed and crippled that were healed.
8. Great joy was in that city.
9. There had been a man named Simon that was from that city, and he was a sorcerer and had previously astonished the nation of Samaria. He claimed that he was a great man.
10. All of the people had previously paid attention unto him, all both great and small. They had said that this man had the mighty power of God.
11. They paid attention to him because for a long time he had been deceiving them.
12. However, when they committed their trust in the message that Philip was preaching, all of the things concerning the kingdom of God, many of the men and the women were baptized in the name of Jesus Christ! (Matthew 28:18; Acts 2:38; Acts 3:19; John 8:31-36; Matthew 18:3; 1 Peter 3:21)
13. Even Simon committed his trust and was baptized and was earnestly continuing according to what was being taught by Philip, seeing the mighty deeds and miracles that were happening, he was amazed!
14. Now when the apostles that were in Jerusalem had received the news that Samaria had now received the message of God, they sent Peter and John to them.
15. They went there concerning why they had not received the spirit of the holy one; *(Jesus)*
16. He had not yet descended upon any of them, though they were baptized in the name of Jesus.
17. But when they laid their hands upon them, they received the holy spirit!
18. When Simon saw that by the laying on of the hands of the apostles the spirit of the holy one was given, he offered them money and said,
19. give me this ability also, so that whomever I lay my hands upon, that they will also receive the spirit of the holy one!
20. But Peter said unto him, take your money with you to hell. The gift of God can not be purchased with money!
21. You shall not receive any participation nor a portion of this because your heart is not right before God. *(If your heart is not right before God, or if the terms of the covenant are not understood at the time of baptism or if the true name of God is not used, there can be no conversion and the spirit of Christ will not come in.)*
22. Repent *(turn away)* from your wickedness and beg God that he might forgive you for the thoughts that were in your heart, (Jonah 3:8-10)
23. because I perceive bitter poison and a great amount of unrighteousness within you.
24. And Simon said, I beg of you to ask of the Lord that none of these things come upon me from what you have spoken.

25. When they had brought the message and earnestly taught the instructions of the Lord, they returned unto Jerusalem after having preached the message unto many of the villages in Samaria.

26. There, a messenger of the Lord spoke to Philip and said, get up! Go down along the south road between Jerusalem and Gaza, of which is a desert.

27. So he rose up and he went; Now look! An Ethiopian man, a powerful eunuch of Candice the queen of the Ethiopians who was the headmaster of all of her treasures, he had come to worship at Jerusalem.

28. He was returning home and was sitting on his chariot reading from the prophet Isaiah.

29. The spirit of God said to Philip (1 John 4:2-3; John 3:5), go unto him and travel with this chariot.
(It was the spirit of God that spoke to Philip, not the bible)

30. As Philip was coming near to him, he heard the man reading from the prophet Isaiah and he said; Are you understanding what you are reading?

31. The man said, how can I be able unless someone explains it to me? Then he called Philip to come up and sit by him.

32. The content of the scripture that he was reading was this: "As sheep going to be slaughtered, as a voiceless lamb going before the shearers, he shall not even open his mouth.

33. Humbly he will be taken and be condemned, but who of his nation shall recognize this? For his life shall be taken from the earth." (Isaiah 53:7-8; Jeremiah 11:19)

34. And the eunuch said unto Philip, what do you have to say about what this prophet says? Is this concerning himself, or someone else?

35. That is when Philip opened his mouth and began from this scripture to preach unto him the gospel of Jesus Christ!

36. As they were going along the way they came upon some water, and the eunuch said; Look, water! Does anything prevent me from being baptized?

37. And Philip said, if you are completely committed in your heart, baptism is <u>necessary</u>. (1 John 4:2-3)
(Greek word - <u>ex-est-in</u> = G-1537 - "<u>from where</u>" + G-1510 (2076) - "<u>I exist</u>" + G-1722 - "<u>in you</u>")
And he said, I do believe that Jesus Christ is the son of God. (Romans 10:9-10)

38. He ordered the chariot to be stopped, and both Philip and the eunuch went down into the water, and Philip baptized him! (Acts 2:38; Acts 3:19; 1 Peter 3:21)

39. When he came up out of the water, the spirit of the Lord plucked Philip up and took him away from that place, and the eunuch did not see him again, but he went on his way rejoicing.

40. Then Philip found himself at Azotus, so he passed through that place and preached the gospel unto all of the cities there, until he made his way into Cesarea.

Acts 9

1. At this time Saul was still speaking threats of murder towards the disciples, so he came to the high priest,

2. and he asked for written permission to go into the synagogues in Damascus, to see if he might find any Christian men or women there, so that he might arrest them and bring them back to Jerusalem.

3. As he was traveling, he began to approach Damascus; Suddenly around him shown a strong light from out of the sky!

4. He then fell to the ground and heard a voice that said unto him; Saul, why are you persecuting me?

5. And he said, who are you master? Then the Lord said, I am the one that you are persecuting, Jesus of Nazareth! Your stubbornness has been like kicking against a thorn tree.

6. By this time he was trembling and completely astonished, and he said, master, what do you want for me to do? Jesus said unto him, get yourself up and go into the city, it will be told to you what you must do.

7. The men traveling with him were speechless because they heard the voice but no one was there!

8. So they lifted Saul from the ground, and when he opened his eyes he could not see anything, so they led him by the hand into Damascus.

9. He was unable to see and did not eat nor drink for three days.

10. There was a disciple in Damascus named Ananias. The Lord said to him in a vision, Ananias. And he responded and said, yes Lord!

11. The Lord said to him, get up and go along the road that is called the straight road, and look for a man of Tarsus named Saul. He will be in the house of Judas and he will be praying.

12. He has also seen a vision of a man named Ananias coming in and taking his hand and making him to see again.

13. And Ananias said, Lord, I have heard from many witnesses concerning this man, that he has done many horrible things unto your saints in Jerusalem.

14. He has authority from the high priests to arrest all that live according to the testimony of your name.

15. But the Lord said to him, Go! He is my chosen delegate (*the apostle to replace Judas Iscariot*) to bring my name unto the foreign nations and the children of Israel.

16. I will show to him how much he must suffer for holding to my name.

17. Ananias went to the house of Simon and he came in and put his hands upon Saul and he said, Saul my brother, Jesus of Nazareth was the one who appeared unto you on the road. He has sent me unto you so that you will be healed to see again and that you also receive the spirit of the holy one.

18. Soon after this, what looked like scales fell off of his eyes and he was able to see again, then he rose up and was baptized!

19. Paul ate some food and began to received his strength back. At that time he began spending his time with the disciples in Damascus.

20. Paul then began announcing Jesus Christ in the synagogues, saying that he is the son of God!

21. Everyone was amazed and all that heard him said, this can not be the man that was destroying those in Jerusalem and then came here to capture them, to take them before the high priests all that were calling upon the name of Jesus!

22. And Saul was full with power, and he confronted the Jews that were living in Damascus by proving that Jesus is the Christ.

23. After many days passed by, the Jews plotted to kill him,

24. but Saul came to know of this plot against him. The Jews began watching the gates night and day so to be able to kill him.

25. But the disciples took him in the night time and lowered him down from the wall in a basket.

Verses 26-28 contradict Paul's account written in Galatians 1:17-24.
Paul states that he did not go to Jerusalem at that time,
but three years later when he did, he only met with Peter, James and John.

26. When Saul arrived in Jerusalem he tried to join with the disciples there but they were all afraid of him and did not believe that he was a disciple. (Galatians 1:17)

27. But Barnabas took him and led him to the apostles and told them of how he saw the Lord and that he spoke to him, and that he spoke the name of Jesus with boldness in Damascus. (Galatians 2:1-2)

28. Saul spent a little time with the apostles in Jerusalem and then left. He continued to boldly speak the name of the Lord Jesus.

29. Then he spoke with the Greek Jews, but they tried to arrest him having intentions to kill him,

30. but the brethren knew of this, so they took him down to Caesarea and sent him to Tarsus.

(Tarsus and Cilicia are towns and Syria and Caesaria are regions)

31. Then the churches throughout Judea, Galilee and Samaria were brought some peacefulness, but they traveled with fear, so the Lord brought them comfort as the holy spirit was growing strong in them.

32. Then Peter happened to come down to the saints that were living in Lydda.

33. While there, he came across a man called Aeneas, who for eight years had been laying on a bed because he had been paralyzed.

34. Peter said to him, Aeneas, Jesus Christ has healed you, so rise up and gather up your bed! Immediately he got up!

35. The people that were living in Lydda and Sharon saw him and they were converted unto the Lord.

36. In Joppa there was a disciple named Tabitha (*Hebrew*), translated (*into Greek*) is called Dorcas, and she was full of good and merciful deeds.

37. But she got sick and she died. So they washed her and placed her in an upper room.

38. Joppa being close to Lydda, the disciples had heard that Peter was there, so they sent two men to him and they begged him to come with them immediately.

39. So Peter got up and he went with them. When they arrived, they led him to the upper room and all of the widows stood by him weeping and showed them the clothing that Dorcas made when she was alive.

40. Then Peter threw everyone outside and he got on his knees and he prayed, and he turned to the body and he said, Tabitha, arise! Then she opened up her eyes and when she saw Peter she sat up!

41. Then he offered his hand and helped her get out of bed, and he called the saints and the widows and he showed that she was alive!

42. This miracle was known throughout Joppa and because of it, many committed themselves to the Lord.

43. And Peter remained with Simon the tanner for a substantial period of time.

Acts 10

1. There was a man of Caesarea by the name of Cornelius and he was a centurion from an Italian group.

2. He was a devout man and he feared God, as did his whole household. He did many merciful deeds to help many people, and he was always praying to God.

3. He saw a clear vision about the ninth hour of the day, an angel of God came to him and said, Cornelius!

4. Then he looked at him in terror, but he said, what is this about? The angel said to him, all of your prayers and your merciful deeds have gone up before God;

5. Send your men to Joppa and request Simon, the one who is nicknamed Peter;

6. He is staying with a man by the name of Simon, a tanner whose house is near the sea. He will give instructions unto you.

7. Then the angel that spoke to Cornelius disappeared. Then he called two of his servants; They were soldiers that faithfully did as he commanded.

8. After he explained everything to them, he sent them to Joppa.

9. The following morning they traveled along a road that was leading to the city, and Peter was up on the roof praying at about the sixth hour of the day (noon).

10. He was getting hungry and he was wanting to eat. While they were preparing it, his mind drifted off

11. and he perceived the sky opening up, and an object like a large linen sail was descending, but at the four corners it was tied up together as it was being let down to the earth.

12. In it were all of the four-footed animals of the earth, the wild animals, small critters and the birds that fly in the sky.

13. Then a voice spoke to him and it said, get up Peter, kill and eat!

14. But Peter said, I will not my Lord, I have never eaten anything common or unclean.

15. Then the voice came unto him again and it said, that which God has cleansed, do not consider common or unclean.

16. Then it happened a third time; Then the large linen was taken back up into the sky.

17. Concerning these things, Peter was confused and he began thinking about it unto himself. What is the meaning of this vision that he had seen? Then the men that were sent from Cornelius arrived and were standing on the entry way of Simon's house;

18. They asked if Simon, the one that is nicknamed Peter was staying there.

19. But Peter was still thinking about the vision, then the spirit said to him, three men are looking for you;

20. Therefore, get up, go down and go with them. Do not discriminate; I have sent them.

21. So Peter went down to the men that were sent by Cornelius and he said, I am the one you are looking for! Why are you here?

22. They said, Cornelius is a centurion and a righteous man that fears our God and he holds a good reputation among all of the Jewish nation. He was told by an angel of God to come unto you and ask that you come to his house, that you have something to speak to him.

23. So Peter called them into the home to offer them lodging. The following morning Peter left with them along with some brethren from Joppa that accompanied him.

24. The following day they entered into Caesarea and Cornelius was waiting for them with all of his family and friends.

25. As Peter was entering the house, Cornelius met him and fell at his feet honoring him.

26. But Peter lifted him up and said, stand up! I am only a man.

27. As they talked, they entered into the house to see the many that were gathered together.

28. Then Peter said unto them, you know that it is unlawful (*according to the Jewish law*) for a man who is a Jew to gather with or come near anyone of another nation; But God has shown unto me that I should not consider anyone, due to their race, to be common or unclean.

29. This is the reason that I did not object when you sent for me. I now ask you, why did you send for me?

30. Then Cornelius said, I have fasted for four days, even until this moment; In the ninth hour of that day, I was praying in my house and a figure stood near me wearing bright radiant clothing.

31. He said, Cornelius, your prayers have been heard, your merciful deeds have been recognized by God.

32. Therefore, send your men to Joppa unto Simon Peter. He is staying in the home of Simon the tanner near the sea. When he comes, he will speak to you.

33. Immediately I sent for you and you did come very quickly. So now we are all gathered together here before God and are awaiting to hear all of the things that our God has ordained for you to speak.

34. Peter opened his mouth and said, I recognize that God does not look to outward appearances of men. (Galatians 3:29)

35. But that in every nation, the ones that are committed to God and living righteous lives are acceptable unto him!

36. The message that he has sent unto the sons of Israel is to preach the message of peace (*with God*) through Jesus Christ, because he is the master of everyone.

37. Are you aware of the things that happened throughout all of Judea, beginning with the baptism that John proclaimed in Galilee;

38. Jesus of Nazareth was anointed by God with the spirit of God and power; That he went around doing good things and healing all who were suffering and oppressed by the devil. This is because God is in him. (1 John 4:1-5)

39. We are witnesses of everything that he did in the nation of the Jews and in Jerusalem; Yet they killed him, hanging him on a cross!

40. But God raised him up on the third day and he was seen by many people. (Matthew 27:52-53)

41. But not unto everyone; Only unto the witnesses that he had beforehand chosen by God; We ate and drank with him after he was raised from the dead! (Luke 22:16; Luke 24:42)

42. He commanded us to announce unto all people and to solemnly testify that it is he who is ordained by God as the judge of those that will eternally live and those that will die. (Revelation 20:12-15)

43. The prophets testified of him, that through his name, deliverance from sins is received by everyone who fully commits themselves unto him. (Acts 2:38)

44. As Peter was speaking these words, the spirit of the holy one came upon all that were listening to the message.

45. All of the faithful Jewish converts that came with Peter from Joppa were amazed, because the gift of the holy spirit was also given unto the gentiles!

46. They heard them speak in foreign languages and worshipping God.

47. Then Peter said; Does anyone object to these people being baptized in water? The holy spirit has been given unto them, just as with us! (Matthew 28:19; John 3:3-5)

48. Then he commanded them to be baptized in the name of the Lord Jesus! (Acts 2:38; Matthew 18:1-4; Acts 3:19; Romans 6:1-23) Then they were asked to remain there with them for several days.

Acts 11

1. The disciples and brethren throughout Judea had heard that the gentiles had received the message of God. (Matthew 28:19)

2. When Peter returned to Jerusalem, many of the Jews disputed with him and said;

3. You went to people not of this nation and you ate with them?

4. But Peter told the whole story from the beginning, and he said;

5. I was in the city of Joppa deeply abiding in prayer; I saw in my mind a vision, an object like a large linen sail was descending, but at the four corners it was tied up as it was being let down to the earth from the heavens and it came near me;

6. I looked closely and I saw, in it were all of the four-footed animals of the earth, the wild animals, small critters and the birds that fly in the sky.

7. I then heard a voice say to me, get up Peter, kill and eat!

8. But I said, I will not my Lord, I have never eaten anything common. Nothing unclean has ever entered into my lips.

9. Then the voice came unto me again and said, that which God has cleansed, do not consider unclean.

10. Then this happened a third time; Then everything ascended back up into the sky.

11. That is when I looked, and there stood three men at the house that I was staying at, and they were sent from Caesarea for me!

12. Then he said to me, go with them. Do not discriminate against them. So six brethren came with me and we entered into the house of this man.

13. He told us that he saw an angel in his house standing there and talking with him and told him, send men to Joppa and request for Simon Peter to come;

14. He will speak a message unto you, and by it you and all of your house shall be brought unto salvation.

15. As I was speaking the message, the spirit of the holy one came upon everyone, just as it did on us in the beginning! (Acts 2:1-4)

16. I remembered the message of the Lord and how he said, John baptized with water, moreover, you will also be baptized in the wealth of God (G-907+G2344+G2316) by the spirit of the holy one.
(John 3:5; John 20:22; Acts 1:5)

17. So if God gave unto them the same gift that he had given unto those of us who have committed our trust unto the Lord Jesus Christ, then who was I to stand in the way of God?

18. When they heard this, they became peaceful together and they honored God and said, God has offered renewed life through repentance unto the gentiles. (Acts 2:38; Acts 3:19)

19. Those that were scattered in foreign nations, because of the persecution that happened concerning Stephen, they had been passing through Phoenicia, Cyprus and Antioch preaching unto only Jews;

20. But there were some who had come to Antioch that were from Cyprus and Syria that spoke to some of the Greeks announcing the gospel of Jesus Christ.

21. The hand of God was with them, and a large number of them believed and turned unto the Lord.

22. This got back to the Christians in Jerusalem, so they sent out Barnabas to go out to them in Antioch.

23. When he came, he saw the presence of God in them. They were cheerful to be taught the necessity of each one's heart to remain faithful unto the Lord. (Romans 6:16; Hebrews 10:26; Numbers 15:28-31)

24. Barnabas <u>was</u> a good man who <u>was</u> full of the holy spirit and faithful unto God in all things.

Verse 24 speaks in the past tense concerning Barnabas, signifying that he was already dead at the time that the book of Acts was being written. The epistle of Barnabas certainly was written early on, well before the book of Acts, giving it much credibility. It is no wonder the early church held the Epistle of Barnabas as part of their cannon.

25. Then Barnabas went to Tarsus to locate Saul (*Paul*);

26. When he found him, they went back to Antioch. And when they were with that assembly for a full year and they had been teaching a considerable amount of people, the disciples in Antioch were first called Christians (*Christ-like*).

27. And at this time, some prophets from Jerusalem came down to Antioch;

28. One whose name was Agabus had stood up and indicated by the spirit that a great famine was about to begin across the entire Roman empire. This happened during the reign of Claudius Caesar.

29. The disciples declared that if anyone was prosperous and could send aid to the brothers living in Judea, that they should aid them. (*this happened at a much later time and is out of context in this place.*)
(2 Corinthians 8)

30. This they truly did, and they sent it in the care of Barnabas and Saul (*Paul*).

Acts 12

1. At that time Herod the king stretched forth his hands to go after some of the Christians.

2. He killed James, the brother of John with the sword. (*this happened in 47 AD or later*)

3. When he saw that this was pleasing to the Jews, he arrested Peter also. This happened during the days of unleavened bread.

4. He was arrested and thrown into prison with four squads of soldiers to guard him, having the intent to bring him out unto the people after Passover.

5. While Peter was being held in prison, there was an earnest effort by the gatherings of Christians to call out to God on his behalf.

6. The night before Herod was going to bring him out, Peter was chained with two chains and was sleeping

between two soldiers and there were also guards protecting the prison outside the gates.

7. Suddenly, an angel of the Lord stood near and his light showed throughout the building and it shined upon Peter and woke him up. Then the angel said, get up quickly, and his chains fell off of his hands.

8. Then the angel said, here, put on your robe and your shoes! So Peter did these things. Then the angel said, now put on your coat and follow me.

9. And he followed him out but he did not know for sure if this was truly an angel with him or if it was a dream.

10. After they passed two guards, they came to an iron gate that gave entrance to the city, and it opened by itself for them. They walked out and went down the first street, immediately the angel disappeared.

11. When Peter had realized all that had happened and that he was awake, he said to himself, now I know that an angel of the Lord was sent to save me from out of the hands of Herod and from all that was being anticipated by the Jews. (Hebrews 1:14)

12. Then he thought about where to go, he came unto the house of Mary, the mother of John who held the nickname Mark, and there were many of the disciples gathered there praying.

13. When Peter knocked on the door, there was a servant girl by the name of Rhoda that came out to answer the door.

14. But when she recognized Peter's voice, she did not even open the door, being so happy she ran to tell the others that Peter was at the door knocking!

15. But those inside said that she is delusional! Yet she continued to insist that it is true. Then they said, it must be his ghost, yet Peter kept knocking.

16. When they finally opened the door, they saw him and were greatly surprised.

17. He signaled unto them to be quiet, then told them of how the Lord brought him out of the prison. Then he said, go and tell James and the others, then he left that house. *(James had recently been killed)*

18. When the daylight arose, there was a great disturbance among the soldiers at the prison concerning what happened to Peter!

19. Herod searched for him but could not find him, and he interrogated the guards and demanded that they be removed from their duties. Peter left Judea and went to Caesarea and remained there.

20. Herod had been extremely hostile unto the Tyrians and the Sidonians, then came to a peaceful agreement with them when he convinced Blastus, the chamberlain of the king to ask for peace, because their country was being supplemented from the bounty of that kingdom.

21. On the appropriate day, the king presented himself in the royal clothing and set himself over a tribunal and then he made a speech to the people.

22. The crowds began yelling out; "This is the voice of a god, not a man!" Immediately the angel of God struck him down, because he did not honor God. Worms began eating him and he died.

23. The message of God was spreading and brought increase.

Verse 25 is inaccurate when compared with Paul's account in Galatians 1-2.

25. Barnabas and Paul returned to Jerusalem when they had completed their appointed services, and John Mark came with them.

Acts 13

1. In Antioch, there were some that were among the existing Christian gathering that were prophets and teachers; Barnabas, Simeon who was called Niger, Lucius of Cyrenia, Manaen the cousin of Herod the king, and Paul.

2. They served the Lord and were fasting when the spirit of the holy one said, now Barnabas and Paul must be taken to do the work that I have called them to do. *(They were already doing the will of God)*

3. Then after fasting and praying with their hands upon them, they sent them off.

4. They were sent by the spirit of the holy one and they went to Seleucia, and then they sailed to Cyprus.

5. When they got to Salmis, they proclaimed the message of God unto the synagogues of the Jews, with John (*Mark*) as an assistant.

6. They traveled through as far as the island of Paphos where they came across a certain Jew who was a sorcerer and false prophet whose name was Barjesus.

7. He was with the proconsul Sergius Paulus, who was a brilliant man. He called Barnabas and Paul unto them so that they could hear the message of God.

8. But the sorcerer tried to turn the proconsul away from the faith (*doctrine*).

9. But Saul, whose name became Paul, was full of the holy spirit and he looked closely at him and said,

10. you are full of great deceptions and you are cunning, but you are the son of Satan and an enemy of righteousness! Will you never stop perverting the ways of God?

11. Now the hand of God is fallen upon you and you will be blind and you will not see daylight for a time.

12. Now when the proconsul saw this occur, he believed and was astonished at the doctrine of God.

13. Then Paul got on a ship and sailed to Paphos and entered into Perga in Pamphylia. John (*Mark*) abandoned them and headed to Jerusalem. (Acts 15:38)

14. As they went through Perga, they finally arrived in Antioch of Pisidian; They then entered into the synagogue on the Sabbath day and sat down.

15. After they read from the old testament scriptures of what the prophets wrote, the synagogue leadership approached them and said, if you have a message of correction and education for the people, speak it!

16. So then Paul stood up and signaled with his hand and he said, Israelites and those who abide in the fear of the Lord, hear these words!

17. The God of the people of Israel chose our forefathers and raised them up from being strangers in the land of Egypt, and with his power he brought them out of that place.

18. For forty years he endured their disobedience in the desert,
(*there were also 40 years from the resurrection of Christ until the destruction of Jerusalem in 70 AD*)

19. then he pulled down seven nations in Canaan and gave unto them an inheritance of the land.

20. For four hundred fifty years he gave them judges, until Samuel the prophet.

21. But then they asked for a king and God gave them Saul, the son of Kish, a man from the tribe of Benjamin and he reigned for forty years.

22. When he was removed, God raised up David as the king, of whom he also wrote concerning him; "I have found David, the son of Jesse, a man who seeks after my own heart, and he will do everything that I ask of him to do." (1 Samuel 13:14)

23. It was of this man that God promised an offspring (*seed*) that would rise up as the savior, Jesus Christ.

24. John (*baptizer*) came before him and preached the baptism of repentance to all of the people in Israel.

25. As John completed his course, he asked, who do you think that I am? I am not the Messiah. But know this, that he who shall come after me, I am not worthy to untie his shoes. (John 1:27)

26. Men and brothers, children of the lineage of Abraham, those of you that fear the Lord our God, the message of salvation has now been offered unto you. (Romans 11:32)

27. Those living in Jerusalem and the rulers of the people, they rejected this man, even though they read the messages of the prophets on every Sabbath day, they fulfilled the prophecies by condemning him.

28. And though they found no reason to kill him, they required Pilate to have him crucified.

29. When they had fulfilled all that was prophesied in the scriptures concerning him, they took him down from the cross and placed him in a tomb.

30. But God raised him from the dead!

31. Then he showed himself many times unto those who had followed him up from Galilee to Jerusalem, and they were witnesses of him unto the people.

32. We now declare unto you this long-awaited good news that our forefathers promised would come.

33. God has now given his promise unto us, through the resurrection of Jesus. This is also written in the second Psalm: "You are my son, and this day I have brought you forth." (Psalms 2:7)

34. And because he has been raised from the dead, he will never turn back again to see corruption (*decay*) just as he said, "I will give unto you the sacred mercy of faithful David." (Isaiah 55:3)

35. In another place he said, "you will not have the holy one be corrupted." (Psalms 16:10)

36. But after serving his people by the instructions of God, David did die along with his forefathers, and he did see decay (*corruption*),

37. but the one who God raises up shall not see corruption (*death and decay*).

38. Therefore let it be known to you my brethren, that through him, it is now announced you can receive deliverance from your sins, from all of the things that under the law of Moses you could not be justified from.

39. But through him (*Jesus Christ*), everyone that fully commits themselves unto him shall be cleared of all charges against them. (Acts 2:38; Acts 3:19; Romans 3:25; Romans 6:7; 1 John 5:16-17; Numbers 15:28-31)

40. So now, take heed of the things spoken by the prophets, that they not come upon you.

41. "Look you heathen, be astonished and then die! For I will do something awful in those days, a thing that you will not believe if anyone tells you of it!" (Habakkuk 1:5; Daniel 9:24-27; Jeremiah 7:29-34; Luke 19:43)

42. When the Jews left the synagogue, the gentiles were begging that they again speak these words unto the people on the next Sabbath.

43. But when their gathering was broken up in the synagogue, many of the Jews and devout converts followed Paul and Barnabas and they continued speaking with them, and they asked them to continue speaking about the charity of God.

44. On the following Sabbath, almost the entire city was gathered to hear the message of God.

45. When the Jews saw the crowds, they were filled with jealousy and they began arguing against the things that were spoken by Paul, contradicting and blaspheming against him.

46. But Paul spoke boldly, and Barnabas said, it was necessary that we first speak the message of God unto you, but since you have rejected it, judging yourselves not worthy of receiving everlasting life, now we have turned to the gentiles!

47. This is what our God has commanded of us, "I have put you to be a light unto the gentiles, so that you might bring my salvation unto the people of the whole earth." (Isaiah 49:6)

48. When they heard this, the gentiles celebrated the message from God and all that chose to live worthy to receive everlasting life also believed. (John 3:16-21; Acts 26:18)

49. The message of our Lord was brought throughout that city.

50. Then the Jews urged upon the elite women, noblemen and the leaders of the city, and they brought persecution against Paul and Barnabas and they threw them out of their city!

51. So they shook off the dust from their feet, then they went to Iconium,
(Luke 9:5; Mark 6:11; Matthew 10:14)

52. and the disciples there were joyful and full of the spirit of holiness.

Acts 14

1. In Iconium they went together and entered into the synagogue of the Jews; When they spoke, a large number of Jews and gentiles believed them,

2. but the Jews that did not believe incited the hearts of the gentiles against the brethren.

3. Yet for a considerable amount of time they spoke boldly concerning the Lord, spreading the message of the power of God and many miracles and wonders were all done through their hands.

4. But the people of the city were divided, some being in agreement with the Jews and others in agreement with the apostles.

5. Then a violent outbreak occurred between the gentile believers and the Jews, so the rulers insulted them and some threw stones at them

6. hoping that they would leave and go to the cities in Lycaonia, Lystria and Derbe and surrounding areas.

7. When they got there, they continued preaching the same message of the gospel of Jesus Christ.

8. There was a certain man in Lystria was unable to use his feet and he sat there being crippled since his mother's womb; He was never able to walk.

9. He heard Paul speaking and he (*Paul*) intently looked at him and saw that the crippled man had the trust and dedication to be healed;

10. Then he said with a loud voice; Stand upright on your feet! The man leaped up and he began walking.

11. And the crowds of people saw what Paul had done and they began raising their voices up in Lycaonian and said, the gods have come down to us in the image of men!

12. They called Barnabas, Zeus and they called Paul, Hermes, because he was the one leading.

13. Then the priests of Zeus went before their city and they brought oxen and wreathes to the gates because the crowds were looking for a sacrifice!

14. But when Paul and Barnabas heard of this, they leaped into the crowd, ripping their clothes and they began crying out,

15. people, why are you doing these things? We are men like you with similar interests as you people have; We are teaching to live accordingly to the good news that we bring you, to turn away from the worthless things and submit yourselves unto the living God who made the heavens, earth, oceans and all that is in them!

16. In past times he allowed every nation to go according to their own ways. (Hebrews 5:2)

17. But he did not forsake you without leaving good witnesses! He gives us the rain and the fruit bearing seasons which fills us with food and happiness within our hearts. (*The way of nature is evidence of God*)

18. When he said these things, he was barely able to settle down the crowds, but he prevented them from sacrificing unto them.

19. But some Jews came over from Antioch to Iconium and they began to deceive the crowds, then they drug Paul outside of the city and stoned him until they thought that he was dead!

20. But the disciples there surrounded him and he stood up, then they entered the city, but on the following morning, Paul and Barnabas went to Derbe.

21. There they preached the message in that city and they made many disciples, then they returned to Lystria, Iconium and then Antioch

22. to help establish the souls of the disciples in those places, urging them to continue in their dedication. They told them that only through many difficulties, hardships and persecutions will we enter into the kingdom of God. (Philippines 1:29; Matthew 5:10-11; John 16:33; 1 Thessalonians 3:4; Isaiah 59:15)

23. After hand picking the elders in every gathering, they took time to pray and fast, then they presented those that believed unto the Lord!

24. Then they traveled through Pisidia and they made their way to Pamphylia.

25. They began speaking the message in Perga and then they came to Attalia;

26. From there they sailed back to Antioch, the place that they originally gave the message of the charity of God; They had then completed what they had begun.

27. When they arrived and called the gathering together, they reported to them all of the things that God had done through them, and that he opened up the foreign nations to faithfulness unto God.

28. They remained there for a long while with the disciples.

Acts 15

1. There were some men from Judea who went down to Antioch and began teaching that if you are not physically circumcised by the custom of Moses, that you are not able to be eternally saved.

2. A massive controversial dispute broke out, Paul and Barnabas among them. So they chose Paul and Barnabas and some others to go to the apostles in Jerusalem concerning this matter.

3. So they were sent by that gathering and they went through Phoenicia and Samaria announcing conversion unto the gentiles. This produced a great amount of joy among the brethren.

4. When they arrived in Jerusalem they were welcomed by the congregation and they announced unto the apostles and the elders all of what God had done through them. (Galatians 2:4-10)

5. But there were some that stood up from a sect of the Pharisee believers that said it is necessary to be circumcised and that they keep the whole Mosaic law. (Galatians 2:4)

Verse 6 contradicts Galatians 2:1-9.

6. The apostles and elders assembled together concerning this matter.

7. This brought about much discussion, then Peter said unto them, brethren, you know that from the ancient times, God chose that the gentiles should hear the message of the gospel from our mouths and that they would commit themselves unto it. (Galatians 2:8)

8. And God, who knows every man's heart, has verified this by giving them the spirit of the holy one, the same as he gave unto us. (Hebrews 4:12) (*only God gives the holy spirit, not any man!*)

9. He has made no difference between us and them, but by the true doctrine they have cleansed their hearts. (Galatians 3:28-29; Galatians 2:14)

10. So now, why do you challenge God, to attempt to put a yoke upon the necks of the disciples, of which our forefathers nor we have had the strength to carry? (Galatians 2:4)

11. But by the power of God, through the Lord Jesus Christ, we truly believe that we shall be saved in the same way as they will. (Romans 2:10-11; Galatians 3:28-29)

12. And the crowd that had gathered became silent to hear the message that Barnabas and Paul told of what God had done through them in the foreign nations, including many miracles and signs.

13. After that, James said; Brethren, hear my words.

14. Simon (*Peter*) has testified that he saw that God took out from the gentile people into his name.

15. And the words of the prophets confirm this, as it is written,

16. "In that day I will return and build up the tabernacle of David that is fallen, and after it has been demolished, I will rebuild and I will make it straight.

17. In this, all men can seek the Lord, even all nations of whom have been called by my name, says the Lord who will do all of these things." (Amos 9:11-12)

18. All of the deeds of each man are known unto God since the beginning, (Romans 2:6)

19. This is the reason that I will not harass (*burden*) the people that turn to God.

Verses 20, 21 and 29 were added by a scribe and contradict many other scriptures.
(Matthew 15:11-18; Galatians 3:1-29; Mark 7:15-20; 1 Corinthians 3:17-20; 1 Corinthians 8:4-10;
Romans 14:2-16; Luke 10:8; Colossians 2:16-18; Romans 10:10-12; Barnabas 14)

What was decided was that the Mosaic law was fulfilled, completed by Christ
and is not valid any longer and that we must now obey the law of God because
we will all be judged by it, based upon each of our actions that we do in this life.

The law of God must be upheld by all true Christians.
(Matthew 22:37-40; Mark 12:30-31; Luke 10:25-28)

22. Then all was settled and seemed good unto the apostles and the elders in all of the assemblies, and they chose men to accompany Paul and Barnabas unto Antioch; Judas called Barsabas, Silas, and some other leaders from among the brethren.

23. And he handwrote a document much like this: Apostles, elders and brethren, unto all those throughout Antioch, Syria and Cilicia, brethren of the nations, we greet you.

24. Since we have heard that some who have gone out from us have agitated you in their message, and have unsettled your spirits saying that you must be circumcised and keep the Mosaic law, we did not give these commands unto them.

25. It seemed right, having come to a unanimous agreement, we chose men to send to you along with the beloved Barnabas and Paul;

26. These men have walked away from their own desires in this life to do the work of Jesus Christ;

27. Therefore, we have sent Judas and Silas with them as they have also committed themselves unto announcing these same things.

28. It is approved by the spirit of the holy one and also unto us that no other burden be put upon you than the necessary things;

30. And when they were on their way unto Antioch, they gathered a large amount of people as they delivered the letter.

31. And as it was read, they joyfully received the comfort.

32. Judas and Silas were also prophets and encouraged the brethren through a long dialog.

33. After they stayed there for a time, they were finally released to go in peace from the brethren and go back to the apostles (*in Jerusalem*).

34. But Silas thought it was necessary to remain there.

35. Paul and Barnabas remained in Antioch teaching and announcing the message of the Lord, along with many of the others.

36. After a period of time, Paul said to Barnabas, maybe we should go back unto all of the brethren in every city in which we have already announced the message of the Lord, to see how they are holding up!

37. Barnabas recommended that they take John Mark with them,

38. however Paul thought that it was not good to take him with them, because he had abandoned them

when they were in Pamphylia and did not continue in the work. (Acts 13:13)

39. There was contention enough to separate them from each other, so Barnabas took Mark and sailed to Cypress.

40. Paul chose to bring Silas and went with the prayers of the brethren that they remain in God's favor.

41. He went through Syria and Cilicia and strengthened the assemblies in those places.

It must be noted:
Chapters 1-15 make up part 1 of the book of Acts.
Up until this point, the narrator has spoken in the third person, often using the term "they".
Beginning in Acts chapter 16 the narrator begins using the term "we",
demonstrating that he was there as a witness of many of the things beyond this point.
It looks like the journals of Timothy were used for chapters 16-28
of which were gathered by a latecomer and non-witness of these events,
who then compiled them with many other notes and testimonials used for the first 15 chapters
to form the book of Acts that we now have. (Philippines 1:1-7; Acts 16:12)

Acts 16

1. Then Paul came to Derbe and Lystria (*in Asia Minor*) and there was a disciple there by the name of Timothy, the son of a certain faithful Jewish woman but his father was Greek. (2 Timothy 1:5)

2. He was well recommended by the brethren in Lystria and Iconium.

3. Paul wanted him to come with him, to take him away from the Jews in those places because they knew that his father was a Greek. (*they would try to force circumcision upon him*)

4. As we made our way through the cities, we delivered the decree concerning how to live, of which was agreed upon by the apostles and the elders in Jerusalem.

5. The assemblies were strengthened in the true doctrine and were increasing in their numbers daily!

6. When we had passed through Phrygia and the country of Galatia, we were prevented from speaking in Asia by the holy spirit.

7. Coming near to Mysia, we tried to go along into Bithynia, but the holy spirit did not allow us.

8. So we passed near Mysia and entered into Troas.

9. Then Paul received a dream at night, a certain man from Macedonia standing there asking him to come to Macedonia because they need your assistance!

10. After seeing this dream, he immediately sought to go out to Macedonia, convinced that the Lord has called us to come and preach unto them.

11. So we then set forth from Troas and ran directly to Samothrace, and the following day into Neapolis.

12. From there we went to Philippi, which is the principal city at the forefront of Macedonia. We were in that city for several days.

13. On the Sabbath day, we went outside of the city near the river where there was a chapel. Sitting down, we spoke to the women that gathered together there.

14. There was a certain woman by the name of Lydia who sold purple fabric in the city of Thyatira and she revered God. As she listened, the Lord opened her heart and she understood the things that were being spoken by Paul.

15. When she was baptized, she demanded of Paul, if you have judged me worthy to be committed unto the Lord, then come to my home and be lodged there. She then continued urging them.

16. After we had come to that chapel, a servant girl approached them who had a spirit of divination and she had gained much wealth for her masters by fortune-telling.

17. She followed us and she yelled out saying, these men are servants of the most high God, and they announce unto us the way to salvation.

18. She did this for many days and it began to frustrate Paul, so he turned towards her and said, spirit, I command you in the name of Jesus Christ to come out of her, and it came out of her!

19. When the masters of that girl saw that their expectation of making more wealth through her was taken away, they arrested Paul and Silas and drug them into the town square before the magistrates.

20. When they brought them near, they said, these men are greatly disturbing our city.

21. Being Jews, they announce customs that are not lawful for us, because we are Romans!

22. The crowd gathered against them and the magistrate tore off their clothes, ordering them to be beaten.

23. They laid many stripes upon them and then threw them into prison, ordering the jailor to secure them.

24. The one that was commanded of this threw them into the inner prison and their feet were fastened into shackles.

25. As midnight approached, Paul and Silas were abiding in prayer and hymning praises unto God and the other prisoners listened to them.

26. Suddenly a mighty earthquake occurred, so strong that it shook the foundations of that prison; Immediately the doors were all opened and their shackles were loosened.

27. The jailer was woken up by this and when he saw that the doors of the prison were opened up, he was about to kill himself, expecting that the prisoners had escaped.

28. But a loud voice called out to him from Paul that said, do not harm yourself, for everyone is still here.

29. So he asked for the torches to be brought in, and he grew weak and fell before Paul and Silas.

30. Then he led them outside and asked, teachers, what shall I do to be saved?

31. They said, fully commit yourself unto Jesus the Christ, both you and your family will be saved *(from their sins)*.

32. And they spoke unto him and all those in his house, the message of Christ Jesus.

33. Then they were taken at that late hour in the night to have their whipping stripes washed (*verse 23*) and they immediately baptized him and his family.

34. Then they brought them (*Paul and Silas*) unto the house and set a table of food before them. The whole house was very joyful having put their trust in God.

35. The following day the magistrates came with the constable and said, release those men.

36. The jailer told this to Paul, that the magistrates have ordered that you be released. Go out in peace.

37. But Paul said to them, you whipped us publicly and threw us in prison, yet we are uncondemned men, and we are Romans! Now you attempt to secretly release us? That is not gonna happen! Let them come here themselves and release us!

38. And when the constables reported these words to the magistrates, they became frightened, knowing that they are Romans.

39. So they came and begged of them to come out and to leave their city.

40. As they went out from the prison, they went to the home of Lydia and they saw their brethren, then they left that city.

Acts 17

1. While traveling through Amphipolis and Apollonia, we came into Thessalonica where there was a synagogue of the Jews.

2. As he regularly did, Paul went on three Sabbaths and there he had a dialog with them from the scriptures.

3. He opened up and brought forth that Christ must suffer and rise from the dead. Then he said, this Jesus that I announce to you is the Christ.

4. Some of them were convinced, so they associated themselves with Paul and Silas. This included a large number of the devout Greeks and many of the prominent women.

5. But the disobedient Jews became jealous and gathered some wicked people from the market place and gathered together a large crowd and brought the city into chaos. First they came unto the home of Jason, and looked to bring the mob upon them.

6. But when they did not find them there, they drug Jason out and some of the other brethren, taking them to the magistrate and they began screaming, those who have turned the habitable world upside down, they have arrived here as well!

7. They testified that Jason had received them into his home, those that are contrary to the practiced laws of Caesar, saying that there is another king, Jesus the Christ.

8. Then they began agitating the crowd and the magistrates that were hearing these things,

9. They took some security (*bail money*) from Jason and the others, then they released them.

10. So the brethren immediately sent Paul and Silas out of that place and sent them to Berea. When they arrived, again they went into the synagogue of the Jews.

11. There, they were much more noble than those in Thessalonica, because they received the message with much anticipation and they examined the scriptures daily to see if these things were true!

12. Truly, many of them committed themselves to believe, even from the prominent Greek men and women there were also many that believed.

13. But when the Jews from Thessalonica found out that Paul was also proclaiming the message of God in Berea, they went there to incite the crowds.

14. Then immediately the brethren there in Berea sent Paul towards the sea, but Timothy and Silas stayed there in Berea.

15. Those that were assisting Paul took him as far as Athens. They then received a command from Paul that Silas and Timothy come to him there, and we quickly departed.

16. While awaiting them in Athens, Paul was uneasy in his spirit as he saw that the city was full of many statues.

17. Then he began addressing the synagogue of the Jews and those that were worshipping. He even approached those in the market place every day until they finally arrived.

18. Some of the Epicureans and the Stoic philosophers encountered him. Some said, what seed might this speaker be trying to announce? He seems to be an announcer of foreign demons because he is proclaiming that this Jesus has been resurrected from the dead!

19. So they grabbed a hold of him and took him to the Aero Pagus (*Mars Hill*) and said, can you explain to us what this new doctrine is that you have been speaking about?

20. You have announced many startling things into the ears of the people and we are interested in knowing what these things are all about!

21. You see, all Athenians and those that are foreigners living here, they make the time to hear or to tell of something that is new!

22. And Paul, standing in the middle of Mars Hill said, men of Athens, I have observed that you respect every possible god!

23. As I have walked through your city, I have seen your objects of worship and I have even seen an alter in which had written upon it, to an unknown God! Though you do not even know him, you honor him. This is the one that I announce unto you.

24. The God that made the entire world and all of the things in it, this one is the master of the heavens and the earth and he does not live in temples that were built by the hands of men,

25. nor do the hands of men bring service unto him. He does not have need of anything. He has created the life and breath in everything.

26. He has made all of mankind from one bloodline, including everyone from every nation on the earth, and he has predetermined the time and the limits of where they live.

27. Even though he is not far from each of us, if we seek after him and happen to find him, we must seek to honor him.

28. Because of him we live, move and exist. This is the same thing that some of your poets have said, because we are also from his kindred.

29. Then, being kindred unto God, we should not think that God is likened unto gold, silver, stone or anything that has been crafted by an artist according to the imagination of a man!

30. Truly God has overlooked the times of the ignorance of men, but now he commands that all people everywhere recognize these things; (Jonah 3:8-10)

31. Because he has set a day when he will judge the entire earth righteously by the one who he has anointed (*Jesus Christ*) (Romans 2:6-11; Revelation 20:12-15) and having raised him from the dead, (Psalms 9:8) now he requires dedication and faithfulness from everyone.

32. When they heard of the resurrection of the dead, some ridiculed, but there were some that said, we will hear more from you another time concerning these things.

33. Then Paul walked away from them;

34. But some of them continued walking with him and believed, of whom were Dionysius and Areopagite and a woman by the name of Damaris and some others with them.

Acts 18

1. After this, Paul left Athens and went to Corinth.

2. He found a certain Jew there by the name of Aquila from the nation of Pontus, having recently arrived there from Italy with his wife Priscilla, because Claudius had ordered that all Jews leave Rome.

3. They became acquainted with each other and because they were workers of the same trade, they lived together and worked together. They were tentmakers by trade.

4. He discussed with the people at the synagogue on every Sabbath and he persuaded many Jews and Greeks.

5. When Timothy and Silas came down from Macedonia, we found that Paul had become distressed in his spirit while earnestly bringing evidence unto the Jews concerning Jesus Christ.

6. This is because they rejected and blasphemed him; So he shook his clothing and he said to them, your blood is on your own heads. I am clean from your blood! I will now go strictly unto the gentiles.

7. From there he went to the house of a man named Justus who worshipped God, and his house was next door to the synagogue.

8. Crispus the synagogue ruler had committed himself unto the Lord with all of his house; Many of the Corinthians that heard the message believed and were properly baptized (G-907 + G-3689).

9. Then the Lord came to Paul in a dream and said, do not fear, continue to speak, do not become silent,

10. because I am with you and no one shall come upon you to harm you. (2 Timothy 4:18) I have many people in this city!

11. So we remained for a year and six months teaching them the instructions of God.

12. But Gallio the proconsul of Achaia, along with the Jews, in one concise effort took Paul and brought him to a tribunal.

13. They testified that he teaches men to worship God against the Mosaic law.

14. But when Paul was about to speak, Gallio said to the Jews, if it was a matter of having done evil or lewd wickedness, I would have a reason to bear with you Jews!

15. But if there is a debate concerning a message of names and your law, you must see to it yourselves. I do not intend to be a judge of these types of things.

16. Then he threw them out of the tribunal!

17. But some of the Greeks arrested Sosthenes, the ruler of the synagogue and they beat him in the presence of the tribunal, but none of this was a concern to Gallio.

18. Paul remained there for quite some time, then he sailed to Syria, unto the brethren that had already left. He took Aquila and Priscilla with him then shaved his head in Cenchrea, because he had made a promise.

19. Then we came down to Ephesus and he left them there. Then he entered into the synagogue and he discussed some things with the Jews.

20. They asked if he would stay for a longer period of time, but he refused.

21. He left them and said, by all means, I must do some shaking (G-4160 + G-4525) at the coming feast in Jerusalem! But I will return back to you, if God is willing. Then he sailed from Ephesus. (Matthew 26:5)

22. He made his way to Caesarea and he went up to offer greetings unto the assembly, then he went to Antioch.

23. After we spent some time there, we departed and passed through Galatia and Phrygia, strengthening the disciples in those places.

24. A certain Jew by the name of Apollos, an Alexandrian by kindred and an eloquent man, came to Ephesus; He was very knowledgeable in the scriptures.

25. He had been taught to live by abiding in the Lord and he was boiling over with passion and he spoke and taught accurately all of the things concerning the Lord, but he only understood the baptism of John.

26. He began to boldly speak in the synagogue, and Aquilla and Priscilla heard him and took him in and more accurately explained unto him the way unto God. (Acts 2:38, 3:19; Matthew 18:10; John 8:31-36; Romans 6:1:1-23)

27. He had the plans to go through Achaia, and being encouraged, the brethren wrote to the disciples there to welcome him. When we arrived we consulted with many of those who completely committed themselves through the power of God;

28. Paul began powerfully proving without a doubt to the Jews publicly, showing through the scriptures that Jesus is the Christ.

Acts 19

1. When Apollos was in Corinth, Paul was passing through the more remote parts, making his way to Ephesus and he came across some disciples and he asked them;

2. Have you received the spirit of the holy one since you have committed yourselves? They said to him, we have never even heard of the spirit of the holy one!

3. And he asked them, into what were you baptized? And they said, the baptism of John.

4. And Paul said, John certainly did offer a baptism of repentance unto the people, but then he told them that they must believe (*be baptized*) in the one who would come after him, that is Jesus the Christ.

5. All those who heard this were baptized into the name of the master, Jesus the Christ. (Acts 2:38; 3:19)

6. Then Paul laid his hands upon them and the holy spirit came into them, and they spoke in languages and prophesied. (1 John 4:3)

7. And the total number of the men there were twelve.

8. Then they went into the synagogue and boldly spoke for over three months, talking and convincing the people of all the things concerning the kingdom of God.

9. But some were hardened in their hearts and disobeyed, they spoke evil of the true way in front of the people and they turned away from them. (Jude 1:4; 2 Peter 2:1; Acts 20:29-30; 2 Thessalonians 2:10-12; Galatians 2:4-5) Paul cast out those false disciples and daily he continued teaching there in the school of a man named Tyrannus. (1 Corinthians 5:5)

10. Over the next two years, everyone living in Asia heard the message of the Lord Jesus, both Jews and Greeks.

11. God did many powerful things through the hands of Paul;

12. Even some of those that were sick were brought handkerchiefs or towels from him and they were healed from diseases, even the evil spirits went out of them.

13. But some of the vagabond Jews that were exorcists called some that had evil spirits, and by the name of the Lord Jesus, they said, we command you, by the one whom Paul preaches to come out! (Matthew 7:21)

14. And they were seven sons of Sceva and a Jewish high priest doing this;

15. But the evil spirits said to them, I know Jesus and I know Paul, but who are you?

16. Then the man with the evil spirit jumped upon them and overpowered them; He beat them so badly that they ran out of that house, both greatly traumatized and naked!

17. This became known unto everyone, both Jews and Greeks. Everyone living at Ephesus was taken by fear and the name of the Lord Jesus was greatly honored.

18. Many who had committed themselves to believe came to acknowledge and speak of these things.

19. Many of those that did practice the magical arts brought together all of their scrolls and burned them in the presence of everyone! They counted the values of them and it was fifty thousand shekels of silver.

20. With much power, the message of the Lord was spreading, and it was powerful.

21. After this, Paul was led by the spirit through Macedonia and Achaia with a plan to go to Jerusalem; After going there, he planned to make his way to Rome.

22. He sent two men into Macedonia to minister unto them, Timothy and Erastus. He put off going to Asia (*Jerusalem*) for a little while.

23. It was about that time when a great disturbance occurred along the way.

24. Demetrius, a silversmith that made silver shrines unto Artemas (*Diana - a Greek goddess*) had brought about a large business for many craftsmen.

25. He said, men, you know that it is by this craft that we have our wealth.

26. You have seen and heard, not only in Ephesus, but throughout all of Asia, this Paul has convinced a large number of people that those things that are made by hands are not gods.

27. You see, not only our livelihood is in danger, but also the temple of the great goddess Diana is considered to be nothing and her greatness is being diminished.

28. After hearing these things they became greatly angered and they yelled out, great is Artemis of the Ephesians!

29. The city went into chaos, and they rushed in, in one assault upon the theater they firmly grabbed Gaius and Aristarchus the Macedonian traveling companions of Paul.

30. Now Paul had the desire to enter into the mob, but his disciples prevented him.

31. Some of the Asiarchs that were his friends transmitted a message to him and begged him to not go to the theater.

32. There were others that cried out and many of the assembly was confused, because most of them did not know why they had gathered together.

33. But they drug Alexander out of the crowd and the Jews pushed him forward. Alexander threw his hands up and tried to defend himself against the mob;

34. But because they knew that he was a Jew, they all yelled together for over two hours, great is Artemas of the Ephesians!

35. Finally, the town secretary quieted the crowd and said, men of Ephesus, who does not know the temple keeper of the goddess Artemis is in the city of Ephesus, because of the great thing that fell from the sky?

36. Being that this is undeniable, it is necessary that you calm yourselves and do nothing before thinking it out first.

37. For these men that you brought are not temple thieves nor are they blaspheming your goddess.

38. If Demetrius and those craftsmen that are with him have a matter against anyone, the courts are open and the proconsuls are there; Bring your complaints to them!

39. If you are upset because of other reasons, it will be settled in a lawful assembly.

40. Today we are also in danger of being accused of insurrection, and without a cause, we will not be able to give a reason for this crowd to have been gathered together.

41. After he had said these things, he dismissed the crowd.

Acts 20

1. After the end of the disturbance, Paul called together the disciples and he spent time to say his goodbyes and then he journeyed to Macedonia.

2. As he passed through the towns, he gave much encouragement unto them, speaking about many things, then he made his way to Greece.

3. Paul spent three months there because there happened to be a conspiracy against him by the Jews, who were about to leave by boat to Syria, so he planned to return to Macedonia.

4. Sopater, a Berean; Aristarchus, and Secundus of Thessalonica; Gaius of Derbe, Timothy of Asia, and also Tychicus and Trophimus accompanied him all the way to Asia, (Hebrews 13:23)
(one of these men is the author of Acts chapters 16-28; Acts 18:5 narrows this down to Timothy)

5. but we went ahead and awaited him in Troas.

6. We sailed from Philippi after the days of unleavened bread and after five days we made our way to Troas and we stayed there for seven days.

7. On one of the Sabbaths, the disciples gathered together to break bread, and Paul discussed some things with them about leaving the following morning. He continued the discussion until midnight.

8. And there were many lamps in the upper room where we had gathered.

9. A certain young man by the name of Eutychus sat on the window sill, and he was overcome by sleep; Paul spoke for quite some time, and being deep in sleep, he fell from the third-floor window and he was thought to be dead.

10. So Paul went down and picked him up, embraced him and said, do not fear, his soul has not left him.

11. So we went up and broke bread and ate and we talked until dawn, then we departed.

12. We brought the boy with us and were greatly comforted by him.

13. We proceeded onward and boarded a ship and set sail for Assos, intending to meet Paul there as we had previously arranged, because he chose to go by foot.

14. When we met with him in Assos, we took him in and we made our way to Mitylene.

15. We sailed out from there and the following day came to the place across from Chios; The following day we crossed to Samos and we stayed in Trogyllium. The following day we made it to Miletus.

16. But Paul had decided to sail past Ephesus, so to not spend time in that part of Asia, because he was eager if it was possible to be in Jerusalem on the day of Pentecost.

17. From Miletus, he sent a message to Ephesus calling for the elders of the assembly there.

18. When they came to him, he said this: You know that from the first day I set foot in Asia, I was with you all of the time.

19. Serving the Lord with complete humility and many tears, I faced much adversity and many difficulties because of the many plots of the Jews;

20. I did not keep anything back from you that is profitable. I taught you publicly and from house to house

21. earnestly testifying unto the Jews and the Greeks of repentance unto God and dedication unto the Lord Jesus Christ.

22. Now, being a servant unto the spirit, I am going to Jerusalem; But those there do not know that I am coming.

23. The spirit of the holy one testifies city by city that chains and much persecution await me there;

24. I do not care about this, as I do not value my life to be precious to myself, though I must finish the race with joy. This ministry that I have received from the Lord Jesus Christ is to announce as a witness, the gospel of Jesus Christ and demonstrate the power of God.

25. And know this! I know that you will never see my face again; You, whom I spent so much time with proclaiming the kingdom of God.

26. Therefore I tell you today, I am clean from the blood of all men.

27. I did not hold back anything from you concerning the counsel of God.

28. Therefore, be careful for yourselves and for the whole assembly, because the spirit of our Lord has placed you to be overseers, to tend to his sheep, those of the gathering of God that he has purchased through his own blood.

29. For I know this; That after my death, grievous wolves will enter in among you that will not care for the people of God. (ekklesia)

30. Even from among yourselves men shall arise and speak corrupt things to draw away disciples after themselves. (Galatians 2:4; Jude 1:4; Isaiah 56:10-11; Ezekiel 22:28; 2 Peter 2)

31. Therefore be awake (*vigilant*) and remember that for three years, both night and day I never stopped admonishing you, even with many tears.

32. But now, I commend you my brethren before God, that the message of his power is established in you and shall give unto you an inheritance among all those that have lived a sanctified life.

33. I have not wanted the silver, gold, or possessions of any man.

34. You know that your hands have ministered unto my needs and unto those that have been with me.

35. I have showed you everything that we must do to assist the feeble ones (*needful*), so remember the words of our Lord, that it is better to give than to receive.

36. After this, he kneeled down and he prayed with all of them.

37. Then there was much crying from everyone there, so they grabbed a hold of him and embraced him and they kissed him in a brotherly way.

38. They were grieving because of the message that he gave and that they would never see his face again; Then they escorted him to the ship.

Acts 21

1. When the time came to sail off and as we were withdrawing ourselves from them, we went directly to Coos, the following day to Rhodes, and from there, Patara;

2. Then we found a ship that was heading off to Phoenice and we got in and set off.

3. We saw Cyprus and we passed by on the left, then we sailed to Syria and came down to Tyre. That is where the ship unloaded its cargo.

4. We found some disciples there and we stayed for seven days; They told Paul to not go to Jerusalem.

5. When the time came and those seven days were over, we set out to again travel, and women and children accompanied us all the way, to just outside of the city. There we placed our knees on the ground and we prayed.

6. Then we began embracing each other, saying goodbye, and we went up into the ship; They went back to their own places.

7. We completed the voyage to Tyre, then arrived at Ptolemais and greeted the brethren there and remained with them for one day.

8. On the following day, those that Paul received assistance from (G-1537 + G-2064 + G-5608) came to Caesarea and we met with them in the house of Philip the evangelist, him being one of the seven, we stayed with him.

9. He had four maiden daughters that prophesied.

10. We remained there for several days when there came a certain prophet from Judea named Agabus.

11. When he came to us, he took his belt and he bound Paul's hands and his feet and said, the spirit of the holy one says this: The man of whom is tied with this belt will in this same way be bound by the Jews in Jerusalem and they will deliver him up into the hands of the gentiles.

(they remembered this happened to Jesus)

12. When we heard these things, we and the people who lived in that place began begging him to not go to Jerusalem!

13. But Paul said, what are you doing by crushing my heart with your tears? I will not only be tied, but most likely be killed for the name of the Lord Jesus!

14. But he would not be persuaded to not go, but said, the will of God will be done.

15. And after preparing for several days, we went up to Jerusalem.

16. Some of the disciples from Caesarea went with us and brought Mnason, an original disciple of Jesus from Cyprus. (*one of the 70 - Luke 10:1*)

17. The brethren joyfully received us in Jerusalem. (Romans 15:25; 1 Corinthians 16:3)

18. The following day, Paul went with James and all of the elders came.

19. After they spent time greeting each other, Paul told of everything that God had done among the gentiles through his ministry.

20. When they heard these things, they glorified God and then said, my brothers, there are a large number of Jews that have committed themselves, yet they are all zealous for the Mosaic law.

(Messianic Judaism - Romans 7:2-5 refutes this doctrinal error)

21. It was made known to them that you teach that the Mosaic Law is apostasy, telling the Jews in all of the foreign nations not to circumcise their children nor live by the customs. (Galatians 3:10)

22. Truly, a gathering must come together when they have heard that you are here.

23. Now, do as we tell you: There are four men with a vow among themselves.

24. Go with them and be purified at their expense, and they will shave their heads; In this they may know that all that they had heard about you is not true, but that you live by keeping the law of God. (Galatians 3:10; Matthew 22:37-40; Mark 12:29-31)

25. Concerning those that have believed while living in other nations, we have communicated in writing that they are not to observe the Mosaic law. (Galatians 3:27-29; Acts 15 - *after the temple in Jerusalem was destroyed it became impossible to continue to fully live by the Mosaic law*)

The final part of verse 25 looks to have been added by a scribe and is in error.
It has been excluded from this text because it contradicts many other scriptures including:
(Matthew 15:11-18; Mark 7:15-20; 1 Corinthians 3:17; Romans 14:2; Luke 10:8;
Colossians 2:16; Galatians 3:28-29; Romans 10:12)

26. The following day Paul was taken by those men, and after they had been purified they went into the temple and declared the completion of the days of purification; An offering was brought on the behalf of each one of them.

27. But when the seven days (*of the feast*) were completed, the Jews from Asia *(Judea)* saw him in the temple, and they threw the crowds into chaos, and they put their hands on him.

28. Then they announced, men of Israel, this is the man that teaches all people everywhere against the Mosaic law, and he has now brought Greeks into the temple and has defiled this holy place!

29. This is because these Jews had earlier seen Trophimus and an Ephesian in the city with him and they assumed that Paul brought them into the temple with him.

30. The whole city was shaken (Acts 18:21), and there was an assembly of the people that quickly gathered together; They, having already arrested Paul, took him outside of the temple, and they immediately shut the doors.

31. They were seeking to kill him, but some sent a message to the colonel (Luke 19:43-44; Daniel 9:25) of the Roman military squad, that there was an outright uproar in Jerusalem;

(Daniel 9:25 – *this brought need for a strong military leader & peace agreement of 7 years - circa 62-63 AD*)

32. Immediately, he brought the soldiers and centurions down to them, and when they saw the colonel and the soldiers, they stopped beating Paul.

33. Then the colonel grabbed a hold of him. He commanded that he be bound by two chains, then he asked, what did he do and who is he?

34. Some in the crowd cried out, not knowing the certainty of the reason for the uproar. Then he was commanded to be brought to the military barracks.

35. When he had come to the stairs, he needed to be carried by the soldiers because of the violence (*done to him*) by the crowd.

36. The crowd had followed them and were screaming out, take him away!

37. As Paul was being brought into the barracks, he said to the colonel, is it lawful for me to speak with you? And the colonel said, are you a Greek,

38. or are you the Egyptian that at an earlier time caused a riot and sent four thousand men into the wilderness to be murdered?

39. Then Paul said, I truly am a Jew from Tarsus in Cilica, not a citizen of an unmarked city! I beg you to allow me to speak to the people;

40. So he allowed him. Paul stood on the stairs and he signaled to the people with his hands, and there was silence. Then he spoke to the people in the Hebrew dialect and he said:

Acts 22

1. My brothers, now hear my defense.

2. When they heard him speak in the Hebrew dialect they showed great calm and quietness unto him.

3. Then he said; Truly I am a Jewish man born in Tarsus in Cilica and I was brought up here in Jerusalem at the feet of Gamaliel (Acts 5:34) and was taught by him in the exactness of the ancestral law, and I have lived zealously before God, as many of you here today also have.

4. I had persecuted (*the followers of Jesus of Nazareth*) even unto death and tied up many, and delivered many prisoners, both men and women unto prison; (1 Timothy 1:13)

5. The high priest can testify for me as well as all of the elders, that I received letters from them to go into Damascus and arrest them and then bring them back to Jerusalem to be punished.

6. It was that while I was traveling, and coming close to Damascus, about the middle of the day, suddenly out of the sky a strong light shined around me;

7. I fell to the ground and heard a voice say to me, Saul, Saul, why do you persecute me?

8. I asked, who are you, Lord? Then he said, I am Jesus of Nazareth and you are persecuting me.

9. Those with me heard the voice and were greatly alarmed, but they did not see the light. (Acts 9:7)

10. And I said, master, what shall I do? Then the Master said unto me, get yourself up and go to Damascus, and there it will be told to you concerning the things that you are appointed to do.

11. I could no longer see due to the powerful light, so I was led by the hand by those that were with me and I went to Damascus.

12. In Damascus there was a man that was devoted unto God and his law (Matthew 22:37-40 Mark 12:29-31) and he was witnessing unto all of the Jews that lived there.

13. He came to me and stood by me and said, Saul my brother, open your eyes and see again! And at that moment I looked up at him;

14. Then he said, the God of our forefathers has appointed me to know his will, and to know the holy one (*Jesus Christ*), and to hear his voice from his mouth.

15. You will be a witness for him to testify of that which you have seen and heard.

16. So now, what are your intentions? Get yourself up and we will baptize you to wash away your sins and to be engulfed with the evidence *(G-1942 + G-4592 + G-3377 - the holy spirit)* in the name of Jesus. (Matthew 28:19; Acts 2:38, Acts 3:19; John 8:31-34; Matthew 18:2-3; Romans 6:1-7; Psalms 145:18)

17. When I returned to Jerusalem, I went to pray in the temple, and while I was praying, my mind drifted,

18. and I saw him (*Jesus*) and he told me, hurry up and get yourself out of Jerusalem, because they will not receive your testimony concerning me!

19. And I said, Lord, they know that I had been imprisoning and beating many that have committed themselves unto you throughout all of the synagogues. (Matthew 10:17)

20. When the blood of Stephen your witness was spilled, I was standing there and I consented to his execution; I watched over the clothing of those who killed him.

21. And he said to me, Go, I will send you to the distant nations.

22. When the crowd that listened to Paul speak heard these words, they again started shouting, take him away from off of the earth, such a man is not fit to live!

23. They continued screaming and began ripping their clothing and throwing dust into the air!

24. Then the colonel commanded that Paul be brought into the barracks and ordered for him to be interrogated by scourging (*whipping*) so that he might find out what crime he had committed to have the crowd speak out against him in such a way.

25. But as they stretched him out with the straps, Paul said to the centurion standing there, if a Roman man has not been found to be guilty, is it lawful for you to scourge him?

26. And when the centurion heard this, he immediately went and reported this to the colonel and said, be careful in what you are about to do, this man is a Roman!

27. Then the colonel came over to him and he asked, are you a Roman? And Paul said, Yes!

28. And the colonel asked him, how much was the fee to become a Roman citizen? And Paul said, I was born a Roman!

29. Immediately those that were about to interrogate him backed away, as well as the colonel and they became fearful, knowing for sure that he is a Roman and that he had him bound!

30. The following day, having the purpose to be certain of the reason that he was accused by the Jews, he freed him from the chains and commanded the high priests and all of the Sanhedrin that had brought Paul in, to stand before him.

Acts 23

1. After Paul had stared at the Sanhedrin for quite some time, he said, my brothers, I have lived unto God with a complete good conscience my entire life:

2. Then the high priest ordered one that was standing near him to punish his mouth;

3. Then Paul said, God shall punish you. You are reserved to be brought to dust; You sit accusing me according to the law of Moses, yet you command for me to be punished contrary to that law?

4. Those that were standing near him said, do you have distain for the high priest of God?

5. Then Paul said I was unaware that he is a high priest my brothers, as it is written, you shall not speak evil against a ruler of the people. (Exodus 22:28)

6. But Paul knew that half were Pharisees and the other half was Sadducees, so he yelled out unto the Sanhedrin, my brothers, I am a Pharisee and the Son of a Pharisee; Is my confidence in the resurrection of the dead why I am being judged? (Daniel 12:2)

7. After he said this, a dissention between the Pharisees and the Sadducees broke out and the people were divided against each other.

8. It is true that the Sadducees pronounce that there is no resurrection of the dead, and they reject that there shall be a messenger. (*Christ*) They also reject the spirit, yet the Pharisees confess these things.

9. Then there was a great outcry that arose; The scribes, which are a division of the Pharisees, were arguing they have found that there is nothing evil in this man, and that if a spirit spoke to him or if it was an angel, we must not fight against God.

10. And there was a great controversy that had happened, but only the fear of the colonel prevented Paul from being torn to pieces! So the colonel commanded that the soldiers go down and take him away from them and to return him back to the barracks.

11. The Lord came to him the following evening and said to him, be cheerful Paul! You have fully testified everything concerning me unto all of Jerusalem, but now you must also testify in Rome!

12. When the daylight came, some of the Jews conspired to neither eat or drink until Paul was killed; They put a curse upon themselves.

13. There were more than forty of those that made this plot.

14. When they came before the high priests and the elders they said, with a curse we have cursed ourselves that we put nothing in our mouths until we kill Paul.

15. Now then, you shall inform the colonel that the Sanhedrin request that he should bring him down tomorrow so that you may gather more information concerning him; Then we will then sneak in closely to him and we will kill him.

16. The son of Paul's sister heard about the ambush and came to him at the barracks and told this to Paul.

17. Paul then told this to one of the centurions and said, please bring this young man up to the colonel because he has something important to report to him.

18. They took him to the colonel and said, the prisoner Paul called me to him and asked me to bring this young man unto you, that he has something important to tell you.

19. The colonel took the boy by the hand and led him into a private place and asked, what is it that you would like to tell me?

20. And he said, the Jews have plotted to ask you to bring Paul before the Sanhedrin tomorrow, so to inquire more information concerning him.

21. Please do not allow this unto them, because more than forty men have cursed themselves to not eat or drink until Paul is dead! They are now ready and waiting for your response.

22. The colonel allowed the boy to leave, but ordered him to not speak to anyone concerning these things that he had reported to him.

23. Then he called two high ranking centurions and said, go and gather two hundred soldiers and seventy horsemen and two hundred spear men to go to Caesarea at the third hour of the night. Get the animals (*horses*) ready and have Paul put on one and bring him to Felix the governor.

25. He wrote a letter that may have read much like this:

26. Claudius Lysias unto the most excellent governor, Felix, greetings.

27. This man was arrested by the Jews and was about to be killed by them; I rescued him with soldiers and I have learned that he is a Roman.

28. While I was trying to apprehend the charges that were against him, I took him before the Sanhedrin.

29. I found that they were accusing him concerning questions in their Jewish law. Nothing was revealed unto me that was worthy of death, nor even keeping him in chains.

30. It then became revealed unto me that there was a plot to kill this man, so I immediately sent him to you; I have also commanded that his accusers bring their charges and their arguments against him before you. Fare well.

31. The soldiers went as they were commanded and brought him in the night to Antipatris.

32. The following morning they allowed the horsemen to take him the rest of the way, and then they returned to the barracks.

33. When they entered into Caesarea, they handed over the letter to the governor and they also turned Paul over unto him.

34. After reading the letter, the governor asked him from which province he was from, and he learned that he was from Cilicia.

35. Then he said, I will hear your words when your accusers arrive. He commanded that he be kept in the court of Herod.

Acts 24

1. Ananias the high priest came down five days later with the elders and a speaker named Tertullus. They came to testify before the governor against Paul.

2. When he was called, Tertullus began his accusation and said: Much peace has been established because of you and excellent things have come unto our nation through your mindfulness;

3. From all places and concerning all things we approve of you most excellent Felix, and we have much gratitude.

4. I will no longer delay, and I beg that you might have patience to hear us in our short testimony.

5. For we have found this man to be a plague, having stirred up the Jews everywhere throughout the empire! He is the ringleader of the Nazarene sect!

6. He also attempted to pollute the temple, so we accordingly arrested and now plan to condemn him according to our Jewish law.

7. However, Lysias, the colonel came and plucked him from out of our hands and commanded all that accuse this man to come before you.

8. Now you have the opportunity to examine him for yourself concerning all of these things that we have accused him of.

9. The Jews also joined in and alleged these things are true.

10. Then Paul answered as the governor gave him a signal to speak; Understanding that you have been a judge unto this nation for many years, I will now happily speak for my own defense.

11. You know this to be true, it has been no more than twelve days since I went to Jerusalem to worship.

12. They did not find me debating with anyone in the temple, nor causing a riotous commotion, nor drawing a crowd, not in their synagogues nor in the city.

13. They can not prove anything of which they now accuse me of!

14. But I do confess unto you that it is true concerning this sect, that I do worship the ancestral God in this way, because I do believe all that is written in the Mosaic law and all that the prophets have written.

15. I have great hope in God, of which those that accuse me may also hold, concerning the resurrection of the dead that shall one day come upon all people, both the righteous and the unrighteous.
(Daniel 12:2; Matthew 27:52-53; Revelation 10:12-15; Romans 2:3-10)

16. With this in mind, I have lived my life with a blameless conscience toward God and unto all of mankind concerning all things.

17. For many years I have offered myself as a sacrifice, to do merciful things for the benefit of my nation.

18. While purifying myself in the temple, without a crowd nor conflict, some of the Jews took me.

19. They should have been brought here before you to present themselves to accuse me if they have anything against me.

20. Can any of these that are standing here of the Sanhedrin accuse me of anything unrighteous,

21. other than this one speaker that has spoken out before the people that have gathered here today? Am I being judged concerning the resurrection of the dead?

22. Knowing that this was the reason that Felix had deferred unto the governor, to know more accurately that which is the right road, he said, when Lysias the colonel comes down I will find out these things about you.

23. Then he ordered a centurion to allow Paul to be at ease and to not prevent any of his acquaintances to attend to him or from speaking to him.

24. Then after several days, Felix had arrived with his wife Drusilla, of whom was a Jew; Then he sent for Paul and they heard him testify concerning faithfulness unto Christ Jesus.

25. And Paul took the time to explain thoroughly concerning righteous living, self-control and the coming judgment that will soon come upon every man.
(Revelation 20:12-15; Romans 2:11; Ezekiel 33:11-20; Jeremiah 32:19)
Then Felix became fearful and he said, that is all for now, but I will call you again later.

26. But with that, he hoped that Paul would give him money in order that he might release him. Therefore, he sent for him often and communicated with him.

27. But the successor of Felix, Porcius Festus chose to show favor to the Jews, so he abandoned Paul in the prison for two years. (*the root of the word "festering"*)

Acts 25

1. Three days after Festus entered into the province, he went up to Jerusalem from Caesarea.

2. At that time the high priest made a request of him that Paul be turned over unto him.

3. He was asking a favor so that he would send him to Jerusalem so they could plot to kill him on the way!

4. But Festus said that he would keep Paul in Caesarea and that he would be leaving Jerusalem soon.

5. Then he said, let those among you that have anything against this man, let them come down to Caesarea and accuse him!

6. Then Festus had stayed among them for more than ten days, but the following morning he left for Caesarea, and he took the judgment seat in a tribunal and he ordered that Paul be brought before him.

7. When Paul was brought up, the Jews that came up from Jerusalem stood around and they brought many heavy charges against Paul, of which they were unable to prove.

8. Paul defended himself and said, I have not sinned against the Jewish law, nor against the temple, nor against Caesar!

9. But Festus wished to show favor unto the Jews, so he responded to Paul and said, do you want to go up to Jerusalem and be judged there?

10. And Paul said, I am standing before a tribunal of Caesar where I ought to be judged. I have done no wrong unto the Jews, and they know this perfectly!

11. For if I have done anything worthy of death, I do not refuse to be put to death; If there are no charges that can be established by those that are against me, then I appeal unto Caesar!

12. Then when Festus conversed with the Sanhedrin he said, you have appealed unto Caesar, and unto Caesar you shall go!

13. Many days passed before King Agrippa and Bernice arrived at Caesarea and they greeted Festus.

14. After they had been there for many days, Festus talked with them about those things concerning Paul, and he said, there is a certain man that was left behind by Felix as a prisoner.

15. Concerning him, the high priests and the Jewish elders made a request that he be sentenced to death,

16. so I answered them and said, it is not a custom of the Romans to freely turn over any man unto death before the one being accused should have his accusers bring their accusation before his face, so that he could bring his own defense concerning the charges.

17. Therefore, they came down here without delay, and I commanded that he be brought the following day for a tribunal.

18. But concerning the charges that his accusers brought, I did not hold any as valid.

19. They debated about his superstitions concerning the man Jesus who had been killed, but Paul claimed was resurrected and is alive!

20. I was confused as to where an injury had been inflicted, so I said, do you (*Paul*) desire to go to Jerusalem to be judged concerning these things?

21. But Paul then brought his appeal that he be kept and brought before Augustus for examination, and I decided to keep him until I could send him unto Caesar.

22. Agrippa then said to Festus, I would also like to hear from the man myself! And Festus said, tomorrow you shall hear him.

23. The following day, Agrippa came with Bernice and they came with great pride. They entered into the auditorium with the colonels and men of prestige of that city. Festus commanded that Paul be brought out.

24. Then Festus said, King Agrippa and all the men that are present with us, here is the man that a large number of Jews begged for, both in Jerusalem and here, screaming out that he must not be allowed to live!

25. But I have not seen that he has done anything worthy of death and he himself has now appealed unto Augustus, so I have decided to send him there.

26. But I have nothing certain to write concerning him unto Caesar, so now I bring him forth unto you king Agrippa, so that I might have something to write concerning my interrogation.

27. It seems unreasonable for me to send a prisoner, yet not have any charges that have been made against him!

Acts 26

1. King Agrippa asked Paul, are you able to speak for yourself? Then Paul affirmed and stretched out his hands and he made his defense.

2. Concerning all of the things that I have been accused of by the Jews, King Agrippa, it is a blessing to be making my defense before you today,

3. because you are an expert, knowing everything concerning the customs and inquiry of the Jews, therefore I ask that you patiently hear my words.

4. The way that I have lived since I was very young, all of the Jews know this, that I was a leader in my nation in Jerusalem.

5. They knew me from the beginning and they will admit that I lived as a Pharisee according to the most exacting sect of our religion.

6. Now I am standing here being judged for holding to the confidence that was promised by God unto our forefathers,

7. of which all of the twelve tribes paid tribute to night and day with the expectation that would soon arrive; It is concerning this hope that I have been accused by the Jews, oh King Agrippa.

8. Why would it be considered unbelievable that God would raise the dead?

9. At one time I did honestly believe that it was necessary to do many things against those that followed Jesus of Nazareth.

10. I did these things in Jerusalem and I delivered many of the saints unto prison. I received authority from the high priests and I cast my vote to put them to death.

11. I punished them often in all of the synagogues and I forced them to blaspheme, I was exceedingly ferocious against them and I even persecuted them away from the city.

12. I went as far as Damascus with the authority and full power of the high priests.

13. But in the middle of the day while I was on my way there, a bright light from the sky that had the brightness of the sun shined around me, of which was seen by all that traveled with me.

14. All of us fell to the ground and I heard a voice speaking to me in the Hebrew language saying, Saul, Saul, why are you persecuting me? Your kicking the poisonous thorns.

15. So I asked, who are you? And he said, I am Jesus of Nazareth and you are persecuting me.

16. Now get yourself up and stand on your feet. The reason that I have appeared unto you is to appoint you as my servant and my witness concerning what you have seen and what I will show unto you.

17. I send you out to be my witness unto all nations;

18. To open the eyes of the blind, to turn them from the ways of darkness *(sin)* unto the Light *(Christ)*, from the deeds *(authority)* of Satan unto the deeds *(authority)* of God; They will be offered remission of their sins (Romans 3:25) and an inheritance among all that are sanctified through faithfulness unto me. (1 John 1:5-7; Psalms 112:4; Ephesians 2:8; Habakkuk 2:4)

19. King Agrippa, I have not been disobedient of the heavenly vision.

20. I announced repentance unto the region near Damascus, then at Jerusalem and unto everyone in the regions of Judea. Then I went unto the foreign nations. I have announced repentance; To turn unto God and live according to him, demonstrating the deeds that are necessary for repentance. (Matthew 3:8; 2 Corinthians 7:9-10; Jeremiah 32:23; John 3:19-21; Jonah 3:8-10; Luke 17:10)

21. It is because of this that the Jews arrested me in the temple and attempted to kill me.

22. It is only because of the assistance of God that I am standing here today as a witness unto the great and the small, and I have not said anything of which Moses and the prophets did not say was going to happen.

23. They prophesied that Christ was going to suffer and that he would be raised from the dead, and that he would be a light unto the people of all nations. (Malachi 1:11; Isaiah 62:2; Isaiah 54:3; Isaiah 59:6)

24. After he finished defending himself, Festus with a loud voice said, you are crazy Paul! You have read too many scriptures and they have turned you into a lunatic!

25. Then Paul said, most excellent Festus, I am not crazy, but I speak truth which I have declared unto you and my words are *(scripturally)* sound.

26. The king understands these things that I declare boldly before you today, and I am convinced that you also understand all of these things that I have said; All of these things were done openly, not secretly.

27. Do you believe the prophets King Agrippa? I know that you believe!

28. Then Agrippa said to Paul, you have almost persuaded me to become a Christian.

29. Then Paul said, I am praying not only you, but also all of those that hear me today, both small and great, to be as I am, with the exception of these chains.

30. After these things were spoken, the king, Bernice, the governor and all those that were there got up and they debated with each other and then said to one another,

31. this man has done nothing worthy of death, nor even of these chains.

32. Agrippa said to Festus, this man would have been released if he did not appeal unto Caesar!

Acts 27

1. It was then decided for us to sail to Italy *(Rome)*, and they delivered Paul and some other prisoners to a centurion named Julius from the military unit of Augustan.

2. We got into a ship at Adramyttium and were about to sail along the Asian coastline, and our brother Aristarchus, a Macedonian of Thessalonica decided to come with us.

3. Then we landed in Sidon, and Julius allowed Paul to go to his friends in that place to receive some hospitality.

4. From there we set sail to Cyprus, because the winds were against us.

5. We sailed through the sea between Cilicia and Pamphylia, and we came to Myra in Lycia.

6. Then the centurion found that there was an Alexandrian ship there that was sailing to Italy, so we were put on it.

7. We sailed slowly for many days and with much difficulty we came to Knidon, because the wind did not help us, so we sailed near Crete, close to Salmone.

8. Again, with much difficulty we sailed to the place called fair havens, that was near the city of Lasea,

9. and we were there for quite some time. That is when the sea became very dangerous and the crew had not been eating, because by this time the food had nearly run out!

10. So Paul said, men, it looks to me like this voyage is about to see much loss and injury, not only of the cargo and the ship, but possibly also our lives.

11. However the centurion was convinced by the ship owner and the helmsman not to trust in what Paul had said.

12. That area was not fit to spend the winter and it was better advised to sail from there and try to pass through to Phoenice for the winter, which is a port at Crete that faced south westerly and north westerly;

13. The south wind blew gently, so thinking that they had gained an opportunity, they raised the anchor and they sailed along the coast of Crete.

14. But not long after this, a typhoon that is called euroclydon seized the ship

15. and they were unable to face the wind, so we gave up and let it drift freely!

16. There was an island that was near there that was called Clauda and we were barely able to master the boat towards it.

17. The crew took chains to try to wrap them under the ship, fearing that we would be pulled into the sand dunes, so we lowered our equipment and we were driven forward.

18. After having been extremely tossed around by the winds, the following day we began throwing the cargo overboard!

19. On the third day we threw all of the equipment overboard.

20. Neither the sun nor stars showed themselves for many days! This storm was pressing hard upon us, and all hope was being taken away that we might survive!

21. None of us had been eating, so Paul stood up in the middle of everyone and said, men, truly you should have listened to me to have not sailed away from Crete. We would not have suffered such injury and loss.

22. But now I tell you to be cheerful, because no one will lose their life, only the ship will be lost.

23. A messenger of the Lord, stood by me in the night

24. and he said, do not fear Paul, you must stand before Caesar! Know that God will protect you and everyone with you;

25. So now be cheerful, because I trust in my God; It will be just as he said that it will be.

26. We must jump off and swim to this island.

27. It was the fourteenth night of which we were being carried about in the Adriatic Sea, and near the middle of the night the sailors thought that we had come near their home country.

28. They measured that we were twenty fathoms deep in the water; Then a short time later they measured fifteen fathoms deep.

29. Then, fearing that we would fall upon the rocks, they threw four anchors from off of the stern of the ship, and they were awaiting the day light to arrive.

30. The sailors were planning to jump from the ship, and they lowered the lifeboat into the sea, they pretended as though they were attempting to drop some additional anchors from the front of the ship,

31. when Paul said to the centurion and the soldiers, if they do not remain on the ship, they will not survive.

32. The soldiers cut off the ropes to the boat and let it drift away.

33. While they were waiting for the daylight, Paul begged that they eat a meal and he said, it is the fourteenth day that we have been without food, the men have eaten nothing!

34. Therefore I highly recommend that everyone eat; It is necessary for us to survive and not one of you will lose a hair from your head.

35. After he said these things, they took the food and gave thanks to God in the presence of all of them.

36. Then they all became cheerful and they ate the food.

37. The number of people that were on the ship were two hundred seventy-six!

38. After they ate the food, they lightened the ship, throwing the grain into the sea.

39. When the day came, they did not recognize the land that they saw, but they did see a bay with a beach, and they planned to get to if they could drive the ship that way.

40. Then they threw the anchors off into the sea and they freed the ropes on the rudder. Then they raised the front sail into the wind and they headed towards that beach.

41. Then they drove the ship between the place where two seas met. That is when the front of the ship became stuck firmly (*in sand*) and it remained immovable, but the stern of the ship was free and was being tossed by the violent waves.

42. Then the soldiers thought to kill the prisoners so that none might swim and escape from them.

43. But the centurion had the necessity to protect Paul and prevented them from their purpose. He commanded that whoever could swim, that they jump overboard and go first, swim to the land.

44. The others grabbed on to planks of wood and some on to broken parts of the ship; It happened that everyone was saved and made it to land!

Acts 28

1. When they were finally safe, they realized that they were on the Island of Melita.

2. The people of that island extended much benevolence and kindness unto us, having lighted a fire and they welcomed all of us; This was appreciated because the rain started again and it was very cold.

3. While Paul was gathering a bunch of wood for the fire, as he put it into the fire, a viper came out of the wood because of the heat and it bit him on the hand.

4. When the people saw the viper hanging from his hand, they said to one another, this man must be a murderer! After being saved from the violent sea, he still is not permitted to live!

5. Then Paul threw the viper into the fire and no harm came upon him. (Mark 16:18)

6. The people expected him to swell up or suddenly fall down dead and they watched him for quite some time, but when they saw that nothing happened to him from this, they changed their minds and said that he must be a god!

7. The head chief of that island lived in that area and his name was Publius, and he welcomed us for three months, hosting us in a friendly way.

8. It happened to be that his father was very sick, having a high fever and bleeding out of his bowels, and he was laid up in a bed; So then Paul entered in unto him and healed him!

9. When this happened, everyone on that island that had infirmities came to him and were healed.

10. We were honored with many honors and upon our setting off to sail, they gave us all of the things that we had need of.

11. We wintered on the island for three months and then we set sail on a ship from Alexandria with the badge (*flag*) of twin brothers that was also wintered there.

12. Finally, we landed in Syracuse and remained there for three days.

13. From there we landed in Rhegium, but after one day, the south wind picked up and on the second day we came to Puteoli;

14. There we found some brethren and we were invited to remain there for seven days. From there we went to Rome.

15. While we were there, some brethren had heard that we were there and some came from as far as the Appii marketplace and Three Taverns! When they saw Paul, they thanked God for his fortitude.

16. When we made it to Rome, the centurion delivered the other prisoners to the commander of the camp, but Paul was able to remain with the soldier that was guarding him.

17. Three days later, Paul was called to come before the highest leader of the Jews. When they came together, he said to them, brothers, men, I did nothing contrary to the ancestral laws nor the people. I have been a prisoner since leaving Jerusalem, having been delivered into the hands of the Romans.

18. They examined me and have decided that I should be set free because there is no cause for you to have me put to death.

19. Because the Jews refused that I be released free, I was compelled to appeal to Caesar, as it is not as though those of my nation had anything to accuse me of.

20. This is why I called to speak to you and see your faces. You see, I have these chains on me for the sake and hope of Israel. (Romans 11:17; Isaiah 6:9-10; verse 28 - *all who would come to Christ, God's Israel*)

21. Then they said to him, we did not receive any letters concerning you from the Jews, nor have any of your brothers arrived to say anything evil against you,

22. however we see that it is necessary to hear what you have to say, because truly this sect (*Christians*) are known to us and are spoken against everywhere!

23. After they scheduled a day, some came unto him in his living quarters. He testified earnestly concerning the kingdom of God and he attempted to persuade them of everything concerning Jesus, by showing them through the books of Moses and through the prophets.

24. Some were truly convinced of what he had to say, but others did not believe;

25. But when they did not agree among themselves, Paul said one more thing before they left that place: Truly the holy spirit spoke unto the prophet Isaiah when he said unto our forefathers,

26. "Go to the people and say this, when you hear this, not all of you will understand, and though you see, not all of you will perceive,

27. because the hearts of these people are heavily hardened and their eyes are closed; They will never perceive with their eyes, nor hear with their ears, nor with their hearts come to understand and be converted, so that I could heal them." (Isaiah 6:9-10)

28. Therefore, know this, the salvation of God has been offered unto the foreign nations, and some of them will hear. (Romans 11:14-26)

29. When Paul had said these things, the Jews went away having much to discuss among themselves.

30. Thereafter, Paul remained in Rome for a full two years in his own rented home and he welcomed all that came unto him.

31. He continued proclaiming the kingdom of God and teaching the things about the Lord Jesus Christ with complete freedom and without any hindrances.

Romans

Chapter 1

1. Paul, a servant of Jesus Christ, called to be an apostle, fully committed and living only according to the gospel of God.

2. The Christ that he promised in the past through the prophets, as it is written in the sacred scriptures,

3. that his son would arise through the offspring of David, concerning lineage.

4. According to his holy spirit, he was appointed son of God in power after he was resurrected from the dead;

5. Jesus Christ is our master, through whom we have been offered the assistance of God and a commission unto obedience and faithfulness proven through testing, that has now been brought unto all people, for the sake of all who shall be named by him,

6. among whom you are also invited by Jesus Christ;

7. Unto all of the beloved that are in Rome and have accepted the invitation of God to be saints, may the grace and peace of our Father God and the Lord Jesus Christ be unto you.

8. Foremost, I thank my God through Jesus Christ for all of you, that your conviction is being made known throughout the world.

9. For God is my witness, of whom I serve with all of my heart through the gospel of his son; I always speak of you in my prayers.

10. I continue to ask if somehow soon I might be able to come unto you, if it be the will of God. (Acts 28:30)

11. I greatly desire to see you, so that I might share the spiritual charisma (*supernatural power*) with you, for confirmation unto you,

12. and that we may be comforted together through the testing of our faithfulness, for both you and also of myself.

13. I do not want you to be ignorant of this my brethren, that I have often planned to come to you, so that your fruit might be complete, the same as is in other nations, but I have been continually prevented even until this present time.

14. I am a debtor unto both Greeks and foreigners, unto both the wise and the foolish;

15. So as for me, I am eager to come to you there in Rome to preach the gospel unto you.

16. I am not ashamed to preach the gospel of Christ, because it offers the ability (*power*) of God that leads to salvation for all that continually put their trust in him. (John 3:16-21)

17. Because the righteousness of God is revealed in you from your conviction until you are proven to be faithful (*through much testing*), just as it is written, "the righteous shall live by faithfulness unto God." (Habakkuk 2:4 - *faithfulness* - H-530)

18. Because the wrath of God is revealed upon all ungodliness and unrighteousness of every man that knows what is right, yet chooses to do that which is unrighteous (*wrong*);
(1 John 5:16-18; Matthew 12:32; Numbers 15:28-31; Hebrews 10:26-27; Luke 12:47-48; Psalms 19:13; Jeremiah 32:23; Romans 7:13; James 4:17; Matthew 18:1-10)

19. Because the truth of God is clearly known unto them, as God makes it known unto all people;

20. The things that were not understood from the beginning of the world have now been made known and are clearly seen, showing both his eternal power and jurisdiction.

21. They shall be without an excuse, because they, having known the ways of God, they refuse to honour him as God and are not thankful for what he has offered; But they become foolish in their thinking and the discernment in their hearts is dimmed. (Isaiah 63:10)

22. They profess that they are wise, though in truth, they have become fools,

23. and they have debased the honorable and uncorrupted creation of God for the corruptible ways of mankind. The flight of the fourth beast creeping upon the earth. (Daniel 7:23)

24. Therefore God has delivered them unto the lusts of their own defiled hearts, unto the dishonoring of their own bodies among themselves;

25. They have changed the truth of God into something false; (2 Peter 2) They adore themselves and they are worshipping (*living for*) the created things instead of the creator, who they should be blessing forever.

26. For this reason, God has turned them over to passions that shall disgrace them, (Ephesians 4:19; Psalms 81:12) as even some of their women have exchanged the physically natural way, unto that which is against the reproduction of offspring;

27. In the same way, some of the men have turned away from the natural contact of a woman, deeply desiring for the forbidden lusts of one another, men with other males, doing very shameful things; But the penalty that they did not consider shall be given unto them in due time.

28. And just as they refused to acknowledge the ways of God, he released them to a corrupted way of thinking, to do the things that are not righteous.

29. And having been filled with much unrighteousness, fornication, wickedness, covetousness, depravity, envy, murder, strife, deceitfulness, mischievousness, slander,

30. and speaking evil, they are haters of God, spiteful, proud, braggarts, inventers of evil things, disobedient and they are foolish (*undiscerning*).

31. They are covenant breakers, hardhearted, unable to reason, and unmerciful;

32. Because they have known the righteous ways that God has ordained, those who do such things are deserving of eternal death, yet they not only do such things, but they approve of and teach others to do them as well!

Romans 2

1. Therefore, you are with no excuses, oh people, everyone making judgments of others; But when you condemn another, you condemn yourself because you are judging the guilt of others, yet you are doing the same things! (Numbers 15:28-30)

2. We know that the judgment of God is according to that which is true (*evidence*) and shall come down upon those that do such things.

3. If you are judging others and doing any of these things, how do you think that you will escape the judgment of God?

4. Do you reject the wealth and kindness of God, and his patience and restraint? Do you not know that the kindness (*grace*) of God is meant to lead you unto repentance?

5. Because of your stubbornness and unrepentant heart, you are gathering unto yourself much anger and punishment for the day of judgment, and the revealing of the righteous judgment of God. (Ephesians 1:11)

6. He will deliver unto every man and woman according to what each had done in their life. (Acts 24:25; James 5:3; Revelation 20:12-15; Isaiah 59:18; Jeremiah 32:19; Ezekiel 33:20; Psalms 62:12; Proverbs 5:21; Proverbs 11:5; Jeremiah 17:10; Ezekiel 7:3)

7. Unto those who live truly continuing patiently in doing that which is good and living incorruptibly, they shall receive wealth, honor and everlasting life. (Psalms 15; Psalms 19:7-11; 2 Timothy 4:1)

8. But unto those that are contentious (*against God*) and disobey his ways, and remain confidently continuing in unrighteousness, they will receive the anger and indignation of God;
(Ezekiel 33:11-18; Psalms 112:10; Hebrews 10:26-27)

9. Distress and fire shall come upon everyone who continues in wickedness. Firstly with the Jews, but the same with the gentiles. (Numbers 15:28-31; Revelation 20:12-15)

10. But honour, wealth and peace unto every one that continues faithfully doing that which is good; First with the Jews and the same with the gentiles. (Numbers 15:28-31; Isaiah 27:5; Luke 14:32; 2 Peter 3:14)

11. Because with God there are no favorites among peoples. (Galatians 3:27-29)

12. For all that commit defiant sin outside of the Jewish law, they will perish without the Jewish law; All that commit defiant sin while being in covenant according to the ten commandments, they shall be judged by the Mosaic law. (Numbers 15:28-31)

13. It was not those who knew the Mosaic law that were justified before God, but those that perform according to the Mosaic law who were to be justified. (*under the old covenant*)

14. Because when those who were not of Israel, not having the Mosaic law, if having done according to the law of God, they are lawful through their actions.

15. They have demonstrated the law of God that is written upon their hearts, (Jeremiah 31:34) being a witness unto themselves in their own conscience. They shall accuse or excuse themselves through their own conscience on the day that God judges the hidden things that men have done,

16. according to the Gospel that I preach through Jesus Christ.

17. Look! You that are called Jews and take comfort in the ten commandments and boast of God,

18. you know what God desires, so be approved in that which you hold, having been instructed from the Mosaic law. (Galatians 3:24)

19. You have persuaded yourselves that you are guides to those that are blind, a light in the darkness,

20. an instructor unto the unlearned and a teacher unto the children, since you have a form of knowledge and truth of the ten commandments;

21. So you go and teach others, but do you have need to reeducate yourselves? You that teach that you shall not steal, do you steal?

22. You that teach to not commit adultery, do you commit adultery? You who teach others to detest idols, do you commit sacrilege?

23. You who boast by the Mosaic law, do you transgress the law of God? Do you dishonor God?

24. You have blasphemed the name of God throughout many nations, just as it has been written: (Isaiah 52:5; Ezekiel 36:20-23)

25. Because circumcision (*coming into covenant with God*) only profits you if you abide within the law of God. But if you transgress against the law of God, your circumcision becomes uncircumcision.

26. If those that have not been circumcised keep the ordinances of the law of God, will their uncircumcised body not be counted as though it was circumcised?

27. The gentiles (*uncircumcised*) that keep the law of God, will they not judge you who are generationally of the circumcision, but transgress the law of God?

28. For a man is not a Jew who is one outwardly, nor is circumcision of the physical body, but of the heart.

29. A true Jew is the man that is inwardly a Jew and is circumcised in his heart, by the disposition (*one's character*) and not by the Jewish law. His praise is not the praise of men, but of God. (Jeremiah 9:26)

Romans 3

1. What is the advantage for those of Judea, or what benefit is there to have been circumcised? (Galatians 5:2)

2. Much, because of many things. First of all, truly we were entrusted with the instructions of God.

3. So, what if some disobeyed? Did their disobedience make void the doctrine of God?

4. It can not be! God is truth but all of mankind have lied. It has been written, "You that are justified by my words, you will overcome when being judged." (Psalms 51:4)

5. If we were to be unrighteous and God was to allow for that unrighteousness, what could be said? God would be unjust (*an unrighteous judge*) to not inflict his wrath upon us! I speak in the ways that men might understand. (2 Timothy 2:13)

6. May it never be; If so, then how shall God judge the world? (Hebrews 9:27; Revelation 20:12-15)

7. You see, the way God deals with us because he is honorable, is, if I was to lie, I will be judged a sinner.

8. I'm not speaking of being wrongly accused, because there are many who make accusations against us; But if we are to do things that are evil, how can we expect something good might come of it? For such people, the righteous judgment of God shall come upon them.

9. So what then? Do we exalt ourselves? No, not at all; For we have already declared that both the Jews and gentiles have all been enslaved by sin! (John 8:31-37)

10. As the scripture says, "no one is righteous, not even one.

11. There are none that have full understanding, no one is fully seeking God;

12. All have turned away and have become worthless; No one has done only things that are useful, not even a single one!" (Psalms 14:2-3) *(Thus the need for conversion)*

13. "With their mouth they dig their own grave, because they speak deceit." (Psalms 5:9) Their lips are as the poison of a viper; (Psalms 140:3)

14. Their mouths are full of cursing and they are fraudulent; (Psalms 10:7)

15. Their feet are quick to go and take vengeance;

16. Their ways are the ways of ruin and misery,

17. and they have not known how to make peace with God! (Isaiah 59:7-8)

18. They can not comprehend the fear of God. (Proverbs 1:7; Psalms 2:11; Psalms 36:1)

19. But we know that all that the Mosaic law says, it says to those who are held to that law and every mouth shall be silenced, and the whole world shall come under the judgment of God! (Revelation 20:12-15)

20. Because by doing the deeds required by the Mosaic law, no man shall be justified before him, because through the Mosaic law the full knowledge of sin is exposed.

21. But now, outside of the Mosaic law, the righteous character of God has been declared, as it was also witnessed (*seen from a distance*) by the Mosaic law and the prophets;

22. The righteousness that is required by God, by faithfulness unto Jesus Christ is now offered to all people and is given unto those who continue living fully committed unto him.

23. For there is no difference between people, (Galatians 3:28) as all have committed sin and have fallen short of the honour of God. (Isaiah 64:6; Psalms 14:3; 1 John 1:8)

24. So now, we can be fully cleansed (*at the time of conversion*) by the charity that he offers through the ransom that was paid by Jesus Christ;

25. God brought him forth to be the expiatory (*the one that pays the penalty*), that through our proven faithfulness and by his bloodshed (Ephesians 2:8-9), all of our past sins can be forgiven (*sins committed previous to conversion*) and we can be presented as righteous (2 Peter 1:9) because of the leniency of God.

26. This is evidence of his righteousness displayed through the new covenant. In this he is honored, by justifying those proven to be faithful unto Jesus Christ (*going forward after conversion*).

27. Then how can we boast? (Ephesians 2:9) It was prevented. But through what law can this be done? The law of works (*Mosaic law*)? No, but through the law of faithfulness unto God that is proven through testing (*new covenant*). (John 8:34)

28. We now know that by complete dedication (*unto God*) a man can be justified without the deeds of the Mosaic law. Is he the God of the Jews only?

29. What about everyone else throughout the world? Yes, he is the God of all people;

30. There is only one God, and he justifies those that are circumcised (*Israelites*) if they have been proven to be faithful unto him and also those that have not been circumcised (*Gentiles*), through their proven faithfulness unto him!

31. So then, shall the law of God be disregarded because of our conviction (*faith*)? No, but we establish the law of God through how we live! (James 2:24)

Romans 4

1. What was it that our forefather Abraham had found through his life?

2. If Abraham was justified by his deeds, he would have something to boast about, but not before God!

3. What does the scripture say? "Abraham confirmed himself to be pious (G-1991+G-2152) unto God, and it was accounted unto him as righteousness." (Hebrews 6:15; Genesis 22:1-2)

4. If one had continued doing the deeds of the Mosaic law perfectly, the promise (*reward - eternal life*) would not be given because of the assistance of God, but because of what would be owed to him.

5. But the one who does not continue doing all things (*deeds of the Mosaic law*), but fully trusts that Christ can justify those that had in the past been ungodly, now his proven dedication (*faithfulness*) is counted unto him as righteousness (James 2:26; Hebrews 6:15)

6. David said; "Blessed is the man that God considers righteous apart from the deeds of the Mosaic law.

7. Blessed are they whose (*past*) lawless deeds are cleansed, and whose unintentional mistakes (sins) shall be forgiven. (Romans 3:25; 1 John 2:1; 5:16; Numbers 15:22-29)

8. Blessed is the man whom the Lord shall in no way take inventory of his unintentional mistakes (*sins*) because in his heart there is no ill will." (Psalms 32:1-2; Numbers 15:28-31; 1 John 5:16)

9. Is this blessedness only for those who had been circumcised (*under the Mosaic covenant*) or is it also for those who have not been circumcised? We have already established that Abraham's dedication unto God was accounted unto him as righteousness.

10. How then was it counted? While he was circumcised, or before he was circumcised? Certainly not after circumcision, but it was before he was circumcised!

11. He received the sign of circumcision, the signet of the righteousness that was previously established by his faithfulness, of which was proven through his being tested when he had not yet been circumcised!
In this, he became the forefather of us all, all of us who remain committed unto God without having been circumcised, which will be recognized unto us as righteousness!

12. He is a father not only unto those that had been circumcised, but also unto all those that remained uncircumcised yet have been proven to be faithful, just as our father Abraham was.

13. Because it was not through the Mosaic law that the promises were made unto Abraham, that through his seed would come those that would inherit the world; But the promises were given unto him through the righteousness of being found to be faithful (*unto God*) through being tested.

14. Because if those that are under the Mosaic law are heirs, then the conviction of each man has become pointless and the promise is worthless; (*freewill*)

15. Because the Mosaic law only brings the wrath of God, and where the Mosaic law is not been established, there can be no transgression against it!

16. This is the reason for faithfulness that is proven through being tested, so that the assistance of God can exist and he can make firm the promises unto all of the offspring of Abraham. (Galatians 3:27-29) The promises are not only offered unto those who were under the Mosaic law, but also unto all who are found to be faithful, just like Abraham was, the forefather of us all!

17. As it is written, "I have appointed you as a father of many nations." (Genesis 17:5) It was because he trusted and obeyed God. He takes those that were spiritually dead and makes them to live; He has also called those who were not his people to be his people. (Matthew 3:9)

18. They who were without hope, now have hope because he became the father of many nations, as it is commonly said, "In this way shall your offspring be." (Genesis 15:5)

19. Abraham did not grow weak in his trust of God and he did not even consider his own aging body was already at that time impotent, being about a hundred years old, and the womb of Sarah also the same!

20. But concerning the promises of God, he did not doubt nor become disobedient, but he was empowered by his trust in God, and having honored God,

21. he was fully persuaded, that which God had promised, he is able to accomplish.

22. For this reason, he was counted to be righteous.

23. But this was not written for him alone; It is not counted only for him,

24. but this is also for us, unto whom it was going to be recognized, unto those of us who completely commit ourselves in God. He is the one who raised the Lord Jesus from the dead,

25. He was given up for our offenses and he was raised up for our justification.

Romans 5

1. So then, by our conviction we can be justified and make peace with God through our Lord Jesus Christ; (Romans 6:1-23; John 3:16-21; Matthew 5:8; 2 Peter 3:14)

2. That through him and through our dedication (*faithfulness* - Ephesians 2:8-9) we have access unto the assistance of God by which we must live, in order to have the hope of receiving the honor of God.

3. Because of this, we can be joyful through afflictions, because we know that if we continue patiently through the afflictions, we are creating evidence. This evidence brings us expectation,

5. and if we have this expectation, we shall not be ashamed. This is because of the affection that God has put in our hearts through his holy spirit, of which he gives unto all who truly convert. (1 John 4:1-3)

6. Christ, at the proper time, was killed for the benefit of the ungodly, while we were yet without ability to overcome; (John 8:31-36)

7. Only with much difficulty would anyone find someone to be willing to die, if only on the behalf of an innocent man. Perhaps for the benefit of a virtuous man one might be found who would courageously die!

8. But because of the love that God has for us, while everyone was yet continuing to be sinners, he allowed for Christ to die on our behalf; (John 3:16-21)

9. But even more, after having been cleansed by his blood, we can be eternally saved from his wrath.

10. For if we who were at one time hostile unto God could be reconciled unto him through the death of his son, now even much more so, because of him, we who have been made right before him shall be saved from sin in this life (John 8:34-36).

11. So now, we can be joyful before our God, that through the Lord Jesus Christ we have been offered restoration unto him.

12. Because of this, just as sin entered into the world by the actions of one man, and because of sin, death also entered the world, death has been passed unto all of mankind, because all have chosen to commit sin.

13. But before the Mosaic law was given, transgressions (*against the law of God*) were already in the world, but at that time transgressions could not be held on record against them, because the Mosaic law had not yet been given. (1 Peter 3:19; Acts 2:27 - *which brought with it disclosure of the penalty for sin*)

14. But death existed from Adam through the time of Moses, even over those that had not committed sin. *(defiance against God)* (Numbers 15:28-30; Hebrews 10:26) The transgression of Adam became the model that was imitated by all that followed.

15. But the pardon (*gift of God*) is not as it was with the transgression. For by the transgression of one man, all men come to die; But now so much more, by the gift of one man (*Jesus Christ*) the grace of God is able to be brought unto many.

16. It is not as though those who defiantly commit sin can receive the gift, for surely such a man is set for judgment and condemnation; But the free gift is only unto those that might commit unintentional sins, yet they may be justified. (*speaking of after conversion* - 1 John 2:1; 1 John 5:16-18; Numbers 15:28-31)

17. By the single offense of one man, death reigned; But now, much more so, by the abundance of his gift, his grace and righteousness can be received, lived and reign in us through Jesus Christ our Lord.

18. So then, because of one offense, all of mankind are subject unto decay *(death)*, but in a similar way through one equitable action, all men are offered the justification of their lives.

19. By the disobedience of one man, many have followed and chosen to become sinners; But now, through the obedience of one man, many shall also follow and choose to live righteously.

20. The Mosaic law was brought in additionally to make known where sin existed, but now the gift of God is offered in abundance; (John 8:31-37)

21. So just as sin reigned unto death, the grace of God is now offered so that he might reign in us, helping us live a righteous life, of which shall lead unto everlasting life, through Jesus Christ our Lord. (Romans 6:16)

Romans 6

1. What then can be said? Shall we *(after conversion)* continue to commit sin so that the grace of God may be multiplied? (1 John 3:9; Jeremiah 32:23; Psalms 119:1-3)

2. No, it is forbidden! How can we who have died to sin still continue in it? (Numbers 15:28-31; Psalms 97:10)

3. Do you not understand, all who have truly been baptized into Jesus Christ have been baptized into his death? (1 Corinthians 12:13; Isaiah 53:11-12; Galatians 3:27-29; Colossians 2:12)

4. This means that we who have been baptized into Christ have been buried with him through baptism, and we have also died with him! So just as Christ was raised up from the dead through the power of the Father, we also must be raised like him to live a truly renewed life. (*reborn* - G-2538 + G-2273) (Matthew 18:1-10; John 13:8; Mark 16:16)

5. Because if we have been buried together with him, we were brought to take part in his death, but we must also be resurrected with him. (Isaiah 53:5)

6. Knowing this, that the former man that we were was crucified with him and our body that had committed those sins was destroyed, now we shall no longer be a slave of sin; (John 8:36; Colossians 2:12)

7. Because he that has died has been made innocent from those past sins. (Romans 3:25; Hosea 14:9)

8. But if we have died with Christ, we must now surely live as him. (Ezekiel 37:27) (1 John 3:3; Ephesians 4:24-27; 2 Corinthians 7:1; 1 Corinthians 10:12-13; 1 Thessalonians 3:13)

9. Knowing that God has raised Christ from the dead, he can never die again; Death no longer holds power over him.

10. And because he died, he died one time for sin; But because he lives, he lives unto God. *(If he lives in us, then we must now live unto God)*

11. So now in the same way consider yourselves completely dead unto sin (*meaning that you must not do it ever*), and now fully live unto God through Jesus Christ our Lord. (1 John 3:3-10; Hebrews 10:26-29)

12. So accordingly, do not allow sin to overcome your mortal body. Do not take orders from the lustful temptations when they arise. (1 Corinthians 10:12-13; Psalms 19:13)

13. Do not even allow yourself to be near the wicked weapons of sin; You must offer yourselves unto God, as though being brought back from the dead, to now live by submitting yourself unto the completely pure ways of God.

14. Sin shall not have power over you, because you shall not live through the Mosaic law, but through the assistance of God! (John 8:31-36)

15. So what then? Shall we continue to commit sin because we are not living by the Mosaic law, but are now living through the assistance of God? No, it is forbidden!

16. Do you not know that whoever you serve and obey, you have given yourself to? You are the servant of whom you obey. So what will it be? Sin that leads unto eternal death or obedience unto God that leads to eternal justification (*righteousness*)? (Matthew 18:4-10; Isaiah 54:17; 1 John 5:16-17; Proverbs 11:5; Psalms 66:19; Proverbs 13:19; 1 John 3:3-10)

17. By the grace of God, we who were slaves to sin have now obeyed from our hearts the instructions which you have previously been given. (John 8:31-36; Matthew 18:1-10)

18. But now, you have been made to be free from sin and you have become the servants of righteousness.

19. I speak in a way that people may understand because of the weakness of your physical bodies:

19. Just as in the past, when you offered your bodies to be a servant unto the things that are impure, from one wicked action unto another wicked action, in a similar way now offer your body to be the servant of righteousness, in which you shall be justified.

20. Because when you were a slave of sin, (John 8:31-34) you were prevented (*exempt*) from being righteous.

21. So why would you choose to do that which you are now ashamed of? In the end, those things bring eternal death. (Matthew 7:17-19; Matthew 12:33; Isaiah 57:21; Psalms 119:21)

22. But now that you have been made to be free from sin, (John 8:36) you have become a servant of God, and what you produce (*your fruit*) must be holy, (Matthew 7:17-19 - *this is what sanctifies you*) and in the end, you shall receive everlasting life. (Isaiah 54:17; Psalms 119:44)

23. Because eternal death is what is earned by committing sin; But God has offered his charisma (a *gift*) that can bring everlasting life through our Lord Jesus Christ.

Romans 7

1. Do you not understand my brethren? I speak unto those who know the Mosaic law. The Mosaic law holds jurisdiction over a man as long as that man shall live. (Romans 6:4 - *To die with Christ ends it*)

2. A woman that has a husband that is alive is bound by the law to her husband; But if her husband dies, she is released from the law concerning her husband. (Matthew 19:9)

3. Therefore, if she gives herself unto another man while her husband is still alive, she is an adulteress. But if her husband is dead, she is free from the requirements of the law unto her husband and she is not an adulteress if she becomes the wife of another man. (1 Corinthians 11:11)

4. So then my brethren, you were made dead unto the Mosaic law by the body of Jesus Christ. *(having been crucified with him)* You have come unto another, unto he that has been raised from the dead, and now we must bring forth good fruit unto God. (Matthew 7:16-19)

5. Because when we were living according to our own cares and desires through the Mosaic law, the passions of sinful acts were made active in us and brought forth fruit that shall lead unto eternal death.

6. But now, we have been made free from the Mosaic law, having died unto that which we were partakers; So now we can be a servant of the new divine way, not in the old way that was written in the scriptures. (*in the old testament*)

7. So then, what shall we say? Is the Mosaic law sin? It can not be! I did not know what was sinful except through the Mosaic law; I would not have known lust. But because the law says you shall not lust,

8. it brought the opportunity for the commandments against sin to cause many lusts to be put into my mind.

9. I did live without the Mosaic law at one time; But when I came to know the commandments of God, sin became established in me and I died *(spiritually);*

10. So that which I found to be the commandments unto eternal life, they in turn brought the death of me,

11. because sin took the opportunity through the commandments to deceive me and it killed me.

12. But the Mosaic law is holy and that which is commanded is holy and righteous and good. (Deuteronomy 6:5; Matthew 22:37-40)

13. So then, did that which was good for me bring death unto me? It can not be! But it was sin, in that I understood that it was sin; (1 Timothy 1:13; Romans 1:18; Hebrews 10:26; Numbers 15:28-31; Galatians 2:17-18) It is because I knew that which is good (*but did not do good*), that is what brought the death of me.

As a result, I became very sinful through knowing that which is commanded unto me. (Deuteronomy 6:5; Matthew 22:37-40; James 4:7; Hebrews 10:26-27; 1 John 5:16-18; Psalms 19:13; Numbers 15:28-31)

14. We must know that the Mosaic law is not physical, but I am physical and I had come under the power of sin. (*a slave to sin* - John 8:31-35)

15. That which I had done, I did not desire to do, because that which I wanted to do I was not able to always do, but that which I hated is what I often did.

16. But if I did that which I did not want to do, I (*in my mind*) am in agreement that the law of God is good,

17. so it was no longer I that did that which was wrong, but the sin that had enslaved me!

18. Understand, that because that which is not good dwelled in me, even though I had the will to do that which is right, I could not come to live in the right way!

19. The good things that I desired to do, I could not continually do, but that which I hated is what I often found myself doing!

20. But if that which I wanted to do I could not do, and I was continuing to do that which I hated, it was no longer I that did those things, but it was the sin that had enslaved me that did them. (John 8:31-36)

21. So certainly, I wanted to do according to the law of God and to do that which is good, but there was evil present within me; (*you can not serve two masters*)

22. In my heart I delighted in the law of God,

23. but there was a different law that had enslaved my body which brought war against the law of God which I knew was good. By the Mosaic law, sin was made evident in my body.

24. Truly what a miserable man I was! Who was able to deliver me from my physical body leading to eternal death?

25. I thank God, that through our Lord Jesus Christ, now I, to the best of my understanding serve the law of God, and my physical body which had served sin has now died with Christ. (Romans 6:4-6)

Romans 8

1. So now there is no condemnation unto those who are in Jesus Christ, if they live in accordance to the spirit of Christ and not according to their own selfish lusts.

2. The law of the spirit of Christ working in my life has made me free from the Mosaic law, of which only exposes sin and brings death.

3. The Mosaic law is powerless because it is weak in dealing with (*against*) the lusts for evil; But God sent his son, who came in the likeness of other men that are sinful, and concerning sin, he prevented it from touching his body. (1 John 3:3; 1:5-6)

4. In this, the righteousness of the law of God can now be accomplished in us, if we do not live according to our own selfish desires, but if we live according to the spirit of Christ.

5. They that live according to their own selfish lusts think about things that are evil. Those who live according to the spirit of Christ have one purpose, of which is the spiritual things of God.

6. The worldly mind lusts for things that are evil and will lead to eternal death. Those who have their mind set upon the spiritual things of Christ shall receive life and peace.

7. The worldly mind is opposed to God and is not able to come in submission unto him. (1 John 2:15)

8. Those that are worldly are not able to please God.

9. But if the spirit of God lives in you, you can not live according to the worldly lusts, but you must live in accordance to the spiritual things of Christ. If any man does not have the spirit of Christ within him, he is not of God. (Philippines 8:19; John 3:3-5 John 14:18-20; 1 John 2:23; 1 John 4:2-3; Acts 19:4-6)

10. If Christ is in you, your body has become dead because of sin, but your spirit is alive because you now live righteously. (Romans 6:4-6)

11. If the spirit of the one who raised Christ up from the dead lives in you, then he has also made your mortal body live again, through his spirit that lives within you. (1 John 3:1)

12. Now my brethren, you do not owe anything to your body and must not live for selfish purposes,

13. because if you live to gratify yourself you shall eternally die; If you live by the spirit of God, you must no longer live according to the selfish desires of your body, but overcome them, and in this you shall eternally live. (1 Corinthians 10:13)

14. Whoever lives according to the spirit of God, these are the sons of God. (1 John 3:1-3)

15. You did not receive the spirit to again become a slave of that which should be feared. (John 8:31-35) But you have received the spirit of adoption, by which we call out, Papa, my Father!

16. The spirit of God is a witness unto the spirit *(soul)* within each of us, if we are the children of God.

17. If we are children of God, then we are also heirs, truly heirs of God and participants in Christ; If we suffer together, we shall also be honored together.

18. I think about all of the hardships that I have suffered, yet they are not even comparable to the coming glory that shall be bestowed upon us;

19. That which has been expected since the beginning of creation is being eagerly awaited, the revealing of the sons of God. All of mankind are subjected unto self-interests and we must choose,

20. because it is only through obedience that we have hope.

21. And each one must choose to be set free from the slavery leading unto destruction, (Acts 2:38) to live as the children of God, free from sin and to be honorable. (John 8:31-36)

22. We know that all of mankind experiences these difficulties and is now awaiting until the resurrection. (Revelation 20:12-15)

23. But we also have the first fruits of the spirit *(of God)* and we struggle within ourselves, eagerly awaiting the adoption and our physical bodies being made whole.

24. It is because of our hope that we are actively being saved. But hope that can be seen is not hope; For why would one hope for that which we already have possession of. *(no one is eternally saved while still alive!)*

25. But if we hope for that which we do not see, we have patient continuance *(faithfulness)* for that which we eagerly await. (Hebrews 1:11)

26. And likewise, the spirit of God also assists within us when we are weak; For when we certainly do not know what to speak, the spirit intercedes on our behalf, speaking that which had been unable to be stated.

27. Search in your heart to know the will of the spirit of God, but he only speaks to those that are holy. *(2 Peter 3:14 - blameless) (John 9:31) (God speaks through your heart if you are fully dedicated to him)*

28. For we know that for all who love God, everything works together for good, in accordance to the offer *(of eternal life)* unto those that heed unto the call.

29. For those that he calls, he has predestined for them to be conformed into the image of his son Jesus Christ. (Psalm 23:3; 1 John 3:3).

30. He is the first reborn of many brethren and those that he is leading, he has called, and those that he is leading, he requires godly character for them to be honored. (John 3:16-20)

31. So now, what can we say concerning these things? If God is watching over us, who can destroy us?

32. He did not even spare his own son, but he committed him unto the cross on our behalf. So how will he at that time not graciously bless us with everything?

33. If God has justified us, who can bring charges against the elect of God?

34. Who can condemn us? Christ died, but more importantly he is risen, (1 Corinthians 1:23) and he sits at the right hand of God and he shall defend us.

35. Who can separate us *(the faithful)* from the love of God? Can stress, or calamity, or persecution, or hunger, or nakedness, or danger, or the governments of this world?

36. It has been written, "for your sake we shall give our lives at any time. We are as sheep on the way to be butchered."

37. But all of these things we shall surely overcome through the one that truly loves us.

38. I have confidence that neither death nor life, nor spiritual beings, nor kings, nor those in powerful places, nor things that exist today, nor things that shall come,

39. nor that which is above, nor that which is below, nor any of mankind is able to separate us *(the faithful)* from the affection of God through the Lord Jesus Christ who lives within us. (John 19:29) *(These are all external things, but it is possible for one to separate one's self from God by choosing to commit sin, to defy God)*

Romans 9

1. I tell the truth of Christ; I do not lie! The holy spirit *(of Christ)* that is within me and my conscience are my witnesses of this.

2. I have great sadness and never-ending pain in my heart.

3. I would sacrifice myself and be cursed by God, if only it would benefit my brethren, my fellow countrymen according to descent, of whom are Israelites.

4. The adoption, the honour, the covenants, the Mosaic law that was given by God, the services and promises, they were all intended for them!

5. God did bless the forefathers forever, from whom Christ was physically descended. He is above all.

6. However the message of God has not been cast away. Not all of those of the descent of Israel (*the ancient nation*) are Israel (*God's people*).

7. They are not all children of God because they are physical descendants of Abraham! As the scripture says," In Isaac shall your seed be." (Genesis 21:12)

8. But this does not speak of the children through descent, the physical offspring as being the children of God, but speaks of those who ascent into covenant (*with God)* that are recognized as the seed. (Galatians 3:27-29)

9. The message of promise was; "At that time I shall come and give a son unto Sarah." (Genesis 18:10)

10. Not only of Sarah, but also a son from out of the womb of Rebecca, having Isaac as a father.

11. "For the children have not yet been generated, neither have they done any good nor evil, but by God, the chosen one shall stand firm; (*We do not inherit sin from Adam but are born sin free* - Matthew 18:1-4)

12. Not by earning it on their own, but by the one that called him." Just as it was said unto her, "The older shall serve the younger." (Genesis 25:23)

13. As it has been written, "Jacob I have loved, but Esau I have hated." (Malachi 1:2-3)

14. What shall we say then? Is God unrighteous? It can not be!

15. For Moses said, "I will have compassion upon whoever I choose to have compassion, and I will assist (*give grace)* whoever I choose to assist." *(based upon God's judgment of each man)* (Exodus 33:19; James 4:6)

16. So therefore, it does not matter what you think the judgment should be, nor is it decided by the one who is competing, but it is only through the mercy of God.

17. Because the scripture says unto Pharaoh, "This is the reason that I have brought you into power, so that I may display my power upon you, in order that my name be made known throughout all of the earth." (Exodus 9:16)

18. So then, unto whoever God decides, he gives compassion; Unto whomever he decides, he allows to become stubborn.

19. You will ask me, then how can God find a man guilty to be condemned, because no one has resisted his will, have they?

20. Now then, are you challenging against the authority of God? Will the thing that is created say to the creator, why did you make me this way? (Isaiah 29:16; Isaiah 64:8)

21. Does the potter not have authority over the clay? From out of the same lump of clay the potter surely makes vessels that are honorable and other vessels that are dishonorable!

22. But if God chooses to bring forth his wrath upon the wicked in order to display his power, they shall receive much suffering and have become vessels unto wrath and are completely ready for destruction.

23. He uses them to make his wealth and honor known unto those who might be vessels of mercy, of whom had earlier demonstrated have been preparing for honor. *(Freewill is demonstrated in us all* - James 4:6)

24. He has called us all, not only the Jews, but all people of all nations!

25. Just as it was written by Hosea, "I will call those who were not my people, and those that were not previously beloved shall become beloved;

26. And in that place where it had been said unto them, you are not my people, there it shall be said unto them, you are the sons of the living God!" (Hosea 2:23)

27. But Isaiah cried out against Israel saying, "Though the children of Israel are as the sands of the sea, only a very few shall be brought to be saved *(eternally).*

28. For they have been shortcoming concerning the required righteousness of the law (*of God*), and I will do a new thing upon the earth and will cut them off *(all who disobey)"* (Isaiah 10:21-23; Luke 19:43-44; Daniel 9:24-27)

29. Isaiah also said, "unless the Lord would leave us a seed, we would have all turned and become as Sodom and Gomorrah." (Isaiah 1:9)

30. What shall be said? The gentiles who did not pursue righteousness, shall find righteousness;
A righteousness that is lived and proven *(tested to be true).*

31. But Israel who pursued the law of righteousness *(Mosaic law)*, they did not meet the righteousness requirements of the law of God.

32. Why? Because they did not live accordingly *(no faithfulness)*, but they tried to manipulate righteousness through the Mosaic law. They stumbled at the stumbling stone.

33. It is written, "Look! I shall place in Zion a stone that shall make them stumble, a rock that shall make the opportunity for them to fall; But all who obey him shall not be ashamed." (Ezekiel 3:20; Isaiah 8:14,15)

Romans 10

1. My Brethren, the true desire of my heart is to ask God on behalf of Israel, that they be eternally saved.

2. I testify that they have zeal for God, but they have no discernment nor understanding.

3. They are ignorant of the righteousness that God requires, but they seek a righteousness unto their own standard; They do not submit unto the righteousness that God demands.

4. But now, Christ is the end of the Mosaic law as the way unto righteousness for everyone who truly believes. (John 3:18-21 - *To believe is to obey)*

5. Moses wrote, "The man who comes under the Mosaic law is required to do all that is in it. (Leviticus 18:5)

6. But the righteousness that comes through one's proven faithfulness says this; "Do not decide in your heart that you shall arise into the heavens." *(Do not say that you are already eternally saved -* Philippines 3:12) That is to have no respect for God. (Deut 30:12-18; 1 Corinthians 10:12; Rev 1:11)

7. Also, do not decide in your heart that you shall descend into the abyss *(hell)*, as that is to reject the death of Christ and make him worthless to you.

8. But what does it say? "The message must be very close to you, in your mouth and in your heart." This is the message of faithfulness *(that is proven)*, of which we proclaim! (Deuteronomy 30:12-18)

9. Because if you make a commitment with your mouth unto the Lord Jesus, and if you completely trust in your heart that God has raised Christ from the dead, you shall be guided to safety; (G-4982+G-5087) (Acts 22:16; Psalms 145:18; 1 Thessalonians 5:27)

10. Because with the heart a man must commit to live a righteous life, and with the mouth a man makes the assent into covenant *(contract)* that leads unto salvation. (G-4982 + G-5083) (Acts 8:37; 2 Timothy 2:25)

11. Because the scripture says, "everyone that continues believing *(trustworthy)* in him shall not be put to shame." (Isaiah 28:16; John 3:18-21)

12. You see, there is no difference, Jew nor gentile! He is the same Lord unto each one and he is wealthy enough for all who live according to the calling. (Galatians 3:28; Acts 15:9; Romans 3:22 Ephesians 2:15)

13. For everyone who ascends, to be called by (G-1941) the name of the Lord shall be reserved. *(unto eternal salvation).* (Acts 2:21; Joel 3:5; Acts 2:39)

14. So then, how may one be of Christ if he is not committed unto him? *(verse 9 beginning)* How can one be committed if he has not come to understand? (G-1990 + G-2151 *knowledge and piety- verse 9 end)* How will they come to understand without it being announced? *(verse 10-11)*

15. How can anyone announce to others if they have not been delegated? It has been written; "How beautiful the feet are of them who bring the good news and show the way unto salvation." (Isaiah 52:7)

16. But not all people obey the gospel! (1 Peter 4:17; Romans 6:1-23)

As Isaiah also wrote: "Lord, which of them have put their trust in your instructions?"(Isaiah 53:1)

17. So then, one's conviction is built upon that which he has come to understand, and understanding is brought by the instructions of God.

18. But I have asked, is there none that have understanding? Surely the message has been brought unto all of the earth, unto the ends of the habitable earth, unto all men! (Psalms 19:4)

19. But I ask; Did Israel truly not know? First Moses said, I will provoke you unto jealousy by a people who have no nation and by an ignorant people I shall make you angry. (Deuteronomy 32:21)

20. Isaiah again boldly said; "I shall be found by those who do not seek me, and I shall be revealed unto those who are not looking for me." (Isaiah 65:1)

21. But unto Israel he has said; "All day long I have reached my hands out unto a disobedient and contradicting *(say one thing do another)* people.

Romans 11

1. I now ask, did God cast away his people? It can not be! For I am also an Israelite, a descendant of Abraham, from the tribe of Benjamin.

2. God did not cast away the people that foreknew him. Do you not know what Elijah said in the scriptures? He plead with God against Israel, saying,

3. "Lord, they have killed your prophets and they have taken down your altars, and I am left alone and they are seeking to kill me!" (1 Kings 19:10)

4. But what did God say unto him? "I have reserved unto myself seven thousand men who have not bowed down a knee unto Baal." (1 Kings 19:18)

5. So even now at this present time, there is a remnant *(small number)* that have come to be chosen by the power of God. (Isaiah 65:8-9; Jeremiah 10:16)

6. And if it is by charity, it is no longer by the deeds of the Mosaic law, otherwise grace would no longer be grace. But if it is by works of the Mosaic law, it can not be by the power of God, where ones previously committed deeds are no longer deeds of record. (Romans 3:25; 2 Peter 1:9)

7. What then? Israel has not obtained what they have been seeking, but the chosen *(elect)* have obtained it and all of the others were hardened.

8. It has been written; "God has allowed them to have a spirit of stupor and eyes that can not see and ears that can not hear; It remains like this even today!" (Isaiah 29:10; Deuteronomy 29:4)

9. David has said, "Let their table *(commerce)* become a snare, a trap and a stumbling block, for recompense unto them;

10. May their eyes be darkened so that they can not see, and may they be afflicted as from behind when kneeling." (Psalms 68:22-23; Isaiah 8:14; Ezekiel 3:20)

11. But then I ask: Shall they stumble so that they might all fall? May it not be! But by their fall, salvation might be offered unto every nation, that they might be provoked unto jealousy.

12. But if their fall brings such a great wealth unto the whole world, and their loss brings great value unto all nations, how much better shall it be if some are made complete?

13. Since I am an apostle to the foreign nations, I honour my ministry and I speak unto all nations,

14. that somehow, I might provoke jealousy in my kinfolk, that I might bring some of them unto salvation!

15. But if the cutting off *(rejection - Daniel 9:26)* of them brings restoration unto the world, what if they reconcile, would that not bring back life from the dead?

16. So if the first part of the sacrifice is holy, so the whole of the sacrifice must be, and if the root is holy, so also must the branches be.

17. If some of the branches have been cut off, (Isaiah 9:14-16) and you being of a wild olive tree are grafted into the good olive tree, (Isaiah 14:1; Isaiah 27:10-11; Jeremiah 11:16; Zephaniah 3:14)

18. do not exalt yourself above the other branches; If you begin boasting against them, remember, it is not you who support the root, but it is the root that supports you.

19. You might say that the branches were broken off so that you could be grafted in! (Isaiah 54:3; 66:12)

20. Well, because of disobedience *(unfaithfulness)* they were broken off, but you stand by your dedication. Do not be arrogant *(haughty),* but be fearful; (Psalms 2:11; Philemon 2:12; Psalms 119:21)

21. For if God did not spare the natural branches, heed the warning or he shall neither spare you.
(Destroys OSAS theology)

22. Take notice of the kindness, but also the severity of God: (Psalms 81:13-15) Surely upon those who have fallen, his severity. But unto you, his kindness, if you continue in his character *(serving him);* Otherwise you shall also be cut off!

23. But if they do not continue in unfaithfulness *(disobedience),* God is able to graft them in again. (Luke 15:24; 2 Samuel 11:1-12:31)

24. Because if you, according to the ways of descent were cut out of a wild olive tree, and against nature were grafted into a good olive tree, how much more shall they, according to the way of descent, be grafted in again into their own olive tree?

25. I do not want you to be ignorant of this hidden truth my brethren, so that you not become conceited; But hardness of their hearts has happened unto many of the nation of Israel and shall remain until the completion *(end)* of the gentiles occupation arrives.
(Daniel 9:26-27 - *the Roman occupation that ended in 70 AD*)

26. And so, all of Israel shall be offered salvation. (Titus 3:5; verse 32) As it is written, "the deliverer will come unto Zion, and unto those of Jacob that turn away from their wickedness.

27. This is my offer (*will and testament*) unto all people, that I might take away their sins." (Galatians 3:14; Isaiah 59:20-21; Romans 3:25) Concerning the gospel, they are enemies of yours;

28. But concerning the chosen, they are beloved because of the forefathers.

29. For the free gift and the invitation of God is unchangeable;

30. For you at one time were disobedient unto God, but now you have obtained mercy because of their disobedience.

31. So they have disobeyed, but because of your compassion, some may also receive the mercy of God.

32. For God has concluded that all have been disobedient, so that he might offer his mercy unto all people.

33. The depths of the wisdom and knowledge of God! In what way are they able to scrutinize his decisions and fully comprehend all of his ways? (Acts 13:26)

34. Who can perceive the mind of the Lord, or who could be a counsellor unto him?

35. Who can first give unto him so that he could compensate?

36. It is because of him, and by him, and for him that all things have been made; (John 1:1-4)
Unto him be the honor forever.

Romans 12

1. Therefore I call unto you, that through the assistance of God you must now exhibit (*offer, present*) your body to be a living sacrifice, blameless and well pleasing unto God. This is your logical responsibility. (Ephesians 5:2; 2 Peter 3:14)

2. Do not be conformed by this world, but be transformed by the renewal of your mind and discern that which is according to the will of God, to be good, well pleasing and perfect in his sight. (Matthew 5:48)

3. Through the power of God that has been given unto me, I say unto everyone who is among you, do not exercise your mind concerning more than that which is necessary to think about. Be sober minded in your thinking, because God tests the faithfulness of each and every man and woman. (James 1:3)

4. Just as we have many parts that make up our bodies and each part has a different function,

5. so also, we who are in Christ make up one body and each one are co-members.

6. But we each have differing gifts (1 Corinthians 12) according to the way God assists each one of us;
If prophecy, use it according to that which shall be proven to be faithful (*true*);

7. If ministering (*helping others*), do so to fill the need; If teaching, do it according to the true doctrine;

8. When calling others to the truth, do so cheerfully and with comfort; When sharing, do so liberally; When standing (*speaking*) before the people, be diligent and compassionate and do so cheerfully!

9. May your affection be equal unto all. Detest those that are evil and grow close to those that are good;

10. Show brotherly affection unto one another and become a family. Value one another and be a good example for others to follow.

11. Be diligent, but do not cause any harm. Serve the Lord with a warm heart.

12. Be happy in that which you have hope for; Patiently endure when you are persecuted and steadfastly continue in prayer. Contribute unto the needs of other saints and be hospitable.

14. Bless those who persecute you; Speak well of others and do not curse them.

15. Be happy with those that are happy and cry with those who are crying.

16. Think upon these things with one another, but do not think too highly of yourself. Yield yourself to become humble. Do not become conceited within yourselves.

17. Do not give evil back unto others if they had done evil unto you. Continually maintain a virtuous appearance unto all people.

18. If it is possible, make peace with all men.

19. Do not avenge yourselves my beloved, but leave room for the wrath of God. For it has been written; "Vengeance is mine, saith the Lord! I will repay." (Deuteronomy 32:35)

20. "So if your enemy is hungry, feed him. If he is thirsty, give him a drink. In doing this you shall be piling heaps of fiery coals upon his head." (Proverbs 25:21-22)

21. We can not gain victory by doing evil, but we gain victory over evil men by doing what is good.

Romans 13

1. Bring everyone who is rational, to become obedient unto the highest authority *(God)*, (Psalms 145:3; 2 Samuel 23:3) because there is no authority except that of God. The only authority that exists are those that are according to God. *(living in the ways of God - 1 Peter 2:13-17; Titus 3:1)*

2. So the ones who reject the authority of God oppose his commandments. Those who oppose him shall receive damnation unto themselves.

3. Because the highest ruler *(God)* does not become fearful unto those who do what is right, but shall be fearful unto those who do what is wicked. Do you not respect his authority? If you do what is good, you shall be commended by him. (Hebrews 11:6)

4. The *(authentic)* ministers of God are there for your own good, but if you do wickedness, you should fear! He *(God)* does not bring judgment for no reason. A minister of God is there to bring forth righteousness *(in you)* before the wrath of God shall fall upon all who do evil. (Hebrews 10:26-29; 13:7; Romans 2:2-11)

5. Therefore, it is necessary for you to submit yourself *(unto God)*, not only because of the wrath, but also because of your moral conscience.

6. This is why you have a responsibility to become completed; *(perfect - 2 Timothy 3:17)* This is the reason the ministers of God persevere, continually attending to you. *(instructing and guiding)*

7. Therefore, this is the way of indebtedness; The one burdened carries the burden; The one that sets out for the goal must attain the goal; The one due respect receives respect, and the one due honour receives honour.

8. Do not be under obligation unto any man, except to love one another; He that has love for others has fulfilled the law of God.

9. Do not commit adultery, do not murder, do not steal, do not bear false witness, do not covet, and if there is any other commandment in this instruction of God it is completely summed up; "You shall love your fellow man *(others)* as yourself." (Exodus 20:13-15; Leviticus 19:18; Matthew 22:40)

10. Love does no evil unto his neighbor. So love is the fulfillment of the law.

11. Furthermore, understand the opportunity that you now have, because now is the time that we must immediately be raised from out of our sleep! Today your deliverance is much closer than at the time you came to understand the instructions of God.

12. The night is coming to its end and the daytime is approaching, so we must cast away the deeds of wickedness and we must put on the tools of the Light. *(speaking to new converts – Acts 26:18)*

13. We must live honestly as in the daylight. We must not become loose nor drunken; Do not do lustful deeds and do not be contentious nor envious.

14. Put on all of the *(qualities of the)* Lord Jesus Christ, (Galatians 5:22-24) and do not even allow for a thought to consider the lusts for that which is evil, nor for anything that is forbidden.

Romans 14

1. Those that are weak concerning the true doctrine, receive them, but not unto the disputing of the teachings.

2. One may truly trust that all things may be eaten, but one who is unlearned eats only vegetables. (Luke 10:8; Colossians 2:16)

3. He that eats must not despise the one who does not eat all things and the one not eating all things must not judge the one that eats all things. God receives each one.

4. Who are you to judge another man's servant? He shall stand or fall before his own master. God is able to help him stand.

5. One man holds one day above another day, but one holds every day as equal to each other. Each man must be completely confident in his own mind.

6. The one who holds the opinion to hold a day, he does so as unto the Lord; He that holds the position to not keep a certain day, he does not keep the day, but as unto the Lord. The one who eats, he does so as to honor the Lord and he gives thanks unto our God; He that does not eat, he does so to honor the Lord and he gives thanks unto God.

7. No one lives unto themselves and no one dies unto themselves;

8. For if you are alive, you must live unto the Lord; But if you die, unto the Lord you die. For he is the Lord of all.

9. This is the reason that Christ died, has risen and now lives in us, (G-326 + G-1524 - *by his holy spirit -*

1 John 4:2; John 14:23) so that he would be the master above all, both the living and those who have died.
10. So why would you condemn your brother? Why would you despise your brother? Everyone shall stand before the judgment seat of Christ! (Romans 2:5-10; Revelation 20:12-15)
11. For it has been written: "As I live, saith the Lord, every knee shall bow and every tongue shall confess unto God." (Isaiah 49:18; 45:23)
12. So then, each one of us shall give an account unto God for the way that we had lived our lives! (Romans 2:6; Revelation 20:12-15)
13. Certainly we must no longer condemn one another. Consider this: (Romans 2:1) You must not trip up your brethren nor allow an occasion for your brethren to fall.
14. But know that I am completely convinced by the Lord Jesus, that nothing (*concerning food*) can be unclean in itself. But unto the one who considers it to be unclean, unto him it is unclean.
15. And if, because of your food, your brother is distressed, then you are not living according to love (*as required*). Do not have your food cause one to defile themselves or destroy one for whom Christ has died!
16. Do not allow your good to be evil spoken of. (1 Corinthians 8:7-13)
17. For the kingdom of God is not for the purpose of eating and drinking, but for righteousness, peace and joy through the spirit of the holy one.
18. For he that is serving Christ must be approved by God, and also be peaceful with others.
19. May we pursue those things that promote peace and the things that help build up one another.
20. Do not undo that which God has done for the sake of your preferred food! All things (*foods*) truly are clean, but for those that would defile themselves because of eating them, they are unclean unto them.
21. It is better to not eat meat nor to drink wine if it was to cause your brother to fall or if it offends him because of his weakness.
22. Do you have dedication? Show it through how you live, in the presence (*eyes*) of God. Do not have anyone condemn themselves by what they approve.
23. But the one who doubts, if he eats, he condemns himself, because of not being faithful. Everything that is not proven to be faithful is sinful.

Romans 15

1. We who are strong must bear those who are weak and incomplete and not use our strength for our own benefit.
2. Let each one be kind unto his fellow man, for his good and his spiritual benefit.
3. Because even Christ did not please himself, but as it has been written, "the contemptuous defamation of those who mocked them of my house shall fall upon me." (Psalms 69:9)
4. These things that were written in the past, were written for our instruction, that through them we might receive encouragement from the scriptures and that we might have hope to patiently continue.
(the words of the bible bring encouragement and instruction, but is not God speaking directly to you!)
5. May God give unto you the same mind of encouragement to patiently continue, the same as Jesus Christ. (1 John 3:3)
6. Together, in one accord and with one voice may you honour our Father God and the Lord Jesus Christ.
7. Continue to be hospitable and accept others, just as Christ also received us unto the glory of God.
8. Because Jesus Christ has become a minister unto those that are circumcised in their hearts according to the truth of God, for the purpose to establish (*fulfill*) the promises that were made unto the forefathers,
9. and also unto all nations according to his compassion, for the glory of God, just as it has been written: "I will give thanks unto you oh Lord, for all nations will praise thy name." (Psalms 18:49)
10. Then again the scripture says; "Put this in your mind, all people of all nations." (Deuteronomy 32:43)
11. And again; "Praise the Lord all nations, praise him all people!" (Psalms 117:1)
12. Then again Isaiah said; "The root shall come out of Jesse, the one who shall rise up and reign over all nations and in him shall all nations receive hope." (Isaiah 11:10)
13. May God bring much confidence, joy and peace unto those that trust in him and that you receive an endless supply of hope through the power of the spirit of the holy one.
14. My brethren, I am convinced that you are full of goodness and that you have been filled with all of this knowledge, so that you are able to keep each other in line.
15. I write boldly unto you, in part, to remind you, because of the assistance that God has given unto me

16. to be a minister of Jesus Christ unto all nations, ministering the truth of the gospel of God, for you to become acceptable and consecrated by the spirit of the holy one.

17. Therefore I have the ability to boast much in Jesus Christ and of God.

18. I would not dare to say anything that I have done was without the assistance of Jesus Christ working through me, of which is for the purpose of teaching obedience unto all nations, both in their words and also in their deeds.

19. Through many powerful signs and fulfilled prophecies, the power of the spirit of God has been proven to be within me; From Jerusalem and in a ring that reaches as far as Illyricum, I have fully delivered the Gospel of Jesus Christ.

20. This is how I have surely strived to preach the gospel everywhere that Christ was not known, and I would not build upon any other foundation.

21. As it is written: "Unto those who it was not announced concerning Christ, they shall see him, and those who had not heard, they shall understand." (Isaiah 52:15)

22. However, I was strongly prevented from coming to you.

23. Now I no longer have the necessity to go to those regions, but I continue to have a longing to come to you, as I have had for many years.

24. When I am able to go to Spain, then I shall come to you; I hope while traveling through, I might see you, but that you might send provisions unto me, so that beforehand I have all of what I need.

25. I am currently heading to Jerusalem to minister unto the saints there. (1 Corinthians 16:3; Acts 21:17)

26. The saints in Macedonia and Achaia thought that it was good to send some gifts to be given unto the poor saints that are in Jerusalem. (1 Corinthians 16:3)

27. They thought that it was necessary and that they owe it to them, because they were made sharers in the spiritual gifts, as with other nations, that they might also help to assist in the physical things that they have need of.

28. When I have completed this, I plan to come through where you are on my way to Spain.

29. I know that when I am there with you, I will come to speak with elegance, the gospel of Jesus Christ.

30. I invite you my brethren, by our Lord Jesus Christ and through the affection of the heart of God, to strive together with me in prayers unto God on my behalf,

31. so that I am protected from those who are disobedient in Judea and that my ministry will be well received by the saints that are in Jerusalem.

32. Pray that I am able to come to you and be joyful with you, by the will of God, that I might be refreshed by you.

33. May our God be at peace with you.

Romans 16

Verses 1-16 were added as a greeting when this letter was forwarded.

1. I commend unto you Phoebe our sister, a servant of the gathering at Cenchrea.

2. Receive her unto the Lord as a worthy saint and assist her in whatever matter that she might need. She has brought many (G-4253+G-4719 - front leader) to Christ, even bringing in many unto myself.

3. Greet Priscilla and Aquila, my fellow workers in Jesus Christ,

4. of whom risked their own lives to save my life, and I offer thanks unto them, and so do all of the gatherings throughout all of the nations.

5. Say hello to the gathering at their home. Greet my beloved Epenetus, of whom is a first fruit of Christ in Achia.

6. Greet Mariam who did many things to assist you.

7. Greetings unto Andronicus and Junias my kinfolk and fellow prisoners who are notable among the apostles, of whom were in Christ at an earlier time than I was.

8. Greet my beloved Amplias in the Lord.

9. Greet Urbanus my fellow worker in Christ Jesus; Also greet Stachys my beloved.

10. Say hello unto Apelles, of whom is approved in Christ. Greet those of Aristobulus.

11. Greet Herodan my kinsman. Greet those of Narcissus who are in the Lord.

222

12. Greet Tryphena and Tryphosa who are working for the Lord. Say hello unto my beloved Persis, who did many things as unto the Lord.
13. Give my best unto Rufus, one of the elect in the Lord, and also the mother of both him and myself.
14. Greet Asyncritus, Phlegan, Hermas, Patrobas, Hermes and all of the brethren that are with them.
15. Say hello unto Philolgus, Juliias, Nereus and his sister, as well as Olympas and all of the saints that are with him.
16. Greet one another with a holy kiss; All of the brethren that are in Christ say hello unto you.

Verses 17-20 were added as an instructional greeting when this letter was sent.

17. I sternly warn you my brethren, watch for those who will try to make divisions and create offenses against the true and pure doctrine that you have learned and are living. Turn away from them! (Acts 20:29-30; 2 Peter 2; 2 Timothy 3:5; Jude 1:4; Matthew 24:4-5)
18. Because such ones do not serve the Lord Jesus Christ, but they serve themselves, feeding unto themselves, and through carefully crafted words and elegance of language, they deceive the hearts of the innocent who are not suspecting such. (Psalms 12:2; 2 Peter 2:3)
19. The news of your obedience has reached everywhere. I rejoice because of you. I desire for you to truly be wise (*aware*) concerning that which is good, and innocent concerning that which is evil,
20. and the peace of God shall soon completely crush Satan under your feet. May the grace of the Lord Jesus Christ be with you.

Verses 21-24 were added by Tertius as an address when forwarding Paul's letter.

21. My fellow worker Timothy greets you, as well as Lucius, Jason and Sosipater who are my brethren.
22. I Tertius greet you, I am the one who has copied (*forwarded*) this letter for the sake of the Lord.
23. Gaius, the host of my gathering greets you. Erastus, the treasurer of the city, and Quartus my brother greet you.
24. The grace of the Lord Jesus Christ be with you all.

Verses 25-27 look to be added by Phebe as an address when forwarding Paul's letter.

25. Now he that is able to establish you according to the gospel and the announcement of Jesus Christ, according to the revealing of the mysteries, having been kept secret throughout the past times,
26. are now made easy to understand through the prophetic scriptures, according to the command of our eternal God, for obedience through the testing of your faithfulness unto all nations is made known,
27. only by the wisdom of our God through Jesus Christ. May the glory be unto him forever.

1 Corinthians

Chapter 1

1. Paul, appointed to be an apostle of Jesus Christ through the will of God, and our brother Sosthenes;

2. To the gathering of God that exists in Corinth who have been purified by Christ Jesus and called out to be saints, along with all others, everywhere that are living according to the calling in the name of our Lord Jesus Christ, both Jews and gentiles.

3. May the grace and peace of our Father God and the Lord Jesus Christ be with you.

4. I always thank my God concerning you for the compassion that God has given unto you through the Lord Jesus,

5. that in all things you are growing to know him in all of his ways and his knowledge.

6. The evidence of Christ in you is proven through how you now live, (1 John 2:3)

7. and you must not be lacking in any of the necessary parts while you are awaiting the manifestation (*coming*) of the Lord Jesus Christ;

8. We shall help establish you until the end, so that you might be blameless on the day of the Lord. (*2 Peter 3:14 - judgment day*)

9. God is trustworthy through the Lord Jesus Christ, of whom you have been called into partnership with.

10. Now I call upon you my brethren, through the name of Jesus Christ, that you also give these same instructions unto everyone and that there is no changes made, but that you are complete, in the exact same understanding and of this same purpose.

11. Now, it has been made known to me by Chloe, concerning you my brethren, that there is contention between many of you.

12. Some of you say, I am of Paul, another says I am of Apollos, and another says, I am of Cephas (*Simon Peter*); But I tell you, I am of Christ! (*I am a Baptist, I am a Methodist, I am a Lutheran...*)

13. I ask, has Christ been divided? It was not Cephas that was crucified for you; It was not in the name of Paul that you were baptized!

14. I give thanks unto God that I did not baptize any of you, except for Crispus and Gaius,

15. so that none might say that they were baptized in my name!

16. I also baptized the house of Stephanus, but I do not remember baptizing any other.

17. Christ did not send me to do baptisms, but to preach the gospel; (1 Corinthians 3:4-10) I was also not sent to be witty in my words, because that would nullify the cross of Christ. (John 4:2) (*as the false preachers often do with their jokes*)

18. The message of the cross is foolishness unto those that will be lost, but for those of us that are being saved, it is the way to receive the power of God.

19. For it has been written; "I will destroy the wisdom of them that are wise, and the understanding of the prudent shall be made worthless." (Isaiah 29:14)

20. Where are they that are wise? Where is the writer? Where are the arguments of this age? Did God not make the wisdom of this world to be foolishness?

21. This is why the world has not known the wisdom of God, but by the wisdom of God, the simple proclamation of salvation is given unto those who continue believing (*living accordingly*). (John 3:18-21)

22. But it is said that the Jews require a sign (*evidence*), and the Greeks are looking for wisdom. (Matthew 16:4)

23. However, we proclaim Christ risen from the dead and living within us. (1 John 4:2; Romans 8:34: Matthew 22:32) This is a great offense unto the Jews and foolishness unto the Greeks;

24. But to those who have heeded the invitation, of both Jew and gentile, Christ is the power and wisdom of God.

25. For the foolishness of God is many times wiser than all of mankind and the weakest part of God is many times stronger than all of mankind.

26. Recognize my brethren, not many who are wise according to the cares of this world, not many that are powerful and not many who are noble have heard the calling. (*the offer, invitation of God*).

27. But God chooses the lowly of this world, so that those who are wise might be shamed by them. God chooses the weak of this world, so that he might make those that are powerful to be ashamed.

28. The unknown of this world and those that are least valued, these are the ones that God continually chooses; Those that are not, so to nullify those that are.

29. This is so that no one can boast when before him (*on judgment day*).

30. Christ Jesus brought us the wisdom of the righteousness of God, through purification (*conversion - Acts 2:38*) and redemption (*living a holy life going forward*), and you are now with him.

31. Just as it has been written, "he that is raised up (Romans 6:4), let him give the glory unto the Lord." (Jeremiah 9:24)

1 Corinthians 2

1. When I came to you my brethren, I did not come to you announcing with a superior way of speaking, nor words of wisdom in order to give you the testimony of God.

2. I was determined to not speak anything unto you but Jesus Christ and that he has risen from the dead and lives within me. (1 John 4:1-5)

3. I came to you in weakness, in much fear and I was greatly trembling.

4. That which I preached was not enticing you with words of the wisdom of mankind, but was with evidence of the spirit of Christ and was powerful,

5. so that your conviction not be according to the wisdom of men, but in the power of God.

6. I certainly speak wisdom that leads unto perfection, but not the wisdom of this world, nor that of the ruler of this world (*Satan*). They will be brought to nothing. (John 16:11; Revelation 12:13; Matthew 4:9)

7. I surely speak of the mysteries of God that have been hidden, because God has predetermined before the creation of the world that we must be honorable.

8. None of the rulers in this world have come to know this, because if they had known, they would not have crucified our honorable Lord.

9. As it has been written; "Since the beginning, their eyes have not seen and the ears have not heard the things that God has prepared for those who love him." (Isaiah 64:4)

10. But God has revealed these things unto us through his spirit, because the spirit reveals all things including the mysteries of God. (John 16:13; Ezekiel 36:27; Jeremiah 31:34-36)

11. Who knows the heart of a man if not for the spirit that is within the man? So also are the things of God, which are not known by anyone except through his spirit. (Jeremiah 31:34; Matthew 16:17; 1 John 4:1-4)

12. But we have not received the spirit of the world, but the spirit of God, so that we might know the things of God that are freely given unto us;

13. These things that we speak are not taught through the wise words of mankind, but in that which is taught by the spirit of the holy one *(Jesus Christ),* bringing the spiritual things unto those that are of the spirit. (2 Timothy 1:14; John 16:13; 1 John 4:2-3)

14. Carnal (*worldly*) men can not receive anything concerning the spirit of God, because these things are foolishness unto them and they can not know, because they are not spiritually inclined.

15. However the man who is spiritually inclined certainly discerns all things, but he is not understood by anyone (*of a worldly mind*).

16. For who knew the mind of the Lord and who can teach him? But we (*who have been converted into Christ*) have the mind of Christ (*in us*).

1 Corinthians 3

1. So I, my brethren, was at that time not able to speak unto you as if you are spiritual, but spoke unto you as though you were carnal, because you were only infants in Christ.

2. I gave you milk to drink and not solid food because you were not able, yet even now you are not yet able!

3. You are still making many mistakes, as there is much contention, dissention and jealousy among you! Some of you are living in the ways as others that do not know Christ!

4. For when one says, I am of Apollos, and another says, I am of Paul, is this not evidence of a worldly mindset? (1 Corinthians 1:12-17)

5. Who is Paul? Who is Apollos? Are they not simply servants through whom you have come to trust in God? Did not both give unto you as the Lord allowed?

6. I planted (*brought the message*), Apollos watered (*baptized*), but it is God who brought the growth!

7. So the one who planted and the one who watered, they are not what matters, but it is the Lord our God who brought the increase.

8. One planted and one did the watering, and each of us shall receive a reward according to each one's work.

9. For each of us are fellow workers in the same field that is owned by God; You are God's construction!

10. As a wise master builder, according to the grace of God that has been given unto me, I laid the foundation, but another one built on top of it. Look and see how each one takes their part in the construction. (1 Corinthians 1:12-17)

11. For no one is able to lay any other foundation that can be built upon, except for Jesus Christ.

12. If anyone tries to build upon this foundation with gold or silver, or precious stones, or wood, or grass, or stubble,

13. the works of each man shall come to be revealed! For there will come a day where all things will be revealed by fire, and the fire will prove the quality of the work of each man.

14. If anyone's work remains through the fire, he shall receive the reward.

15. If any man's work shall be consumed, he shall be lost and he shall be reserved for destruction unto the eternal fire.

16. Do you not know that you are the temple of God if the spirit of God lives in you? (1 John 4:1-4; 1 Cor 11:29)

17. If anyone corrupts the temple of God, God will destroy him; For the temple of God is to be holy, if you belong to him. (1 John 3:3)

18. Do not allow anyone to deceive themselves; If anyone among you thinks that he is wise according to the ways of this world, he must forget everything that he knows in order to become wise;

19. Because the wisdom of this world is foolishness unto God; For it has been written, "He takes those that are wise by way of their own trickery." (Job 5:13)

20. Then again, "The Lord knows the imaginations (*ways of thinking*) of the wise of this world and that they are worthless." (Psalms 94:11)

21. Therefore none of us can boast of ourselves, for we have all been given unto you by God.

22. Whether Paul, Apollos or Cephas *(Simon Peter),* whether life, or death; Concerning things that are present or that which is in the future; We are all here for your sake if you are in Christ, because Christ is of God.

1 Corinthians 4

1. Suppose that certain men are called to be assistants of Christ and stewards of the mysteries of God.

2. The remainder of the people are searched by these stewards to see if there are any faithful that can be found.

3. For me it is the smallest concern that I might be judged by you or by any other man, on any day; I do nothing that might condemn myself. (Hebrews 10:26; Numbers 15:28-31)

4. There is nothing that I am aware of (*that I do wrongly*), but that in itself does not justify me; It is only the Lord that is examining me. (Revelation 1:11)

5. So do not condemn before the proper time. When the Lord comes, he will reveal the things that have been hidden away from others and also the intents of the heart; At that time, the honor shall be given by God unto each one that is deserving. (Romans 2:1-10; Revelation 20:12-15)

6. These things I have applied to myself and Apollos for your sake, so that you might learn from us, not exceeding what we have instructed you to understand, so that no one becomes prideful above any other.

7. Which of you have any contention against this? What do you have that you were not first given? So if you have been given it, why do you boast as though you have not been given it?

8. Having already been given this, you have already received this wealth (*understanding*). But some of you did what you wanted without us there! Oh, and how you force us to bring stern correction unto you!

9. This is why I think that God has made his apostles to be the lowest of his chosen, as though appointed unto death, as we have become a spectacle unto the world, unto both men and angels.

10. We have become as fools because of Christ, yet some of you look as though you are prudent in Christ. We are weak, so that you might be strong; You appear glorious, but we are disrespected.

11. Even at this very moment we are hungry and thirsty and are not dressed well, and we are often beaten, and we are homeless,

12. and we work hard with our own hands, and while we are being cursed we bless others, and when we are persecuted, we endure it.

13. When we are spoken evil of, we are inviting. We are cleansed from the things of this world, even unto the present time we remain polished before God.

14. I do not write these things to shame you, but as unto my own children, this is a beloved warning.

15. Because, though you have many teachers in Christ, you do not have many fathers; For in Jesus Christ, I have fathered you through the gospel.

16. I urge you to become imitators of me.

17. This is why I sent Timothy unto you, as he is my beloved son and faithful in the Lord. He will remind you of the ways of Christ that I have taught unto you, the same as I teach in every gathering that is in Christ, everywhere.

18. And as for my not coming unto you, some of you were very upset. (2 Corinthians 2:4)

19. But I will come unto you soon, if the Lord allows, and I will not allow a word with any that have reverted back (*fallen away*); But they shall see the power (*of God*).

20. Because the kingdom of God is not in word, but in power. (Acts 1:8; 2 Timothy 3:5)

21. What do you desire? Should I come unto you with a rod of correction or in the spirit of love and of meekness?

1 Corinthians 5

1. Everywhere it has been made known that there is a fornicator among you, and such fornication that is not even spoken of among the heathen, so that one had taken unto himself, his father's wife!

2. I have come to understand that you are living in a very proud way, and you have not come to be grieved by this! This man must be thrown out of your gathering because of the deed that he has done!

3. I am physically absent, but I am there in spirit and I have already made the judgment as though I were physically there with you concerning this man who is living in such a way.

4. In the name of the Lord Jesus Christ, in the spirit that I have shared with you and with the authority of the Lord Jesus Christ,

5. cast this man away from you unto Satan for destruction because of his evil lusts, so that the vital principals (*of God*) may be preserved (*within your gathering*) unto the return of the Lord Jesus. (Acts 19:9)

6. Your boasting is not good. Do you not know that a little yeast (*sin*) leavens (*spoils*) the whole mass (*church*)?

7. So now cleanse yourselves thoroughly from such leaven (*sin*) and become a fresh lump; Become unleavened, because Christ is our Passover and he was sacrificed for us.

8. So may we surely keep the feast, but not with the old leaven (*sinful ways*), not with the leaven of malice and wickedness. You must be unleavened (*without sin*) and be sincerely in truth. (Galatians 5:9; Hosea 7:4)

9. I had previously written a letter unto you in which I told you to not associate with fornicators; *(where is this letter now?)*

10. Not telling you to altogether not communicate with fornicators, nor with thieves, nor with idolaters, because you have need to go out into the world to bring them the gospel.

11. But I told you to not associate intimately with these types of people. So if anyone that is a brother is known to be a fornicator, or as covetous, or an idolater, or an evil talker, or a drunkard, or a thief, do not even eat with such a man! (2 John 1:10)

12. Why would I judge those outside of the gathering? Why would you not judge those inside?

13. Those on the outside shall be judged by God, however "you must put that evil one away from you." (Deuteronomy 17:7)

1 Corinthians 6

1. Are any of you so bold to have a matter against another and take it before the wicked to decide the matter? Why not take it before the saints to decide?

2. Do you not know that the saints shall be judging the entire world?

3. If you shall judge the whole world, why are you unwilling to judge such small matters?

4. Do you not know that we shall certainly judge the angels, so why not the things of this life? (Romans 2:1) If you have the need to make such judgments in this life concerning those that are the least from among your gathering, choose some of the elders to hear such matters.

5. I say, shame on you! Is there not a single wise man among you that is able to discern these things concerning the brethren that are there in your midst?

6. But instead, you have taken brother against brother to be a spectacle before unbelievers!

7. Certainly, you have already failed in that you have lawsuits against yourselves! Why not just allow yourselves to be wronged?

8. You are wicked to take those that are your brothers before unrighteous men!

9. Do you not know that the unjust shall not inherit the kingdom of God? (1 John 3:8-9; Romans 2:1-10) Do not be misled; No fornicator, nor idolater, nor adulterer, nor homosexual, nor sodomite, (Proverbs 6:32)

10. nor thief, nor covetous one, nor drunkard, nor evil talker, nor plunderer shall inherit the kingdom of God.

11. Some of you did these things in the past (Romans 3:25; Romans 6:17-18), but since you have been baptized into Christ (Galatians 3:27; Romans 6:1-23), you began to live a holy life and you are justified by the name of the Lord Jesus through the spirit of our God! (Acts 2:38)

12. I test all things, because not everything is beneficial; I test all things, because I will not be overcome by anything. (2 Peter 2:19)

13. Food is for the belly and the belly needs food, but in the end, God shall change this. The body is not for fornication, but the body is meant to be the house of the Lord. (1 Corinthians 3:16; John 2:21; 2Thess 2:4)

14. Just as God has raised our master, he will also raise us up through his mighty power. (Romans 6:4)

15. Do you not know that your bodies are a part of the body of Christ? So will you now take the body of Christ and join it with the body of a harlot? God forbids such! (Romans 6:1)

16. Do you not know that the one who joins himself with a harlot, he becomes of one body with her? As the scripture says, "the two shall be joined together and become one body." (Genesis 2:24)

17. But he that is joined with the master is of one disposition (*purpose*) with him.

18. Run away and escape from the temptations of fornication. Every sin that a man might commit is external from the body, but if a man commits fornication, he commits defiant sin against his own body. (1 John 5:16-17)

19. Do you not know that your body is the temple of the spirit of the holy one (*Jesus Christ*), of which you have been given from God?

20. You are not your own, but you were purchased at a high price! Now honor God with your body and with your whole spirit, because they are God's.

1 Corinthians 7

1. Now concerning that which you wrote to me, it is good for a man to not touch a woman.

2. It is because of indulgence that God has allowed each man to have a wife and each woman to have her own husband.

3. The husband is under obligation unto his wife to give unto her accordingly, and likewise the wife is also under obligation unto her husband.

4. Concerning this matter, the wife does not hold complete authority over her own body, but her husband does; Likewise, the husband does not have complete authority over his own body, but the wife does.

5. Do not deprive one another, unless there is an agreement for a short time, but only for the reason of fasting and prayer; Then to come together again so that Satan does not overcome you through temptation when you are weak.

6. The following I say as a fellow brother and not by command;

7. I would recommend that all men be as I am; Yet each man has his own ability that is given by God, to have a wife or to not have a wife.

8. I tell you, that if you do not have a wife or if you are widowed, it is good to remain as I am (*celibate*).

9. But if you have no self-control, then it is good to wed. It is better to be wed than to burn! *(lake of fire)* (Matthew 18:5-10)

10. But to those who are wed, I have a message, not of myself, but from the Lord; A woman must not be separated from her husband.

11. But if she leaves, she must remain celibate or be reconciled unto her husband. The husband must not leave his wife.

12. Now the following I tell you is not directly from the Lord; If a brother has a wife that is not a believer, if she consents to remain with him, he must not leave her.

13. If a wife has an unbelieving husband, if he consents to remain with her, she must not leave him.

14. For the unbelieving husband might be brought unto God (*converted*) by the believing wife, and the unbelieving wife might be brought unto God through the believing husband. Otherwise the children will end up being wicked, but in this way they may become righteous. (Genesis 6:1-2)

15. But if the one who is not believing chooses to separate, let them separate. The believing brother or sister does not remain obligated to the first (*spouse*) in such cases, but God releases us to be at peace. (Romans 7:2-3)

16. This is because you do not know if the unbelieving husband or wife would be brought unto Christ.

17. Only those that God allows, each one that the Lord draws near, they must live accordingly. I have instructed the same unto all of the gatherings of God.

18. Those living as circumcised should not want to be uncircumcised. Those that are living as uncircumcised, do not choose to be circumcised.

19. Physical circumcision is nothing and physical uncircumcision is nothing; What matters is keeping the commandments of God. (Matthew 22:37; Luke 10:27; Mark 12:30-31; Deuteronomy 6:5; Leviticus 19:18)

20. Each one should remain satisfied as they are.

21. Are you desiring to be a slave? Does it matter to you? If you are able to become free, then use that freedom. (*from the Mosaic law*)

22. Because the one that the Lord has called, having been a servant (*of the Mosaic law*), he becomes the Lord's freeman (*free from the Mosaic law*); And likewise, he that is free (*from the Mosaic law*) is called to become a servant of Christ. (Romans ch.9-11)

23. You were purchased at a very high price; Do not become the slave of men.

24. My brethren, everyone must choose to abide near to God.

25. Concerning the unwed, I do not have a command from the Lord; Yet I will offer my judgment as living faithfully in the compassion of the Lord.

26. I recommend that this should be valuable because of the present world we live in; It is good for a man to remain this way (*unwed*):

27. Are you betrothed unto a woman? If so, do not desire to be released from her. If you have been released, it is good to not look for a wife.

28. But if you take a wife unto yourself, you do nothing that is wrong. If you wed a young woman, she does nothing that is wrong either, but in this world you shall have many difficulties. I will not much further speak of this;

29. But I tell you my brethren, the time of death quickly approaches and those that have wives, think as how not having one might be.

30. Those that are weeping, look at how much they are weeping. Those that are cheerful, they are not very cheerful. Those that buy things, they are not able to keep them;

31. Those who live for this world, they live in an abusive way! The condition of this world is decaying!

32. I do not want you to be anxious, but the one who us unwed cares only for the things of the Lord and how to please him.

33. He that has a wife must also think about some concerns of this world, in order to care for his wife.

34. There are also differences between a wed woman and an unwed woman. The unwed woman cares for the things of the Lord and she lives in complete pureness, both physically and spiritually; The woman that is wed must also care for some of the things of this world, in order to please her husband.

35. I tell you this to assist you, not to put a snare in front of you. It is proper to be completely committed unto the Lord without any distractions.

36. Let's suppose someone physically abuses an unwed woman; In the case that this happens, and if she is physically mature, he is under obligation if she becomes pregnant, if he is determined to do as he pleases, it is not a sin unto death for her if it happens in this way (*forcibly*).

37. But she must stand firm in her heart, that it was forced upon her, not having the freedom unto herself to choose her own will. If she discerns in her heart to protect herself from him, she does something good.

38. So the man who takes a wife, he does well; He who does not take a wife, he is greatly advantaged.

39. A wife is bound unto her husband for as long as her husband shall live; But if her husband dies, she is free from the law of her husband, (Romans 7:1-3) and she is free to be wed unto whomever she desires, but only if he is in the Lord.

40. However, she will be better off if she remains unwed, at least according to my judgment; I suppose the spirit of God might also agree.

1 Corinthians 8

1. Concerning idolatrous sacrifices, you know that I have complete understanding. This understanding can make one proud, however offering it in love is constructive.

2. If anyone thinks that he knows something, he usually does not understand what he thinks he knows;

3. But if anyone loves God, he will be brought to know through his spirit. (Jeremiah 31:34; John 16:13)

4. Now concerning the eating of idolatrous sacrifices, we know that an idol is nothing and that there is no other God except for one.

5. But if they (*pagans*) presently bring forth their gods, (*in the sky or on the earth*) it is no different than them having many rulers and many jurisdictions;

6. But for us there is one Father, God, of whom created all things and we are of him. There is one master, Jesus Christ, through whom all things exist and we live because of him. (John 1:1-3)

Verses 7-10 clearly contradict and disprove Acts 15:20 & 29

7. But all men do not have this knowledge; Some conceive a false god and even today they eat food that is sacrificed unto their idols. Their consciences are weak and they have become defiled.

8. But food does not prove (*establish*) us before God. So we do not become excellent if we do not eat, and we do not become defiled and fall away if we do eat. (Romans 14:14; Mark 7:14-23; Matthew 15:10-20)

9. But I warn you, watch that your liberty of eating does not put a stumbling block before others who are weak; (Romans 14:15)

10. Because if anyone sees you, knowing that you were seated to eat at a place that idols are worshipped, there is no way that their weak consciences will be rebuilt if you eat that which was sacrificed unto idols!

11. Do you not think that a weak brother for whom Christ has died would be destroyed because of your knowledge?

12. So if you cause a brother to commit an unpardonable sin by wounding his weak conscience, you may have committed an unpardonable sinful act against God as well!

13. Therefore, if your food might cause your brother to fall, you should not eat that food, so that you not cause your brother to fall (*be scandalized*). (Romans 12:15)

The proper placement of 10:19-33

19. Then, what shall I say? Is an idol anything? Is what is sacrificed unto an idol anything?

20. But the things that the nations sacrifice, they sacrifice unto idols and not unto God! (Deuteronomy 32:17) I do not want for you to become sharers with demons!

21. You can not drink of the cup of God and also of the cup of demons, nor are you able to partake of the table of God and from the table of demons. (Matthew 6:24)

22. Would that not surely make the Lord angry? Are we more powerful than he is?

23. All things unto me are lawful to eat, but not all things are beneficial. All things are lawful to eat, but not all things are healthy.

24. No one should seek after pleasing themselves, but each should care for the needs of others.

25. When you go to the butcher who is selling meat, do not ask him anything concerning this, for the sake of your own conscience.

26. For the whole earth is the Lord's and so is everything that is in it. (Psalms 24:1)

27. But if anyone who is an unbeliever happens to invite you for dinner and you wish to go, eat whatever is set before you and do not ask questions for conscience sake.

28. But if anyone tells you that this meal was a killed sacrifice unto idols, do not eat it for the sake of the conscience of the one who has told you this; For the earth is the Lord's and so is all that is within it. (Psalms 24:1)

29. But I do not say this for your own conscience sake, but for the sake of others; Why should my freedom be judged by another man's conscience?

30. Yet if I, due to grace choose to eat, why would I be blasphemed for that which I have given thanks for?

31. Whether you eat or drink, give thanks unto God and honor him.

32. Do not be offensive unto Jews nor Greeks, nor unto the people of God; (Galatians 3:27-29)

33. We must make every effort to be at peace with all people and not look for our own advantage (*gain*), but for the concerns of others, so that they might find salvation.

1 Corinthians 9

1. Am I not an apostle? Am I not free? Have I not seen our Lord Jesus Christ? Is it not by my work that you have come to know our Lord?

2. If I am not considered an apostle by others, surely I am an apostle unto you, because you that are in the Lord are my seal of apostleship!

3. My defense unto those who are questioning me is this:

4. Do I not have the freedom to eat and drink?

5. Do I not have the freedom to take a sister (*in Christ*) to show as a wife, the same as all of the other apostles and our brethren in the Lord, and also Cephas (*Simon Peter*)?

6. Is it that only Barnabas and I do not have such freedom to take time for rest?

7. Who has ever served as a soldier without compensation? Who plants a garden and does not eat of the fruit of it? Who shepherds a flock and does not harvest the milk in which to drink?

8. I speak according to the ways of mankind. Does the Jewish law not also say these things?

9. For in the law of Moses it has been written, "You shall not muzzle the oxen that are threshing! (Deuteronomy 25:4) Is it that the oxen are of special interest unto God or did he write this for our sakes?

10. It is written for us! It is because of hope that one plows a field, and the one that threshes does so in hope that he might share in the production!

11. For if we have planted spiritual things in you, is it such a great thing that we shall receive the needed food, clothing and shelter from you.

12. If others have power over you to have a share of your gain (*taxes*), shouldn't we also much more? However, we have not used this authority and we have truly endured many hardships so not to create an obstacle unto anyone to whom we might offer the gospel of Jesus Christ.

13. Do you not know that those who work in the temple eat from the holy things of the temple? Those who work at the alter eat from that which is offered!

14. So the Lord also ordained that those who announce the gospel unto others may live of the gospel.

15. Yet, I have not claimed any of this for myself! I do not write these things so that I might be provided for properly. I would much rather die than for anyone to nullify my positive boasting.

16. If I preach the gospel, is it not an honor unto me? In how I present myself, the necessities are laid upon me *(I take the burden upon myself),* and woe it is unto me if I do not offer the gospel!

17. If I do this willingly, I have an eternal reward; If I do it unwillingly, it is only a stewardship that I have been entrusted with.

18. So why should I receive a reward? Because I preach the gospel without charge, I lay down the gospel of Jesus Christ and I do not use my full authority in doing so.

19. I am free from all obligation, but I have willingly become enslaved so that I might gain many more souls.

20. I became as a Jew when among Jews, so that I might gain more of them; To those who hold themselves under the Mosaic law, I become as they are (*while with them*), that I might gain more of them;

21. Unto those who were without the Jewish law, I was unto them as without the Jewish law, but yet subject unto the law of God, so that I might gain those not under the Jewish law.

22. Unto those that are weak in their conscience, in the same manner I did accordingly so that I might gain those that are weak. Unto each of these I have accommodated; I made myself to be many things so that I might bring some unto salvation. (Romans 11:14)

23. I do this so that I might do my part according to the gospel.

24. Do you not know that in a race there are many that run, but only one receives the prize? So I run the race in the way that I might be able to win!

25. Everyone that competes must control himself in everything; Truly, there are many who strive to receive the temporary crown which decays; But we strive for the eternal crown.

26. This is why I run the race with determination; So I fight, but not as throwing punches at the air!

27. I bring my body into complete subjection unto God and make it a captive, so that while proclaiming the gospel unto others, I myself am not cast away by God! (*This verse destroys OSAS theology*)

1 Corinthians 10

1. I do not want you to be ignorant my brethren. Our forefathers were under a cloud and they all passed through the sea;

2. All were baptized by Moses in the cloud and by the sea;

3. They all ate the spiritual food that he (*Moses*) offered;

4. They all drank the same spiritual drink that was given; They were drinking of a spirit that would be produced by the bedrock that would come in the future; And that bedrock is Christ Jesus. (Matthew 16:18)

5. But most of them were not pleasing unto God, so they were made to remain in the desert.

6. These things are examples for us to consider, that we must not lust after that which is evil, as some of them surely did;

7. We must not become idolatrous as some of them were, as it has been written, "The people sat down to eat and drink and stood up to play." (Exodus 32:6)

8. Do not commit fornication as some of them did, and in one day twenty-three thousand were killed. (Numbers 25:9)

9. Neither put Christ to the test, as some of them had tempted and they were killed by serpents. (Numbers 21:6)

10. Neither complain as some of them did and they were destroyed by the destroyer. (Numbers 11:1)

11. All of these things are examples, and this was all written as a warning unto us and all others that shall live from now until the end of the world has arrived. (Barnabas 14)

12. So if you think that you are already saved, beware and open your eyes or you will fall! (Romans 10:6)

13. Your temptations must not overcome you, such as is common with mankind; But God is faithful, as he will not allow you to be tempted beyond what you are able to overcome, because with the temptation he will also have an exit way for you to escape the temptation so that you can continue to endure faithfully. (James 1:12; Hebrews 2:18; 2 Peter 2:9; Psalms 97:10; Psalms 106:3; Psalms 119:1-3; Numbers 15:28-30)

14. Therefore my brethren, run away from all evil. (Revelation 21:7)

15. I offer you wise instruction; Seriously consider what I tell you.

Verses 16-19 were added by a scribe and are not a part of the original text.
They promote false doctrine of religious practice and rite,
Therefore, they have not been included in this text.

Verses 20-33 were errantly moved into this place by a scribe.
These verses were taken from the original placement after 8:13.
This was done so to promote a false religious rite.
These verses have been properly placed in chapter 8.
(Matthew 20:23-25)

1 Corinthians 11

1. Become imitators of me, the same as I am of Christ.

2. I applaud you my brethren, because most of you have remembered everything that I taught you on the subject and you have held strongly unto the precepts.

3. But I also want you to know that the head of every godly man is Christ; The head of every woman is her husband and the head of Christ is our God.

4. Every man that prays or prophesies with something on his head, shames his own head.

5. But every married woman that prays or prophesies without something on her head, she shames her own head; It is the same as if her head was completely shaved.

6. For if a woman is not covered then she is as if she were shaved clean; Though it is shameful for a woman to be shaved clean or have short hair, this is the reason she should be covered.

7. But a man must surely not cover his head, because he is the likeness and the honor of God; However, the woman is the glory of her husband.

8. Because man was not created from his wife, but the wife was created from the man. (Genesis 2:21-22)

9. But the man was not created for the woman, but woman was created for the man.

10. For this reason, a wife should show this subjection unto her husband by wearing a covering on her head, to make this clear to others; *(if the woman is covered, lust will not tempt other men of God.)*

11. So that in the Lord, the man will not be separated from his wife and the wife will not be separated from her husband. (Romans 7:3)

12. For just as the woman was formed from the man, so also, men are brought into this world by the woman. But all things are brought by God.

13. Judge these things among yourselves; Is it proper for a woman to pray unto God uncovered?

14. Does not nature itself conclude, if a man has long hair it is dishonorable for him?

15. If a woman has long hair instead of a veil, that it is glorious unto her!

16. If anyone thinks that this is contentious, there is no order concerning this in any of the gatherings of God.

17. In this message I do not praise you; You do not properly care for each other! (G-4905+G-2066)

18. For I hear that there are many divisions among the people when they are gathered together, and I believe what I have heard is true! (Luke 14:12-32; John 6:27-60)

19. There also have been some heresies that have crept in among you while bringing in new members. (Acts 20:29; Jude 1:4)

20. When you gather together, your people eat, but not as unto the Lord. *(they don't eat as a family)*

21. But each one brings and eats his own food in front of others that are hungry, yet they are ignorant of it!

22. Do you not have your own houses in which to eat and drink? Do you not care about the people of God so you go and shame those who do not have? What should I say? Should I praise you in this? I do not commend you!

23. I have received from the Lord that which I now give unto you: The night that the Lord Jesus was betrayed he took the meat, *(the Passover lamb)*

24. and he gave thanks for it and divided it and said, take this and eat it, this is a symbol of my body, *(the lamb of God)* and for your sake it *(my body)* shall be broken. Whenever you eat remember me.

25. And after the dinner, in the same way he took the pitcher and said, my blood shall establish the new covenant; (Jeremiah 31:31-34) Do this now and whenever you drink remember me. (Luke 22:19-20; John 7:37-39)

26. But whoever determines (chooses) to defile (G-2309 + G-2274) the bread and the cup thereafter their death *(baptism, rebirth – Romans 6:1-5)* derides the Almighty and there is no possibility remaining for that one to accompany him *(Christ)*. (Numbers 15:28-31; Hebrews 10:26-27; Hebrews 6:4-6)

27. Whoever of you should eat of this bread *(Christ - Luke 14:26)* or drink of this cup *(John 6:54-60 - to begin to follow Christ)* in an unworthy way, he will be guilty of the body and the blood of the Lord. (Hebrews 10:26; John 6:51-56; 1 John 3:6; 34; Matthew 12:31-32; 2 Peter 2:20-21)

28. But every man must examine himself, then choose whether to eat of the bread and drink of the cup. *(to convert to Christ - Acts 2:38; Luke 14:12-32; John 6:27-60)*

29. For the one who eats and drinks *(the way one lives after conversion)* unworthily brings damnation upon himself for not discerning the body of the Lord. (Hebrews 10:26-39; 2 Peter 2:20-22; 1 Corinthians 3:16)

30. Because of this, many among you have not received the power of God, have no passion and many have spiritually died.

31. For if we live in discernment, we will not be condemned. (Romans 2:5-6)

32. But if we continually judge our own actions, we will be taught by the Lord (Jeremiah 31:34), so that we not be condemned with the rest of the world. (1 John 5:16)

33. So my brethren, when you come together to eat, share with each other!

34. And if anyone is famished, let him eat at home so that no guilt come upon you when you are together. For all else, I will set in order when I come.

1 Corinthians 12

1. Concerning spiritual things my brethren, I do not want for you to be ignorant.

2. You know that you gentiles had been carried away by meaningless idols in which you were led.

3. Therefore I make it known unto you that no one having the spirit of God in him can say that Jesus Christ is worthless; No one is able to conform unto Jesus Christ except by his holy spirit. (1 John 4:3-13)

4. But concerning the spiritual gifts of God (Romans 12:6), there are many differences, though they are given by his spirit.

5. There are also different ministries that are all from our master.

6. There are varieties of things to be done, but our God is effectively working through each one to accomplish all of the necessary things.

7. Each one (*converts*) is given a bestowment of the spirit of God, that each may contribute. (1 John 4:2-3)

8. Unto one, the spirit gives a message of wisdom, but to another, a message of knowledge is given.

9. Unto another, the true doctrine is given, again by the same spirit; Another receives the gift of healing by the spirit;

10. Unto another, the ability to do miracles. Unto another, the gift of prophecy, but another shall receive the discernment of spirits (*dispositions and intents of others*); Another receives the gift of languages and unto another, the interpretation of languages.

11. Through all that are in Christ, all of the necessary actions are accommodated by the same spirit who distributes privately unto each one as he chooses.

12. For just as you have one body and there are many parts of that body, all parts combine to make one body, so also is the body of Christ.

13. For it was by one spirit that each of us have been baptized into one body (John 3:5; Romans 6:1-23; Acts 2:38; Acts 3:19), whether Jew (*by blood*), or gentile, whether a slave or if you are free; (Galatians 3:27-29) All are given of the same spirit to live by.

14. The body is not only made up of one part, but is made up of many parts.

15. If the foot says, because I am not a hand I am not a part of the body; How would it not be a part of the body?

16. If an ear says, because I am not an eye I am not a part of the body; How would it not be a part of the body?

17. If all of the parts of the body were eyes, then where would the hearing come in? If all parts were ears, then how would the body sense smell?

18. But God has set each one to be a part of the body, accordingly where he has desired to place them.

19. If all were for the same purpose, then how could there be a body?

20. But we know that there are many parts, but only one body.

21. So now, the eye can not say unto the hand, I do not need you; Or unto the feet, I have no need of you;

22. Because those parts that seem to be less esteemed, they are also very necessary.

23. Those that we think are less honorable are still a vital part of the body. Unto these, we surely must surround them with much more respect; Those parts that are not glamorous surely do have abundant abilities that must be recognized.

24. Those that are beautiful do not have need, but God has combined together all parts of the body, that the one who is lacking receives more abundant honor.

25. There must not be division in the body. Each part must care for one another as part of the same body.

26. Whenever one is suffering, all of the other members feel his pain; If one is honored, all of the other members rejoice with him.

27. Now, each of you are only one part of the body of Christ

28. and God has placed each into the body; First are apostles, then prophets, thirdly are teachers, then those who do miracles, then those with the gift of healing, then some are helpers, some are organizers and some have languages (tongues).

29. Not all are to be apostles; Not all are to be prophets; Not all are to be teachers; Not all can do miracles;

30. Not all receive the gift of healing; Not all shall speak in languages (tongues). Not all interpret.

31. You should desire the gifts that are more honorable. The more excellent ones I have demonstrated unto you.

1 Corinthians 13

1. If I speak in the languages of mankind and also the language of the angels, if I do not have affectionate benevolence (love), then I become as a bell that is ringing or a drum that is struck.

2. If I have the gift of prophecy and if I know all of the mysteries and have complete knowledge of all things; If I have complete conviction that I could move mountains, yet if I do not have affectionate benevolence (love), I am nothing.

3. If I give away all that I have and if I deliver my body to be burned alive, if I do not have affectionate benevolence (love), I am benefited nothing.

4. True affection (love) is longsuffering and is benevolent (kind, giving) unto others. Love is not envious and love does not self-promote, nor is it prideful.

5. Love does not misbehave, nor does it take for itself and it is not provoked easily. Love does not consider to do evil,

6. nor does it rejoice in that which is wrong, but it rejoices in truth.

7. It is patient in all things, trustworthy in all things, has hope for everyone and endures all things.

8. Affectionate benevolence (love) shall never be non-valuable. If there are prophecies, they shall be fulfilled; (Luke 22:37 - come to their conclusion) If there are languages, they shall come to their end; If there is understanding, it shall grow old and fade away.

9. We only know fractionally and we prophesy only a portion;

10. But when the completion (fulfillment) comes, then all that is in part will be made known.

11. When I was a child, I spoke as a child, I thought as a child and I had the reasoning of a child; But when I became a man, I turned away from those childish ways.

12. For we now only see through a dimmed window (prophecy), but then (at the return of Christ) we will be face to face; Now I know partly, but at that time I will know him fully, as he fully knows me.

13. But now we have conviction, and hope, and love; Of these, the greatest of these things is love. (affection and benevolence for others)

1 Corinthians 14

1. Continue to be affectionate and greatly desire the spiritual things, but much more, desire that you receive the gift of prophecy.

2. The one who speaks in foreign languages does not speak unto men but unto God; This is because no one can understand what he says, but he speaks mysteries through his spirit.

3. But the one who prophesies speaks to other people and does so to build up, bring encouragement and comfort.

4. The one who speaks in a foreign language builds himself up, but the one who prophesies builds up the whole gathering.

5. I would desire that all of you speak in languages which are foreign, but I would rather that you prophesy; The one who prophesies is greater than the one that speaks in tongues, aside from an interpretation so that the gathering might receive it and be encouraged by it.

6. My brethren, if you speak in a foreign language, what profit does it offer unto others if you do not also speak the meaning, offer knowledge, a prophecy, or a teaching?

7. Many lifeless things offer a sound, whether a harp or a pipe, yet they give different notes that sound

distinct from each other. Without a difference of sound, how would it be known what was being played?

8. For if a trumpet gives an uncertain sound, who would gather themselves to be ready for war?

9. It is the same if you speak a foreign language, if it is not understood, how could it be known what was said? For you would be speaking unto the air!

10. There are also many languages in the world, yet none is without its own sounds.

11. So if I do not know the meaning of the sound, I will be a foreigner unto the one speaking and he that is speaking will also be a foreigner unto me!

12. Since you are very zealous for the earlier instructions of those things that are spiritual, seek to build up each other so that you may prosper.

13. Therefore, he that has the gift of languages, let him pray so that he be able to also interpret;

14. Because if I pray in a foreign language, it is my spirit that prays, but my understanding is barren.

15. So then, what is the purpose? I can pray in the spirit or I can do so with my intellect. I can sing in the spirit or I can do so while using my intellect.

16. When you offer a blessing in the spirit (*tongues*), at the completion of it, how would one that does not know the language say that they agree to what you have given thanks for, since he would not know what you have said?

17. You might sincerely be grateful, but others are not built up by it.

18. I thank my God that I am able to speak many more languages than any of you;

19. But when gathered together, I would rather offer five words that are spoken by my intellect, in which I may offer instruction, than tens of thousands of words in a foreign tongue that no one would understand.

20. My brethren, do not be as children in your thoughts; Concerning wickedness, you must be innocent, but you must be mature in your intellect.

21. In the scriptures it is written, "by other languages and on other shores I will speak unto these people, but in like manner, these people will not hear me, saith the Lord" (Isaiah 28:11-12)

22. Tongues (*languages*) are for a sign, but not for those that are unbelieving. They are a sign for those that are believing. Prophecy is not a sign for those who are believing, but for those that are unbelieving.

23. If the whole assembly gathered together and everyone spoke in foreign languages, if some unbelievers and the unlearned were to come in, would they not say that you are all insane?

24. But if all were to prophesy and an unbeliever or uneducated one comes in, they will be corrected by everyone and examine themselves fully;

25. In this way, the secrets that are hidden away in their hearts would be revealed to them; Then they are likely to fall on their faces and worship God, announcing that God truly is among you!

26. What should it be like then? When you come together, each one of you has a psalm, or a testimony, or a language and a revelation or the interpretation! All of these are for the building up of each other. It must be this way.

27. So if one speaks in a foreign language, no more than two or three at the most, one at a time and there must be an interpretation.

28. But if there is no interpreter, they must remain silent when gathered together and each one should speak within himself unto God.

29. When a true prophet speaks, do not allow more than two or three, and let the others discern (*judge*).

30. If there is one that is there that uncovers falsehood, then the first must be silent.

31. For by one prophet, you are able to know everything that is to be prophesied. In this, all may learn and be encouraged.

32. The disposition (*spirit*) of a prophet must be in accordance with all other true prophets;

33. For God does not bring confusion, but he does bring doctrinal harmony throughout all of the gatherings of the saints. (*Doctrinal harmony does not exist in the modern churches*)

Verses 34-36 look to have been added by a scribe and are out of context, of which is speaking about prophets. These verses are certainly not a part of the original 1Corinthians text, therefore they have been deleted from this text. Verses 34-36 contradict what other scriptures tell us concerning godly women including Priscilla and Phebe. (Acts 18:26; Romans 16:1-2; Galatians 3:28-29)

37. If anyone desires to be a prophet or to be spiritually inclined, he must recognize what I write unto you, and be instructed only by the Lord. *(it must come from God)*

38. If any have not heard from God, they will be wrong.
(This is evidence that identifies the many false prophets)

39. So my brethren, eagerly seek the gift of prophecy but do not prohibit the speaking in foreign languages.

40. Just keep in mind, all things must be done honestly and be according to proper character.

1 Corinthians 15

1. Brothers, I make known to you that the gospel that I have brought unto you, of which you have trusted in and have now begun to live is how you are clothed with protection,

2. if you hold completely dedicated to the message; Otherwise you have not truly believed and your efforts will be of no effect. (John 3:18-21)

3. I delivered unto you the foremost things of which I have been shown by Christ Jesus, who died for our sins, for our benefit, in accordance to the scriptures.

4. He was buried and he was raised from the dead after the third day, again a fulfillment of the scriptures.

5. Then he appeared unto Cephas (*Simon Peter*), then unto the other ten;

6. Afterward he appeared unto more than five hundred brethren at one gathering, of whom, most remain alive even today, though some have died;

7. He appeared unto James and then all of the apostles;

8. Finally, last of all, because of my untimely birth, he also appeared unto me. *(The road to Damascus)*

9. For I am the least of all apostles, though I am not worthy to be called an apostle, because I had previously persecuted the people of God.

10. But through the compassion of God, I am what I am, and through his grace, I have not been fruitless; But I have worked much more abundantly, more than all the others, yet not of myself, but by the assistance of God through me.

11. So whether it was myself or any of the other apostles, we proclaimed the truth and you believe.

12. So if Christ is proclaimed to have been raised from the dead, how can some of you say that there is no resurrection of the dead? (Matthew 22:23)

13. If there is no resurrection of the dead, then Christ has not been raised!

14. If Christ has not been raised, our proclamation is worthless, and so is your conviction,

15. and we are then found to be false witnesses of God, because we have witnessed accordingly that God has raised Christ, of whom he could not be raised if the dead shall not be raised!

16. If those that are dead will not be raised, then Christ has not been raised!

17. If Christ has not been raised, your conviction is foolish and you are still in your sins!
(John 8:31-36; Acts 2:38; Romans 6:1-10)

18. If that is the case, then all those who have died have been eternally lost!

19. And if in this life we do not have hope in Christ, then we are the most miserable of all people.

20. But Christ has been raised from the dead and he is the first fruit of those who have physically died.

21. Through one man, death entered the world; But through one man, the resurrection from death.

22. For just as in Adam, all things shall see death, but in this, through Christ all things will be resurrected and judged.

23. But each one in their own order, first is Christ Jesus; But afterwards those that are in Christ at the time of his return (*coming*). (1 Thessalonians 4:14; Matthew 24:29-31)

24. Then the conclusion (*end*) shall come and at that time he will establish the kingdom of God our Father, and he will abolish all (*earthly*) rulers, jurisdiction and all other powers, (Revelation 19:19-21; Matthew 26:29)

25. For it is necessary for him to reign, and he shall put all of his adversaries under his feet. (Malachi 4:3)

26. The final adversary that shall be destroyed is death;

27. Yet he has made all things to be subject under our feet when he says, "all things have been made subject unto mankind" (Genesis 1:26) but it is clear that exempts the one who has given the subjection of all things unto us. (*God is exempt from the jurisdiction of mankind*). (Hebrews 2:6-9; Psalms 8:4-8)

28. If he has subjected all things unto us, then we ourselves, his sons must be subject unto him in all things, so that all may be subject unto God in everything.

29. Otherwise why are we presently performing these baptisms for people to be raised up from death?

If those who have died are not going to be resurrected (1 Thessalonians 4:14-18 - *at the return of Christ*), why then would we baptize them into his death? (Romans 6:4; Galatians 3:27)

30. Why then would we place ourselves to be in danger at all times?

31. The day that I die, I have you to glory about before our Lord Jesus Christ.

32. For as much as I was spoken against by men that were seeking to destroy me there in Ephesus, what benefit is there for me if the dead are not going to be raised? "certainly, eat and drink today because tomorrow we shall die." (Isaiah 22:13)

33. Do not be deceived; Wicked morals (*actions*) will destroy a good relationship (*with God*).

34. Awaken unto righteousness and continually choose to not commit sin. But some have a lack of knowledge of God's values (Hebrews 10:26-27, 1 John 5:16-18) I speak to your confusion on the matter.

35. But there are some that will say, how can the dead be raised? And what type of body shall they receive?

36. You are ignorant. Do you not know that the seed that you plant, it is not brought back to life unless it first dies!

37. When it is planted (*buried*), it is not the body that is caused to continually live, but it is the naked seed. It will grow into good grain or of some other type of seed.

38. But it is God that shall give to each one a body as he chooses, and every seed shall receive a body.

39. But all people are not the same. Certainly, the people within mankind are different from one another; Just as there are different types of animals, and different types of fish, and different types of birds;

40. There are bodies in the heavens and bodies on the earth. There are certainly differences in the heavens, and differences in that which is earthly.

41. The glory of the sun, a different glory of the moon, a different glory in each of the stars, and each star differs in glory (*brightness*) from all of the others.

42. So also it is in the resurrection of the dead. Each is planted (*buried*) and decays, and shall be raised immortal;

43. Planted (*buried*) without honor, but raised unto honor; Planted without life, but is raised with life;

44. It is planted as a physical (*natural*) body, but raised a spiritual (*supernatural*) body. There certainly is a physical body and also a spiritual body.

45. Just as it has been written, "The first of mankind, Adam became a living body." (Genesis 2:7) However the final man (*Christ*) shall restore life.

46. By the first, it was the physical which was produced, thereafter the spiritual is produced;

47. The first was made from the earth, but the second is of the master in the heavens.

48. Just as the one from the ground is also like the ones of this world, (*before conversion*) so also the spiritual man shall be as those in the heavens (*after conversion*). (Romans 6:5-8; 1 John 3:3)

49. And even as we have in the past been in the likeness of the earthly man, we shall now also have the requirement to take on the image of the heavenly man (*Jesus Christ*). (Romans 6:17; 1 John 3:1-3)

50. This I tell you my brethren, that the physical bodies and blood are not able to receive an inheritance of the kingdom of God, nor can that which decays inherit an eternal existence.

51. Understand that I reveal this mystery unto you; Everyone shall not die, but all shall be changed.

52. In the smallest moment, in a blink of an eye, at the final trumpet, the trumpet will announce and those who have died will be raised immortal, and those of us that are in Christ who are alive at that time shall be changed. *(through the idea of fermentation)* (Hebrews 12:19; 1 Thessalonians 4:16; Revelation 10:7)

53. Because that which is decayed must put on that which is incorruptible and not feeble; That which is mortal must put on that which is immortal and not weak.

54. When that which is decaying (*our bodies*) shall put on that which can not decay, and the mortal puts on that which can not die, then those that knew the instructions (*of God*) that have been written and then also lived by them, unto these, death shall be conquered. (Isaiah 25:8)

55. Where is your sting, oh death? Where is your victory Hell? (Hosea 13:14)

56. The impalement (*poison*) that leads to death is sin, and the power (*ability, strength*) of sin is the Mosaic law. (Numbers 15:28-31)

57. But may God be gracious, as he has offered unto us the way to defeat death through our master Jesus Christ.

58. So as my beloved brethren, be steadfast and immovable; Be superabundant in the deeds of the Lord at all times, knowing that your efforts are not worthless.

1 Corinthians 16

1. Concerning the offerings for the saints, as I instructed the gatherings at Galatia, so also you should do.

2. On one of your days of rest, by his own choice, may each one of you offer what he has been saving up, that which he is able, so that when I come the collection shall already be there.

3. When I arrive, whomever you approve concerning the content of this topic, have him then copy this epistle (*letter*) and with the assistance of God, deliver it unto those in Jerusalem (*with your donations*);

4. But if it is possible for me to go, we might go there together. (Acts 21:17; Romans 15:25)

5. When I come to you, I will go through Macedonia, for I have need to go to Macedonia.

6. I hope to stay there with you and possibly spend the winter, and that you might aid my travel wherever I may go from there.

7. For I do not want to only see you in passing; Therefore, I am hoping to be able to spend some time there with you, if the Lord permits.

8. However, I will remain here in Antioch until Passover; (*Paul did not keep the feast as some claim*)

9. Then a large door of opportunity looks to have finally open up, as many times I have been prevented.

10. But if Timothy arrives, see that he remains with you without fear; Because he truly does the deeds of the Lord, the same as myself.

11. Do not allow anyone to treat him poorly. Assist him in his travels, to give him peace of mind (*comfort*) so that he might arrive before me. (*earlier*)

12. Concerning Apollos our brother, I have strongly urged him to come unto you and accompany the brethren; Though it was not his desire to come at this time, he will come when he has the opportunity.

13. Remain awake! Stand in the true doctrine. Be strong men!

14. Everything must be done in love.

15. I encourage you my brethren, the house of Stephanas is the first fruit of Achaia, and they have appointed themselves to take care of (*house and feed*) the saints while we are there.

16. Submit yourselves unto them to assist all who have worked with me that are fatigued.

17. I am very happy at the assistance of Stephanas, Fortunatus and Achaicus. Help supplement them with anything that they might be lacking.

18. They have refreshed my spirit and will do the same for them; Make sure to appreciate them.

19. Greet all of the gatherings in Asia. Priscilla and Aquila often think of you, as well as the whole gathering in their home.

20. Greet all of our brethren. Greet one another with an innocent kiss.

21. I write this greeting with my own hand, Paul.

22. If anyone does not love the Lord Jesus Christ, he shall be cursed. (1 John 2:23; John 14:15; John 3:18-21) Our Lord is coming soon.

23. May the grace of the Lord Jesus Christ be with you.

24. My love is with you, all of you that are in Jesus Christ.

2 Corinthians

Chapter 1

1. Paul, an apostle of Jesus Christ by the will of God, and Timothy our brother: To the gathering of God that is in Corinth and unto all of the saints that are in Achaia;

2. May grace and peace be unto you from God our Father and our Lord Jesus Christ.

3. Blessed be God our Father and our Lord Jesus Christ, Father of compassion and God of all assistance;

4. He is the one calling us near unto him, to lay all of our troubles upon him. He also enables us to comfort all who are having hardships through the same assistance that we ourselves are comforted by through our God; (Psalms 34:19)

5. This is because of the many sufferings for the sake of Christ are always surrounding us and against us; But through Christ his comfort and assistance also surrounds us.

6. If we are troubled by those that are corrupt, know that it is for your deliverance that your faithfulness remain alive and active through the same kinds of sufferings that he also suffered. Your patient endurance is being proven through your sufferings, of which we also endure; But if we draw the corrupt ones unto ourselves, know that it is for the purpose that you draw near unto God and for your eternal salvation.

7. But our hope is firm regarding you, knowing that you are also sharers in the sufferings (*of Christ*), but also in his comfort and assistance.

8. We do not want you to be ignorant my brethren as to the difficulties that we have had, of which came upon us in Asia; They were so excessive, we were certainly burdened well beyond our abilities, bringing us to great distress just to continue living.

9. We ourselves certainly have a death sentence, in that we do not trust in our own ambitions, but upon God who raises the dead;

10. From out of such an extensive threat of death he delivered us, and we that are in him have hope that he will continue to deliver us.

11. Join your hearts together on our behalf in prayer, that by many people (*praying*), the charisma (*miraculous power of God*) may remain within us. I offer gratitude unto you on the behalf of all of us.

12. For my glorying is this: The testimony of my conscience is, that by the simplicity and sincerity of God, and not by worldly wisdom, I have lived in this world and through me, the grace of God has been much more abundant unto you.

13. We certainly do not write more than what you need to understand; We expect that you will acknowledge him (*remain faithful*) until the end.

14. Because you have also encouraged us, we now rejoice because of you, just as you will of us on the day the Lord Jesus returns. (1 Thessalonians 4:14-18)

15. In this, know that I had planned to come to you previously in order that you may receive a second measure of the assistance of God through me; (1 Corinthians 16:1-7)

16. I was going to come through you on my way to Macedonia, and from Macedonia to again come back unto you; Then have you supply me so that I might go to Judea.

17. When I planned this, it was not to be lightly profitable, yet that which I purposed I did according to my own desires, that I might know whether certainly yes, or no (*concerning you*).

18. But God is faithful and our message unto you did not become no, but yes!

19. For by Jesus Christ, the son of God, the one who we proclaim to you through Silvanus, Timothy and myself, we did not need to question a yes and no answer; But yes! We are certain that you are in Christ!

20. For all of the instructions of God are certainly living in you and you are doubtlessly in Christ; Unto God be the glory that he did this through us.

21. He has confirmed this with us that you are in Christ and God has comforted us.

22. He has reserved us, having come with the pledge of his spirit into our hearts. (Acts 2:38)

23. As God is my witness to testify for my soul, if we do not come to you there in Corinth,

24. as we certainly do not lord over the testing of your faithfulness, we know that we are fellow workers and are satisfied with you because you stand with sincerity.

2 Corinthians 2

1. Because of the difficulties that I had, I decided not to come to you.
2. For if I was to burden you, then who shall remain to lift up my spirit? Certainly not the one whom I have burdened!
3. I have written this for you so that when the difficult times come, I can trust you make it easy for me to rejoice, because I receive joy from all of you.
4. It was with much sadness and distress in my heart that I wrote to you through many tears, that you not be burdened by this. But the love that I have for you is now much more abundantly known unto you.
5. Though I brought grief unto you, I am not grieved, though partially; But not that I be overbearing unto you. (2 Corinthians 7:8-12 – *proves the reason for writing the first letter*)
6. It is enough that the correction was brought in this way unto the majority.
7. Now, in their presence, you should bring graciousness and comfort to those that are weak (*unlearned*), that sadness not overtake them.
8. Therefore I instruct you to confirm your love unto them. (*third person plural*)
9. For this is the reason that I wrote unto you, that you receive the knowledge to challenge yourselves, that you might be obedient in everything.
10. It was so that some of you might become hot. (Revelation 3:15) I wrote that you not make worthless his grace! You must avoid making the grace worthless; Do this by remaining in the presence of Christ,
11. that we not be overtaken by Satan; For we are not ignorant of his ways. (1 John 3:3)
12. But a door was opened unto me by the Lord, so I went to Troas with the gospel of Jesus Christ.
13. I could not find rest in my spirit there, nor could I find Titus my brother, so I went to Macedonia.
14. But God be thanked, because he leads us to victory in Christ. Having tasted his understanding of which was further revealed unto us in that place,
15. we have become a sweet-smelling fragrance unto God. Christ is in those who are actively being saved.
16. But for those who are perishing, they smell of death and they shall receive death; But those of you that have the fragrance of life, you will go unto eternal life. But who has not comprehended these things?
17. We are not as many as those who are corrupting the instructions of God; Because we sincerely live in the ways of God, we announce Christ while in the sight of God.

2 Corinthians 3

1. Do they think that they can again pollute themselves and remain established (*in Christ*)? Do they not truly need correction by introductory epistles that we had previously sent unto you or those sent out by you?
2. You have our letters surely engraved in your hearts, being clearly understood by all of you.
3. It is declared that you are living the instructions of Christ, teaching the godly way, having been engraved not by ink (*by the letter*), but by the spirit of our living God; Not on tablets of stone, but on the tables of our own hearts. (Jeremiah 31:31-36)
4. And we have this confidence of our God, through Christ.
5. Not that we have this ability in ourselves to account that anything is of ourselves, but that our abilities are because of the assistance of God
6. who has also made us to be ministers of the new covenant (*contract offer*), which is not of the letter (*ten commandments*), but is by the spirit; Because the letter brings death, but the spirit brings life.
7. But if the ministry of death by the letter that was engraved in stone was so glorious, that the sons of Israel could not look upon the face of Moses because of the brightness upon him, of which is now abolished, (Exodus 34:34-35)
8. how then will the ministry of the spirit (*of God*) not be established to be much more glorious?
9. For if the ministry that brought condemnation was glorious (*Mosaic law*), how much more abundant shall the ministry of righteousness be glorious?
10. And for nothing but glory (*power*), those who were abiding in that glory participated (*in the first covenant*), because of the extremely high glories that they could partake of.
11. For if that which is now taken away was glorious, how much more is that which remains alive to be glorified? (Hebrews 8:13)
12. Therefore, having such an expectation, we can now have boldness through our decaying bodies;

13. Not as Moses, who put the veil over his own face so that the sons of Israel could not look upon him to see, that in the end, that way of living would all be taken away;

14. But their understandings (*comprehension*) were hardened; Even today the same veil remains upon them in reading of the old testament, as they remain veiled to that which Christ has now abolished;

15. But even today when Moses is being read, there lies a veil upon their hearts.

16. Though, whenever one might turn unto the Lord, the veil is taken away.

17. The spirit of Christ lives and is, there is freedom. (*from the Mosaic law*)

18. But unto us, all has been unveiled and we see the face of the Lord mirrored in us, as we are being changed, from hoping to be glorified, unto being glorious, exactly as the spirit of the Lord. (1 John 3:3)

2 Corinthians 4

1. Because of this ministry we shall surely receive compassion (*from God*), if we do not grow tired.

2. As we have turned away from the shameful hidden things and are not living in deceiving ways nor corrupting the instructions of God, but the revealing of the truth that is exhibited in us is before the eyes of everyone and in the eyes of God.

3. But truthfully, if our gospel is hidden, it is only in those that are perishing that it is hidden,

4. of whom the god of this world (*Satan*) has blinded (John 12:31; 14:30; 16:11; 1 Cor 2:6; Ephesians 2:2; Matthew 4:9) through the desires of those who are unfaithful; They do not come into the light, the illuminated gospel of the glory of Christ, who is the physical representation of God. (John 3:19-21)

5. We do not proclaim ourselves, but we do proclaim Jesus Christ our Lord; We are only his servants unto you, on the behalf of Christ Jesus.

6. Our God has said, "out of darkness the Light shall shine" (Isaiah 60:1-3) and he shines into our hearts through the illuminated knowledge of the glory of God, until the coming (*return*) of Jesus Christ.

7. So we have wealth (*knowledge*) in our earthly bodies because of the exceeding power of God, not because of ourselves; (Ephesians 2:8-9; Romans 3:25)

8. In everything we are living with many hardships, but we are not living as though we are distressed; As having no options and perplexed, we are not living in despair.

9. We are often persecuted, but not living as though we have been forsaken; We are continually rejected, but not destroyed.

10. At all times we are carrying around with us in our bodies the suffering of the Lord, in this we live the life of Christ Jesus.

11. For we continually live near death; We are turned over unto those that are corrupt because of him (*Jesus*), so that his life might be made evident in our mortal bodies.

12. Truly in this same way, death works against us, yet we have life.

13. Have this same spirit through the testing of your faithfulness, according to that which is written; "I have trusted so therefore I speak truth." (Psalms 116:10) We have completely trusted and therefore we speak truth;

14. Because we know that he that raised the Lord Jesus will also raise us up through himself and we will stand beside you. (Romans 6:5)

15. For all that we do is for your sake, so that God's grace may be extremely abundant unto many and the receiving of you may bring much glory unto God.

16. Therefore do not faint (*quit*); Truly the bodies of all men are aging and will decay, but your inner spirit is being renovated day by day.

17. For the present afflictions are an easy burden for us when we think of the much more exceedingly better eternal glory that will be poured out upon us

18. if we do not consider the things that we do see, but think on the things that are not yet seen. (Hebrews 11:1); For the things that are being seen are temporary; But those things that are not yet seen are everlasting.

2 Corinthians 5

1. For we know that if the earthly house of our body is destroyed, that our God is building for us an eternal home that is not made with hands, of which is in the heavens.

2. But because of this, we must continue looking forward to our home in the heavens that we have been investing in and we intensely crave for.

3. If indeed we are investing now (*in this life*), we shall not be naked but find wealth. (*in the eternal life*)

4. For truly while living in this body we have many hardships and we are living with many burdens. We must overcome, because we do not want to be naked, but be clothed with the treasure that we have invested in when this mortal life comes to its end.

5. God is working in us for the same purpose, as he has given unto us the pledge of his spirit.

6. Therefore, now we can be courageous, because we know that while we are yet in our physical body, we will soon be there at home with the Lord;

7. We must live by our conviction, not through what we currently see. (Hebrews 11:1)

8. We must be courageous and know that it is to our benefit, so that when we physically die, we will go to our home with the Lord.

9. Therefore, we must seek to be honorable; Whether we are at home or away from home, we must always seek to be pleasing unto him;

10. Because we will all give an account of the things that we have done (*in this life*) when we are made to stand before the judgment seat of Christ, (Romans 2:1-11) in order for each one to be given accordingly to what each had done while alive in their physical body, whether good or wicked. (Revelation 20:12-15)

11. Therefore, because we understand why to have fear of the Lord, (Proverbs 1:7) we make every effort to persuade others how we have come to know God and hope that he is also made known in their consciences.

12. Not as to repeat ourselves, but we approve of you. Having an opportunity to bring forth unto you the joyfulness in us, in order that you might be able to present yourselves confident before others; But do not become prideful in your hearts.

13. Therefore you are truly living lawfully before God, because we have made these things clear unto you.

14. For our love for Christ holds us together; So understand, that if he died for all of us, we must also die.

15. But he died for everyone, so that all who would no longer live for themselves, but for him, could live (*eternally*). Because he died for us, we will also be raised up as he is.

16. So we who fully understand, do not continue living according to our own worldly lusts; If we have truly perceived Christ, we can no longer continue to live according to our own selfish desires.

17. Therefore, if anyone is in Christ, they are a new creation; The old ways are to be turned away from and all of our ways must be renewed. (Matthew 18:3-4; John 8:34-36; Acts 2:38; Romans 6:1-23)

18. All of this is through God, having offered reconciliation unto us through Jesus Christ and has now given us the ministry to bring forth the way unto reconciliation.

19. In the same way that God was in Christ, he offers reconciliation unto the world through himself, a way to no longer continue to hold their trespasses against them. He has now placed in us (*the apostles*) the message of the way unto reconciliation with him (*God*).

20. Therefore, we are ambassadors of Christ in the manner that God has instructed, that through our invitation, others might be reconciled unto God.

21. He caused the one who did not commit sin to pay the ransom for our sins, that we might be reborn righteous before God, through him. (John 3:16-21; Matthew 18:1-10)

2 Corinthians 6

1. Continue working together with Christ (*synergy* – 1 Cor 3:9; Ephesians 2:8) and draw near to him, so not to have received the assistance (*grace*) of God in vain.

2. As it is written, "In an acceptable time I have heard you, and in the day of salvation I will help you." (Isaiah 49:8) Take notice; Now is the acceptable time; Look, today is the day to come to the deliverer.

3. Do not allow yourself to commit sin and the relationship with God will not be damaged. (1 John 3:8)

4. Do that which is approved in all that you do, as a servant of God, by patiently continuing through many difficulties, through distress and in anguish,

5. when being wounded, when taken into prison, when in disarray, when beaten up, when extremely tired and when not having enough food;

6. Always be pure and have a clean conscience; Be longsuffering and be Christ-like, through the spirit of the holy one, unto sincere affection (*love*);

7. Live only according to these instructions and by the power of God, by living in the ways of righteousness, in the eyes of those on the right (*obedient*) and also those on the left (*disobedient*); (Matthew 25:32)

8. Unto those that are highly esteemed and those that are not highly esteemed; Through being well spoken of, or being evil spoken of; By those who are deceivers and those who are truthful;

9. Unto those who are ignorant, and also those who are living in understanding; We live as though we are continually dying, but having the knowledge that we shall live eternally; We teach to not continue in anything that will bring (*eternal*) death;

10. We are always distressed, but must also be joyful; We live without many things (*as poor*), but are building great wealth (*eternal*); We live as having nothing, yet shall possess all things.

11. Our mouths have announced this unto you and our hearts have been greatly strengthened by those of you there in Corinth.

12. Do not be distressed concerning any of our hardships; You are distressed in your own afflictions.

13. I speak as though we are children holding the same eternal reward, of which you are also building up.

14. Do not be unequally joined together with those that are unfaithful: What fellowship do the righteous have with those that are lawless? What relationship does light have with darkness?

15. What do Christ and Belial have to agree upon? What part has a believer with an unbeliever?

16. What principle does the temple of God have with idolatry? (1 Corinthians 3:16-19; 1 Corinthians 6:19; Revelation 11:1; 2 Thessalonians 2:4)
For you are the temple of the living God, as is written, "I will be among them and I will live in them, (2 Timothy 1:14; 1 John 4:2) and I will be their God and they shall be my people." (Ezekiel 37:27)

17. "Therefore, come out from among them, you must separate yourselves from them, says the Lord; Touch not anything impure, and I will accept you. (Isaiah 52:11; Ephesians 5:11; 2 Timothy 2:19)

18. I will be a Father unto you, and you will be sons and daughters unto me, says the highest Lord." (2 Samuel 7:8-14)

2 Corinthians 7

1. Beloved, now having these promises, continually live in purity, apart from all filthy lusts and for things that are evil, but continue to perfect yourselves unto the character of holiness, in the fear of our God. (Ephesians 4:24-27; James 1:12; 1Corinthians 10:12-13; 1 John 3:3; 1Thessalonians 3:13; Psalms 2:11; Proverbs 8:13)

2. Hold a place within your heart for us, as we have not wronged any of you, nor have we corrupted any of you, nor have we taken anything from you.

3. I do not say these things to condemn you, as I have said before, you are in our hearts. We would rather ourselves to die, so to be together with Christ.

4. I have much boldness toward you, though great is my boasting because of you. I have been greatly filled with comfort and I am overflowing with joy, even through all of our troubles.

5. Since having come to Macedonia, none of us have had rest in our bodies, but we have been living with many troubles concerning everything. Outwardly, unto much controversy and inwardly afraid.

6. But God sent much comfort unto us who were beaten down, with the arrival of Titus.

7. And not only by his coming, but also in the comfort which came from you, in that he told us of your longing, sadness and great zeal that you have for us; In this, he has brought much joy unto us.

8. Because now, even though I grieved you by the earlier letter, I do not regret sending it, though I did regret sending it because I heard that you did grieve for a short time; (2 Corinthians 2:5-10)

9. But now I rejoice, not in that you were grieved, but that you were brought unto repentance (*correction*), and because you grieved unto God so that you might not suffer the loss of anything taught by us.

10. For godly sorrow brings sincere repentance (*change of actions*) that in the end will lead unto eternal salvation. (John 3:16-21; Acts 2:38; 3:19) However the sorrow of the world (*insincerity*) leads unto eternal death. (Matthew 18:1-10; Matthew 3:8; Acts 26:20)

11. Those things that grieved you before God brought about in you an earnestness, an apology, displeasure, fear, an eager desire, zeal and correction. *(all of these make up Godly repentance)*

245

You have cleansed yourselves and made yourselves prudent in the matter.

12. Therefore, I did write unto you concerning the wrong doing, but not concerning myself having been wronged, but for the revealing of our earnestness for your benefit in the presence of God. (James 1:12-16)

13. Therefore we are abundantly comforted by your presence (*in Christ*) and even more joyful because Titus has been refreshed by all of you.

14. If I have boasted anything unto him of you, I am not ashamed, because all that I had said is true which we spoke of you and all that Titus spoke to us is the evidence.

15. He is emotional toward you, knowing that you are obedient, and that with fear and trembling you received him. (Psalms 2:11)

16. So now, we are joyous in all that he has assured unto us concerning you.

2 Corinthians 8

1. We make it known unto you our brothers, that the assistance of God has been brought unto the people of Macedonia;

2. Even through their testing, while having many hardships, their joy is abundant; And due to the depth of their poverty, they are sincerely increasing in the wealth of God.

3. Because according to their ability, I testify that even more than what they are able, they voluntarily do.

4. With much comfort they received us, asking for the assistance of God and fellowship of our ministry.

5. Though it was not as we had expected; Through the will of God, they gave themselves unto the Lord first, then they received us.

6. Now we desire to send Titus, because he was there before, that he might now receive the gift in this way

7. so that you are made complete in everything; In doctrine, instruction, knowledge and care, and that you are abundant in the charity and affection that we also have.

8. I do not command this upon you, but expect that because of your care for others and the trueness of your love, that you will be found to be genuine. (2 Corinthians 2:5)

9. For you know that through the assistance of the Lord Jesus Christ, for your sake he became poor, though he is greatly wealthy, but that you through his poverty would be made wealthy;

10. But in this I offer my judgment, because it is beneficial for you; There is the need to do this, as I have been wanting to do this for a long time, even since last year, so that you will be made complete.

11. I know that you are eager and willing, so give as you have the ability. (2 Corinthians 2:9)

12. Therefore, if the willingness is there within you, do according to your ability, this is how you are proven to be acceptable. But do not give what you do not have. (2 Corinthians 2:5-10)

13. We do not bring ease unto others so that you might be without, but for equality;

14. In the presence of your abundance we can fill their needs; If they have abundance, they will fill your needs so that all may have what is needed;

15. "As it has been written, "He that gathers much shall have nothing left over, and he that has gathered little has no need." (Exodus 16:18).

16. But thanks be unto God, that with such willingness you should give from your hearts unto Titus.

17. He truly brought comfort and earnest value unto you and he went out unto you voluntarily.

18. We sent him out unto you because he is commendable, according to the gospel throughout all of the gatherings of God;

19. But not of ourselves; He was appointed by the people of God as a traveling companion for us and as a charitable helper. He has ministered and is honored by us before our Lord. But only if you are willing.

20. Avoid dwelling on this, so not to have someone blemish us in the great things that this ministry is abundantly doing through him;

21. Begin preparing in advance concerning these virtuous things, not only before the Lord, but also as an example before others.

22. Now that we have been earnestly assured concerning you, we sent a group with our brother who have been proven many times and in many things have been diligent.

23. Whether my partner Titus, your fellow worker or our brethren, they are ministers unto the people of God and they all glorify Christ.

24. Therefore the evidence of the affection that we have for you is the boasting of you unto all of the gatherings of God.

246

2 Corinthians 9

1. Concerning the ministering unto the saints, it is excessive for me to write unto you,

2. because I know of your eagerness. I have boasted unto Macedonia, because Achaia has also gotten ready as early as last year, but your zeal brings a greater amount.

3. Therefore I sent the brethren, so that the boasting that I brought concerning you not be in error when I said that you would be ready.

4. So that if some come unto you from Macedonia and find that you are prepared, we will not be ashamed, due to of the assurance unto them given through our boasting of you.

5. Therefore, I thought it was necessary to send the brethren to bring encouragement when they come unto you. Prepare beforehand the blessing which you have committed, in this, it may clearly be a blessing and not appear as greed.

6. Know this, that the one who sows the seed lightly will harvest a small amount, but the one who plants much seed is looking for an eternal reward and he will harvest plentiful.

7. Let each one give according to the intentions of his own heart, not grudgingly nor by force, because God loves one who gives cheerfully.
(tithing is not in the new covenant, but giving unto the needy if you are able truly is required)

8. God is also able to bring an abundance of assistance unto you, that in everything, you will always have what you need in order to be abundant unto every good deed.

9. As it has been written, "he scattered and gave unto the poor, his righteousness lives forever."
(Psalms 11:2-9)

10. He brings the needed seed unto the sower and he supplies food to eat; He multiplies your seed and increases the fruits of your righteousness;

11. He enriches us with all that we need so that we bring thankfulness unto God for everything;

12. For his assisting service not only brings that which is lacking unto the saints, but is also multiplied through our thankfulness unto God;

13. Through your assistance, God is glorified. In their acknowledgement unto the gospel of Christ, there is sincerity. Because of this partnership, they have offered a special thanks unto every one of you,

14. greatly caring for you because of the exceedingly abundant assistance of God through you.

15. Thanks be unto God because of his indescribable gift.

2 Corinthians 10

1. I Paul personally call on you through the humility and appropriate behavior of Christ. When I am among you, according to appearance, I am very meek; Though presently absent, I am bold unto you;

2. I ask, though not there with you, that you be bold in the confidence that I have supposed you have, and be courageous toward those who have accused us to be living according to our own fleshly desires.

3. For living in this world, we have waged war to not live unto the selfish desires.

4. Because our weapons used to fight are not physical, but are through the power of God that break down the previous strongholds in our consciences;

5. We are demolishing all barriers that stand against the knowledge of God that had brought us into slavery, now with every thought according to obedience unto Christ.

6. He is prepared and able to bring discipline upon all that have not fully understood, until obedience is perfected in you. (Numbers 15:28-31; 1 John 2:1; 1 John 5:16-17)

7. Those things that are easily seen, you notice: But if anyone is persuaded to be of Christ, let him continually examine his own self to see whether he is of Christ, as we are of Christ.

8. For even though I might be able to boast much more about the authority which the Lord gave unto us to build you up (*conform you*), not for your destruction, I will not have my value to be put to shame.

9. I am hoping that I do not terrify you through these letters,

10. because these letters are said to be burdensome and powerful; Yet when I am present with you, I am weak and my speech is continually impotent.

11. Let such a man think, that as we are in our letters when we are not there with you, so we shall be when we are working there with you face to face.

12. For we do not dare to rank ourselves nor compare ourselves with those that are presently commending themselves, because they measure themselves against themselves and compare one to another, but they are not able to understand.

13. But we are not boastful beyond measure, but according to the amount of which God has chosen to apportionately give, to reach even as far as you.

14. For it is not as though we reached you by overstretching ourselves, because we were even able to go to the distant places of where we are needed to bring the gospel of Christ.

15. But we are not beyond a measure of boasting unto others of the work we have done. We have hope concerning your growing faithfulness and that you are magnified, filling our needs abundantly.

16. We preach the gospel in regions beyond you, not according to the ways that others often boast,

17. but we abide by boasting in the joy of the Lord.

18. For it is not the one who commends himself whom the Lord approves, but only unto whom the Lord exhibits as approved.

2 Corinthians 11

1. I would now have you endure a small amount of foolishness, so please bear with me.

2. I have strongly zealous feelings for you before God; For I brought you together unto Christ to present you as a pure young woman unto her husband.

3. I had feared that somehow, as the serpent beguiled Eve by his craftiness (lies), that in like manner you might have been spoiled through your thoughts, away from the simplicity that is in Christ. (Acts 20:29-31)

4. For truly there are many that will come to proclaim another Jesus, one whom we have not spoken of; (They have come and have taken over Christianity throughout the world) They will also bring other spirits that you might receive (a false holy spirit), of which you have not received from us, and also another gospel of which you have not heard from us; (Galatians 1:7-9) (a different picture of Christ Jesus, one that allows for sin and says that everyone is a sinner, and comforts the people in their sin, of which is widespread throughout the world today)
Beware of these types of people and stand strong against them.

5. For I do not believe that I have fallen short in anything when considering the foremost of the apostles.

6. Even though I am unskilled in my public speaking, certainly not in understanding, I have revealed all things unto you.

7. Did I commit a trespass by humbling myself so that you might be uplifted, because I taught unto you the gospel of God at no charge?

8. I took rations from other gatherings before I came to minister unto you;

9. While I was with you, I did not have the needed things, yet I was not a burden unto anyone. But my lack was filled by the brethren who came from Macedonia and in no way did I burden you. I kept myself.

10. This is the truth before Christ and my boasting shall not be silenced in any of the regions of Achaia.

11. Why? Do you think that I do not love you? God knows!

12. But what I have done, I will continue to do, so to cut off any opportunity for those who are looking for an opportunity. They boast so that they might appear as us (true apostles).

13. For they are false apostles, deceitful workers that have disguised themselves as apostles of Christ, (Psalm 74:4-9; Matthew 24:4-5; 2 Peter 2:1-3; Jude 1:4; Acts 20:29-30; 2 Thess 2:10-12; Galatians 2:4-5; Mark 13:6; 1 Timothy 4:1; 2 Timothy 3:5; 4:3-4; Jeremiah 23; Ezekiel 22:28; Isaiah 56:10-11)

14. Do not be surprised, because even Satan makes himself appear as an angel of light. (John 10:12-13)

15. Why then is it any great thing for his servants to transform themselves into the image of ministers of righteousness, of which their end judgment will be according to their deeds. (1 Timothy 4:1)

16. Again I tell you, there is no one who thinks that I am foolish, but if there are any, and even if I act foolishly, they receive me. In this I may boast a little.

17. This that I speak, I do not speak according to the Lord, but I speak this boast in boldness as a fool.

18. Since many boast of themselves, I will also boast (of the Lord),

19. because you gladly endure a fool, in that you are wise.

20. For you endure if anyone enslaves you, if anyone devours you, if anyone steals from you, if anyone rises up against you, or if anyone hits you in the face!

21. Concerning honor, I tell you, be as if you are weak. But if someone is courageous, I am also courageous. Again, I speak foolishness.

22. Are they (*the other apostles*) Hebrews? I am also! Are they Israelites? So am I! Are they of the offspring of Abraham? I am as well!

23. Are they ministers of Christ? I stand beside myself as I speak! I have been more abundant then them in my work and in wounds, beyond measure! In prison many more times, in threat of death much more often.

24. Of the Jews, five times I received forty lashes less one.

25. Three times I have been beaten with rods! Once I was stoned (*and left for dead*)! Three times I suffered shipwreck; I spent a night and a day in the depths of the sea (*within a sunken ship*).

26. I have often traveled and have been in dangerous waters, in danger of thieves, in danger of my own countrymen and in danger of foreigners; I have been in danger in the cities and in the wilderness; I am always in danger of false brethren;

27. I have been worn out (*tired*) and suffered much pain; Many times I have been sleepless and in need, hungry and thirsty, often not having food to eat; I have been cold and not properly clothed.

28. Besides all of these external things, I have had the responsibility for the caring of all of the gatherings of the saints.

29. Who is weak? Am I not weakened? Who has reason to stumble? Do I not burn by fire?

30. If being boastful is deserving, those things that have caused difficulty upon me, I will tell.

31. Our Father God and the Lord Jesus Christ knows all of this. He is blessed forever. I am not lying.

32. In Damascus, the ethnarch, king of Aretas guarded the city of Damascenes, having the desire to arrest (*kill*) me; But I was lowered in a basket through a window and escaped from their hands!

2 Corinthians 12

1. It is not profitable for me to boast, though I have come to see visions and many things are revealed unto me by the Lord.

2. I was shown the appearance of the man (*Christ*) fourteen years ago, if in body or without body I do not know; (Acts 9:3-6) Only God knows. I was caught up to the third part of the heavens.

Verse 3 is a scribe's error, repeating most of verse 2 again.
Therefore, it has been left out of this text.

4. I was taken up unto a park like setting (*paradise*) and I heard unspoken words that are not possible for any man to speak. (*on the road to Damascus*)

5. For God's benefit I will joyfully tell of that experience; For my benefit I will not speak except of my weakness.

6. But if I have the desire to boast, I would not be foolish, for I speak truth. But I will spare you that, so that no one might see or hear me as more than I am.

7. The revelations are all extremely clear and abundant, but so that I not become prideful, I was given a thorn in the flesh (*physical disability in my body*). A messenger of Satan beat me badly, and because of that, now I am not arrogant (*prideful*).

8. However, on three occasions I did seek the Lord for it to depart from me (*that he heal me*).

9. Yet he said unto me, my grace (*assistance of God*) is appointed unto you, for my power is made perfect in you through your weakness.

10. Therefore, I would rather boast in my weakness, so that the power of Christ might overshadow me. For this reason, I take pleasure in physical pain, in injury, when I am in need, when I am persecuted or in anguish for Christ's sake: For when I am weak, then I receive power.

11. I have become foolish through boasting; But you compelled me, because I ought to be commended by you; I lack nothing in comparison to the most prominent of the apostles, yet I am nothing.

12. Surely, the signs of my apostleship were demonstrated in your continuance, your endurance and in the miracles, wonders and powerful deeds.

13. For what does it matter anyway if you received less than the other gatherings, because I myself did not burden you? Please forgive me if this was wrong.

14. So know this, that I am readying to come unto you a third time, though again I will not burden you, for

I do not seek that which you have, but I seek you. For the children are not to build up treasures for the parents, but the parents are to build up wealth for the children.

15. I will gladly spend that which I have and also extend of myself for the benefit of you, even if I am not loved in return to the degree that I love you.

16. But so that I not burden you, I will be hard working and I will not take from you subtly.

17. Did I send anyone unto you that took advantage of you?

18. I asked Titus and the dispatched brother; Did Titus take advantage of you? Do we not walk in the same spirit? Do we not live in the same ways?

19. Do you think that we are being defensive against you? Before God in Christ we are clarifying everything on your behalf, that you might be built up.

20. Because I fear that when I come, I might not find you as I have determined that you are, and that I am found by you to be other than that which you might desire; Such would create strife, envy, anger, rivalry, evil words being spoken, gossiping, pride, and disturbances;

21. But if I do come again, may God not humiliate me with you, that I be mourning because of some having returned unto sin, not having turned away from their previous uncleanness, fornication and lustfulness that they had previously done. (Colossians 1:22; 2 Peter 3:14; Titus 2:12; 1 John 2:3-6)

2 Corinthians 13

1. This third time that I come to you, "In the mouths of two or three witnesses, every matter shall be settled." (Deuteronomy 19:15) (*false doctrines are often established by only one misinterpreted scripture*)

2. I told you previously and I forewarn you, as when I was with you the second time, and now I make it known by writing you, tell those who have returned to their sin, all of them, that if I come to you again, I will not spare them. (2 Cor 12:21; Titus 2:12; 1 John 3:3; 2 Corinthians 2:5-10 *corruption in most bibles*)

3. This, since you require evidence that I speak the message of Christ powerfully and not impotently unto you (*as in the past*);

4. Even though he was crucified in weakness, yet now he lives in me through the power of God. (1 John 4:2) For we are often weak, but we must live through him by the power of God.

5. So examine yourselves to see if you are in the true faith (*doctrine*). Recognize that if Jesus Christ is in you, you are not reprobate (*returned to your sin*).

6. I trust that you are not reprobate.

7. I also pray unto God that you do nothing that is evil, so that you are easily approved; Otherwise you will surely be rejected. (Matthew 5:48; 7:21-24; Titus 2:12; Romans 6:16; 2 Peter 1:3-9; Ephesians 4:27)

8. For we must not do anything against the truth, but only that which is according to truth.

9. For we are joyful when we are weak but you are strong. And this we pray, that you might be brought to perfection. (Matthew 5:48)

10. This is why I write these things while not there with you, so when I am there with you, I will not have need to deal sharply with any of you in the authority in which the Lord gave to me; So in this, I might build you up and not pull you down.

11. For everything else, my brethren, be joyful, encourage yourselves and perfect one another unto his singular mindset. Be at peace and may God's affection and peace be with you.

12. Greet one another with a purely innocent (*holy*) kiss. Greet all of the saints.

13. May the grace (*assistance*) of the Lord Jesus Christ and the affection of God through fellowship with the spirit of the holy one be with you all.

Galatians

Chapter 1

1. Paul, an Apostle, (*ordained*) not of men nor through the ways of mankind, but through Jesus Christ and Father God who raised him from the dead.
2. I write unto all of the brethren of the gatherings in Galatia:
3. Grace and peace be with you from our Father God and the Lord Jesus Christ.
4. He gave himself to pay for our sins, so that he could help us overcome wickedness in this present world, according to the will of our Father God, (1 Corinthians 10:13; Matthew 7:21)
5. unto whom receives the honor and praise at all times.
6. I am surprised that you so quickly have turned away from the one who called you into the grace of Christ, to now serve another gospel;
7. Though it is not another gospel, but that there are some there with you that agitate you and have perverted the gospel of Jesus Christ. (2 Corinthians 2:17; Acts 20:29-30)
8. But if anyone, or even an angel from the heavens was to bring unto you a message that is different than that which we have already taught unto you, he shall be cursed. (Matthew 25:41; 2 Peter 2:14)
9. As we have said before and I shall again repeat myself; If anyone brings unto you any set of doctrines that is different than that which you have already received from us, he shall be cursed! (2 Corinthians 11:4)
10. Who shall we serve? God, or men? Do we seek to please men? For if we are to serve men, we would not be servants of Christ!
11. I have already made it known to you that the gospel that I preach is not according to other men.
12. I did not receive it from any man, nor was I taught it by any other man, but I received it by revelation given unto me by Jesus Christ.
13. For you have heard of my past life when I was in Judaism, that with great zeal I had persecuted the people of God and tried to destroy them. (Acts 7:58)
14. I advanced greatly in Judaism, far beyond many others like myself of my country, because I was much more zealous unto the traditions of my ancestors.
15. But when it pleased God, he separated me from my ancestral worthlessness and called me unto the power of God,
16. to reveal his son within me, (1 John 4:2) so that I would preach him among many nations; Therefore, I immediately no longer associated with my own countrymen;
17. I did not go to Jerusalem to see the apostles, but I went away unto Arabia then returned to Damascus.
18. Then after three years I went to Jerusalem to converse with Peter and I remained there with him for fifteen days. (Acts 9:26)
19. I did not see any other of the apostles, except James, the brother of our Lord. (Matthew 13:55; Acts 1:13)
20. That which I write to you, know before God that I do not lie.
21. Then I went to the different parts of Syria and Cilicia.
22. My face has been unknown to the gatherings of Judea that are in Christ;
23. They only heard that the one that was persecuting them now preaches the gospel of dedication unto that which he had earlier destroyed.
24. They glorify God because of me.

Galatians 2

1. Then after fourteen years, Titus, Barnabas and I went to Jerusalem.
2. We went for the purpose to make certain that the gospel that we have preached unto many nations was correct by them (*the other apostles*), and to be sure that we had not fallen into, nor supported anything worthless. (Acts 15:2)
3. But not even Titus, being Greek was compelled to be circumcised;
4. As it had occurred that false brethren had crept in without being noticed (Jude 1:4), like spies, looking at the freedom (*from the Mosaic law*) that we now have in Christ, because they have the desire to again enslave us all; (2 Peter 2:1; Acts 20:29-30; Matthew 24:4-5, 11, 24; 2 Thessalonians 2:10-12; Jude 1:4; Isaiah 56:10-11; Ezekiel 22:28)

5. Of those, we did not subject ourselves unto them not even for one hour, so that the truth of the gospel might remain firm within you.

6. But those that appeared on the surface to be strong in Christ, whatever kind they were of does not matter to me, because God does not look at nor accept the outward appearances of men. For those that looked good outwardly, we did not associate with them, not even one of them;

7. But to the contrary, knowing that I have been entrusted with the gospel unto the gentiles, just as Peter was to the Jews.

8. The apostleship of Peter was in good effect unto some Jews as I also was unto the gentiles.

9. Knowing the assistance that God has given unto me, Peter, James and John who looked to be solid pillars in truth, they offered Barnabas and I their company, because we have been to the gentiles what they were to the Jews.

10. They focused on keeping the poor in mind, of which we were also eager to do the same.

11. But when Peter came to Antioch, I came against him opposing him face to face, because he was surely in great error.

12. You see, in the past, James came and he sat and ate with the gentiles; But when they all came here together, he feared the others who were converted Jews.

13. They all turned away from the gentiles to eat among their fellow Jewish converts, even Barnabas was led away with them!

14. But when I noticed that they did not do what was right according to the truth of the gospel, I said unto Peter in front of all of them, if you are a converted Jew why do you live as one of the heathen? Why do you force the customs of Judaism upon us? (Acts 15:9)

15. We are Jews by birth and not sinners as the heathen;

16. But you know that a man is not justified by the works of the Mosaic law, but through being tested and having been found to be faithful unto Jesus Christ, because we also trust in Jesus Christ so that we might be justified by our faithfulness unto him and not by the works of the Mosaic law; No one shall be justified by the deeds of the Mosaic law!

17. Therefore, while we are seeking to be justified in Jesus Christ, if we are found to choose to commit sin, certainly Christ is not the minister of sin! God forbids such! (Romans 6:1; Numbers 15:30-31)

18. For if that which I have turned away from I again choose to do, I would again establish myself as a transgressor *(in violation)* against God. (2 Peter 2:20-22; John 8:31-34; Hebrews 10:26-27; John 5:14; John 8:11; John 9:41; Romans 2:6; John 3:18-19; Numbers 15:28-31)

19. So through the law of God, we have become dead unto the law of Moses, that we might live unto God.

20. I have been crucified with Christ, therefore though I live, though it is not I that lives, but Christ that lives through me! With the life that we live in our bodies, we must obey the doctrine of the son of God, the one that loves us and offered himself on our behalf.

21. We are not to annul *(throw away)* the assistance that God has given unto us (Matthew 12:31); For if through the Mosaic law we are made righteous, then Christ died for no reason!

Galatians 3

1. You of Galatia, you are so foolish! Who has deceived you to not obey truth? In the eyes of Jesus Christ, which of you have the evidence to prove that you have been crucified with him? (*by living faithfully* - Romans 6)

2. I ask you, did you receive the spirit of God by the works of the Mosaic law or by being tested and found to be faithful, being demonstrated before many witnesses? (Romans 6:16)

3. Are you so foolish to think that you, having begun by living according to the spirit, that you will now be made perfect through the physical deeds of the Mosaic law?

4. So much you have done for nothing! Indeed, it is for nothing!

5. Did God give you of his spirit and did he work miracles in you through the Mosaic law, or by the evidence of your faithfulness unto him?

6. The same as Abraham walked closely unto God's ways and so he was approved by God, in this he became righteous.

7. Know then that those who are found faithful through being tested, these are the sons of Abraham.

8. And through the scriptures, foreseeing that by being found to be faithful, the foreign nations would be justified by God, in that it was spoken unto Abraham that in you, all nations shall be blessed.

9. So then, those that are found to be faithful unto God, these are those that are blessed along with faithful Abraham.

10. Because all that are doing the works of the Mosaic law, they are under a curse. For it has been written within the books of the Mosaic law that they must continue to fully live by them; (Deuteronomy 27:26) (*of which is impossible today, with no temple for sacrifices*)

11. And that by the Mosaic law, no one shall be justified before God. This is clear, because the scriptures also say, the just shall live by being proven to be faithful. (Habakkuk 2:4; Romans 1:17)

12. The Mosaic law is not of being found to be faithful through testing, but is contrary to this. (*doing sacrifices to cover over sin*) Those that live in these things must live by them perfectly! (Leviticus 18:5)

13. But Christ rescued us from that curse of the Mosaic law, as he was cursed; As it has been written, "Cursed is every man that hangs upon a tree." (Deuteronomy 21:22-23)

14. In this, the blessings given unto Abraham shall be offered unto the people of all nations, (Romans 11:26) that through Jesus Christ, the promise of the spirit of God might be received in each of us through our faithfulness unto him (*of which must be proven through being tested*).

15. Brethren, I say this in comparison to that which is of men; Even with mankind, when they make a covenant, no one takes away from it or adds to it; (*a covenant is an agreement, a contract*)

16. But to Abraham, these promises were spoken of his seed. It does not say seeds, as with many! But it says seed, as in one, and that seed is Jesus Christ! (Hebrews 11:18; Genesis 21:12; Matthew 13:37)

17. And this I tell you, that covenant that was ratified by God which points to the promise of Christ, can not be annulled four hundred and thirty years later when the Mosaic law came into being! The Mosaic law can not possibly abolish the promise given unto Abraham by God!

18. Because if it was by the Mosaic law that the inheritance is given, then it is no more by the promise! But Abraham was given the promises from God.

19. So why did we have the Mosaic law? It was given for the purpose of dealing with sin; It was added until the seed (*Jesus Christ*) would come, in whom the promise was established. He (*Jesus Christ*) was confirmed by the hands (*writings*) of the prophets (*messengers*). (Matthew 11:13)

20. We know that there was not only one prophet, but there is only one God.

21. So then, is the Mosaic law against the promise of God? It can not be! For if the Mosaic law could have given (*eternal*) life, surely it would have produced righteousness; (John 8:31-36)

22. But to the contrary, as it is conclusive in the scriptures that all have violated God's ways, and this is the reason for the promise, that by faithfulness it might be offered unto those that remain fully committed and are faithful unto Jesus Christ. (Daniel 9:24)

23. But before the new covenant (*of faithfulness*) was established, they were under the Mosaic law, looking forward but prevented from receiving of the soon to come new covenant (*of faithfulness*) that would at that time later be revealed.

24. Therefore the Mosaic law was a tutor of sorts, bringing us to Christ, who established faithfulness that must be proven through testing as the way to be justified.

25. But when faithfulness is established, there no longer is a need for the tutor (*Mosaic law*).

26. So now we can all become sons of God through having been tested and being found to be faithful unto Jesus Christ. (1 John 3:1-2)

27. Because all that are properly baptized into Jesus Christ receive (*the spirit of*) Christ within them. (Romans 6; Acts 2:38; John 14:18; 1 John 4:1-5)

28. For in the body of Christ there are neither Jews nor are there non-Jews; There are no slaves nor freemen; There are not males nor females. You see, you are all coming into Jesus Christ in the same way. (Acts 15:9; Romans 10:12; Romans 3:22; Ephesians 2:15; Colossians 3:11)

29. So then, if you are in Christ, then you are of Abraham's seed and surely you are equal heirs according to the promises. (Isaiah 59:21; Zephaniah 3:14; Psalms 69:36)

Galatians 4

1. But I will tell you that for quite a long time, the heir is much like an immature child, no different than a slave unto the Lord in everything, (John 8:31-36)

2. except that they are under guardians and overseers until the time set by the Father.

3. So also, when we were infants, we were held down by the ways of the world, of which we had been enslaved. (John 8:31-34 – *slaves of sin*)

4. But when the time came, God sent forth his son, born of a woman and he lived perfectly according to the law of God; (1 John 1:5)

5. He did this so that he could purchase us, so that we might receive the adoption as sons; (1 John 3:1)

6. And because you are now sons, God sent forth the spirit of his son (*Jesus Christ*) to enter into your hearts to alert each of us unto him, Daddy, Father! (1 John 4:2; John 14:17-20; John 14:23)

7. So then, you no longer are a slave, but a son, and if a son, then also an heir unto God through Christ Jesus. (John 8:31-36; 1 John 3:1-2; Romans 8:16)

8. But before (*conversion*) you surely did not know God and you were a slave unto Satan, who was not created to be a god. (John 8:31-36, 44; Acts 26:18; Romans 6:16)

9. Now you have come to know God, even more importantly, now he knows you. So how could you choose to return to the diseased and unvalued ways that again renew you to be a slave? (Hebrews 10:26-29; 2 Peter 2:20-22; John 8:31-36)

10. You are observing days and months and seasons and years! (*under the Mosaic law*)

11. I fear for you! God forbid if I worked with you for nothing! (1 Thessalonians 3:5)

12. I beg of you, be like me, I once was like you. You did not wrong me in any way,

13. but you know that I taught the gospel unto you while I was physically suffering greatly in my body.

14. Concerning the challenge (*infirmity*) in my body, you did not hate nor turn away from me. But you received me as a messenger of God and you even heeded the calling of Jesus Christ (*through me*).

15. In this, goodness was demonstrated by you. I testify on your behalf, that if you were able, you would have plucked out your own eyes and given them to me! (2 Corinthians 12:7)

16. So have I now become your enemy because I spoke truth unto you?

17. They (*the false teachers*) are zealous for you, but not in truth nor in honesty. They desire to exclude you from us, that you only trust in them.

18. It is always good to be zealous for virtue, not only when I am present with you.

19. My children, I shall labor greatly until Christ is formed in you.

20. I would like to be there and speak differently to you, because I am in doubt whether you are in Christ.

21. Tell me, those who desire to be slaves to the Mosaic law, do you not understand the scriptures?

22. It is written that Abraham had two sons; One from out of the slave woman and one out of the free woman. (Isaiah 54:1; John 8:34; Genesis 16:5; 21:2)

23. The one that was born of the slave woman was born because of selfishness, but the one that was born unto the free woman was a fulfillment of God's promise unto Abraham. (Hebrews 11:11)

24. These things are an allegory for the two covenants; The first of Mount Sinai that brought them into slavery, this is representative of the slave woman Hagar. (Deuteronomy 33:2)

25. Hagar is Mount Sinai in Arabia, which represents the present-day Jerusalem who are now slaves along with their children.

26. But the Jerusalem from above is free, of whom is now the mother of all of us (*who have been converted into Christ*). (Revelation 21:2)

27. It has been written, "be happy those of you who are not able to have children; Break and cry if you do not bring forth children, because the children of the unwed are many more than the children of the woman that has a husband." (Isaiah 54:1)

28. But we my brothers are in the order of Isaac, the children of promise.

29. Know that the one that was born according to selfishness (*Esau*) persecuted the one that was born of the spirit (*Jacob*), and it is also this way now for those that live according to the spirit.

30. But what does the scripture say? Cast away the slave woman and her son (Malachi 1:2-3); For the son of the slave woman shall not inherit, but the son of the freewoman shall inherit (*everlasting life*). (Genesis 21:10; John 8:31-36)

31. So then my brothers, we are not to be the children of the slave woman, but of the free woman. (John 8:36)

Galatians 5

1. So now, persevere in the freedom in which Christ has made you free and do not be entangled again in the slavery of the past (*Mosaic law, sin* - Romans 7:13- 8:2).
2. Understand this, I Paul tell you, that if you are of the circumcision (*unconverted Jews*), Christ shall benefit nothing unto you. (John 14:6)
3. I am a witness unto every man that is of the circumcision (*living by the Mosaic law*) that they are a debtor of the whole Mosaic law and must live by it completely flawless.
4. They are not associated with Christ; All who are justified by the Mosaic law have no way to receive the grace of God! (John 14:6)
5. Through the spirit of Jesus Christ, we eagerly await with expectation to be called righteous by our faithfulness unto God. (Ephesians 2:8-9)
6. Because in Jesus Christ, neither those who have been physically circumcised nor those that have not been physically circumcised have any advantage; But only through dedication and faithfulness that is established unto affection and benevolence (*love*).
7. You were doing so well! Who held you back, preventing you from obeying the truth?
8. Certainly they (*those deceiving you*) are not of the one who is calling you (*Christ Jesus*).
9. A little amount of yeast raises the whole mass (*of dough*)! (1 Corinthians 5:6; Hosea 7:4)
10. I trust if you are truly in Christ, that you will consider the doctrine of no one else. Whoever has provoked you into such error shall receive damnation, whoever they may be.
11. My Brothers, if those of the circumcision (*unconverted Jews*) continue to teach truth, what is the reason that I continue to endure persecution from them? If what they teach is true, then the hardship endured on the cross is for no purpose!
12. I wish that those who have caused you to err would castrate themselves! (*walk away from you*)
13. My brothers, you have been called unto freedom (*from the Mosaic law*). Do not use your freedom to bring gain unto yourselves, but use your freedom from the Mosaic law to care for one another.
14. For all of the law of God is fulfilled in one word (*Love*); You shall have love (*affection and benevolence*) for one another! (Luke 10:27; Deuteronomy 6:5; Lev. 19:18; Matthew 22:37; Mark 12:30)
15. If you were to take from and feed off of one another, don't you see that would destroy you?
16. Live according to the spiritual and you shall not commit the carnal lusts;
17. For the carnal lusts are against the spiritual and spiritual are against the carnal, as they are contrary to each other; You must not do what you might have done.
18. But if you are led by the spirit of God, you are not under the jurisdiction of the Mosaic law.
19. Now the deeds of the flesh (*carnal*) are clear to recognize and they are adultery, fornication, filthiness, lustfulness, (Proverbs 5:1-23; Proverbs 6:32)
20. idolatry, sorcery, hatred, strife, covetousness, passionate rage, self-promotion, double mindedness, heresies,
21. ill will towards others, murder, drunkenness, verbal abuse, and other like things; As I have already warned you and clearly told you in the past, those that do any of these things shall not inherit the kingdom of God. (Revelation 21:8; Ezekiel 3:19; Ezekiel 18:10-32; 1 John 3:8)
22. But that which is produced by the spirit of God are these things; Love (*affection and benevolence*), joy (*joyfulness*), peace (*peacefulness*), patient continuance in truth, kindness (*gentleness*), goodness,
23. conviction, meekness (*humility*), self-control, and there is no law against such things.
24. Those that are in Christ have extinguished their own selfishness (Matthew 16:34) and the longing for that which is forbidden by God, through many hardships and sacrifices.
25. If we live in the spiritual, we must also conform ourselves unto the spiritual ways of God.
26. May we not be self-conceited, but challenge one another to desire these things.

Galatians 6

1. Brothers, if a man has unintentionally or unknowingly committed a sin, those that are fully mature in Christ that can see the error that he committed must make it known to him and help him correct his error, but they must do so in the spirit of meekness, as it could have been you that had made an error.
(1 John 2:1; Hebrews 10:26-27; Numbers 15:28-31; John 5:16-17)
2. Bear the hardships of one another and in this you shall fulfill the law of Christ.

3. If a man thinks too highly of himself, if he is not in truth, he deceives himself.

4. It is the deeds of each man that will bring them as individuals to be approved and then only unto himself may he boast, but not to anyone else.

5. Each man shall bear that which is put upon him. (*speaking of being tested*)

6. Speak the truth unto others that which you have learned and the instructions of how to succeed in similar circumstances.

7. Do not deceive yourself, because God will not be mocked; Whatever a man plants (*his actions*), he shall also harvest accordingly (*on judgment day*).

8. If a man plants (*lives his life*) unto his own desires and the lusts of his own body, he shall harvest damnation; If a man plants (*lives his life*) through the disposition (*qualities*) of Christ, by the spirit of God he shall receive everlasting life.

9. Let us not become tired in doing good, for in due time we shall reap if we faint not. (Hebrews 10:36)

10. So when we have opportunity, do good unto all people, but to the greatest degree do so unto those who are also being tested to be found faithful before God.

11. Know that I have written this long letter by my own hand.

12. Those that try to push you to be circumcised, they do so in order that they are not persecuted for the cross of Christ;

13. But those that are of the circumcision (*the cut off ones*), they do not keep the law of God, but they want you to be circumcised, so that because of your obeying them, they might be able to boast.

14. But as far as I am concerned, there is nothing for us to boast about other than our having been cleansed by our Lord Jesus Christ, by whom the cares of the world are now dead to us; We must now be dead to the temporary cares of this life.

15. In Jesus Christ, there is no power nor benefit in being physically circumcised nor in remaining uncircumcised;

It is only to be a new creation that matters. (Acts 2:38; Romans 6:5 - *the evidence of a true conversion*)

16. Unto all who live by these instructions, may peace and mercy be upon the Israel of God. (*spiritual Israel*).

17. For all others, they will not even communicate with me, because I bear on my body the marks of the Lord Jesus Christ.

18. May the grace of our Lord Jesus Christ be with your spirit, my brothers.

Ephesians

Chapter 1

1. Paul, an Apostle of Jesus Christ through the will of God, unto the saints that are in Ephesus and the faithful everywhere that are in Christ Jesus;

2. Grace and peace unto you from our Father God and our master, Jesus Christ.

3. May God, the Father of our Lord Jesus Christ be blessed, as he has given unto us every spiritual blessing from above through Christ.

4. Before the foundations of the world were laid down, we were chosen to be holy and perfectly unblemished in Christ; To be in his presence through affection for him. (2 Peter 3:14; Colossians 1:22)

5. He predetermined that we could become his children through Jesus Christ, according to that which he has offered, unto his satisfaction,

6. of which will be given unto those who are deserving (*commendable*) of the honor through the power of God, for those of us that he has called, all who truly love him;

7. In him we have the ability to be ransomed through his blood (*converted* - Acts 2:38; Romans 6:1-7), and receive a pardon from our past trespasses, according to the wealth of the power of God. (Romans 3:25) (Numbers 15:28-31; Hebrews 10:26-27; 1 John 5:16; 1 John 1:9-2:6)

8. He has given unto us an abundance of all the necessary wisdom and understanding,

9. and is making known unto us the mysteries of his instructions, according to his satisfaction, of which he exhibited in himself.

10. He is the administrator of the completion of the times (*end of the world*), to gather together all things unto God, all things both in the heavens and upon the earth.

11. We who will be chosen by him shall receive an inheritance. It has been predetermined that all that we have done will be shown before the eyes of God and he will judge each of us according to that which each one deserves, based upon his judgment.
(Romans 2:1-10; Revelation 20:12-15; Revelation 1:8 - *Jesus will decide who is deserving*)

12. Those of us that put our trust in Christ must be worthy of his honor.

13. It is of him that you yourselves heard the message of truth, the gospel of our saviour, in whom when you were converted (Acts 2:38; 3:19; Matthew 18:2-4; Romans 6:1-23), you were given the signet, the spirit of the holy one (*Christ Jesus*) of which was promised,

14. which is the security deposit of our inheritance, until we receive that which shall be delivered and possess it unto much praise and honor. (*eternal life*)

15. I have come to understand that there is great dedication among you unto the Lord Jesus Christ and that you have great affection towards all of the ones that are holy through faithfulness (*the elect, saints*).

16. I do not stop giving thanks for you and I always speak of you in my prayers.

17. May our master Jesus Christ, the father of all honor, may he give unto you the spirit of wisdom and the full understanding of his knowledge.

18. With such enlightenment and vision in your understanding, you will know the fullness of what we anticipate through obeying his calling and all of the wealth and the honor of the inheritance that he shall give unto his faithful ones (*saints*);

19. The extreme magnitude of Christ's power that is given unto those of us who are fully committed unto him is shown through the working of his dominion and strength through each of us; (*miracles*)

20. He established this in Christ, raising him from the dead and seating him at his right hand in the heavens.

21. He is placed far above all others in power, strength, authority and jurisdiction. (Revelation 1:11)
He has been made known and named in not only this world, but also in the world to come.

22. Everything was created to serve under his feet (*authority*). He is the head of the faithful people of God that are of his body,

23. unto the completion of everything, when all is accomplished.

Ephesians 2

1. At one time you were dead in your trespasses and defiant sins;

2. Because at that time you lived according to the ways of this world, according to the ruler of this world who holds jurisdiction all around you (*circumambient*), which is the spirit that is now active in all of the sons of disobedience, (John 12:31; 14:30; 16:11; Daniel 11:36-45; Matthew 4:9; Revelation 12:12)

3. of whom in past times we also served, conducting ourselves at that time according to the lustful desires for that which is evil. We must understand that we had grown up to be the children of wrath as everyone else; (Psalms 119:21)

4. But God who is abundantly wealthy in mercy and his overwhelming affection, that he chose to love us.

5. Even though we were dead in our sins, he made a way that by working together (*conjointly, synergy*) we could be made alive in Christ. It is this compassion of the Lord that is actively healing you,

6. and has raised you from death. (Romans 6:1-6; Acts 2:38; Acts 3:19; Matthew 18:2-4) Now a seat in the celestial places with Jesus Christ is being reserved for you.

7. He will show in the world to come, the extensive wealth of the power of God and the kindness that he has toward us, through Christ Jesus. (Proverbs 28:13)

8. It is by the compassion of God and through being tested and found to be faithful unto him, that you are actively being saved. (Habakkuk 2:4) It is not something that you can do on your own, but it is a gift from God (*grace is the gift - having past sins forgiven unto those who convert unto him*). (James 1:21; Romans 3:25)

9. Good works can not make up for past sins that you had committed, and no one can be boastful of not having committed any. (Romans 3:27; John 8:34-36; 1 John 1:8-10)

10. Because we are his creation and were created to do good deeds, of which was ordained by God that we must surely live accordingly.

11. Therefore, remember that you at one time were foreign in your heart, surely being called uncircumcised by those that were called circumcised physically at the hands of men. (*Jews*)

12. Because at that time you were without Christ and alien to God's Israel, a stranger to the covenant of promise, having no hope and you were without God. (Galatians 3:28)

13. But now through Jesus Christ, you who were at one time distanced, have come to be close by through the blood shed of Christ (*the free gift*); (Acts 2:38; Romans 6:1-6)

14. For he has created peace between us, by making of both, now one, and the wall that separated us has been dissolved. (Galatians 3:28; Romans 2:11) By the hostility done unto his body (*on the cross*),

15. he has brought an end to the Mosaic law and the authority of the ordinances (*Jewish law*), so that of the two (*gentiles and Jews*), he has created unto himself one new people, creating peacefulness with God.

16. He is reconciling both into one body through the cross, destroying the opposition that was between them. (Galatians 3:28-29; Romans 10:12; Acts 15:9; Romans 3:22)

17. He came and announced peace unto those that were far away, and unto those close by;

18. Because through Christ, everyone now has access unto the Father by one spirit. (Galatians 3:29)

19. Now thereby, you are no longer strangers nor tenants, but of the family of the saints that are of the household of God.

20. You have built upon the foundation of the prophets and the apostles, Jesus Christ is the cornerstone linking the two. (Matthew 21:42; Mark 12:10; Luke 20:17; Acts 4:11; 1 Peter 2:6-7; Isaiah 28:16)

21. In him, the construction is fitted together and grows into a holy temple by the master.

22. In him, you also are being constructed to be a dwelling place for God through his spirit. (1 Cor. 3:16)

Ephesians 3

1. Because of this, I Paul have become a slave of Jesus Christ on the behalf of the foreign nations.

2. If you have heard of the stewardship of the power of God that has been given unto me

3. by manifestation, the mysteries have been made known unto me, of which I have already written unto you. You are able to easily see the knowledge that I have concerning the mystery of Christ.

4. You are able to easily see the knowledge that I have concerning the mystery of Christ.

5. All of this was not made known unto the past generations of the children of Israel, but now the spirit of the prophecies has been made known unto his blameless apostles;

6. Now the people of all nations can be participants in common, be of the same community and joint sharers of his promises through the gospel of Christ, (Galatians 3:27-29)

7. of which I have become a minister according to the gift of the power of God that has been given unto me to accomplish his purposes.

8. I am lesser than the least of all of the saints, yet I was given his grace to teach the gospel unto all nations, the untraceable wealth in Christ,

9. and to bring a light unto everyone as to the mystery of the partnership (Ephesians 2:8) that has been hidden throughout the ages within God, the one that all things were created by, Jesus Christ; (John 1:3)

10. Now, the commencement of the authority in the heavens could finally be revealed unto the people of God along with the great diversity of the wisdom of God.

11. Concerning the reason for the world that he created through Christ Jesus our master, (John 1:1-3)

12. we can now have confidence and access to approach him because of our proven faithfulness to him.

13. Therefore I call for you to not be disheartened when you hear of the many troubles that I suffer on your behalf. I suffer for your benefit.

14. Because of this, I bow my knees before the Father of our Lord Jesus Christ,

15. of whom every family in the heavens and on the earth is called,

16. that he may give unto you of his wealth, honor and the strength to become mighty in his name and through his spirit of which is given unto the hearts of men; (*power* - Acts 1:8)

17. May Christ dwell within you through the faithfulness within your own hearts and through your love, having truly been rooted and completely made perfect, (Matthew 5:48; 2 Peter 3:14)

18. that you might be entirely competent to obtain (*eternal salvation*) along with all of the saints,

19. and to know the fullness of the breadth, length, depth and height of the knowledge of the love of Christ, so that you can be made completely perfect unto all things; That you may be fitted perfectly, completely filled by God. (2 Peter 3:14)

20. But unto he that is able to go beyond all these things and exceedingly above what we ask, according to the power that is working in us,

21. unto him be the glory from the people that are in Christ Jesus, unto all generations, forever and ever.

Ephesians 4

1. Therefore I call for you to be servants unto the Lord and to live appropriately to that which is necessary for that which you have been called; (Romans 6:16-23)

2. Do so with complete humility and gentleness with much patience and be sure to interact with each other affectionately.

3. Be diligent to keep peaceful unity and be strongly bonded with the spirit of Christ.

4. There is one body, one spirit, and one hope unto which you have been called.

5. You have also been called unto one master, one truth, one baptism,

6. and one God, the Father of us all, who is above all, and through all and in all of you that have been converted. (1 John 4:1-5)

7. But the gift of grace has been offered unto every one of us, according to the amount appropriated by Christ.

8. Ask therefore, because he has ascended into the heavens and he has made a way for the captives (*by Satan*) to be set free. He has offered this gift unto mankind. (John 8:31-36; Acts 2:38; Isaiah 58:6)

9. But in that he has now ascended, what does it matter that he had also descended to participate with us upon the earth? (John 1:10)

10. He that came down is also the same who has now ascended far above all of the heights, so that he may surely bring everything unto completion.

11. He has made some to be apostles, and some to be prophets, and some to be evangelists, and some to be shepherds and some to be teachers, for the perfection of the faithful,

12. for the needs of ministering and to construct the healthy body of Christ,

13. until each one shall come to be unified with Christ, through the testing of each of our faithfulness, to become completely perfect and unto the full knowledge of the son of God, and grow unto the same degree of maturity as Christ; (1 John 3:3)

14. This, so that we may no longer be immature and fluctuating back and forth, being tossed around in all directions by the doctrines of men (Matthew 15:9 - *the modern churches*), through their deceitfulness of the many men who are frauds, lying in wait looking for the opportunity to defraud and deceive you. (Matthew 24:4-5; 2 Peter 2:1-3; Jude 1:4; Acts 20:29-30; 2 Thess. 2:10-12; Galatians 2:4-5; Mark 13:6; 1 Timothy 4:1; 2 Timothy 3:5; 4:3-4; Jeremiah 23; Ezekiel 22:28; Isaiah 56:10-11; 2 Corinthians 11:15)

15. We who are mature in Christ must speak the truth in love for you to grow in Christ in all things, because he is the head,

16. of whom the whole body is being built up and united together, with every ligament contributing according to the operational purposes of every part, to increase the healthy body that is being built through a structure of affection (*love*).

17. Therefore, I tell you this and I stand by it before the Lord, that you shall no longer live your lives the way that the people who do not know God live. In the depravity of their own minds,

18. they become obscure in their understanding, (Romans 1:28) and alienated away from the life God has intended, because of their ignorance, because of the hardness within their hearts; (Romans 1:18)

19. They give themselves over unto lasciviousness (*their own lusts, without care of consequences*) and they do that which is impure because of their covetousness. (Romans 1:28; Jude 1:4)

20. If you have heard from Christ and if you were taught by him, you were taught not to continue to live in such a way, but to live according to the truth in Christ Jesus;

21. You were taught to turn away from the former behaviors of which you had in the past committed, by which you were completely corrupted because of the deceitfulness of your own lusts;

23. But now, be renovated in your mind and through the spirit of God in you,

24. and invest in living as a new man (Romans 6:4) that is created to live in righteousness, holiness and truth, according to God. (2 Corinthians 7:1; James 1:12; 1Corinthians 10:12-13; 1 John 3:3)

25. Therefore, completely turn away from lying and now speak the truth unto everyone.

26. If you become angry (*exasperated*) do not commit sin (*defiance of God's way*) (Hebrews 10:26-29; Numbers 15:28-31) Do not allow the sun to set while you are still angered.

27. Do not allow the devil to take occupancy within you. (John 8:31-36; 1 John 3:8-10; Romans 6:16)

28. He that was a thief, do not steal any more, but you must work hard and do good work so that you may have more than you need, so that you can give and help others in need.

29. Do not allow any corrupt communication to come out of your mouth, but use constructive words of goodness that encourage those that are in need of encouragement, that you might bring peace unto those who hear.

30. Do not bring grief unto the holy spirit, (Matthew 12:3; Numbers 15:28-31; 1 John 5:16-17- *blasphemy of the holy spirit*) of whom you have been offered a reservation for the day of deliverance.

31. All poison, fierceness, malignity, passionate violence and speaking out evil things, be sure to remove from you.

32. Grow to be kind to one another, tenderhearted and forgive one another, in the same way that God through Christ Jesus has forgiven you.

Ephesians 5

1. Therefore become imitators of Christ as a beloved child; (Matthew 18:1-3; 1 John 3:3; 1 Peter 2:1-2)

2. In all that you do, do it through a heart of affection for others, the same as Christ has loved us and gave himself on our behalf. You now must present yourself as a sacrifice unto God to be pleasing unto him. (Romans 12:1)

3. Do not allow, not even one time, fornication or any other type of uncleanness to be committed by any of you; Live as is necessary in order to be blameless. (1 John 3:3-10; Numbers 15:28-30; Hebrews 10:26; Proverbs 5:3-23; 2 Peter 3:14; Matthew 5:48; Romans 6:1)

4. Also all obscenity, moronic speaking (*foolish talk*), witty words and joking around, these things are not proper. It is much better for your speech to be full of thankfulness unto God.

5. You already know that no fornicator, nor anyone who is impure, nor anyone that is covetous (*which is idolatry*), none of these shall enter into the kingdom of God; (Galatians 5:19-21)

6. Do not allow anyone to deceive you with words that are not true, because it is these kinds of things that shall bring the wrath of God upon all who are disobedient. (Romans 1:18-32)

7. Do not share in the coming wrath with them!

8. You did live in darkness, but now the Lord has brought you into the light, so live as a child of the Light! (Romans 6:16-23; John 1:1-5)

9. The fruits of the spirit (*of Christ*) are for you to be completely virtuous, righteous and in all truth;

10. Become approved through your testing, (*be proven to be faithful*) because this is what is pleasing unto the Lord;

11. Do not participate in (*touch*) any of the unfruitful deeds of darkness, but refuse to do them. (2 Corinthians 6:17; Romans 6:6-16)

12. It is shameful to even speak of the things that are being done by others in darkness.

13. All things that are rejected will be revealed by the light and everyone that is approved is of the light. (John 3:18-21)

14. Therefore, ask and rise up if you are asleep; Be raised up from the dead (Romans 6:3-4, 17) and you will be enlightened by Christ.

15. Therefore be careful and watch how you live, not as those that are foolish, but live as those that are wise! (Proverbs 24:7; Proverbs 18:2)

16. Be sure to be thrifty with how you spend your time, because time is running out.

17. This is why you should not be foolish, but come to understand what the will of the Lord is.

18. Do not become intoxicated with alcohol, because to do so is to be completely given in to licentiousness. Instead, be filled by the disposition (*character*) of Christ.

19. Speak unto each other with joy and peacefulness in your words; You should have spiritual songs singing with music in your heart as unto the Lord.

20. Always give thanks unto our master for all that you have been given. Be thankful unto Jesus Christ our God and Father,

21. and be accountable unto each other, having fear for our God. (Philippines 2:12; Proverbs 8:13)

22. Wives, subject yourselves unto your own husbands, as unto the Lord.

23. The husband is the head of his wife, just as Christ is the head of the people of God and he is also the saviour of the body.

24. But just as the people of God are subject unto Christ, so the wives are also to be unto their own husbands in everything.

25. Husbands, love your own wife just as Christ also loves the people of God, giving himself up for their sake;

26. As he has cleansed us and has purified us (*made us holy, blameless*) through the command of water baptism, (G4487+G5099+G3067 - Mark 16:16; Acts 2:37-38; Romans 6:1-23; 3:25; Matthew 28:18-19)

27. that he present unto himself a glorious body, not having blemish nor need to be hidden, nor any such kind of thing; But that the body of Christ be blameless and completely pure. (2 Peter 3:14; 1 John 3:3)

28. In this same way, each husband is to love his own wife.

29. No one hates his own body, but we all feed and cherish ourselves, just as the Lord also does with his people;

30. We are part of his spiritual body, each of us make up the various parts, flesh and bones.

31. In the same way, a man shall leave his mother and father and shall cling together with his own wife creating something of value together; And of the two, they shall be joined to become one body. (*with one purpose*)

32. I tell you that this is a great mystery, concerning Christ and his people (*body*).

33. Yet each one accordingly, each man must love his own wife, because she is a part of himself; Wives, you must have respect and reverence for your own husbands.

Ephesians 6

1. Your children shall obey their parents according to the ways of the Lord, for this is right.

2. Honor your father and mother, of which is the first commandment of promise (Exodus 20:12)

3. so that you shall be well and live a long life on the earth.

4. Fathers, do not be provoking unto your children, but cherish them and use discipline to bring their attention unto knowing the Lord.

5. Servants, obey those that you serve in this world with fear and respect, with sincerity in your heart, as unto Christ.

6. Do not please them only when they are watching or to impress others, but as servants of Christ who are doing the will of God from your heart.

7. Serve with good will unto the Lord.

8. Know that whatever you do that is good, you will be returned the same from the Lord, whether you are a slave or a freeman. (Galatians 3:27-29; Romans 2:5-10)

9. The Lord will also do the same unto them, whether they are easy or menacing, because the Lord is above you and also above them and he does not play favorites between men. (Romans 2:11)

10. For all else, my brothers, strengthen yourselves in the Lord and remain under the jurisdiction of his power.

11. Put on all of the armor of God so that you will be able to stand against the methods (*trickery and deception*) used by the devil;

12. Because it is not for us to physically struggle against the flesh and blood of others, but it is for us to struggle against magistrates, the jurisdictions of the rulers in this world of darkness and against evil spirituals that are operating in high places of power.

13. Because of these, take unto yourself the whole armor of God so that you will be able to resist those that are malicious when that time comes, having truly accomplished all that is necessary to firmly remain standing.

14. Therefore firmly strap the truth on to your belt and stand thereon and put on the armor of righteousness.

15. Just as you wear shoes on your feet, be prepared to bring the gospel of peace (*with God unto others*);

16. Above all, gather up the shield of having been tested and proven to be faithful; You must be able to extinguish all of the fiery assaults brought by the devil. (1 Corinthians 10:13)

17. Take the helmet of defense and the sword, which are the spirit of Christ; This is a command of God.

18. Pray always and approach God with humility, according to the character of Christ; Petition (*pray unto*) the Lord concerning all of the saints. Continually watch with complete perseverance.

19. On my behalf, ask the Lord that I might be able to be given the ability to speak and to open my mouth in boldness, to make the mysteries of the gospel to be known;

20. Because I have been a representative enchained (*not able to be a bold speaker in public*); In this, that I may gain the ability to speak boldly that which it is necessary for me to speak.

21. So that you may know about me and how I am doing, Tychicus our beloved brother and faithful minister in the Lord, he will tell you everything.

22. I recently sent him to come to you for these reasons; That you may know how we are and that he might comfort your hearts.

23. May the peace and love of our Father God and the master Jesus Christ be with you all my brethren, through the testing of your faithfulness.

24. In all sincerity, may the gift of God be with you, all who love our Lord Jesus Christ.

Philippines

Chapter 1

1. Paul and Timothy, slaves of Jesus Christ; We write unto all the saints in Christ that are of Philippi, including overseers and assistants;

2. Grace and peace unto you from our Father God and our master Jesus Christ.

3. I thank my God every time I think of you,

4. You are always in our prayers. On the behalf of all of you we always joyfully make our request unto God

5. concerning your partnership in the gospel, from the beginning until today. (Acts 16:12)

6. I am confident in this, that because he (*Christ Jesus*) has begun to dwell in you, a good thing is being accomplished (*in you*) unto the day of the judgment of Christ. (Revelation 20:12-15; Romans 2:5-10)

7. It is right for me to think of you in this way and I know that I have also been on your mind concerning both my chains (*imprisonment*) and the defense of the gospel, since you are sharers with me in the power of God.

8. For God is my witness, I know that you are in the tender mercies of Jesus Christ.

9. I pray that your love may continue to abundantly grow in discernment and judgment

10. so that you may be approved through that which you are enduring and that you continue to be found to be genuine and blameless unto the day of the judgment of Christ. (1 Corinthians 1:8; 1 Timothy 5:7; 2 Peter 3:14; Luke 1:6; Ephesians 4:13; James 2:22)

11. Having been completely filled with the fruits of righteousness through the assistance of Jesus Christ, you will receive the honor and praise of God.

12. My brethren, I want you to know much more about me for the purpose of spreading the gospel.

13. My chains (*charges against me*) have clearly revealed Christ throughout the court room and everywhere I am brought. (Acts 23)

14. Most of the brethren in the Lord are convinced that my chains are too tightly bound for them to gather the courage to fearlessly speak a word on my behalf.

15. Some men have testified through their jealousy and contention against me, but there are some that have delightfully proclaimed the gospel of Jesus Christ.

16. There have been some who have brought the message of Christ contending against it, making the efforts to add more trouble unto my chains.

17. But others know that I am well prepared to bring a strong defense of the gospel.

18. What is the reason for this? So that in everything, whether by attempt to vilify or in a true testimony, Christ is being proclaimed!

19. For I know that I will go on to victory because of your prayers and the assistance of the spirit of the holy one. (*Jesus Christ*) (Romans 8:9; John 14:18)

20. I anticipate and hope that I shall be disgraced in nothing, and in bluntness, as always, through my victory (*not having been put to death),* the power of Christ shall be seen by many;

21. Because for me, to live is for Christ, but to die is gain!

22. That if I remain alive, this is the fruit of my labors, because I am not interested in gain unto myself.

23. I am torn between the two, desiring to depart and be with Christ which is much better for me,

24. or to remain alive which is much more beneficial for you.

25. But know this for certain, that I know that I shall not die at this time, but I will continue with you unto your perfection and joy, while your faithfulness is being tested.

26. Your happiness shall be established in Jesus Christ through me while I am with you.

27. Keep your conduct only unto that which is suitable unto Christ, so that whether I come to see you, or if I remain away, that I shall hear only good things about you and that you are standing in one accord, with one heart, striving together in the true doctrine of the gospel.

28. Do not be afraid of anything that comes against you, because that is evidence unto them that they have destroyed you; But know that your rescue is of God.

29. Such difficulties are necessary for the sake of Christ, not only that you trust in him, but also that you suffer for his sake, (Acts 14:22; 1 Thessalonians 3:4; John 16:33; 2 Corinthians 7:4)

30. This is the same struggle that you have seen me go through and has now been made known to you.

Philippines 2

1. If there is any comfort in Christ, if there is encouragement in love (*affection*), if you have a partnership with the spirit of Christ (Ephesians 2:8) and if you have any sympathy and compassion;

2. Bring joy unto me if you are likeminded, if you have the same heart, if you are of the same desire and if you are all working together;

3. Do not do so unto rivalries nor self-promotion, but unto humility, always caring for each other more than for your own self.

4. Do not look to what you might need, but always look unto the needs of each other.

5. For this is the way that you must think, as this is the way of Christ, who exists as a form of God.

6. He did not think it to be theft to be equal with God; (John 10:30; John 1:1-4)

7. Yet he emptied himself to take the form of a servant and became in the likeness of a man and in body he was recognized as a man.

8. He humbled himself, being obedient until he was killed upon the cross. (1 John 1:5)

9. Because of this, God raised him up (*from the dead*) and gave him a name above every name;

10. So that in the name of Jesus, every knee shall bow in the heavens, on the earth and under the earth.

11. Every tongue shall confess that the master is Jesus Christ, unto the honor of our Father God.

12. My beloved, just as you have continued to obey, not only in my presence but even more so in my absence; Work out (*accomplish*) your own salvation with fear and trembling. (Psalms 2:11; Proverbs 1:7; Proverbs 8:13; Proverbs 16:6; Ephesians 5:21)

13. If God is working in you, it is for you to serve him and to accomplish his will.

14. Do all things without complaining nor argument,

15. so that you may be blameless and innocent, the children of God, without a fault, while living among people that are corrupt and perverted. You must shine among the people of this world as the stars in the sky. (Daniel 12:3)

16. Hold up the true message of eternal life, so that I might be overjoyed on the day of judgment, that I did not work for nothing nor take this course worthlessly.

17. But if it is necessary that I be killed because of my work and service so to bring you through unto faithfulness, then I shall be joyous and I shall celebrate with you,

18. and you shall also be joyous and shall celebrate with me.

19. But I have confidence in the Lord Jesus, that I will soon be sending Timothy to you to uplift your spirit and that I may be able to know how you are.

20. I have no one else available other than him who is like-minded and will genuinely care for you.

21. Most men seek for gain unto themselves and not for the things of Jesus Christ.

22. But you already know that he is proven; And like a child unto his father, he has served with me to bring the gospel.

23. I expect to send him as soon as these things concerning me have been finished;

24. I have been convinced by the Lord that I myself shall also come.

25. I think that it is necessary for our brother and co-worker, Epaphroditus, my fellow servant and assistant to also come to you;

26. He has been missing you and was troubled because you had heard that he was very sick.

27. He sure was sick and was near death, but God had mercy upon him; Not only him, myself also, so that I did not receive sadness upon sadness.

28. Therefore I have chosen to send him to you, that you can see him again and you may be abundantly joyful and less concerned.

29. Therefore, receive him as unto the Lord with much joy and hold him as honorable.

30. Through the work of Christ, as close to death as he was, it brought forth his spirit and he shall fill you up on my behalf, whatever you are lacking.

Philippines 3

1. My brethren, for that which remains, be cheerful in the Lord. For these things that I write unto you are not meant to be frustrating, but are for your security. (*OSAS is a false doctrine*)

2. Beware of the dogs (*those looking only to feed unto themselves*), beware of those who do wickedness and beware of the cut off ones (*Jews who reject Christ*);

3. Because we are the circumcision (*of the heart* - Colossians 2:11; Romans 2:28; Romans 4:10), who live by the spirit of God and are glorified by Jesus Christ. Do not have confidence in the physical things of this world;

4. I do trust in my abilities and if anyone else thinks that they can rely on themselves, I would have more reason than they!

5. I was circumcised on the eighth day, from the offspring of Israel and of the tribe of Benjamin, the highest of the Hebrews; According to the Mosaic law, a Pharisee;

6. Whereas I had so much zeal that I persecuted the true people of God; According to the righteousness of the Jewish law, I lived perfectly blameless. (verse 18-19)

7. But of all of these things that were a gain to me, I now consider them worthless (a *detriment*) because of Christ Jesus.

8. No, but let me correct myself, I count all things to be worthless compared to the supremacy of the knowledge of the Lord Jesus Christ, my master. For his sake I have suffered the loss of all things and consider them to be garbage, so that I could gain Christ;
(*he threw all he knew away to become established in Christ*)

9. That I might be found with him, not possessing my own righteousness through the Mosaic law, but through my proven faithfulness unto Jesus Christ. I have established the righteousness according to God and according to truth. (*by how I live* - John 3:21; John 4:24)

10. I know him and his power of rebirth from the dead (Romans 6:1-6), and I have shared in his sufferings.

11. I have been conformed into his image through my death with him (Acts 2:38; Romans 6:1-23) in hope that I might attain an eternal resurrection from death. (Acts 9:18)

12. Not that I have already received (*eternal life*), nor that I have already completed (*the race*); But I press onward, so that I might grasp a hold of that which is offered by Jesus Christ. (Romans 10:6-8)

13. Brothers, I do not count myself to have already attained (*eternal salvation*) with certainty, but I have certainly abandoned those things that are in the past and I stretch forward unto the things that are in the future, focusing on the goal (*eternal life*).

14. I press on toward the reward which is only through the invitation of our God through Jesus Christ.

15. Unto all that think of themselves as perfect, consider this: Do not do anything different, but it is God that shall decide (*reveal those that are approved* - Revelation 1:11; Revelation 20:12-15).

16. May we live with this certainty in mind, no matter what we have come to anticipate.

17. Brothers, become imitators of me and regard those who live in such a way; You have us as a model.

18. For there are many that live as enemies of the cross of Christ, of whom I have told you many times before and I tell you again, that I have great sadness for them;

19. Because for them, their end is damnation. They serve and honor themselves, disgracing themselves before God. They only concern themselves in the things of this temporary world.

20. But for us, our home is in the heavens from where our saviour, the Lord Jesus Christ shall be revealed;

21. He will transform our feeble bodies into the likeness of his glorified body; According to his working plan, he will put everything under his authority. (1 Corinthians 15:52; 1 Thessalonians 4:13-18)

Philippines 4

1. As my beloved brothers, I ask that you persevere as unto the Lord, to be my joy and my crown.

2. I ask that Euodia and Syntyche be of the same mind in the Lord.

3. I also ask of you as fellow co-workers, that you help all of those, who concerning the gospel worked with me and also with Klemes, and all of my fellow workers whose names are written in the book of life.

4. Always be cheerful in our Lord. I will say it again, be cheerful!

5. Your politeness shall be made known unto all people. The master is coming soon.

6. Do not worry about anything, but in everything continue to pray and approach God with humility and thankfulness, then whatever your requests are, make them known unto God.

7. The peace of God that surpasses all of our comprehension will guard your hearts and minds unto the return of Jesus Christ.

8. For everything else my brethren, that which is true, that which is honorable, that which is just, that which is pure, that which is acceptable and whatever has good reputation, if it is virtuous and commendable, meditate on these things.

9. Of these, you have learned, received, heard and have seen them in me, so continue in them and our God shall be at peace with you.

10. Have much joyfulness in the Lord, now that you are flourishing greatly, of which you also thought but were unable to verify until now (*lacking opportunity*).

11. Though it is not necessary that I tell you, I have come to understand that we should be satisfied with whatever we have.

12. Learn how to remain humble; Learn how to handle having an abundance. We must know how to go hungry and also to eat well, both to have and to be lacking.

13. I can prevail in anything, because Christ is who strengthens (*assists*) me.

(Mark 10:27; 1 Corinthians 10:13)

14. You explained everything well in sharing all of your difficulties with us.

15. All of you in Philippi should know this; When I began teaching the gospel, I went out from Macedonia, and not one gathering communicated with me in the giving and receiving of messages except for you.

16. Even when I was in Thessalonica, both the first and the second time, you sent correspondence, because you had need of me.

17. Not that I seek this from you, but I seek to have word from you that your fruit is multiplying.

18. I have all that I need and I have been filled with excess, having received from Epaphroditus that which you have given, of which is a pleasant smell and a sacrifice that is well pleasing unto our God.

19. Our God shall also fill your needs according to the wealth and glory of Jesus Christ.

20. Unto our God and Father be the honor, forever and ever.

21. Say hello unto every saint that is in Christ Jesus. Greet my brethren that are there with you.

22. Say hello unto all of the saints; Do not forget those living in the home of Caesar.

23. May the grace of the Lord Jesus Christ be with you all.

Colossians

Chapter 1

1. Paul, an Apostle of Jesus Christ through the will of God, and Timothy our brother,

2. we write unto the saints and faithful brothers in Colosse that are in Christ; May the gift and peace of our Father God and the Lord Jesus Christ be abundant in you.

3. We give thanks unto our God, the Father of our Lord Jesus, always praying for you.

4. We have heard of your dedication unto our Lord and the affection that you have for all of the saints. (Matthew 22:37; Luke 10:27; Deuteronomy 6:5; Leviticus 19:18)

5. Because of this, there is hope in you to attain that which is awaiting you in the heavens, which you already know is the message of the gospel.

6. It shall appear unto you and also unto all of those in the world that are fruit bearing in the same way that it has been established in you since the day that you first heard and came to fully know the gift of God in truth.

7. You learned this from Epaphras our beloved fellow servant, who is a faithful minister of Christ unto you.

8. He has expressed unto us concerning your spiritual affection.

9. Because of this, since the day that we came to know this, we always remember you in our prayers. We ask that you might be filled with the knowledge of his will, with complete wisdom and spiritual understanding,

10. and for you to live worthy unto the Lord and pleasing unto him unto only good deeds; To be fruit bearing and grow into the full knowledge of our God.

11. We pray that you shall be empowered with the complete ability, according to his dominion and honor and that you patiently continue with fortitude and joy;

12. We give thanks unto our Father who has made us qualified to share in the inheritance of the saints, of which has now been brought to light.

13. He delivered us out of the jurisdiction of darkness and transformed us into the realm of his son, unto his love. (Acts 26:18; John 3:18-20; 1 John 1:5)

14. In him, we shall be able to find complete deliverance through his blood for the forgiveness of our transgressions (*committed in ignorance*).

15. He is the representation of our invisible God, the first to be brought forth (*redeemed*) in all the world.

16. He created everything, all that is in the heavens and all things on the earth, both that which is visible and that which is invisible, including his throne and his dominion, including all things from the past and all that is presently existing; All things are through him and he created them for himself. (John 1:3)

17. He is the headmaster of all things and everything works together according to his plan. (John 1:1)

18. He is the head of the body, which is the elect people of God; He is the first of the resurrection of the dead, and in everything he is preeminent. (Revelation 1:11)

19. It pleased God that the fulfillment of all things be with him *(Jesus Christ),*

20. that he (*the Father*) might reconcile all things through Christ unto himself; To make peace through his blood on the cross, whether things on earth or things in the heavens.

21. And you, who in the past were distant and hostile in your mind because of the evil deeds that you did, you now have reconciled with him (Isaiah 27:5; 2 Peter 3:14; Luke 14:32; Romans 2:10; Romans 6:17)

22. through the death of his physical body. (Romans 6:1-7) So now present yourselves pure and without blemish, to be blameless in his sight. (2 Peter 3:14; 1 John 3:3-10; Matthew 5:8; Romans 5:1; 2 Cor 12:21)

23. If you continue in the true doctrine, you will be building a strong foundation, so be immovable, not moving away from the gospel that you have heard that has been announced throughout all of the world (*Roman empire*), of which I Paul am a minister. (Matthew 24:14)

24. Be appreciative of the hardships that I have suffered on your behalf and strive to be completed in the things that you have not yet perfected; The persecutions that I have suffered on my body are on behalf of the body of Christ, these are the faithful ones of God.

25. I am a minister concerning the stewardship that has been given unto me, of which is to make complete your knowledge concerning the instructions of God.

26. The mystery that has been hidden from all generations until this time is now revealed unto his saints.

27. God now desires to make this mystery known unto all nations concerning his wealth and honor, of

which is Christ in us. (1 John 4:2) He is our hope and glory;

28. We announce, we warn and we teach every man of this wisdom of which we hope might bring every man to come to be mature in Christ Jesus.

29. This is why I work and struggle according to his plan and he is working powerfully through me.

Colossians 2

1. I want you to know the great struggles that I have suffered for you and also those in Laodicea. All that have never seen my face, be comforted in your hearts, because we are joined together by our love.

2. So hold all of this wealth with full assurance, unto the full knowledge of the mystery of God our Father and the Lord Jesus Christ;

3. In him all wealth, wisdom and knowledge is established.

4. This I tell you, let no one deceive you with persuasive words.

5. Though I am absent physically, I am with you in spirit and I am overjoyed at being able to see your orderly way and your steadfastness through the testing of your faithfulness unto Jesus Christ.

6. Therefore, in the way that you were taught concerning the Lord Jesus, continue to live in the same way.

7. Now that your roots are growing and you are gaining maturity in Christ and are being confirmed through your faithfulness in the true doctrine in the same way that you were taught, continue solidly therein with thankfulness.

8. Be careful so that no one shall steal what you have gained through their philosophy and self-conceited deceptions according to the doctrines *(traditions)* of men, because they are according to the principals of this world and are not the way of Christ. (Jude 1:4)

9. Because in his *(Christ's)* physical body, he lived the fulfillment of divinity

10. and you have been filled by him; He is the head of all power and authority; (Revelation 1:11; Romans 13:1)

11. You were circumcised by him with the circumcision that is not done by the hands of men and you have turned away from the sins of the flesh *(lusts for that which is evil)*, by the circumcision of Christ.

12. You were buried with him through baptism (Romans 6:1-23; Acts 2:38), and with him you were also raised from the dead through your conviction *(faithfulness)*, of which is according to the plan of God. (John 16:33; Acts 14:22; 1 Thessalonians 3:4)

13. And you, who were *(spiritually)* dead because of your trespasses against God, because you could *(at that time)* not stop committing the lustful sins, he has now made you alive with him by bringing assistance unto your lifeless body! (G-3844 + G-4430 - Romans 3:25; 1 Peter 1:9)

14. He has obliterated those things that were written in the ordinances *(of the Mosaic law)* of which were set against us, and he has taken them out of the way, nailing them to the cross;

15. He has stripped away all authority from all rulers and he put them to an open shame and triumphed over them. (Romans 13)

16. Therefore, do not allow anyone to judge you concerning what you eat, or what you drink, or concerning holidays, or concerning new moons or sabbaths. (Luke 10:8; Romans 14:2-3)

17. For these are only shadows of that which was to come, but only those that are firmly sound in truth are in Christ. *(true doctrine matters - Galatians 1:8-9; 2 John 1:9)*

18. Do not allow anyone to steal away your eternal salvation, but choose to submit yourself to and observe *(learn from)* the messengers *(apostles and prophets)* concerning everything that you have not experienced nor come to understand. Turn away from your pride.

19. Does not the head *(Christ)* empower the whole body? Through the joints and ligaments *(true holy men of God)* they continue to keep you nourished and bound together, to increase your growth unto God.

20. If you have died with Christ (Romans 6:4) from the arrangements of this world, why would you live according to the statutes of this world?

21. Touch not, taste not, associate not; These are all things that are worthless and temporary

22. and are according to the commandments and doctrines of men. (Matthew 15:9; Mark 7:7; Hebrews 13:9)

23. In such words there is wisdom concerning the appearances of holiness, submission and self-denial; However, you should not value the cares of this world. *(outward appearances before men.)*

Colossians 3

1. If you have been raised with Christ (Romans 6:4-5), then seek the things above where Christ is, at the right hand of the Father.

2. Set your mind upon the things that are above, not upon the things of the earth;

3. Because you died, and your life was given to be the possession of Christ unto God. (Romans 6:16, 22)

4. When Christ is revealed through your life, then you shall also appear with him in his glory. (Hebrews 10:36)

5. Therefore, make your body dead unto fornication, impurity, lustful passions, evil lust and all covetousness, which is idolatry; (Romans 6:16; John 3:19; 1 John 3:3-10)

6. Such things shall bring the wrath of God down upon all who disobey him;

7. In the past, you lived in such ways, (Romans 6:17)

8. but now you must turn away from all of those things: Wrath, passionate anger and hatred, remove them from out of your mouth as well as the vilification of others and all perverse talk.

9. Do not lie unto anyone; Completely commit yourself to put off the old man and the things that you previously did,

10. and put on the new man and be renovated according to the complete knowledge of the image of Christ, the one who created you, where there is neither Jew nor gentile,

11. circumcision nor uncircumcision, foreigner nor savage, freeman nor slave; Christ is now offered unto all. (Galatians 3:27-29; Romans 3:22; Romans 10:12; Acts 15:19)

12. Therefore, as the elect of God, live a life of holiness and be tenderhearted; Be full of mercy and kindness, humility and meekness;

13. If anyone has a complaint against someone, have patience and forgiveness with one another; Just as Christ has forgiven you, also do the same.

14. Above all of these, have affection for one another, of which brings perfection. (Matthew 22:37; Mark 12:30; Luke 10:27)

15. May the peace of God reign in your hearts, because you have been called to be a healthy body. Be thankful.

16. May the instructions of God live within you abundantly and in complete wisdom, teach and encourage each other. Keep psalms, hymns and spiritual odes with graceful singing in your hearts unto the Lord.

17. In everything that you do, whether speaking or working, do everything in the name of the Lord Jesus and give thanks unto God our Father through him.

18. Wives, be submissive unto your own husbands, because this is the way that God has instructed.

19. Husbands, love your wives and do not be made bitter against them.

20. Children, obey your (*godly*) parents in all of these things, because it is pleasing unto the Lord.

21. Fathers, do not provoke anger in your children, so that they do not lose their spirit. (*to not become discouraged and lose their purpose*)

22. Servants, obey your masters in all that is right, not only to look good before them, but also with a good heart, while keeping the fear of God.

23. Do all that you do with all of your heart and work with zeal to please the Lord and not to please men,

24. knowing that it is from the Lord you shall receive the reward of inheritance; Because it is he, Christ Jesus whom you serve.

25. If you do what is wrong you shall receive accordingly, because God does not favor one more than another. (Verse 11; Ephesians 6:9; Romans 2:11)

Colossians 4

1. Masters, give that which is due and right unto those that serve you, knowing that you also have one that you serve who is above, he that is the master of us all.

2. Persevere continually in prayer and always look to that which you can be thankful for.

3. Pray also for us, so that God may open the door, that I might be able to speak well in public, the message of the mystery of Christ, for which I have also been praying for,

4. so that I could make it known unto others, as it ought to be spoken.

5. Walk in wisdom towards those on the outside, but do not waste time.

6. May your speech always be charitable, season it with salt and know what is the best way to give an answer to each one.

7. How I am shall be made known unto you by Tychicus, our beloved brother, faithful minister and fellow servant unto the Lord,

8. of whom I sent to you for this reason; That he might know how you are and that he might offer comfort unto your hearts.

9. I also sent Onesimus, our faithful and beloved brother who is of your family. They will make everything here to be known to you as well.

10. Aristarchus, my fellow servant, and Marcus, the cousin of Barnabas, from whom you have received the instructions of God; If they come to you, receive them.

11. Also Jesus, nicknamed Justus who is a Jewish convert; These are the only fellow workers for the kingdom of God that have (*recently*) been a comfort to me.

12. Epaphras says hello, as he is also from your family and a servant of Christ. He is always striving for you in prayer, so that you might be made fully mature and stand perfectly in the will of God.

13. I testify that he has zeal for the good of you as well as those in Laodicea and Hierapolis.

14. Lucas the beloved physician also says hello, and also Demas.

15. Say hello unto the brethren in Laodicea, and also unto Nymphas and his whole household gathering.

16. When you have read this letter in your gathering, make sure that the Laodicean gathering also reads it.

17. Tell Archippas to look at the ministry that you have built up in the Lord.

18. I offer this greeting with my own hand. Always keep my chains (*imprisonment*) in your thoughts. May the grace of God be with you.

1 Thessalonians

Chapter 1

1. Paul, Silvanus and Timothy, we write unto the gathering in Thessalonica who are in accordance to our Father God and our Lord Jesus Christ; May the grace and peace of God our Father and our Lord Jesus Christ be upon you.

2. We continually give thanks unto God concerning you, always speaking of you in our prayers.

3. Always remember that your faithfulness unto God is being tested, so continue your hard work, and through affection, patiently continue in the hope of our Lord Jesus Christ, knowing that you are always in the eyes of God.

4. Know this my beloved brethren, you are truly loved by God, the one who has called you.

5. The gospel that we have received did not come to you in word only, but also in the power of the holy spirit, with much evidence. You know what type of men we were while we were there assisting you. (Acts 1:8; Luke 24:49; 2 Peter 1:16; 2 Timothy 3:5)

6. You have become imitators of us and of the master, in that you welcomed the correction while enduring much affliction, yet you remained cheerful according to the holy character (*qualities*).

7. Now you are examples unto all that are in Macedonia and Achaia.

8. The instructions of the Lord have been made known not only in Macedonia and Achaia, but also in many other places in which your conviction unto God has also been made known. There is no need that we say anything to anyone concerning you, for you yourselves have made it known

9. through the kind of reception they received of you. They have turned unto God from their past idolatry, to now serve the living God in truth.

10. They are now awaiting the Son of God coming in the heavens, Jesus, of whom was raised from the dead, the one who shall deliver us from the coming wrath of God. (Matthew 24:29-31)

1 Thessalonians 2

1. My brethren, you know that our coming unto you was not in vain (*to no effect*);

2. As you already know, even though we were insulted and suffered much when we were in Philippi, we were bold in speaking the gospel of our God unto you, though it was with many challenges and much difficulty.

3. Because the doctrine that we bring does not stray from truth, nor is it unclean, nor is it deceitful;

4. We have truly been proven by God. We are entrusted with the gospel and so we speak it, not to please other people, but to please God who knows our hearts.

5. We have at no time used flattering words, as you well know, nor have we at any time looked for gain unto ourselves. God is our witness!

6. We have not looked for the honor of men, not from you nor of any others;

7. But surely, we placed great burdens upon ourselves while we were with you, as a nurse cherishing her own children;

8. So while we were caring for you, we not only taught unto you the gospel, but we also gave of ourselves, because we have come to love you.

9. My brethren, you surely remember all of the work and the efforts; Night and day we worked so not to put a burden upon any of you and we spoke unto you the gospel of God.

10. Both you and God are our witnesses of how holy, righteous and blameless we lived while with all of you who have chosen to believe.

11. As you well know, we corrected, comforted and challenged each of you, as a father does unto his own children, so that you would live appropriately unto God.

12. He has now called you unto his kingdom and honor.

13. This is the reason that we give thanks for you unto God continually, because you have received the instructions that you have been given by us and that you did not receive them as only the words of men, but as they truly are, the instructions that are given to all of us by God, of which now also are working in all of you that have chosen to believe.

14. Because you have become imitators of and now brothers with those in Judea that are in Christ Jesus, and you now also suffer similar things by your own fellow countrymen as they have of the Jews

15. who killed both their own prophets and also the Lord Jesus, and have also been persecuting us; They have no interest in pleasing God and they are antagonistic towards all of mankind.

16. They tried to prevent us from speaking unto the gentiles so that they might be eternally spared as well. They continue to pile up sin upon sin unto themselves, awaiting the final day (*judgment day*), when the wrath of God shall be poured out upon them. (2 Thess 1:8; Hebrews 10:30; Romans 12:19; Deut 32:35)

17. My brethren, we have been taken away from you for a short time, though we are with you in our hearts. Know that we are very eager, wanting to come to you so we can see your faces.

18. This is why, I Paul have tried on two occasions to come to you, but both times Satan prevented me.

19. For what other reason would we have hope and joy and a crown of honor to be given unto us, if you are not to be presented worthy before the Lord Jesus Christ at his return?

20. Surely it is you who are our honor and our joy.

1 Thessalonians 3

1. When I could no longer continue, we thought that it was a good thing that I stay in Athens alone.

2. That is why I sent our brother Timothy, a teacher of God and co-worker of ours in the gospel of Jesus Christ, to strengthen you and encourage you concerning the testing of your faithfulness,

3. so that none of you might fall by those afflictions, as you know that we are appointed unto them. (Acts 14:22; Matthew 10:24; 13:21; John 16:33; Romans 5:3; 2 Corinthians 1:4, 7:4; Revelation 1:9)

4. For even when we were with you, we told you that you shall suffer much affliction, just as it began to happen unto you. (Matthew 5:11; John 16:33; Acts 14:22; Psalms 34:19; Psalms 11:2; Isaiah 59:15; Revelation 1:9)

5. This is the reason that when I was no longer able to travel, I sent him to know of your faithfulness, hoping that you did not fall while you were being tested, of which all of our work would have been in vain. (Hebrews 6:4-6; 10:26-39)

6. But now, Timothy has returned unto me and told me the good news of your faithfulness and your love, and that you have a good memory of what we taught unto you and that you strongly want to see us, the same as we also want to see you;

7. My brothers, in all of this, we have been greatly comforted and have overcome our concerns, that through all of your afflictions, you have been found to be faithful.

8. Truly you are spiritually alive if you continue to stand firm in the Lord.

9. What thanks can we return unto God concerning the joy that we now receive from you in the presence of our God?

10. We have continued praying both night and day to be able to again see your faces and to complete all of the things that may still be lacking in you.

11. May God our Father and the Lord Jesus Christ make a way for us to come to you.

12. May the Lord bring you to be greatly abundant and have extreme affection toward one another, and even for all people, even as we also have shown unto you, so that you will firmly build up your hearts.

13. Be sure to remain blameless and completely holy before our Father God, until the return of the Lord Jesus Christ, so you can be among all of his saints. (2 Peter 3:14; Ephesians 4:24-27; 2 Corinthians 7:1; James 1:12; 1 Corinthians 10:12-13; 1 John 3:3)

1 Thessalonians 4

1. For all else my brethren, we ask and invite you who are in the Lord Jesus, that just as you have been instructed by us, to live in a way that pleases God; Do so ever increasingly.

2. You know the commands that we gave unto you of the Lord Jesus;

3. They are according to the will of God and they are the way that you shall become sanctified; You must abstain from fornication.

4. Each one of you must live your life in purity and honor,

5. not in the passions of lust, as those who do not know Christ.

6. Do not begin to be covetous in anything against a brother, because the avenger concerning all things is the Lord; Just as we have told you in past times and you have seen in us.

7. For we are not called by God to continue in wickedness, but to be completely pure. (1 John 1:6; 3:3)

8. Therefore, those who violate these things despise God and his spirit, of which he has given to us. (Numbers 15:30-31; Matthew 12:30-33; 1 John 5:16-17)

9. But concerning brotherly affection, there is no need to write unto you, for you yourselves are taught by God to love one another. (Jeremiah 31:34)

10. Surely you show your affection unto all of the brethren in Macedonia and in you we expect this to be growing in abundance.

11. Be diligent to stay out of trouble and mind your own business. Continue to assist with your own hands in the necessary work that is needed to be done, the same as we did when we were there with you.

12. Live in a good way towards those that do not know God and there is nothing more that you have need of.

13. But I desire that you not be ignorant my brothers concerning those that have died in Christ. Do not be sorrowful as you would be for those that have no hope. (John 3:16-17)

14. Because if we believe that Jesus died and then was raised, those that have died in Christ will come with him when he returns. (Zechariah 14:5)

15. This we tell you, just as God has spoken it to us, that those of us that remain alive at the time of the return of the Lord, they shall surely not be received by him before those that have died in Christ.

16. Because the Lord himself, at the announcement given by the archangel and the trumpet call of God, he will come down from the sky, and those that have died in Christ shall arise together first; (1 Corinthians 15:52; Hebrews 12:19; Revelation 10:7; Zechariah 1:16)

17. Then we that remain alive shall be taken up with our fellow brethren into the clouds to meet the Lord in the air, and we will be with our Lord forever. (Matthew 24:30; 26:64; Mark 13:26; Revelation 1:7)

18. So now comfort each other with these words. (Verse 13)

1 Thessalonians 5

1. But concerning how long until that time and concerning exactly when this will happen, my brethren you have no need for me to write unto you;

2. Because you already know that the day of the Lord shall come as a thief would come in the night; *(unannounced)* (verse 4; 2 Peter 3:10)

3. When they say that there is peace on earth and safety for all, that is when their unexpected punishment shall come upon them, like the pains come unto a woman about to give birth, with no way to escape.

4. But you my brothers are not unaware, that that day might overtake you as a thief! (Matthew 24:33; John 16:13)

5. You are the sons of Light and sons of the day. (John 3:19; 12:36; Isaiah 50:10; 1 John 2:9) You are not of the night nor of darkness. (1 John 1:5-6)

6. So make sure that you do not grow tired and lazy as most others do, but make sure to pay attention and be sure that you remain sober. (aware)

7. Because those that sleep, do so in the darkness; Those that are drunken, do so in the darkness.

8. But we are of the Light and of the day, so let us be sober, having put on the breastplate (*armor for the chest*) of having been tested and found to be faithful and having affectionate benevolence *(love)* for others; The anticipation of eternal salvation shall be a helmet unto you.

9. Because God has not appointed us (*the faithful*) to receive of his wrath (Revelation 8:1-10:6), but unto the preservation and safety given by our master, Jesus Christ. (Revelation 7:13-14)

10. He was put to death for our gain; So whether we (*the faithful*) are alive and watching, or if we will have died, either way, we shall be together with him.

11. So continue to encourage and help build up one another as you already do.

12. Additionally, we ask of you brethren, that you be sure to acknowledge those that work among you and also the apostles in Christ that are teaching and correcting you. (Romans 13:1-5)

13. Respect and appreciate them exceedingly with strong affection because of the work that they do. Be peaceful among yourselves.

14. We call unto you our brothers, to warn those that are insubordinate, encourage those that want to give up, support those who are weak and have great patience with all people.

15. See that no one returns evil for evil unto anyone. Always pursue that which is good towards one another and unto everyone.

16. Always be cheerful.

17. Pray continually.

18. Be thankful for everything, for this is the will of God.

19. If Jesus Christ is in you, do not take action against the spirit of God;

(blasphemy of the holy spirit - Numbers 15:28-31; Matthew 12:30-33; 1 John 5:16-17)

20. Do not reject prophecy,

21. but test everything and hold tightly unto that which is proven to be valuable.

22. Abstain from every type of wickedness

23. and God will make peace with you, and you will be completely clean. Your whole spirit, soul and body must be preserved to be blameless at the return of our master, Jesus Christ.

24. He that is calling you is trustworthy and he will do as he promises.

25. Keep us in your prayers, my brothers.

26. Greet all of the other brethren with an innocently pure kiss.

27. I order you, by your oath unto the Lord (*covenant*) to read this letter to all of the mature and blameless brethren.

28. May the grace of our master Jesus Christ be with you.

Verse 27 speaks of your oath unto the Lord. (Greek word 3726)
This is speaking about coming into covenant with God.
A covenant is a contract agreement where both parties involved have certain responsibilities
and also certain benefits, but only if the agreement is not broken by either party.
God can not break his word. Therefore only we, as individuals have the ability
through our own freewill to honor him by faithfulness and obedience,
or break our covenant with God if we were to choose to defy him.
This is what happened with ancient Israel and Judah!
After truly being converted, we must remain completely faithful to God
to the best of our understanding if we want to receive the inheritance of eternal life.
Yes, it is possible, because you can do all things through Christ who strengthens you.
This is only possible by the power of God active and alive in you;
But it takes great effort and sacrifice!

If you have chosen to commit sin after you were converted,
it is most likely that you were not properly converted
and were never told of the terms of the covenant (contract),
therefore you still have hope and can still be converted and
come to God for real! I pray that you will.

2 Thessalonians

Chapter 1

1. Paul, Silvanus and Timothy, write unto the gathering in Thessalonica who are in the Father God and Lord Jesus Christ;

2. May the grace and peace of God our Father and the Lord Jesus Christ be with you.

3. We always give thanks unto God concerning you our brethren, because it is right, because your dedication has been greatly multiplied, and because of the abundance of affection that you all have for one another;

4. We even speak of you as an example unto the other gatherings of God, speaking about all of the affliction and persecutions that you have faithfully endured,

5. which is the indication that you shall be judged to be righteous by God, so to be counted worthy to enter into the kingdom of God. This is the reason that you have suffered!

6. It is a good thing with God to repay those that have been persecuting you, to bring unto them their own punishment,

7. and those of you who have been persecuted, as we surely have, know that when the Lord Jesus returns with his angels and his mighty power,

8. in a flaming fire he shall deliver his full vengeance upon those that do not know him, all who did not obey the gospel of our master Jesus Christ. (1 Peter 4:17; Romans 10:16; Isaiah 66:15-17; Hebrews 10:30)

9. They will pay the penalty of eternal destruction, away from the presence of the Lord and away from his honor and strength.

10. When he comes, he will be honored by his saints and be revered by all of those that have been found to be faithful unto him, because of the testimony that both us and you shall give on that day.

11. We also pray for these things concerning you, that you may be judged worthy of the calling of God that we have brought unto you and that you might be perfected unto every kindness and good deed while you succeed through the testing of your faithfulness.

12. So in this, the name of the Lord Jesus might be glorified in you and you in him, through the grace of our God, the Lord Jesus Christ.

2 Thessalonians 2

1. And brothers, we must comfort you concerning the coming of our Lord Jesus Christ and our gathering together unto him.

2. Do not easily be shaken or disturbed in your thoughts or in your spirit, nor by words, nor by letter, thinking that the day of the Lord has already come. (*As some have taught*)
(2 Timothy 2:18; Matthew 24:29-31; Matthew 27:52-53; Daniel 12:2; 1 Thessalonians 4:16-17)

3. Do not allow anyone to deceive you, because that day shall not come until after there is a great apostasy and mankind is revealed to be very sinful, the damnable children of the adversary (*Satan*).

4. They shall exalt themselves above all who remain faithful unto the instructions of God, making themselves the object of their own worship, so to take residency in the temple of God, showing themselves as though they are gods. (1 Corinthians 6:19; 1 Corinthians 3:16-17; 2 Corinthians 6:16; Revelation 11:1)

5. Do you not remember that I told you these things when I was with you?

6. And now this is what holds him back (*Jesus Christ from returning*), you now know that they will be exposed in their appointed time. (*they are now being exposed and he will return very soon*)

7. Truly the silent ways of wickedness are already active, but that which is currently holding him (*Christ*) back, will do so, until from out of themselves their wickedness shall become much more established and grow. (Romans 1:19 - 2:10)

8. Then will be the revealing of those who are precious unto God; Yet the wicked ones will come, (Daniel 12:10; Revelation 13:15-17) of whom the Lord will destroy with his mouth (*as he speaks*) and they will be made useless by the manifestation of his coming. (2 Corinthians 11:15)

9. They are those who continue to be close to that which is according to the operations of Satan. Deceived by his power and signs (Revelation 13:2-4 & 13) and false omens (*false fulfillment of prophecy*)

10. And because of much deception (Revelation 13:14; Matthew 24:24) that will lead to unrighteousness committed by those that shall be lost, they shall be completely destroyed, because they had no interest in receiving the truth, that they might be preserved. (Isaiah 56:10-11; Ezekiel 22:28)

11. And for this reason, God shall allow them a strong delusion, so that they believe a lie; (Genesis 3:4; 2 Peter 2:2; Acts 20:29-30; Matthew 24:24, 11; Galatians 2:4-5; Jude 1:4; Isaiah 66:3-4)

12. So they all might be damned, all who did not believe the truth, but had pleasure living unrighteously.

13. But we are under obligation to always be thankful unto our God for you our brethren who are loved by the master, because you continue to choose God's way since the beginning of your deliverance, by purity through the spirit of God and true doctrine.

14. Of this, he has called you through the gospel that we preach, to live accordingly until you receive the honor from our Lord Jesus Christ.

15. Therefore my brethren, persevere and hold on to the precepts that you have been taught, both by the spoken word and by the letters that we have sent.

16. Our Lord Jesus Christ and our Father God loves us and offers unto us an everlasting comfort and a good expectation through his compassion.

17. May he comfort your hearts as your faithfulness is proven through every good word and good deed that you do.

2 Thessalonians 3

1. Furthermore my brethren, pray for us, that the instructions of the Lord may continue to be brought unto everyone and that they may be made honorable, just as you.

2. Also pray that we not be harmed by perverse or malicious men, because our credence is not received by all men.

3. The Lord is faithful and he will make you completely perfect and strong, and he will guard you from evil.

4. We have confidence that the Lord will bring you unto maturity, as the things that we have surely taught unto you, you already do and will continue to do.

5. May the Lord guide your hearts unto the love of God and into the consistent endurance that is in Jesus Christ.

6. We instruct you brothers, in the name of our Lord Jesus Christ, withdraw yourselves from every brother that is insubordinate to this message, those who live outside of the instructions that you have received from us. (2 John 1:10)

7. For you already know that it is right to do as we have taught and as we live, as we were not disorderly while among you.

8. We did not even take food from anyone without proper compensation, but we worked until we were exhausted; Both night and day we worked so not to bring any burden upon any of you;

9. Not that we do not have authority to do so, but we offer ourselves as an example so that you might imitate us.

10. Even while we were with you, we taught this to you, that if anyone does not work, he should not eat.

11. Though we have surely heard that there are some among you who do not do anything but walk around meddling in other people's affairs. They accomplish nothing but waste their time and cause trouble.

12. For them, we instruct you to bring stern correction unto them through (*the guidance of*) the Lord Jesus Christ.

13. And for you our brothers, do not lose heart in doing good unto others.

14. If anyone does not obey the words that I have written through this letter, mark him and do not associate with him, so that he might be ashamed. (verse 6; 2 John 1:10)

15. Do not hold him as an enemy, but warn him as a brother.

16. The Lord shall give you guidance to handle this properly in every instance. May the Lord be with you.

17. By my own hand, I Paul greet you, which is a symbol of every letter that I write.

18. May the grace of our Lord Jesus Christ remain with you always.

1 Timothy

Chapter 1

1. Paul, an Apostle of Jesus Christ, according to the authority of God and our savior who is our hope.
2. Unto Timothy, a genuine child in the true doctrine; Grace, mercy and peace from our Father God and Jesus Christ our master.
3. When I went to Macedonia, I had asked you to remain in Ephesus and instruct that no one teach any other doctrine,
4. nor listen to fables or undeterminable genealogies because they breed doubt more than the doctrines of the plan of God. (1 Timothy 4:7; 2 Timothy 4:4; Titus 1:14; 2 Peter 1:16)
5. But in the end, the command is to love (*affection and benevolence*) from a pure heart and to have a clean conscience brought by genuine faithfulness unto God.
6. But there are many who have erred, who have fallen during their testing, who speak nonsense,
7. desiring to be teachers of law, yet they do not even understand what they are talking about, nor do they comprehend that which they stand strongly by.
8. We know that the law of Moses was valuable if it was used properly.
9. But know this, that the Mosaic law was not applicable except for those that were lawless and undisciplined, for the ungodly and sinners; For those that were unholy and wicked;
10. It was for fornicators and sodomites, and for those that kill their parents; For all murderers, all liars, oath breakers, and all other things that oppose the wholesome (*true*) instructions of God.
11. According to the gospel of our God that I have been blessed and honored to be entrusted with,
12. I thank Jesus Christ our Lord, who gives me strength and considers me faithful to put me into this ministry.
13. Even though I had at one time been a blasphemer and persecuted the people of Christ, I received the grace of God abundantly and I received forgiveness, because what I did, I did in ignorance. (John 9:41; Hebrews 10:26; 1 John 5:16-18; James 4:17; Romans 1:18; 7:13; Matthew 18:6-10; Numbers 15:28-31)
14. But the power of God is now greatly abundant in me, because I have been proven to be faithful through adversity and because of the affection I have for Jesus Christ. (Psalms 119:1-3)
15. This instruction is faithful and completely deserving and acceptable; Jesus Christ came into the world to save sinners, of which I formerly was chief. (verse 13)
16. But it was because of this that I obtained mercy, that through my past, the patience of Jesus Christ might be clear for all to see and be a pattern unto others that will put their trust in him, in hopes of receiving eternal life.
17. But the eternal King is not corruptible and he is able to be seen in us (G-1 + G-517); He is clearly the only God and unto him be the honor and the glory forever and ever.
18. I order one thing of you my son Timothy, according to the prophecies that were given at an earlier time, you must fight the good fight,
19. stand firm in your dedication and keep a good conscience, of which some have sadly rejected concerning dedication and faithfulness; Many have been thrown overboard! (Matthew 7:21-23; 2 Peter 2)
20. Hymenaeus and Alexander are two examples, of whom I have surrendered unto Satan, because that which they teach is blasphemy.

1 Timothy 2

1. Therefore I instruct, first of all, when you pray, ask for the Lord's favor for others and bring a request on behalf of all people; (1 Peter 2:13-17)
2. For kings and all of those that are in authority positions, that we may live a quiet and peaceful life of complete godliness and honesty. (*that they don't harass us* - Romans 13:1-5)
3. It is good and acceptable unto our God and savior, (1 Peter 2:15)
4. that all people might desire to receive the knowledge of the truth and be saved. (Romans 13:1)
5. Because there is only one God and one mediator between God and mankind, Jesus Christ.

6. He offered himself as a ransom for the sake of all of us; This is evidenced in me,
(Matthew 20:28; Mark 10:45; Hosea 13:14; Isaiah 35:10; Isaiah 51:10; Jeremiah 31:11)

7. of which I was appointed to be a preacher and apostle of the truth that I speak of Jesus Christ, and I do not lie, as I am a teacher unto the nations in true and honest doctrine.

8. Therefore I order that husbands everywhere seek God and lift up clean hands, without violent anger nor debate.

9. Likewise also that the women wear modest clothing with bashfulness and sobriety, to not braid their hair, nor wear golden jewelry, nor pearls, nor expensive apparel,

10. but to live as is necessary to profess the fear of God through good deeds. (Titus 2:12; 2 Peter 1:3-9; James 1:12-22)

11. The women should learn in quietness in complete subjection.

12. But a woman is not allowed to instruct nor to hold authority over an elder man (*her husband*), but must remain submissive.

13. This is because Adam was created first and then Eve.

14. Adam was not deceived, but the woman was deceived and became a transgressor.

15. However, she (*Eve*) was pardoned for the purpose of childbearing, but only if she remained in the truth according to love, through holiness and self-control. (Genesis 3:4)

1 Timothy 3

1. This message is faithful and true: If anyone desires to be an overseer, it is a good thing that he desires.

2. It is necessary that an overseer must be the head of his own unrebukable family. (*if he has one)* He must be sober, self-controlled, modest, hospitable and a good teacher;

3. He must not be a drunkard, not quarrelsome and must not be greedy. He must be patient and peaceful; He must not be concerned with gain unto himself.

4. He must rule over his own household well and his children must be obedient and reverent.

5. If anyone does not know how to keep his own house in order, how can he care for the people of God?

6. He must not be a young convert, so that he not be self-conceited and fall into the condemnation of the devil.

7. He must also have a good reputation among the gathering, so that he not be spoken of as evil and fall into the snare of the devil.

8. In the same way, the helpers and assistants must also be honorable, not double minded, not drunkards, and not interested in self gain.

9. They must remain completely faithful in all things, at all times and hold a clean conscience before God.

10. They must be thoroughly proven first, only then may they be put into service if they are found to be blameless.

11. Also, their wives must be reverent and not slanderers, but they must be sober and faithful in everything.

12. Helpers and assistants must keep their own wives in subjection; If they have children, they must be well behaved. They must rule over their own households well.

13. For if they have done well as the head of their own household, they shall also have firmness in the doctrines of Jesus Christ.

14. I write these things unto you expecting that I will soon be there with you.

15. If I am delayed, you already know in what way the family of God is expected to live, because they are a living pillar in the house of God that rests upon a foundation of truth. (Revelation 3:12)

16. Admittedly, the mystery of holiness surely is great; God himself comes physically into us. (*the spirit of Jesus Christ*) (1 John 4:2; Acts 2:38; 3:19) He was justified by the spiritual ones (*prophets*), was seen by messengers (*the disciples*), spoken of unto the nations *(by the apostles),* was believed on by many throughout the world and he has ascended in honor (*at the right hand of the Father*).

1 Timothy 4

1. The spirit of God clearly spoke this to me:
In the final times, most people will fall away from living a faithful life of dedication unto God;
They will attach themselves to imposters that will deceive them and to the doctrines of demons;
(2 Corinthians 11:14; Ephesians 4:14; Matthew 24:4-5; 2 Peter 2:1-3)
2. They will be hypocritical liars, distorting that which they perceive as truth, and their moral consciousness will be cauterized (*welded in place*). (Ecclesiastes 8:11)
3. They will prevent men and women to be joined together in holiness before God (*substituting government for God in a different form of union*) and will restrict the consumption of food that God created for eating. (*replacing it with chemical garbage and GMO's*). But the faithful shall thankfully know the truth.
4. All that God has created is good (*to be eaten*) and nothing should be rejected, but to be received with thankfulness;
5. For all that God has created is holy through sincere prayers spoken unto God.
6. Put these things into your memory my brothers and you will continue to be a good servant of Jesus Christ. Be educated by these words and stand by the teachings that you have followed in order to remain faithful through all difficulties.
7. Reject the Jewish stories and unbelievable fables and commit yourself to holy living (*godliness*).
(1 Timothy 1:4; 2 Timothy 4:4; Titus 1:14; 2 Peter 1:16; 1 John 3:3)
8. Physical exercise is somewhat beneficial, but living a holy life is beneficial in many ways, both in this present life and also in your hope for eternal life. (James 1:22)
9. These words are true and faithful and completely deserving to be accepted;
10. It is for this reason that we do the hard work and suffer being spoken evil of, because we have surely put our hope in the living God, who is the savior of men throughout the world, specifically the faithful.
11. Declare these things and teach them.
12. Do not allow anyone to despise new converts, but be an example unto them in your speech, in conduct, in affection, in spirit, in doctrine and in purity.
13. Until I get there, continue with the reading for clarity in the instructions.
14. Do not be neglectful of the charisma (*assistance of the holy spirit*) within you, which committed unto you the gift of prophecy, and continue laying your hands upon the elders (*sincere prayer*).
15. Continue in these things and take care of them diligently so that because of you, the advancement of the Gospel may be known publicly unto all.
16. Pay attention to yourself and to the doctrine. Continue in truth. Doing so will bring benefit unto yourself and also unto those that hear you.

1 Timothy 5

1. Do not chastise an elder, but gently speak to him as a father, with respect. Treat the younger ones as brothers. (1 Timothy 2:11-15)
2. You shall treat the older women as mothers and the younger women as sisters, in complete purity.
3. Honor widows if they truly are widows;
4. But if any widow has children or grandchildren, teach them to most importantly get those in their own house to respect God, and there will be blessings that shall return unto them. Because this is good and expected by the Lord.
5. In contrast, a true widow is surely desolate and has her hope only in God, and she must continue in prayer night and day for her needs to be met.
6. The widow that lives for pleasure (*fornication*) is dead while she is yet alive!
7. This is the command so that there will not be any among you that can be accused.
8. But if anyone does not care enough for his own family (*to teach them truth*), he has rejected the teachings of Christ and is worse than an unbeliever.
9. Do not allow a widow to live with your gathering if she is less than sixty years old, being the wife of only one dead husband.
10. Only if she has a reputation of good deeds, if she has brought up children, if she is a good host, if she has washed the feet of the saints (John 13:14), if she has helped those in need, and if she follows after everything that is good.

11. Younger widows you must refuse (*to live in your home*), as they will grow lustful against the ways of Christ, because they desire to be wed.

12. Have good judgment, because they tend to put aside the established teachings

13. and they also become idle, they go around to the homes of others, not only being idle, but also gossiping and being meddlesome, speaking things that should not be spoken.

14. Therefore I instruct the younger women to be wed, bear children and manage the home, allowing for no opportunity to the adversary to speak evil of her.

15. There are some that have already turned back unto Satan.

16. If any faithful man or faithful woman has a widow in the family, they must assist them and not burden the whole gathering so that those who are true widows may receive assistance.

17. The elders that bring forth excellence shall be entitled to receive double appreciation, specifically those that do physical labor concerning the teaching of the true doctrine;

18. Because the scriptures say, you shall not prevent the ox from eating when he is grinding the grain. But the one that works is deserving of his keep *(food and other needful things)*. (Deuteronomy 25:4)

19. Do not accept accusations against an elder, unless there are at least two or three witnesses against him.

20. Those who willfully commit sin (Numbers 15:28-31; Hebrews 10:26-27; 1 John 5:16-18), condemn them openly in the presence of all of the people so that all of the others might have fear of the same. (1 Corinthians 5:5; Psalms 119:21)

21. I honestly testify before God and the Lord Jesus Christ and his elect messengers, that you must obey these things without playing favorites and do not ever show favor one above another.

22. Never quickly lay a hand on anyone, nor talk about (*gossip*) the sins that others have committed, but keep yourself pure.

23. My son Timothy, do not drink only water, but drink a little wine because of your stomach problems and your frequent weakness.

24. The sins of some men are evidenced before the judgment shall come, but for others they shall be made known at the time of judgment.

25. In the same way, the good deeds of some men are obvious and easy to see, but for others they are hidden and can not be seen. (Matthew 6:3)

1 Timothy 6

1. Whoever is under the obligation of being a servant, give of yourself all of the value that is due unto your master, so that the name of God and the true doctrine not be spoken evil of.

2. Those that have faithful masters, do not despise them, because they are brethren; Serve them well as good servants, because they are faithful and are beloved and you shall receive good in return. Teach these things and do them.

3. If anyone teaches otherwise, they do not teach the true message of our Lord Jesus Christ, nor the doctrine of holiness;

4. Such people are self-conceited and understand nothing and they are not right. Their many disputes and arguments stir up envy, strife, blasphemy and vicious thoughts.

5. Through complete perversion they shall corrupt the minds of many people who are depraved of the truth. There are some that think that earning money is the way of godliness. Remove yourselves from these kinds of people. (*the prosperity gospel*)

6. That which is great gain is to be satisfied with living a holy life (*godliness*).

7. Because we brought nothing into this world and it is easy to recognize that we shall not take anything with us when we die!

8. If we have food, shelter and clothing, we should be content.

9. Those who make their goal to become wealthy fall into a time of testing, unto the snare of many foolish and injurious desires (*lusts*) that cause men to fall into damnable ways and unto eternal destruction. (Luke 18:24)

10. It is the love of wealth *(lusts for things of this life)* that is the root of all wickedness. (Matthew 6:24; 16:13) There are many who have lusted after wealth and were drawn away from faithfulness unto God; They have completely devastated many others in their quest for wealth.

11. But you that are of God, run away from these things; Pursue being righteous and living a godly life of faithfulness, benevolence, patience and meekness. (2 Peter 1:3-9; Titus 2:12; James 1:12-27)

12. Hold firmly unto the things that lead unto the everlasting life, of which you are now called unto, so that you have a good record before many witnesses.

13. I command you in the sight of God, the one that gives life unto everything, and Jesus Christ, of whom Pontius Pilate gave a good testimony, (Matthew 27:24)

14. that you must keep this instruction perfectly and be blameless until the return of the Lord Jesus Christ.

15. He will be revealed in the proper time, the blessed and only powerful ruler, the king of the kingdoms and the Lord of all existence. (Romans 13:1; Revelation 20:12-15)

16. Remain holding unto the immortal and the light shall remain alive within you. He is not able to be approached or to be seen by anyone that is worldly, nor can they see his value, but his strength is forever trustworthy.

17. Those who are wealthy in this life, do not be arrogant and do not set your trust in the riches that are temporary, but put your trust in the living God, the one who has given us all things for our use;

18. We are to do that which is good and to be wealthy in good deeds, always ready to do them and to be generous;

19. Build up a strong foundation of treasures in the coming world, so that you may receive eternal life. (Matthew 6:19-20)

20. Timothy my son, these are the instructions that I have entrusted unto you. Preserve and protect the congregation and keep them from the worthless discussions of the wicked ones and those who hold opposing theories of what is often called science,

21. by which some who had professed the true doctrine have fallen into great error. May the grace of the Lord be with you always.

2 Timothy

Chapter 1

1. Paul, an Apostle of Jesus Christ, through the will of God, unto the promise of life in Christ Jesus;

2. Timothy my beloved son, may grace, mercy and peace be with you from our Father God and Jesus Christ our master.

3. I thank God, of whom you have honored with a pure heart since you were a child; I continually have thoughts of you in my mind, praying for you both night and day, reminded of your sadness.

4. I am looking forward to seeing you soon so that we might again be cheerful together.

5. I remember talking sincerely with you about the testing of your faithfulness, of which was first confirmed in your grandmother Lodi and then in your mother Eunice, and I am assured that you shall also stand firm and not fall. (Acts 16:1; Hebrews 10:38 - *the possibility of falling destroys OSAS theology*)

6. This is the reason that I remind you to keep the gift of God (*charisma*) alive within you, of which abides in you the same way that it is working through my hands.

7. God did not give us the spirit of being timid, but of ability, affection and self-control. (*freewill*)

8. Therefore, do not be ashamed of the evidence of our Lord, nor for being his servant; But when you suffer hardships for the gospel, do so with that same power of God that is alive within you.

9. He that has offered salvation has called us to live a holy life, not according to the things that we might have chosen to do for our own purposes, but to live in this life for his purposes, with the ability that is given to each one of us who are in Jesus Christ, that we must now live before the eternal times.
(Acts 1:8; Titus 2:12; Mark 8:34; Matthew 16:24; Luke 14:27)

10. Through this evidence of our Lord and savior Jesus Christ, God is revealed in us. He has made death truly meaningless, in that he has brought light, life and immortality through the gospel.

11. This is the reason that I have been appointed as a preacher, an apostle and a teacher unto all nations.

12. This is why I suffer, though I am not ashamed; For I know whom I have put my trust in and I am convinced that he is able to help me continue to persevere until that final day.

13. Repeat the message that you have heard from me without any deviation, concerning the true doctrine. Do so with affection unto Jesus Christ. (Galatians 1:8-9)

14. Stay true to the calling that has been given unto you through the spirit of the holy one that lives within you. (1 John 4:2; 2 Corinthians 6:16)

15. Know this, those that turned me away in Asia are Phygellus and Hermogenes.

16. May the Lord give mercy to the house (*gathering*) of Onesiphorus because they took care of me when I was in prison, and they were not bashful.

17. They searched diligently for me in Rome and with much difficulty they found me.

18. May the Lord see their assistance and give much mercy unto them on the day of judgment. You also know of the assistance that they gave to me in Ephesus.

2 Timothy 2

1. Therefore my son, be strengthened in the compassion of the Lord Jesus Christ.

2. Those things that you have learned from me, commit them unto people that are faithful, those that will be competent to teach others.

3. Truly you will suffer much hardship as a valuable warrior of Jesus Christ.
(Matthew 10:22; Matthew 24:9; Philippians 1:29; 1 Thessalonians 3:4; 1 Peter 3:14)

4. No one that serves Christ entangles himself with the concerns (*affairs*) of this life, so that he might focus on pleasing the one that he is committed to.

5. If anyone chooses to enter this calling, he shall not receive the reward unless he strives lawfully.

6. It is necessary for hard working caretakers (*ministers*) to first be bringing forth only good fruit from within themselves.

7. Understand my words! The Lord shall give unto you understanding in all things. (John 14:26)

8. Always remember that Jesus Christ was raised from the dead. He was of the offspring of David, according to that which I know to be true.

9. For this, I have suffered being jailed, as though I had done something evil; But yet the message of God is not prevented from being distributed abroad.

10. I endure all things that I must suffer on the behalf of the elect, that they might obtain eternal salvation in Jesus Christ, with everlasting honor. (*If salvation was as easy as saying a little prayer, why did he need to suffer?*)

11. This word is true: That if we have truly died with Christ (Romans 6:3-4), then we must also live as he lived. We must continue to endure faithfully, (1 John 3:3)

12. and if we do, we shall surely reign with him. But he will certainly deny those that contradict him.

13. If one is found to be unfaithful, Christ is unable to bring a contradiction against himself; Only those who are found to be faithful shall remain. (Romans 3:5)

14. Put these things firmly into your thoughts, surely everything is being witnessed by the Lord; It is not useful to argue with anyone about these things, but all those who will not hear will be destroyed.

15. Make every effort to present yourself approved, to show unto God that you are a worker who has nothing to be ashamed of and having made the right decisions in life, according to his instructions.

16. But turn away from all wicked and fruitless talk, because such will increase ungodliness.

17. Such words are like an infectious cancer, of which Hymenaeus and Philetus have become;

18. Concerning the truth, they have deviated into great error, claiming that the second coming of Christ and the resurrection of the dead have already happened.
(Daniel 12:1-2; Matthew 27:52-53; 2 Thess. 2:2 - *as errantly placed & falsely translated by most bibles*) They have undermined the dedication and faithfulness of some.

19. However the foundation of God stands firm in this single mark of genuineness; "The Lord knows who are his, everyone who professes the name of Christ must turn away from all sin."
(2 Corinthians 6:17; Isaiah 52:11; Numbers 15:28-31; 16:7; Hebrews 10:26-27; 1 John 3:3-10)

20. Because in a great house, there are many kinds of vessels (*people*), some are of gold and silver, and others are made of wood and some are clay. Some are valuable and some are disgraceful.

21. If anyone therefore is thoroughly cleansed, he shall be a vessel of value, having then become holy and now useful unto the master and shall be made ready to do only that which is good.

22. Turn away from all youthful lusts (*desires*). Pursue righteousness, faithfulness, affection, peacefulness and at all times, appeal unto the Lord with a pure heart. (Proverbs 28:13)

23. Avoid the foolish questions of those that are unwilling to learn, knowing that they are looking to create controversy.

24. A servant of the Lord must not strive against others in such a way, but must be gentle toward all people, willing to patiently teach them.

25. With humility, instruct those that are only set in opposition looking to dispute, only having the faint hope that God might allow some of them to come to repentance (Romans 10:9-10) and that they might come to understand the complete knowledge of the truth,

26. hoping that they might regain their senses and turn away from the devil's snare, of which they have been captured by, which is set to bring about his will. (John 8:31-37)

2 Timothy 3

1. I tell you the truth; In the last days difficult times shall come.

2. Men will be lovers of themselves and will be covetous. They will be proud, braggarts, blasphemous, disobedient, ungrateful and they will be wickedly unholy. (Proverbs 30:11-14)

3. They will lack natural affection for others (Matthew 24:12) and be trucebreakers, false accusers and have no self-control. They will be fiercely savage and hostile towards anyone that is virtuous.

4. They will be traitors, self-willed, self-conceited and they will love recreation (*pleasure lovers*) much more than they will love God.

5. Some will have the appearance of godliness, but they will reject the ability (*power*) of living a godly life. Be sure to turn away from these types of people; (*those that say that we are all sinners and always will be*) (Acts 1:8; 2 Corinthians 13:4; Acts 26:18; Romans 16:17; Zephaniah 3:4; Jeremiah 12:10; Isaiah 59:2)

6. Because such are they who sneak their way into the homes of foolish women, leading their hearts into captivity, continuing to pile up their sins. They are led by a variety of lustful desires;

7. They are always trying to learn, but are never able to come to acknowledge the truth.

8. They continue in the way of Jannes and Jambres of whom opposed Moses, in that they stand opposed to the truth. They are men and women of corrupt minds and completely worthless concerning faithfulness and dedication unto God;

9. But they shall not continue forever. For their error shall be easily seen by all, just as the error of those men was made to be.

10. But you have clearly followed the teachings, the conduct, the purpose and the true doctrine with determination, affection and patient continuance (*faithfulness*).

11. The persecutions and suffering that I endured in Antioch, Iconium, and in Lystria, so many persecutions that I needed to endure, yet out of all of them I was delivered by the Lord.

12. Truly, all who desire to live a godly life in Christ Jesus will be persecuted.
(Acts 14:22; 1 Thessalonians 3:4; Matthew 10:24; Revelation 1:9; John 16:33; Revelation 13:7)

13. But evil people and imposters (*false men of God*) will be greatly increased and grow worse and worse, continuing to deceive and surely being greatly deceived. (Matthew 24:5, 11, 24; 2 Peter 2:1-4; 2 Cor. 11:15)

14. But continue in that which you have learned and assuredly trust as true, knowing from whom you have learned these things.

15. Since you were a child, you have known the sacred writings (*scriptures of the old testament*), as they are able to bring you wisdom that will lead you unto your deliverance (*eternal salvation*), by being proven to be faithful unto Jesus Christ.

16. All that I have written is for you to stand firmly upon God's spirit {"theopneustas"}
(G-2316- "theo" = *God* + G-4151- "pneu" *spirit* + G-4714 - "stas" *to stand firmly upon*)
(Romans 7:6; 1 Peter 1:22; 1 John 4:2; Acts 2:38; Acts 3:19; John 3:5; Joel 2:28)
and is helpful for teaching, for evidence, for correction and for the instructions of how to be righteous.

17. In them, the people of God may learn how to be made completely perfect and fully equipped to only do that which is good.

2 Timothy 4

1. Now I earnestly testify before God and the Lord Jesus Christ, that he will soon return and establish his kingdom and he will judge all that are at that time still alive and also all who have previously died.
(Romans 2:6-11; Revelation 20:12-15 - *the kingdom of God is the eternal kingdom that will soon come*)

2. Announce the instructions! When the opportunity arises, rebuke, challenge, encourage, and teach with much patience. Write letters when you can not be there in person.

3. For the time will come (*has come*) when many will not continue in the true (*uncorrupted*) doctrine, but according to their own lustful desires, they will gather unto themselves teachers to teach what their itching ears want to hear. (Isaiah 30:9-10; Acts 20:29-30; Jude 1:4; 2 Peter 2:1-3; Matthew 24:5, 10, 24)

4. They will turn their ears away from hearing the truth and they will be turned to believe many myths and lies. (1 Timothy 4:7; Titus 1:14; 2 Peter 1:16; Isaiah 30:10 - *relativism*)

5. But you must be sober (*mindfully aware*) in everything. You will suffer many difficulties and persecutions, but continue to do the work of preaching the gospel and you will completely accomplish your duty as a servant of God.

6. I am now coming to my end and the time of my death is approaching.

7. I have fought the good fight. I have finished the race and I have remained dedicated and faithful.

8. Now there has been appointed unto me, a crown of righteousness that will be given unto me by the master on judgment day, because he is a righteous judge. Not only unto myself, but also unto all who live, looking forward unto his appearance. (*those that heed the calling and faithfully live for the eternal*)

9. Hurry and come to me very soon.

10. Demas has abandoned me, having loved this present life (*world*) and he went to Thessalonica. Crescens went to Galatia and Titus went to Dalmatia.

11. Only Lucas is with me. Bring Marcus with you when you come, he is useful as a helper.

12. I have sent Tychicus to Ephesus.

13. When you come, please bring the coat that I left at Troas with Carpus and bring the books; Do not forget the parchments (*notes*).

14. Alexander the coppersmith brought forth much harm unto me; May the Lord give unto him as he deserves, according to his deeds.

15. I warn you of him so that you protect yourself against him, as he strongly opposes our words.

16. In my first defense (*plea to clear oneself*) no one came to assist me, but all had abandoned me. May their record not be kept to be held against them on judgment day;

17. Yet the Lord stood close to me and gave me strength, so that the preaching might be established through me and that all of the nations might hear the truth. I was rescued from out of the mouth of the lion.

18. The Lord will protect me from every malicious action taken against me and he shall preserve me unto his celestial kingdom. Unto him be the honor forever and ever.

19. Say hello unto Priscilla and Aquilla and all of the Onesiphorus household.

20. Erastus remained in Corinth. I left Trophimus in Miletus because he was very sick.

21. Be sure to get here before winter arrives. Eubulus says hello, and also Pudins, Linus, Claudia and all the rest of the brethren.

22. May the Lord Jesus Christ be with you in spirit. Grace be unto you.

Titus

Chapter 1

1. Paul, a servant of God and an apostle of Jesus Christ, according to the faithfulness and dedication of the elect of God by the full understanding and knowledge of the truth, which is to live unto godliness; (*a godly life* - 1 John 3:3)
2. This is what gives us the hope of the eternal life, of which was in the past promised by God and he can not lie.
3. He has revealed his instructions unto us in our times and has called for us to announce unto others. Therefore, I have heeded the call of our saviour God.
4. I write unto Titus, a true son according to the dedication that we share; May the grace, mercy and peace of God the Father and the Lord Jesus Christ our saviour be with you.
5. This is the reason that I left you there in Crete, so that the things that they lacked, you might set in order and that you appoint elders in each city as I instructed for you;
6. They must be blameless, the husband of only one wife and whose children must be faithful, not wild nor insubordinate. (1 Timothy 3:2)
7. It is necessary for the overseers to be blameless stewards of God; They must not be focused on pleasing themselves, not easily angered, not a drunkard, not a fighter, not looking for ill-gotten gain.
8. They must be hospitable and love that which is good. They must be self-controlled, righteous, pure before God and masterful in his ways.
9. They must be standing firmly upon the true doctrine and faithful unto the message, so to be able to teach the true doctrine strongly and to convince even those that dispute against them.
10. For there surely are many disobedient men who are senseless and misleading, that try to seduce you into error, especially those that were cut off from God. (*circumcision - Jews that reject Christ* - 2 Peter 2:1-4; Galatians 2:4)
11. These men (*stewards of God*) must be able to put them (*the false teachers*) to silence, because they subvert entire gatherings, teaching that which is not right for the sake of ill-gotten gain unto themselves.
12. One of the prophets said that the Cretians are always liars, evil animals, gluttonous and lazy.
13. This claim may be true, but it is for this reason that you must convince them thoroughly, so that they may come to soundness in the true doctrine.
14. Do not listen to the Jewish myths and doctrines of men that have turned many away from the truth; (1 Timothy 1:4; 1 Timothy 4:7; 2 Timothy 4:4; 2 Peter 1:16; Galatians 1:6-9)
15. Indeed, in everything, those that are pure must remain clean. But in those that defile themselves, nothing can be pure, because their mind (*desires*) and their understanding is corrupt.
16. They may profess to know God, but by their deeds (*way that they live*) they deny him, being abhorrent and disobedient unto all that is true; Unto good deeds they are worthless.

Titus 2

1. Therefore, teach only that which we have established as true doctrine;
2. The older men must be alert, honorable, self-controlled and completely dedicated to the true doctrine; They must do so continually in affection *(love)*.
3. The aged women likewise must be in the same behavior, reverent, not being slanderers nor a drunkard, but they have need to be good teachers
4. so that they may teach the young ones to love their own husbands and children.
5. They must be self-controlled, innocently pure, keep their home in good order and be all around good people. They must be subject unto their own husbands, so the message of God will not be blasphemed;
6. The younger men likewise are called to be calm in nature and hold themselves as a model unto others by doing good deeds;
7. They must apply the true doctrine in complete purity, honesty, and incorruptibly;
8. When talking with others, they must be sincere and be without condemnation, so that the one who is opposed might come to be ashamed, having nothing bad to say.

9. Servants, be in subjection unto your own masters and in everything you do, do it to please them, not to come against them.

10. Do not take unto yourself, but show complete goodness unto all that you do, so that the doctrine of our God and saviour may be seen as appealing unto others.

11. Because the grace of God that can bring eternal life shall appear unto all men,

12. of which instructs us to reject ungodliness and corrupt lusts; We must live our lives with a clear conscience and be righteous and Godly in this present world (1 John 3:3; 2 Peter 1:3-9; 2 Cor 12:21)

13. while we await that which we hope for (*eternal life*), of which will be revealed at the appearance of our great God and saviour, Jesus Christ, in his power and honor. (*no one is eternally saved before judgment day*)

14. He gave his life for us as a ransom for the lawlessness that we had done in the past and to purify unto himself a special people that are now zealous to do that which is right. (Romans 3:25)

15. Speak these things and call others unto them and convince them with all authority, so that no one shall think otherwise.

Titus 3

1. Remind them, even the powerful ones and the privileged, to be subject unto God (Romans 13:1-5) and that we must all be obedient; So be ready unto every opportunity. (1 Peter 2:13-17)

2. Do not vilify anyone and do not be quarrelsome, but be gentle and moderate to show complete meekness unto all people.

3. For we were all at one time senseless and disobedient, having been led astray, the slaves unto our own lusts and various pleasures; (Romans 6:17; John 8:31-34) We were wicked, lived in jealousy, were vicious and despised one another.

4. But when the kindness toward mankind appeared through our saviour Jesus Christ, our God

5. offered salvation unto us (Romans 11:26, 32), but not because of the righteous deeds that we may have done, but because of his mercy, through the baptism of regeneration (Romans 6:1-23; Acts 2:38, 3:19; Mark 16:16; Matthew 18:1-4) and the remolding of us by his holy spirit,

6. of which he has poured out unto us abundantly through Jesus Christ our saviour.

7. Now having been justified by his good will, we become heirs according to the hope of an endless life.

8. This message is faithful and true and through these things that I have written unto you, be willing to conform unto them completely. Continue to believe in God and to be careful to maintain only good deeds. These are the things that are good and beneficial unto mankind;

9. But avoid absurd challenges (*debateful questionings*), genealogies, arguments and debates of law; They are vain and not beneficial.

10. Reject those that remain as heretics after the first and then second warning (*instruction*);

11. Know that such people are corrupted and that they continue to choose to commit sin, having already condemned themselves.

12. When I send Artemas and Tychicus to you, be quick to come to me at Nicopolis; I have decided to spend the winter there.

13. Bring Apollos and Zenas the lawyer with you so that they shall lack nothing (*in understanding*)

14. Also maintain your charitable contributions for those who are in need, so that they will not be lacking.

15. All of those with me greet you. Greet those that are dedicated and all who affectionately care for us. May the grace of the Lord God be with you all.

Philemon

Chapter 1

1. Paul, a slave of Jesus Christ and Timothy our brother, we write unto Philemon our beloved fellow worker in Christ,

2. and unto Apphia and Archippas, beloved fellow workers of ours, and to the assembly in your house:

3. Mercy and peace from God the Father and our Lord Jesus Christ.

4. I thank my God for you when I pray.

5. I have heard of the affection and the dedication that you have shown unto the Lord Jesus and unto all of the saints,

6. in which your partnership with God (*synergy*) concerning the testing of your faithfulness shall produce a full understanding in you of all that is good in Jesus Christ.

7. For we have much joy and encouragement concerning your benevolence, in that you are meeting the needs of the brethren and that they have been kept faithful unto God through you my brothers. (2 Corinthians 8)

8. Therefore, I have a strong desire to come and join you, so to do that which is needed,

9. though I would rather have you come to me, except for my affection to see those of your gathering. Now I Paul am an old man, yet I remain a servant of Jesus Christ.

10. I beg of you concerning one of my (*spiritual*) children of whom I have brought unto regeneration through much effort, Onesimus;

11. In the past he was useless unto you, but now he has become useful unto both myself and also for you,

12. thus I plan to send him back unto you. He is like my own son, so receive (*accept*) him.

13. I have considered keeping him myself, for him to assist me in my responsibility unto the gospel;

14. Therefore, without your consent, I will not send him; Do not think it is a necessity that you accept him, but only if you are willing.

15. Perhaps this is the reason that he was taken from you for a time, so that you may now receive him on a permanent basis,

16. though no longer as a servant, but now as a brother who is beloved, especially unto me and now much more he shall also be unto you, both with his physical presence and also spiritually unto the Lord.

17. Therefore if you consider me to be a partner, then receive him as if he were me.

18. If he wronged you in the past in anything or if he owes you anything, attribute it to me;

19. I Paul have written this with my own hand and I will repay, though I do say this in truth, that truly you are also indebted to me.

20. Therefore my brothers, if you have appreciation for me in the Lord, then may he be rejoined unto you with the compassion of the Lord.

21. I have written this unto you, having been convinced of your obedience unto God, knowing that you will do even more than I have asked of you.

22. Also, prepare a place for me to stay, as I hope that through your prayers, I will be able to come unto you soon.

23. Greet Epaphras a fellow brother of mine in Jesus Christ;

24. Also, Marcus, Aristarchus, Demas and Lucas who are also fellow brothers of mine.

25. May the grace of our Lord Jesus Christ be with your spirit.

Hebrews

Chapter 1

1. In many pieces and in many ways, God formerly spoke through the prophets by the prophecies,

2. In these final days, he has spoken unto us through his son, whom he has appointed to be the heir of everything. Through him the world was created. (Genesis 1; John 1:3)

3. He (*Jesus Christ*) is the radiance of the glory and the exact copy of the essence of God, upholding everything by the commands of his power. Through himself, he has offered that our sins may be cleansed, then he sat down on the right side of the highest greatness. (Psalms 110:1)

4. He is so much more noble than the messengers (*angels*), as he has inherited a much more excellent name then they.

5. To which of the messengers (*angels*) did he ever say, "You are my son, this day I have begotten you", or "I will be unto him as a father, and he will be a son unto me"? (Psalms 2:7; 2 Samuel 7:16; Matthew 3:17)

6. And again when he brought forth the firstborn son unto the earth and he said, "Let all of the angels of God worship him."

7. Unto the angels, he said, "What are his spiritual messengers but his servants, just as flames to a fire." (Psalms 104:4)

8. But concerning the son, "Your throne God is forever and ever. Your staff is righteousness and your staff is your kingdom.

9. You have loved righteousness and have hated wickedness, and because of this, God has anointed you with the oil of joy; You are above all others." (Psalms 45:6-7)

10. And you oh Lord, in the beginning, you laid the foundations of the earth, and the heavens are the creations of your hands. (Genesis 1:1-28; John 1:3)

11. They will disappear, but you will remain. Everything shall grow old, just as a piece of clothing;

12. But you will roll them up as a cloth and all shall be made different; But you are always the same and your time shall never end." (Psalms 102:25-27; Revelation 6:14; Isaiah 34:4)

13. But to which of the angels did he ever say at any time, "Sit at my right hand until I put your enemies under your feet"? (Psalms 110:1)

14. Are they (*all of the angels*) not ministering spirits meant to serve, being sent forth for assistance unto those who shall receive an inheritance of eternal life? (Psalms 104:4)

Hebrews 2

1. Because of this, should we not more earnestly pay close attention to the things that we have heard of him, so that we do not let it (*eternal life*) slip away from us?

2. Because through the words of the prophets, if their testimony is true, then every transgression *(violation of God's law)* and disobedience *(choice to willingly defy God's law)* is to receive a just penalty. (Romans 2:4-11)

3. How shall we then escape such a life of drunkenness if we neglect such a great opportunity for deliverance? In the beginning, this was offered through the words of the Lord and then was brought unto us by those that had heard him speak. (*the apostles*)

4. We were given evidence of this by the miracles that he did and the fulfillment of all of the prophecies, and many other various works of power. We also have received the distribution of the spirit of the holy one (*Jesus Christ*), according to his will. (John 14:16-18; 1 John 4:1-3)

5. He did not give unto the angels the world to come, of which we speak.

6. But one did earnestly testify, "What is mankind that you would think of him or the sons of mankind that you look upon them?

7. You made them (*mankind*) a little below the angels in honor and glory, but you gave unto them crowns, and you set them over your creation. (Psalms 144:3-4; Genesis 1:26; 1 Corinthians 15:27-28)

8. You have put all things under the feet of mankind. For all things are subject unto us; You left nothing not subjected unto us." (Psalms 8:4-8) But now, though we may not see it, all things have surely been made subject unto us.

9. But we who are lower than the angels, in a short while we shall surely see Jesus, because of the hardships that we have suffered; Upon our death we will receive honor and rewards and we shall be crowned. It is because of the charity of God that we can have victory over the experience of death. (Psalms 8:4-9)

10. It is fitting because we are the reason all things were made, to bring some of us to firmly stand in purity, to rescue (*save*) the foremost of us by being perfected through many hardships.

11. He also cleansed us, and all who are pure are not in danger. For this reason, he is not ashamed to call us brethren (*family*).

12. He said, "I will declare thy name unto my brethren: In the midst of the people, I will sing praises unto you." (Psalms 22:22)

13. And again, "I will always obey him, I and the children whom God has given to me." (Isaiah 8:17-18)

14. Since the children have emptied themselves of lustful desires and bloodshed, likewise not even through death did Christ take part in those things (*anything evil*), so that he might annul the one holding power over death. (*the devil*) (1 John 1:5-6)

15. In this, now he offers to free all those who held the fearful expectation of (*eternal*) death, because throughout their past, they were held as slaves (*to sin*). (John 8:31-36; Romans 6:17)

16. He certainly did not come for the purpose of the angels, but he did come for the offspring of Abraham. (Galatians 3:27-29)

17. Therefore, all of the brethren are under obligation to become the same as he is (*Christ - 1 John 3:3*) so that he might be merciful and faithful to complete the purposes of God, to be the ransom for the sins of his people. (Matthew 1:21 - *Jesus paid the ransom to Satan for us.*)

18. Because we know that he (*Christ*) suffered and he was tested and found faithful, it is now possible for those of us who are being tested to receive his assistance. (*to help us overcome*) (1Corinthians 10:13)

Hebrews 3

1. Therefore my blameless brethren, participants of the heavenly invitation, consider the fullness of our ambassador and high priest whom we acknowledge, Jesus Christ;

2. He is faithful to perform, as Moses was with all that God gave unto him. (Numbers 12:7)

3. Yet Christ is deserving of much more glory than Moses, accordingly he also possesses much more honor than the house that Moses had built.

4. For every house is built by someone; But God has created all things.

5. Moses was a faithful servant over all of his house and there is much evidence of this to be offered.

6. But Christ is the son over his own house, of which we are, if we continue to remain completely trustworthy and glorious unto that which we anticipate at the time of the end. (*The promise of eternal life*)

7. Therefore, this is why the spirit of the holy one said, "today if you will hear my instructions,

8. do not harden your heart as those who have provoked me in the time when they tested me in the wilderness." (Psalms 95:8)

9. Your forefathers were defiant, so I did not approve of them and they saw my discipline for forty years.

10. I was greatly angered at that nation and I said, "they always err in their heart, and they refused to know my ways;

11. Just as I swore in my anger, that from that moment, they would surely not come to peace with me." (Psalms 95:11) (*they had at that early time already broken the covenant* – Barnabas 2:7; 3:7)

12. So watch my brethren, that any of you do not in some way allow unfaithfulness to slip into your heart and fall away from the living God. (Hebrews 6:4-6)

13. So encourage each other every day (*to remain faithful*) until the time you are called home, so that your heart not be hardened (*against God*) by the delusions of sin. (Numbers 15:28-31; Hebrews 10:27-29)

14. If we have truly become partners with Christ, we must continue to be stable in the truth, from the commencement (*coming into covenant with Christ - conversion*) until the end of life.
(Acts 2:38; Acts 3:19; Romans 6:1-22; Hebrews 6:4-6; Hebrews 10:26-29; Matthew 18:6-10)

15. It has been said, "Today, if you can understand this offer unto you (*the terms of the new covenant*), do not harden your heart as they did when they provoked me." (Psalms 94:7-8)

16. For there were some, who after having heard the instructions then went and provoked him, but it was not all who came out of Egypt with Moses that had provoked God.

17. With whom was he angry with for forty years? Was it not those who sinned that eventually died in the desert?

18. And unto whom did he swear would not come to make peace with him? Was it not those who disobeyed?

19. We should now see that those who were not able to enter (*the promised land - a picture of the eternal life*), they were those who were unfaithful.

Hebrews 4

1. We must be fearful of abandoning the promises of entry into peace with God, so that none of you may fall short of the goal, making your efforts to no effect. (G-5302 + G-2758)

2. For we were given the instructions of God with precision, but the message was not profitable unto those who had fallen, because it was not combined with dedication and faithfulness.

3. But unto them who entered into that peace but then believed the adversary, (Matthew 13:20-22) it shall be just as he said, "As I swore in my anger, they shall in no way enter into my peace, except through living in the way that has been instructed from the beginnings of the world." (Psalms 95:11) (*law of God*)

4. For it has been said, concerning the seventh day, "God did rest on the seventh day;" (Genesis 2:2)

5. And also, in this place it is again said (Psalms 95:11) "They shall not enter into my rest."
(*the eternal life* - Epistle of Barnabas 15:1-6)

6. Therefore, otherwise some of the forsaken would have entered therein; But those who long ago were given the instructions, they did not enter because of disobedience!

7. Therefore he limits the time, saying through David, "today, if you hear (*understand*) his instructions, do not harden your heart." (Psalms 95:8; Malachi 1:2-3)

8. By keeping them (*the instructions*), Joshua came in (*to the promised land - symbolic of the eternal life*), but no others did, speaking of those at that time. (Matthew 7:20-24)

9. So the Sabbath rest (*eternal life*) remains for the faithful people of God.

10. In the same way, he (*Joshua*) entered therein and he colonized the land because his deeds were righteous, just as God had promised.

11. We must be diligent therefore to enter into that peace, that we not fall into disobedience in the same way as those who are now our examples.

12. Because living according to the instructions of God, operational (*in us*) cuts deeper than a double edged sword; As deep as to separate the rational mind (G-5590 - *psyche*) from the spiritual (*mind*), and joins us together (*with God*), (1 John 1:7) instructing us to be fully cleansed (G-3453 + G-3068) and to discern in our thoughts and in our hearts, moral wisdom from what brings wrath. (Jeremiah 17:10)

13. Because there is nothing in the world that is not fully known by God. All things are as though they are naked, and are completely exposed before his eyes and every one of us shall give an account unto him. (Matthew 18:10; Romans 2:6-10; Revelation 20:12-15)

14. Therefore, having such a powerful high priest, have fear whenever (*you think of*) the freedom (G-1167 + G-1658 + 3752) brought by Jesus Christ, the son of God in the heavens. For we must firmly remain faithful according to the covenant in which we have ascended. (Proverbs 1:7)

15. However, we do not have a high priest who is unable to have compassion concerning our lack (*of understanding* - 1 John 2:1; Numbers 15:28; 1 John 5:16) but as he was certainly tested and remained without sin, we must also remain in his likeness. (1 John 3:3-10; Romans 6:1-2, 16)

16. So may we be able to approach him with confidence when we come before the throne of God's power, so that we may receive mercy. May we receive the assistance of God at all times when it is needed. (1 Corinthians 10:13)

It is important to understand that chapter 5 begins a comparison and contrast between the old covenant and the new covenant, between the high priests under the Mosaic law and the eternal high priest we now have in Christ Jesus, and explains many of the differences.

Hebrews 5

1. Certainly, every high priest that was raised up by men was designated to do that which is according to God, intending to bring forth both offerings and sacrifices for the purposes of dealing with sin. (*under the Mosaic law* - Malachi 2:1-9)
2. Compassion was possible for those who did not know better and those who had gone astray, because the people were surrounded by many weaknesses; (*Hebrews 6:4-6 - presents a contradiction to this. This is explained by understanding these chapters are a comparison between the old and the new covenants*)
3. Therefore, he (*Christ*) was obligated for the sake of the people, to offer himself up for the reason of sin.
4. But no one can take the honor unto himself, yet he has surely been called (*to be high priest*) by God, just as Aaron.
5. In like manner, Christ did not glorify himself to become a high priest, but it was from the one that spoke unto him, "This is my beloved son in whom I am delighted. This day I have assuredly empowered him." (Psalms 2:7; Matthew 3:17; Hebrews 1:5)
6. Even as it is said in another place, "You are a priest in the order of Melchisedek." (Psalms 110:4)
7. In the days that he (*Melchisedek*) lived, he greatly sought through prayer, a longing for favor, so that he be saved from death; Through many tears and much weeping that he offered, he was heard because of his fear of God.
8. Nevertheless, he (*Christ*) was a son and he understood the importance of obedience through many sufferings.
9. He (*Jesus*) lived completely perfect unto God and he established the way unto eternal salvation for all who obey him; (Romans 6:16)
10. He was called out by God to be the high priest according to the arrangement of Melchisedek.
11. Concerning Christ, I have much to say, but can be difficult to explain since you are sluggish in your understanding. (2 Peter 3:16)
12. Therefore, as the arrangements are set, you are obligated to be teachers, but you have the need for someone to teach you again with the principles of the law of God; Currently you are in need of milk, not of solid food. (1 Corinthians 3:2)
13. For everyone who is in need of milk is ignorant of the message of righteousness, much like an infant.
14. But for those who are fully grown they have need for solid food, as they have formed the ability to continually exercise discernment, to recognize that which is good from that which is evil. (Hebrews 4:12)

Hebrews 6

1. Therefore, having already presented the beginning of the instructions of Christ, let us now move on to maturity; May we reach the fuller depths of understanding because we do not again need to lay the foundation of conversion from evil deeds that lead to (*eternal*) death, unto being proven to be faithful which is revealed through testing before God. (Romans 6:16)
2. The doctrine of baptism (Romans 6), the laying on of hands, the resurrection of the dead and the eternal judgment,
3. if God allows, we will surely present these things unto you again.
4. For those that have been illuminated (*those who have entered into the new covenant*), if they have truly experienced of the heavenly gift (1 Corinthians 12:1-31), having become partners with the holy spirit of Christ, (1 John 4:2; 2 Timothy 1:14; 1 Corinthians 2:13; 2 Corinthians 6:16; Ezekiel 37:27; Acts 19:6; John 16:13)
5. and if they have experienced the goodness of the instructions of God (1 Peter 4:17; 2 Thessalonians 1:8; Romans 10:16) and the abundant power (Acts 1:8) and held the expectation of the world to come,
6. if they fall away (*to contradict* - G-3844 + G-3979 + G-473), it is impossible to renew them again unto repentance (Acts 2:38; 3:19); As they would need to re-crucify themselves and put the son of God to an open shame. (Romans 6:3-8; Hebrews 10:29; Numbers 15:30-31; Matthew 12:32; 1 John 5:17)
7. The earth drinks in the rain that often comes and it brings forth vegetation that is good for those who work the ground, it is a blessing from God.
8. But if the ground brings forth thistles and thorns, it is deemed to be unfit ground and is cursed and it is now ready to be burned. (*similar to those who defy God, they will in the end also burn in hell*)

9. But concerning you, you are dear unto me and I am convinced of better things for you, that you might have the ability to remain unto salvation, and I am speaking to you as if this is the case:

10. God is not unjust to forget all of the work that you have done, and the labors of love that you have done in his name, as you have in the past and continue to minister unto the saints.

11. But we expect that each one of you will show the same eagerness *(faithfulness)* that leads to the complete confidence of the expectation *(eternal life)*, until the end *(of your lives)*.

12. Do not become sluggish, but imitate the ones that have been proven to be faithful and have patiently endured much difficulty and are now heirs unto the promises.

13. For God has truly made promises unto Abraham, and because there is no one greater to swear by, he swore by himself.

14. He said, "Surely, I shall bring blessings unto you and I will multiply you." (Genesis 22:16-17)

15. And because he *(Abraham)* was faithful through being tested, he obtained the promises. (Romans 4:3-5)

16. For men swear by something greater than themselves, and an oath is the confirmation of this and is held as the end of all argument.

17. This is why God chose to make an oath, in order to more trustfully declare unto the heirs of the promise that his word *(vow, agreement)* is true and unchangeable.

18. But through two unchangeable things, the other being that it is impossible for God to lie, we might have strong comfort *(confidence)* to run unto him and take hold of the hope that is being offered unto us.

19. This is the anchor *(security)* that we have for our souls, of which is both secure and firm, that we might enter into the holy place,

20. where the forerunner Jesus entered on our behalf, according to the likeness of Melchisedek, truly having become a high priest for all ages.

Hebrews 7

1. The king of Salem, Melchisedek, a priest of the most high God, when he met with Abraham as he was returning from the slaughter of the evil kings, he *(Melchisedek)* blessed him *(Abraham)*. (2 Peter 2:3)

2. A tenth of all that he had, he gave unto Abraham. He was previously known as the king of righteousness, but thereafter was also called the king of Salem, which means the king that makes peace. (Genesis 14:17-20 - *the king of Sodom also offered unto Abraham, of which was rejected due to his evil*)

3. He was without a record of father and mother and without his birth having been recorded, he did not have a known age or even a known time of death; In this, he was very similar to the son of God *(Christ Jesus)*, who shall continue to be the high priest forever. (Psalms 110:4)

4. Look at how great this man was, that a tenth of all that he owned he gave unto Abraham the Patriarch!

5. But the children of the priesthood of Levi have received the commandment to take a tenth from the people according to the Mosaic law; They take from their own brethren who have also come out of the line of Abraham;

6. But the one without pedigree *(Melchisedek)* gave a tenth unto Abraham, unto the one whom the blessed promises were given.

7. And without any dispute, the less wealthy one *(younger)* was blessed by the one that was more wealthy *(elder)*. (*Christ, the greater, blesses us, the lesser, offering a way to be cleansed and be saved eternally, the same as it was under the arrangement of King Melchisedek.*)

8. But among yourselves *(those under the Mosaic law)*, in truth, men who die received tithes; But now there is evidence that he *(Christ)* continues to live!

9. But as these words are spoken through the descendants of Abraham, Levi received the tithes that are brought in by the people;

10. Yet, with the ancestor, the forefather *(Abraham)*, it was when he came to meet Melchisedek (*that he received a tenth*).

11. So with complete certainty, if perfection was through the Levitical priesthood in which the people were given the Mosaic law, then there would be no need for another to rise up according to the order of Melchisedek and not be called according to the order of Aaron.

**Melchisedek gave a tenth (*tithe*) unto Abraham, but under the Levitical priesthood
and Mosaic law this was reversed and the people paid a tenth to the priests.
In the new covenant it is again according to the first priesthood of Melchisedek
where Christ is the high priest and he offers tithes (*wealth*) unto the people,
of which is the offer of the covenant and the remission of all past sins at conversion.
With the slavery of sin broken, this brings with it the freedom from sin
through the assistance of the holy spirit of Christ Jesus, the helper.
(John 14:16; Romans 6; Acts 2:38; 3:19)**

12. But with the priesthood now changed, there is also a necessity of the law to also be changed. *(from the Mosaic law unto the law of God)*

13. The one in whom these things were spoken of (*Christ Jesus*) is from a different tribe, from which no one has offered tithes unto at the altar. (*tithing is not part of the new covenant*)

14. It is clear that from out of the tribe of Judah our Lord has arisen and Moses spoke nothing about a priesthood concerning this tribe. (*nor tithes from it*)

15. It is also abundantly clear that if another priesthood was to arise according to the order of Melchisedek,

16. it would not be according to that which is commanded by the Mosaic law, which pertained to the temporal physical things. Now (*the priesthood*) is according to an endless life. (Matthew 6:19-21)

17. Here is a witness for you, "that unto you a permanent priest according to the order (*way*) of Melchisedek shall soon arise." (Psalms 110:4)

18. For truly an annulment of the preceding commandments (*Mosaic law*) had become necessary, because they had been without strength and they were unable to assist anyone; (Galatians chapters 3:19-5:26)

19. For the Mosaic law did not perfect anyone (*it did not put an end to sin - Daniel 9:24*), but the bringing in of something better did, by which we can now draw near unto God. (John 16:13; 1 Corinthians 10:13)

20. And accordingly, how many have become a high priest without an oath? Truly they have all become high priests without taking an oath.

21. But he (*Christ Jesus*) did so with an oath, through the one who said unto him, the Lord has sworn and he can not change, "You are a priest forever according to the order (*way*) of Melchisedek." (Psalms 110:4)

22. Jesus has now brought in a much better assurance through a much better covenant (*contract offer*).

23. Certainly there have been many priests who were prevented from continuing as priests because of their own deaths.

24. But he (*Jesus*), because he shall remain a priest forever, the priesthood can not be passed on to another;

25. Because of this, he is able to be the saviour until the end. He (*Christ*) is able to bring them (*the people of God*) to remain close unto God through himself (*through his spirit - John 14:16; Acts 2:38; 1 Corinthians 10:13*) and is able to intercede on their behalf. (1 John 2:1)

26. This is because such a high priest is necessary, he is holy, without any evil, undefiled, separated from sinfulness and has become higher than the heavens. (1 John 1:5-6)

27. So now there is no need for the high priests to continue their sacrifices day after day (*70 AD temple destroyed*), as they have done, first for their own sins and then for the sins of the people; Because he (*Jesus Christ*) died once for all people when he offered himself up. (*written before the temple was destroyed*)

28. The Mosaic law appoints high priests from mankind, each one having weaknesses (*imperfections*); But because of the oath that was taken (*by God*), it is the Law of God that has now appointed his own Son to truly complete and perfect everything, and he shall remain forever.

Hebrews 8

1. Now a summary over the things that I have just explained: It is true that we have a high priest. He has sat down at the right hand of power upon the throne of almighty God in the heavens.

2. He is the minister of the eternal places of occupancy and is empowered by the Father, not by mankind.

3. Because every high priest is appointed to continue to bring gifts and sacrifices upon which it is necessary to have something in which he can offer them upon.

4. If he were truly on the earth he could not be a priest, in that those priests offered gifts according to the Mosaic Law;

5. But that was only a shadow that served as an example the things that are heavenly. Moses was warned when he intended to build the tabernacle, "See that you make all things according to the pattern that was shown unto you on the mountain." (Exodus 25:40)

6. Now a much more excellent administration has been established by a much better covenant, (*contract offer unto everyone*) of which he is the mediator of, on which better promises have been established.

7. For if the first (*covenant*) was perfect, there would be no need for a second to replace it. (Jeremiah 31:31-34)

8. But when he found certain fault with them he said, "Behold the days are coming when I (*the Lord*) will bring the house of Israel and the house of Judah to an end, and make a new covenant;

9. not according to the covenant that I made with their fathers when I took them by the hand out of the land of Egypt; They did not continue faithfully in covenant with me, (*breach of contract*) so I could not remain with them, says the Lord." (Jeremiah 31:31-34; Daniel 9:24-27; Malachi 2:1-3:18)

10. "Because this is the contract (*covenant*) that I will offer unto the house of (*spiritual* - Romans 11) Israel at that time, says the Lord, I will give my laws into their minds and I will write them upon their hearts, and I will be their God, and they shall be my people.

11. They (*the faithful*) will not have need to instruct their neighbor or their brother, saying, know the Lord; Because they will all know me (*personally*), from the lowest of them unto the greatest of them.

12. I will be merciful unto their unrighteousness, unto their sins and unto their transgressions, and I will no longer hold their sins against them." (Jeremiah 31:33-34 - *speaking of past sins previous to conversion and unaware sins after conversion* - Romans 3:25; 1 John 5:16-17)

13. In these previously quoted words it says "new" and he has now made the first to be obsolete and is growing old (*worn out*) and is near death and is about to be taken away (*abrogated*).

The Mosaic law was abolished by God a few years after the book of Hebrews was written, with the destruction of Jerusalem in 70 AD, having no temple and no way to continue the sacrifices. In the New covenant, the people of God are the temple of God. (1 Corinthians 3:16-17) Jesus cut off the old covenant when he was 12 years old in the temple. (Luke 2:40-49; Daniel 9:26; Luke 19:43-44; Matthew 3:10; notes on pages 160-161) The sacrifices are now done through us by the sacrifices that we make in this life, to live as Christ.

Hebrews 9

1. Truly the first covenant had required ordinances and services, the sanctuary was physically in this world.

2. For the tabernacle was first (*originally*) prepared with a lampstand and a table, and the setting out of the loaves (*show-bread*) of which are called holy;

3. Then beyond the second veil (*curtain*) there was a tabernacle that was called the holy of holies,

4. of which had a golden alter and where the ark of the covenant rested. It was covered in gold on all sides and within it was a golden pot full of manna, the staff of Aaron and the tablets of the covenant (*contract - the ten commandments*).

5. On the top of it were the glorious cherubim of which overshadowed the lid of the ark; But now is not the correct time to explain it piece by piece.

6. And this is how it was done: The priests went into the first area completing all of their services.

7. But once a year, only the high priest was to go beyond the second veil (*curtain*), but not without blood, of which he offered on behalf of himself and for the shortcomings of the people.

8. At that time, while the tabernacle was in its physical existence (verse 1), the holiest way was not yet fully revealed, of which we now know is the manifestation of the spirit of the holy one. (*Christ in us* - 1 John 4:2)

9. The tabernacle is a foreshadowing of what is now established in the present time. At that time, gifts and sacrifices were offered, but they were never able to completely make perfect the consciences of those that offered them (*concerning sin*),

10. except concerning foods, drinks, diverse washings and the ordinances concerning the physical body. It was this way until the time would come when things would be set right. (*at the time the new covenant was established*).

11. But Christ was made to be the high priest for the purpose of the good things that were coming through the greater and more perfect tabernacle which is not made by the hands of men, nor of this present world. (verse 1, 8; 1 Corinthians 3:16-17)

12. It is not by the blood of bulls and goats, but through his own blood that he entered into the holy of holies, taking hold of eternal redemption (*ransoming*).
(we access his blood to be redeemed - Romans 6:1-23; Acts 2:38; Acts 3:19; Matthew 18:1-10; John 8:31-36)

13. Because the blood of bulls and goats, and the sprinkling of the ashes of heifers upon those that had been defiled only sanctifies (*makes holy*) the purity of their physical bodies (*not the spiritual*).

14. But by his own blood, through eternal principals (*the law of God*) he offered himself spotless before God. Now how much more shall he cleanse you from the deeds that were leading you to eternal death, to now have you fully serve the living God! (Titus 2:12; Matthew 18:6-10)

15. And by this, he has become the mediator of the new covenant (*contract offer*), so that through his death, the transgressions that were committed under the first covenant might be redeemed (*ransomed*), and those who are now called might receive the promise of an eternal inheritance. (Isaiah 55:3; 61:8 - *not eternally saved yet*)

16. For where there is a testament (*a will, an inheritance*), death is necessary to be offered by the one offering the covenant (*contract*).

17. For a testament (*will - inheritance*) is only enforced when one has died, otherwise it does not hold power while the one offering the covenant has not died.

18. Whereby, the first covenant was not dedicated without bloodshed.

19. For every commandment according to the law of Moses had the need to be made known unto all of the people, of whom had to take the blood of bulls and goats, with water, scarlet wool and hyssop, with which he sprinkled all of the people as well as the book. (Barnabas 6)

20. Then he said, "this is the blood of the covenant which God has commanded unto you." (Exodus 24:3-8)

21. He also sprinkled the blood upon the tabernacle and all of the vessels used for the services of the people.

22. Almost all things are able to be cleansed by blood. According to the eternal principles, without the shedding of blood, no remission of sin can occur. (Romans 6:1-7 - *we access his blood through baptism*)

23. It is now necessary for those examples of the things that are heavenly to be cleansed in a similar way, but for the heavenly things, it is necessary for a much better sacrifice than those of bulls and goats.

24. For Christ did not enter into the holy of holies that was made by the hands of men, as such is only representative of that which is true in the heavens in the presence of God, but he did appear unto mankind on our behalf.

25. But not that he might offer himself frequently, as the high priests did many times, entering into the holy of holies year after year with another's blood; (Romans 6:10)

26. For in that way, he would have needed to have suffered many times since the foundation of the world; But only once, at the consummation of that age, he was manifested to bring an end to sin through the sacrifice of himself. (Romans 6:3-6; Daniel 9:24)

27. It is appointed for a man to die only once, (Romans 2:6) then the judgment of God shall come upon him.

28. So in this, Christ offers to cleanse the sins of many and he shall appear the second time unto those who will be without sin (Romans 6:1,16-23; 1 John 3:1-3) and living according to what is expected in order to receive eternal salvation. (*apekdechomenois* = G-575 + G-1537 + G-2192 + G-3306 + G-3634 = *hereafter from this point hold to living in such manner*)

Hebrews 10

1. For the Mosaic law is only a shadow of the good things that were to come, but not the exact image of those things. Year by year they continued to offer sacrifices, but those who were approaching God were never able to come unto complete maturity and perfection.

2. Otherwise why would they not have stopped offering sacrifices? Would they not have ended their sacrifices if their consciences had been made clean from the sins that they had committed, if they had surely been cleansed? *(Why would they continue to make sacrifices for sins if they no longer committed them?)*

3. But the sins remained with them (*a continuance due to slavery of sin* - John 8:31-34) year after year.

4. Because it is impossible for the blood of bulls and goats to take away sin. (*free them from slavery to sin*) (Numbers 15:28-31; Leviticus 4-5)

5. Therefore, coming into this world he said, "Sacrifice and offerings are not desirable, but give unto me a

healthy (*pure*) body." (Matthew 9:13; 1 Samuel 15:22, Micah 6:6-8; Proverbs 21:3; Matthew 12:7 Deuteronomy 11:26 - *Do not make amends for sin, but live righteously before God from a pure heart*)

6. But God was not pleased by the sacrifices and the burnt offerings. (Malachi 1:1-14; Isaiah 61:8)

7. Look and see, it is written in the book, "do the will of God." (Psalms 40:6-8)

8. Earlier in the book it also says, "You did not desire nor were you pleased with the sacrifices and offerings concerning sins," of which were brought according to the Mosaic law. (Proverbs 21:3; Matthew 9:13; 1 Samuel 15:22; Micah 6:6-8)

9. Then it is said, "behold, I come to do your will, my God. He shall abolish the first (*covenant*) so that he could establish the second (*new covenant*)." (Jeremiah 31:31-34)

10. By this decree, we shall be cleansed through the sacrifice of his body, the one-time sacrifice of the body of Jesus Christ. (Romans 6:1-23; Romans 3:22-27; Acts 2:38)

11. And yet, day after day every priest continued to perform (*until the temple was destroyed at 70AD*) and they often offered sacrifices that were never able to take away the sins of the people!

12. But when he (*Christ*) offered one sacrifice for sin, he sat down at the right hand of God.

13. From that time forward he expectantly awaits until his enemies are put down under his feet.

14. For in his one offering, he has perfected forever all who would come to be purified,

15. and his holy spirit is also a witness unto us, as it is written;

16. "This is the covenant that I will give unto them in those days, says the Lord, I will put my laws in their hearts (*those who enter into covenant with Christ*) and I will write them in their consciences;

17. and their sins (*past sins before conversion* - Romans 3:25; 2 Peter 1:9) and their transgressions (*unaware mistakes*) will no longer remain in my mind." (Jeremiah 31:33-34; Ezekiel 33:12-16)

18. And where there is freedom from sin (*from slavery to sin* - John 8:31-36; Acts 2:38; Romans 6:3-6), there is no more need for sacrifices and sin offerings. (*because there is no further sins being committed* - 1 John 3:3)

19. Therefore brethren, have confidence by entering the holy of holies through the blood of Jesus Christ, (Romans 6:1-23)

20. because he has brought this new way of living for our sake, doing away with the veil through his body,

21. he has become the high priest over the house of God.

22. So let us approach him with a sincere and honest heart and with complete confidence while our faithfulness is being tested.

23. May we accept the acknowledgment of this hope without wavering, because he that has brought it is faithful.

24. Let us strengthen and inspire one another unto affection and benevolence (*love*) for others.

25. Do not turn away from gathering together, (Hebrews 13:17 - *with true brethren, those of the true doctrine* - 1 John 2:19) as is the practice of some, but comfort each other in a real way (James 2:14-17), even much more as you see the day (*the return of Christ*) approaching; (1 Thessalonians 5:4-5)

26. Because if we (*the converted*) willfully commit sin after we have come to understand the true way (*that it is sin*), there is no longer a sacrifice remaining for such defiance against God, (*sin*) (Numbers 15:28-31; 1 Corinthians 15:34; 1 Timothy 1:13; Luke 12:47-48; Mark 9:42-43; Romans 1:18; Romans 7:13; James 4:17; John 9:41; Matthew 18:6-10; Luke 23:34; 1 Samuel 15:23; Psalms 19:13; Psalms 68:6-21; Hosea 14:9; Psalms 69:27-28; Leviticus 4&5; 1 Peter 1:14; Numbers 14:23-24; Proverbs 5:21-23; Proverbs 8:30-36; Psalms 51:17; James 5:19)

27. but there is a certainty of terrifying judgment and the fiery anger of God that shall consume all that defy him. (Galatians 2:17-18; John 5:14; John 8:11; John 9:41; John 3:18-19; Romans 2:6-10; Romans 6:16; Acts 26:18; Revelation 20:12; Ezekiel 33; Proverbs 14:9-16; Malachi 4:1-2; Psalms 21:8-9)

28. Anyone who disregarded the law of Moses was put to death without pity, at the testimony of two or three witnesses; (Numbers 15:35)

29. How much harsher of a punishment is then due if someone pushes the son of God down under their feet and chooses to defile the blood of Christ and the covenant (*contract*) by which they had been cleansed, (Acts 2:38; Romans 6:1-23) and also chooses to defy the spirit that has brought unto them the assistance of God? (*blasphemy of God, the holy spirit* - Matthew 12:31-32; Numbers 15:30-31; 1 John 5:16-17)

30. For we know that he has said, "Vengeance is mine, I will bring recompense (*repay*), says the Lord; The Lord will judge his people. (Romans 2:7; 12:19; 1 Peter 4:17)

31. It is a fearful thing to fall into the hands of the living God!" (Deuteronomy 32:35-36; Psalms 94:1-3)

32. But bring into your mind the former days when you were converted, when you endured much hardship and many difficulties; (*speaking to those who have truly been converted into Christ*)

33. Surely you were exposed and being poorly spoken of, with many people persecuting you, and through those hardships you have become a sharer with the others who have chosen to live in the true way.

34. In this, you also shared in my difficulties; We suffer together and you have accepted with God's assistance, the plundering of your own possessions, knowing that you shall have a much better wealth awaiting you above.

35. Therefore, do not throw away your confidence, because with it comes great reward.

36. You must continue to patiently endure (Matthew 10:22, Mark 13:13), because after you have accomplished the will of God, you shall obtain the promise (*eternal life*). (Colossians 3:4; Matthew 7:21; 1 Peter 4:17 - *this destroys the doctrine that we do nothing for our own salvation, that Christ did it all!*)

37. "Because in a little while, the one who shall return will come and he will not delay." (Habakkuk 2:3)

38. "The righteous shall live by their faithfulness; If someone turns back (*falls away* - 1Thessalonians 3:5) I will not be pleased with him" (Habakkuk 2:4; Hebrews 6:4-6; Luke 8:13)

39. But we (*the faithful*) are not of those who turn back (*fall away*) unto those damnable ways, but we remain faithful, even through difficulty (*testing*) of which will lead unto the preservation of our souls. (Psalms 26:1; Romans 6:9-22)

Hebrews 11

1. So now conviction (*faith*) is confidence in that which we anticipate, and the physical evidence (*proof*) of what is not yet seen. (*demonstrated in how we now live* - verse 40)

2. For this is the way that the forefathers received their good testimony (*reputation*).

3. It is because of our conviction that we know that the world was created by God and that we know that it did not just appear from nothing.

4. It was because of his conviction that Able presented a much better sacrifice unto God than Cain, that by his sacrifice which was demonstrated (*proven*), it was made known that he was righteous. Even though he was killed, he continues to speak. (Genesis 4)

5. Because of his convictions, Enoch was taken by God and did not see death, because God removed him. Certainly it was established that before he was taken, he had obtained the testimony that he was pleasing unto God. (Genesis 5:21-24)

6. Without faithfulness, it is impossible to please God. For one to believe, it is necessary to grow close to God and know that he rewards those who seek to please him. (John 3:19-21; Romans 13:3)

7. Because of his trust in God, Noah was warned by God of the things that were soon to happen. Being greatly motivated, he prepared an ark that would save his family from which the remainder of the world was destroyed. Because of his righteous dedication unto God, he became an heir. (Genesis 6-7)

8. Because of his dedication unto truth, Abraham obeyed God and left his homeland and came to the place that he would receive as an inheritance. This is why he left his home without knowing where the Lord would take him. (Genesis 12)

9. Because of his trust in God, he lived there as a foreigner. He lived in tents with Isaac and Jacob, who are co-heirs of the promise of God. (Matthew 8:11)

10. He saw into the future, a city with foundations that would be designed and created by God.

11. Because of her trust unto God, Sarah was given the ability to conceive many years beyond the time of normal child bearing age; She gave birth because she knew God to be faithful to bring about that which he had promised. (Genesis 21)

12. Therefore from just one, many were brought forth, and even though these forefathers have died, their descendants are countless, like the stars in the sky and the sand grains along the seashore. (Genesis 22:17)

13. These men were faithful, yet they still died not having received the promises. They were able to see them from a distance, and they were convinced by them and embraced them because they were only foreigners and strangers upon the earth.

14. In their writings, they make it clear that they were seeking the eternal home.

15. But truly, if they had longing for that which they had left behind, they might have made the opportunity to revert back, but they gave all that they had to a much better hope, a hope that is celestial. (*as we must also*)

16. Therefore, God is not ashamed to be called their God, so he is preparing a better living place for them.

17. Because he trusted in God, Abraham was tested and offered up Isaac, the one in whom the promises were to come through,

18. of whom it was told unto him by God, "through Isaac, your seed shall descend." (Genesis 21:12)

19. Abraham trusted God, knowing that he was able to raise Isaac from the dead, of which is a prefigured comparison (*unto Christ*) that he understood.

20. Because of his trust in God, Isaac blessed Jacob and not Esau. (Genesis 27:27-40; Malachi 1:2-3)

21. Because of his trust in the Lord, when Jacob was dying, he put the end of his staff over him, paid homage to him and offered a blessing upon him (*Jacob*). (Genesis 27)

22. Because of his trust in God, Joseph, speaking about the then future exodus of the people of Israel, when he was dying, he gave commands concerning his bones. (Genesis 50:25)

23. It was because of what they trusted to be true, the parents of Moses hid him for three months. Because they knew that he was a special child, they did not obey the decree of the king of Egypt! (Romans 13:1)

24. Because of what Moses trusted to be true, he became powerful but refused to be called the son of the daughter of Pharaoh,

25. but he chose that it was better to suffer persecution with the people of God for a time, than to temporarily have the benefits that would accompany doing that which was sinful.

26. He considered the hardships of serving God to be much better than all of the treasures of Egypt, because he was looking forward unto the eternal rewards. (2 Timothy 2:12; 3:12; Philippines 1:29)

27. Because of what he trusted to be true, he left Egypt and he did not fear the fierceness of the king of Egypt; He continued as though he could see that which is invisible. (verse 1)

28. Because of what he trusted to be true, he accommodated the passover with the spreading of blood (*on the doorposts*), so that the firstborn would not be touched by the destroyer. (Exodus 12)

29. Because of what he trusted to be true, they were able to cross the red sea as though it were dry land, of which when the Egyptians tried to cross, they were drowned. (Exodus 15)

30. Because of what they trusted to be true, the walls of Jericho fell after circling them for seven days. (Joshua 6)

31. Because of what she trusted as true, Rahab the harlot was not killed with the others that were disobedient, because she received the spies in secret. (Joshua 2)

32. What more is there to say? For the sake of time, I will not further tell about Gideon, Barek, Samson, Jephthah, David, Samuel and the prophets; Of whom,

33. because of their dedication unto what is true (*their conviction*), they overcame kingdoms, committed themselves unto righteousness, were given the promises of God, and even stopped the mouths of lions!

34. They overcame the power of fire, escaped those with swords and were given much power through weakness. They became strong in warfare and made strong foreign armies yield unto them.

35. Looking forward unto the (*eternal*) resurrection, the women received those who died; Some were tortured to death, but they remained faithful; Not accepting (*temporary, worldly*) safety, that they might receive a better life after the (*eternal*) resurrection. (Daniel 12:2; Revelation 20:12-15; Romans 2:7-10)

36. There were also many who were mocked and whipped and were tried in court as criminals; Some were put in chains and thrown into prison;

37. There were some that were stoned to death and some cut in two. (*beheaded*) Some were murdered by sword; There were many that died. They wore sheepskins and goatskins and were in great need; They had many troubles and were treated poorly; (*a picture of the coming times for the faithful*)

38. The ways of this world were not suitable for them, so they wandered through wildernesses and in the mountains; They hid themselves in caves and caverns within the earth.

39. Yet they received a complete record of faithfulness through their difficulties (*testing*), even though they had not at that time obtained that which was promised by God;

40. But God planned something better for us. However, we shall not be perfected by God in any different way than they were. (Galatians 3:27-29)

Hebrews 12

1. Therefore, we also have all around us a large mass of witnesses (*people looking at us*); So overcome every temptation and the sin that surrounds us, and through patient continuance may we run the race that is set before us. (1 Corinthians 9:24; Philippines 2:16; Galatians 2:2)

2. Look to the faithfulness that our master leader, Jesus had through much difficulty and testing. (John 14:26) Because of the power of God that was presented through him, he endured the cross and the shame of being despised, and he sat down at the right hand of God.

3. Think on the one (*Jesus*) who endured all those sinners speaking evil against him; So do not grow tired in your heart and do not give up.

4. Because you have not yet resisted unto bloodshed, wrestling against sin.

5. Have you forgotten the encouragement that he gave unto you, calling you sons, as he spoke, "My sons, do not hate the training (*testing*) of the Lord, and do not give up when you are being corrected by him.

6. Because those that the Lord loves, he has need to teach them. He educates every son that he shall receive." (Proverbs 3:11-12; Psalms 11:5)

7. Therefore if you receive correction (*education*), then God is dealing with you as a son. What father does not teach his own children?

8. But if you are without correction and education, of which every son must share in, then God does not treat you as a son, but as fatherless!

9. Furthermore, certainly we have all had paternal fathers in this world who have taught and corrected us, and we respected them. Why then would you not respect the spirit of the Father above so that you might eternally live?

10. But surely, the paternal fathers in this world dealt with us for a short time according to what they thought was needed for their purposes. But our Father above deals with each of us for our benefit, so that we might be able to partake in his holiness.

11. No discipline (*training*) is joyful while suffering through it, but it is grievous; However, afterward the rewards of having made peace with God and to be righteous are brought forth in the ones who faithfully suffer through it.

12. "Through it, the weak hands and feeble feet have been strengthened,

13. and the pathway for your feet shall be made straight so that the weak ones not be turned away, but that they be made whole. (*completely perfect* - Proverbs 4:26; Isaiah 35:3)

14. Eagerly pursue peace (*with God*) and holiness, because without such, no one shall see God.

15. Beware and pay attention so that you are not lacking; Do not allow any roots of poison to begin to grow within you, which will defile you; Such has defiled many.

16. Do not let any fornicator or wicked man come in among you (*your gathering, home or church*);
(1 Corinthians 5:2) As in Esau, who for the sake of one meal, gave up his birthright.
(*this is representative of trading away the inheritance of eternal life for a single sinful desire in this life*)

17. You know, afterwards he desired to inherit the benefit, but he was rejected. Though he tried to repent, there was no opportunity for him to take back that which had been lost (*no second repentance*).
(Hebrews 6:4-6; Malachi 1:2; Genesis 27:36-39)

18. For he did not draw near unto the higher way, to be changed and have a fire kindled within him; But he was as the gloom and darkness of a storm. (Malachi 1:2-3)

19. But at the sound of the trumpet and when the announcement is given (*judgment day*), those that would not obey (*in life*) shall be rejected and nothing that they can say shall be admitted to help them;
(1 Corinthians 15:52; 1 Thessalonians 4:16; Revelation 10:7)

20. They could not uphold that which was necessary (*commanded unto them*), but refused to turn away from that which was prohibited. "If a disobedient man tries to handle the higher things (*of God*), he will be stoned to death or killed with a spear." (Exodus 19:12)

21. It was such a fearful thing that even Moses said, "I am terrified and I am trembling." (Deut. 9:19)

22. But you have drawn near to the higher things of God, the heavenly Jerusalem, the city of God. There shall be many angels that shall gather together an assembly of the people of God, (Matthew 24:30-31)

23. the firstborn people that are enrolled, their names written in the book of life are known in the heavens. You shall be set before your God; He is the judge of us all. The spirits of the righteous ones that are being perfected through the shed blood of Jesus,

24. the mediator of the new covenant (*contract offer*), whose blood is much more precious than the blood of Able. (Isaiah 55:3)

25. Beware that you not reject the one who is offering. For if anyone, while living on earth, rejects the divine warning, so much more will he turn them away from the heavens;

26. His voice shook the earth at that time when he promised, "Yet once, I will shake the heavens and the earth." (Haggai 2:6)

27. Now the words "yet once" makes it clear that it shall be for the removal of all of creation, so that the things that are not shaken shall remain.

28. Therefore, associate yourself with the kingdom that is unshakable and may we receive the assistance of God with great reverence and fear (Proverbs 1:7), through which we shall be well pleasing unto him. (Psalms 2:11)

29. "For surely our God is a consuming fire." (Deuteronomy 4:24)

Hebrews 13

1. May brotherly love remain. Do not forget to be hospitable,

2. because some have unknowingly hosted messengers of God. (Matthew 10:11)

3. Be mindful of those who have been thrown into prison, as if it were you in there with them; Toward those that have been treated poorly, consider it to have been done unto your own body.

4. It is honorable for every man to take a wife, but he must keep the bed undefiled; Because God will condemn all fornicators and adulterers. (Proverbs 6:32)

5. Live your life without coveting and be satisfied with what you have. For he has said, "I will never fail you nor abandon you." (Deuteronomy 31:6; 1 John 5:14-15; James 4:3)

6. In this we shall confidently say, "the Lord is my helper and I will not fear that which men might do to me!" (Psalms 118:6)

7. Remember the elders who brought you the instructions and imitate their faithfulness unto God.

8. Jesus Christ is the same yesterday, today and forever. (Malachi 3:6)

9. Do not be deceived by different and strange new doctrines. For it is necessary that your heart be solidly established in love (*compassion, charity*), not in what is forbidden, it was not beneficial for those who did so in the past.

10. We truly have the ability to bring a sacrifice in which to partake of, that those in the temple have no authority to rule over.

11. For the blood of the animals that are brought in by the high priests unto the holy of holies concerning sin offerings, their bodies are burned outside of the city.

12. Therefore, Jesus, to purify the people with his own blood also suffered outside of the gates of the city. (*this refutes* Luke 13:33)

13. So let us now go forth, outside of the city that speaks evil of him. (*Jerusalem*)

14. For the present-day city (*Jerusalem*) is not a permanent city, but we look forward to the permanent city that is to come. (Revelation 21:10)

15. Through him, may we offer up a sacrifice of thankfulness unto God for all that he has given unto us; May we offer up good fruit and acknowledge his name through the way we live our lives.

16. Do not forget about doing good and sharing with others; Such sacrifice is pleasing unto our God.

17. Obey the living elders that are above you, but only those that are truly in Christ. (Romans 13:1-4) Submit unto them; For they watch carefully on behalf of your souls and they will give an account unto God; (Romans 13:4) May they work joyfully because of you, not grieving because of you as that would not be beneficial for you.

18. Pray for us, as we are convinced that we have a good conscience, because in everything, we desire to do what is right before God.

19. I ask that I might be able to come unto you much sooner if God allows. (Acts 21:10-15)

20. May the peacefulness of our God, he who is raised from the dead, the great shepherd of the sheep, (Isaiah 40:11; John 10:1-27) through the blood of the everlasting (*new*) covenant, the Lord Jesus Christ,

21. may he perfect you unto every good deed, for you to do only his will and may he do through you that which is pleasing unto him through Jesus Christ; Unto him be the honor forever and ever.

Verses 22-25 were added by Paul before sending one of the copies of this letter.

22. I encourage you my brothers, endure this message of education and correction; Surely it was I that has added these few words, unto you.

23. Know that our brother Timothy has been freed from prison, and if he comes soon, I will bring him with me when I come.

24. Greet all of the leading elders among you. All of the saints that are in Italy say hello.

25. May the gift of God (*the spirit of the holy one*) be with you all.

It looks as though Paul wrote this letter and sent it to several different Jews
that were in Judea at a time just before he was planning to make his final return to Jerusalem.
This letter is the clear evidence through the old testament scriptures that Jesus is the Christ and that
he brought in the new covenant. Outside of his final visit to Jerusalem, this letter was the final call
and last warning unto the Jews that Paul cared for, before the destruction of Jerusalem.
Paul did bring Timothy with him when he went to Jerusalem, as is recorded in Acts 20:4
It looks as though the book of Hebrews was written between 58AD - 61AD.

James

Chapter 1

1. James, a slave unto God and the Lord Jesus Christ, I write unto the twelve tribes that are scattered abroad and I greet you. (Revelation 7:4) (*most likely written by the Apostle James, brother of John*)

2. Count it all joy, my brethren, when various temptations come upon you.

3. Know that the proving of your faithfulness leads to patient continuance; (Romans 12:3)

4. The deeds that lead to patient endurance perfect you so that you may become perfect and complete, lacking nothing. (Matthew 5:48)

5. But if any one lacks wisdom, let him ask of our generous God who freely gives unto those who do not defy him. (Matthew 11:19; Proverbs 9:10) Ask, and it will be given.

6. One must ask in truth and have no doubt, because one who doubts is like a wave in the sea that is driven by the wind, being tossed about with no direction.

7. Such a man should not expect to receive anything of the Lord.

8. For a man that changes his mind back and forth is not trustworthy nor stable in what he does.

9. May the one who is lacking be joyful when he is elevated.

10. May the wealthy man be joyful when he is brought down; Because just as the flower of the grass, even he shall pass away.

11. The sun rises and its glare dries out the grass and the flowers fall off and the appearance of beauty is lost. So shall wealthy men because of their lewd ways also come to their end.

12. Blessed is the man who endures temptation; When he is tested and proven to be faithful, he shall receive the crown of eternal life which is promised by the Lord for all who love and obey him.
(Hebrews 10:36; 1 John 3:3; Ephesians 4:24-27; 2 Corinthians 7:1; 1 Corinthians 10:12-13; Romans 6:8; Romans 6:16; Matthew 5:48; 2 Peter 1:3-9; 1 Peter 4:19; Titus 2:12; 1 Timothy 2:2-10)

13. Do not say when you are tempted that God is tempting you. God does not tempt anyone to do evil;

14. But every man is tempted by that which appeals to him in the flesh (*his body*); Each one is enticed and is surely being seduced;

15. When lust is conceived, it produces sin; If sin is consummated (*committed*) it brings forth (*eternal*) death. (Hebrews 10:26-27)

16. Do not give in to your temptations my beloved brethren. (Psalms 106:3; 1 Corinthians 10:13)

17. Every good gift and everything that is given unto you that is from above is perfect (*holy*) and comes from the Father in light (*in truth, uncorrupted*). With him there is no variability, and no gray area (*corruptness*) exists when he gives.

18. He purposed for us that we bring forth (*live according to*) truth as he has instructed, so that we might be fruitful and the elect (*chosen*) of all of his creation.

19. In this my brethren, let every man be quick to hear, slow to speak and not commit passionate violence;

20. Because the wrath of man does not comply with the righteousness that is required by God. (Psalm 22:31)

21. Therefore you must turn away from all filth and wickedness. In meekness, receive and implant within you these instructions that I bring unto you, of which are able to help save your soul. (Proverbs 28:13)

22. Do not only hear these instructions as those who deceive themselves do, but be of those that live according to that which is commanded;

23. Because if a man is a hearer of the truth but not a doer, he is like a man that observes his own face closely in a mirror;

24. He discovers the truth of his heritage, then immediately neglects the kind of man he was meant to be.

25. But we, after having looked at the complete law of God, that of freedom from sin and remaining pure, we must not be a hearer unto forgetfulness, but of those who do that which is required. Only these shall be blessed because of how they live.

26. If any man thinks that he is doing as required by God and he does not bridle his tongue, he deceives his own heart. This one's efforts to be pious are to no effect, but done in vain.

27. Pure piety is to be unblemished before God our Father, to visit orphans and widows in their difficulty, to remain unspotted, completely undefiled and to keep ourselves from the world.
(Titus 2:12; 2 Peter 1:3-9)

James 2

1. My brethren, hold unto your dedication and faithfulness as unto our Lord Jesus Christ without playing favorites among men. (1 Peter 1:17; Proverbs 24:23)

2. If a man comes into your assembly wearing an expensive gold ring and is very well dressed, and another comes in wearing tattered clothing;

3. If you look upon the one wearing the expensive clothing and say to him, you can come over here and sit in this comfortable seat, but then you say to the poor one, you stand over there or come sit on the floor;

4. Did you not differentiate between the two men and become as a judge because of your evil intentions?

5. Listen to me my brethren, God chooses the poor of this world who were wealthy in God's truth. They are heirs of the kingdom that he has promised; He gives to those who love and obey him.

6. But in this instance, you would have dishonored those who were poor! Is it not the wealthy who oppress you and drag you in before their courts?

7. Do they not blaspheme the good name by which you are called?

8. If you fulfill the law of God according to the scripture; "You shall love your neighbor as yourself" then you shall do well. (Leviticus 19:18; Matthew 19:19)

9. But if you show partiality (*play favorites*), you commit sin, being guilty of transgressing the law of God.

10. For whoever shall live according to these principals but stumbles on one thing, he is guilty of violating the law as a whole.

11. God said, do not commit adultery and he also said do not murder; If you do not commit adultery but you commit murder, you have become a transgressor of the law of God. (Exodus 20:13-14)

12. So that which he speaks, you must also live if you are to abide within the law of God. Our God will judge all who think they are free to do as they please.

13. The judgment will be without mercy unto all that do not offer mercy unto others. Mercy triumphs over judgment.

14. Brethren, what is the benefit if a man says he has dedication, but does not do the deeds? Is his dedication able to save him?

15. If a brother or sister is naked or are lacking the necessary daily food, (Matthew 15:42)

16. and one of you say to them, go in peace be warmed and filled, but then does not assist them to fill their need, what is gained? (1 John 3:17-18)

17. In the same way, if one is dedicated but does not do the necessary actions, his dedication is worthless and is dead.

18. Though a man may say, you have dedication but I have action; How will you show me your dedication without the action? I will show you my dedication (*faith*) by my actions.

19. If you believe that there is only one God, you are right; But the devils also believe that there is only one God, yet they are afraid. (*because they do not obey*)

20. Are you willing to know the truth, oh vain man. Dedication without actions is worthlessly dead!

21. Was our ancestor Abraham not justified by his actions? He offered up Isaac his son and put him upon the altar! (Genesis 22:9)

22. Do you see that his conviction (*faith*) worked with his actions, and by his actions, his dedication (*faith*) unto God was established and proven?

23. In this, the scripture was fulfilled which states, Abraham believed God and by his obedience proven through his actions, he was validated and justified before God. In this he was called a friend of God. (Genesis 15:6; Isaiah 41:8)

24. Do you now see that by your actions you are proven (*justified*) unto God and not by your conviction (*faith*) alone?

Verse 25 was added by a scribe and is out of context.

25. *In the same way Rahab was also justified by her actions when she showed hospitality unto the messengers and let them out another way.*

26. As the body without the spirit is dead, so likewise, conviction (*faith*) without action (*works*) is also dead.

James 3

1. Do not allow there to be many teachers my brethren; Know that they will be held to a higher standard.
2. We all surely often make mistakes. If anyone does not stumble when he speaks, he is a perfectly mature man. He that is able to bridle his tongue is also able to bridle his whole body.
3. We put bits in the mouths of horses so that they obey us and therewith we can turn their whole body.
4. Ships, as big as they are, of which are driven by the strong winds, yet they are steered by a very small rudder, going the direction the pilot desires.
5. So also, the tongue is a small part of the body, though it speaks mighty things. Surely a small fire can burn an entire forest.
6. The tongue is a fire, a world full of many injustices. Though the tongue is placed among our other body parts, it corrupts the entire body, setting ablaze the true way and set aflame by the fires of hell!
7. Every kind of animal, the beasts of the field, birds, reptiles and snakes have been tamed by the ability of the mind of mankind,
8. yet no one is able to tame his own tongue; It is an unrestrainable wicked thing that is full of poison and is deadly. (Philippines 4:13 - *But I can do anything through Christ who strengthens me.*)
9. With it we speak kindly unto our Father God, but then we turn around and curse men that were created in the image of God!
10. Out of the same mouth comes out blessings and curses. It is not proper my brothers for it to be this way!
11. Does one fountain put forth both salty water and fresh water?
12. My brethren, can a fig tree produce an olive? Can a vine produce a fig? Surely a fountain can not produce both salty water and fresh water! (Matthew 7:16-20)
13. Who is wise and able among you? Can he show by his good behavior and deeds that he has meekness and wisdom?
14. But if you have bitterness, contention and jealousy in your heart, do not pretend you are what you are not by lying against what is true.
15. Such is not the wisdom that comes from above, but are of the ways of this world; These types of people are instinctive and animal like; Such is the way of devils.
16. Where jealousy and contention are, there is disorder and all kinds of wicked things occurring.
17. The wisdom from above is above all, pure, peaceable, patient, and always compliant with God's ways.
18. That which is produced of it is righteous, peaceful and is planted in those who make peace with God. (Isaiah 27:5; Luke 14:32; 2 Peter: 3:14; Romans 2:10)

James 4

1. From where do the battles and fighting among you originate? Not from what I have taught you, but from each of your own lusts, showing themselves through your actions.
2. You have desires, but you do not have what you desire, so you desire to do harm and are zealous to get it, but you are not able to obtain. You fight and battle, but you do not have because you do not ask.
3. But when you ask, you do not receive, because you ask for the wrong reasons, that you might receive that which you have lust for. (John 16:24)
4. You who are adulterers and adulteresses, do you not know that having relationships with the ways of the world is hatred against God? Whoever is a friend of the world is also an enemy of God! (Proverbs 6:32)
5. Do you think that the scripture says it for no reason, that jealousy greatly desires that which is in opposition to the spirit (*of God*) that is within us?
6. But he gives us more power to overcome; Therefore it says, God sets himself against those that defy him because they are determined to please themselves, but he gives his assistance unto those that are humble before him. (Matthew 5:3; Hebrews 10:26; Numbers 15:30-31; Romans 9:15-23)
7. Submit yourselves therefore unto God. Resist the devil and he will run from you.
8. Sincerely approach God, and he will come unto you. Those of you who are sinners, cleanse that which you do (John 8:11 - *go and sin no more*) and all of you who are wavering, purify your hearts!
9. Be distressed, mourn and cry, or your laughter will be turned into mourning and your joy into shame.
10. So humble yourself before the Lord and he will raise you up.

11. Brethren, do not speak against one another. He who slanders his brother or condemns his brother, he does so against God's ways and challenges the law of God. If you judge the law of God, then you are not a doer of the law, but a judge.

12. There is only one lawgiver; He is able to protect or destroy. Who do you think you are, that you can judge him?

13. There are some that might say, come now, tomorrow we will go to the city and spend some time there so that we can trade and make some profits;

14. Yet you do not know what tomorrow will bring. What is your life? A mist appears for a little while, but then it disappears. You are no different.

15. Instead, you should say, if the Lord allows and we live, we will do this or that.

16. But you are boasting in your arrogance. All such boasting is evil.

17. Therefore, unto he that knows to do what is right and does not do it, unto him it is sin unto eternal death. (Numbers 15:28-31; Hebrews 10:26-29; 1 John 5:17-18; Psalms 19:13; Matthew 18:6-10; Romans 7:13; Romans 1:18-21; Luke 12:47)

James 5

1. Come now, you who are wealthy, weep and cry loudly, because great misery is soon coming upon you.

2. Your wealth is corrupt and your clothing is of low quality;

3. Your gold and silver (*money*) is being devalued and is a witness against your treachery. Your flesh shall be consumed by fire. You have built up treasure against yourself for judgment day. (Romans 2:5)

4. Look at the wages of the workers who have reaped your fields, now you are keeping it from them and they cry out! The cries of them have been heard in the ears of the Lord and he is readying for war!

5. You have lived luxuriously on the earth and have lived in self-gratification; (Revelation 18) You have fed your own desires, of which is leading you unto the day of slaughter.

6. You have condemned and killed those who were righteous, though they do not fight back to resist you.

7. Be patient through your endurance my brethren (Matthew 10:22; Mark 13:13) unto the coming of the Lord. Surely the farmer awaits the precious fruit of the earth, being patient for it until it has received the early and the latter rain.

8. You must also be long suffering. Make your hearts firm, the coming of the Lord is near!

9. Do not grudge against one another, my brethren, that you will not be condemned. Look at the hardship my brethren, look unto the longsuffering of the prophets who spoke in the name of the Lord.

11. Take notice, we truly are blessed (*by their writings*) because they endured. You have heard of the patience of Job; You are aware of the final result! The Lord is full of compassion and is merciful.

12. I tell you my brethren, do not swear an oath; Not by the heavens (*spiritual*) or the earth (*physical*), nor by anything else. Say yes when you mean yes and say no when you mean no, so that you are not condemned.

13. Do any among you suffer hardship? If so, then speak sincerely unto God. Are any of you cheerful? If so, let him sing praises unto the Lord.

14. Are any among you sick? If so, then call the elder brethren and have them pray over him. Anoint him with oil in the name of the Lord.

15. The prayer of the one who has been tested and found to be faithful unto God shall cure those that are sick and the Lord shall restore him. If he has committed unintentional mistakes, he may be forgiven. (1 John 5:16, Hebrews 10:26-29; Numbers 15:28-31)

16. Confess your unintentional mistakes unto one another my brethren and pray for one another so that you may be healed. The prayer of one righteous man holds great power. (1 John 1:9; 1 John 5:16)

17. Elijah was a man that had feelings the same as we do and he asked God for it to not rain; Therefore, it did not rain upon that land for three and a half years! (1 Kings 17:1)

18. When he prayed again, the heavens gave rain and the ground sprouted its fruit.

19. Brethren, if any among you make an unintentional mistake, turning away from what is true, and one of you turns him back unto the truth; (Numbers 15:28; Heb 10:26; Romans 1:18; 4:8; 1 Tim 1:18; Psalm 32:2)

20. Know that the one who turns him from his sinful ways, he shall help keep his soul from eternal death and will prevent a great many additional transgressions. (1 John 5:16)

1 Peter

Chapter 1

1. Peter, an apostle of Jesus Christ; I write unto the elect foreign nationals that are dispersed in Pontus, Galatia, Cappadocia, Asia and Bithynia;

2. According to that which we have learned from our Father God, we must live unto obedience with a pure conscience unto the shed blood of Jesus Christ, so that your grace and peace may be full. (Psalm 119:1-3)

3. Adoration unto our Father God and the Lord Jesus Christ; According to his great mercy he has regenerated us to a hope, by living our lives through the resurrection of Jesus Christ; (Romans 6:4-8)

4. Unto an inheritance that is undecaying, undefiled and forever, of which is awaiting you in the heavens

5. by the power of God that is truly being reserved for all of you that are proven to be faithful, of which shall be revealed on the final day. (*judgment day* - Revelation 20:12-15; Romans 2:1-11)

6. At that time you will be greatly joyous, though now, for a short while it is necessary that you are suffering through many difficult temptations, because the proving of your faithfulness

7. is much more precious than gold. When you have been proven through the fire (Matthew 3:11), you shall be received unto praise, honor and glory at the revealing. (Revelation 20:12-15)

8. Jesus Christ, of whom you have not yet seen, yet you love; Though you have not yet come to a full understanding, you believe in and adore him with unspeakable joy, having been reborn.

9. Make sure that you remain faithful and you shall receive the deliverance of your soul. (1 John 3:3-10; Ephesians 2:8-9; Proverbs 28:13)

10. Of this deliverance the prophets craved and searched diligently for, and they prophesied about the mercy that you have now received.

11. They were seeking for it, and for when it would be declared through the spirit of Christ, surely having testified of Christ, of his sufferings and then later, his honor.

12. This was not declared for them, but it was for us of which they spoke these things, which have now been made known unto you by those who have preached the gospel unto you by the spirit of the holy one that is sent unto us from above, of which the prophets long desired to see. (1 John 4:2)

13. Therefore, build yourself up and solidly establish it in your mind, be sober and do not waiver. Have confidence in what is offered to you, that by his grace you shall be received at the coming of Jesus Christ.

14. Be children of obedience and do not return unto the former ways of your own lusts and desires that you did in ignorance; (2 Peter 2:20-22; Hebrews 10:28; Romans 6:16; Numbers 15:28-31)

15. In all that you do and in all of your ways, be holy, as he that has called you is holy. (1 John 3:3)

16. Because it is written, you must be holy (*perfectly blameless*), because the Lord your God is the holy one. (Leviticus 19:2; 1 Thessalonians 3:13; Romans 6:22; Matthew 5:48)

17. If Father calls you, he does not play favorites, as he shall judge every man and woman, according to each one's own deeds. (Romans 2:6-10) So pass your time as a stranger in this world, in fear! (Psalm 2:11; Psalm 119:19; Proverbs 24:23; Proverbs 1:7)

18. Know that it is not by things that are decaying, not even silver or gold by which you have been ransomed from the worthless way of life that was handed down by the forefathers;

19. But you were ransomed by the blood of the precious Jesus Christ, who as an unblemished and unspotted lamb was killed, (Jeremiah 11:19) of whom was known before the creation of the world,

20. and has now been revealed unto you in these recent times.

21. Now you, because of him, believe in God who raised him from the dead. He has made a way for you to have complete dedication and a hopeful expectation that now exists through God.

22. Your souls are now being purified through obedience unto the truth, through the spirit of God, unto sincere care for others from a pure heart. So love one another deeply.

23. Now that you have been regenerated, do not live for that which is temporary and which fades, but unto that which is forever, through living as God has instructed and abiding in it unto the end of your life. (Matthew 6:19)

24. Because all that is of the physical body is like grass, and all honour given by mankind is like the flower that is produced by the grass. But the grass shall soon dry up and the flower fades away. (Isaiah 40:6-8) But the instructions of the Lord must surely remain in you unto the end of your life.

This is the message and the good news (*gospel*) that we declare unto you.

1 Peter 2

1. So put off all wickedness, all deceptions, all envy, all slander and all else that would condemn you, and become as a newborn baby. (to *have a clean record, innocent* - Matthew 18:3; Acts 3:19; 2:38; John 8:31-34; Romans 6:1-23; Psalm 119:21)

2. Be rational and desire completely pure milk (*doctrine*) so that you may grow;

3. That is, if you have taken part in the grace of our Lord.

4. Draw near unto him and surely become solid and alive within the one that was rejected by men, but was chosen by God to be precious.

5. Now you must live firmly, as building a spiritual temple and a holy priesthood; So offer up spiritual sacrifices that are acceptable unto God, through Jesus Christ.

6. This is also contained in the (*old testament*) scriptures: "Behold, I lay in Zion an elect corner stone, a firm foundation that is precious. (Matthew 16:18; 1 Corinthians 10:4) Those that continue believing upon him shall not be dishonored." (Isaiah 28:16)

7. Unto you that believe, he is precious. But unto those that disobey him, he is the stone that the builders rejected. However, he has become the head (*foundation stone*) of the corner (*where two walls join*).

8. He is the stumbling stone and the rock of entrapment unto all those who defy his instructions (Hebrews 10:26-27) and those who are disobedient, unto whom the commandments were also given. (Psalms 118:22; Isaiah 8:14)

9. But you are chosen, the children of the king, a nation of holy people. To be preserved, you must demonstrate the virtues, having been taken out of darkness and called into his wonderful light; (Acts 26:18)

10. In past times, you were not a nation, but you have become the people of God; In the past, you were not offered mercy, but have now been offered mercy. (Hosea 1:10)

11. Beloved, I sincerely beg you, abstain from all fleshly lusts that continually inflict war against your soul.

12. Your behavior among the heathen (*unbelievers, disobedient*) must always be proper before God, because they slander all Christians as though they are criminals; But by the good behavior that they see in you, they might come to glorify God on the day that he shows himself unto them.

13. Therefore, bring every man unto obedience unto the Lord; Whether it is the king who is supreme or leaders in government; (Titus 3:1; 1 Timothy 2:1; Romans 13:1-5)

14. Do so as unto the Lord who shall surely bring punishment unto those that do evil, but rewards unto those that do what is right. (Romans 13:4)

15. For this is the will of God, (Matthew 7:21; 1 John 2:17) to do what is right and silence the ignorance of foolish men. (Mark 3:35)

16. You have been made free from sin (Romans 6:18; John 8:36), so do not use your freedom to conceal evil actions, but be as a servant of God.

17. Care about all people and have affection for the brethren. Fear God and honor him as king. (Romans 13:1; Psalms 2:11; verse 9)

18. Submit unto all that hold jurisdiction over you. Have respect unto your masters, not only unto those that are good to you, but also unto those that are hard on you and are crooked.

19. It is a pleasure to suffer unjust persecution and difficulty because of having a clean conscience to do what is right before God.

20. What benefit is there if you patiently endure while you are punished for doing what is wrong? But if you do what is right and suffer for it while you are patiently enduring, this is the grace (*the assistance*) that is given by God.

21. For this is what you have been called unto, so remember that Jesus Christ did suffer on our behalf, leaving behind an example for us, so we now must follow in his footsteps. (Matthew 10:24; Luke 6:40)

22. Jesus did not commit sin, nor was there any deceit in his mouth; (Isaiah 53:9; 1 John 1:5-6)

23. When he was spoken evil of, he did not slander in return. When he suffered, he did not threaten, but he reserved himself unto the one that judges righteously.

24. He bore the penalty for our sins upon his body on the wooden cross, so that we who were made dead to sin could now live righteously, by whom, through his suffering, you might be restored. (Acts 2:38; 3:19 - *Peter explaining the true method of conversion* - Romans 6:1-23 - *details by Paul*)

25. Because you were as sheep that had gone astray, but you have converted unto the shepherd (*Christ*), the overseer of your soul. (Acts 3:19; 2:38; Matthew 18:2-4; John 8:31-34; Romans 6:1-23; Isaiah 53:5)

1 Peter 3

1. Wives, submit yourselves unto your own husbands. If any (*husbands*) do not obey Christ, through the behavior of the wife they might be won.

2. They would surely have seen your chaste behavior, having fear of the Lord. (Psalms 2:11; Proverbs 1:7)

3. Do not be outward, in braiding your hair or wearing jewelry, or attractive clothing;

4. But be concealed from the lustful hearts of mankind, having an incorruptible meekness and quiet way, which is of great value before God.

5. Because the holy women of old times who had hope in God, they placed themselves under their own husbands.

6. Sarah was subordinate unto Abraham, calling him master. Now you have become her children, and if you do what is right you have no reason to fear.

7. In the same way, husbands live together through proper understanding that she is weaker than you, so give her respect, as you are both heirs of the graciousness of God; So do not frustrate your common goal in this life.

8. Be of one mind and have sympathy for others, love the brethren, be tenderhearted and be friendly.

9. Do not return evil unto those that did evil unto you and do not slander the one that slandered you. Do the contrary and you will be blessed; Know that this is what you have been called unto and in this you shall be commended.

10. If you desire to live a life of love and see good days, restrain your tongue from speaking evil and do not speak anything treacherous against anyone.

11. Turn away from evil and do that which is good; Seek for peace and pursue it;

12. Because the eyes of the Lord see all who are righteous and his ears shall hear what they ask of him. (Psalms 34:12-16; John 9:31)

13. Who shall want to harm you if you follow these instructions well?

14. If you suffer because of having lived righteously, you are blessed; So do not be afraid of those that threaten you and do not be troubled.

15. Purify your heart unto the Lord your God, and always be ready to explain unto every man that asks, the reason for your hope; Do so with meekness and fear.

16. Hold a clear conscience; When they speak evil against you as though you had done something wrong, they may be ashamed by the proper way that you handle yourself according to the ways of Christ.

17. Because it is better that you suffer for doing good, if God chooses that for you, than for you to suffer for doing evil.

18. Because Christ also suffered concerning sin, for both the righteous and the unrighteous, so that he might bring us to God. Having been put to death in his body, he was made alive in spirit. (John 14:17-18)

19. He also went unto the spirits that were held in prison (*hell* - Psalms 16:10; Acts 2:27; Isaiah 61:1)

20. to proclaim unto those that had in the past disobeyed, those who once suffered patiently for God, awaiting in the days of Noah while the ark was being built, in which only a few, only eight souls were saved by the waters. (*from the filthy people*)

21. This is representative of how baptism cleanses us (*from our past deeds that were sinful-Romans 3:25*); Not in the removal of dirt and grime from off of your body, but in receiving a pure record unto the day of the judgment of God, through baptism into the resurrection of Jesus Christ; (Romans 6:1-23; Acts 2:38) (*As the 8 people were cleansed from the evil that surrounded them at the time of the great flood, so also baptism cleanses those with a pure heart from all evil that we had done. The evil is washed away as the evil people also were. We start over with a clean record, much like a newborn baby enters the world* – Matthew 18:1-4)

22. He now sits at the right hand of the Father God, having returned unto the heavens, now holding all power and jurisdiction.

1 Peter 4

1. Therefore, Christ, having suffered for us upon his body, you must also expect the same of yourselves; Because he suffered upon his body, he put an end to sin; (Isaiah 53:5)

2. So now, each man must no longer live according to his own desires, but each one must live according to the will of God as long as he is alive. (Romans 6:1; Matthew 7:21)

3. In past times you have lived your lives according to the ways of the heathen, in that you were lascivious (*wildly reckless*) in your lustful desires, drunkenness, parties, banquets and abominations of idolatry;

4. Of these things, they (*the heathen*) are now surprised that you no longer gather together with them unto the things of which lead to eternal damnation and they continue to speak evil of you.

5. They shall give an account of themselves unto the one that is waiting to judge both those who have been regenerated (*quickened*) and those who are eternally dead.

6. The reason that this message is offered unto those that are spiritually dead is so that they may indeed be judged as men of the world or that they might convert and live according to the spirit of God.

7. But the end of all things is close at hand, so be disciplined and always sober in your prayers.

8. At the foremost of all things, have exceeding affection and benevolence among yourselves, because such love looks past (*forgives*) many offenses.

9. Be a people that show hospitality (*kindness*) without complaining;

10. Those that have offered the gift of themselves serve as good stewards, giving much charitable assistance as though they do so unto God.

11. If anyone preaches, it must contribute unto God; If anyone offers assistance, let him do so as with the power of God; In this, may everything you do bring honour unto God, through Jesus Christ. Unto whom the glory and the power shall forever be.

12. Beloved, do not be surprised when a fiery hardship is brought upon you.

13. But understand that you share in the sufferings of Christ, so be happy, that at the revealing of his glory, you may surely welcome him with great joy.

14. If you are spoken evil of because of Christ living in you, you are blessed. In this, you honor the spirit of God that is in you.

15. Do not have any of you be accused of being a murderer, a thief, doing any evil activity. Do not even meddle in the affairs of others.

16. But if any of you suffer for being a faithful follower of Jesus Christ, do not feel ashamed, but thank God because of this.

17. Because now is the time to begin the judgment of the temple *(body)* of God. (1 Corinthians 6:19). And if it is first unto us, what shall be the final result for those who do not obey the gospel of God?
(Romans 10:16; 2 Thessalonians 1:8; Acts 2:38; 3:19; Matthew 18:1-10)

18. And if the righteous are being saved through much hard work and difficulty, in what way shall the ungodly and the sinner appear before God? (Isaiah 57:21; Psalm 104:35)

19. Therefore, those that suffer according to the will of God, may they commit their souls unto living properly as unto their faithful creator. (Deuteronomy 6:5; 2 Peter 1:6-9; Titus 2:12)

1 Peter 5

1. Unto the elders (*mature leaders*) that are among you, know that I am a fellow elder and a witness of Jesus Christ and his sufferings, and also a sharer in the honor that is soon to be revealed.

2. Tend to the gathering of God that is among you and continually oversee them, not because it is your duty, but because you care for them; Do not look for personal gain from them, but do so because you love them.

3. Do not exalt yourself above them as master of the inheritance, but be a perfect example unto the gathering.

4. When the chief shepherd (*Christ*) appears, you shall receive the eternal crown of honor. (Daniel 12:3)

5. In the same way, you that are younger in the doctrine of Christ, submit yourselves unto those that are elder. Be subject to one another and be engulfed in humility, because God sets himself against those that are proud within themselves, but unto those that are humble he gives mercy.

6. Submit yourselves therefore under the powerful hand of God so that he may lift you up in the proper time.

7. Give all of your anxieties to him, because he cares about you.

8. Be of a sound mind and watch, because the adversary (*Satan*) is as a roaring lion that is seeking all that he can devour;

9. Resist him by standing firm in the true doctrine and know that your fellow brethren throughout the world are suffering in similar ways.

10. Our God is full of mercy. He is the one who is calling us unto his everlasting honor through Jesus Christ and he knows that you will suffer for a time; But through it he shall perfect you, confirm you, strengthen you and set you firmly in Christ. (Revelation 1:9)

11. Unto him be the glory and the power, now and forever.

The following is a greeting or a cover page
from one of the copies that was sent out. (verse 1:1)

12. Unto Silvanus, you are a faithful brother as I understand it; Through these few words that I have written unto you, I have explained that which is expected of a true Christian and I further attest that this is possible by the grace of God in which you stand.

13. Your fellow elected brethren of Babylon greet you, as does my son Marcus.

14. Welcome everyone with an innocent kiss of affection. Peace unto all of you that are in Jesus Christ.

.

2 Peter

Chapter 1

1. Simon Peter, a slave and apostle of Jesus Christ. We have received the precious doctrine which is the pursuit of the righteousness that is required by our God and our saviour Jesus Christ.

2. May grace and peace be abundant unto you through the full understanding of God and master Jesus Christ.

3. All things that pertain to this pursuit of godliness have been given to us by his divine power, through the complete understanding of the one that has called us to be honorable and virtuous;

4. Through this, he has given unto us the very precious promises; That through these things, you might become partakers of the godlike disposition *(way of living)*, escaping from the lustful corruption of the world.

5. But besides this, with all diligence, in addition to the doctrine, add excellent virtue; With such virtue, add to your knowledge;

6. And with knowledge, add self-control; With self-control, add patient endurance *(consistency)*; And with all of this, add godliness.

7. With godliness, add unto your brotherly affection *(love)* towards one another. Unto your brotherly affection, add benevolence.

8. For if these things are in you abundantly, you will not be idle nor unfruitful and you will come to know the full knowledge of the Lord Jesus Christ. (Matthew 7:20; James 1:22; Titus 2:12; 1 Timothy 2:2-10; 4:7-8)

9. But he that does not have these things within himself, he is blind and is short-sighted and forgets that his past sins have been forgiven. (Romans 3:25)

10. So my brethren, be sure to be diligent in order to make your calling firm so that you will also be chosen. Because if you continue to do these things, you shall not fall. (Hebrews 10:26-39; Hebrews 6:4-6)

11. In this, the entrance into the everlasting kingdom will be granted through our Lord and Savior Jesus Christ. (*You are not currently saved, but have an inheritance if you qualify*)

12. Therefore I will never regret continually reminding you of these things, because by your knowledge of them, you shall be confirmed *(tested and found faithful)* in the present truth.

13. Yes, and I think it is right, that as long as I live in this temple *(body - 1 Corinthians 6:19)*, I shall continue to remind you of these things,

14. because I know that I shall soon be leaving this body, surely, as the Lord Jesus has already made it clear unto me;

15. I will be continuing my efforts to do so, so that after my departure these things will continue to be in your memory.

16. Because we have not followed after the cleverly crafted fables, as others do. But we have made the truth known unto you, all that is of the Lord Jesus Christ, having been eyewitnesses of his mighty power. (1 Timothy 1:4; 1 Timothy 4:7; 2 Timothy 4:4; Titus 1:14)

17. He received glory and honor from God the Father, when there came a voice that we heard from out of the sky, when we were with him on that holy mountain which spoke unto him the magnificent honor:

18. "This is my son, my beloved, in whom I am greatly delighted." (Matthew 17:1)

19. And we truly have the fulfillment of what was brought forth by the words of the prophets, of which you will do well to listen to, as a lamp that shines upon a murky place before the day dawns and the light rises in your hearts.

20. But before anything else, know this first; That there has never been a prophecy in the scriptures that has been written based upon the writer's own desires.

21. Because no prophecy of God was established by the will of any man, but was borne by the spirit of God and was carried along and spoken by holy men of God *(the prophets)*.

2 Peter 2

1. But there were false prophets among them, as there will also be many false teachers among you, of whom will secretly bring in damnable heresies of destruction, living in a contradicting way unto the Lord who redeemed them, of which they lead themselves unto eternal damnation. (Acts 20:29-30; Matthew 24:4-5,11; Jude 1:18; Mark 13:6; 2 Thessalonians 2:10-12; Galatians 2:4-5; Jude 1:4; 2 Corinthians 11:15; Ephesians 4:14; 2 Timothy 3:5-13; 4:3-4; Ezekiel 22:28; 28:18 Isaiah 30:10; 56:10-11; Proverbs 14:9; Jeremiah 23:1-40)

2. There will be many who will follow their damnable ways, of whom will speak evil of the true way. (Proverbs 21:16; Zephaniah 3:4; Ezekiel 34:2)

3. And through extortion *(tithes),* due to carefully crafted words, they will use you for their own personal gain. *(Isaiah 42:22; take money from you - Hebrews 7:1-4 corruption in most bibles)* The judgment of these people has already been decided and their eternal damnation shall never be ended. (Jeremiah 9:3; Romans 16:17-18; Psalms 12:2)

4. Know that God did not offer leniency unto the angels that chose to commit sin, but placed them in chains in the deepest darkness of hell awaiting the day of judgment. (Jude 1:6)

5. God did not spare the ancient world, but preserved only eight with Noah, a preacher of righteousness, but the flood destroyed the whole world of the ungodly. (Genesis 6)

6. The cities of Sodom and Gommorah were burnt to ashes as an example unto others that we must live a godly life. (Genesis 19)

7. But Lot was oppressed by the lawless lustful behavior of those cities, yet he was saved!

8. He did see and hear many lawless things and his righteous soul was tormented day after day while he lived among them.

9. For the Lord knows how to save the godly from evil, but the ungodly are kept for the day of judgment to be punished; (Romans 2:5-10; 1 Corinthians 10:13; Revelation 20:12-15)

10. For they are those that lust to defile the bodies of others and they despise the authority of God; (Romans 13:1-5) They commit defiant sins against him (Numbers 15:28-31; Hebrews 10:26-27; Acts 26:18; Psalms 19:13) and are self-pleasers who do not tremble, but bring glory unto themselves in their blasphemy.

11. But even angels who have miraculous power and strength, being greater than men, (Hebrews 2:8) yet they do not even bring a slanderous charge against themselves before the Lord;

12. Yet these men are like mindless instinctive animals; They were created to take unto themselves and to destroy everyone that is ignorant, blaspheming due to their own corruption; But in the end, they will all be destroyed. (Isaiah 65:12-15; Psalm 144:8)

13. They will receive what is due for doing that which is wrong, seeking to pleasure themselves with debauchery during the daytime. They are spotted with filth and full of blemishes, sporting themselves in their own doctrinal errors while they are certainly feasting upon you;

14. They have eyes full of adulterous lusts and they never stop committing sin. They entice those with unsettled souls and their hearts are full of covetous practices. They are cursed children. (Psalms 106:39-40; Malachi 2:2)

15. They have forsaken the true way and they went astray, following the way of Balaam, the son of Beor, who loved the rewards for doing that which is wrong. (Jeremiah 10:21)

16. He was rebuked for his own transgressions by a mute donkey that spoke with the voice of a man, telling the words of the angel of God. (Numbers 22:28)

17. They are springs with no water, squall clouds blown unto the darkest blackness to be kept there forever.

18. They speak great swelling words of vanity to attract others by the lusts for that which is evil, bringing forth unbridled lusts and they allow for them to live in error.

19. While they promise them freedom *(from the penalty of sin)*, they themselves are slaves unto damnation; This is because, by whatever a man is overcome, the same is he also enslaved. (John 8:31-34)

20. Therefore if one has escaped the defilements of this world by the full knowledge of our savior Jesus Christ, but if they are again entangled and overcome, the last state for them is worse than in the beginning. (Hebrews 6:4-6; Hebrews 10:26-27; Matthew 12:43-45; Numbers 15:30-31)

21. For it would have been better for them to have not come to know the way unto righteousness, than for them to understand and then turn away from the command to live a holy life. (Hebrews 6:4-6)

22. What has then happened is as the proverb states; The dog returns again unto his vomit, and the pig after having been washed, returns again unto the mud! (Proverbs 26:11)

2 Peter 3

1. My beloved, this is the second time that I have written unto you. I now sincerely hope to awaken in your memory,

2. that the words spoken by the holy prophets and apostles are the instructions unto our saviour and Lord.

3. But know this is certain; In the last days, many false teachers shall arise; According to their own lustful desires they will go forth and say (*to themselves*), (1 Timothy 4:1-3)

4. where is the evidence concerning his promise to return? The forefathers have died and things remain the same as they were since the beginning.

5. However, such things are hidden from them because of their own choice to be ignorant; The old world stood in water, but then again was brought out of the water;

6. Thereby, those that were of the world died by the waters of the flood.

7. But now, the earth and the sky are reserved for fire. By that same command of God, they are kept for the day of judgment and the destruction of all ungodly men.

8. Beloved, do not allow this one thing to be hidden from you, that one day with the Lord is equal to a thousand years unto us. (Psalms 90:4)

9. So know that the Lord is not slow to fulfill his promise, in the way that some might count slowness; But he is very patiently awaiting for our sake, not wanting any to die eternally, but having the hope that everyone would come to repentance before his return. *(The mark of the beast puts an end to the waiting - being that all who take it are damned and all who don't will die, with the exception of the faithful 144,000)*

10. But when the day of the Lord has come, it will be like a thief in the night (1 Thessalonians 5:2-4 - *horribly shocking)*, wherewith there will be a great and mighty noise that approaches and the natural arrangement of this world shall be set afire and everything shall be completely destroyed. (James 5:3; Matthew 13:30; Isaiah 1:31; Psalms 97:3-5, 19)

11. Now that you know what the end of all things shall be, what type of people do you suppose that you must be? Why would you not live your lives according to holiness before God?
(1 John 3:3; Psalms 104:35; Isaiah 24:1-6; Nahum 1:5)

12. So look forward unto the quickly approaching return of our God; The day in which the sky will be enflamed and the natural arrangement of all things shall all be consumed by fire and destroyed.
(Amos 9:5-13)

13. Look forward unto that which he has promised, when we will be brought unto the place where the sky and the earth are renewed afresh.

14. Therefore my beloved brethren, look forward unto these things, be diligent and spotless, completely spotless, and be found to have made peace with God. (Colossians 1:22; Ephesians 1:4; 3:17; Matthew 5:48)

15. Think about the patience that the lord has for each of us to come into his place of safety! It is the same as our beloved brother Paul and all of the wisdom that has been given unto him;

16. In all of his letters he spoke of these things, some of which are difficult to understand for those that are unlearned, (Hebrews 5:11) and they are not able to be understood by those that are unstable, so they pervert them, as they do with all of the other writings (*scriptures*), of which shall lead them unto their own eternal destruction. (2 Peter 2:1-3)

17. But you my beloved, now that you know before hand, watch carefully so that you are not led away into lawless error that will annul your covenant with God and the promises thereof. (Hebrews 10:26-27)

18. Continue to grow more and more deeply into his favor and also in the knowledge of our Lord, our saviour Jesus Christ. Because the glory is his, both now and forever.

1 John

Chapter 1

1. I write unto you concerning the one who was from the beginning, who we heard speak, saw with our own eyes and our hands touched; The message of Life. (*Jesus Christ*)

2. The life he lived was witnessed by us and is the way that we now live. We are teaching you of the eternal life that is of the Father, of which was revealed unto us, according to the will of God. (John 1:1)

3. That which we have seen and heard, we now share with you so that you could have the ability to fellowship with him; It truly is a partnership, each of us with our Father and his son, Jesus Christ.

4. I write these things unto you so that your understanding may truly be complete.

5. This is the message that we heard from him and now declare unto you, that God is light, and there is absolutely no darkness (*sin*) in him at all. (John 1:4-5; Psalm 92:15)

6. If we claim to be in fellowship with him, but participate in evil, we are a liar and not bringing forth truthfulness. (Matthew 7:17)

7. But if we live in the light as he is in the light, (1 John 3:3) we have a relationship with each other and the blood of Jesus Christ can cleanse us from all sins. (*past sins at the time of conversion*)
(Romans 3:25; 2 Peter 1:9; Romans 6; Ephesians 2:8-9; Hebrews 4:12)

8. If we claim that we have never committed any sins, we truly deceive ourselves and we are not in truth. (Romans 3:23)

9. If we acknowledge our sins (*at the time of conversion*), he is trustworthy and just to free us from all (*past*) sin and purify us from all wrongful character. (*moving forward*)
(John 8:31-36; Acts 2:38; Romans 6:1-23; Proverbs 13:19; Proverbs 14:9; Proverbs 28:13)

10. If by all means we are not truly living unblamable, we are lying and his message does not abide in us. *(Greek words: 1437 1513 3754 3756 2248 5037 273 5583 2532 3588 3056 2076 3756 1722 2254)*

1 John 2

1. Those young in the faith (*doctrine*), I write unto you these things so that you do not choose to commit sin. But if anyone does make an unaware mistake, we have an advocate with the Father, Jesus Christ, the righteous judge; (Proverbs 28:13; 1 John 5:16-17; Numbers 15:28-31; Hebrews 7:25)

2. He is the atonement concerning our transgressions; Not only ours, but he offers this unto everyone in the world. (Genesis 18:18; Malachi 3:12)

3. In this, we know that we know him: If we live by his instructions. (1 Corinthians 1:6)

4. Whoever says they know him, but do not live as he has instructed, they are a liar and there is no truth in them. (2 Corinthians 12:21; 1 John 3:8)

5. But whoever lives as he has instructed, in him the affection of God has been established.

6. This is how we know that we are in Christ: Whoever says that they are in Christ must live as Christ lived. (1 John 3:3)

7. Brethren, I do not write to give you any new instructions, but to emphasize that which has been since the beginning.

8. Furthermore, a new commandment I do write unto you, of which is true in myself and also in you, because the darkness (*doing evil*) is in the past and the light truly shines through you. (Romans 6:16-23)

9. Anyone that says that they are in the light, yet despises one of the brethren, he remains in darkness.

10. He who lives in the light must have a deep affection for the brethren and he does not make such an error.

11. Whoever hates his brother remains in darkness and lives in darkness and does not understand he is in error, because the darkness has blinded his eyes.

12. I write unto you who are young in the doctrines of Christ, because you have turned away from your sins by his name.

13. I write unto you who have been long established in truth, because you knew Christ (*when he walked the earth*), the one who is above all. I write unto you younger men (*men under 40*) because you are valiant, and Jesus Christ lives in you and because you have overcome all wickedness.

14. I write to the children because you have knowledge of the Father.

15. Do not love the ways of the world and in no way become as the world; Because if any man loves the world, the love of the Father is not in him. (John 12:25)

16. Because all that are of the world lust after evil things that the body desires, the lust of the eyes and boasting of oneself (*self-exaltation is opposite of humility*);

17. These things are not of the Father, but are the ways of the world. But the things of the world and the lusts thereof shall come to an end. Those who do the will of the Father shall live forever. (Matthew 7:21; Mark 3:35; 1 Peter 2:15)

18. I call unto you, because it is the last days. You have heard that the antichrist shall come, but there are already many antichrists, and by this we know that it is the final times.

19. Turning away from us, they turned from the straight way, (G-1813+G-2116) because they were not the same as us; If they were as we are, they would have remained with us. In this it is revealed that they are not all our brethren. (*the true brethren are faithful unto Christ and love those who live a holy life*)

20. But you have the charisma of the Holy Spirit of Christ and you understand all of these things.

21. I have not written unto you because you do not know the truth, but because you do know truth! You know that no liar is of the spirit of God. (Revelation 21:8)

22. So a man is a liar if he denies (*by word or action - Titus 1:16*) that Jesus is the Christ. The one who denies the Father and the son is antichrist. (John 5:23; John 12:45)

23. The one who denies the son does not know the Father. (John 8:44 - *most religious Jews reject Christ*) He who assents into covenant with the son also has the Father. (John 15:24; 1 John 4:1-3; Romans 11)

24. Continue to keep that which you have heard from the beginning living within you. If that which you have heard from the beginning remains in you, you shall remain in the son and the Father.

25. That which he promised unto us is everlasting life.

26. I write these things unto you to warn you of those who are trying to lead you astray.
(2 Peter 2:1; Acts 20:29-30; Matthew 24:4-5, 11; Mark 13:6; 2 Thessalonians 2:10-12; Galatians 2:4-5; Jude 1:4; 2 Corinthians 11:15; Ephesians 4:14; 2 Timothy 3:5-13; 4:3-4; Jeremiah 23; Ezekiel 22:28; Ezekiel 28:18; Isaiah 30:10; Isaiah 56:10-11; Proverbs 14:9; Jeremiah 23:1-40)

27. But if the charisma that you have received of God through his spirit remains in you, then you have no need for any man to teach you: (John 16:13; Jeremiah 31:34.) This same charisma of the spirit of God teaches you all things and is true, and does not lie; All that you are taught by him, keep firmly within you. (John 16:13)

28. Again, those who are young in the true doctrine, remain according to Christ, so that when all is determined, you will have complete assurance that you will not be ashamed at his coming.

29. If you know that he is righteous, know that everyone who is living a fully righteous life has been regenerated by him.

1 John 3

1. Look at the amount of affection that the Father has for each of us, in that we may be called the children of God! (Galatians 3:26) Those who are of the world do not understand us because they do not know him.

2. Beloved, we currently are the children of God, though it has not yet been declared as to who shall be (*on judgment day*); But when he appears, we do know that it shall be announced that we are like him, because he will see each of us as we are (*how we live*). (Romans 2:6-10; 1 Thessalonians 5:5; John 1:12)

3. Everyone that has this hope in him must purify himself, to be as pure as Christ is pure. (verse 8)
(2 Timothy 2:11; Psalm 119:1-3, 44; Matthew 5:48; 1 Peter 1:16; 1 Thessalonians 3:13; 1 John 2:6; Romans 6:8, 16, 22; James 1:12; Revelation 1:7; Revelation 20:12-15; Psalms 91:15; Psalms 19:7)

4. Whoever chooses to commit sin also chooses to do wickedness, because sin is wickedness.

5. And you know that Christ came in order to remove our sins. (Matthew 1:21; Psalms 66:18) Sin can not be in him. (Hebrews 10:26-29; Numbers 15:28-31; 1 John 5:17)

6. Whoever is in Christ can not continue to commit sin. (Hebrews 10:26; 1 John 1:5; Isaiah 55:7) Whoever chooses to commit sin has not seen him and does not know him. (Numbers 15:28-31)

7. Unto all that are young in the faith (*doctrine of truth*), do not allow anyone to deceive you: It is the one who chooses to always do righteousness, it is he who is righteous, the very same way that Christ is righteous. (Romans 6:16; Jeremiah 32:23)

8. He that chooses to commit sin is a servant of the devil (Jeremiah 31:30; John 8:31-36, 47)
(commit = G-4160 ποιῶν = to commit - present participle active – "a single action moving forward") because the devil has chosen to commit deadly sin from the beginning. It is because of this that Christ manifests himself in us (*by his spirit*), so to destroy the deeds of the devil. (Acts 26:17-20; Ezekiel 3:20; 18:10-32; John 14:23; Acts 2:38; 3:19; Zephaniah 3:13; Proverbs 12:19; Hosea 14:19)

9. Whoever is regenerated by God must not choose to commit sin, because God's seed (*The spirit of Jesus*) lives in him; (1 John 4:2) He is not permitted to commit sin, because he is regenerated by God. (Numbers 15:28-31; Psalms 119:1-3; Zechariah 3:13; Romans 6:1)

10. It is by this, that the children of God are made known, but so are the children of the devil. Everyone who does not live a righteous life and anyone that does not love the brethren, they are not of God. (Isaiah 58:7-9; Isaiah 39:2)

11. This is the message that was established in the beginning, to have love for one another. (Matthew 22:39; Luke 10:27; Mark 12:33)

12. Not as Cain who was evil, as we know that he killed his brother. And why did he kill him? Because his deeds were evil but his brothers were righteous. (Genesis 4)

13. Do not be surprised my brethren if those of the world hates you. (John 15:18)

14. We know that we have been raised from being dead, to now be of the living, (Romans 6:4-8) because we love the brethren. Whoever does not love the brethren remains (*spiritually*) dead.

15. He that detests his brother is a murderer and you know that no murderer will receive eternal life.

16. By our love we truly demonstrate the affection of God, because he laid down his life for our sake; Therefore, we ought to also lay down our own lives for the brethren.

17. Whoever has the ability in this present world to offer help and sees one of his brothers have a need, if he does not offer assistance to help him, how is the love of God living in him? (James 2:14-16)

18. My beloved children, do not offer your affectionate care unto those in need by giving advice or encouragement only, but by your actions and truly meeting the need. (James 2:24)

19. By this we know that we are in truth, because beforehand he will surely put in in our hearts to give help where it is needed. (*Do not give to feel that you did something, but only give as God leads you to give, to fill a need.*)

20. If our heart accuses us of doing wrong, beware; But God is much more knowing than our own heart, as he knows all things.

21. Beloved, if our heart does not accuse us, then we can have confidence with God.

22. Whatever we have certain need of, he will supply, because we obey his commandments and all of the things that he desires of us, we do. And this is the instruction that he gave unto us;

23. To fully commit ourselves unto the name of the son of God, Jesus Christ, and to have affectionate benevolence for one another, just as he commanded of us. (Matthew 22:37; Mark 12:30; Luke 10:27)

24. Whoever keeps this commandment is in compliance with God and has Christ living in him. By this, we know that he lives within us through his spirit that he has given unto us. (1 John 4:2)

1 John 4

1. Beloved, do not believe every one that is spiritual, but test the spirituals to see whether they are of God; Because there are many false prophets and false teachers that have stood up in the world. (2 Peter 2:1-3)

2. By this, you shall know who has the spirit of God: Every soul that has come into covenant with Jesus Christ and has received his spirit into his own body, it is he that is of God. (1 Peter 1:12; 2 Timothy 1:14; 1 Corinthians 2:13; 2 Corinthians 6:16; Ezekiel 37:27; Acts 19:6; John 16:13; Hebrews 6:4; 9:8)

3. Every soul that does not come into covenant with Jesus Christ, not having the spirit of God come into his own body, this one is not of God. This one is antichrist, of which you have heard would come and is now already in the world. (2 John 1:7)

4. But if you are of God, beloved, you have conquered over them, because he that is in you (verse 2) is more powerful than he that is of the world. (Philippines 4:13; John 16:33)

5. They that are of the world, they speak of things of the world, and because of this the world understands them and recognizes them.

6. But we are of God and those who know God hear us; He that is not of God does not understand us. In this we can discern who is in truth and who is in error.

7. My beloved children, may we love one another, because love is of God; All that have been regenerated

by God and are born of God, they love one another.

8. All who do not have affection for others, they are not of God, because God is truly loving. (*affectionate*)

9. God showed his love toward each of us in sending his only begotten son into the world, so that we could actively live through him. (Titus 2:12; John 3:16-21)

10. By this, that love is demonstrated, not that we first loved God, but that he first loved us, by sending his son to pay the penalty incurred by our sins.

11. Brethren, if God has loved each of us in such a way, we must also love the brethren in the same way.

12. No one has ever fully comprehended God. But if we have affectionate benevolence for one another, then God lives in us and his love is truly demonstrated through us.

13. Because he has given each of us of his spirit, we know that we live in Christ and he lives in us. (1 John 4:2)

14. We (*apostles and older people*) witnessed and have surely seen with our own eyes that the Father sent his son into the world.

15. The one that assents into covenant with him and lives faithfully unto him, God lives in him and he in God, because Jesus Christ is the son of God.

16. And we continually see and surely know the love that God has for each of us. He that lives in God's love is demonstrating the same affectionate benevolence. He lives in God and God in him.

17. In this, the love of God is established in us and we can have confidence that on the day of judgment, that as Christ is, we also are the same in this present world. (Titus 2:12; 1 John 3:3; 1 John 1:7)

18. There is nothing to fear when in his love, and when we are perfectly mature in his love there is no reason to fear. (*concerning judgment day*). There is fear for that which the punishment will bring, because the one who is not demonstrating his love surely has reason to fear. (Proverbs 1:7)

19. So we love him because he first loved us.

20. If anyone says that they love God but they despise the brethren, they are a liar. How can he that despises the brother that he can see, have love for God who he can not see.

21. This is the instruction that we have from him: Every one that loves God must also love the brethren.

1 John 5

1. All that continue believing that Jesus is the Christ and love (*obey*) him, these are regenerated by God. (John 3:16-21) Everyone that is regenerated by God also loves others that have been regenerated by him,

2. and by this, we can be sure that those young in the faith love God; If we love God, we surely live by his instructions.

3. In this, we demonstrate our affection for God; We truly live in the way that he has commanded for us to live and that his instructions are not burdensome to us.

4. Everyone that is born of God must overcome the world; Our conviction and dedication is what brings the victory that overcomes the world. Who is it that overcomes the world?

5. No one but those that commit themselves fully unto Jesus Christ, the son of God.

6. They are the ones that pass through the water and shed blood of Jesus Christ. (Romans 6; John 19:33) Not by water only, but by the water and the sacrifice (*baptism and living in obedience thereafter*). (John 3:5) The spirit of God is the witness, because the spirit is the truth.

7. There are three witnesses in the heavens; The Father, the instructions and the spirit; These three are one. (*make up the whole*)

8. And there are three that are witnesses on the earth; The spirit of God, water of baptism and blood of sacrifice (*faithful endurance through testing*), and these three are one. (*make up the whole*)

9. If we have witnesses that are men, God's witness is greater. This is because they are the witnesses of God by multiple testimonies through his son (*spirit*).

10. Those that believe (*obey*) unto the son of God have themselves as a witness; Those that do not believe, accuse God of being a liar, because they do not believe the testimony that is seen of God through his son.

11. And those that obey are a witness that God offers everlasting life unto us; And this life is in his son.

12. He that has the son (*Christ Jesus*) has life; Anyone that does not have the son does not have life.

13. I write these things unto those who believe (*obey*) in the name of the son of God, so that you might know that you shall receive everlasting life, if you continue faithfully unto the name of the son of God.

14. And this is the assurance that we can truly depend upon, that if we have need of anything, according to his will, he hears us;

15. If we know that he hears us, whatever we have need of, we know that we shall receive that which is needed, given by him. (James 4:3)

16. If anyone becomes aware of his brother having committed a sin not unto death (Numbers 15:28-31 - *unaware sin*), they shall ask God for forgiveness and God will give life unto those that commit a sin not unto death. There is a sin that is unto death, for such, I do not say that you should pray for it!
(Numbers 15:28-31; James 5:20, Hebrews 10:26-29; Matthew 18:15; Psalm 19:12-13)

17. All wickedness is sin, but there is a type of sin not unto death (*unaware sin* – Psalm 32:2).

18. We know that whoever is regenerated of God does not choose to commit sin, because he that is regenerated by God guards himself and the devil does not corrupt him.
(1 John 3:3; 1 Corinthians 10:13; Romans 6:16; Psalm 19:12-13)

19. By this we truly know that we are of God, though the majority of the world lives in wickedness (*sin*).

20. And we know that the son of God is with us and he has given us an understanding that we know the truth and that we are in the truth of his son, Jesus Christ. He is the true God and the only way unto everlasting life.

21. Children, beware; Protect yourselves from all idolatry.

(idolatry - anything that is chosen above God, held as more important than God or anything that prevents one from remaining faithful unto him)

2 John

1. I the elder, write unto my favorite woman and her children of whom I truly love, and not only I, but you are also loved by all others who have known the truth.
2. This is because the truth remains in us and will be with us until the end.
3. May grace, mercy and peace be with you from God the Father and the Lord Jesus Christ, in truth and affection.
4. I am very happy to have found that your children are living in the true way, just as we had received the instructions from the Father.
5. Now I instruct you, not as a new commandment from the Father, but that which has been from the beginning, that we must care greatly for one another.
6. Our affection and benevolence (*love for God*) is that we live according to his instructions; This is the instruction that you have known from the beginning, that you must live in this way.
7. Because there are many deceivers in the world who do not assent into covenant with Christ Jesus, nor believe that he comes into each of us. (John 14:23) Such people are deceivers and antichrist. (1 John 4:3)
8. So watch yourselves that you not lose that which you have already gained, but bring forth the full amount of what is necessary.
9. Whoever violates and does not remain within the doctrine of Christ does not have God. He who does remain according to the doctrine of Christ, he is of the Father and the Son. (Colossians 2:17)
10. If anyone that you come across does not uphold this instruction, do not allow them into your house and do not be happy to see them, nor speak kind words to them. (1 Corinthians 5:11; 2 Thessalonians 3:6)
11. Because if you speak kindly to them, you endorse their evil deeds (*and doctrines*).
12. I have many things to tell you, but do not intend to write with pen and paper, so I am hoping to come unto you and speak to you face to face, so that we might have complete joy.
13. The children of your favorite sister say hello unto you.

3 John

1. I write unto Gaius the beloved, of whom I love because you are morally in truth. (Acts 20:4)
2. Beloved, concerning all things, I pray that you succeed in your work and that you are in good health, just the same as your soul is well.
3. I am very happy that the brethren came and told me that you live according to the true way.
4. There is no greater happiness for me, than to hear that my children are living in the truth.
5. Beloved, you have been faithfully doing that which is necessary for the brethren and also strangers,
6. and they brought a good loving testimony unto the gatherings; Concerning them, you have done well in bringing them forth properly unto God.
7. For his name sake, they went out, taking nothing from the gentiles.
8. We certainly applaud the character of these men because we are co-workers in bringing forth the truth.
9. I wrote a letter unto the church, but Diotrephes, who loved to be the leader would not allow us to teach.
10. Because of this, if I am able to come, I will remember the evil that he does and that he spoke evil against us, and that he would not accept us as brothers, and that he prevents those who would, by throwing them out of the church. (*A christian church that is corrupt? Yes, even at such an early time!*) (Acts 20:29)
11. Beloved, do not do as those who are worthless do; Always do that which is proper in the eyes of God. Those who live in complete compliance unto God, they are of God; But those who do what is evil, they have not come to understand God's ways. (1 John 3:8, Romans 2:3)
12. Demetrius has had a good report by everyone, and also by his own words that are in truth; We also have seen for ourselves and you know that our testimony is true.
13. I have many things to tell you about, but I do not wish to write them all unto you,
14. but I am hoping to see you soon and we will speak face to face. Peace be unto you. Your friends here say hello. Say hello unto our friends that are there.

Jude

1. Jude, a slave unto Jesus Christ, the brother of James, (Acts 1:13; Galatians 1:19) I write unto all those who are in God the Father, having been made holy and called unto Jesus Christ.

2. May you receive mercy, peace and love, and be increased by the words that I send unto you.

3. I care deeply for you, and I have given all earnestness to write unto you about the deliverance in Christ that we share. I had the need to write unto you in order to remind you to work hard and strive to uphold the doctrines that were delivered unto us in the past by the saints;

4. Because some men have crept into the churches without being noticed, those that in the past have been written about and they will receive damnation. (Jeremiah 23) They are ungodly men that are corrupting the grace of God, perverting it to allow for their own lusts; They contradict and deny (*by teachings and deeds*) our only God and the Lord Jesus Christ. (Titus 1:16; 2 Peter 2:1; Acts 20:29-30; Galatians 2:4-5; Jeremiah 23; 2 Thessalonians 2:10-12; Matthew 24:4-5, 11, 24; Isaiah 30:10; Isaiah 9:16; Zephaniah 3:4)

5. My purpose is to remind you, because at one time you knew this, that the Lord who rescued his people from Egypt, he later destroyed those who did not remain faithful unto him.

6. And the messengers (*angels*) that did not keep their original purpose but deserted their calling, God has put them in eternal chains of darkness awaiting the final judgment. (2 Peter 2:4)

7. Just as Sodom and Gomorrah and the cities near them committed fornication and chased after forbidden flesh, these in a similar way received the judgment of God unto everlasting fire.

8. Surely in the same way today, these corrupt men now dream of defiling the bodies of others; They despise the leadership (*of Christ*) and speak evil of the honorable ones. (*saints*)

9. When the false accuser opposed the chief messenger Michael, disputing about the legitimacy of Moses, he did not dare bring a blasphemous accusation, because Michael said, the Lord will bring judgment against you. (Numbers 13:13; Deuteronomy 19:16-21)

10. These evil men speak evil about that which they are unlearned of. The things that they do understand in nature, they, like the irrational animals that they are acquainted with, bring ruin upon themselves.

11. Woe unto them! They have gone the way of Cain; They have made the same error as Balaam and they bring judgment upon themselves by the same disobedience as Korah. (Numbers 16)

12. They bring a stain upon the charity that you give to those in need, because they, without having need, take from what you have given, feeding themselves without embarrassment nor fear. They are clouds without water that are carried about by the wind. They are as trees in the autumn that have brought forth no fruit; They shall be uprooted and die two deaths. (*physical & eternal*)

13. They are as raging waves in the sea that bring up the foam, of which is the shame that they bring upon themselves. They are as shooting stars that are reserved unto the gloom of darkness forever.

14. As Enoch, seventh from Adam said about these types, the Lord will come with thousands of his saints,

15. and bring judgment unto all and rebuke all who are ungodly, for all of the ungodly deeds that they had committed and for all of the harsh things that ungodly people spoke against the holy ones. (Romans 2:10)

16. They are murmurers and complainers living according to their own lusts. Their mouths speak proud things, complementing the appearances of others for the purposes of gain unto themselves.

17. But you beloved, remember the words that were spoken at an earlier time by the apostles of our Lord;

18. Because I did tell you that in the last times there would be mockers who would chase after ungodly things and they will live for that which they have lust for. (2 Peter 2:1-22)

19. They are moved away from God to set their own boundaries (G-575 + G-2203 + G-3724), setting their own distinctive differences between themselves (G-5591 = *like different kinds of animals - the many different churches all teaching their own form of doctrine*) they do not have the spirit of God.

20. But you my beloved, build yourselves up by the most holy doctrine and pray for spiritual purity.

21. Keep yourselves within the love of God and do not waste the mercy of the Lord Jesus Christ, but remain faithful unto eternal life. (Hebrews 10:38-39; Romans 6:16-23)

22. For some of them have compassion, but use good judgment.

23. But unto others, use fear to bring them unto salvation, forcefully taking them out of the fire while detesting the clothes they are wearing that are stained by their recent lust for evil.

24. There is one who is able to help keep you from falling and to set you in front of his throne without blemish and with extreme joy; The only wise God and our saviour Jesus Christ; (*through his spirit*)

25. Unto him be the glory, and greatness, and power, and authority, both now and forever.

The Revelation of John

Chapter 1

**Verses 1-3 are an introduction that was added by a scribe
and is not a part of the original text.**

1. A telling of Jesus Christ that God gave to John, to show his servants the things that must soon come to pass, to indicate and delegate unto his messenger, his servant John;

2. He testified of the instructions of God and the witness of Jesus Christ, all of which he did see.

3. Blessed be the reader and those that understand the words of this prophecy and keep to all of the things that have been written (within); Know that the time is drawing near.

The original beginning of the book

4. John, unto the seven gatherings of the called-out people that are in Asia Minor (*the western shores*), may grace be given unto you and peace, from the one who was and is, and is to come again; And from the seven spirits who are in front of his throne;

5. From Jesus Christ, the faithful witness, the first born of those who have died; He is above all of the kingdoms of the earth. He loves us and has washed away our (*past*) sins through his blood; (Romans 3:25)

6. He shall make us kings and priests of our Father God. Unto him, the glory and all of the power, forever.

7. Watch, he will come in the clouds and every eye shall see him, and those who have pierced (*rejected*) him and all people of the earth shall greatly mourn because of him, truly. (Matthew 24:30; Acts 1:11)

8. I am the beginning and the end, the highest power and the final authority says our supreme God, the one who was, is, and is coming, almighty God. (Isaiah 44:6; Isaiah 48:12)

9. I John, am your brother and co-sharer in the tribulations, in the Kingdom of God, and in the patient endurance in (*the doctrine of*) Jesus Christ; I am on the island of Patmos for the instructions (*truth*) of God and for my testimony (*record*) in Jesus Christ. (Isaiah 59:15; Psalms 119:63)

10. I humbled myself to spend time before the Lord and I heard behind me a loud sound much like a trumpet.

11. He said, I am the beginning and the end, the foremost and the final authority, and what you see, write down on paper, and send to the seven gatherings of the called-out people which are in Asia; Send to Ephesis, Smyrna, Pergamos, Thyatira, Sardis, Philadelphia and also unto Laodicea.

12. And I turned toward the voice who spoke to me, and having turned, I saw seven lamp stands of gold.

13. In the midst of the seven lamp stands, one like the son of man wearing a robe down to the foot; Along the belt line and about the chest he wore a golden vest. (Zechariah 4:2)

14. His head and his hair was white as wool, as snow; His eyes were as flames of fire.

15. His feet were the color of fine brass, as in a burning furnace. His voice was as the sound of many waters (*large waterfall*). (Ezekiel 8:2)

16. In his right hand were seven stars and out of his mouth went forth a double-edged sword. His face was as bright as the midday sun. (John 1:7)

17. When I saw him, I fell at his feet as though I was dead. He put his right hand upon me and said, do not fear; I am the foremost and the final authority.

18. I am he who was alive but was killed. But look, I am now alive forevermore; And I have the keys of hell and death.

19. Write the things which you have seen (*past*) and the things that are (*present*) and the things which are to come (*future*). (Isaiah 46:10)

20. That which you did not know of the seven stars that you saw on the right of me and the seven lamp stands of gold are thus: The seven stars are the shepherds of the seven gatherings of the called-out ones and the seven lamp stands are the seven gatherings.

Revelation 2

Ephesus

1. Unto the shepherd/messenger of the Ephesian gathering write this: These things saith the one who is holding the seven stars in his right hand and walking in the midst of the seven lamp stands:

2. I know your deeds, your efforts and your patient continuance. I know that you can not bear the wicked ones and that you have tested those who pretend to be apostles but are not, and that you have found them to be liars.

3. You have removed them and have patiently endured, and for my name sake you have worked diligently.

4. Yet I have this against you, that you have forgotten your first love.

5. Remember from where you have slacked off and reform yourselves, and do the first (*initial*) deeds. (Acts 2:38) But if you do not, I will come soon and I will remove your lampstand unless you reform.

6. This you do have; You hate the deeds of the Nicolatians (*those who promote the doctrine of lasciviousness*) which I also hate.

7. He who has an ear, let him hear, that which the Spirit (*of God*) has said unto the gathering. For he who overcomes, I will give unto him to eat of the tree of life which is in the center of the paradise of God.

Smyrna

8. To the shepherd/messenger of the Smyrna gathering write this: He that is the highest and foremost authority, he that was killed, but now lives says this:

9. I know your deeds, your tribulations and your poverty, but you are wealthy. I know the blasphemy of those who claim to be Jews but are not, but are an assembly of Satan.
(Romans 2:28; Matthew 21:43; 1 John 2:23; Zephaniah 2:1-5; John 8:44)

10. Do not fear the things that you will suffer; Be aware that false accusers *(workers of the devil)* shall throw some of you in prison so that you may be examined. You will be afflicted for ten days, but be faithful unto death and I will give you the crown of eternal life.

11. He who has an ear, let him hear what the spirit of God has said unto the gathering. He who continues to overcome shall not be hurt by the second death.

Pergamos

12. To the shepherd/messenger of the Pergamos gathering write this: These things saith he that holds the sharp two-edged sword:

13. I know your deeds and where you live, where the throne of Satan is, yet you hold my name and have not denied dedication in me. Even in the days of Antipas who was a faithful witness unto me, he was killed in your midst, there where Satan lives.

14. Yet I have a few things against you, because you have some there who teach the doctrines of Baalam, who taught Balak to throw a snare before the sons of Israel, to eat meat sacrificed to idols and to commit fornication.

15. Some also hold the doctrines of the Nicolatians *(those who promote the doctrine of lasciviousness)*, which I hate.

16. Reform yourselves or I will come unto you very quickly and will make war against you.

17. He who has an ear, let him hear what the Spirit of God has said unto the gathering. To those who overcome, I will give to eat of the hidden manna and will give him a clean slate (*This is what happens through a true conversion* - Acts 2:38; Matthew 18:1-10; Romans 6; John 8:31-36) and on it written a new name of which no man shall know but he whom it is written upon.

Thyatira

18. To the shepherd/messenger of the Thyatira gathering write this: These things saith the Son of God, whose eyes are as flaming fire and his feet are like polished brass:

19. I know your deeds, your love, your service, your faithfulness, your patient endurance and that your deeds now are more than at the beginning,

20. however I have a few things against you; You allow the woman (Revelation 17) Jezebel, calling herself a prophetess that teaches lies among my servants, causing them to be in error, (*spiritual*) fornication and partaking of things that are idolatrous.

21. I gave her time to be turned away from of her fornication, but she did not.

22. Truly, I will cast you into a bed and those who have committed adultery (*held false doctrines*) with her into great affliction, if they do not turn away from their wicked deeds (*convert*).

23. I will kill them and bring them eternal death. All of the gatherings will know that I am the one who knows the depths of the heart. I will give unto every one according to their deeds. (Romans 2:6)

24. Unto you I speak and unto all others of Thyatira; All who do not hold any false doctrines and have not known the depths of Satan, I say to you, I will not put on you any other burden;

25. But that which you do have, hold firmly until I come.

26. He who overcometh (*this world*) and keepeth my deeds until the end, I will give you authority over the nations; (1 Corinthians 10:13)

27. I will be a shepherd with a staff of iron; As clay vessels, they shall be broken (*and remolded*).

28. I will give these the morning star.

29. He who has an ear, let him hear what the Spirit of God has said unto the gathering.

Revelation 3

Sardis

1. To the shepherd/messenger of the gathering in Sardis, write this: These things says he who holds the seven spirits of God and the seven stars: I know your deeds and that you hold a living name, yet you are dead. (*spiritually*)

2. Wake up and establish the remnant that are near death. I have found that your deeds are not being done unto God. (*because they are serving themselves*)

3. Remember that which you received and heard, keep it and turn around. If you do not awaken, I will come as a thief and you will not know when I will come upon you. (*speaking of his return*) (2 Thessalonians 5:2-4; 2 Peter 3:10; Revelation 16:15; Matthew 24:43)

4. There are a very few of you in Sardis who have not defiled yourselves. Only these shall walk with me in purity (*white*), for only they are worthy. (Revelation 6:11; 19:8)

5. He who overcomes he shall be clothed in white robes and I will not take away his name from the book of life. These I will acknowledge before my Father and the witnesses/messengers/angels.

6. He who has an ear, let him hear what the spirit (*of God*) has said unto the gathering.

Philadelphia - the 144,000

7. And to the messenger/shepherd of the gathering of Philadelphia, write this: These things says the holy one, the true one, the one who holds the keys of David; The one who opens and no man shuts and the one who shuts and no man opens.

8. I know your deeds. Look, I set before you an open door, no man can shut it: You do have some ability/power, and you have kept my instructions and you have not denied my name.

9. Take notice, I will bring those who are of the gathering of Satan, those who say that they are Jews but are not, but they lie; (Zephaniah 2:1-5; Romans 2:23; Matthew 21:43; John 8:44) I will make them come and bow down before you and make them know that I have loved you,

10. because you have kept my commandments continuously and faithfully. I will keep you from the time of purification (*testing*), that will come upon the whole earth (Matthew 24:21 - *great tribulation*), that will test/examine all that live upon the earth. (Revelation 7:3)

11. I shall come suddenly: Hold strongly to what you have so no one might steal your reward.

12. He who overcomes, I will make a support in the temple of my God, and he shall not be abandoned; And I will write upon him the name of my God and the name of the city of God, the new Jerusalem that will come down out of the heavens from my God.

13. He who has an ear, let him hear, what the spirit (*of God*) has said unto the gathering.

Laodicea

14. And to the messenger/shepherd of the gathering of Laodicea, write: This is what the trustworthy witness, the faithful and true head master of creation says.

15. I know your deeds; You are neither hot nor cold. You are better to be hot or cold.

16. So because you are lukewarm, neither hot nor cold, I will spit you out of my mouth.
17. You say that you are wealthy and that you have need of nothing, but you do not know that you are wretched, miserable, poor, blind and naked.
18. I advise you to purchase of me gold purified in the fire, that you might become wealthy, and white clothing that you might be clothed, that your nakedness not reveal your shame;
Anoint your eyes with poultice that you might be able to see.
19. All whom I love, I rebuke and bring correction. (Hebrews 12:6-11) Be zealous and reform yourselves.
20. Behold, I stand at the door and knock; If any man hears my voice and open the door, I will come in unto him and sit with him and he with me.
21. To he that overcomes, I will allow to sit with me at my place of power (*throne*), just as I also overcame and now sit with my Father at his throne.
22. He who has an ear, let him hear, what the Spirit (*of God*) has said unto the gathering.

**Note: The names of the seven churches hold meanings,
and when put in the order as they appear in chapters 2 & 3,
they speak an important message.**

gatherings	Greek word	the message given in the names:	
Ephesus	G-2181	The discoverer	
Smyrna	G-4668	of the anointed (Christ)	
Pergamos	G-4010	is renewed (reborn)	(Matthew 18:3)
Thyatira	G-2363	as a fragrance before the Lord	
Sardis	G-4556	as a precious gemstone	(Malachi 3:17)
Philadelphia	G-5359	through brotherly love	
Laodicea	G-2993	to be judged in truth & justice	(Malachi 3:18)

The discoverer of the anointed (Christ) is renewed (reborn) as a fragrance before the Lord, as a precious gemstone, through brotherly love to be judged in truth & justice

----

Revelation 4

1. Then, I (*John*) saw a door that was opened up in the sky and the foremost voice that I heard was loud like a trumpet speaking to me, and it said come up here and I will show you what will happen hereafter.
2. Immediately, I became as a spirit, and behold a throne was in the heavens and there was one that was sitting on the throne. (Ezekiel 1:26)
3. He that sat on the throne looked like a jasper stone, a gem, and a rainbow was around the throne which looked like an emerald. (Ezekiel 1:28)
4. And sitting all around the throne were twenty-four thrones; On the twenty-four thrones were sitting twenty-four elders wearing white robes, and on their heads they wore each a crown of gold.
5. Out of the throne came forth bright lights and thundering and voices. There were seven lamps burning in front of the throne, of which are the seven spirits of the supreme God.
6. In front of the throne there was a sea of glass much like crystal. (*a glass floor in the heavens*) In the vicinity of the throne, gathered around the throne there were four living creatures having eyes in the front and back. (Revelation 15:2)
7. The first living creature was like a lion, the second like a calf, the third had a face like a man and the fourth was like an eagle. (Ezekiel 1:10)
8. Each living creature had six wings all around them and their undersides were full of eyes. They did not rest day nor night; They sang, Holy, Holy, Holy, Lord God Almighty, who was, is and is to come.
9. Then the living creatures gave glory, honour and gratitude to the one that sat on the throne, he that lives forever and ever;

10. Then the twenty-four elders fell down before he that sat on the throne and they worshipped the one that lives forever. They cast their crowns before the throne saying:

11. You are worthy O Lord, to receive glory, honour and power, because you created all things and because they were created for your pleasure.

Revelation 5

1. And I saw in the right hand of he who sat on the throne, a book having been written within and on the covers, having been sealed with seven seals.

2. Then I saw a strong angel proclaiming with a loud voice, who is worthy to open the book and to break open the seals on it?

3. No one in the heavens, on earth or under the earth was able to open the book to see what was in it;

4. So I cried greatly because no one was found worthy to open and read the book.

5. One of the elders said to me, do not cry: Behold the Lion of the tribe of Judah, the root of David shall break open the seals and open the book. (*Jesus the Christ*)

6. I saw, take notice, in the vicinity of the throne and the four living creatures among the elders stood a Lamb as though it had been slain, having seven horns (*powers*) and seven eyes, which are the seven spirits of God, having been sent out across all of the earth.

7. And he came and took the book out of the right hand of him who sat on the throne.

8. When he had taken the book, the four living creatures and the twenty-four elders kneeled down before the lamb, each one having a harp and bowls made of gold full of incenses, which are the prayers of the saints.

9. They sang a new song, singing, worthy are you to take possession of the book and to open the seals upon it. It is because you were killed and you purchased (*offer a ransom for*) of us by your blood; Everyone from every family, every language, every people and of every nation.

10. You have made us (*the faithful*) kings and priests unto our God, and we shall reign on the earth.

11. And I saw and heard the sound of many voices of the living creatures and the elect, standing around the throne. The number of them was innumerable, thousands upon thousands, (Daniel 7:10; Revelation 7:9)

12. They spoke with a loud voice and said, worthy is the Lamb that was sacrificed to give to us the ability, wealth, wisdom, strength, honour, glory and blessing.

13. I heard every created thing that is in the sky, on the earth, underneath the earth and in the sea saying unto the one sitting on the throne and unto the Lamb, blessing, honour and glory, forever and ever.

14. And the four living creatures said, truly. And the twenty-four elders kneeled down before the one who lives forever and ever.

Revelation 6

1. Then I saw the Lamb open one of the seals, and one of the four living creatures as loud as thunder said, come and see.

2. And I saw a white horse (Revelation 19:11); The one sitting on it had a bow (*simple fabric coat*) and a crown was given to him and he went forth to overcome so that he would gain victory. (*Christ*)

3. He opened the second seal, and I heard the second living creature say, come and see.

4. There came a red horse, and the one sitting on it was given ability to take peace from the earth, that they might kill one another, and a large sword was given unto him.

5. And when he opened the third seal, I heard the third living creature say, come and see. And I saw a black horse, and the rider who sat upon him had a pair of balances in his hands.

6. I then heard a voice coming from the four living creatures say; A certain amount of grain for a denarius (*an amount of money*) and three amounts of barley for a denarius; Do not waste the oil or the wine.

7. When he had opened the fourth seal, I heard the voice of the fourth living creature say, come and see.

8. And I looked and I saw a light green horse: And the name of the rider of the horse was Death, and hell followed with him. Jurisdiction was given to him to destroy a fourth of the earth with the sword, with famine, with disease and by the wild animals on the earth.

9. When he opened the fifth seal, I saw below the altar, the spirits of all who have been killed for the gospel (*instructions*) of God and each of their records of which they lived. (Psalms 116:15)

10. They cried with loud voices saying, oh Lord, holy and true, how long will you not avenge and vindicate our blood upon those living on the earth? (Revelation 18:20; 7:9-10; 13:15)

11. Each one was given a white robe and it was said to them that they be patient just a little longer until all of their other fellow servants and brethren that are meant to be killed, shall be, as they also were, of which shall soon be accomplished. (Matthew 24:21 - *the great tribulation*)

12. I looked when he opened the sixth seal, and I saw a great earthquake that occurred, and the sun became black (*like garments worn to show mourning*) much like fur, and the moon became red in color; (Isaiah 13:9-13; Isaiah 29:6-7; Ezekiel 32:7; Joel 3:15; Matthew 24:29; Revelation 8:5-12)

13. The stars in the sky become alighted as though falling, even as a fig tree drops her unripe figs when shaken by a strong wind.

14. And the skies were separated, much like a scroll that is being rolled up. And every mountain and Island were shaken. (Ezekiel 38:20; Matthew 24:29-31)

15. And the leaders on earth and the influential people, the wealthy, military leaders, the capable ones, servants and every free man all hid themselves in the caves deep in the earth; (*bunkers*)

16. They said to the mountains and rocks, fall upon us and hide us from the face of the one who sits on the throne; Even from the wrath of the Lamb. (Hosea 10:8; Micah 7:17; Isaiah 42:13-16; Isaiah 34:8)

17. The great and dreadful day of the Lord and his wrath is come! Who is able to face him?

Revelation 7

1. After these things, I saw four messengers (*angels*) standing on the four extremities of the earth (*north, south, east and west*), holding power over the four winds that they should not breathe upon the earth, nor on the sea, nor on any tree.

2. And I saw another angel coming up like the sunrise, holding the seal of the living God; He announced with a loud voice unto the four angels to whom it was given unto, to harm the earth and the sea, and he said:

3. Do not harm the earth, nor the sea, nor the trees, until we have protected the servants of our God, to seal each one of them on their face. (Ezekiel 9:4)

4. And I heard the number of those who are truly living genuinely (G-2229 + G-4973 + G-3306), 144 thousand truly living genuinely from out of every race of the family of Israel.
(*Includes those who have been grafted in.- Romans 11:17*)

5. Of the tribe (*sprout*) of Judah, twelve thousand that are truly living genuinely. Of the tribe (*sprout*) of Reuben, 12 thousand that are truly living genuinely. And of the tribe (*sprout*) of Gad, 12 thousand that are truly living genuinely.

6. Of the tribe (*sprout*) of Asher, 12 thousand that are truly living genuinely. Of the tribe (*sprout*) of Naphtali, 12 thousand that are truly living genuinely. And of the tribe (*sprout*) of Manasseh, 12 thousand that are truly living genuinely.

7. Of the tribe (*sprout*) of Simeon, 12 thousand that are truly living genuinely. Of the tribe (*sprout*) of Levi, 12 thousand that are truly living genuinely. Of the tribe (*sprout*) of Issachar, 12 thousand that are truly living genuinely

8. Of the tribe (*sprout*) of Zebulun, 12 thousand that are truly living genuinely. Of the tribe (*sprout*) of Joseph, 12 thousand that are truly living genuinely. And of the tribe (*sprout*) of Benjamin, 12 thousand that are truly living genuinely.

Mid chapter note:
Verses 5 through 8 speak of the tribes of Israel. There is a secret message hidden that is revealed through the Hebrew meanings of each of the names, in the order that they are given above. Each tribe is listed in such a way which shows the message of the gospel of Jesus Christ, the New Covenant and the generalized pathway for one to become a son of God. The message is the true message of the Gospel of Jesus Christ and reads as follows:

Tribe name	Greek	Hebrew	the message revealed:
Judah	G-2448	H-3194	the calling
Reuben	G-4502	H-7205	for those who can see
Gad	G-1045	H-1410	through his prophet
Asher	G-768	H-836	to be happy
Naphtali	G-3508	H-5321	through hardship
Manassah	G-3128	H-4519	their sins are forgiven (forgotten)
Simeon	G-4826	H-8095	they hear and obey
Levi	G-3017	H-3878	holy spirit comes (attachment)
Issachar	G-2466	H-3485	helps to attain reward
Zebulun	G-2194	H-2074	through faithful living
Joseph	G-2501	H-3130	that they may be added
Benjamin	G-958	H-1144	to become a son of God

The calling, for those who can see, through his prophet, to be happy through hardship, their sins are forgiven, they hear and obey, the holy spirit comes, to help attain the reward, through faithful living, that they may be added, to be a son of God.

Revelation 7 continued:

9. And after this, I saw a large gathering of people that no one could number, of all nations and families, and peoples and languages, standing in front of the throne before the Lamb. They were all wearing white robes and holding palms in their hands; (Revelation 6:9-11; Revelation 19:8)

10. They called out with a loud voice saying, the salvation of our God sits on the throne, he is the Lamb.

11. The messengers stood around the throne, and also the elders and the four living creatures. They fell in front of the throne on their faces and worshipped God and they said:

12. Truly, blessings, glory, wisdom, thanksgiving, honour, jurisdiction and strength shall be unto our God forever and ever, truly.

13. Then one of the elders asked me, who are these that are wearing white robes? Who are they and from where have they come?

14. And I said unto him, you know. He said to me, these are those coming out of the great tribulation; (Revelation 6:9-11) They washed their robes and whitened them through the blood of the Lamb. (Zephaniah 2:3)

15. This is why they are in front of the throne of God. They shall serve him day and night in his temple. He that sits on the throne shall live with them. (Zechariah 2:10)

16. They shall hunger no more, nor thirst any more, neither shall the sun shed its light on them to burn them.;

17. Because the Lamb who is in the midst of the throne shall take care of them and will lead them to sources of live water, and God shall wipe away every tear from their eyes. (Isaiah 25:8; Isaiah 60:20)

Revelation 8
The judgment of God - (8:1-10:6)

1. When he opened the seventh seal, there was a silence in the heavens for half an hour.

2. Then I saw seven angels stand before God and they were given seven trumpets. (Jeremiah 10:10)

3. Another angel came before the altar, holding a golden censor *(a vessel to burn incense in)*; There was given to him a large amount of incense and he offered it, of which is the prayers of all of the saints. He offered it upon the altar before the throne of God.

4. The smoke of the incense and prayers of the saints ascended up to God from out of the angel's hands.

5. Then the angel took the censor, lit it on fire from the altar and he cast it to the earth; And there were voices, thunder, lightning and a great earthquake. (Revelation 16:2 - *the impact of a comet*)

6. The seven angels with the seven trumpets prepared to inhale *(readying to blow their trumpets)*.

7. The first angel sounded, and there came hail and fire mixed with blood, and it fell to the earth. One third of the trees were burnt up and all of the green grass was burned up to the ground. (Isaiah 42:15)

8. The second angel sounded, and something like a mountain of great burning fire had fallen into the sea. One third of the sea became as blood *(poisoned/dead/reddened)*. (Revelation 16:4)

9. One third of the creatures in the sea that had life died and one third of the ships were destroyed.

10. The third angel trumpeted and there fell out of the sky a great burning star, like a lamp, and it fell and corrupted a third of the rivers and sources of waters *(springs and wells)*. (Isaiah 34:9; Psalm 144:5-6)

11. The name of the star is called Wormwood. It caused a third of the waters to be poisoned. Many men shall die from the waters because they will be poisoned. (Luke 21:29; Revelation 16:4)

12. When the fourth angel sounded, A third of the sun was darkened, a third of the moon and a third of the stars, so that a third of the day would be darkened and a third of the night likewise. (Revelation 16:8)

13. Then I saw and heard an angel flying in the middle of the sky saying with a loud voice, woe, woe, woe to them living on the earth, because of the remaining trumpets of the three remaining angels are about to sound.

Revelation 9

1. When the fifth angel sounded, I saw a star fall from the heavens *(sky)* to the earth. It was given the key to the deepest abyss. (Revelation 16:10)

2. It opened the pit and smoke went up out of the pit, like the smoke of a great furnace. And it darkened the sun and air due to the smoke out of the pit. (Isaiah 9:19; Isaiah 34:10)

3. Out of the smoke came forth that which is like locusts *(on the tip or top)* onto the earth and great ability was given to them, as the power of a scorpion on the earth.

4. It was commanded that they not harm the grass of the earth, nor anything green, nor tree, but only the men who do not have the seal of God on their foreheads.

5. It was not allowed for them to kill them, but that they be tormented for five months. Their torment is as that of a scorpion when it stings a man.

6. In those days, men will seek death and will not find it. Men will desire to die and death will not be found.

7. The form of the locusts look like horses that are prepared for battle. Their heads look like golden crowns and their faces were similar to the faces of men.

8. Their hair was like the hair of women and their teeth looked like the teeth of lions.

9. Their chests were like chests of iron. The sound of their wings was like the sound of many horses running to battle.

10. They had tails like scorpions and they stung with their tales and they had power to harm men for five months.

11. They have a king over them, the angel of the abyss whose name in Hebrew is Abaddon; In Greek his name is Apollyon.

12. One woe is past, surely there are two more woes hereafter.

13. The sixth angel sounded and I heard a voice of the four horns of the golden altar that was before the throne of God.

14. He said to the sixth angel who had the trumpet; Go and loose the four evil spirits that have been caged by the Euphrates river. (Revelation 16:12)

15. The four evil spirits were loosed who were prepared for one year, one month, one day and one hour, to kill one third of mankind.

16. The numbers of the army of horsemen were two hundred million. I heard the number of them.

17. And I saw their horses in the vision, and those sitting on them had fiery breastplates of deep blue and sulfur, and the heads of the horses were like the heads of lions. Out of their front edge comes lightning and smoke with a flash.

18. By these three things was a third of mankind killed, from the lightning, smoke and a flash coming out of the front of them.

19. Their power is in their front edge and in their tails; Their tails are like snakes, having head and they do harm with them. *(some form of a military tank)*

20. And the remaining men who had not been killed by this plague did not repent of their deeds, but they continued to worship devils, and idols of gold, silver, brass, stone and wood, of which are not able to see, nor hear, nor walk. (Isaiah 42:25)

21. Yet they did not repent of their murders, nor sorceries, nor their fornication, nor their thefts.

Revelation 10

1. And I saw another mighty messenger come down from the sky wrapped in a cloud: A rainbow was on his head, his face was like the sun, and his feet were like pillars of fire.

2. He had in his hand a little book that was opened up: Then he set his right foot upon the sea and his left foot upon the land, (Revelation 13:15-18)

3. and he announced with a loud voice, much like a lion roaring. When he spoke, seven thunders sounded.

4. When the seven thunders sounded, I was about to write, when I heard a voice in the sky saying: Seal up the things which the seven thunders uttered and do not write them. (Daniel 12:4)

5. The messenger that I saw that was standing on the sea and the earth lifted up his hands to the heavens

6. and he swore by him that lives forever, he who created the heavens and all things therein, the earth and all things therein, and the seas and all that is within them, that there shall be no more time hereafter! *(this is the fulfillment of - Daniel 12:7 prophecy --- Revelation 16:17; Isaiah 62:11; Ezekiel 7:6)*

7. But in the days of the voice of the seventh messenger, when he shall begin to announce, the mystery of God shall be finished, as he has spoken it to his servants and the prophets.
(1 Corinthians 15:52; 1 Thessalonians 4:16)

8. And the voice that I heard from the heavens spoke to me again and said, go and take the little book which is opened in the hand of the messenger who stands on the earth and the sea.

9. I then went to the messenger and said to him, give me the book. He then said to me, take it and eat it; It will make your stomach bitter, but in your mouth it will be as sweet as honey. (Ezekiel 2:9; Isaiah 34:16)

10. I took the book out of his hand and I ate it. In my mouth it was as sweet as honey, but as soon as I had eaten it my stomach was made bitter. (Ezekiel 3:3)

11. He then said to me, you must prophesy before many people, nations, languages and kings.

Revelation 11

1. I was given a measuring stick, much like a staff: The angel stood and said, arise and measure (*count*) the temple of God, the altar and all who worship within.
(1 Corinthians 3:17; 6:19; Zechariah 2:1; 2 Corinthians 6:16)

2. Leave out those which are outside of the temple, do not measure (*count*) them; For they are heathen and they shall desecrate it for forty-two months. (*they will kill those who do not take the mark* of *the beast -* Revelation 6:9; 1 Corinthians 3:16-17 - *the people of God are the temple of God*)

3. I will give my two martyrs, and they shall be prophets for a thousand two hundred and sixty days, clothed in sackcloth.

4. They are the two olive trees that are the two candlesticks standing at war against the god of the earth. (*Satan* - John 12:31; 14:30; 16:11; 1 Corinthians 2:6; Revelation 12:12; 19:20; 20:2; Zechariah 4:14)

5. If any man shall try to harm them, fire shall come forth from their mouths and kill their enemies; If any man shall try to harm them, he must be killed in this way.

6. They shall have the ability to close the sky that it not rain in the days of their prophecy. (Malachi 4:5; James 5:17) They shall have power over the waters to turn them into blood, and to harm the earth with plagues as often as they choose. (Isaiah 42:15)

7. When they shall have completed their testimony, the beast that had risen up out of the deep abyss (*pit*) shall make war against them, and shall take them and kill them. (Jeremiah 26:15)

8. Their dead bodies lay in the street of the great city, that is spiritually called Sodom and Egypt, where our Lord Jesus was crucified (*Jerusalem - Daniel 11:45*).

9. And the people of all races, nations and languages will see their dead bodies for three and a half days, not allowing them to be put into graves.

10. They that live on the earth will be overjoyed and shall celebrate, and shall send each other gifts, because these two prophets had tormented all of them that live on the earth.

11. After three and a half days, the spirit of life from God entered into them, and they arose upon their feet and great fear came upon all of the people who saw them.

12. They then heard a mighty voice from the heavens call to them, come up here. They then ascended up into the sky, in a cloud as their enemies watched.

13. In that same hour, there was an earthquake, and one tenth of the city fell; Seven thousand men were killed due to the earthquake. Those remaining were terrified but they refused to give honor unto the God of the heavens.

14. The first two woes are past, surely the third will come without delay.

15. The seventh angel then sounded and there were great voices in the heavens saying: The kingdoms of this world have become the kingdoms of our Lord and his Christ. He shall reign forever and ever. (John 16:11)

16. The twenty-four elders that were in front of God sitting at his throne, they fell on their faces and worshipped God and they said;

17. We thank you Lord God Almighty; The one who was, is, has now appeared and is alive, because you took your great power and you reign; (Revelation 10:6; Revelation 16:7; Matthew 24:29-31)

18. The nations are enraged because your wrath is come. It is the time of the judgment of the dead; To give reward unto your servants, the prophets, the saints and to all who fear your name; Both, the small and great, to destroy the ones who destroy the earth. (Revelation 20:12-15; Malachi 4:1; Daniel 12:2)

19. And the temple of God in heaven was opened and the ark of his covenant was seen in his temple. There was much lightning, the sounds of thunder, a mighty earthquake and great hail.
(Ezekiel 38:22; Revelation 16:21)

Revelation 12

1. And there appeared a great sign in the sky, a woman (*the faithful of Ancient Israel*) wrapped in the sun (*Light/truth*), and the moon (*evil/darkness*) is under her feet, and upon her head a crown of twelve stars. (*the 12 Apostles of Christ/representing the 12 tribes*)

2. And she, being pregnant, cried, experiencing the pains of birth, was distressed to be delivered.

3. Then there appeared another sign in the sky, and look, a strong fiery dragon, having seven heads, ten horns and seven crowns (*jurisdictions*) upon his heads (Daniel 7:24; Revelation 13:1; *early form of* 17:3)

4. and his tail drew one third of the stars of heaven and did throw them down to earth (*the fallen*). And the dragon stood in the presence of the woman which was ready to be delivered, for the purpose to kill her son as soon as he was born. (Matthew 2:13 - *King Herod*).

5. And she (*the faithful of ancient Israel*) brought forth a son who is going to rule all nations with a staff of iron: (Revelation 2:27) And her son was taken up unto God, unto his throne. (Mark 16:19)

6. And the woman escaped into the wilderness (*uninhabited place*), where she hath a place prepared by God, that there they should eat (*live*) for a thousand two hundred sixty days (*1260 years*).

7. And there was a war in the heavens: Michael and his helpers fought against the dragon and the dragon fought with his demons (*fallen angels*), but they could not win;

8. There was no place found for them in the heavens. (*they had fallen*)

9. And the powerful dragon was thrown down, that malicious snake called the devil and Satan, which deceives and causes the whole world to go astray: He was thrown to the earth, and his demons were thrown down also. (*with the resurrection of Jesus Christ*)

10. I heard a loud voice saying in the heavens, now is come (*present tense*) salvation from sin and the powerful ability, (2 Timothy 3:5) the kingdom of our God (*highest divinity*) and the power of Christ: The accuser of our brethren is thrown down, he that accused them before our God day and night.

11. And they (*the faithful*) overcome him by the blood of the Lamb (*Christ*) (Romans 6:1-23; Acts 2:38) and by the word of their testimony (*living faithful unto Christ*); They love not their lives even unto death.

12. Therefore rejoice ye heavens and all that dwell in them. Beware to the people living on the earth and sea! For Satan has come down to you with great rage because he knows that he only has a little time. (John 12:31; John 14:30; John 16:11; 1 Corinthians 2:6; Ephesians 2:2; Acts 26:18; Matthew 4:9)

13. When the dragon saw that he was cast unto the earth, he chased the woman (*faithful of ancient Israel*) which brought forth the Son (*Christ*).

14. The woman was given two wings (*sails & protection*) (Matthew 23:37) of a powerful eagle (*air/wind*), that she might be taken unto an uninhabited place (*wilderness; North America - Revelation 17:3;*

Isaiah 35:8; Isaiah 51:10-11), where she shall eat (*live*) for a time, and times and a half a time (*1260 years - verse 6*), away from the presence of the enraged serpent.

15. And the serpent (*Satan*) cast out of his mouth (*at his command*) water (*a great mass of people*) like a flood after the woman, that he might cause her to be destroyed by the flood.

16. But the earth helped the woman and opened-her-mouth and swallowed up the flood which the dragon cast out of his mouth.

17. The dragon was enraged with the woman and went to make war with the remainder of her seed (Romans 9:8); those who keep the commandments of God and have a testimony (*proven faithfulness*) unto Jesus Christ. (*her seed are the martyred saints from the past 2000 years*)

Revelation 13

1. And I stood on the sand of the sea and saw a beast rise up, having seven heads and ten horns; Upon his horns ten crowns and on its heads it held many blasphemous names.
(Revelation 17:3,12; Daniel 7:7, 23 – *see note page 346*)

2. The beast which I saw was like a leopard and his feet were as the feet of a bear and his mouth as the mouth of a lion. The dragon gave him his power, his seat and much authority. (Daniel 7:3-7)

3. I saw one of his heads (*chief leader - the antichrist*) that received a deadly injury and his deadly wound was publicly healed; All the world followed after (*served*) the beast.

4. They served the dragon (*Satan*) that gave authority unto the beast and they served the beast. They said, what can be compared to the beast? Who is strong enough to make-war against it?

5. There was given unto it a voice speaking many great things and blasphemies. Authority was given unto him to perform for forty and two months. (Revelation 11:2; Daniel 7:25)

6. And he opened his mouth in blasphemy against God, to blaspheme the name of God, his temple and those that dwell in the heavens. (Ezekiel 35:12; Daniel 7:25; Daniel 11:36)

7. It was given unto him to make war against the saints and to kill them: And jurisdiction was given to him over all races, languages and nations. (Psalms 116:15; Daniel 7:21; Ezekiel 35:5)

8. All that live upon the earth shall serve him, all whose names are not written in the book of life of the Lamb, all who have lived as a living sacrifice since the founding of the world.

9. If any man hath an ear, let him hear.

10. He that leads into captivity shall go into captivity: He that kills with the sword must be killed by the sword. This is the patient endurance and the faithfulness of the saints.

11. And I saw another beast, arising upon the earth: (*a false prophet with Vatican ties*) It had two horns like a lamb (*in the image of Christ - Matthew 24:5*), but it speaks like a dragon. (Daniel 2:40)

12. And he holds all the jurisdiction and authority of the first beast in his presence, and he causes the land and the people that are alive to serve the first beast whose deadly wound was healed. (*through taxes*)

13. And he does powerfully fearful things, in that he makes fire come down (*descend*) from the sky unto the earth in the sight of mankind.

14. He deceives all that live upon the earth by the power of those deeds that he committed, of which he did in the presence of the first beast: He shall command and instruct that all who live on the earth make themselves a resemblance of the beast, which had the wound by the sword but did live.

15. He had the ability to give a spirit unto the images of the beast, so that the resemblances of the beast should both communicate and cause as many as would not humble themselves unto the resemblance of the beast, that they be killed. (Revelation 6:9-10; Revelation 7:9-10; Psalms 116:15; Daniel 11:32-35)

16. And he mandates that all, both small and great, rich and poor, free man and all slaves must receive (*accept*) a mark (*implanted technology*) in their right hand or in their foreheads, (Daniel 11:31)

17. so that no man will be able to buy or sell (*speaking of entering into commerce*), unless each has the mark (*the implantable technology*), and the name (*surname - your all capital letter name*) of the beast, and the number of its name (*social security # or the equivalent*).

18. Here is wisdom. Let him that has intellect compute the number of the beast, for it is the number mankind, and its number is six hundred, threescore and six. (666)

(In Hebrew: 666 = vav vav vav = WWW = world wide web - in you)
(Daniel 11:31; Matthew 24:15)

Revelation 14

1. I John, looked and saw the Lamb (*Christ*) standing on the mountain of Zion (*spiritual high place*), and with him was the hundred and forty-four thousand who had the name of the Father written upon their foreheads. (Revelation 7:3; Revelation 3:7-12)

2. I then heard a voice from the heavens and it was loud like the sound of a large waterfall, and the voice spoke like thunder. I also heard the sound of harps being played.

3. They played a song that was never before heard, playing in front of the throne of God and in the presence of the twenty-four elders. No man could learn the song but for the hundred forty-four thousand which were purchased, abiding upon the earth. (Revelation 7:1-8)

4. These are they that do not defile themselves with the woman (Revelation 17:1-7) and before God they are as pure as virgins. They follow after (*obey*) the Lamb wherever he goes. They were redeemed (*purchased*) from all of mankind to be the first fruits unto God and the Lamb.

5. There is no evil spoken by them and they are without fault before the throne of God. (*they are completely mature in Christ*)

6. I saw a messenger flying across the mid-heavens (*spiritual high place*), holding the eternal gospel to give unto them on the earth, unto every nation and tribe and language and people.
(Matthew 24:14; Isaiah 42:1-3; Malachi 4:5; Daniel 12:1)

7. He said with a loud voice, fear God and give him respect; The hour of his judgment is now come. Serve him who made the heavens, the earth, the sea and the fresh water springs. (Isaiah 42:6)

8. Another messenger followed him and he said; Babylon is fallen! (Revelation 16:19; 18:1-24; Jeremiah 50:23-51:58) The great city is fallen, because she made all nations drink of the wine of the wrath of God, because of her fornication. (*evil ways*)
(Revelation 18; Zephaniah 3; Ezekiel 26; Isaiah 47; Isaiah 13; Ezekiel 38-39)

9. There was a third angel that followed and he said with a loud voice; If any man worships (*serves*) the beast, holds his image and receives the mark in their forehead or in their hand, (Revelation 13:15-18; Daniel 11:31; Matthew 24:15)

10. they will drink of the wine of the wrath of God, undiluted in the cup of his furious anger; They will be tormented with fire and brimstone, with the holy angels and the Lamb overseeing;

11. The smoke of their torment shall ascend up forever and ever, and they will have no peace day or night; This shall be upon all who worship (*serve*) the beast and his image and whoever receives his mark.

12. Here is the way that the saints will remain alive: They keep the commandments of God and are completely faithful (*in how they live*) unto Jesus Christ. (verse 4; Zephaniah 3:13)

13. Then I heard a voice from the heavens say unto me, write this: Blessed are those who die in Christ from now until the end. Yes, their spirits may rest and their righteous deeds will remain as their record.
(Revelation 6:9; Revelation 13:7; Revelation 17:6)

14. Then I looked and saw a cloud, and on the cloud sat one who looked like the son of man, (*Christ Jesus*) having on his head, a golden crown and in his hand, a sharp sickle. (Matthew 24:31; Mark 13:24; Acts 1:11)

15. An angel then came out of the temple saying with a loud voice unto him who sat on the cloud: Thrust in your sickle and reap the harvest of the earth; For the time of harvest is at hand.
(Revelation 11:18; Zephaniah 3:20; Revelation 20:12; Daniel 12:2; Romans 2:6)

16. He who sat on the cloud thrust his sickle upon the earth and the earth was harvested.
(Matthew 9:37; Matthew 13:39; Matthew 24:29-31; 1 Thessalonians 4:17)

17. Another angel came out of the temple in the heavens and he also had a large sharp sickle.

18. Another angel came out from near the altar, of whom had the power over fire. He announced with a loud voice unto him who had the sharp sickle, thrust in your sharp sickle and gather the clusters of the vine of the earth, her grapes are fully ripe. (Joel 3:13)

19. The angel thrust his sharp sickle upon the earth and gathered the vine of the earth and cast it into the great winepress of the wrath of God. (Isaiah 24:22; Isaiah 63:3-6; Zechariah 14:12)

20. The winepress was pressed outside of the city and the blood flowed as tall as a horse's bridle, covering the area of sixteen hundred furlongs.

Revelation 15

1. I saw a sign in the heavens, great and marvelous; Seven angels having the seven final plagues; In them is the completion of the wrath of God. (Revelation 16; Isaiah 42:13-15)
2. Then I saw as if it were a sea of glass, mingled with fire (Revelation 4:6): They who had gotten victory over the beast, over his image, his mark and over the multitude in his name, were as though they were standing on the sea of glass, having the harps of God.
(the sea of glass is a floor in the heavens looking down upon the earth)
3. They sang a song of Moses, the servant of God and the song of the Lamb, saying, great and marvelous are your works. Lord God Almighty, righteous and true are your ways; You are King of the saints.
4. Who will not have fear for you and glorify your name, Oh Lord? Only you are holy. All nations shall come and stand in front of you, because your judgments are soon to be made known.
(Revelation 20:12; Romans 2:6)
5. Then I looked and saw that the temple of the tabernacle and the testimony in heaven was opened up.
6. The seven angels came out of the temple, having seven plagues, all clothed with pure and white linen, having on their chests golden girdles.
7. One of the four beasts gave to the seven angels, seven golden vials that are full of the wrath of God; He lives forever and ever.
8. And the temple was filled with smoke from the glory of God and from his mighty power; No man was able to enter into the temple, until the seven plagues of the seven angels were completed.

Revelation 16

1. Then I heard a loud voice out of the temple saying to the seven angels, go your way and pour out the vials of the wrath of God upon the earth. (Isaiah 24:1-23; Isaiah 29:6-7; Jeremiah 10:25)
2. And the first went and poured out his vial upon the earth, and there fell an evil and painful sore upon the men who had received the mark of the beast and worshipped his image. (Isaiah 24:1-23; Isaiah 29:6-7; Jeremiah 10:25; Revelation 8:5 - *EMP due to the impact*)
3. The second angel poured out his vial upon the sea (*Atlantic Ocean*) and it became as blood, and all in it died. (Rev. 8:8)
4. The third angel poured out his vial upon the rivers and fountains of waters, and they became as blood. *(poisoned)* (Revelation 8:10-11)
5. I heard the angel of the waters say, you are righteous oh Lord, who is, and was, and shall be, because you have judged in this way;
6. For they have shed the blood of the saints and the prophets, and you have given them blood to drink, for they are deserving. (Revelation 6:9; Revelation 13:7; Matthew 24:21)
7. I then heard another angel out of the alter say, even so, Lord God Almighty, true and righteous are your judgments.
8. And the fourth angel poured out his vial upon the sun; And it was brought about that men would be scorched as with fire. (Revelation 8:12)
9. So the people were scorched with great heat, therefore they blasphemed the name of God, because he had power over all of these plagues, yet they did not repent nor give him glory.
10. The fifth angel poured out his vial upon the seat of the beast and his kingdom was full of darkness. (Isaiah 24:23; Matthew 24:29) They gnawed at their tongues, because of the great pain. (Revelation 9:1)
11. They blasphemed the God of the heavens because of their great pains and sores, and they did not repent of their deeds.
12. The sixth angel poured out his vial upon the great river Euphrates and the water thereof dried up. In this, the way of the kings of the east could be prepared.
13. And I saw three unclean spirits like frogs come out of the mouth of the dragon, the mouth of the beast and out of the mouth of the false prophet.
14. For they are the spirits of devils who do mighty things and go forth unto the kings of the earth to gather them to the great battle of the great day of the Lord God Almighty. (Isaiah 34:8)
15. Behold, I come as a thief. Blessed is he who watches and keeps himself pure or he will walk naked and his shame shall be seen. (1 Thessalonians 5:4; 2 Peter 3:10; Revelation 3:3; Matthew 24:43)

16. And he gathered them together into a place that in the Hebrew language is called Armageddon. (Ezekiel 38:1-15; Revelation 9:6; Revelation 14:9; Revelation 19:19)

17. The seventh angel poured out his vial into the air, and immediately a loud voice came from out of the throne in the temple of heaven that said, it is finished. (Ezekiel 7:6; 39:15; Joel 3:2; Revelation 10:4-6)

18. There were voices, thundering and lightnings, and then there was a great earthquake, such as has not been at any time since men were upon the earth. Such a mighty earthquake, so strong!

19. The great city (*Rome*) was divided into three parts and the cities of the nations fell. Mighty Babylon came into remembrance before God, to give her the cup of the wine of the fierceness of God's wrath.

20. Every Island disappeared and the mountains were flattened to no longer be evident.

21. There fell great hail out of the sky, and the stones weighed about a hundred pounds. Men blasphemed God because of the plague of the hail; For the plague was very severe. (Isaiah 30:30; Ezekiel 38:22)

Notes:

To properly understand chapter 16, it must be first recognized that these are the plagues upon mankind that are derived from the wrath of God being poured out, as stated in chapters 8, 9 & 10. Each vial is the result of a trumpet from those chapters.

The sore that is received by all who take the mark of the beast is due to the censor being cast to the earth, creating an electromagnetic pulse which burns up the microchip implant in the hands and foreheads of all who had received the mark of the beast. This burn is said to be very painful and also causes cancer in many.

The second vial upon the sea is because of the large land mass that is thrown into the ocean due to the impact of the censor, which is the result of the impact of the first comet fragment.

The third vial is the result of the second impact which hits the fresh waters and poisons the fresh water in that region.

The fourth angel poured out his vial upon the sun and scorches men with fire, which is the result of the impacts having thrown smoke and dust into the sky to darken the sun. This is because the ozone is destroyed due to the impacts.

The fifth vial is the result of the third impact of the comet which opens up the great abyss. Yellowstone caldera erupts due to the third impact. This spreads darkness across the whole land due to the eruption.

The sixth vial will then kill one third of the people on earth in little over 13 months.

The seventh vial pours out in the air. This corresponds to Revelation 10 which states that this is sealed and not to be written. (Revelation 10:4)

Revelation 17

1. One of the seven angels who had the seven vials came and talked with me and said, come here and I will show you the judgment of the great whore that sits on many waters, (*Babylon – USA – Rev 18:9-17*)

2. with whom the kings of the earth have prostituted themselves and the inhabitants of the earth have been made drunk with the product of her corruption. (Isaiah 47:9; Isaiah 14:26; Isaiah 23:17)

3. So he carried my spirit away into the wilderness; (Revelation 12:14) There I saw a woman sitting upon a red colored beast, and she was full of many blasphemous names and she had seven heads and ten horns. (Revelation 13:1; Daniel 7:7 – *the woman and the beast are two different entities*)

4. The woman was dressed in purple and red colors, decked with gold, precious stones and pearls, holding a golden cup in her hands that is full of abominations and the filthiness of her fornication. (Daniel 11:38; Zephaniah 3:1)

5. Upon it's forehead, a name was written: "The Secret Powerful Babylon", the mother of prostitutes and the abominations of the earth." (*secret or mystery = not recognized as Babylon by most people - a secret*) (Isaiah 57:3)

6. And I saw the woman drunken with the blood of the saints and with the blood of the martyrs of Jesus Christ: When I saw her, I was greatly curious about her. (Revelation 6:9-10; 13:1; 18:24; Isaiah 47:6)

7. The angel said to me, why do you marvel? I will tell you the secret of the woman and the beast that is carrying (*serving*) her, which has seven heads and ten horns. (Revelation 13:11)

8. The beast that you saw was, and is not, yet it will ascend out of the abyss and go to destruction. They who live on the earth will serve it when they see it, all whose names are not written in the book of life from the beginning of creation. (Revelation 13:8)

9. Here is for the mind that has wisdom: The seven heads are seven mountains on which the woman sits.

10. There are seven kings; Five have become relaxed (G-2261+G-5607), one is, and another will come, and when he does, he will continue for a short time. (*these may be Bush, Clinton, Bush, Obama, Trump, Biden, ? and one of these is the eighth. Bush 41 established the NWO.*)

11. The beast that was, and is not, he is the eighth and is also one of the seven; He shall be set to destroy.

12. The ten horns that you saw are ten kings (*10 reps from 10 regions*) which have not yet received a kingdom, but will receive power as kings for a period of time with the beast. (Daniel 7:7, 24; Rev 13:11)

13. They will be of one mind and they will give their power and strength to the beast.

14. They will make war against the Lamb, but the Lamb will overcome them: For he is Lord of lords and King of kings: All those that are with him are called, chosen and faithful. (Ephesians 2:8; Rev 13:15)

15. And he said unto me, the waters that you saw where the whore lives are many peoples and multitudes and nations and tongues.

16. The ten horns which you saw upon the beast shall hate the whore and shall make her desolate and naked; They will consume her flesh and burn her with fire. (Jeremiah 50 - 51; Ezekiel 26:3)

17. For God has put it in their hearts to fulfill his will and for them to agree with and give their kingdoms to the beast, until the will of God shall be completed.

18. And the woman which you saw is the great city who reigns over the kings of the earth. (Washington DC)

Notes:
The beast of Revelation 17:3, the first beast of Revelation 13 and the dreadful beast of Daniel 7 are all speaking of the same entity: The world government, the new world order (through US leadership)

The eighth king of Revelation 17:10-11, the head of the first beast that was slain in Revelation 13:3 and the little horn of Daniel 7 are the same entity: A man with Israeli/Jewish affiliation, the antichrist.

The second beast of Revelation 13 is a man, religious leader, the false prophet and a commander having affiliation with the Vatican. (Revelation 19:20)

The woman of Revelation 17 and Babylon of Revelation 18 are the same entity: The USA

The other beasts of Daniel 7 are Great Britain (the EU), Russia and China

Revelation 18
1. After these things, I saw another angel come down from the heavens, having great power, and the earth was lighted with his glory.

2. He announced with a strong and loud voice, Babylon the great is fallen, is fallen, and is now the habitation of devils and the home of every evil spirit, and the cage of every unclean and detestable bird. (Jeremiah 51:8, Revelation 14:8; Ezekiel 26:7; Isaiah 13:19-21; Isaiah 47; Zephaniah 2:15; Barnabas 9:4)

3. Because all nations have drunk of the wine of the wrath of her corruption and the kings of the earth have committed fornication with her. (Isaiah 14:26) The merchants of the earth have grown rich because of the

abundance of her delicacies. (Jeremiah 51:7; Nahum 3:4; Ezekiel 27:9-33)

4. And I heard another voice from the heavens saying, come out of her my people, that you not be partakers in her sins and that you receive not of her plagues. (Zechariah 2:6; Jeremiah 50:8; Jeremiah 51:45)

5. For her sins have reached into the heavens and God knows of her iniquities.

6. Give unto her, even as she has given unto you, and double unto her according to what she has done. In the cup that she has filled, double it unto her. (Ezekiel 7:27; Psalms 75:8; Jeremiah 25:15-38)

7. How much she has glorified herself and lived deliciously; Give unto her so much torment and sorrow. For she has said in her heart, I sit as a queen, I am not a widow and I will see no sorrow. (Psalms 10:6; Ezekiel 28:2; Isaiah 12:11-14; Isaiah 47:7-10; Zephaniah 2:15)

8. Therefore, her plagues come in one year, death, mourning and famine; (Ezekiel 7:26-27) Then she will be utterly burned by fire. Strong is the Lord who judges her. (Jeremiah 51:46; Revelation 6:12-13; Revelation 17:16; Ezekiel 28:28; Zephaniah 3:8)

9. The kings of the earth have committed fornication and lived deliciously with her, and they will cry for her and sulk when they see the smoke of her burning. (Ezekiel 27:30; Isaiah 23:17)

10. They will stand far off, for the fear of her torment, saying, alas, alas, the great city Babylon, the mighty city! In one hour is thy judgment come. (Isaiah 14:16)

11. The merchants of the earth will weep and mourn over her; For no one will buy their merchandise any more: (Isaiah 47:15; Nahum 3:16)

12. The merchandise of gold and silver, precious stones, pearls, scarlet, all types of wood and vessels, brass, iron and marble, (Ezekiel 27:9-24; Ezekiel 26:12; Zephaniah 1:18)

13. cinnamon and other fragrances and ointments and frankincense and wine, oil and fine flour, wheat and animals, sheep, horses (*vehicles*), slaves and the souls of men.

14. The fruits that your soul lusted after have been taken away from you and all things that were good and dainty are no longer yours, and you will not find them again.

15. The merchants of these things that were made wealthy by her will stand far off because of the fear of her torment, weeping and wailing. (Ezekiel 27:36)

16. They will say, oh, oh, that great city that was clothed in fine linens, purple, scarlet, decked with gold, precious stones and pearls! (Isaiah 14:4)

17. For in one hour such great riches have been brought to nothing. Every shipmaster and all of the ships, sailors and those that trade by sea stood far off.

18. They cried when they saw the smoke of her burning, saying, who is like this great city?

19. They cast dust on their heads (*tradition of the Jews*) and they cried, weeping and wailing, saying, Oh my god! The great city, the one who made all of the ships in the sea wealthy because of her highly paid prices. For in one hour she is made desolate. (Isaiah 14:7-8, Isaiah 9:14)

20. Be happy over her oh heavens, holy apostles and prophets, for God has avenged you upon her. (Revelation 6:10)

21. The mighty angel took up a giant millstone and cast it into the sea saying, with this violence shall the great city Babylon be thrown down and shall not be found again at all.

22. The voice of harpers, musicians, pipers and trumpeters shall be heard no more at all in you; The craftsman and the crafters shall be found in you no more. The sound of the millstone will never be heard again within you. (Zephaniah 3:6)

23. The light of the candle will never shine again in you; Your merchants were the great men of the earth, for because of your sorceries (*corruptions, poison*), all of the nations were deceived. (Revelation 17:2)

24. In her was found the blood of all of the prophets and all of the faithful ones that were killed upon the earth. (Revelation 13:15)

Revelation 19

1. After these things, I heard a loud voice of many people in heaven saying, alleluia; Salvation, glory, honour and jurisdiction unto the Lord our God. (Daniel 2:44)

2. True and righteous are his judgments; For he has judged the great whore that did corrupt the earth with her corruptions, and has avenged the blood of his servants at her hand. (Revelation 6:9; 13:7)

3. Then again, they said Alleluja (*praise be to Jehovah*). And her smoke rose up forever and ever.

4. The twenty-four elders and the four beasts (*living animals*) fell down and worshipped God as he sat on the throne, saying Alleluja. And a voice came out of the throne, saying,

5. praise our God all of his servants. Fear him everyone, both small and great.

6. I heard as if it were the voice of a great multitude, as the voice of many waters, and as the voice of mighty thundering saying, alleluia; For the Lord God omnipotent reigns.

7. Let us be glad and rejoice and give honour to him: For the wedding of the Lamb is come and the people of God have made themselves ready. (Matthew 22:14)

8. And unto them was granted that they would wear fine linen, clean and white; For the linen is the righteousness of the saints. (Revelation 7:9; Matthew 22:12)

9. Then he said to me, write this; Blessed are they which are called to the wedding feast of the Lamb. These are the true sayings of God.

10. And I fell at his feet to worship him, but he said to me, do not worship me, for I am your fellow servant and your assistant; To keep the testimony of Jesus Christ, worship God. The testimony (*witness*) of Jesus Christ is the spirit of this prophecy.

11. And I saw the heavens opened up, and behold, a white horse, (Revelation 6:1) and he that sat on him was called faithful and true, and in righteousness he did judge and make war. (Daniel 7:13; Matt. 24:29-31)

12. His eyes were as a flame of fire, and on his head, he wore many crowns; He had a name written that no man knew but he himself. (Daniel 7:9)

13. He was clothed with a cloth soaked in blood, and his calling (*purpose*) is his name (*Yehowshuwa = Yehovah's salvation*), and he is the way unto God. (John 1:1-12)

14. The armies which are in the heavens followed him on white horses, clothed in fine white linen.

15. Out of his mouth goes a sharp sword, that with it he shall smite the nations and rule them with a rod of iron. He shall compress the winepress of the fierceness of the wrath of Almighty God.
(Psalms 97:3; Isaiah 34:2; Psalms 110:5)

16. He has on his vest and on his thigh a name written, King of kings and Lord of lords.

17. And I saw an angel standing like the sun, and he announced with a loud voice, saying to all of the birds that fly in the midst of the heavens, come and gather yourselves together unto the supper of the great God, (Ezekiel 39:17-20)

18. that ye may eat the flesh of kings, the flesh of captains, the flesh of mighty men, the flesh of horses, those that sit on them and the flesh of all men, both free and slave, both small and great.

19. And I saw the beast and the kings of the earth, and their armies gathered together to make war against he that sat on the horse and against his army. (Revelation 16:16)

20. Then the beast was taken and with him the false prophet that wrought wonders before him, (Revelation 13:13) with whom he deceived all those that had received the mark of the beast, and them that worshipped his image; They were cast alive into the lake of fire burning with brimstone.

21. And all of the remaining ones were killed by the sword of him that sat upon the horse, which sword proceeded from out of his mouth, and all of the birds were filled with their flesh.

Revelation 20

It looks as though verses 1-10 may have been altered from the original script.

1. I saw an angel come down from the sky, having the key to the abyss and a strong chain in his hand.

2. He laid hold of the dragon, that old serpent, which is the devil, Satan, and bound him a thousand years, and cast him into the bottomless pit (Isaiah 27:1)

3. and locked him up, and set a seal upon him, that he should deceive the nations no more till the thousand years should be completed, but after that he shall be loosed for a short time.

4. Then I saw thrones and those that sat upon them, and judgment was given, and I saw the souls of them that were beheaded (killed) for the witness of Jesus (Revelation 6:9), and the gospel of God, of whom had not worshipped the beast, neither his image, nor had received his mark upon their foreheads or in their hands; And they lived and reigned with Christ a thousand years. This is the first resurrection.

5. But those that remained dead did not live again until the thousand years were completed.

6. Blessed and Holy is he that has part in the first resurrection; For unto these the second death has no

power, but they shall be priests of God and of Christ, and shall reign with him a thousand years.
7. And when the thousand years are completed, Satan shall be loosed out of his prison,
8. and he will go out to deceive the nations which are in the four quarters of the earth, Gog and Magog, to gather them together to battle: The number of whom is as the sand of the sea.
9. And they went from the entire earth and circled the camp of the saints and the beloved city: Then fire came down from God out of the heavens and it destroyed them.
10. The devil that deceived them was cast into the lake of fire and brimstone where the beast and the false prophet are, and they shall be tormented day and night forever and ever.

11. And I saw a great white throne and the one that sat on it, from whose face the earth and the sky fled away and there was no place for them.
12. And I saw the dead, both the small and great stand before God, and the books were opened: (Daniel 7:10) Then another book was opened, which is the book of life: And the dead were judged out of those things that were written in the books, each one according to their own deeds. (Jeremiah 17:10; Psalm 75:2; Matthew 13:37-52; Matthew 25:32-33; Daniel 12:1; Daniel 7:10; Romans 2:6-10; Proverbs 11:5-6; Psalms 19:7-11; Psalms 9:7-8, 16-17; Psalms 69:28; Ezekiel 38:11-20; Isaiah 59:18; Jeremiah 25:14; Jeremiah 32:19)
13. And the seas gave up the dead that were in them, and death and hell delivered up their dead that were in them, and they were judged, every man according to each one's own deeds. (Ezekiel 7:8; Romans 2:5-10)
14. Death and hell were cast into the lake of fire. This is the second death.
15. Whoever was not found written in the book of life was cast into the lake of fire. (Malachi 4:1)

Revelation 21

1. Then I saw a new sky and a new earth; The first sky and the first earth were passed away and there was no more sea. (Isaiah 60:1-22; Isaiah 65:17-25; Psalm 75:3)
2. I John saw the holy city, new Jerusalem of God coming down from the heavens (*sky*), prepared as a bride adorned for her husband. (Isaiah 54:5-13)
3. I heard a loud voice out of the heavens saying, behold, the tabernacle of God is with mankind and he will dwell with them. They shall be his people and God himself shall be with them and be their God.
4. And God shall wipe away all tears from their eyes and there shall be no more death, neither sorrow, nor crying, neither shall there be any more pain: (Revelation 7:17) The former things are passed away.
5. Then he that sat upon the throne said, behold, I make all things new. Then he said to me, write this, for these words are true and faithful.
6. Then he said unto me, it is completed. I am the alpha (*beginning*) and omega (*end*), the highest and final authority. (Revelation 1:11) I will give unto those that are thirsty, to drink of the fountain of the water of life freely.
7. He that overcomes shall inherit all things (1 Corinthians 10:13; Revelation 2-3) and I will be their God, and they shall be my children. (1 John 3:1)
8. But the fearful, unbelieving, abominable, all murderers, whoremongers, sorcerers, idolaters and liars shall all find themselves in the lake which burns with fire and brimstone, which is the second death. (Galatians 5:21; Exodus 20:12-17)
9. Then there came to me one of the seven angels which had the seven vials full of the seven last plagues; And he spoke with me saying, come here and I will show you the bride, the lamb's wife.
10. And he carried me away in the spirit unto a great and high mountain and showed me that great city, the holy Jerusalem, descending out of the heavens of God, having the glory of God.
11. Her light was like a most precious stone, even as a gemstone, even as clear as crystal.
12. It had a large and high wall and twelve gates, and at the gates were twelve angels, and names written thereon are the names of the twelve tribes of the children of Israel: (Revelation 7:5-8; Ezekiel ch.40-48)
13. On the east there are three gates; On the north there are three gates; On the south there are three gates, and on the west, there are three gates.
14. And the wall of the city had twelve foundations, and in them the names of the twelve apostles of the Lamb. (*not Judas Iscariot, but Paul*)
15. The one that spoke with me had a golden reed to measure the city, its gates and the wall thereof.
16. The city is laid out with four corners, and the length is as large as the breadth: Then he measured the

city with a reed, twelve thousand furlongs (*fifteen hundred miles*) The length and the breadth and the height are equal.

17. Then he measured the wall thereof, a hundred forty-four cubits, according to the measure of a man. *(nearly 500 feet tall)*

18. The construction of the wall was jasper and the city was of pure gold, transparent like clear glass.

19. The foundations of the walls of the city were garnished with all types of precious stones. The first foundation was jasper; The second sapphire; The third was chalcedony; The fourth was emerald; (Isaiah 54:12)

20. The fifth was sardonyx; The sixth was sardius; The seventh was diamond; The eighth was beryl; The ninth was topaz; The tenth was chrysoprasus; The eleventh was jacinth; The twelfth was amethyst.

21. And the twelve gates were each a pearl. Each gate was one large pearl and the streets of the city were pure gold, it was like transparent glass.

22. I did not see a temple therein: For the Lord God Almighty is the temple.

23. The city had no need for the sun, nor the moon to shine on it, for the glory of God lighted it, and the Lamb is the light thereof. (Isaiah 60:19-20; Zechariah 14:7; John 1:4-6)

24. The nations of those that shall be eternally saved shall walk in his light, and the kings of the earth do bring their glory and honour unto him.

25. The gates of the city shall not be shut at all by day, and there shall be no night there;

26. They shall bring glory and honour into it.

27. And there shall in no way enter into it anything that is defiled, neither anyone that commits an abomination or makes a lie; But only those who are written in the Lambs book of life. (Isaiah 60:21)

Revelation 22

1. And he showed me a pure river of the water of life, clear as crystal proceeding out of the throne of God and of the Lamb. (Psalm 65:9; Zechariah 14:8)

2. In the midst of the street of it and on both sides of the river there was a tree of life which bears twelve types of fruits, of which yield their fruits each month;
The leaves of the tree were for the healing of the nations.

3. And there shall be no more curse, but the throne of God and the Lamb shall be there and his servants shall serve him, (Zechariah 14:9)

4. and they shall see his face and his name shall be on their foreheads.

5. There shall be no night there and they will not need a candle, nor the light of the sun; For the Lord God gives them light and they shall reign forever and ever. (Isaiah 60:19-20)

6. And he said unto me, these words are faithful and true. The God of the holy prophets sent his messenger (*John*) to show unto his servants the things that will surely soon happen.

7. Behold, I will come suddenly! Fortunate are those who keep the words written by the prophets.

8. I John saw these things and heard them. When I had heard and seen all of these things, I fell down before the feet of the angel that showed me these things.

9. Then he said unto me, do not do that, for I am your fellow servant and one of your brethren, just as the prophets and all of them which keep the words of this book. Worship God alone.

10. Then he said unto me, do not seal the words of the prophecy of this book, for the time is drawing near.

11. Those that are unjust, they will remain unjust; Those that are filthy, they will remain filthy; Those that are righteous, will remain righteous. Those that are holy, will remain holy. (Matthew 18:18)

12. Be aware! I shall come suddenly and my rewards are with me. I will give unto everyone according to their deeds; So shall it be.

13. I am the Alpha (*beginning*) and the omega (*end*), the foremost and the final authority, the first and the last.

14. Blessed are those who obey his instructions (*precepts*), that they may have right to the tree of life, and may enter in through the gates into the city.

15. For outside are dogs and sorcerers, whoremongers, murderers, idolaters and all that enjoy making lies.

16. I Jesus have sent my messenger (*John*) to testify of these things and give them to the people of God. I am the root and the offspring of David and the bright morning star.

17. The spirit and the bride say, come. Let he who hears these words come, let those that are thirsty come;

Whoever will, let him take the water of life freely.

18. For I testify unto every man that hears the words of the prophecy of this book, if any man shall come against what is written, God shall add unto him the plagues that are written in this book:

19. If any man shall fall short of the words written by the prophets, God shall take away his part out of the book of life and out of the holy city.

20. He who testifies these things says, surely, I will come suddenly. Even so, come Lord Jesus.

21. May the grace of our Lord Jesus Christ be with you all.

It must be noted that the book of Revelation is written in the Hebrew style, of which is to give an overview, then to circle back around repeatedly to fill in more details. This differs from the modern method of telling a story in a narrative order of events.

Barnabas

Chapter 1

1. Blessed are you my sons and daughters in the name of the Lord Jesus Christ who loves those of us that are at peace with him.

2. Having now seen the abundant knowledge of the message of God abiding in you, I am extremely joyous that your honorable souls have received of this grace of which has now been made a part of you.

3. This is the reason that I am full of joy, now having the hope (*expectation*) of eternal salvation for you. I truly see his spirit infused in you, as the pure fountain of God.

4. Being convinced of this, since I first began to speak to you I have come to understand many additional things. The Lord has much more thoroughly showed me the depths of the knowledge of righteousness.

5. Know that I am bound to the highest, to love you even more than my own soul, because of your faithfulness and the great amount of love that is living in you while you await the life that he has promised.

6. Therefore, consider that if I take the time to communicate some part of what I received, I shall receive a reward for serving you concerning the accommodation of your souls. I have diligently written this letter unto you so that along with your faithfulness, this knowledge might help perfect you.

7. Therefore, there are three things that are dogmatic: The hope for eternal life, the commencement of it (*conversion* – Acts 2:38; 3:19) and the completion of it. (*living according to the covenant until death -* 1 John 3:1-10).

8. For the Lord has announced through the prophets in past times, all of the things that were to come. We have now come to see that these things (concerning Christ) have been accomplished.

9. Now each one of us as individuals must come into the greater wealth of faithfulness and draw near unto him in true reverence.

10. Therefore, I, not as a teacher, but as a fellow brother shall take upon myself to lay out a few of the things that might assist you in many ways and may bring joy unto you.

Barnabas 2

1. Now the days are full of evil, because Satan holds jurisdiction over this world. (John 14:30; John 12:31; John 16:11; 1 Corinthians 2:6; Ephesians 2:2; Daniel 11:36-45) Therefore we must diligently seek to live according to that which will be judged to be righteous by the Lord.

2. Having patience and the fear of the Lord help us to remain faithful. To be long suffering and to have patient endurance also help us.

3. Wisdom, science, understanding, and knowledge always remain pure in everything that relates to the Lord, so rejoice in this.

4. For God made it known to us through the prophets that he had no interests in our sacrifices, burnt offerings and oblations, when it was said: "Thus saith the Lord, unto what purpose are the many sacrifices that you offer unto me? (Isaiah 1:11-14)

5. I am not interested in the fat of lambs and the blood of bulls and goats. I have had enough of your burnt offerings.

6. Who has required this of you when you appear before me? You shall never again enter into my courts."

7. "Do not bring your worthless offerings; Incense is an abomination unto me. Your new moons and your Sabbaths, the calling of assemblies; I can not take any more of them, as they are iniquitous, as are your solemn meetings. My soul hates your new moons and your appointed feasts!" (Isaiah 1:11-14; Hosea 2:11)

8. God therefore has abolished these things so that the new covenant of our Lord Jesus Christ be established (Jeremiah 31:31-34; Hebrews 8:8-13), of which is without yoke of any such necessity, (works of the Mosaic law) that he might receive a personal, spiritual offering, each man of themselves.

9. For the Lord again said; "At the time when I brought your forefathers out of the land of Egypt, I did not speak nor did I command them concerning burnt offerings and sacrifices.

10. What I did command of them was, obey my voice and live according to the ways that I have ordered of you and I will be your God and you shall be my people." (Jeremiah 7:22-23) "Allow not one of you to think of committing an evil act against another and be sure to not make a false oath." (Zechariah 8:17)

11. Therefore, as we are not without understanding of these things, we must comprehend the gracious intentions of God our Father. These scriptures speak to us, that those of us who have also been in the same error concerning the sacrifices might seek and find how to properly approach him.

12. This is the way that the scriptures instruct us concerning this: "The sacrifice that God desires is a broken spirit, a broken and contrite heart that will not contradict (*defy*) him."
(Psalms 51:17; Numbers 15:30-31)

13. This is why my brethren, we ought to be much more diligent to inquire concerning the things that are necessary for our salvation, so that Satan not be allowed entrance into us of which would deprive us of our true life. (the eternal life)

14. It is again written unto us concerning these things; "Your fasting is done for strife, debate and for wicked reasons. You shall no longer fast as you presently do, because you make it known in the streets!

15. This is the fast that I have required: A day for a man to search his own soul and to humble himself with sackcloth and ashes. Will you not come in unto the fast that is acceptable unto the Lord?"
(Isaiah 58:4-5)

16. But he also said this; "Is this not the fast that I require, to loosen the bands of wickedness and undo the heavy burdens, to allow the oppressed to go free and for you to break every yoke (*chain*)?

17. Is it not to offer your food to those that are hungry and to bring the poor into your home? That when you see one that is naked, you offer him clothing while not having concern about providing for yourself?

18. Do this and a new dawn shall be brought forth, a new day of healing shall spring forth immediately, and righteousness shall be brought forth from you and the glory of God shall be your reward.

19. Then you shall call upon the Lord and he shall answer. When you shall cry out, he will say, here I am! Put away from yourself the bondage of pointing the finger and speaking vanity. Offer your own goods unto those that are needy so to satisfy the needs of those that are suffering hardship.

20. In this, God manifests his divine providence and love for us, because the people that he has purchased through his beloved son, demonstrate that they truly believe with sincerity." (Isaiah 58:6-10; John 3:16-21) This is why he has shown these things unto us through the prophets, so that we do not continue in error as the proselytes of the Jewish law do.

Barnabas 3

1. This is why it is necessary concerning all of the things that we do every day, that we search ourselves diligently and continue in that which will lead unto salvation.

2. We must now completely turn away from all iniquity (*evil deeds*) and hate the errors of this present world. Be satisfied with setting your focus on the world to come. (*eternal life*)

3. We must not give ourselves the liberty to associate with sinners and wicked people, or we will become like they are.

4. For the end of sin is come, (2 Thessalonians 2:1-3) as it is said by one of the prophets, "to finish the transgressions, to put an end to sin, make atonement for past wickedness and bring in everlasting righteousness" (Daniel 9:24)

5. I beg of you my brethren, as I love you all beyond my own life, you must then also understand this: You must be very careful to preserve yourselves and not become like those who compound their sins, of whom say that the first covenant (*Mosaic*) is the same as ours (*the new covenant*). You must know that they have forever lost that which Moses had received.

6. The scripture says, Moses continued fasting for forty days and forty nights on the mountain before he received the covenant from the Lord of which was written upon two stone tablets that were engraved by the hand of God. (Exodus 31:18)

7. But the people turned themselves unto idols (*the golden calf*) and they broke it (*the covenant*). That is when the Lord said to Moses, "go down quickly, for the people that I have brought out of the land of Egypt have defiled themselves and have rejected to live in the way that I have commanded of them."
(Exodus 34:28) Moses threw down the tablets of stone from out of his hands, smashing them. In this, their covenant was broken. But now, the love of Jesus can be sealed within your hearts, having hope through faithfulness unto him. (Deuteronomy 9:12; Exodus 32:7)

8. Therefore we must be careful every day until the end of our lives. In our past, if we lived according to righteousness and have done what is right, having complete faithfulness, all of this will profit us nothing unless we continue to hate all that is evil and overcome every temptation that will come upon us in the future. This is why the son of God said, "you must resist all iniquity and hate it." (Psalms 97:10; Proverbs 8:13)

9. Do not allow the evil one to gain entrance into you. Be sure not to withdraw yourselves from others in the faith, as though you have already been justified (*as though you have finished the race*). (Hebrews 10:25) But gather together with those that are faithful and see what you can do to tend to the general welfare of the brethren. As the scripture states; "Woe unto those that are wise in their own eyes and prudent in their own sight." (Isaiah 5:21; Romans 10:5-7)

10. Each of us must be spiritually minded and become a perfect temple unto God. With all that is in us, we must keep our focus upon the fear of God. (Proverbs 1:7) We must strive to always keep his commands (Matthew 22:37-40) so that when judgment day comes, we may have confidence and rejoice in our victory;

11. Because God will judge the whole world, each one, with no favorites among peoples. Everyone will receive accordingly, based upon what they have done in this life. (Revelation 20:12-15; Romans 2:5-11)

12. If a man lives righteously in all that he does, he shall receive good on the day of judgment. But if a man does any wickedness, he shall receive accordingly the punishment for that which is due unto him.

13. You must be careful so that you do not come to be at ease where you might slip and in your rest find that you have again defiled yourselves with sin, having the wicked one (*Satan*) again gain control over you, thrusting you away from the inheritance of the kingdom of God. (Hebrews 6:4-6)

14. You must much more attend to this my brethren, when you reflect upon all of the mighty things that have recently occurred in the nation of Israel (the destruction of 70 AD). You must keep in mind that they were cut off. In this, we can reflect upon the scripture, as it is written, "many are called, but few are chosen." (Matthew 22:14; Matthew 7:13-14)

Barnabas 4

1. This is the reason that our Lord offered up his body unto death; That through forgiveness of our sins, we could be sanctified through the shedding of his blood.

2. Concerning those things that are written about him, some are directed unto the Jews and some unto us.

3. As it is written; "He was wounded for our transgressions and bruised for our iniquities, and by his blood we can be made whole." (Isaiah 53:5-7) He was led as a lamb to be slaughtered; Just as a sheep does not speak when it goes before the shearers, he did not open his mouth.

4. Therefore, we should give much thanks unto God, for he has fulfilled those things that were written in the past and he has given us wisdom through them about how we must now live. He has not left us without understanding concerning the things that will happen in the future. *(due to the prophetic scriptures)*

5. Now the scripture says, "it is not unjust that the nets are stretched out for the birds." (Proverbs 1:17)

6. This means that a man shall (*eternally*) perish if he understands the way of righteousness, nevertheless he does not prevent himself from the deeds of darkness. (Romans 1:18-19; James 4:17; 2 Peter 2:20-22)

7. This is the reason that the Lord decided to bring suffering upon himself, even though he is the highest above everything! He did so for us, when at the beginning of the world he said, "I will make man in my own image and likeness." (Genesis 1:26 – *that image is purity, innocence and holiness*) (1 John 3:1-3)

8. So he suffered for us, at the hands of the people that he created. Let me show you something.

9. The prophets had received the gift of prophecy from him and they spoke concerning Christ:

10. But so that he might abolish death and bring about the resurrection of the dead, he was satisfied to physically manifest himself in this world, as was necessary. In this, he made good on his promise unto the forefathers to build for himself a new people and explain to them while he walked the earth, that after the resurrection of the dead he will judge the world. (Revelation 20:12-15; Daniel 12:2; Romans 2:5-10)

11. So he taught the nation of Israel and he fulfilled the prophecies and he did many miracles while he was among them. While he preached to them, he showed exceedingly great love towards them.

12. When he chose his apostles who were afterwards to publish (*spread*) his gospel, he took men that had been very great sinners, so that by them, he would show that he came to call even the worst of sinners unto repentance. (Matthew 9:13)

13. He clearly manifested himself to be the son of God. But if he had not physically come into the world, how could the people look unto him so that they might be saved?

14. If men were to look at the sun, a creation of God that will one day no longer exist, they can not even bear to look upon it. (*its glory is too bright*)

15. This is why the son of God came physically into this world, so that he could bring an end to the iniquity of those that had persecuted and killed his prophets. This is the reason that he also suffered.

16. For God had said through a prophet, "the strokes against his body shall be done by them. When the shepherd is struck down, the sheep will be scattered." (Zechariah 13:6-7)

17. Thus he suffered because it was necessary for him to suffer on the cross.

18. For there was one that prophesied concerning him that has said, "spare my soul from the sword." (Psalm 70:1-5)

19. Then he again said, "fasten my body with nails. For the assemblies of the wicked have risen up against me, they have pierced my hands and my feet." (Psalms 22:16)

20. Then again it was written, "I gave my back to the whippers and I set my cheeks for them to pluck out my beard and I did not hide my face from those that spit upon me." (Isaiah 50:6)

Barnabas 5

1. So therefore, since he fulfilled the commandment of God, what does he say? "He that justifies me is near me. Who can contend against me. Let us stand together. If the one that is my adversary comes against me, the Lord God will help me. Who is it that can condemn me? But woe unto you who are soiled as a tattered cloth, the moth shall eat you up." (Isaiah 50:8-9)

2. Then the prophet said, "He had put forth a stumbling stone" (Isaiah 8:14) "I lay in Zion a precious foundation stone, a choice corner stone that is honorable." (Isaiah 28:16) Then what does he say? "He that puts their strength (*hope*) in him shall live forever." (Psalms 133:1-3)

3. What then, is our hope in a building stone? God forbids! But because the Lord has hardened his body against those sufferings, it is said, I have built upon a solid rock. (Isaiah 1:7; Matthew 7:24; Matthew 16:18)

4. Then again the prophet adds, "the stone that the builders rejected has now become the headstone between the two walls." (Psalms 118:22) Then again it is written, "This is the great and wonderful day that the Lord has made." (Psalms 118:24) I will now write these things more simplified so that you understand, because of the great love that I have for you.

5. The prophets have said, "The council of the ungodly (*wicked*) have encircled all around me. They came upon me like bees surrounding the hive and they cast lots for my clothing." (Psalms 22:18)

6. In this, it was prophesied that our Saviour would present himself in the likeness of a man and that he would suffer greatly. In this, his passion was foretold.

7. The prophet again spoke against Israel: "Woe unto their souls, for they have taken council wickedly against one of their own, saying, let's lay a snare against the righteous one, because he is not profitable unto us." (Isaiah 3:9)

8. Moses also in much the same way spoke of this; "Behold, this is what the almighty God says; Enter into this good land of which God swore unto Abraham, Isaac and Jacob, that he would give it to them for a possession, a land full of milk and honey." (Exodus 33:1)

9. Now what was the spiritual meaning of this? Understand, it is as if it was said, put your trust completely in the one that would physically come (*Jesus*). Mankind is of the earth and suffers, being of the same substance of the earth that Adam was formed of.

10. Therefore, what does it mean when it is said, a land flowing of milk and honey? Blessed be our Father God who has given us wisdom and a heart to understand his secrets.
As the prophet said, "who shall understand these difficult sayings of the Lord? Only those that love the Lord and have been given the wisdom and intelligence." (Proverbs 1:2-7)

11. Now if we understand that he has renewed each of us through the remission of our sins, he also remolds each of us. Having cleansed our souls, as pure as little children, he now begins to form us by his spirit. (Matthew 18:1-4; 1 Peter 2:1-2; John 14:26)

12. The scriptures say this concerning us, where it shows the Father speaking to the Son: "I will make man in my own image and give him dominion over the beasts of the earth and the birds of the air and the fishes of the sea. (Genesis 1:26)

13. And when God saw the man that he had formed, he said, he is very good. Increase and multiply, and replenish the earth. This he spoke to the son for our sake.

14. Now I will show you how he made us (*the converted*) to be a new creature in these latter days.

15. The Lord said, "I will make the last as the first." (Isaiah 43:18-19) a prophet also wrote, "Enter into the land flowing with milk and honey, and you shall have dominion over it." (Exodus 33:1-3)

16. This is the way that we are reformed anew. Again he spoke through another prophet: "Thus saith the Lord, I will take from those who the spirit of the Lord foresaw, and I will remove their hearts of stone and replace them with hearts of flesh. (Ezekiel 11:19)

17. This refers to Christ being in the physical form (*flesh*), that he would be made to come into our own hearts and live within us. (1 John 4:1-3 – *the holy spirit of Christ*)

18. My brethren, the habitation of our hearts is a holy temple for the spirit of God. As it is written, "Where shall I appear before the Lord my God to be glorified?" (Psalms 42:2)

19. Then he answered, "I will confess unto you through the congregation that is in the midst of your brethren (*their hearts*), and I will sing unto you in the gathering of the saints." (Ephesians 2:21-22)

20. Therefore, we are those people that he has brought into that good land.

21. But what does the milk and honey signify? It is this: As a child is first nourished with milk and then later with honey, we are kept alive by trust in the promises that he spoke, that we shall receive dominion over the land. (Matthew 18:1-10)

22. But earlier it was said of these things, "be fruitful and multiply and have dominion over the beasts of the field and the fishes of the sea and the birds of the sky." (Genesis 1:28)

23. But is there any that have full power over all of the wild animals? You know that to rule is to have power and that a man should have authority over what he rules.

24. But for all that we do not presently have at this time, yet he has promised it to us; But specifically, when will this happen? When we become perfect (*converted and mature in Christ*) and become inheritors of the covenant of God.

Barnabas 6

1. Now understand this my brethren, that our God has previously made these things known unto us, so that we would always know unto whom to give our praise and thankfulness.

2. Therefore, because the son of God had suffered, by his stripes we might live; We know that he will come to judge the quickened and those that are eternally dead. We know that the son of God would not have suffered except for us. But when he was crucified, they gave him vinegar and gall to drink.

3. I will tell you how the priests of the temple did foreshadow this: By the commandment of the Lord that was written, "I have declared that whoever did not fast the appointed fast would be brought to death." (Leviticus 23:29) This was because, one day he was to offer up his body for our sins. In this, the example of what was shown in Isaac, when he was offered upon the altar it would be fulfilled.

(Genesis 22 – *Christ is the lamb that was sacrificed.*)

4. What was it that was said by the prophet? They will eat the goat that was offered on the day of the fast, for all of their sins. Listen carefully my brethren, "all of the priests only ate the inner parts that are not washed with vinegar." (Numbers 29)

5. Why is this? "because I know that I shall hereafter offer my body for the sins of a new people, but you will give me vinegar to drink, mixed with gall. Therefore, eat alone while the people fast and mourn in sackcloth and ashes." (Psalms 69:21-22)

6. This was given so he might foreshow that he was going to suffer for them. This is how he appointed it:

7. He said, "take two goats that are of good quality and similar to each other, and offer them. The high priest will take one and offer it as a burnt offering for sin." (Leviticus 11) So what was to be done with the other? It is accursed!

8. Let us now see how this exactly shows in what happened to Christ Jesus. "And let all of the congregation spit on it, pierce it and encircle its head with scarlet wool, then take it and leave it in the wilderness."

9. After this was to be done, the one that took the goat to the wilderness then took off of it the scarlet wool and then put its body upon a thorn bush, of which we are accustomed to eat the fruit of. Only the fruits of this thorn bush are good to eat.

10. So what was the finality of the ceremony? Consider that one was offered upon the alter and the other

was accursed.

11. So why was the one that was accursed crowned? Because they saw Jesus having the scarlet cloth wrapped around his body; They shall say, isn't this the one that we crucified? We despised him, pierced him and mocked him. For sure, this is he, the one that said that he was the son of God!

12. So, just as the way that it would happen to him on the earth, so hereto, the Jews were also commanded to take two goats, both good quality and equal. So that when they will see him, our Saviour coming in the clouds in the sky, they will be amazed at the similarity to the goats.

13. So in this, we see a similitude of Christ Jesus who was to suffer for us.

14. So what does the wool being put on the thorn bush represent?

15. This is also a similitude that is sent out to those in the new covenant with God. So just as one that would take away the scarlet wool must undergo much hardship because the thorns were very sharp, and it was difficult to attain it, "so they that will see me and come into my kingdom must go through many hardships and difficulties to attain unto me, says Christ Jesus." (Acts 14:22)

Barnabas 7

1. What similitude do you suppose it is, where it is commanded to the people of Israel, the people that were very wicked should offer up a heifer and after they had killed it, to then burn it.
(Numbers 19; Hebrews 9:13)

2. Then the young men should take the ashes and put them in jars, and then tie a piece of scarlet wool and hyssop on a stick and sprinkle the ashes upon all of them so that they could be cleansed of their sins.

3. Now consider that this was also a pre-figurement unto us.

4. The heifer represents Jesus Christ. The wicked men that were to offer it were those that put him to death, who afterwards have nothing to do with it.

5. The young men that performed the sprinkling signify those whom the Lord gave authority to teach us of the forgiveness of our sins and purification of the heart. At the beginning there were twelve apostles, of whom signify the twelve tribes of Israel. (Romans 11:17)

6. But why was there three young men that were appointed to sprinkle? This is to denote the patriarchs Abraham, Isaac and Jacob who were great before the Lord our God.

7. Why was the wool put on a stick? Because the kingdom of Jesus was founded upon a cross, and that those who completely commit themselves to him shall live forever.

8. But why was the wool and hyssop put together? To signify that in this world, the times here would be evil and filthy through which we will be saved. (Psalm 23:4) Hyssop is a cure for many diseases.

9. Therefore, through these things it is now evident unto us, but unto the Jews, they refuse to see because they have been hardened against the voice of God.

Barnabas 8

1. The scriptures also speak to us concerning circumcision, how God has circumcised our ears and our hearts. For the Lord spoke through the prophets, "when they understand what they hear, they obey me." (Isaiah 43:8)

2. Then again it was said, "Those that are far away shall hear and understand the things that I have done." (Isaiah 33:13) And yet again the Lord said, "circumcise your hearts." (Jeremiah 4:4)

3. Again it was written, "Here this oh Israel." Again the spirit of God prophesied, "who is it that will live forever? Only those that hear the voice of my son." (Psalm 37:28)

4. Then it is again written, "hear my words oh ye heavens, and understand all ye on the earth, for the Lord has spoken these things as a witness unto you." (Isaiah 1:2)

5. Then it is written, "hear the voice of the Lord, all ye rulers of the people." (Isaiah 1:10) "Hear me oh my people, the voice of the one crying in the wilderness." (Isaiah 40:3) These are all evidence!

6. Therefore circumcise your ears so that we might understand and commit ourselves to him (*believe*). Because the circumcision that the Jews trusted in has been abolished! The circumcision that God spoke of is not of the physical body, but of the heart.

7. But they broke his commands, because the evil ones deceived them. (Malachi 2:8) This is what the Lord your God says: Here is the new law: "Do not plant your seed among thorns, but circumcise yourselves unto the Lord your God." (Jeremiah 4:3-4; Matthew 13:7) Submit yourselves unto the Lord.

8. Then again he said, "cut off (*circumcise*) the hardness of your hearts; Do not become hardhearted or stiff-necked." (Jeremiah 4:4) Then it is said again, "Thus saith the Lord, all of the foreign nations are uncircumcised physically, but these people (*of Israel*) are uncircumcised in their hearts." (Deuteronomy 10:16)

9. But there are some that say the Jews were physically circumcised as a sign. But so are all of the Syrians, Arabians and all of their idolatrous priests; Even the Egyptians physically circumcise themselves! Are they also included in the covenant with Israel?

10. My brethren, understand these things much more fully, as it was Abraham that brought in physical circumcision. He did so looking forward to the spirit of Jesus of which was circumcised, having received the mystery of three letters.

11. The scriptures tell us that Abraham circumcised three hundred eighteen men of his own house, but what was the mystery that was made known unto him?

12. First take the eighteen and then the three hundred. The number letters of ten and eight are "IH", and these denote Jesus.

13. Because the cross is the way that we might find grace; Therefore he adds three hundred, of which is denoted with a "T", symbolizing the cross.

14. He that puts the engrafted gift of genuine doctrine within each of us, knows that I never taught unto anyone a more certain truth. But I trust that you are worthy of it.

Barnabas 9

1. So why did Moses say that you shall not eat of the swine, nor the eagle, hawk or crow, nor any fish that does not have scales on them? The answer is, that in the spiritual sense, he gathered the doctrines that could be attained by them.

2. In Deuteronomy, the Lord is quoted to have said to them, "I will establish my ordinances with this people." (Deuteronomy 4:1) So it was not commanded of God that they must not eat these things, because Moses spoke in the spiritual sense unto them.

3. Now he forbade them to eat from the pig, but this means that they should not join themselves to people that are like swine. While they live in pleasure, they forget God; Yet when they have need, they run to God. It is also like this with the pig, who does not want to know her master, but when she is hungry she cries to him. When she is fed, she no longer wants to know him.

4. Then it says, "thou shall not eat of the eagle, nor the hawk, nor kite, nor the crow;" That means that you shall not keep company with those types of people. Such do not know how by their own labor and sweat, to get food for themselves, but they injuriously ravish food from others; They also look for opportunity to lay snares for them, while at the same time they give the appearance that they live in perfect innocence.

5. These birds, while they sit idle, they look for ways to devour the flesh of others, proving themselves to be pests unto all. They are destructive through their wickedness.

6. He also said, "do not eat of the lamprey, the polypus, nor the cuttlefish." That means that you must not be like such men who are wickedly ungodly and are in the end accursed, because those fish are accursed; Wallowing in the mire, they do not swim like other fish, but they flop along the soil at the bottom of the sea.

7. Then he said, "you shall not eat the meat of the rabbit (*hare*)." What does that signify to us? It means that we must not be an adulterer and not place ourselves in the company of such types of people. For every year a rabbit sets its den in a different place to bring conception of its young. For every year that it lives, it also has a different mate.

8. Then it is written, you must not eat from the hyena; That means to not associate with an adulterer nor a corrupter of others. It also means to not become such. For they are known to change their kind, sometimes being a male, and other times being a female.

9. For a just cause he also taught to hate the weasel. It was so that they not be like such people who commit wickedness with their mouths through unclean talk. It was also that they not join themselves with impure women that commit wickedness with their mouths.

10. Moses therefore spoke concerning meats to deliver three important precepts unto the people of which have spiritual significance. But they, according to the desires of the flesh, understood him as though he had only meant it concerning meat. (Deuteronomy 4)

11. This is why David justly took this understanding of the three-fold command and spoke in this way:

12. "Blessed is the man that does not walk in the counsel of the ungodly" (Psalms 1:1) This speaks to the fish that were earlier mentioned that live on the bottom of the deep dark sea.

13. "nor stand in the ways of sinners" (Psalms 1:1) referring to those that look outwardly to fear the Lord, but yet are sinners concerning what they do and how they live.

14. "and does not sit in the seat of scorners" (Psalm 1:1) referring to those birds that sit looking for someone to devour.

15. In this, David perfectly demonstrates that he understood the laws concerning meat perfectly, in accordance to the true understanding of what was intended.

16. But Moses said, you shall eat of the meat of the animals that have a divided hoof and chew the cud. This signifies those that take up their own food and know the one who feeds them and they put their trust in him and are thankful unto him.

17. In this, he spoke well, having respect for the commandment. What was it that he then said? That we should stand strongly with those that fear the Lord, with those that meditate on the message of instruction that they have received in their hearts and with those who declare the righteous judgments of the Lord and keep his commandments.

18. For these, to meditate on the Lord is a great desire, so they then spend their time dedicated and completely living in the ways of the Lord.

19. But why is it that they could eat of the animals with the split hoof? Because those that are righteous live in this present world, yet hold their focus upon the next world. *(the grass is greener on the other side)* Now my brethren, do you now see how much thought Moses put in the commands of these things?

20. But how is it that we can know all of this and have understanding of it? We know that the commandments of the Lord speak concerning how we are meant to live, and he has circumcised our ears and our hearts so that we could understand these things.

Barnabas 10

1. Now we should ask if the Lord cared to make anything known beforehand concerning water baptism and the cross.

2. Now concerning water baptism, it is written to the people of Israel that they would not receive the baptism that brings forgiveness of sins, but that they would institute another that can not forgive sins.

3. It was written by Jeremiah the prophet, "be astonished in the heavens and let the earth tremble, because these people have done two greatly wicked things: They have left me, the fountain of living water and they have dug for themselves cisterns that can not hold water." (Jeremiah 2:12)

4. "Is my holy mountain (*Zion*) a desolate wilderness? You shall be as a young bird when its nest is taken away." (Isaiah 16:1-2)

5. Then again the prophet said, "I will go before you and will flatten the mountains (*obstacles*) and will break down the strong gates; I will break through the bars of iron and I will give unto you the secret hidden and invisible treasures so that you will know that I am the Lord God almighty!" (Isaiah 45:2)

6. Then it is said again, "he shall live in a high den on the strong rock." (Isaiah 33:16-17) Then again the same prophet said, "his water is faithful and you shall see your king in his glory and your soul shall learn the fear of the Lord."

7. Then again through another prophet, "he that does these things shall be like a tree that is planted by the waters of a river that will bring forth its fruit in due season. Its leaf will not whither and whatsoever he does shall prosper.

8. But for the wicked it will not be like this, but shall be like the chaff that the wind drives away.

9. Therefore the ungodly will not remain when the judgment comes and sinners will not remain in the council of the righteous. The Lord knows the doings of those that are righteous, but those that are ungodly shall perish." (Psalms 1)

10. Do you see how he (*David*) joins the water of baptism with the cross of Christ together?
(We access the cross through baptism. Romans 6:1-23)

11. Then he said, "blessed are those who commit their trust in the cross and descend into the water, for they will have their reward in due time and I will give unto them accordingly." (Isaiah 12:3; John 3:5)

12. Concerning our times he said, "their leaves shall not fall." This means that those words shall go forth from us through faithfulness and charity, and will bring conversion and hope unto many.

13. In a similar way another prophet also spoke, "the land of Jacob shall be the praise of all the earth" This was speaking of the body of Christ and of the holy spirit.

14. Then what follows? "And there was a river flowing on the right side with beautiful trees growing up by it; Those that eat of them shall live forever." This signifies that we are to go down into the water full of sin and pollutions of the present world, but when we come up we must bring forth good fruit, having within us the fear and hope that is in Jesus through his spirit. Whoever shall eat of him (*Christ*) shall live forever. (John 6)

15. That means, that whoever shall believe (John 3:16-21) and obey him when he calls, they shall live forever. (Mark 16:16; Romans 10:9-10)

Barnabas 11

1. In a similar way he speaks concerning the cross through another prophet; "When shall these things be fulfilled?

2. Then the answer was given: "When the tree that has fallen shall arise and when blood flows down from the tree." (Esdras 5:4 – *of the apocrypha*) In this you have the mention of the cross and the one that was to be crucified on it.

3. Yet again it was said by Moses, "when Israel attacks and then beats a man that they do not understand"; God put it in mind, that it was because of their sins that they would be delivered unto death. Yes, the holy spirit put it in the heart of Moses to represent the sign of the cross and the one that would suffer on it. He did this so that they might know that if they did not commit themselves unto him, they would be destroyed forever.

4. Moses then piled up the armor on the top of the hill and stood on the top of it; Standing above all of them he stretched out his arms so that Israel again might win the battle.

5. But as soon as he let down his hands they began to be killed and be defeated. Do you understand what this means? It was so that they might know that unless they believe in him they can not be saved.

6. Through another prophet it is said, "I have stretched out my hands all day long unto a disobedient and double speaking people." (*say one thing but do another* – Isaiah 65:2)

7. Then again Moses makes the symbol of Jesus, signifying that it was necessary for him to suffer, to become the author of salvation unto another people when they (*a falling Israel*) would think that they had destroyed him on the cross.

8. This was symbolized when God caused all kinds of serpents to bite them and they died, similar to how the serpent caused Eve to transgress. But in this, it was shown that because of their transgression, they would be delivered unto a painful death.

9. Then Moses who commanded them said, "you shall not make for yourselves any graven or molten image to be your god." Yet he himself did so, that he might represent unto them a figure that would point to the Lord Jesus. (Deuteronomy 17:15)

10. That is when he made a serpent constructed of brass and he set it high up and then called the people together. When they came they begged of Moses that he might make an atonement for them and ask God that he might restore (*heal*) them. (Numbers 21:9)

11. Then Moses said to them, when any of the people are bitten by a serpent, if they would come before the brass serpent that was on the pole, if they might truly trust in him, though it was not alive, he is able to offer life and they would be preserved (*saved*). They did so. Do you now see that this points to the glory of Jesus, and that in him and for him all things exist. (Colossians 1:16)

12. What was it that Moses said to Joshua the son of Nun at the time that he gave him the name of the only prophet that all of the people would look to? The Father did manifest these things concerning Jesus unto the son of Nun. He gave him that name when he went to spy out the land of Canaan.
(Exodus 17:14) He said, "Take a book in your hands and write upon it what the Lord God tells unto you." There Jesus, the son of God, in the last days will cut off the roots of the house of Amalek. You see, here it is, Jesus, the son of God, not the son of man that was shown that he would come in physical form.

(In Hebrew Joshua and Jesus are the same name)

13. Hereafter it would be said that Christ would be the son of David; Therefore David, having fear and knowing very well the ways of wicked people said, "The Lord saith unto my Lord, sit at my right hand until I make those that are your enemies to be under your footstool." (Psalms 110:1)

14. Again Isaiah spoke in this way: "The Lord said unto my Christ, my Lord, I have laid hold of his right hand that the nations shall obey before him and I will break the power of the kings." (Isaiah 45:1)

15. So how is it that both David and Isaiah call him Lord and the son of God? (Matthew 22:44)

Barnabas 12

1. Now let us go further to see if it will be the Jews that will be the heir or if it will be us. Let us also see if the *(new)* covenant will be with them or with us.

2. So now, concerning the Jews, hear what the scriptures have to say:

3. Isaac prayed for his wife Rebecca because she could not have children, then she conceived. (Genesis 25:21) Later, she went before the Lord to ask him of this;

4. The Lord said to her, there are two nations in your womb and two people shall come from your body. One shall hold power over the other and the greater shall serve the lesser. Now understand who Isaac was and who Rebecca was, and to whom it was foretold concerning who the greater was and who the lesser was.

5. In another place Jacob speaks more clearly unto his son Joseph when he said, "the Lord did not prevent me from seeing your face; Bring unto me your sons so that I may bless them." So Joseph brought his oldest and next oldest sons, Manasseh and Ephraim, hoping that he would bless Manasseh because he was the oldest. (Genesis 45:3)

6. Joseph brought him to the right hand of his father Jacob, but Jacob in his spirit foresaw the figure of the kind of people that would come from him.

7. What does the scripture say? "And Jacob crossed his hands and then he put his right hand upon Ephraim, the younger son and he blessed him. Then Joseph said unto his father Jacob, put your right hand upon the head of Manasseh, for he is my eldest son! Then Jacob said to Joseph, I know that my son, I do know it, but the greater shall serve the lesser, though he will also be blessed." (Genesis 48:18)

8. You see who he laid his hands upon, that those would be the first people and heir to the covenant.

9. But if the same was initiated through Abraham we would understand perfectly.

10. What then does the scripture say concerning Abraham? That when he believed, it was counted unto him as righteousness. He believed upon the Lord while he was not yet circumcised and was made a forefather of many nations that will believe upon the Lord while not physically circumcised. (Romans 4:11)

11. Now we will look to see whether God fulfilled this covenant that he gave to our forefather in the nation of Israel. Yes, truly he did; But they were not worthy to receive of it because of their sins.

12. The prophet said, "And Moses continued fasting for forty days and forty nights on Mount Sinai to receive the covenant from the Lord." (Exodus 24:18; Exodus 31:18 – *the forty days represents the forty years before entering the promised land. The forty nights represents the forty years from the death of Christ to the destruction of Jerusalem and their eviction from the promised land*)

13. And he received from the Lord two tablets, written by the finger of God in the spirit. When Moses had received them, he brought them down so that he could give them to the people. (Deuteronomy 9:10)

14. Then the Lord said to Moses, get yourself down from the mountain quickly, for the people that you brought out of the land of Egypt have done wickedly.

15. Moses had understood that they again had set up a molten image, so he threw the two tablets from his hands, and the tablets of the covenant were broken! You see, Moses received them but they were not worthy. (Exodus 32:7; Deuteronomy 9:12)

16. Now come to know how we received them: Moses was a servant and he took them, but the Lord himself had given them to us, (Hebrews 3:5-6) that we might be the people of inheritance and that he would suffer for us.

17. He was manifested on the earth so that they would make complete *(end)* their sins and that we might be made heirs by him and receive the *(new)* covenant of the Lord Jesus Christ. (Daniel 9:24)

18. Then again the prophet said, "Thus saith the Lord who shall redeem you *(Christ)*, I have set you to be a light unto the gentiles, to be a Savior unto all of the earth." (Isaiah 49:6)

19. He was prepared for this very reason, so that by his appearing, he could redeem our hearts that were already surrounded in death and deliver us from the errors of darkness, and establish a covenant with us.
20. For it is written that the Father commanded him to deliver us from darkness and prepare for himself a holy people.
21. This is why the prophet wrote: "I the Lord your God have called you unto righteousness and I will take you by the hand and will strengthen you. I offer a covenant unto all people, and will offer a light unto the gentiles. (John 1:4) To open the eyes of the blind and bring the prisoners out from the prison, and those that sit in darkness may be brought into the light." (Isaiah 42:6-7)
22. Now consider from where we have been redeemed. Then again the prophet said, "The spirit of the Lord is upon me because he has anointed me. He has sent me to preach the good news unto the lowly and heal the broken in heart; To proclaim the acceptable year of the Lord and the day of restitution and to comfort those that mourn." (Isaiah 61:1-2; Luke 4:19)

Barnabas 13

1. Concerning the Sabbath, it is written in the ten commandments that God gave to Moses on Mount Sinai, when Moses spoke face to face with God; "Sanctify the Sabbath of the Lord with clean hands and a pure heart." (Exodus 20:8)
2. In another place it is said, "if your children shall keep my Sabbath, then I will put my mercy upon them." (Jeremiah 17:24)
3. But even in the beginning of creation he speaks of the sabbath; "God made the world and all that is in it in six days, and on the seventh day he rested and sanctified it." (Genesis 2:2)
4. Consider what this signifies, that he finished in six days. This means that in six thousand years God will bring an end to all things.
5. For with God one day is as a thousand years, as it is testified to this; "Behold, a day is as a thousand years." (2 Peter 3:8) Therefore, in six days, of which is six thousand years, all things shall be accomplished (*completed*).
6. So what does it mean that he rested on the seventh day? That the Son of God shall return and abolish the time of the wicked one and judge the ungodly; He will alter the sun, moon and stars and then he shall rest on the seventh day.
7. The scripture says, "you shall sanctify it with clean hands and a pure heart." (Exodus 20:8) Therefore we are deceived if we think that we can sanctify a day that the Lord has made holy, if we do not have a pure heart (*clean conscience*) in everything.
8. Therefore, he will sanctify it with a blessed rest when we come to sanctify it by making ourselves holy.
9. Then again he said to them; "Your new moons and your sabbaths, I can not bear them." (Isaiah 1:13) Now consider what this means: "The sabbaths that you are now keeping are not acceptable unto me, as they are not as I have intended. When resting, I shall begin the eighth day, that is, the beginning of the eternal world."
10. This is the reason that we observe the eighth day (*Sunday*) with gladness, being the day that the Lord Jesus rose from the dead. Then after he showed himself to his disciples and he ascended into the heavens.
11. Now it is necessary that I explain unto you about the temple, and how these miserable men (*Jews*) have been deceived in that they put their trust in the building, as though it was the living place of God, but they do not put their trust in the God that made them. (*Do you put your trust in a book or use the book to direct you to God?*)
12. Much in the same ways that the pagans worship in a temple, they (*the Jews*) also do.
13. Now listen closely to how the Lord spoke concerning the worthlessness of the temple (*building*): "Who has measured the heavens with a rod and the earth with his hands? Is it not I, saith the Lord?
(Isaiah 40:12) The heavens are my throne and the earth is my footstool. What meaning is there for a house that you might build for me? Where is it that I shall rest?" (Isaiah 66:1) Know that all of their hope is in vain (*worthless*).
14. Then again he speaks in the same way: "They have destroyed the temple and built it up again"; And it came to pass that through war it was destroyed by their enemies and as servants of their enemies they rebuilt it again. (*after the Babylonian captivity*)

15. Furthermore it has been made known unto us through a prophet, that the city and the temple would be given up. As the scripture says, "And it shall come to pass in the final times that the Lord will deliver up the sheep of his pasture and the entire fold, and their towers will be destroyed." (Zephaniah 2:6) Then it came to pass as it was prophesied. (*70 AD*)

16. So let us ask, is there a true temple of God? Yes! He himself declared that he would make it and perfect it. It is written: "As soon as the time is at hand, the temple will be gloriously built." (1 Peter 2:4-5)

17. I find that there is a temple. But how will it be built in the name of the Lord? I will show you.

18. Before we believed in God, the habitation of our hearts were corrupt and feeble, just as the physical temple built by the hands of men has shown to be.

19. It was a house full of idolatry and a house of devils. This is because the goings on of what was in our hearts at that time was contrary to God. But it shall be rebuilt in the name of our Lord.

20. This is how the temple of the Lord will be gloriously built;

21. Having received remission of our (*past*) sins (Romans 3:25) and then committing ourselves unto the Lord, we are renewed, as being created (*born*) again (Matthew 18:1-4) like it was when we entered into this world. Now God truly lives in our house, that is, within us. (1 Corinthians 3:16)

22. But how does he live in us? The message of faithfulness, the expectation of his promise, the wisdom of his righteous judgment and the commands of his law. He himself prophesies in us, by speaking to our soul (*heart*); He lives in us and opens the doors of the temple unto us who were enslaved by death. That is the mouth of wisdom which strengthens us to turn from our old ways and he introduces unto us an incorruptible temple.

23. Then those who want to be saved no longer need to look to other men for guidance, but unto the one that lives within themselves, (*Christ in us -1 John 4:1-4*) and he (*the spirit of Christ*) speaks to him personally. (Jeremiah 31:31-34) One might be amazed, having never heard such words spoken before by anyone, nor ever having even considered them. (John 16:13)

24. The people of God are the spiritual temple that are being constructed unto the Lord. (1 Corinthians 3:16)

Barnabas 14

1. Now here is a summary of how a true Christian must live: I hope that I have declared unto you in a simple way, the things that may lead to your salvation. I hope to have not omitted anything that might be a prerequisite thereunto.

2. For if I explain further of the things that are now and of the things to come, you would not understand them, as they are explained in parables.

3. So I will now go on to knowledge and doctrine. There are two ways of doctrine and power; One of the Light and the other of darkness. (*good and evil*)

4. There is a great deal of difference between the two ways. Over one, the messengers of God are appointed to lead unto the way of Light; Over the other, the messengers of Satan. (2 Corinthians 11:15) Over the one, the everlasting Lord, our God; Over the other, Satan, the prince of unrighteousness in these final times. (1 Corinthians 2:6; John 16:11)

5. Now the way of Light is this: If anyone desires to attain unto the place appointed for him, he must be very zealous in his deeds. The knowledge given for each of us that chooses to live in such a way is as follows: You will love your maker; You will glorify the one that redeemed you from death. (*Christ Jesus*)

6. You must be simple in heart but rich in spirit. You must not be close to those that live according to the ways of death. You will hate anything that is not pleasing unto your God. You will hate all hypocrisy. You shall not neglect the commandments of God.

7. You must not exalt yourself, but you must be humble. Do not bring honor unto yourself. You must not plan evil against your neighbor. You must not be over-confident in your heart.

8. You shall not commit fornication nor shall you commit adultery. You shall not corrupt the young ones. You must not teach the message of God with any impurity (*no corruption in doctrine*).

9. You must not play favorites among people when it comes to correcting one of a transgression (*mistake*). (1 John 5:16) You must be gentle. You must be meek and peaceable. You will tremble at the things that you have heard. You must not keep hatred in your heart against any of the brethren. You must not be double-minded. (James 1:8)

10. You must not take the name of the Lord in vain. You must love others more than your own life.

11. You must not kill a child by means of an abortion, nor shall you slay the child after it is born.

12. You must not withdraw your hand from your sons or daughters, but you shall teach them from their youth, the fear of the Lord.

13. You must not covet what others have. You must not be greedy. You must not be reckoned with proud men, but must be seen as righteous and lowly. Whatever things may come upon you, you must accept them as good for you.

14. You must not be double minded nor double tongued. A double tongue is the snare of death. You must submit yourself unto the Lord in all things. You shall also submit yourself with fear and reverence unto earthly masters that are in the Lord, as they are representatives of God. (Romans 13:1-7)

15. Do not give bitter orders unto your servants or underlings that are committed unto God. To do so is to not be reverent unto God, in that he is above both you and them. Because he came to call all people, without having favorites among people based upon earthly status (*outward appearances* – Ephesians 6:9), but according to whoever the spirit of God has prepared. (Romans 8:29-30)

16. You shall communicate with others all that you have been given (*have come to understand*). You must not call your possessions your own. For if you are sharers in common of the things that are eternal, how much more should you also be willing to share in the things that are temporary (*of this world*)?

17. You must not be quick with your tongue; For the mouth is a snare of death. Strive for your soul with all of your might. Do not be extending your hands to take while you are retracting them to give.

18. You shall love as the apple of your eye, anyone who speaks unto you the authentic message of the Lord. Always, both night and day be thinking on the approaching day of judgment.

19. Every day you should be seeking out others that are righteous. Bring correction when needed, by explaining through the scriptures. Such will save a soul.

20. You shall also give unto those in need as though it is for the redemption of your sins. You must not hesitate to give and do not complain or brag when you do. Do not deliberate whether to give unto someone that is in need.

21. Give something unto everyone that asks. You know that God is your rewarder.

22. Keep what you have received concerning true doctrine. You shall not take away from it, nor add to it.

23. Finally, you must repel yourself from the wicked. You must use righteous judgment. Never bring dissention from these things (*true doctrine*). Make every effort to pacify others and bring them together.

24. You must confess your mistakes (*sins committed unaware*) and always come to God in prayer with a clean conscience (*do not defy God by choosing to commit sin*).

25. This is the way of Light.

Barnabas 15

1. The way of darkness is crooked and is cursed. For it is the way unto eternal death and will bring punishment. Those that do any of these things destroy their own souls.

2. Idolatry, overconfidence, the arrogance of power, hypocrisy, double-mindedness, adultery, murder, rape, pride, transgressions, deceit, malice, arrogance, witchcraft (*drug abuse*), covetousness, and a lack of the fear of God.

3. Many that live according to this way persecute those that are good; They hate truth and love lies. They reject the reward of righteousness because they reject to do what is right.

4. Some do not administer righteous judgment unto widows nor orphans. They seek out doing wickedness and do not fear God.

5. Gentleness and patience are far off from them. Many love vanity and look for rewards. Most have no compassion for the poor. Many do not ease the pain of those that are heavily burdened or oppressed.

6. Most are always ready to speak evil, because they do not know the one who made them. Some are murders of children and some corrupt the creatures that God has created. Many turn away from the needy, and oppress the afflicted; Many are advocates of the rich and unjust judges of the poor. They are altogether, sinners.

Barnabas 16

1. It is fitting, that we know the commandments of the Lord and live accordingly, because those that live in the ways of Light shall be glorified in the kingdom of God.

2. The one that chooses against the way of Light will be destroyed along with their deeds. This is the reason that there will be a resurrection and a judgment. (Daniel 12:2-3)

3. I beg of all that might hear my words that I have offered unto you, if there are others among you that desire to live in the way of Light, do not forsake them. (Hebrews 10:25)

4. For the day is approaching when everything will be destroyed, along with all that are of the wicked one (*Satan*). The Lord is coming and his rewards are with him.

5. I beg of you, again and again, be good lawgivers unto one another and become faithful counselors unto each other. Remove from yourselves all hypocrisy.

6. May God, who is above all, give you wisdom, knowledge, counsel, and understanding concerning his judgments. Be patient. (*faithful*)

7. Be taught by God; (Jeremiah 31:34) Seek out what it is that the Lord requires of you and do it, so that you may be saved on the day of judgment.

8. If there is any remembrance of that which is good within you, think of what I have written and meditate on these things.

9. I beg of you, that while you remain in your physical bodies, do not be lacking any of these things. But seek them without ceasing and fulfill every command. Because these things are fitting and are necessary to be done.

10. **This is why I have been diligent to write (*this book*) for you, according to my limited ability, so that you might find peace with God. Fare well my brethren. Love and Joy.**

11. **May our glorious master bring grace unto your spirit.**

The Epistle of Barnabas, the companion of the Apostle Paul,
was included in the bible canon for the first 200 + years of the early church.
Written about 72-75 AD.

The current state
of the world and the churches

"Many will come and claim to be of me, they will even say that I (Jesus) am the Christ,
yet they will deceive many and lead them into great error.
You will hear of many battles and reports of war.
Nation will arise against nation, and uprisings with kings against their own people!
There will be shortages of food and plagues and earthquakes in many various places.
But all of these will be the beginning of sorrow. People will hate and betray one another.
Wickedness shall be greatly multiplied and the natural affection and care that people
have for one another will evaporate and disappear."

Matthew 24

"I tell you the truth, in the last times, difficult times shall come.
For the people will be lovers of themselves and will be covetous.
They will be proud, braggarts, blasphemous, disobedient, ungrateful
and they will be wickedly unholy. They will lack natural care for others and be
trucebreakers, false accusers and have no self-control.
They will be fiercely savage and hostile towards anyone that is virtuous.
They will be traitors, self-willed, self-conceited and they will love recreation
much more than they will love God. Some will have the appearance of godliness,
but they will reject the ability of living a godly (holy) life.
They will always be learning but will never be able to recognize the truth."

2 Timothy 3

"these men (false teachers, lying preachers and false prophets) are like
mindless instinctive animals; (2 Corinthians 11:13-15)
They were created to take unto themselves and to destroy everyone that is ignorant,
blaspheming in their own corruption; But in the end they will all be destroyed.
They are spotted with filth and full of blemishes,
sporting themselves in their own doctrinal errors while they are feasting upon you;
They have eyes full of adulterous lusts and they never stop committing sin.
They have forsaken the true way and have gone astray. They speak great swelling
words of vanity to attract others by the lusts for evil things, bringing forth unbridled lusts
in them, and they allow for them to live in error. While they promise them freedom from
the penalty of sin, they themselves are slaves (of sin) unto damnation..."

2 Peter 2

"Come now, you who are wealthy, weep and cry loudly,
because great misery is soon coming upon you.
Your wealth is corrupt and your clothing is of low quality;
Your money is being devalued and is a witness against your venom.
Your flesh shall be consumed by fire.
You have built up treasure against yourself for judgment day.
Look at the wages of the workers who have reaped your fields;
You are keeping it from them and they cry out!
Their cries have been heard in the ears of the Lord
and he is readying for war!
You have lived luxuriously on the earth and have lived in self-gratification;
You have fed your own desires, of which is leading you unto the day of slaughter.
You have condemned and killed those who were righteous,
though they do not fight back to resist you.
Be patient through your endurance my brethren, unto the coming of the Lord."

James 5

"The day of the Lord is near and approaching quickly...
That day will be a day full of wrath, distress and anguish.
It will be a day of darkness and gloom. The fortified cities shall fall.
The people will walk like blind men because of their sin.
Their silver and their gold (money) will not save them.
In the fire of his jealousy, the whole earth will be consumed.
There will be a sudden end for all that live on the earth."

Zephaniah 1

Do you have eyes that can see?

Do you recognize that the time is near?

The Prophecies Revealed
These things will soon happen

Part 1
The times leading up to and including the great tribulation:
(The great tribulation is Satan's wrath against the people of God)

Food shortages due to weather, disease, poor management and production problems will be a great challenge in the coming years. In some places, governments will help to create the problem and some will take from the people all that they had stored up and hoarded. Food prices will escalate significantly. Plagues and diseases will give opportunity for governments to restrict travel and access. People will be pushed to impersonal and online services more and more. Cash will be discouraged and looked down upon until everyone is made to use non-physical currency. Personal interaction will become less and less personal. People will increasingly become more and more dependent upon government.

People will become increasingly volatile and divided. Most people will grow more vicious and selfish, looking out for themselves and having less and less care for others. Lying, theft, rape and murder will increase. We are entering a time when the line in the sand is being drawn. Every man and woman will need to choose which side to take. Those who reject Christ will become more and more evil, selfish and corrupt; Yet those that are drawn to Christ will grow to become more Christ-like, having great care and love towards others, especially those that are likeminded.

The doctrines brought forth through this book will be condemned by the churches and governments. The media will treat the true doctrine of Christ and true Christians as though they are a plague that is a great threat to society. Freedom of religion will still exist in many places, as long as it is not keeping firm to nor teaching faithfulness unto Jesus Christ. Many that come to the true Christian faith will be persecuted, tortured, imprisoned and killed. Endure faithfully until the end and you will be eternally saved.

A world government body will be created before the year 2030, of which will be made up of 10 leaders that give their power to one leader.

There will be a world-wide mandate that will require every man, woman and child to receive a technological device implanted within their hand or forehead. This will be the rolling out of the mark of the beast, spoken of in the book of Revelation. No one will be able to enter into commerce or take part in society without it. It will be mandated that all who do not receive the mark of the beast implant must be killed. (Matthew 24:22) All that do receive it will be eternally damned. This will be done before the year 2030 is completed. When this begins it will be the beginning of the great tribulation, a 3 ½ year persecution upon all that reject the mark of the beast, of which will be the greatest genocide that the world has ever seen. There will be two types of devices that will be mandated to be implanted into the bodies of the people. First will be the generic device that will go in the right hand and will give access to commerce, banking, records and a wide variety of other possible applications. The second will be an upgrade that will have many additional applications and seeming benefits for those that receive it. It may connect the brain to the internet (*computer-human interfacing / transcendence / transhumanism*). The first may be free to the public but the upgrade may be very costly, intended for the elites.

Those that do not receive the mark of the beast will be gathered up, set before tribunals, pressured to take the mark, and killed. First the population areas will be assaulted, then they will spread out to the suburbs, then the countryside and eventually to the more desolate areas. Drones, satellite and other apprehension methods will be used to gather and destroy nearly all those who refuse to come in to the system.

As things unfold, each man and woman will be tested as to whether they truly believe in what Jesus Christ offers. To truly believe is to fully commit your trust and then take the appropriate action, demonstrating it through how you live.

Part 2
The judgment of God and his soon return:

A large comet made up of multiple fragments will impact the earth at a time between 2032-2034. The impacts will bring devastation upon the entire world. The first impact will bring an end to the great tribulation. (Matthew 24:22)

144000 faithful people from all nations will be sealed by God and be protected from the coming judgment. They are chosen by God, being mature in the faith, standing perfect and blameless in the eyes of God.

Many people will be hidden in caves and bunkers all around the world, to try to protect them from the results of the impacts brought by the comet. This is the reason for the seed vaults and underground facilities that were, and are being built all around the world.

A large mass of earth will be thrown into the Atlantic Ocean; It will cause a massive tsunami of which will send forth great devastation upon the coastlines and even inland many miles throughout the regions surrounding the Atlantic Ocean. Life in the water and many ships will be destroyed.

Those that had received the mark of the beast will receive much torment and pain due to an EMP created by the strike of the first impact. The device will give a bad burn and create cancer in many people.

Due to one of the impacts, a large expanse of fresh water will be made poison of which will kill many people in that region.

The Yellowstone volcano will erupt due to tectonic plate shifting caused by the impacts. It will spread ash that will darken the sky throughout most of North America.

Mystery Babylon, the nation that controls the worlds commerce, will be destroyed by a nuclear attack brought by many nations. This will happen about a year after the eruption, when that nation is greatly weakened. (Revelation 18; Jeremiah 51:46)

Jesus Christ will return very soon after these events are completed.

The evidence of the prophetic timeline
is from understanding the prophecies in Daniel.

Daniel chapters 11-12 speak of a prophecy of the end times leading up to judgment day. Evidence of this is clear in chapter 12. Verse 2 is a parallel of Revelation 20:12-15, judgment day. Verse 4 gives us two signs of the times of the end of this prophecy. These signs can not reasonably be speaking of any other time in history except for today: It states that in these times, the people would travel extensively and that knowledge would be greatly increased. In the history of the world, travel has never been more frequent, and with computers and the internet, incredible knowledge on practically every possible subject is now at your fingertips, of which could not even have been imagined at any time in the past.

Verse 6 asks the question; How long will it be until all of the things in this prophecy are completed? The angel states in verse 7; "*It will be a time, times and a half of a time and he will scatter the power of the holy people, then all will be completed.*"

Scatter	= H-5310	= cut into pieces, discharge, kill
hand/power	= H-3027	= to be, to exist, ability to, the alive hand
holy people	= H-5971	= those who are of God, the righteous, the elect

In this, we should see that the elect people of God will be killed. Revelation 20:4 states that many will be killed for their testimony in Christ, those that do not take the mark of the beast. This is a parallel account of Revelation 13:14-18. If we can gain the understanding as to the meaning of a "time" and have the specific time as to when the Daniel 11-12 prophecy was written, we can then gain the understanding as to know when all things in the prophecy will be completed.

First, the evidence for when this was written is gained from Daniel 9:24-27. (*Please refer to page 160*) "Seventy weeks" refers to 70 periods of 7 years, 490 years. This is a precise prophecy that was completed at 70 AD. Knowing this, it then becomes easy to conclude that the Daniel 9 prophecy would have begun at 420 BC with the command to rebuild the temple. The writing of the Daniel 9 prophecy would have been just a short time (*2-5 years*) after that command was given, in that Daniel referred to it in the prophecy; The Daniel 11-12 prophecy was written only weeks later. Therefore, the date of the writing of the Daniel 11-12 prophecy would have been about 418-415 BC. Furthermore, historically there were Persian kings named Cyrus and Darius that ruled at about that time, of which is given in the Daniel text.

After seeking the key to the meaning of a "time" for many years, and then asking God for the wisdom to know the key, asking him every day for 9 months, God finally showed me the answer in a dream. The meaning of a "time" is 700 years! Therefore, a time, times and a half a time (3 ½ times) would equal 2450 years, in which the prophecy was to be completed. If we work from 418-415 BC, the time of the writing of the Daniel 11-12 prophecy, this gives the date of somewhere between the year 2032 and 2035 to be the time of the completion of the prophecy!

Furthermore, God then reaffirmed this time period again through Revelation 12. The woman (*faithful of ancient Israel*) was protected for 1260 days (Revelation 12:6), of which represent 1260 years. This started at the destruction of Jerusalem in 70 AD, the completion of the Daniel 9 prophecy. This takes us to 1330 AD. Now if we add in the key to Daniel 11-12 prophecy (*700 years*), we come to the year 2030! This will be the approximate beginning of the great tribulation!

The decaying world

Evolution is impossible in a world of decay, where everything breaks down by nature. Evolution is touted by many people today as the way of nature, despite that there has not been evidence demonstrated that would prove the theory. The world that we live in is a world that is degenerating and not growing more evolved. This is the way that it was designed to be. Here is the evidence:

Examples:
* Men grow old and die, just as all animals and plants also do.
* Objects like buildings, bridges and streets decay and are ripped down or need fixing.
* Things that we use wear out and most things either rust away or decay.
* Even mountains erode away and stars eventually fall.
* Everything that we can observe is in a constant state of decay, including all animals and plants.
* The character of mankind is also decaying with each new idea.
* Fire consumes and then burns out.
* The strongest and most talented people grow old, wear out, break down and die.

In this world, everything has its beginning and its end, breaking down along the way. This can not be denied as it is easily demonstrated and proven, being seen by all. So how can we believe that through this process of breakdown and decay, that physical things, whether they be animals, plant life or people, are also growing more and more evolved, making them better, stronger and more enduring? Doesn't this contradict what we already recognize and know to be true? The truth is that God created everything perfectly, just as the scriptures tell us. What we should see and understand is that if things are evolving, making them better, then isn't that evidence that God did not make them perfect to begin with? (Genesis 1)

We should see from the scriptures that Adam lived over 900 years and Shem lived over 600 years, and Abraham lived over 150 years; What we generally see is that men have devolved, becoming more and more frail, living shorter lives as time has gone on. This has only changed somewhat in recent times due to modern technology and medicine. We should understand that if we are to trust in the unproven theory of evolution, this is to deny what the bible says is true and to deny what is clearly observed by all of us! It is to contradict by one's belief, that which has been clearly demonstrated and the way things are easily observed to be; It is to deny reality! It is to believe a lie!

Sure, there have been incredible scientific discoveries that have been made which have extended the lives of many people in recent decades. There have even been numerous discoveries which allow for incredible growth in food production by means of manipulation of the environment of the plant or animal. Pesticides, herbicides and other chemicals can kill the diseases and pests which would have damaged the crop, but there is always a price to be paid. At best it is a tradeoff, taking the immediate benefit for the long-term penalty. But all these things only put up a fight against the inevitable, never completely defeating this process of decay, only extending it. They never change the laws of nature, the law of decay or the evidence of degeneration and de-evolution.

For the scientific evidence, see the book: *The case for a creator* – Strobel 2004

There is currently a great hope in the scientific community for what they believe will give people an indefinite lifespan. It is the interfacing of technology into our bodies; It is called transhumanism. With super computers connected to our bodies through internet connections, working through implanted technologies within the bodies of people, possibly working along with nanotechnologies that may also be put within the body, even the slightest risk of a potential health problem will be recognized before it becomes a problem that would damage or kill the body, giving time to repair and correct the potential problem before damage is done. This might sound great to many, but is only a means to control the masses by a very few. It will promise you a greatly extended life, but there will be strings attached!

Picture this, those controlling the system will put laws in place, intended for control, of which have already been designed, written and in many cases already put into law. They will allow the few who rule to control, manipulate and much, much worse. If you consent to be a part of such a system, how much control is possible for the elites to have over you, if the threat is to let you die if you do not completely comply with their laws, no matter how evil they might be? They might say, that through their technology, you can live indefinitely, but that you must comply perfectly with the demands of those running the system. This is the recipe for a nightmare that would enslave the world. It will make you a slave to the fullest degree! Because they own the technology in you, they own you! This type of power will be the sledge hammer that will be used to dictate to what degree you are to be used and for what purposes, forcing you to comply because they can end your life by shutting off the technology that keeps you alive and allows you to take part in society and commerce. This will be the ultimate in a one world government and population control, and it will happen very soon.

But even with such technology, the process of decay is not stopped, changed nor ended in any way, but only the ways of dealing with such will be altered. Degeneration, aging and decay do prove that the world is not evolving nor getting better. No matter the technology, this can not and will not change. You will grow old and eventually die, just as your children will and all those who came before you also did. Things are not evolving into higher forms of life and things are not getting better, though because of technology, on the surface it might seem this way.

The theory of evolution is a hoax, a scam that is used to deceive and manipulate the people, getting most to turn away from traditional trust in God and put their trust in science or government. It is also used to pull trust away from the validity of the scriptures, knowing God and having a personal relationship with him. It is meant to create a world view instead of an eternal perspective. It is to expand the viewpoint that humans are the ultimate authority in all things and that everything revolves around them. The theory of evolution was created to take God out of the picture, and through secular society and other corruptions, they generally have for most people.

"Keep that which is committed to thy trust, avoiding profane and vain babblings,
and oppositions of science falsely so called, which some who had professed
the faith have erred and fallen away from the faith (true doctrine). Grace be with thee."

1 Timothy 6:20-21

"The condition of this world is decaying" - 1 Corinthians 7:31

Help in time of need

This is how to live through what is coming in this world
and requirements to be one of the 144,000 first fruits of God

Spiritually:

Each one of you must be certain that you are properly converted into Christ. There is power in a true conversion that will give you the ability to overcome every temptation of sin brought by the devil, but you must also be determined to overcome. (*synergy*) A false conversion will not bring the power to overcome sin but will bring with it many false doctrines. (Acts 2:38, Romans 6)

Following a true conversion, you must live a life to the best of your understanding, always doing the right thing and being obedient to God in everything. This includes loving God with all of your heart, mind, soul and strength, and always treating others the same way that you would want to be treated by them. You must be conformed into the image of Christ and grow to become mature in Christ. Innocent mistakes can be forgiven, but defiance will not be. (Numbers 15:28-31; 1John 5:16-17; Matthew 12:32)

Do not stockpile food or weapons or medical supplies. That said, there are things that may be good to have on hand, though hoarding is not going to help you or your loved ones, but will only make you a target. Be content with what you have, both now and throughout your life. God will provide for those that are his. There is no need to continue building that financial nest-egg, as it will distract you and soon be worthless.

Physically

You need to get healthy and in great physical condition. Get the dental procedures done ASAP. Loose the weight. Get physically motivated and active. Gain the ability to do what you have never before done. Work at it and do not give up, keep bettering yourself and motivate those around you.

Mentally

It will be a great challenge to watch the things that you have worked so hard for and accumulated in this life be taken away from you. We must also be able to mentally deal with loss of friends, family and loved ones, both those that have turned away from the truth, but also those that will die. We must prepare ourselves now to deal with these types of hardships. Living conditions and other hardships that will soon come will also be a great mental drain and could lead to depression without preparing in advance and also the encouragement of other brethren. We must keep our focus on the eternal goals at all times.

Educationally

Having the proper education will be extremely necessary. This subject is multi-dimensional. It will consist of knowing how to function in a world that excludes and bans you from everything while you are being hunted down. This includes legal understanding, traditional medical practices and herbal medicine, traditional food procurement and preservation, nutrition and the knowledge of skills - how to do many things in the ancient ways.

- Legal understanding -

Understanding jurisdiction and how the world system works will be very important. Understanding the different kinds of laws and whether they apply to you, or not, and being able to handle yourself properly when before a tribunal will be necessary. Having knowledge of these things will be a great asset, but know that the spirit of God will guide you to speak in the moment of necessity. For those that do not have knowledge of legal matters, calmness, submission and a quiet mouth will be an asset. It is suggested that you test jurisdiction in every place. Make those who assault you prove that they have jurisdiction and do not just allow them to presume it. Make them prove that the law applies to you and that it is valid, backed up by actual laws, and not just a false interpretation that acts against the spirit of a law. Do no harm to anyone and do not attack. Jesus went before his accusers as a lamb going to the slaughter and we are to present ourselves in much the same way, but only as the spirit of God leads. Foul language and personal attacks must not be used for any reason.

- traditional medicinal practices -

Education of how to treat medical needs and emergencies while working with herbal medicines and traditional methods will be a necessity. Being aware of ancient herbal cures as well as what parts of the plants to use, what time of year they can be harvested and how to prepare and administer them will also be important. The knowledge of diagnosing health problems properly and an understanding of what plants will cure specific types of sicknesses and injuries will be a great benefit. Through nature, God has provided the cures for us, but it is up to us to gain that understanding and use it properly.

- traditional food procurement -

Understanding the time to harvest each part of a plant and naturally extend the usage through methods of drying, salting, pickling or other preservation methods, all being done in a natural environment with limited resources. Understanding simple trapping, primitive hunting and gathering methods will also be very necessary, as will proper butchering, food preparation and primitive cooking methods. The knowledge of how to manufacture and use of primitive tools may also be necessary. Our ancestors lived by such methods for thousands of years and it is still possible today if we take the time to learn, practice and teach ourselves and others. We must also learn to eat things for necessity in order to continue to live, and not be so concerned with taste. We should also learn and train our bodies to go without. I suggest to go without eating when food sources are low so that another can eat, of which demonstrates brotherly love.

- skills -

Having the knowledge to purify water, travel without detection, make a fire that will not give a heat footprint or make smoke, boil water with a rock, know what to use for toilet paper when there is none and knowing how to deal with other hygiene concerns. These are all skills that may be very important to know; Knowing how to hide in plain sight, fit into a crowd without being noticed and evasion tactics may be necessary. These are only a few of the things that are recommended to be learned in advance that will make life more tolerable during the great tribulation. Knowing of hidden cave systems, mines and tunnels may be something of interest. Understanding different climatic environments and knowing where to find resources in any environment will also be necessary. Knowledge may not save you, but without knowledge you will not have a chance.

Summary:

Know that Babylon has all of the technology, but we have God to assist us. Technology will fail, but God will never fail. You must remember that we must not violate God's law at any time. We are not to steal or lie to anyone at any time, or kill anyone. You must keep your focus on the eternal goal at all times so that you are able to overcome and properly deal with the hardships that will soon come.

The mental challenge that will be presented when we come to realize that we will not be able to partake in commerce will be grueling and may dissuade some. We will be prevented from using money, checks, credit cards and trading. Travel will not be able to be done by car or other motorized methods. Understanding ways to deal with these great restrictions and hardships, both strategically and also mentally will be of great value. The time to prepare is now!

You will need to know how to do many things, many of which you might never think of until you have the need. Spiritual, mental, physical and educational preparation in advance will be very valuable.
Having the ability to deal with mental, physical and heartfelt pain, as well as being able to go without will be necessary. Improvising will be a plus.

Each one that will be a part of the 144,000 must have a mindset, heart-set and then act upon caring for the brethren in Christ. Each one must be willing to give themselves up, even unto death, for the benefit of another - if it becomes necessary, but that does not mean to be suicidal. (*Greater love has no man than he that gives up his own life for his friends. John 15:13*) Such love is necessary for one to be a first fruit of God.

All of these recommended preparations are considerations and not mandates, and each of you must choose for yourselves which of these preparations you will prepare for, if any. The most important of these are the spiritual and having a strong mind to remain faithful, being completely focused on the eternal goal, while enduring many hardships and even death.

WARNINGS:

If you choose to make plans for what is coming, do so in secret. Start today, but think it out well and commit yourself to proper responsible planning. You will be demonized by most people and pay a high price for it if you tell others about what you are preparing for. Share with others that are dedicated fully to Christ and be an encouragement. Though the times will be very difficult, your hope must not be in what you currently see, but in what you do not yet see but have hope for in the eternal world. People will not understand your thinking and you will be called crazy. Some of you may be institutionalized by family members that think that you have lost your mind. Watch your words concerning all planning, but spread the Gospel unto others whenever the spirit of God leads you to do so.

Do not trust any lawyer, banker, investor, councilor, government, agency, agent, professor, doctor or corporation when it comes to preparing for what is coming. Do not trust commentators, talk show hosts, news organizations, news reports, experts or preachers who are not completely faithful unto God. They are a part of the system and will guide you into the system and they will become aware that you are making efforts to remove yourself from it, of which should be a serious concern. Do not trust anyone that is not completely dedicated to the same mindset and plan. Choose your confidants and friends wisely. (Matthew 10:16-17)

The scriptures tell us that brother will betray his own brother, father will betray his own children, and children will betray their own parents. If you have a family member or friend that is not committed to Christ but on board with preparing with you, they will betray you when the time comes. Share the Gospel with them and give them a copy of this book, but do not give up what your plans are or you will endanger yourself and those that will be with you when you are betrayed.

If you have the ability, get out of Babylon ASAP! (Revelation 18).

The pleasures of this life are set to deceive and entrap you. Food is for the preservation and health of your body and enjoying what you eat may become a luxury and a rare thing that each one of us will need to overcome.

At some point, you will be hunted down. Remaining in one place for too long is going to be very dangerous. Traveling may be even more dangerous. Moving undetected will become very necessary. Expect to die as a martyr. If God allows you to be one of the very few, allow it to happen without having that expectation. It is only the humble that will succeed. Plan for and have hope that your death will be honorable and for the benefit of another while remaining completely faithful unto God in all things.

No matter how difficult and hopeless things get, know that there is someone out there that is suffering a much more difficult hardship than you. Know that your saviour also suffered greatly for you and think about his suffering on the cross while you endure your hardship. Know that God does love you, as do all of the other faithful brethren. If you have a serious need, ask God and he will provide it for you. Keep your chin up and win this race of life. Keep your focus on the eternal promises to overcome this world and you will gain eternal victory.

For those that are apprehended for not having received the mark of the beast, you will not have it easy. It may be easier to die than to live in the coming times, but it will not be that simple. You will be set before tribunals and coerced, threatened and worse. They will do all that they can do, to get you to accept the mark of the beast. That is their goal. Killing you will only come after they see that you will not give in. You may be tested for 10 days. You must remain faithful to God no matter what you must suffer.

374

The Watchman

My son, speak to the children of thy people and say unto them;
When there is a threat of war upon your land, the people of the land take a man of their border
and set him for their watchman: If when he sees the sword come upon the land,
he blows the trumpet and warns the people, then whosoever heareth the sound of the trumpet,
and taketh not warning, if the sword comes and take him away, his blood shall be upon his own head.
Because he heard the sound of the trumpet and did not take warning, his blood shall remain upon him.
He that taketh warning shall deliver his soul.

But if the watchman sees the sword come,
And does not blow the trumpet and the people be not warned;
If the sword come and take any, they are taken away in their iniquity,
but his blood will I require at the watchman's hand.

Now my son, I have set you to be a watchman over the house of Israel (Romans 11:17-19);
Therefore, thou shalt hear the instruction from my mouth and warn them from me.
When I say unto the wicked, whoever is wicked, thou shalt surely die;
If you do not speak to warn the wicked of his way, that wicked one shall die in his iniquity,
yet his blood will I require at thine hand.
Nevertheless, if you warn the wicked of his way to turn from it,
if he does not turn from his way, he shall die in his iniquity, but you have protected your soul.

Therefore my son, speak unto the house of (*spiritual*) Israel;
This ye shall speak:
If our transgressions and our sins be upon us and we turn away from them, how shall we live?
Say unto them; As I live, saith the Lord God, I have no pleasure in the death of the wicked;
But if the wicked turn from his evil ways, he shall surely live:
So then, turn ye, turn ye from your evil ways;
For why will ye die, O house of Israel?

Therefore, now say unto the people;
The righteousness of the righteous shall not deliver him in the day of his transgression:
As for the wickedness of the wicked, he shall not fall thereby in the day that he turns from his wickedness;
Neither shall the righteous be able to live for his righteousness in the day that he chooses to commit sin.

When I say to the righteous that he shall surely live, if he trusts to his own opinion that he is righteous,
and then chooses to commit iniquity, all his righteousness shall not be remembered;
But for his iniquity that he has then committed, he shall die for it.

Now when I say unto the wicked, you shalt surely die,
then if he turns from his sin and does that which is lawful and right; If he restores the pledge,
returns that which he had robbed and then walks according to the law of God
without again committing iniquity, he shall surely live and shall not die.
None of his sins that he hath committed shall be remembered unto him:
(*You shall receive a clean slate at conversion.*)
He that lives accordingly to that which is lawful and right, he shall surely live.

I will judge each one of you according to your ways.

(Ezekiel 33:2-20)

A prayer for the end times

Oh Lord, have mercy upon us and see our needs. Send your fear upon all people who do not worship you nor seek after you. Lift up your hand against the nations and make them know your power. Make yourself be known, to be raised up above all people. Let them know you as I have known you, that there is no other God but you. Show the signs and great wonders. Strengthen your right hand to go forth with mighty deeds. Raise up your indignation and pour out your wrath; Take away the adversary and destroy the devil. Make the time until that day to be short and remember the covenant which a few obedient servants have entered into with you. Declare your mighty ways. Let those who escape your wrath be consumed by fire and make all who oppress your people to perish. Cut in pieces the rulers of the nations that say there is no higher than they. Gather your people together to receive their inheritance, as was intended from the beginning. Oh Lord, have mercy upon your people of whom are called your elect. Bring down your holy city, heavenly Jerusalem. Fill the holy place within each of your people with your spirit. Honor the testimony of all who have been faithful unto you from the beginning and raise up the prophet who shall bring forth truth in your name. Reward all who patiently wait for you and make the words of your prophets to be found reliable. Oh Lord, hear the prayer of your servant, that all who live upon the earth will know of your offer of salvation and that you are the Almighty God.

Taken from Chapter 36
of the book:

"The Wisdom of Jesus"
Of the Apocrypha